FORTRAN
With Engineering Applications

FIFTH EDITION

Elliot B. Koffman

Frank L. Friedman

Temple University

Addison-Wesley Publishing Company
Reading, Massachusetts ▪ Menlo Park, California
New York ▪ Don Mills, Ontario ▪ Wokingham, England
Amsterdam ▪ Bonn ▪ Sydney ▪ Singapore ▪ Tokyo
Madrid ▪ San Juan ▪ Milan ▪ Paris

Sponsoring Editor	*Lynne Doran Cote*
Production Supervisor	*Loren Hilgenhurst Stevens*
Assistant Editor	*Andrea M. Danese*
Design, Editorial, and Production Services	*Quadrata, Inc.*
Copy Editor	*Laura Michaels*
Text Designer	*Joyce Cameron Weston*
Illustrations	*Tech-Graphics*
Cover Art Director and Designer	*Peter M. Blaiwas*
Manufacturing Supervisor	*Roy Logan*

Library of Congress Cataloging-in-Publication Data

Koffman, Elliot B.

    Fortran / Elliot B. Koffman, Frank L. Friedman. — 5th ed. with engineering applications.

      p. cm.

    Includes index.

    ISBN 0-201-55875-0

    1. FORTRAN (Computer program language).   I. Friedman, Frank L.

II. Title.

QA76.73.F25F63 1993

005.13'3—dc20
                                            92-18188

                                                  CIP

The programs and applications presented in this book have been included for their instructional value. They have been tested with care but are not guaranteed for any particular purpose. The publisher does not offer any warranties or representations, nor does it accept any liabilities with respect to the programs or applications.

Many of the designations used by manufacturers and sellers to distinguish their products are claimed as trademarks. Where those designations appear in this book, and Addison-Wesley was aware of a trademark claim, the designations have been printed in initial caps or all caps.

1 2 3 4 5 6 7 8 9 10—HA—9695949392

To our families
Caryn, Richard, Deborah, and Robin Koffman
and
Martha, Shelley, and Dara Friedman

Preface

This is a textbook for a first course in problem solving and programming methods using the Fortran language. It assumes no prior knowledge of computers or programming. A course in high-school algebra is sufficient mathematics background for most of the material in this textbook, except for a few scattered examples (marked as optional) and sections of the last chapter that require some elementary knowledge of calculus.

Although the language of the text is Fortran, its primary goal is to teach effective problem-solving and program-design techniques that are independent of the programming language used. For this reason, the text emphasizes a software engineering approach to program design and carefully applies a five-step problem-solving approach: problem specification, analysis, design, implementation, and testing/verification. This approach is applied uniformly to the solution of 26 case studies, many of which are more ambitious in scope than one normally finds in a programming text, extending over several pages. The longer case studies integrate material introduced over several chapters and more closely resemble real-world problems. The techniques used in their solution will serve the programming student well regardless of the language that he or she uses in the future.

Engineering Emphasis

Fortran is a general-purpose language, and there are many Fortran programs in use today that perform vital operations in a variety of disciplines, from business and the humanities to engineering and science. Many of today's Fortran programming students, however, are engineering or science majors. Thus a major goal of this edition was to increase the emphasis on engineering and science applications of Fortran. We accomplished this by introducing 12 Fortran in Focus commentaries that describe how Fortran is used by engineers and scientists working in private industry and the government to solve today's pressing technological problems. We have also inserted over 50 new engineering/science projects, examples, and case studies. Finally, Chapter 2 now covers all aspects of using Fortran for computations, including the use of library functions. So that the book would continue to appeal to students in other fields, we have retained many of the general applications and examples.

Modularization   We firmly believe that learning how to write and use independent subprogram modules is one of the most important skills that a student can take away from an introductory programming course—particularly for a course in Fortran whose popularity is enhanced by its rich libraries of special-purpose routines. Thus we stress modularization in this textbook by introducing the use of Fortran's intrinsic functions early (Chapter 2) and by showing students how to write and call their own subprograms (Chapter 6). Each function and subroutine includes informal preconditions and postconditions as part of its interface section. Chapter 6 introduces the structure chart as another documentation tool that is useful for specifying the flow of control between a main program and its subprograms.

Arrays   Our coverage of arrays in Chapter 7 begins with five sections that do not use subprograms. This will enable instructors who prefer to cover arrays early to introduce the essentials of arrays at any point after Chapter 4 ("Repetition and Loops"). Chapter 8 discusses additional features of arrays such as multidimensional arrays, searching, and sorting, and includes a case study on image processing.

Fortran 90   Although Fortran 90 has been approved, it is still not in widespread use and Fortran 77 will continue to exist as an alternative standard. For this reason, we decided to use Fortran 77 in the main body of the text and to discuss Fortran 90 features only in separate, clearly distinguishable sections at the end of each chapter. These sections introduce those features of Fortran 90 that are relevant to the programming topics discussed in the particular chapter and may also include Fortran 90 features introduced in earlier chapters. These sections will be valuable for reference when Fortran 90 usage becomes more widespread.

The WHILE loop has been an important control structure for teaching structured programming in Fortran since the first edition of this book was published in 1977. For the convenience of those students who are unable to use the WHILE loop, we discuss in Appendix D how to write it in standard Fortran 77, and we include standard Fortran 77 code in all complete programs with WHILE loops.

Other Organizational Changes   Many of the organizational changes in this new edition have been motivated by a desire to reduce emphasis on the spiral approach. The long introductory chapter of the previous edition has been split into separate chapters: "Introduction to Computers and Programming" (Chapter 1) and "Problem Solving and Fortran" (Chapter 2). Chapter 2 begins by introducing the software engineering method and applies it to a case study solution. The remainder of the chapter introduces the Fortran language, discusses the data types INTEGER, REAL, and CHARACTER, and provides thorough coverage of computation in Fortran through intrinsic functions. Chapter 3 covers all aspects of decisions, including a discussion of the LOGICAL data type. Chapter 4 describes loops and repetition, and Chapter 5 covers FORMAT statements and introduces files.

The remainder of the text corresponds closely to the previous edition with a few exceptions. Chapter 6 describes user-defined subprograms. Chapter 7 introduces arrays and includes new sections on searching and sorting. (Recall that Sections 7.1–7.5 may be studied earlier.) Chapter 8 completes the discussion of arrays (multidimensional arrays) and discusses additional features of subprograms (COMMON, the SAVE statement, and using random functions).

Coverage of Advanced Topics

Chapters 9–12 consist of advanced topics. The topics selected for study will depend on the time available and the students' abilities and backgrounds. For classes with predominantly engineering and science students, Chapters 11 and 12 discuss graphing, computer-aided design, and numerical methods. For classes with a general audience, Chapters 9 and 10 discuss additional aspects of file usage and string processing.

Pedagogical Features

We employ many pedagogical features to enhance the usefulness of this book as a teaching tool. Some of these features are discussed below.

End-of-Section Exercises   Most sections end with a number of self-check exercises. These include exercises that require analysis of program segments as well as short programming exercises. Answers to these exercises appear at the back of the book.

End-of-Chapter Exercises and Projects   Each chapter ends with a set of quick-check exercises with answers. There are also chapter review exercises whose solutions appear at the back of the book. Finally, there is a set of programming projects whose solutions appear in the instructor's manual. The icons in the left margin denote particularly challenging projects.

Examples and Case Studies   The book contains a large number and variety of programming examples. Whenever possible, examples contain complete programs or subprograms rather than incomplete program fragments. There are also substantial case studies that help a student integrate and apply concepts studied over several chapters.

Syntax Display Boxes   The syntax displays describe the syntax and semantics of each new Fortran feature and also provide examples.

Program Style Sections   The program style sections discuss issues of good programming style.

Error Discussions and Chapter Reviews   Each chapter ends with a discussion of common programming errors. A chapter review includes a table of newly introduced Fortran statements.

Appendixes and Supplements

A reference table of Fortran statements appears on the inside covers of the book. We have also included appendixes on Fortran library functions and character sets, MS-DOS, the Microsoft Fortran 77 compiler, and the Lahey Personal Fortran compiler, and on implementing the WHILE loop in Fortran 77.

Supplements include an instructor's manual with a program disk, which includes all the programs that appear in the book. Use the reference number below to order the supplement from your Addison-Wesley sales representative.

Instructor's Manual with Program Disk: 0-201-91395-X

We are very grateful to Thomas Cunningham at Indiana University of Pennsylvania for his work on producing the instructor's manual.

Acknowledgments

Many people participated in the development of this book. A number of faculty members prepared a host of engineering examples, exercises, case studies, and programming projects for inclusion in the book. Their help was invaluable in increasing the number of engineering and science applications presented. They include Betty Barr, *University of Houston*; Bart Childs, *Texas A&M University*; Thomas Cunningham, *Indiana University of Pennsylvania*; Jerry Dunn, *Texas Tech University*; Tom Kisko, *University of Florida*; and George Leach, *St. Petersburg Jr. College*.

The principal reviewers were most essential in suggesting improvements and finding errors. They include William Beckwith, *Clemson University*; John D. Carpinelli, *New Jersey Institute of Technology*; John J. Goda, Jr., *Georgia Institute of Technology*; Dr. Rick Lejk, *University of North Carolina*; Philip Liu, *Cornell University*; Mary Louros, *University of Southern California*; Migri Prucz, *West Virginia University*; Howard Saltsburg, *University of Rochester*; Frazer Williams, *University of Nebraska*; and Michael Zeiger, *Eastern Michigan University*.

Finally, a number of practicing engineers and scientists described how they use Fortran at work in the Fortran in Focus commentaries. They include John

Cagney, *Cummins Engine Company;* Jerry Dusinski, *Triangle Package Machinery Company;* Howard Fishman, *HMF Associates;* Warren James, *McDonnell Douglas Space Systems Company;* Jeffrey J. Jelicks, *Somerset Technologies, Inc.;* R. M. Jones, *John V. Volpe National Transportation Systems Center;* Rocky Nelson, *McDonnell Douglas Space Systems Company;* Robert Panoff, *North Carolina Supercomputing Center;* Mark Potapczuk, *NASA Lewis Research Center;* Sal Profeta, *Glaxo Pharmaceuticals;* and Dan Wang, *Metcalf & Eddy.*

We are grateful to everyone listed above for their significant contributions.

We would also like to acknowledge the contribution of Professor Richard Epstein of West Chester University, who helped with the preparation of much of the material in Chapters 11 and 12.

The personnel at Addison-Wesley responsible for the production of this book worked diligently to meet a very demanding schedule. Our sponsoring editor, Lynne Doran Cote, was closely involved in all phases of the manuscript preparation and provided much help and guidance. Her assistant, Andrea Danese, was very effective in contacting reviewers and keeping the review process on schedule. She also helped coordinate the Fortran in Focus commentaries. Loren Hilgenhurst Stevens supervised the design and production of the book, while Martha Morong and Geri Davis coordinated the conversion of the manuscript to a finished book. We are grateful to all of them for their considerable efforts on our behalf.

E.B.K.
F.L.F.

Contents

1 Introduction to Computers and Programming   1

2 Problem Solving and Fortran   25

3 Decisions and the IF Statement   91

4 Repetition and Loops   152

5 FORMAT Statements and Introduction to Files   220

6 Top-Down Design with Subprograms   274

7 Arrays   336

8   More Arrays and Subprograms   406

9   Sequential and Direct Access Files   478

10 String Manipulation   522

11 Plotting Functions and Computer-Aided Design   566

12 Introduction to Numerical Methods   600

Application Areas

Mechanical Engineering

Natural and Physical Sciences

CHAPTER 1
Introduction to Computers and Programming

Since the 1940s, the development of the computer has spurred the growth of technology into realms only dreamed of at the start of the century. The computer has dramatically changed the way we live and how we do business. We depend on computers to send rockets into space, design and build cars and machines of all types, control chemical plants and nuclear reactors, help us do our shopping and banking—and the possibilities seem endless.

A computer system consists of two major components. The first is *hardware*, that is, the equipment used to perform the necessary computations. Hardware includes various parts such as central processing units, keyboards, monitors (display devices), and printers. We will discuss the hardware components of a computer system shortly. The second essential major component is *software*, that is, *programs*. Programs enable us to communicate with the machines by providing the computer with the instructions it needs to operate; without them, a computer is virtually useless. These instructions are usually written in special computer programming languages such as Fortran, which is the subject of this book.

In this chapter, we introduce you to the computer and its components and review its history. We also describe the different categories of computers and programming languages.

1.1 Electronic Computers Then and Now

It is difficult for people to live today without having some contact with computers. But it wasn't always this way. Not long ago, most people considered computers to be mysterious devices whose secrets were known by only a few computer wizards. However, as advances in solid-state electronics led to large reductions in the size and cost of electronic computers, more of the general populace have been willing and able to use them. Today, a common sight in most offices and many homes is the personal computer (see Fig. 1.1), which can cost less than $2000 and sit on a desk, and yet has as much computational power as one that 10 years ago would have cost more than $100,000 and filled a 9- by 12-ft room. (This price reduction is even more remarkable when we consider the effects of inflation over the last decade.)

Brief History of Computers

If we accept the literal definition of a computer as being a device for counting or computing, then the abacus might be considered the first computer. Table 1.1 lists some of the important milestones along the path from the abacus to modern-day computers and programming languages.

Well into the twentieth century, computers were large and laborious devices. Advancements in their development were slow. The first major improvement was in the form of a computer that used electronic switching

Figure 1.1. *IBM Computer with Mouse*

circuits. Designed in the late 1930s by Dr. John Atanasoff at Iowa State University, this computer enabled graduate students to perform the calculations necessary for nuclear physics research.

In 1946, the first large-scale, general-purpose electronic digital computer was built at the University of Pennsylvania with funding supplied by the U.S. Army. Called the Electronic Numerical Integrator And Computer, or ENIAC for short, it weighed 30 tons, occupied a 30- by 50-ft space, and could perform 300 multiplications per second (see Fig. 1.2).

As its switching component, the ENIAC used vacuum tubes. Electronic computers such as the ENIAC built between 1939 and 1957 typically used vacuum tubes and are usually referred to as *first-generation* computers. They were used primarily in scientific and mathematical contexts, such as for ballistics tables computation, weather prediction, and atomic energy calculations. Unfortunately, these computers operated very slowly and the vacuum tubes tended to overheat and burn out quickly. Consequently, the computers in this generation were expensive and highly unreliable. They soon gave way to the next generation of computers.

The *second generation* began in 1958 with the changeover from vacuum tubes to transistors as the switching component. Transistors generated less heat, were more compact, and were more reliable than vacuum tubes, resulting in computers that were faster, smaller, and less expensive than those of the first generation. Consequently, this generation marked the first time that business became the primary user of computers and soon accounting, payroll, and other business applications were being run on the machines.

Figure 1.2. *The ENIAC Computer (Photo courtesy of Unisys Corporation)*

The *third generation* followed quickly when in 1964, integrated circuits were introduced. This advancement resulted in increased miniaturization in computer circuitry and faster computational capability. An *integrated circuit* is an electronic component with the functionality of several transistors and their interconnections whose overall size is comparable to that of a single transistor.

Then, in 1975, the *fourth generation* was ushered in with the advent of large-scale integration. *Large-scale integration* enables semiconductor device manufacturers to package computer processors in a single electronic component (called a *computer chip*) about the size of a postage stamp. The affordability and small size of these devices enable computer chips to be installed in pocket calculators, watches, automobiles, microwave ovens, and, of course, personal computers. As you can see, each generation of computers has been faster, smaller, and less expensive than the generation that preceded it.

Programming, too, has undergone significant changes over the years. Initially, it was very difficult to program computers. Programmers for the ENIAC computer constructed their programs by running wires between connection points on special circuit boards. Other early programmers wrote program instructions as long binary numbers (zeros and ones). Today it is much easier to program because we can use high-level programming languages like Fortran or MATLAB. Table 1.1 lists some of the key developments in programming languages; we discuss categories of programming languages in Section 1.3.

Table 1.1. *Milestones in Computer Development*

2000 B.C.	The abacus is first used for computations.
1642 A.D.	Blaise Pascal creates a mechanical adding machine for tax computations. This machine is unreliable.
1670	Gottfried von Leibniz creates a more reliable adding machine that adds, subtracts, multiplies, and divides, and calculates square roots.
1842	Charles Babbage designs an analytical engine to perform general calculations automatically. Ada Augusta (a.k.a., Lady Lovelace) is a programmer for this machine.
1890	Herman Hollerith designs a system to record census data. The information is stored as holes on cards which are interpreted by machines with electrical sensors. Hollerith starts a company that will eventually become IBM.
1939	John Atanasoff designs and builds (with graduate student Clifford Berry) the first electronic digital computer. His project was funded by a grant for $650.
1946	J. Presper Eckert and John Mauchly design and build the ENIAC computer. The ENIAC used 18,000 vacuum tubes and cost $500,000 to build.
1946	John von Neumann proposes that a program be stored in a computer in the same way that data are stored. His proposal, called ''von Neumann architecture,'' is the basis of modern computers.
1951	Eckert and Mauchly build the first general-purpose commercial computer, the UNIVAC 1.
1957	John Backus and his team at IBM complete the first Fortran compiler.
1958	IBM introduces the IBM 7090 series, the first computer series to use the transistor as a switching device.
1958	Seymour Cray builds the first fully transistorized computer, the CDC 1604, for Control Data Corporation.
1962	Fortran IV is first introduced for IBM computers. Its standard is approved by the American National Standards Institute (ANSI) in 1966.
1964	IBM announces the IBM 360, the first computer using integrated circuits.
1975	The first microcomputer, the Altair, is introduced.
1975	The first supercomputer, the Cray-1, is announced.
1976	Digital Equipment Corporation introduces its popular minicomputer, the VAX 11/780.
1977	Steve Wozniak and Steve Jobs found Apple Computer.
1978	Fortran 77 is approved by ANSI and the International Standards Organization (ISO).
1981	IBM introduces the IBM PC.
1981	Apollo Computer ships the first Domain workstation.
1988	MathWorks, Inc., develops the MATLAB software package for solving engineering and scientific numeric calculations.
1991	Fortran '90 is approved by ANSI and ISO.

Categories of Computers

Computers are classified according to their size and speed. The four categories of computers are microcomputers, minicomputers, mainframes, and super-computers.

Many of you have seen or used microcomputers such as the IBM Personal Computer (see Fig. 1.1) or the Apple Macintosh. Microcomputers are also called personal computers or desktop computers because they are self-contained, used by one person at a time, and small enough to fit on a desk. The largest microcomputers, called *workstations* (see Fig. 1.3), are commonly used by engineers to produce engineering drawings and to create and test mathematical models of new products they are designing.

Minicomputers are the next larger variety of computers. Compared to microcomputers, they generally operate faster and can store larger quantities of information. They also can serve more than one user simultaneously. A small- or medium-sized company might use a minicomputer to perform payroll computations and to track its inventory. Engineers often use them to control production plants and processes.

The next largest computer is the mainframe. A large company might have one or more mainframes at a central computing facility. Mainframes are often used as "number crunchers," that is, to generate solutions to systems of equations that are characteristic of engineering or scientific problems. A mainframe can solve in seconds equations that might take hours to resolve on a minicomputer or even days on a microcomputer.

Figure 1.3. *SUN Microsystems SPARCstation 370 (Photo courtesy of Sun Microsystems, Inc.)*

The largest computer is the supercomputer. Possessing the computing power of several mainframes, it can solve the most complex systems of equations. For example, a supercomputer could be used to solve the equations describing the motion of atomic particles. Because they generally are too expensive for individual companies or universities to purchase, several supercomputer centers have been established in the United States to make this equipment more accessible to those who need their computational power.

Tremendous changes in the speed and size of computers have occurred over a relatively short time; consequently, the boundary lines between computer categories are constantly shifting. For example, in the late 1950s, mainframes could perform only fifty instructions per second. Today, there are much smaller workstations that can perform over twenty million instructions per second.

1.2   Components of a Computer

Despite significant variations in cost, size, and capabilities, modern computers resemble each other in many basic ways. Essentially, most consist of the following components:

- Main memory
- Secondary memory, which includes storage devices such as hard and floppy disks
- Input devices, such as keyboards and mouses
- Central processing unit
- Output devices, such as display devices (monitors) and printers

Figure 1.4 shows how these components would be connected in a computer system; the arrows connecting the components show the direction of information flow.

All data to be processed by a computer first must be entered into the computer's *main memory* via an *input device*. The data in main memory are then manipulated by the *central processing unit*, with the results of this manipulation stored in *secondary memory*. Information in main memory can be displayed through an *output device*.

In the next several sections that follow, we define these components and describe in more detail how they interact.

Memory

Memory is an essential component to any computer. Before discussing the types of memory—main and secondary—let's first look at what it consists of and how the computer works with it.

Figure 1.4. *Components of a Computer*

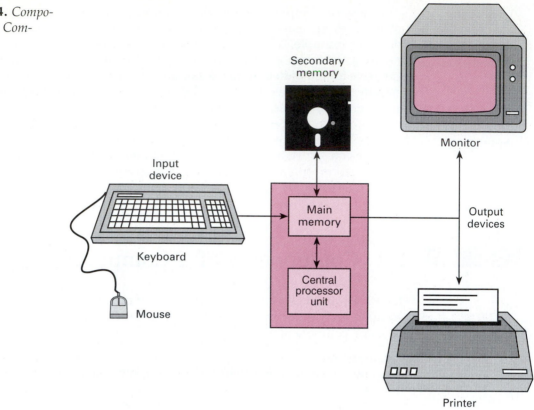

Secondary memory

Input device

Keyboard

Mouse

Main memory

Central processor unit

Monitor

Output devices

Printer

Anatomy of Memory Picture the memory of a computer as an ordered sequence of storage locations called *memory cells* (see Fig. 1.5). To store and retrieve (access) information, the computer must have some way of identifying the individual memory cells. Therefore each memory cell has associated with it a unique address that indicates its relative position in memory. Figure 1.5 shows a computer memory consisting of 1000 memory cells with addresses 0 through 999. Most large-scale computers have memories consisting of many millions of individual cells, while most personal computers have one million memory cells or less.

The data stored in a memory cell are called the *contents* of the cell. Every memory cell always contains some contents, although we may have no idea what they are. In Fig. 1.5, the contents of memory cell 3 is the number -26 and the contents of memory cell 4 is the letter H.

A memory cell is actually an aggregate, or collection, of smaller units called bytes. A *byte* is the amount of storage required to store a single character, such as the letter H used in our figure. The number of bytes a memory cell may contain will vary from computer to computer.

A byte is a collection of even smaller units of storage called bits. The term *bit* derives from the words **bi**nary dig**it** and is the smallest element a computer can deal with. *Binary* refers to a number system based on two numbers, in this case, 0 and 1; therefore a bit is either a 0 or a 1. Generally, there are eight bits to a byte.

Each character or set of characters, or *value*, is represented by a particular pattern of zeros and ones, that is, bits. A computer can either *store* a value or *retrieve* a value. To store a value, the computer sets each bit of a selected memory cell to either 0 or 1; storing a value replaces the previous contents of the cell, that is, the contents are destroyed and cannot be retrieved. To retrieve a value from a memory cell, the computer copies the pattern of 0s and 1s stored in that cell to another storage area, the memory buffer register, where the bit pattern then can be processed; the copy operation does not destroy the bit pattern currently in the memory cell.

This process is the same regardless of the kind of information—character, number, or program instruction—stored in a memory cell.

Main Memory   Main memory is used to store programs and certain data such as those used for arithmetic and logical operations. For example, in most computers, there are two types of main memory: *random access memory* (*RAM*), which offers temporary storage of programs and data, and *read-only memory* (*ROM*), which stores certain data permanently.

Figure 1.5. *A Computer Memory with 1000 Cells*

Memory

Address	Contents
0	−27.2
1	354
2	0.005
3	−26
4	H
.	.
.	.
.	.
998	X
999	75.62

RAM is used for temporarily storing programs while they are being executed by the computer. It also temporarily stores such data as numbers, names, lists, and even pictures while you are manipulating them. RAM is usually volatile memory, which means that when you turn off your computer, you will lose everything in RAM unless you first store it in secondary memory, which provides for a semipermanent storage of data.

ROM, on the other hand, stores information permanently within the computer. The computer can read this type of memory but cannot write to it—that is, it prevents you from making changes to the data stored there, hence its name, read-only. Because it is not volatile, the data stored in ROM memory do not disappear when you shut off the computer. Usually ROM is used to store the information needed to get the computer running, among other possible information.

Secondary Memory and Storage Devices   Secondary memory, via secondary storage devices, provides semi-permanent data-storage capability. For example, a common secondary storage device for today's personal computers is a *disk drive*, which stores data on a storage medium called a *disk*.

There are two kinds of drives: hard (also called fixed) and floppy. A computer may have one or more drives of each kind. A hard drive records data onto a hard disk, which normally cannot be removed from its drive; therefore the storage area on a hard disk can be shared by all the users of the computer. However, each user may have his or her own floppy disks that can be inserted into a floppy disk drive (see Fig. 1.6). Hard disks can store much more data than can floppy disks and the CPU can retrieve data from and store it to a

Figure 1.6. *Inserting a Floppy Disk into a Floppy Disk Drive*

hard drive much faster than it can with a floppy. However, hard drives lack the portability that floppy drives offer.

Comparison of Main and Secondary Memory   The computer can manipulate only data that are in main memory; therefore data in secondary memory must be transferred to main memory before they can be processed. For this reason, the computer manipulates data already in main memory faster than it does that in secondary memory. Further, data in main memory are volatile and disappear when you switch off the computer, while that in secondary memory are permanent and do not disappear when the computer is switched off. Main memory is limited in size, but secondary memory is unlimited.

Central Processor Unit

The *central processor unit*, or CPU, follows the instructions contained in a computer program to coordinate all activities of the computer. It determines which operations should be carried out and in what order and then transmits coordinating control signals to the various computer components.

The CPU retrieves information, which may be either data or instructions for manipulating data, from secondary memory, that is, from a hard or floppy disk, and brings it into main memory. Once the instructions and data are in main memory, the CPU then performs the actual manipulation, or processing, of the data. The CPU stores the results temporarily in main memory, but it can also store them back in secondary memory for later use.

The CPU can perform a variety of arithmetic operations, including addition, subtraction, multiplication, and division. A typical CPU can perform an arithmetic operation in about a millionth of a second. The unit also consists of electronic circuitry to compare information and to make decisions based on the results of the comparison.

Input and Output Devices

Input and output (I/O) devices enable us to communicate with the computer. Specifically, I/O devices provide us with the means to enter data for a computation and to observe the results of that computation.

A common I/O device used with computers is the computer terminal. A *computer terminal* is both an input and an output device. A terminal typically consists of a *keyboard*, which is used for entering data, and a display screen, or *monitor*, which is used for displaying the results of data manipulation. The keyboard and monitor are connected to a computer by cables.

A computer keyboard resembles a typewriter keyboard. When you press a letter or digit key, that character is sent to the computer and is also displayed on the monitor at the position of the *cursor*, a moving placemarker. A keyboard has extra keys for performing special functions. For example, on the IBM PC/AT keyboard shown in Fig. 1.7, the 12 keys in the top row labeled F1 through

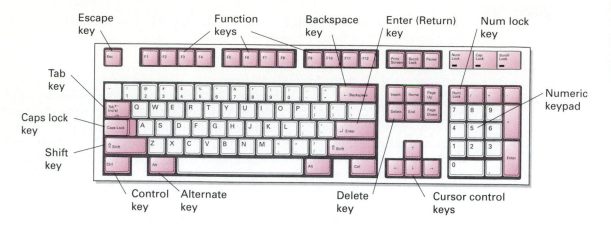

Figure 1.7. *Keyboard for the IBM PC/AT*

F12 are *function keys.* The activity performed by pressing a function key depends on the program currently being executed; that is, pressing F1 in one program will usually not produce the results of pressing F1 in another program. Other special keys enable you to delete characters, move the cursor, and "enter" a line of data you typed at the keyboard (see the highlighted parts of Fig. 1.7).

Another common input device is a mouse (see Fig. 1.1). A *mouse* is a handheld device that attaches to the computer with a cable and contains a rubber ball. You use the mouse by moving it around on your desktop, which causes the rubber ball to move. As the ball moves, so does an arrow on the monitor's screen. You can use the mouse in this way to select an operation by moving the arrow to an *icon,* which is a picture on the screen that represents the operation you want performed, or to an item displayed in a menu. You then *select* the icon or menu item by pressing one of the mouse's buttons.

Another type of output device is a printer. The information displayed on a monitor screen does not represent a permanent record of the information shown; when you turn off the computer, this information is lost unless you either store it in secondary memory or send your computational results to a printer. A *printer* produces *hard copies,* or printed versions, of whatever data you send to it.

EXERCISES FOR SECTION 1.2

Self-check

1. What are the contents of memory cells 0 and 999 in Fig. 1.5? What memory cells contain the letter X and the fraction 0.005?
2. What is the purpose of main memory, secondary memory, the central processing unit, the disk drive, and a disk? What input and output devices will be used with your computer?

1.3 Overview of Programming Languages

So far we have discussed computer hardware. It is the computer's software, or programs, that enable it to do useful work. A *program* is a list of instructions to be carried out by the computer. Often, we separate software into two categories: system software and application software. *System software* performs tasks required for the operation of the computer system; *application software* is written to perform a particular task for the person who is using the computer. The software (programs) in this book are all applications software.

We use programming languages to write computer programs. Although there are many different programming languages, the most commonly used today are the high-level languages.

A *high-level language* enables us to write programs in everyday language. To understand the importance of this feature to program writing, it is necessary first to understand how a computer communicates.

The native tongue of a computer is *machine language*. Each machine language instruction is a binary string of 0s and 1s that specifies an operation and the memory cells involved in the operation. For example, a sequence of instructions in machine language might look like the following:

```
0010 0000 0000 0100
0100 0000 0000 0101
0011 0000 0000 0110
```

Translated into English or into Fortran, this sequence would read:

```
PRICE = COST + PROFIT
```

which means add COST to PROFIT and store the result in PRICE. As you can see, what is easiest for a computer to understand can be very difficult for a person. Similarly, the English language can be just as difficult for a computer to understand, unless we happen to be using a high-level language, such as Fortran.

Using such a language, we can reference data that are stored in memory using descriptive names—for example, NAME, RATE, RADIUS, WEIGHT—rather than numeric memory-cell addresses. We can also use familiar symbols to describe operations we would like performed. Hence, writing programs using a high-level language is much easier than writing programs with other types of languages.

Common high-level languages include Fortran, BASIC, COBOL, Pascal, C, Ada, and MATLAB. Each of these languages was designed with a specific purpose in mind. Fortran is an acronym for FORmula TRANslation; its principal users have been engineers and scientists. BASIC (Beginners All-purpose

Symbolic Instructional Code) was designed to be easily learned and used by students. COBOL (COmmon Business Oriented Language) is used primarily for business data-processing operations. Pascal was designed as a language for teaching structured programming techniques (we'll have more on this later). C is a very powerful and flexible language that programmers often employ to write system software. Ada is a language developed by the Department of Defense for use by their contractors; for example, an Ada program could be used to control missiles. MATLAB is used to perform engineering and scientific numeric computations and is much easier to use for this purpose than any of the other languages described above.

Recall that a computer can execute only programs that are in machine language. Therefore a high-level language program first must be translated into machine language. This process is described in the next section.

FORTRAN in Focus

A Tool for Engineering

CUMMINS ENGINE COMPANY

Cummins Engine Company, headquartered in Columbus, Indiana, is the number-one producer of diesel engines and related components (such as turbochargers) in the world. They design and manufacture diesel engines ranging up to 2000 HP, and their products are used in over-the-road trucks, Dodge pickup trucks, and farm and industrial equipment, among others.

Many departments at Cummins use Fortran to solve engineering problems. Most Fortran users work at the Cummins Technical Center (CTC) or perform work affiliated with CTC. Modeling physical systems is an important part of the engineering design and development

work that the center undertakes, and probabilistic dynamic analysis is one of the applications for which Fortran is used.

A series of Fortran programs running on Sun Sparc workstations simulate actual engine assembly and operation. Analysts seeking to predict the performance of an engine gather information from the assembly line, engineering drawings, and solid modeling software, and then input operating conditions and engine characteristics, both geometric and mass, into the engine simulation. The programs draw on the numerical relationships underlying the simulation to produce a set of data on engine performance.

**EXERCISES FOR
SECTION 1.3**

Self-check

1. What do you think the high-level language statements below mean?

```
X = A + B + C
X = Y / Z
D = C - B + A
X = X + 1
```

2. Which high-level language was designed for teaching programming? Which for business applications? Which for translating scientific formulas?
3. Which type of language has instructions such as $X = X + Y$? Which type has instructions that are binary numbers?

Although there are Fortran programmers on staff to maintain the local area network and provide support to the engineers, the programs to simulate physical systems are generally written by the engineers themselves. A large part of developing the application is working out the theory behind the engine's operation and selecting the appropriate numerical techniques for the simulation. To program a complex physical system effectively, it is important to understand both the theory and Fortran. Most of the engineers select Fortran both because of its suitability for engineering work and because they are familiar with it. A small number of people also program in C.

For John Cagney, Senior Engineer, Fortran is a logically created tool that he can use to communicate his ideas to the computer. For him, there are no real advantages to using any other language for engineering analy-

ses. For students, he feels Fortran presents some real advantages. It is relatively easy to learn, and has an internal logic well-suited to engineering applications. Just as important, the large number of people who know and use Fortran give a beginning programmer or engineer many sources of information as his or her knowledge of the language "ramps up." In the workplace, these sources of information can be a significant advantage.

We would like to thank John Cagney, Senior Engineer for Structural Components Design in the Cummins Technical Center, for telling us about the use of Fortran in his work.

1.4 Preparing a Program for Processing and Execution

The first step in preparing a Fortran program is to write it and then enter it (type it in) at the terminal using the keyboard. Part of this process includes using an *editor* program, which is part of the system software designed specifically for entering the program statements. You then would save the program as a source file on a disk. A *file* is a collection of data that pertain to a specific application. You must give each file a unique name when you first save it on disk so the computer can retrieve it later. A *source file* is a file that contains a program.

A Sample Fortran Program

Before beginning our in-depth study of Fortran, we will examine a short program. Don't worry about understanding the details of this programs yet; they will all be explained later.

EXAMPLE 1.1

Figure 1.8 contains a Fortran program (its last line is END) followed by a sample execution of that program. Note that the information entered by the user of the program is in color in the sample execution.

The program user enters the cross-sectional area (its value is 25.5) and length (its value is 65.0) of a steel beam. The program then computes the beam's volume (volume = area × length) and weight (weight = volume × density, where the density of steel is assumed to be 0.28 lb/cu in.). The beam's volume and weight are displayed in the last two lines of Fig. 1.8.

Figure 1.8. *Sample Fortran Program*

```
PROGRAM BEAM
REAL DENSTY
PARAMETER (DENSTY = 0.28)
REAL AREA, LENGTH, VOLUME, WEIGHT

PRINT *, 'Enter cross-sectional area in square inches'
READ *, AREA
PRINT *, 'Enter beam length in inches'

READ *, LENGTH
VOLUME = AREA * LENGTH
WEIGHT = DENSTY * VOLUME

PRINT *, 'Volume in cubic inches is ', VOLUME
PRINT *, 'Weight in pounds is ', WEIGHT
```

```
        STOP
        END


Enter cross-sectional area in square inches
25.5
Enter beam length in inches
65.0
Volume in cubic inches is      1657.50
Weight in pounds is      464.100
```

Preparing a Program for Processing   Preparing a program for execution involves the following steps:

1. After you save your program in a source file, the computer must translate it into machine language (see Fig. 1.9) using a *compiler program,* which processes the source file. The compiler will attempt to translate each statement, but often, one or more statements in the source file will contain a *syntax error,* or grammar error, which means that these statements do not correspond exactly to the syntax (grammar) of the high-level language. When this happens, the compiler will display pertinent error messages to warn you of the problem. At this point, you can make changes to your source file and have the compiler process it again.
2. Provided that there are no more errors, the compiler next will create an *object file,* which contains your program translated into machine language and which is generally stored in secondary memory.
3. A *linker program* then will combine the object file with any additional object files (for example, programs for input and output) that may be needed into a *load file,* or *executable file,* which is a file that is ready for execution.
4. Finally, a *loader program* will place the load file into main memory.

This process is shown in Fig. 1.9. The editor, compiler, linker, and loader programs are part of the system software.

Executing a Program   Executing a program involves the following steps:

1. The CPU examines each program instruction in main memory and sends out the command signals required to carry out the instructions. Normally, the instructions are executed in sequence; however, as we will see in later chapters, the CPU may skip over some instructions or execute some instructions more than once.
2. During execution, data may be entered into memory and manipulated in some specified way. Then, the result of this data manipulation is stored temporarily in main memory and may be displayed on your monitor.

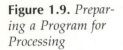

Figure 1.9. *Preparing a Program for Processing*

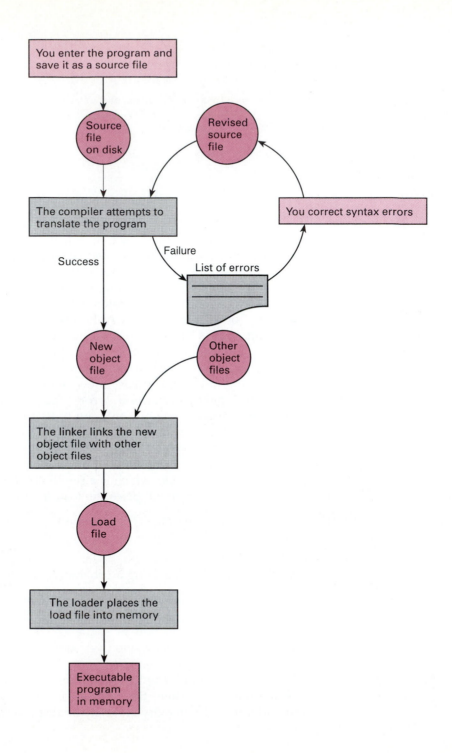

Figure 1.10 shows the effect of executing the program shown earlier for computing the volume and weight of a steel beam. First, the cross-sectional area and length of the beam were entered. Then, those data were manipulated by the CPU as directed by the program, with the results of the computations stored in main memory. And finally, the computational results were displayed on the screen.

**EXERCISES FOR
SECTION 1.4**

Self-check

1. What is the role of the compiler? What is a syntax error? Which file can contain syntax errors?
2. What is the source file? An object file? A load file? Which do you create and which does the compiler create? Which does the linker create and which is processed by the loader? What do the linker and loader do?

Figure 1.10. *Flow of Information During Program Execution*

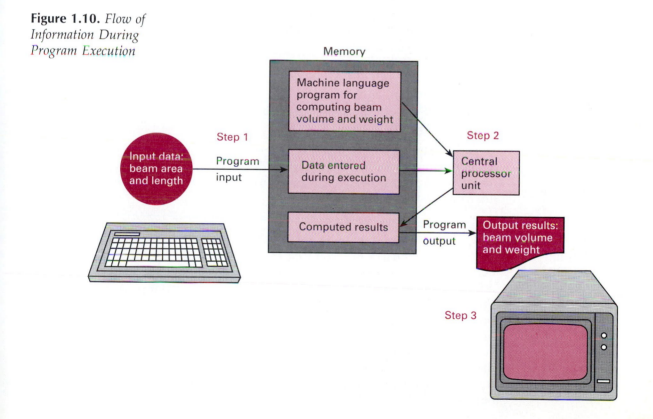

1.5 Using a Computer

We discussed the process of preparing and executing a program in the last section. The mechanics of doing this differ on each computer system; we provide a general description of the process in this section.

Operating Systems

As you work with the material in this book and later as you use Fortran in your work and studies, you will probably be using either of the following types of computers: a personal computer (PC) or a time-shared computer, where many users are connected by terminals to one central computer and all users share the central facilities. (Universities often use these computers for instructional purposes.) Regardless of the type of computer you use, you will need to interact with a supervisory program, called the operating system. The *operating system* performs many tasks, such as

- making the editor, compiler, linker, or loader programs available,
- allocating memory and processor time,
- providing input and output facilities,
- retrieving needed files,
- saving new files,
- validating user identification and account number (applies only to a time-shared system), and
- allocating the central resources among many users (applies only to a time-shared system).

Each computer has its own special control language for communicating with its operating system. We cannot provide the details here, but we will discuss the general process next. Your instructor will provide the specific commands for your system.

Booting or Logging On

Before you can use a PC, you first must *boot*, or start up, the computer. On computers with a hard disk, you need only switch on the computer. To boot a PC without a hard drive usually involves inserting a floppy disk containing the operating system into disk drive A and switching on the computer. Once booted, the operating system displays a *prompt* (for example, A>, if you booted using a floppy, or C>, if you booted from a hard drive), which indicates the computer is ready to accept commands. Figure 1.11 demonstrates the result of booting an IBM Personal Computer using a floppy drive and the MS-DOS (the Microsoft Disk Operating System) operating system. The computer user enters the characters that are in color; the other characters are those that the

Figure 1.11. *Booting a Personal Computer*

```
MS-DOS Version 3.3
Current date is Tue 1-01-1980
Enter new date: 4-05-92
Current time is 0:01:43.53
Enter new time: 10:30
A>
```

operating system displays. (See Appendix C for more information on MS-DOS.)

Before you can use a time-shared computer, you must *log on,* or connect, to the computer. To log on, you enter your account name and your password (given to you by your instructor). (Note that for security reasons, your password is not displayed.) Figure 1.12 demonstrates this process for the Digital Equipment Corporation VAX computer. The computer user enters the characters that are in color; the other characters are those the operating system displays. Observe that the time-shared operating system VMS Version 5.1 used in this figure displays the symbol $ as a prompt.

**Creating a
Source File**

Once you have booted your personal computer or logged on to a time-shared computer, you can begin to create your program. In most cases, you will use the editor program to enter your Fortran program and save it temporarily in main memory. If you want a record of the program once it is entered, you must save it as a permanent file on disk in secondary memory; otherwise, your program will disappear when your session with the editor is over. Follow these steps to create and save a program file:

1. Log on to a time-shared computer or boot up a personal computer.
2. Access the editor program.
3. Enter each line of the program you have written.
4. Name your file and save it as a permanent file in secondary memory.
5. Exit from the editor.

Figure 1.12. *Logging On to a Time-shared Computer*

```
Username: Koffman
Password: (Password is not displayed when you enter it.)

CIS Department Vax-11/780 VMS V5.1

Last interactive login on Friday, 28-April-1992 10:20

$
```

Make sure you remember to perform step 4. The file created by the editor program will be stored in main memory; however, unless you save your editor file in secondary memory, it will be lost when you exit the editor program.

Running the Program

Once you have entered your program and you are satisfied that each line is correct, you can attempt to compile, link, load, and execute it, as explained in Section 1.4. On some systems you must give three separate commands to initiate this sequence of operations; on other systems one command, such as RUN, will suffice to initiate the sequence.

If your program will not compile because it contains syntax errors, you must edit, or correct, the program. Follow these steps to correct and reexecute a program file:

1. Reaccess the editor program.
2. Retrieve your program file.
3. Correct the statements containing syntax errors.
4. Save your edited program file.
5. Compile, link, load, and execute the new program file.

EXERCISES FOR SECTION 1.5

Self-check

1. Will you be using a personal computer or a time-shared computer? What model computer? What operating system? What is the operating system command to enter the editor, to compile a program, to link a program, to load and run a program?

Programming

1. Try to enter and save the program shown in Fig. 1.8 as a source file on your computer system. Each Fortran statement should begin in column 7, so move the cursor to column 7 by pressing the space bar or Tab key on your keyboard. Press the Enter or Return key after you type in each statement. After you save the program on disk, attempt to compile and run it.

Chapter Review

In this chapter, we briefly reviewed the history of computer and software development. We discussed the four generations of computers and described the different categories of computers: microcomputers, minicomputers, mainframes, and supercomputers. We learned that larger computers are generally faster and more powerful than smaller computers. We also introduced the basic components of a computer: main memory, secondary memory, the central processing unit (CPU), disks and disk drives, and input and output devices. The following facts are important to remember about computers:

1. A memory cell is never empty, but its initial contents may be meaningless to your program.
2. When data are *stored* in a memory cell, the current contents of that cell are destroyed and replaced with the new data. When data are *retrieved* from a memory cell, the contents are copied and the original contents in the cell remain as they were.
3. Programs must first be placed in the main memory of the computer before they can be executed.
4. Data cannot be manipulated by the computer until they are first brought into main memory.
5. A computer cannot think for itself; you must instruct it how to perform a task by writing a program.
6. Programming a computer can be fun—if you are patient, organized, and careful.

We also described the differences between high-level languages and machine language and gave an example of a program in the high-level language, Fortran. We described the following basic steps involved in working with Fortran:

1. Entering a program using an editor program
2. Preparing a program for processing and execution

Finally, we discussed how to use a computer and its operating system to accomplish these tasks.

In the remainder of the text, we introduce you to features of the Fortran language and provide rules for using these features.

Quick-check Exercises

1. The _____ translates a(n) _____ program into _____.
2. After a program is executed, all program results are automatically displayed. True or false?
3. Specify the correct order for these four operations: execution, linking, translation, loading.
4. A high-level language program is saved on disk as a(n) _____ file.
5. The _____ finds _____ errors in the _____ file.
6. A machine language program is saved on disk as a(n) _____ file.
7. The _____ is used to create and save the source file.
8. The _____ creates the load file.
9. The _____ places the _____ file into memory.
10. Computers are becoming (more/less) expensive and (bigger/smaller) in size.
11. The _____ was the first large-scale, general-purpose electronic computer. It (was/was not) a stored-program computer.

12. Indicate whether each characteristic that follows applies to secondary memory or main memory.

   a. Provides permanent storage of files
   b. Is used by the editor program for temporary storage of a new file
   c. Provides storage of data and program results during program execution
   d. Provides relatively inexpensive storage
   e. Provides limited quantity of storage
   f. Is accessed by the CPU during program execution

Answers to Quick-check Exercises

1. compiler, high-level language, machine language
2. false
3. translation, linking, loading, execution
4. source
5. compiler, source
6. object
7. editor
8. linker
9. loader, load
10. less expensive, smaller
11. ENIAC, was not
12. secondary, main, main, secondary, main, main

Review Questions

1. List at least three kinds of information stored in a computer.
2. List two functions of the CPU.
3. List two input devices, two output devices, and two secondary storage devices.
4. A computer can think. True or false?
5. List two categories of programming languages.
6. Give three advantages of programming in a high-level language such as Fortran.
7. Differentiate between system software and application software.
8. What processes are needed to transform a Fortran program to a machine-language program ready for execution?
9. Describe the purpose of the following computer components: main memory, secondary memory, central processing unit.
10. Which memory component provides permanent storage for program files? Which is less expensive? Which is limited in size?

CHAPTER 2
Problem Solving and Fortran

PROGRAMMING IS predominantly a problem-solving activity. Therefore if you are an effective problem solver, you can probably become a good programmer. One important goal of this book is to help you improve your problem solving ability. Because we believe each programming problem should be approached in a systematic and consistent way, we show you in this chapter how to apply the software engineering method of problem solving to programming.

This chapter also introduces Fortran, the first high-level programming language. Developed in 1957 by a programming team led by IBM's John Backus, Fortran originally was used primarily for scientific computation; it has since evolved into a language suitable for many different kinds of programming applications. For example, more recent versions have been designed to facilitate writing *structured programs*—programs that are relatively easy to read, understand, and keep in good working order.

A *language standard* describes all Fortran language statements and specifies their syntax, thus ensuring that a Fortran program written on one computer will execute on another computer. Currently, there are two standard versions of Fortran—Fortran 77 and Fortran 90. Fortran 90 is so new only a few compilers can now translate its programs. However, all Fortran 77 programs can be translated by either a Fortran 77 or a Fortran 90 compiler. For this reason, we stress Fortran 77 in this book; however, we describe new features of Fortran 90 in separate sections of the book so you will know what changes to expect.

2.1 Problem Solving and Programming

To succeed in academics or in the real world, you must be able to solve problems. Students in many subject areas receive instruction in specific problem-solving methods; for example, business students are taught a *systems approach*, while engineering and science students are encouraged to follow the *engineering and scientific method*. Programmers use a widely practiced technique for solving programming problems called the *software engineering method*, which we describe next.

Software Engineering Method

The software engineering method of problem solving uses the following five steps:

1. Specify the problem requirements.
2. Analyze the problem.
3. Design the algorithm to solve the problem.
4. Implement the algorithm.
5. Test and verify the completed program.

Specifying the problem requirements forces you to state the problem completely and unambiguously and to gain a clear understanding of what its solution requires. This may sound easy, but it can be difficult. You must be able to recognize and define the problem precisely, to eliminate unimportant aspects and zero in on the root problem. As needed, you should request more information from the person who posed the problem.

Analyzing the problem involves identifying the problem (a) *inputs*, i.e., the data you have to work with; (b) *outputs*, i.e., the desired results; and (c) any additional requirements for or constraints on the solution. At this stage, you also determine the required format in which the results should be displayed (for example, as a table with specific column headings) and develop a list of problem variables and their relationships. (These relationships may be expressed as formulas.)

These first two steps are the most critical; if they are not done properly, you will be trying to solve the wrong problem. Read the problem statement carefully, first, to obtain a clear idea of the problem and second, to determine the inputs and outputs. (You may find it helpful to underline phrases in the problem statement that identify them.)

Once you know the inputs and outputs, you should then develop a list of formulas that specify relationships between them by selecting theories or scientific principles that apply to the problem. For example, if the problem inputs are *distance traveled* and *time* and the desired output is *average speed,* the formula that applies is

speed = distance/time.

In some situations, you may have to make certain assumptions or simplifications in order to derive these relationships. This process of extracting the essential variables and their relationships from the problem statement is called *abstraction.*

Designing the algorithm to solve the problem requires you to write step-by-step procedures and then verify that these procedures—the *algorithm*—solve the problem as intended.

Writing the algorithm is often the most difficult part of the problem-solving process. Don't attempt to solve every last detail of the problem at the beginning; instead, discipline yourself to use *top-down design.* In top-down design, you first list the major steps (called *subproblems*) that need to be solved. Most computer algorithms consist of at least the following subproblems:

1. Read the data.
2. Perform the computations.
3. Display the results.

Also, don't try to list each and every step imaginable. Instead, concentrate on the overall strategy. Once you know the subproblems, you can attack each one individually. For example, step 2 is generally the most difficult and may need to be broken down into smaller steps called *algorithm refinements*. This process of solving a problem by breaking it up into its subproblems is also called *divide and conquer*. *Note:* Always verify that your algorithm is correct before proceeding further.

Implementing the algorithm involves writing it as a program. Doing this requires you to know a particular programming language. You must convert each algorithm step into a statement in that language.

Testing and verifying the program calls for you to test the completed program to verify it works as desired. Don't rely on just one test case—run the program several times using different sets of data.

EXERCISES FOR SECTION 2.1

Self-check

1. List the five steps of the software engineering method.
2. In which phase is the algorithm developed? In which phase do you identify the problem inputs and outputs?

2.2 Applying the Software Engineering Method

In this textbook, we provide case study solutions for several programming problems using the software engineering method outlined above. We begin each case study with a statement of the problem. As part of the problem analysis, we then identify the problem inputs and desired outputs as a list of problem variables. Next, we develop and refine the initial algorithm and then implement this algorithm as a Fortran program. Finally, we provide a sample run of the program and discuss how we might perform a more complete test of the program.

Below, we walk you through a sample case study, in which we provide a running commentary on the process being followed so that you will be able to apply that process to other situations.

Case Study: Converting Units of Measurement

PROBLEM STATEMENT

You have a summer job as a receiving clerk for an electronics parts distributor that imports large quantities of wire and cable produced abroad and sold in the United States. Most of the wire you receive is measured in meters; however, your customers order wire by the foot. Consequently, your supervisor wants you to compute the length in feet of each roll of wire or cable that you stock. You need to write a program to perform this conversion.

ANALYSIS

The first step in understanding this problem is to determine what you are being asked to do. You must convert from one system of measurement to another, but are you supposed to convert from meters to feet, or vice versa? The problem statement says that you receive wire measured in meters; therefore the problem input is *wire length in meters*. Your supervisor wants to know the *equivalent amount in feet*, which is your problem output.

To solve the problem, we need to know the relationship between meters and feet. Examining a table of conversion factors, we find that one meter equals 39.37 inches. We also know that there are 12 inches in a foot. These two numbers are the constants we use for this program. The data requirements and relevant formulas are summarized below. We use the name WMETER to identify the memory cell, or *variable*, that contains the problem input and the name WFEET to identify the variable that contains the program result, or the problem output.

Data Requirements and Formulas

> *Problem Input*
>
> wire length in meters (WMETER)
>
> *Problem Output*
>
> wire length in feet (WFEET)
>
> *Additional Program Variable*
>
> wire length in inches (WINCHS)
>
> *Relevant Formulas or Relations*
>
> 1 meter = 39.37 inches
> 1 foot = 12 inches

The relationships set forth above point out the need for an additional variable, one that represents the wire length in inches. This variable, named WINCHS, is included in our data requirements summary given above. Note that we often need to introduce additional variables to hold computational results that are not problem outputs.

DESIGN

Next, we formulate the algorithm we must follow to solve the problem. We begin by listing the three major steps, or subproblems, of the algorithm. This algorithm follows the general form described earlier (read the data, perform the computations, display the results).

Algorithm

1. Read the wire length in meters.
2. Convert the wire length from meters to feet.
3. Display the wire length in feet.

We then must decide whether any steps of the algorithm need further refinement or whether they are perfectly clear as stated. Step 1 (reading data) and step 3 (displaying a value) are basic steps and require no further refinement. It would help to add some detail to step 2, however. The refinement of step 2 that follows shows how to perform the conversion.

> *Step 2 Refinement*
> 2.1 Convert the wire length from meters to inches.
> 2.2 Convert the wire length from inches to feet.

The complete algorithm with refinements is shown below. The algorithm resembles an outline for a research paper in that the refinements of step 2 are indented under that step.

Algorithm with Refinements

1. Read the wire length in meters.
2. Convert the wire length from meters to feet.
   2.1 Convert the wire length from meters to inches.
   2.2 Convert the wire length from inches to feet.
3. Display the wire length in feet.

Our next step is to implement the algorithm as a Fortran program, test it, and verify its correctness. To do this, you must first convert each algorithm step or its refinement (if it has been refined) into equivalent Fortran statements. We will do so now and explain the Fortran statements in Section 2.3.

IMPLEMENTATION

Figure 2.1 shows the Fortran program for the units conversion problem. The line END indicates the end of the Fortran program; a sample run follows the program. Each line of the program is a Fortran statement. Don't concern yourself with understanding these statements just yet; we will describe the meaning and syntax of these statements after we complete the solution to the case study. In the sample run, the number 12 is a data item entered by the program user.

TESTING AND VERIFICATION

The last step in the software engineering method is to test the program and verify that it is correct. To do so, you must compare the program results with those that you compute manually or by using a calculator.

Figure 2.1. *Converting Wire Length from Meters to Feet*

```
      PROGRAM CONVRT
C Converts wire length from meters to feet.
C The program user enters the wire length in meters.

C Declarations
      REAL INCHMT
      PARAMETER (INCHMT = 39.37)
      INTEGER INCHFT
      PARAMETER (INCHFT = 12)
      REAL WMETER, WFEET, WINCHS

C Read the wire length in meters.
      PRINT *, 'Enter the wire length in meters'
      READ *, WMETER

C Convert the wire length from meters to feet.
      WINCHS = WMETER * INCHMT
      WFEET = WINCHS / INCHFT

C Display the wire length in feet.
      PRINT *, 'The wire length in feet is ', WFEET

      STOP
      END


Enter the wire length in meters
12
The wire length in feet is      39.3700
```

The sample run in Fig. 2.1 shows that the program converts a wire length of 12 meters to 39.37 feet. You can easily compute the length in feet of a wire length of 12 meters. You multiply the conversion constant 39.37 by 12 and divide that product by 12, so the result will be 39.37 feet as shown. To complete the testing of the program, you should run it with several other values of wire length.

EXERCISES FOR SECTION 2.2

Self-check

1. Show the problem statement, analysis, and design phases for a program that converts a weight in pounds to a weight in kilograms.
2. Show the problem statement, analysis, and design phases for a program that computes the sum and average of three numbers.
3. Show the analysis and design phases for a program that solves the problem: Compute the discounted price for an item given the list price and the percentage of the discount.

2.3 Overview of Fortran

In this section, we describe the meaning and syntax of seven kinds of Fortran statements: the type declaration, PARAMETER, assignment, READ, PRINT, STOP, and END statements. They will appear in most of the programs that you write. As each new statement type is introduced, you should refer back to Fig. 2.1 to see where it appears in a Fortran program.

PROGRAM Statement

The first statement in every Fortran program is a PROGRAM *statement* that specifies the name we give to the program. The statement

```
PROGRAM CONVRT
```

gives the name CONVRT to our program. Generally we choose a program name that is indicative of the operation performed by the program (in this case, CONVeRTing units of measurement). We discuss why the name consists of only six letters later.

Comments and Declarations

The next program lines are sentences preceded by the letter C typed in column 1. These lines, called *comments,* describe what the program does. Comments are essentially ignored by the Fortran compiler and are not translated into machine language. Their sole purpose is to make it easier for someone to read and understand the program. We say more about comments in Section 2.4.

The comment line

```
C Declarations
```

precedes the program's *type declaration statements.* The type declaration statements tell the Fortran compiler what variables are used in the program and the *data type* of each variable. A type declaration statement always begins with a data type. For example, the statement

```
REAL WMETER, WFEET, WINCHS
```

tells the Fortran compiler that type REAL data will be stored in each of the three variables (WMETER, WFEET, WINCHS) used in the unit conversion program. A variable can store only one type of data.

The Fortran data types we will study are REAL, INTEGER, and CHARACTER, representing data that are either a real number with a decimal point and fractional part (e.g., 0.123, −943.25), an integer (e.g., 10, −999), or a series of characters (e.g., Sally Smith, R2D2). We discuss these data types again in Section 2.5.

We must also declare any special constants that appear in relevant formulas. For example, the numbers 39.37 and 12 are constants for the units conversion problem. The type declaration statement and PARAMETER *statement*

```
REAL INCHMT
PARAMETER (INCHMT = 39.37)
```

specify the data type (REAL) and value (39.37) of *parameter* INCHMT (abbreviation for INCHes in a MeTer). The statements

```
INTEGER INCHFT
PARAMETER (INCHFT = 12)
```

specify the data type (INTEGER) and value (12) of *parameter* INCHFT (abbreviation for INCHes in a FooT). As shown above, the data type of a parameter should be declared in a type declaration statement that precedes the PARAMETER statement.

Only data values that never change or change very rarely should be associated with a parameter. (*Note:* It is illegal to change the value of a parameter in a Fortran program.)

You have considerable freedom in selecting names (called *identifiers*) to use in Fortran programs. The syntactic rules are given below.

Rules for Fortran Identifiers

1. An identifier must always begin with an uppercase letter (A – Z).
2. An identifier must consist of only uppercase letters (A – Z) or only upper-case letters and digits in combination.
3. An identifier must consist of one to six characters.

Some valid and invalid identifiers are listed below.

Valid Identifiers

```
LET1, LET2, WINCHS, CENT, CPERIN, HELLO
```

Invalid Identifiers

```
1LET, TWO*FOUR, JOE'S, CENTPERINCH
```

The PROGRAM, data type declaration, and PARAMETER statements introduced so far are summarized in the following displays. Each display describes the syntax of the statement and provides examples and an interpretation of the statement. Each of the elements in italics is described in the interpretation section.

SYNTAX DISPLAY

Program Statement

SYNTAX: PROGRAM *programname*

EXAMPLES: PROGRAM CONVRT
         PROGRAM BUDGET

(*continued*)

INTERPRETATION: The PROGRAM statement is the first statement of a Fortran program. It identifies the name, *programname,* of the program; *programname* must follow the syntax rules for a Fortran identifier.

NOTES: The PROGRAM statement is not required in Fortran 77; however, we recommend you use it to name each Fortran program. You also should use *programname* in the name given to the source file containing that program. On many systems, the source file name should have the form *programname*.FOR. The extension part of the file name (called *file extension*), .FOR, identifies the source file as a Fortran program. Following this convention will help you remember which source file contains a particular Fortran program.

SYNTAX
DISPLAY

Type Declaration Statement

SYNTAX: REAL *variable-list*
       INTEGER *variable-list*
       CHARACTER **length variable-list*

EXAMPLES: REAL X, Y, Z
         INTEGER COUNT
         CHARACTER *12 UNITS

INTERPRETATION: A memory cell is allocated for each identifier in the *variable-list.* The type of data—(REAL, INTEGER, or CHARACTER)—to be stored in each variable (or parameter) is specified at the beginning of the statement. Commas are used to separate the identifiers in the *variable-list.* If the type is CHARACTER, the length of each character data item is specified as an integer value after the symbol *. The example above declares UNITS as a variable that can store 12 characters.

SYNTAX
DISPLAY

PARAMETER Statement

SYNTAX: PARAMETER (*parameter-list*)

EXAMPLES: PARAMETER (PI = 3.141593)
        PARAMETER (CPERIN = 2.54, FMONTH = 'JANUARY')

INTERPRETATION: The *parameter-list* consists of one or more parameter definitions separated by commas. Each parameter definition has the form

parameter = value

where *parameter* becomes the name of the constant represented by *value.* A *parameter* cannot be redefined by any subsequent program statements. The data type of each *parameter* should be declared first in a type declaration statement.

Implicit Data Typing of Identifiers

If you forget to declare the data type of an identifier, Fortran will make an assumption as to its type. If the identifier begins with the letter I – N, Fortran assumes it is type INTEGER; if the identifier begins with any other letter, Fortran assumes it is type REAL. We strongly suggest that you explicitly declare the type of every identifier used in a program rather than relying on Fortran's implicit data typing to do this for you. Explicit typing enhances program readability.

Program Style: *Choosing Identifiers*

We discuss program style in sections like this throughout the text. Program style is a very important consideration in programming. A program that "looks good" is easier to read and understand than one that is sloppy. Most programs will be examined or studied by someone other than its author. In the real world, only about 25 percent of the time spent on a particular program is devoted to its original design or coding; the remaining 75 percent is spent on maintenance (i.e., updating and modifying the program). A program that is neatly stated and whose meaning is clear makes everyone's job simpler.

To make your programs easier to read and understand, choose meaningful identifiers and declare them explicitly at the beginning of the program. For example, SALARY would be a good name for a variable used to store a person's salary; the identifiers S, X1, and BAGEL would be bad choices.

If you mistype an identifier, the compiler may or may not detect this as a syntax error. Sometimes mistyped identifiers look like other variable names. For this reason, avoid picking names that are very similar to each other.

Many compilers permit long identifiers (more than six characters) that may include lowercase characters. On these compilers, you could use the name circumference instead of the six-letter name CIRCUM. Your instructor may prefer that you do this to enhance program readability. However, keep in mind that doing so is not standard in Fortran 77 and will reduce program portability. *Note:* Fortran 90 allows longer identifiers and lowercase characters.

Program Style: *Avoiding Keywords as Identifiers*

What about words that have special meaning in Fortran (*keywords*) such as PROGRAM, REAL, READ, PRINT, STOP, and so on; can they be used as identifiers? The answer is yes; however, we strongly recommend you avoid doing this as it will lead to programs that are difficult to understand. The Fortran compiler can determine from the context in which it is used whether a word such as REAL is being used as a Fortran keyword or as an identifier; however, we humans are more easily confused.

Executable Statements

The executable statements follow a program's declarations. They are the Fortran statements used to write or *code* the algorithm and its refinements. The

Fortran compiler translates the executable statements into machine language; the computer executes the machine language version of these statements when we run the program.

In Fig. 2.1, the lines

```
C Read the wire length in meters.
      PRINT *, 'Enter the wire length in meters'
      READ *, WMETER
```

show algorithm step 1 as a comment followed by two Fortran statements that implement it. If the algorithm step was refined, we code its refinements in Fortran. The two Fortran statements used above, PRINT and READ, are described next.

Displaying Results: The PRINT Statement

To see the results of a program execution, we must have some way of specifying what variable values should be displayed on your computer monitor. In Fig. 2.1, the statement

```
PRINT *, 'The wire length in feet is ', WFEET
```

causes the line

```
The wire length in feet is     39.3700
```

to be displayed. There are actually two separate items displayed by this statement

- the *character string* enclosed in apostrophes:

  ```
  'The wire length in feet is '
  ```

- the value of the REAL variable WFEET

When a PRINT statement is executed, each item in the output list is displayed on the screen. For character strings, the characters enclosed in apostrophes are displayed but the apostrophes are not. For variables, the current value of the variable is displayed.

SYNTAX DISPLAY

The PRINT Statement

SYNTAX: PRINT *, *output-list*

EXAMPLE: PRINT *, 'Age is ', AGE

INTERPRETATION: The value of each variable or constant is displayed in the order in which it appears in *output-list*. A string is displayed without the quotes. After the entire output line is displayed, the cursor advances to the start of the next line.

Reading Data: The READ Statement

The first PRINT statement in Fig. 2.1

```
PRINT *, 'Enter the wire length in meters'
```

is used to display a *prompt* or *prompting message*. A prompting message is a string that is displayed just before a READ statement is executed to prompt you to enter data. The prompt may describe what data are needed and the kind of data (e.g., real number or integer). You must precede each READ statement with a PRINT statement that displays a prompt; otherwise, the program user will have no idea that the program is waiting for data or what data to enter.

The READ statement

```
READ *, WMETER
```

in Fig. 2.1 reads a real number entered at the terminal into the variable WMETER for storage. To enter the number, simply type it at the cursor, then press either the Return or Enter key (which one you press will depend on the configuration of your keyboard). The effect of this READ statement is shown in Fig. 2.2.

You can also use a single READ statement to read in multiple data items. In this case, be sure to leave at least one space between data items. Figure 2.3 shows the effect of the statement

```
READ *, X, Y
```

assuming that X and Y are declared as type REAL variables.

Figure 2.2. *Effect of READ *, WMETER*

Figure 2.3. *Effect of READ *, X, Y*

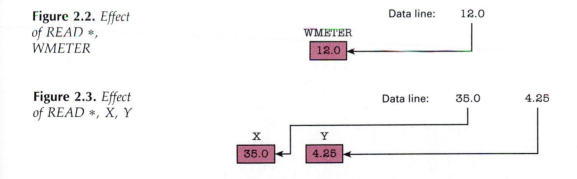

**SYNTAX
DISPLAY**

READ Statement

SYNTAX: READ *, *input-list*

EXAMPLES: READ *, WINCHS
          READ *, AGE, GENDER

INTERPRETATION: Data are entered into each variable specified in the *input-list*. Commas are used to separate the variable names in the *input-list*. When a READ statement is executed, program execution is suspended until the required data items are entered and the Return or Enter key is pressed. There must be one data item for each variable in the *input-list*, and the order of the data must correspond to the order of the variables in the *input-list*. At least one space should be left between data items. Do not type a comma between data items nor inside a data item.

**Assignment
Statements**

A primary function of a computer is to perform arithmetic computations. *Assignment statements* are used to specify such computations.

You use an assignment statement to assign a specific value to a variable. For example, the assignment statement

```
WINCHS = WMETER * INCHMT
```

in Fig. 2.1 assigns a value to the variable WINCHS. In this example, the value assigned is the product that results from multiplying (the symbol * means to multiply) the variable WMETER by the constant 39.37 (the value of parameter INCHMT). Valid information must be stored in WMETER before you execute the statement. As shown in Fig. 2.4, only the value of WINCHS is affected by the assignment statement; WMETER retains its original value.

The symbol = is the assignment operator in Fortran and should be read as "gets" or "is assigned the value of" rather than "equals." Other Fortran operators appearing in assignment statements include the familiar mathematical operators +, −, and /, as described in Table 2.1. The general form of the assignment statement is shown after the table.

Figure 2.4. *Effect of WINCHS = WMETER * INCHMT*

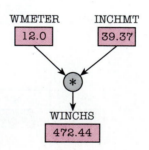

Table 2.1. *Fortran Arithmetic Operators*

ARITHMETIC OPERATOR	MEANING
**	exponentiation (e.g., X ** 2 is X^2)
*	multiplication
/	division
+	addition
−	subtraction

SYNTAX DISPLAY

Assignment Statement (Arithmetic)

SYNTAX: *result = expression*

EXAMPLE: Z = Y + X − 3

INTERPRETATION: The variable specified by *result* is assigned the value of *expression*. The previous value of *result* is destroyed. The *expression* can be a single variable, parameter, or constant, or involve variables, parameters, constants, and the arithmetic operators listed in Table 2.1.

EXAMPLE 2.1

In Fortran, you can write assignment statements of the form

SUM = SUM + ITEM

where the variable SUM is used on both sides of the assignment operator. This is obviously not an algebraic equation, but it illustrates something that is often done in programming. This statement instructs the computer to add the current value of the variable SUM to the value of ITEM; the result is then stored back into SUM. The previous value of SUM is lost in the process, as illustrated in Fig. 2.5; however, the value of ITEM is unchanged. ■

Figure 2.5. *Effect of SUM = SUM + ITEM*

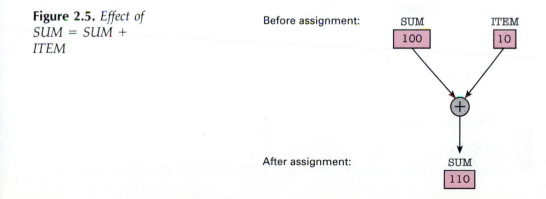

EXAMPLE 2.2   Assignment statements can also be written with an expression part that consists of a single variable or value. For example, the statement

NEWX = X

instructs the computer to copy the value of X into NEWX. The statement

NEWX = −X

instructs the computer to get the value of X, negate that value, and store the result in NEWX (e.g., if X is 3.5, NEWX becomes −3.5). Neither of the preceding assignment statements changes the value of X.   ■

**STOP and
END Statements**   After the program computations are performed and the output results are displayed, program execution should stop. Use the statement

STOP

to halt program execution.
    The last statement in every Fortran program is

END

which marks the end of the Fortran source program during translation; the translation phase terminates when the END statement is processed by the compiler. If the STOP statement is omitted, program execution terminates when the END statement is reached.

**SYNTAX
DISPLAY**   **STOP Statement**

SYNTAX: STOP

INTERPRETATION: Terminates the execution of a running program.

**SYNTAX
DISPLAY**   **END Statement**

SYNTAX: END

INTERPRETATION: Indicates the end of a program unit during translation.

**Storing Data
in Memory**

Data cannot be manipulated by a computer unless they are first stored in main memory. We have discussed three ways in which to place a data value in memory: associate it with a parameter, read it into memory, or assign it to a variable. We summarize the differences between these three methods next:

- *Associating a constant value with a parameter:* Used to store constants that do not change from one run of the program to the next.
- *Reading a data value into memory:* Used to read a program's data into its input variables.
- *Assigning a value to a variable:* Used when the variable is a problem output or an intermediate result whose value is determined through a computation.

**Programs
in Memory**

Figure 2.6 shows an area of main memory occupied by the machine language version of the units conversion program. Figure 2.6(a) shows the program data area before execution of the program body. The constants 39.37 and 12 are stored in parameters INCHMT and INCHFT. The question marks in variables

Figure 2.6.
*Memory
Before and After
Execution of a
Program*

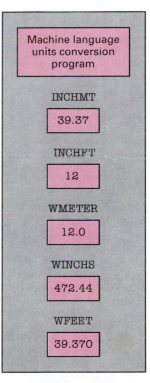

(a) Before execution (b) After execution

WMETER, WINCHS, and WFEET indicate that these variables are undefined (value unknown) before program execution begins. During program execution, the data value 12.0 is read into variable WMETER and the assignment statements shown earlier are used to compute values for WINCHS and WFEET. After program execution, all variables are defined as shown in Fig. 2.6(b).

Parameters versus Literal Constants

You may be wondering why we used parameters INCHMT and INCHFT to represent the constants 39.37 and 12 instead of writing them as *literal constants* directly in the assignment statements:

```
WINCHS = WMETER * 39.37
WFEET = WINCHS / 12
```

There are two reasons. First, using names like INCHMT and INCHFT makes a program more readable because an identifier conveys more meaning than just a number. Second, after further study, we might determine that a more exact approximation to the number of inches in a meter is 39.368 instead of 39.37. If this were the case, it is much easier to change a single PARAMETER statement at the beginning of a program than it would be to find and change all occurrences of a literal constant in a program. *Note:* Because Fortran reads commas as separator symbols, be sure to avoid typing a comma inside a number (e.g., type 10000, not 10,000).

EXERCISES FOR SECTION 2.3

Self-check

1. Which of the following identifiers are Fortran keywords? Which are valid identifiers?

```
END  READ  BILL  PROGRAM  SUE'S  RATE  OPERATE  START
BEGIN  STOP  XYZ123  123XYZ  THISISALONGONE  Y=Z
```

2. Which are valid Fortran statements?

```
    a. X + Y = Z
    b. Z = X +* Y
    c. PROGRAM FORTRN
    d. PROGRAM FORTRN.FOR
    e. READ *, X, Y
    f. PRINT *, X, Y
    g. READ *, X, 3.14159
    h. PRINT *, X, 3.14159
    i. REAL (PI = 3.14159)
    j. PARAMETER (PI = 3.14159)
    k. X = X + 2
```

    l. `2 = X + Y`
  m. `X = Y + 2Z`
   n. `X = 100,000.056`

3. Correct the syntax errors in the program below and rewrite it. What does each statement of your corrected program do? What is printed?

```
PROGRAM MIXUP
REAL *, X, Y, X
15.0 = Y; Z = -Y + 3.5
Y + Z = X
PRINT *, x; Y; z
STOP
END
```

4. Show the output displayed by the program lines below when the data entered are 5 and 7.

```
PROGRAM TWOINT
INTEGER M, N
PRINT *, 'Enter two integers:'
READ *, M, N
M = M + 5
N = 3 * N
PRINT *, 'M = ', M
PRINT *, 'N = ', N
STOP
END
```

5. Show the output displayed by the lines below.

```
PRINT *, 'My name is: '
PRINT *, 'Doe, Jane'
PRINT *
PRINT *, 'I live in Ann Arbor, MI '
PRINT *, 'and my zip code is ', 48109
```

Programming

1. Write the `PRINT` statement that causes the line

```
The value of X is _____ pounds.
```

   to be printed where the value assigned to variable X is inserted in the blank space.
2. Write the program for Self-check exercise 1 of Section 2.2.
3. Write the program for Self-check exercise 2 of Section 2.2.
4. Write the program for Self-check exercise 3 of Section 2.2.

2.4 Style and Format of Fortran Programs

In the preceding section, we described seven types of Fortran statements. In this section, we elaborate on the formatting of Fortran programs, such as how to position data within columns, the effective use of blank spaces and lowercase letters, and taking advantage of comments.

Rules for Positioning Fortran Statements

As you type in Fortran programs, make sure that you begin each new statement on a separate line. Furthermore, do not begin a statement before column 7—always ensure you press the space bar at least six times before you type in the statement. On some systems, pressing the tab key will advance you to column 7.

Another constraint is that a statement cannot extend past column 72 on any line. Any characters typed beyond column 72 are ignored by the compiler; however, you can continue a long statement on the next line. Do this by placing any symbol *other than zero* in column 6 of that next line. Do not leave column 6 blank; you must enter a symbol. We recommend you use the symbol +. In the following statement, the + in column 6 indicates that the output list for the PRINT statement is continued on the second line:

```
      PRINT *, 'The distance travelled in miles is',
     +          DISTNC
```

Column 1 can be used as either a comment designator or a statement label. If a line contains C or * in column 1, Fortran assumes that the line is a comment and does not attempt to translate or execute that line. For example,

```
C This line contains a C in column 1 and is ignored.
* So is this one.
```

If Fortran does not find C or * in column 1, but does find a number anywhere in columns 1 through 5, it assumes the rest of the line is a regular Fortran statement and that the number in columns 1 through 5 is the statement label (an integer). For example, the following line has the label 10:

```
10    PRINT *, 'This PRINT statement has label 10'
```

We will discuss comments later in this section. The Fortran rules for column use are summarized in Table 2.2.

Table 2.2. *Use of Columns in Fortran*

COLUMN	USE
1	C or * indicates that the line is a comment.
1–5	May contain the statement label. Labels are always numbers.
6	If it contains any character except a zero, the line is a continuation of the previous line.
7–72	Contains the Fortran statement.
73–	May be ignored by the compiler (system dependent).

Program Style: *Use of Blank Space and Lowercase Letters*

The consistent and careful use of blank spaces can significantly enhance the style and readability of a program. Beyond column 6 of a line, blanks not inside strings are ignored by the compiler, so you may insert them as desired to improve the program's appearance. For example, as shown in Fig. 2.1, we always leave a blank space after a comma and before and after arithmetic operators such as *, −, =. Blanks inside strings, however, are not ignored but are used to make program output more readable. We also use blank lines to separate sections of the program, again, to make it easier to read and understand.

The standard Fortran character set does not include lowercase letters. However, most compilers permit lowercase letters to be used inside strings in Fortran programs. The use of lowercase in prompting messages and strings that are displayed makes the program output easier to read. Consequently, we use lowercase in strings even though this use is not standard. Check whether your Fortran compiler allows lowercase before you follow this practice.

These measures, taken to improve the style and, hence, the clarity of the program, do not affect the meaning of the program so far as the computer is concerned.

Comments and Documentation

The program in Fig. 2.1 contains some phrases on lines that begin with the letter C in column 1. These phrases are examples of *comments*. Comments are an important part of any program because they help people read and follow the program. For example, those in Fig. 2.1 make the program easier to understand by describing the purpose of the program (the first comment line) and the purpose of each program step (the other comments). Comments are ignored by the compiler and are not translated into machine language. They may be designated not only by the letter C but also by an *. The next two displays describe the syntax and use of comments.

Comment

SYNTAX: C comment
       * comment

EXAMPLE: C This is a comment
        * So is this

INTERPRETATION: A c or * in column 1 indicates that the current line is a comment. Comments are listed with the program but are otherwise ignored by the Fortran compiler. Lowercase is permitted in comments. A blank line is also considered a comment.

Program Style: *Using Comments*

Comments make a program more readable by describing the purpose of each program section. Generally, there will be one comment in the program for each major algorithm step.

Each program should begin with a series of comments that specify

- the programmer's name,
- the date of the current version,
- a brief description of what the program does,
- a description of the program inputs and outputs, and
- a list of any program variables and what they represent.

Although space considerations prevent us from doing this in the text, we strongly recommend you follow this practice. The program in Fig. 2.1 could begin with the following comments:

```
C Converts wire length from meters to feet.
C The program user enters the wire length in meters.

C Programmer: Ethan Waldman
C Date: July 15, 1993
C Instructor: Dr. F. Tran

C Data Requirements
C Inputs : WMETRS — the wire length in meters
C Outputs: WFEET — the wire length in feet
C Other  : WINCHS — the wire length in inches
```

Self-check

1. What is the purpose of including comments in Fortran statements?

2. Each line of the Fortran program below begins in column 1. Respace this program so that it is correct.

```
PROGRAM SPACES
REAL X, Y
* Assign values to X and Y
10 X = 10
15 Y = 15
C Display X and Y
PRINT X, Y
STOP
END
```

2.5 INTEGER, REAL, and CHARACTER Data Types

So far in this chapter, we have written programs that manipulate INTEGER, REAL, and CHARACTER data. In this section, we formally introduce these data types and discuss their differences.

INTEGER and REAL Formats

In most of this text, we use two Fortran numeric types: REAL and INTEGER. Type REAL variables are used to store data containing a decimal point and a fractional part (for example, 3.14159, −15.0, 0.000123, 1234567.90). Type INTEGER variables can store only integer values (for example, 1000, 0, −999). For this reason, type INTEGER variables are more limited in their use; they are used more often to represent a count of items (e.g., a count of coins).

You may be wondering why Fortran has two numeric types. Can the data type REAL be used for all numbers? For example, couldn't we represent the integer 13 as the real value 13.0? The answer is yes, but on many computers, operations involving integers are faster. Further, integers need less storage space. And while operations with integers are always precise, there may be some loss of accuracy when dealing with real numbers.

These differences result from the way real numbers and integers are represented internally in memory. All data are represented in memory as binary strings—strings of 0's and 1's. However, the binary string stored for the integer 13 is not the same as that stored for the real number 13.0. Although the actual internal representation used is computer dependent, generally an integer data item is represented as a single binary value whereas a real number

Figure 2.7. *INTE-GER and REAL Formats*

Integer format

| binary number |

Real format

| mantissa | exponent |

is represented by a binary mantissa and exponent, which are stored and processed separately. (See Fig. 2.7.)

In addition to its ability to store fractions, the type REAL format can represent a range of numbers that is considerably larger than can the INTEGER format. For example, on Control Data Corporation Cyber series computers, real numbers range in value from 10^{-294} (a very small fraction) to 10^{+322}, whereas the range of positive integers extends from 1 to approximately 10^{15}.

Fortran Scientific Notation

A real number appearing in a Fortran program or entered as a data value may be written in *Fortran scientific notation*. A number in Fortran scientific notation has the form

$$mantissa\mathrm{E}^{exponent}$$

where the *mantissa* may be an integer or real number and the *exponent* must be an integer. Both the *mantissa* and the *exponent* may have a sign. If no sign is given, it is assumed to be +.

Fortran scientific notation is like normal scientific notation except that it is written on a single line. Consequently, the value of a number written in Fortran scientific notation is

$$mantissa \times 10^{exponent}$$

Those of you familiar with normal scientific notation will recognize that 1.234E−5 is the Fortran form of 1.234×10^{-5}, or 0.00001234. This value is obtained by shifting the decimal point five positions to the left. Similarly, the value of 3.98E6 is 3980000. This value is obtained by shifting the decimal point six positions to the right. Normally, only very large numbers (i.e., greater than 1000) or very small fractions (i.e., less than 0.0001) are written in scientific notation.

Table 2.3 shows some numbers in Fortran scientific notation and their equivalent values. As shown by the last real number in Table 2.3, 1.15E−3 means the same as 1.15×10^{-3}, where the exponent −3 causes the decimal point to be moved left three digits. A positive exponent causes the decimal point to be moved to the right; the + sign may be omitted when the exponent is positive.

Although there are no restrictions on the numbers you may write in Fortran scientific notation, most Fortran compilers display numbers in scientific nota-

Table 2.3. *Fortran Scientific Notation*

$-15.0E-08$	(value of -15.0×10^{-8} or -0.00000015)
$-2.345E2$	(value of -2.345×10^2 or -234.5)
$1.2E+6$	(value of 1.2×10^6 or $1,200,000$)
$1.15E-3$	(value of 1.15×10^{-3} or 0.00115)

tion using a mantissa value between 0.1 and 1.0 (or -0.1 and -1.0, for negative numbers). This means that if you entered $-15.0E-08$ as a data value, Fortran might display this value as $-0.15000000E-06$.

Numerical Inaccuracies

One of the problems we encounter in processing real numbers is the occasional error in representing real data. Just as there are certain numbers that cannot be represented exactly in the decimal number system (e.g., the fraction 2.0/3.0 is 0.666666 . . .), there are numbers that cannot be represented exactly in type REAL format on a computer. In fact, many decimal fractions cannot be represented exactly in the internal binary format used for real numbers. The representational error will depend on the number of bits used in the mantissa: the more bits, the smaller the error.

The number 0.1 is an example of a real number that has a representational error. Although this error is quite small, its effect can become magnified through repeated computations. Therefore, on some computers, the result of adding 0.1 ten times will not be 1.0.

Other problems occur when manipulating very large and very small real numbers. On some computers, when a large number and a small number are added, the larger number may "cancel out" the smaller number (a cancellation error). For example, if X is much larger than Y, X may cancel out Y so that $X + Y$ and X have the same value, as in 1000.0+0.000001234 is equal to 1000.0.

If two very small real numbers are multiplied, the result may be too small to be represented accurately and so will be zero. This is called *arithmetic underflow*. Similarly, if two very large real numbers are multiplied, the result may be too large to be represented. This is called *arithmetic overflow* and is handled in different ways by different computers. Arithmetic underflow and overflow also can occur when very large and very small integer values are processed.

CHARACTER Data Type

Type CHARACTER variables store string values consisting of combinations of letters, digits, and special characters. For example, the data type declaration statement

```
CHARACTER *9 OBJECT, ARTICL
```

identifies `OBJECT` and `ARTICL` as variables that can contain a string of exactly nine characters. The assignment statement

```
OBJECT = 'ABCD12345'
```

stores the nine characters `ABCD12345` in variable `OBJECT`. The apostrophes used to mark the beginning and end of a string are called *string delimiters.* They are not considered part of the string, so they are not stored in `OBJECT`.

Suppose we want to store the nine characters `Joe's hat` in `ARTICL`, where the fourth character is an apostrophe and the sixth character is a blank. Because Fortran uses apostrophes as string delimiters, we must use something else, for example, two consecutive apostrophes, to tell Fortran that we want to store an apostrophe *inside* a string. We can use the assignment below to accomplish this.

```
ARTICL = 'Joe''s hat'
```

In the character variable `ARTICL` (`CHARACTER *9`) below, we let the blank character be represented by the symbol □:

```
ARTICL
```

Joe's□hat

The length specifier for a `CHARACTER` declaration does not have to follow the reserved word `CHARACTER`. Instead, it can come after each variable listed in the `CHARACTER` declaration. For example, the statement

```
CHARACTER NAME *10, ZIPCOD *5
```

declares two character variables of different lengths, `NAME` (length 10) and `ZIPCOD` (length 5).

SYNTAX DISPLAY

CHARACTER Declaration

SYNTAX: CHARACTER *len variable list
CHARACTER *variable1 *len1, variable2 *len2, . . .*

EXAMPLE: CHARACTER *10 NAME1, NAME2
CHARACTER STATE *10, CITY *10, ZIP *5

INTERPRETATION: The first form allocates memory space for each of the character variables specified in the variable list. Each variable has the capacity for storing *len* characters, where *len* is an integer constant. The second form allocates memory space for one or more character variables. The integer constant appearing after each variable name specifies separately the length of each character variable. *Note:* The symbols *1 may be omitted when declaring a character variable that stores a single character.

Character String Storage

You can use assignment statements or READ statements to store strings in CHARACTER variables according to the rules below.

Rules for Storing Strings in CHARACTER Variables

- If the CHARACTER variable and string length are the same, then all characters in the string will be stored in the character variable.
- If the CHARACTER variable is longer than the string, then blank padding will be added to the right of the string to equalize the lengths.
- If the CHARACTER variable is shorter than the string, the string will be truncated, that is, the extra string characters will be removed from the right end of the string.

EXAMPLE 2.3

Assuming the type declaration

```
CHARACTER ALPHA *10, BETA *12, GAMMA *3
```

then the assignment statements

```
ALPHA = 'ABCDEFGHIJ'
BETA = ALPHA
GAMMA = BETA
```

yield the results

ALPHA	BETA	GAMMA
ABCDEFGHIJ	ABCDEFGHIJ□□	ABC

As shown above, the character string is padded with two blanks (indicated by the symbol □) before being stored in BETA and is truncated before being stored in GAMMA.

The same rules for padding and truncation apply when the string value being read is not the same length as the CHARACTER variable receiving it.

EXAMPLE 2.4

The statements below read a string and a numeric value into the variables NAME (type CHARACTER *10) and RATE (type REAL).

```
PRINT *, 'Enter the employee name and rate:'
READ *, NAME, RATE
```

To satisfy the input-list NAME, RATE, we need to enter a character string and a number as data when the READ statement executes. The data line

```
'JOHNNY JONES' 3.50
```

would result in the following variable values:

```
    NAME            RATE
 JOHNNY□JON         3.50
```

Numeric Strings

Numeric strings consist of digit characters only, for example, '123' or '345'. Arithmetic operations cannot be performed on numeric strings (e.g., '123' + '345' is illegal). These strings can be manipulated only in the same way as other character data.

EXERCISES FOR SECTION 2.5

Self-check

1. Identify the data type of each valid value below. Indicate which of these are invalid. If NAME is a type CHARACTER *4 variable, what would be the effect of assigning the last value in the list to NAME? The last four characters are apostrophe, apostrophe, double quote, apostrophe.

   ```
   15   15.5E-2   10E10   '*'   "X"   '3.45E-5'   3.45E-5   '*+'''"'
   ```

2. Rewrite the numbers in exercise 1 that are in scientific notation as real numbers in normal decimal notation.
3. Show what string is stored in memory for each assignment or READ statement below. Represent a blank character by using the symbol □.

   a. CHARACTER *8 CITY
      CITY = 'NEW YORK'
   b. CHARACTER *5 TRIP
      TRIP = 'HONEYMOON'
   c. CHARACTER *6 FIRST, LAST
      READ *, FIRST, LAST
      data: 'Bill' 'Smith'
   d. CHARACTER *12 LASTNA
      LASTNA = 'JACKSON'
   e. CHARACTER *9 TEAM
      TEAM = 'ORIOLES'
   f. CHARACTER *9 TEAM
      TEAM = 'RED STOCKINGS'

Programming

1. Write an appropriate sequence of type declarations and READ statements for entering the data shown below. The first line of data contains a student ID number, name, class, and major. The next group of lines will be read into the same three variables. The data items in each line are the course ID, number of credits, and grade.

```
700007 'J.A. OSHEA' 'SENIOR' 'ENGINEERING'
'SOC101' 3 'A'
'CIS120' 4 'C'
'MAT201' 3 'B'
```

2.6 Arithmetic Expressions

Thus far, most of the expressions we have used in programs have been relatively simple. To write more complicated expressions correctly, we must know the Fortran rules for evaluating expressions. For example, in the expression A + B * C, is * performed before + or vice versa? Is the expression X / Y * Z evaluated as (X / Y) * Z or as X / (Y * Z)?

Rules for Expression Evaluation

Fortran follows the normal rules of algebra in evaluating expressions, as set out below:

a. All parenthesized subexpressions are evaluated first. Nested parenthesized subexpressions are evaluated inside out, with the innermost subexpression evaluated first.

b. Operator precedence: Operators in the same subexpression are evaluated in the following order:

Operator	Order of Evaluation
**	first
*, /	next
+, −	last

c. Left associative: Operators in the same subexpression and at the same precedence level (such as + and −) are evaluated left to right. The only exception to this rule is that consecutive exponentiation operators are evaluated right to left (e.g., X ** Y ** 2 is evaluated as X ** (Y ** 2)).

Consider the following two expressions with multiple operators:

```
1.8 * CELSUS + 32.0
(SALARY − 5000.00) * 0.20 + 1425.0
```

In both cases, the multiplication is performed before the addition. The use of parentheses in the second expression causes the subtraction to be done first.

EXAMPLE 2.5   The formula for the area of a circle, $A = \pi r^2$, is written in Fortran as

```
AREA = PI * RADIUS ** 2
```

where PI is the parameter 3.14159. The evaluation tree for this formula is shown in Fig. 2.8. In this tree, the arrows connect each operand with its operator. The number to the left of each operator shows the order of operator evaluation. The rules that apply are shown to the right. ■

Figure 2.8. *Evaluation Tree for AREA = PI * RADIUS ** 2*

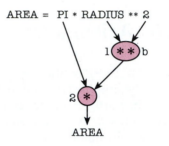

EXAMPLE 2.6   The formula for the average velocity, v, of a particle traveling on a line between points p_1 and p_2 in time t_1 to t_2 is

$$v = \frac{p_2 - p_1}{t_2 - t_1}$$

This formula is written and evaluated in Fortran as shown in Fig. 2.9. ■

Figure 2.9. *Evaluation Tree for $v = (p_2 - p_1)/(t_2 - t_1)$*

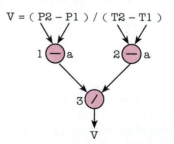

Inserting parentheses in an expression affects the order of operator evaluation. You should use parentheses freely to clarify the order of evaluation, as demonstrated in the next example.

EXAMPLE 2.7   Consider the expression

```
Z - (A + B / 2.0) + W * Y
```

The parenthesized subexpression (A + B / 2.0) is evaluated first [rule (a)] beginning with B / 2.0 [rule (b)]. Once the value of B / 2.0 is determined, it is added to A to obtain the value of (A + B / 2.0). Next, the multiplication operation is performed [rule (b)] and the value for W * Y is determined. Then the value of (A + B / 2.0) is subtracted from Z [rule (c)], and finally, this result is added to W * Y. The evaluation tree for this expression is shown in Fig. 2.10. ∎

Figure 2.10. *Evaluation Tree for*
Z − (A + B / 2.0) + W ∗ Y

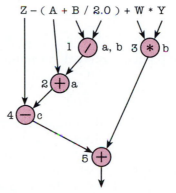

Writing Formulas in Fortran

There are two problem areas in writing a mathematical formula in Fortran: one concerns multiplication and the other, division.

First, multiplication can often be implied in a mathematical formula by writing the two items to be multiplied next to each other; for example, $A = bc$. In Fortran, however, the ∗ operator must always be used to indicate multiplication, as in

```
A = B * C
```

The second difficulty arises in formulas involving division. We normally write the numerator and denominator on separate lines:

$$m = \frac{y - b}{x - a}$$

In Fortran, however, all assignment statements must be written on one line. Consequently, we often need to use parentheses to separate the numerator from the denominator and to clearly indicate the order of evaluation of the expression's operators. We would write the formula above, for example, as

```
M = (Y - B) / (X - A)
```

EXAMPLE 2.8   This example illustrates how several mathematical formulas can be written in Fortran.

Mathematical Formula	Fortran Expression
a. $b^2 - 4ac$	B ** 2 - 4.0 * A * C
b. $a + b - c$	A + B - C
c. $\dfrac{a + b}{c + d}$	(A + B) / (C + D)
d. $\dfrac{1}{1 + x^2}$	1.0 / (1.0 + X ** 2)
e. $a \times -(b + c)$	A * (-(B + C))

The points illustrated are summarized next.

Rules for Writing Fortran Expressions

- Always specify multiplication explicitly by using the operator * where needed. (See Example 2.8a.)
- Use parentheses as required to control the order of operator evaluation. (See Examples 2.8c and d.)
- Never write two arithmetic operators in succession; they must be separated by an operand or parentheses. (See Example 2.8e.)
- Do not mix integer constants with real variables in expressions (called *mixed-mode expressions*). The only exception is that you may use an integer constant as an exponent. (See Examples 2.8a and d.)

The next examples show how to write the Fortran forms of some formulas found in engineering problems.

EXAMPLE 2.9   The heat loss through a brick furnace wall in joules per second is expressed by the equation

$$q = \frac{kA(T_2 - T_1)}{L}$$

where T_2 is the inside temperature, T_1 is the outside temperature, L is the furnace wall thickness, A is the surface area affected, and k is the thermal conductivity constant. We implement this equation in Fortran as

```
Q = K * A * (T2 - T1) / L
```

EXAMPLE 2.10   The general equation for pressure loss due to pipe friction is

$$\Delta P = f \rho \frac{L}{D} \frac{v^2}{2}$$

where f is the friction factor, ρ is the density of fluid flowing in the pipe, L is pipe length, D is pipe diameter, and v is velocity. We implement this equation in Fortran as

```
DELTAP = F * RHO * (L / D) * (V ** 2 / 2.0)
```

EXAMPLE 2.11   The deflection of a cantilevered flat parallel spring is given by the equation

$$\delta = \frac{2}{3} \frac{sL^2}{Et}$$

where s is the tensile stress, E is the modulus of elasticity, L is the length, and t is the thickness of the spring. We implement this equation in Fortran as

```
DEFLEX = (2.0/3.0) * (S * L ** 2) / (E * T)
```

The preceding example used the subexpression `(2.0/3.0)` to represent the fraction 2/3. We did this because the result of dividing two integers in Fortran is always an integer (e.g., 2/3 is 0 in Fortran). We will explain this next.

Type of an Arithmetic Expression

All the arithmetic operators (`+`, `−`, `*`, `/`, `**`) can have either INTEGER or REAL operands. If both operands are the same type, then the result of an arithmetic operation has the same type as its operands. This means that the result of `3.0 * 4.0` is the real number `12.0`; the result of `3 * 4` is the integer `12`. If one operand is type REAL and the other is type INTEGER, the type INTEGER operand is converted to type REAL, and the result will be type REAL (e.g., the expressions `7.0/2` and `7/2.0` are evaluated as `7.0/2.0`).

In Fortran, the result of a division operation must be type INTEGER when both operands are type INTEGER. This means that the value of `7/2` cannot be the same as the value of `7.0 / 2.0`. The value of the latter expression is `3.5`; the value of the former expression is the integral part of this result (i.e., the integer `3`). In general, when two integers are divided, the result is the integral part of their quotient; the fractional part is lost. Therefore, the value of the fraction `2/3` is `0` in Fortran; whereas, the value of the fraction `2.0/3.0` is `0.66666....`.

EXAMPLE 2.12   In Fig. 2.11, the expression

    3 * 6 / 4

involving three integer operands is shown to evaluate to the integer 4. In Fig. 2.12, the expression 3.0 * 6 / 4 is shown to evaluate to the real number 4.5. The reason for this discrepancy is that the left operand of the division operator in Fig. 2.12 is a real number (18.0) due to the prior multiplication. Consequently, the result of the division is also a real number.   ■

Figure 2.11. *Evaluation Tree for 3 * 6 / 4*

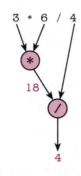

Figure 2.12. *Evaluation Tree for 3.0 * 6 / 4*

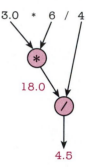

We can conclude from Example 2.12 that expressions involving the division operator and mixed-type operands often lead to unexpected results. For this reason, you should avoid using mixed-type expressions, especially when division is involved.

Mixed-Type Assignment Statements

When an assignment statement is executed, the expression is first evaluated and then the result is assigned to the variable listed to the left of the assignment operator (=). Recall that only an integer can be stored in a type INTEGER variable, and only a real number can be stored in a type REAL variable. Consequently, if the expression and the value being assigned are the same type, the expression value will be stored directly; however, if they are not the same type, a type conversion occurs and the value stored may not be what is intended.

EXAMPLE 2.13   The expression in the assignment statements

    X = 3.0 * 6 / 4
    I = 3.0 * 6 / 4

evaluates to the real number 4.5, as shown in Fig. 2.12. If X is type REAL, the real number 4.5 is stored in X, as expected. If I is type INTEGER, only the integral part of the expression value (the integer 4) is stored in I.

The expression in the assignment statements

```
X = 3 * 6 / 4
I = 3 * 6 / 4
```

evaluates to the integer 4, as shown in Fig. 2.11. If I is type INTEGER, the integer 4 is stored. If X is type REAL, the integer 4 is converted to its equivalent real value (4.0) before being stored in X. ∎

A common error is to assume that the type of X (the variable being assigned) causes the expression to be evaluated as if its operands were that type too. Remember, the expression is evaluated before the assignment is made, and the type of the variable being assigned has no effect whatsoever on the expression value.

EXERCISES FOR SECTION 2.6

Self-check

1. Draw the evaluation trees for the expressions below.

```
1.8 * CELSUS + 32.0
(SALARY - 5000.00) * 0.20 + 1425.00
```

2. Given the declarations

```
REAL PI, X, Y
INTEGER MAXI, A, B, I
PARAMETER (PI = 3.14159, MAXI = 1000)
```

find the value of each of the statements below that are valid. Also indicate which statements are invalid and why. Assume that A is 3, B is 4, and Y is −1.0.

a. I = A * B
b. I = (990 − MAXI) / A
c. I = A * Y
d. X = PI * Y
e. I = A / B
f. X = A / B
g. X = A * (A / B)
h. I = B / 0
i. I = A * (990 − MAXI)
j. I = (MAXI − 990) / A
k. X = A / Y
l. I = PI * A
m. X = PI / Y
n. I = B / A
o. I = (MAXI − 990) * A
p. I = A * 0
q. I = A * (MAXI − 990)

3. What values are assigned by the valid statements in exercise 2, assuming A is 5, B is 2, and Y is 2.0?

4. Assume that you have the following variable declarations:

```
INTEGER COLOR, LIME, STRAW, YELLOW, RED, ORANGE
REAL BLACK, WHITE, GREEN, BLUE, PURPLE, CRAYON
```

Evaluate each of the statements below given the values: COLOR is 2, BLACK is 2.5, CRAYON is −1.3, STRAW is 1, RED is 3, PURPLE is 0.3E1.

a. WHITE = COLOR * 2.5 / PURPLE
b. GREEN = COLOR / PURPLE
c. ORANGE = COLOR / RED
d. BLUE = (COLOR + STRAW) / (CRAYON + 0.3)
e. LIME = RED / COLOR
f. PURPLE = STRAW / RED * COLOR

Programming

1. Let A, B, C, and X be the names of four type REAL variables and I, J, and K the names of three type INTEGER variables. Each of the statements below contains a violation of the rules for forming arithmetic expressions. Rewrite each statement so that it is consistent with the rules.

a. X = 4.0 A * C   d. K = 3(I + J)
b. A = AC   e. X = 5A / BC
c. I = 2 * −J   f. I = 5J3

2. Implement the equations below in Fortran.

a. Euler's formula for maximum buckling load on a long, slender column,

$$Load = \frac{\pi^2 AE}{(l/r)^2}$$

where *Load* is the largest safe load, pounds; *A* is the cross-sectional area, square inches; *E* is the modulus of elasticity, pounds per square inch; *l* is the effective length of column, inches; and *r* is the radius of column, inches.

b. Pump Power Equation

$$Horsepower = \frac{QW(TDH)}{550E}$$

where *Q* is the flow of water in cubic feet per second; *W* is the water density, 62.4 pounds per cubic foot; *TDH* is the Total Delivered Head in feet (pressure measurement); and *E* is the pump efficiency in %.

c. Tool Cutting Speed

$$R = \frac{12C}{\pi d}$$

where R is the spindle rpm; C is the cutting speed, feet per minute; and d is the work diameter, inches.

2.7 Using Functions in Fortran

In this section, we describe the use of Fortran functions to perform numerical computations. A *function* is a separate module of code that may be provided as part of the compiler (called an *intrinsic* or *library function*) or may be written by the programmer. Each function performs a different mathematical operation (square root, cosine, etc.) and computes a single value. Functions are referenced directly in an expression. When the expression is evaluated, the function code is executed and the value computed by the function is substituted for the function reference.

EXAMPLE 2.14   Assume that SQRT is the name of a function that computes the square root of a positive value. If X is 16.0, the assignment statement

```
Y = SQRT(X)
```

is evaluated as follows:

1. X is 16.0, so function SQRT computes the $\sqrt{16.0}$ or 4.0.
2. The function result, 4.0, is assigned to Y.

The expression part of the assignment statement above specifies the name of a function, SQRT, followed by the function *argument*, X, enclosed in parentheses.

A function can be thought of as a "black-box" to which one or more input values are passed and which automatically returns a single output value. Figure 2.13 illustrates this concept for the call to function square root above.

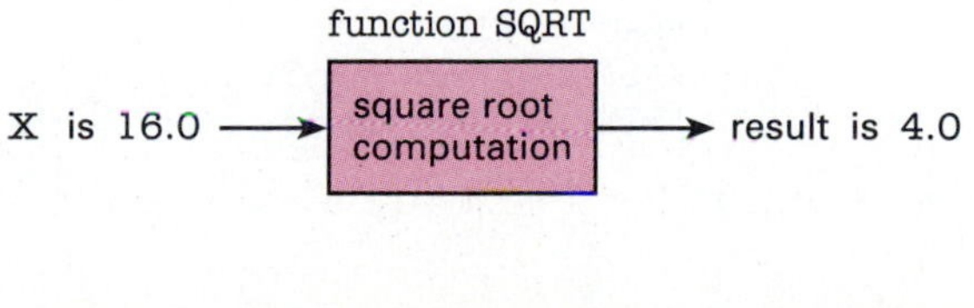

Figure 2.13. *Function SQRT as a "Black-box"*

The function input is the value of X (16.0), and the function result or output is the square root of 16.0 (result is 4.0).

Functions are *called* into execution by writing a function name and argument in an expression. After the function executes, its result is substituted for the function name. For example, if W is 9.0, the assignment statement

```
Z = 5.7 + SQRT(W)
```

is evaluated as follows:

1. W is 9.0, so function SQRT computes the $\sqrt{9.0}$ or 3.0.
2. The value of 5.7 and 3.0 are added together.
3. The sum, 8.7, is stored in Z.

The two calls to function SQRT discussed so far have different arguments (X and W). We will illustrate this capability of functions again in the next example.

EXAMPLE 2.15   The program in Fig. 2.14 displays the square root of two numbers that are provided as input data (FIRST and SECOND) and also displays the square root of their sum. To accomplish this, it must call the function SQRT three times:

```
ANSWER = SQRT(FIRST)
ANSWER = SQRT(SECOND)
ANSWER = SQRT(FIRST + SECOND)
```

For the first two calls, the function arguments are variables (FIRST and SECOND). The third call shows that a function argument can also be an expression (FIRST + SECOND). For all three calls, the result returned by function SQRT is assigned to variable ANSWER and then displayed.   ■

Figure 2.14. *Using Function SQRT*

```
      PROGRAM SQROOT
C Uses function SQRT to perform three square root computations.

C Declarations
      REAL FIRST, SECOND, ANSWER

C Get first number and display its square root.
      PRINT *, 'Enter the first number'
      READ *, FIRST
      ANSWER = SQRT(FIRST)
      PRINT *, 'The square root of the first number is ', ANSWER
```

```
C Get second number and display its square root.
      PRINT *, 'Enter the second number'
      READ *, SECOND
      ANSWER = SQRT(SECOND)
      PRINT *, 'The square root of the second number is ', ANSWER

C Display the square root of the sum of both numbers.
      ANSWER = SQRT(FIRST + SECOND)
      PRINT *, 'The square root of their sum is ', ANSWER

      STOP
      END


Enter the first number
9.0
The square root of the first number is 3.00000
Enter the second number
16.0
The square root of the second number is 4.00000
The square root of their sum is 5.00000
```

Functions and Reusability

A primary goal of software engineering is to write error-free code. One way to accomplish this is, whenever possible, to reuse code that has already been written and tested. In software engineering, this is called *reusability*. Stated more simply, "Why reinvent the wheel?"

Fortran promotes reusability by providing several predefined functions like SQRT that can be used to perform complicated mathematical computations. The names and descriptions of some commonly used predefined functions are given in Table 2.4. The function name is always followed by one or more arguments enclosed in parentheses and any valid arithmetic expression of the proper type may be used as an argument for these functions. A complete list of Fortran library functions appears in Appendix A.

The names used in this table are fairly descriptive of the operation performed by the function. Also, the type of result returned by each function is determined using the implicit type convention: A function whose name begins with the letters I through N returns a type INTEGER result; otherwise, the function returns a type REAL result. This is the reason for having two similar functions named ABS (type REAL result) and IABS (type INTEGER result) and for function names such as ALOG and AMAX1 instead of LOG and MAX1.

The type of argument(s) required by each function is also listed in Table 2.4. Note that using a type REAL argument where a type INTEGER argument is specified may cause a syntax error or incorrect results.

Table 2.4. *Table of Fortran Library Functions*

FUNCTION REFERENCE	OPERATION	ARGUMENT TYPE	RESULT TYPE
INT(*arg*)	Converts *arg* to an integer by dropping the fractional part	REAL	INTEGER
NINT(*arg*)	Rounds *arg* to nearest integer	REAL	INTEGER
REAL(*arg*)	Converts *arg* to a real value	INTEGER	REAL
ABS(*arg*)	Finds absolute value of *arg*	REAL	REAL
IABS(*arg*)	Finds absolute value of *arg*	INTEGER	INTEGER
SQRT(*arg*)	Computes square root of *arg* ($arg > 0.0$)	REAL	REAL
EXP(*arg*)	Computes e^{arg}	REAL	REAL
ALOG(arg)	Computes natural logarithm, $\ln(arg)$ ($arg > 0.0$)	REAL	REAL
ALOG10(*arg*)	Computes logarithm, $\log(arg)$ ($arg > 0.0$)	REAL	REAL
SIN(*arg*)	Computes sine of angle *arg* in radians	REAL	REAL
COS(*arg*)	Computes cosine of angle *arg* in radians	REAL	REAL
TAN(*arg*)	Computes tangent of angle *arg* in radians	REAL	REAL
MOD(*a1*, *a2*)	Computes remainder of *a1/a2*	INTEGER	INTEGER
MAX0(*a1*, . . . , *an*)	Selects largest value from list *a1*, . . . , *an*	INTEGER	INTEGER
AMAX1(*a1*, . . . , *an*)	Selects largest value from list *a1*, . . . , *an*	REAL	REAL
MIN0(*a1*, . . . , *an*)	Selects smallest value from list *a1*, . . . , *an*	INTEGER	INTEGER
AMIN1(*a1*, . . . , *an*)	Selects smallest value from list *a1*, . . . , *an*	REAL	REAL

The first three functions listed in Table 2.4 convert a value of one numeric type to the other numeric type. The function INT converts a type REAL value to an integer value by truncating it, that is, removing the fractional part.

EXAMPLE 2.16   The functions INT and NINT are used to convert a REAL value to an integer, as shown below. The function INT always removes the fractional part, whereas the function NINT rounds a real value to the nearest integer.

```
INT(5.3) is 5        NINT(5.3) is 5
INT(5.8) is 5        NINT(5.8) is 6
INT(-5.3) is -5      NINT(-5.3) is -5
INT(-5.8) is -5      NINT(-5.8) is -6
```

EXAMPLE 2.17   The function REAL converts an integer value to a real number. If TOTAL and NUMITM are both type INTEGER and AVE is type REAL, the assignment statement

```
AVE = REAL(TOTAL) / REAL(NUMITM)
```

stores the value of TOTAL divided by NUMITM in AVE, including any fractional remainder. For example, if TOTAL is 7 and NUMITM is 2, the value of AVE becomes 3.5. What would be stored in AVE by the following assignment statement?

```
AVE = TOTAL / NUMITM
```

The last few functions in Table 2.4 have multiple arguments. The function MOD must always have two arguments, while the functions MAX0 (pronounced "max zero"), AMAX1, MIN0, and AMIN1 may have any number of arguments.

EXAMPLE 2.18   If I is 5 and J is –7, the function reference

```
MAX0(3, 6, I + J, I - J)
```

returns the largest value in its argument list, which is the value of I – J, or 12. The function reference

```
MIN0(3, 6, I + J, I - J)
```

returns the smallest value in its argument list, which is the value of I + J, or –2.

EXAMPLE 2.19   The MOD function determines the integer remainder of an integer division. The value of the expression

```
MOD(N, 3)
```

is the integer remainder of N divided by 3. The only possible values for this expression are the integers 0 (no remainder), 1, or 2. The value of MOD(17, 3) is 2, as shown below:

$$
\begin{array}{r}
5 \leftarrow \text{quotient} \\
3\overline{)17} \\
15 \\
\hline
2 \leftarrow \text{remainder}
\end{array}
$$

However, the function reference MOD(3, 17) is not the same as the one

Fortran in the Programmer's Portfolio

JOHN V. VOLPE NATIONAL TRANSPORTATION SYSTEM CENTER

The Volpe National Transportation System Center supports the U.S. Department of Transportation by providing research and systems and software development to its subgroups, such as the FAA, and other government agencies. The center works with many different languages, and its programmers are all cross-trained in more than one language. Fortran is one of their programming languages; Pascal, COBOL, C, and BASIC are used as well.

Railroad track analysis and LORAN long-range navigation signal calibration are two examples of projects for which Fortran is used. The scientific or numerical nature of a project will generally motivate the use of Fortran, but for smaller, ad hoc programs, the preference of the investigator or programmer will point to Fortran. In addition, the center makes use of a number of existing applications, or "legacy" systems, which are frequently written in Fortran. In the absence of a good reason for converting the application to another language, the Fortran code is used and maintained.

The "CARF" system is an example of an older application originally written in Fortran on a Digital Equipment Corporation PDP-10 computer. The CARF system tracks air traffic and weather nationally and can be used to specify a flight path that is free of inclement weather and other aircraft. When the space shuttle is flown from California to Florida, for example, CARF is used to ascertain an uninterrupted path for it that avoids storms and precipitation. Since CARF was created, it has been converted to the VAX's VMS Fortran and then to the Fortran available on Apollo workstations.

above. The value returned by this function reference is 3, which is the integer remainder of 3 divided by 17.

The MOD function is often used to determine whether one integer is an exact divisor of another. If integer M is a divisor of N, the value of MOD(N, M) will be zero. ■

EXAMPLE 2.20   Einstein's theory of relativity demonstrates that mass increases with speed, that is,

$$m = m_0/(1 - (v/c)^2)^{1/2}$$

Despite the use and availability of other programming languages, Fortran remains a valuable part of the programming portfolio available to the programmers and investigators. Aside from its numerical procedures, Fortran's option of externally specifying input/output formats for data is a very useful one. In the commercial environment, where recompiling a large program after making adjustments to the input/output can cause unacceptable delays, this feature makes it possible to modify a Fortran application for a new use without recompiling.

Richard Jones, Project Programmer Analyst at the Transportation System Center, recommends that students learning Fortran today also learn to use another language. He suggests studying Fortran, Pascal, and C, because they all have a solid following and are block-structured

VNTSC Central Altitude Reservation Function (CARF)
Automated Airspace Allocation System

Program discovers that planned flights show a conflict zone in time, location, or altitude.

tured procedural languages that have been extended to parallel processors. But more important, he would follow this training with the work experience that acquaints the programmer with the unstructured nature of real-world problems and the importance of initiative and self-discipline. For Jones, whose livelihood is problem analysis and selection of an appropriate programming approach, the programming task includes everything from goals, through requirements analysis, logical and physical design, coding, multipurpose documentation (online, user, maintainer, programmer, reference), error reporting, and maintenance. A student who starts developing a methodology for programming will be more successful, and will be more likely to write code, Fortran or otherwise, that will be around to be called a "legacy" system one day.

Many thanks to Richard Jones of the John V. Volpe National Transportation System Center in Cambridge, Massachusetts, for explaining how Fortran is used by his colleagues, and for providing his perspective on the role of Fortran in the programmer's toolbox.

where m_0 is the mass of an object at rest, v is the velocity with respect to the observer, and c is the speed of light. We implement this equation in Fortran as

```
M = MO / SQRT(1.0 - (V/C) ** 2)
```

where the SQRT function raises its argument to the power 1/2 (its square root). We also can use the assignment statement

```
M = MO / (1.0 - (V/C) ** 2) ** (1.0/2.0)
```

to compute the mass, M. However, it is more efficient and more accurate to call the SQRT function. Note that the exponent 1/2 must be written in Fortran as (1.0/2.0), not (1/2). Fortran evaluates (1/2) using integer division, so (1/2) is zero in Fortran. ◼

EXAMPLE 2.21   The quadratic formula

$$\frac{-B \pm \sqrt{B^2 - 4AC}}{2a}$$

may be used to compute the roots of a quadratic equation in x:

$$Ax^2 + Bx + C = 0 \qquad A \text{ not equal to } 0.$$

The two roots are defined as

$$root_1 = \frac{-B + \sqrt{B^2 - 4AC}}{2A} \qquad root_2 = \frac{-B - \sqrt{B^2 - 4AC}}{2A}$$

when the discriminant $B^2 - 4AC$ is positive. If we assume that this is the case, we can use the following assignment statements to assign values to ROOT1 and ROOT2:

```
DISC = B ** 2 - 4.0 * A * C
ROOT1 = (-B + SQRT(DISC)) / (2.0 * A)
ROOT2 = (-B - SQRT(DISC)) / (2.0 * A)
```

We use parentheses to set off the numerator and the denominator in the expressions for ROOT1 and ROOT2, which causes the division to be performed last. Without parentheses, the division would be performed too early and the root values would not be correct. ◼

Program Style: *Computing and Saving Intermediate Results*

The assignment statements given above illustrate the correct way to write a complicated formula in Fortran. Rather than recompute the value of the discriminant each time, we compute it once and save it in DISC. Then, whenever we need the discriminant value, we reference the variable DISC. Doing this is not only more efficient but also reduces the chances of error because the resultant formulas for ROOT1 and ROOT2 are much simpler. We could introduce another variable to store the value of 2.0 * A, which appears in two assignment statements, but don't because the expression is so simple.

EXAMPLE 2.22

If we know the length of two sides (*B* and *C*) of a triangle (see Fig. 2.15) and the angle between them in degrees (*Alpha*), we can compute the length of the third side (*A*) using the formula

$$A^2 = B^2 + C^2 - 2BC \cos Alpha$$

To use Fortran's cosine function (COS), we must express its argument angle in radians instead of degrees. To convert an angle from degrees to radians, we multiply the angle by $\pi/180$. Assuming PI represents the constant π, the assignment statement below computes the unknown side length, *A*:

```
A = SQRT(B ** 2 + C ** 2 - 2 * B * C * COS(ALPHA * PI / 180.0))
```

Figure 2.15. *Triangle with Unknown Side A*

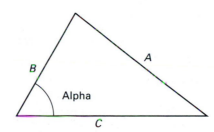

EXAMPLE 2.23

A very important function in biology and physics is the exponential function

$$f(x) = e^x$$

where *e* is the constant 2.718282 rounded to six decimal places. An equation of the form

$$population_{new} = population_{old} \times e^{ct}$$

describes the growth or increase in microorganisms over time *t* when *c* is a positive constant.

Figure 2.16. *Computing Radioactive Decay*

```
        PROGRAM DECAY
C Computes the decay of a radioactive substance.

C Declarations
        REAL C
        PARAMETER (C = 0.693 / 28.0)
        REAL SUBNEW, SUBOLD, TIME

C Read initial population and time.
        PRINT *, 'Enter the initial amount of Strontium 90'
        READ *, SUBOLD
        PRINT *, 'Enter the time in years'
        READ *, TIME

C Compute new population amount.
        SUBNEW = SUBOLD * EXP(-C * TIME)

C Display result.
        PRINT *, 'The amount remaining is ', SUBNEW

        STOP
        END


Enter the initial amount of Strontium 90
10.0
Enter the time in years
28.0
The amount remaining is 5.00074
```

The equation

$$\text{substance}_{new} = \text{substance}_{old} \times e^{-ct}$$

describes the decay (exponent of e is negative) of a radioactive substance over time due to its emission of radioactive particles. The program in Fig. 2.16 uses this formula to compute the amount of Strontium 90 remaining after a given time period, assuming the constant c is 0.693 / 28.0. The sample run shows that an initial mass of 10.0 grams would decay to 5.0 grams, or half its mass, after 28 years. This means that 28 years is the *half-life* of the Strontium 90 isotope. ◼

EXAMPLE 2.24   Archaeologists use carbon dating to determine the age of an object based on the proportion of carbon 14 (a radioactive substance) remaining in the object. The formula is

$$age = -\log_e(carbon14) / .0001216$$

Figure 2.17. *Carbon Dating Program*

```
      PROGRAM DATING
C Computes the age of a substance by carbon dating.

C Declarations
      REAL AGE, CARB14

C Enter the proportion of carbon 14.
      PRINT *, 'Enter proportion of carbon 14 as a decimal fraction'
      READ *, CARB14

C Estimate the age.
      AGE = -ALOG(CARB14) / .1216E-3

C Display the age.
      PRINT *, 'The approximate age in years is ', AGE

      STOP
      END


Enter proportion of carbon 14 as a decimal fraction
0.8
The approximate age in years is      1835.06
```

where *carbon14* is the proportion of carbon 14 remaining expressed as a fraction. Figure 2.17 uses this formula to compute and display the estimated age of an object.

Using Data Type INTEGER and Function MOD

The next case study uses type INTEGER variables and the function MOD.

Case Study: Finding the Value of a Coin Collection

PROBLEM STATEMENT

Your little sister has been saving nickels and pennies for quite a while. Because she is getting tired of lugging her piggy bank with her whenever she goes to the store, she would like to trade in her collection for dollar bills and some change. To do this, she needs to know the value of her coin collection in dollars and cents.

ANALYSIS

To solve this problem, we must know the count of nickels and the count of pennies in the collection. First, we determine the total value of the collection in cents. Next, once we have this figure, we can do an integer division using 100 as the divisor to obtain the dollar value; the remainder of this division will be the loose change your sister should receive. In the data requirements below, we list the total value of her collection in cents (TOTVAL) as a program variable because that variable is needed as part of the computation process but is not a required problem output. Note that we also specify the data type (INTEGER) of each variable.

Data Requirements and Formulas

Problem Inputs

the count of nickels (INTEGER NICKEL)
the count of pennies (INTEGER PENNYS)

Problem Outputs

the number of dollars she should receive (INTEGER DOLLAR)
the loose change she should receive (INTEGER CHANGE)

Additional Program Variables

the total value in cents (INTEGER TOTVAL)

Relevant Formulas or Relations

one dollar = 100 pennies
one nickel = five pennies

DESIGN

The algorithm is straightforward and is displayed next.

Algorithm

1. Read in the count of nickels and pennies.
2. Compute the total value in cents.
3. Find the value in dollars and loose change.
4. Display the value in dollars and loose change.

Steps 2 and 3 may need refinement. Their refinement follows:

Step 2 Refinement

2.1 TOTVAL is 5 times NICKEL plus PENNYS.

Step 3 Refinement

3.1 DOLLAR is the integer quotient of TOTVAL and 100.
3.2 CHANGE is the integer remainder of TOTVAL and 100.

IMPLEMENTATION

The program is shown in Fig. 2.18. The statement

```
TOTVAL = 5 * NICKEL + PENNYS
```

Figure 2.18. *Value of a Coin Collection*

```
      PROGRAM COINS
C Determines the value of a coin collection.

C Declarations
      INTEGER PENNYS, NICKEL, DOLLAR, CHANGE, TOTVAL

C Read in the count of nickels and pennies.
      PRINT *, 'Enter number of nickels'
      READ *, NICKEL
      PRINT *, 'Enter number of pennies'
      READ *, PENNYS

C Compute the total value in cents.
      TOTVAL = 5 * NICKEL + PENNYS

C Find the value in dollars and change.
      DOLLAR = TOTVAL / 100
      CHANGE = MOD(TOTVAL, 100)

C Display the value in dollars and change.
      PRINT *, 'Your collection is worth ', DOLLAR, ' dollars'
      PRINT *, ' and ', CHANGE, ' cents.'

      STOP
      END

Enter number of nickels
30
Enter number of pennies
77
Your collection is worth 2 dollars
and 27 cents.
```

implements algorithm step 2.1. The statements

```
DOLLAR = TOTVAL / 100
CHANGE = MOD(TOTVAL, 100)
```

use integer division and the function MOD to implement algorithm steps 3.1 and 3.2.

TESTING AND VERIFICATION

To test this program, try running it with a combination of nickels and pennies that yields an exact dollar amount with no change left over. For example, 35 nickels and 25 pennies should yield a value of 2 dollars and no cents. Then increase and decrease the amount of pennies by one (26 and 24 pennies) to ensure that these cases also are handled properly.

Self-check

1. Rewrite the following mathematical expressions using Fortran functions.

 a. $\sqrt{U + V} \times W^2$
 b. $\log_n (X^Y)$
 c. $\sqrt{(X - Y)^2}$
 d. $|XY - W/Z|$

2. Evaluate the following:

 a. `INT(-15.8)`
 b. `NINT(-15.8)`
 c. `NINT(6.8) * ABS(-3.0)`
 d. `SQRT(ABS(NINT(-15.8)))`
 e. `NINT(3.5)`
 f. `REAL(7 / 2)`
 g. `REAL(7) / REAL(2)`

Programming

1. Write a statement that computes and displays the *absolute difference* of two real variables X, Y. If $X > Y$, then the absolute difference is $(X - Y)$; if $Y > X$, then the absolute difference is $(Y - X)$. Use function ABS.
2. Using the NINT function, write a statement to round any real value X to the nearest two decimal places. *Hint:* You will have to multiply by 100.0 before rounding.
3. Write a complete Fortran program that prompts the user for the Cartesian coordinates of two points (X_1, Y_1) and (X_2, Y_2) and displays the distance between them computed using the formula below

$$distance = \sqrt{(X_1 - X_2)^2 + (Y_1 - Y_2)^2}$$

4. Write a program that uses the formula for microorganism growth shown in Example 2.23. Use a value of 1.386 for c. Prompt the user for the initial microorganism population and the elapsed time in hours.

2.8 Common Programming Errors

One of the first things you will discover in writing programs is that a program rarely runs correctly the first time. Murphy's Law regarding whatever possibly can go wrong, will, seems to have been coined with the computer programmer or programming student in mind. In fact, errors are so common that they have their own special name—*bugs*—and the process of correcting them is called *debugging* a program. To alert you to potential problems, we provide a section on common errors at the end of each chapter.

When an error is detected, an error message is printed indicating you have made a mistake and its probable cause. Unfortunately, error messages are often difficult to interpret and are sometimes misleading. As you gain experience, however, you will become more proficient at understanding them.

Although we don't like to see error messages, it's worse when errors occur with no indication that they exist. For example, a program may compute results that appear perfectly reasonable but that are, in fact, incorrect. We may have no idea that the program results are wrong and might use these results as the basis for a decision.

Be forewarned that such errors can happen—don't assume a result is correct just because it was generated by a computer. You should manually verify all computational results using representative data. You may not be able to do the computation with the same degree of accuracy as the computer, but you can derive approximate results for comparison purposes.

Debugging a program can be time-consuming. Your best approach: Plan your programs carefully and desk check them beforehand to eliminate bugs before they occur. If you are not sure of the syntax for a particular statement, look it up in this text or on the inside front cover. If you follow this approach, you will be much better off in the long run.

Several types of errors can occur, which we discuss below. Common ones to watch out for include

- syntax errors,
- run-time errors,
- line-position errors, and
- arithmetic expression errors.

Syntax Errors

Syntax errors are detected by the compiler as it attempts to translate your program. If a statement has a syntax error, the compiler cannot translate it and your program will not be executed.

Figure 2.19 shows a compiler listing of a payroll program with errors from the Digital Equipment Corporation VAX Fortran compiler. Line numbers are on the left, and each error message is shown directly beneath the line in error.

The program contains the following syntax errors:

- PARAMETER misspelled (line 3)
- missing * after PRINT (line 5)
- apostrophes used with READ statement (line 6)
- assignment statement with transposed variable and expression part (line 10)
- transposed comma and apostrophe in PRINT statement (line 11)
- missing apostrophe in PRINT statement (line 12)

Your compiler may display error messages that differ from those shown in Fig. 2.19. Some compilers list all error messages after the program or in a

Figure 2.19. *Compiler Listing of a Program with Syntax Errors*

```
0001 PROGRAM MESSUP
0002 REAL TAX
0003 PARAMATER (TAX = 25.00)
%FORT-F-MISSDEL, Missing operator or delimiter symbol

0004 REAL HOURS, RATE, GROSS, NET
0005 PRINT, 'Enter hours worked'
%FORT-F-MISSVAR, Missing variable or constant
%FORT-F-IOINVFMT, Format specifier in error

0006 READ *, 'HOURS'
%FORT-F-IOINVLIST, Invalid I/O list element for input statement

0007 PRINT *, 'Enter hourly rate'
0008 READ *, RATE
0009 GROSS = HOURS * RATE
0010 GROSS - TAX = NET
%FORT-F-INVLEFSID, Left side of assignment must be variable or array
element

0011 PRINT *, 'Gross pay is $,' GROSS
%FORT-F-MISSDEL, Missing operator or delimiter symbol

0012 PRINT *, 'Net pay is $, NET
%FORT-E-MISSAPOS, Missing apostrophe in character constant

0013 STOP
0014 END
```

separate file altogether. If there are one or more errors, your compiler may be unable to translate your program and may not create an object file.

The error messages generated by a compiler do not always provide a clear indication of what is wrong. For example, in line 5 of Fig. 2.19, the actual error is due to a missing * after the word PRINT. The first error message

```
%FORT-F-MISSVAR, Missing variable or constant
```

gives no hint of this error. The second error message

```
%FORT-F-IOINVFMT, Format specifier in error
```

is a little better, but only if you understand that the symbol * serves as a format specifier (explained in Chapter 5).

One very common syntax error is caused by the improper use of double quotes as string delimiters. Make sure you always use a single quote or apostrophe to begin and end a string; double quotes are not allowed. Also, ensure there are no missing or extra apostrophes in a string; for example, if the apostrophe at the end is missing, the compiler is unable to determine where the string stops (see line 12 in Fig. 2.19). Another frequent error when working with string delimiters is transposing a comma with an apostrophe in an output list (see line 11).

Misspelling a variable name is an often-seen error. For example, if you misspell NET as NST in an assignment statement, Fortran will not tell you that you have an undeclared variable—it will simply allocate a new variable named NST. If NST appears in the expression part, some Fortran compilers may warn you that NST was not defined before it was used. If NST appears on the left of an assignment (e.g., NST = . . .), there will be no warning and the expression value will be incorrectly assigned to NST, not NET, when the program executes.

Run-time Errors Run-time errors are detected by the computer during program execution. They occur because the computer was directed to perform an illegal operation, such as dividing a number by zero or manipulating undefined or invalid data. When a run-time error occurs, the computer stops executing your program and displays a diagnostic message that indicates the line where the error occurred. Sometimes it also displays the values of all variables.

Figure 2.20 shows a program with a run-time error. The program compiles successfully, but the assignment statement

```
Z = X / Y
```

attempts to divide a real value by zero (value of Y). This causes the computer to stop execution at line 6 and to display a message such as

```
Attempted division by zero
```

Figure 2.20. *Program with a Run-time Error*

```
PROGRAM ERROR
REAL X, Y, Z
PRINT *, 'Enter X'
READ *, X
Y = 0.0
Z = X / Y
PRINT *, 'Z is ', Z
STOP
END
```

```
Program terminated at line 6
Attempted division by zero
```

Line-positioning Errors

Line-positioning errors can cause either syntax or run-time errors. For example, sometimes errors are caused by lines that start in the wrong column or that are too long.

If you start a line in column 6 instead of column 7, Fortran assumes that the new line is a continuation of the previous line. This most likely will cause a syntax error. Lines that are too long can cause either syntax errors or run-time errors. For example, if the apostrophe at the end of a string appears after column 72, some Fortran compilers will ignore the apostrophe and display a missing-apostrophe syntax error.

If the name of a variable used in a long expression happens to begin in column 72, Fortran may ignore all but the first letter of that variable name. Fortran will assume that there is a new variable with a one-letter name and will allocate a memory cell for that variable (for example, variable W instead of variable WEIGHT). When evaluating the expression, Fortran will use whatever value happens to be stored in variable W instead of the value of variable WEIGHT. This may cause a run-time error or lead to incorrect program results.

Errors in Arithmetic Expressions

This chapter described how to declare the names and data types of variables and parameters used in a program. Errors in type declarations are generally caused by spelling mistakes or failure to declare a variable used in a program. In either case, the compiler will assume incorrectly that the misspelled or undeclared identifier is the name of a new variable. It will determine this variable's type by the implicit type convention and allocate a memory cell for its storage. If type REAL or INTEGER data are stored in the implicitly declared variable, no error message will be printed; however, the program results may be incorrect.

The type of each data value entered during program execution must correspond to the variable in which it is stored. If the data type required is not obvious, your program should print a prompting message with appropriate instructions for the program user. If a character string is being entered as a data item, your program prompt should remind the user that the string must be enclosed in apostrophes.

Be careful to use the correct type of operator with each operand in an expression. And recall that the arithmetic operators can be used only with type INTEGER or REAL operands. If a type REAL expression is assigned to a type INTEGER variable, the fractional part of the result will be lost. Also, the fractional remainder is lost when two integers are divided. Fortran does not consider the occurrence of either of these events an error, but it could cause your program to compute incorrect results.

Exercise care when working with complicated expressions. It is easy to inadvertently omit parentheses or operators, especially the * operator. If an operator or a single parenthesis is omitted, a syntax error will be detected; however, if a pair of parentheses is omitted, then the expression, although syntactically correct, may compute the wrong value.

We recommend you break a complicated expression into subexpressions that you assign separately to temporary variables and then manipulate these temporary variables. For example, instead of writing the single assignment statement

```
Z = SQRT(X + Y) / (1.0 + SQRT(X + Y))
```

you could write the three assignment statements

```
TEMP1 = SQRT(X + Y)
TEMP2 = 1.0 + TEMP1
Z = TEMP1 / TEMP2
```

which has the same effect. Using three assignment statements is also more efficient because then the square-root operation is performed only once; it is performed twice in the single assignment statement. During debugging, you can display the values of the temporary variables (TEMP1 and TEMP2) to verify that the computations are correct.

Finally, be careful to use the right type and number of arguments in a function call. A type REAL argument cannot be used with one of the functions MOD, REAL, IABS, MAXO, and MINO. A negative value cannot be passed as the argument of SQRT, ALOG, or ALOG10.

Other Kinds of Errors

In addition to the errors mentioned above, you may encounter the following other kinds of errors:

1. *Logic errors.* These are errors in the logic of your program, such as using the wrong variable name in an equation. Very common and very dangerous, these errors are difficult to detect and are usually found when the program generates strange-looking results.
2. *System problems.* Even though your program may be perfect, it may, on rare occasions, not run correctly because of problems with the computer system. Examples of this type of problem include when the disk drive is malfunctioning or when your program is writing an output file, but there is insufficient room on the disk for the new file.
3. *Compiler problems.* Sometimes the Fortran compiler has bugs and cannot translate your program properly. Beginning programmers often blame their difficulties on a faulty compiler. These errors are extremely rare, however, and occur mostly with new equipment.

Chapter Review

You saw how to perform some fundamental operations using Fortran. You learned how to instruct the computer to read information into memory, perform some simple computations using assignment statements, and print the results of the computation. All of this was done using symbols (punctuation marks, variable names, and special operators such as *, −, and +) that are familiar, easy to remember, and easy to use. You do not have to know very much about your computer to understand and use Fortran.

The Fortran language enables your computer to manipulate different types of data. We have introduced three of these types—INTEGER, REAL, and CHARACTER—in this chapter.

All information is stored in the computer as a binary string whose format is determined by the type of data being represented. In order for the Fortran compiler to generate the correct machine language instructions for a program, it must know the types of all data being manipulated. Thus you must clearly indicate the types of all constants and variable names used in a program. You specify the types of variable names either by using data type declaration statements or by allowing the compiler to assign a type to each name according to the implicit typing convention. This latter method is not recommended; if you elect to use it, all variable names beginning with the letters I through N will be automatically typed as INTEGER while names beginning with A through H or O through Z will be automatically typed as REAL.

Constants in programs are typed according to the way in which they are written. Real constants are numbers that contain a decimal point; integer constants are numbers that do not contain a decimal point. Character-string constants consist of a string of legal Fortran characters enclosed in apostrophes.

In this chapter, we also provided rules for forming and evaluating arithmetic expressions, which are useful when dealing with numerically oriented problems. Knowledge of these rules will enable you to apply Fortran correctly to perform calculations. One useful guideline to keep in mind when transforming an equation or formula to Fortran is when in doubt of the meaning, insert parentheses.

We also discussed integer arithmetic. Of the basic arithmetic operators, +, −, *, /, and **, only the slash (division) produces different results when used with integers instead of reals. This is because the internal format used for storage of integers does not permit the representation of a fractional remainder.

We also introduced Fortran library or intrinsic functions. Using these functions will enable you to perform numerical calculations more efficiently because calling a function to compute a result is much faster and easier than trying to perform the calculation using the basic arithmetic operations.

Fortran Statements   The Fortran statements introduced in this chapter are described in Table 2.5.

Table 2.5. *Summary of Fortran Statements for Chapter 2*

STATEMENT	EFFECT
Type Declaration	

`REAL X, Y, Z`
`INTEGER ME, IT`
`CHARACTER *20 NAME`
	Allocates memory cells X, Y, and Z for storage of real numbers; allocates ME and IT for storage of integers; allocates NAME for storing a character string of length 20.

PARAMETER Statement	
`PARAMETER (TAX = 25.00)` `PARAMETER (STAR = '*')`	Associates the parameter TAX with the value 25.00 and the parameter STAR with the value '*'.
Assignment Statement	
`DISTNC = SPEED * TIME`	Assigns the product of SPEED and TIME as the value of DISTNC.
`I = J / K + MOD(L + 5, N)`	Adds the result of J / K to the integer remainder of (L + 5) divided by N. L and N must be type INTEGER.
READ Statement	
`READ *, HOURS, RATE`	Enters data into the variables HOURS and RATE.
PRINT Statement	
`PRINT *, 'Net = ', NET` `PRINT *, X, Y`	Displays the symbols Net = followed by the value of NET, then prints the values of X and Y on the next line.
STOP Statement	
`STOP`	Terminates program execution.
END Statement	
`END`	Indicates the end of a program during translation and terminates program execution if STOP is missing.
Comment	
`C This is a comment` `* So is this!`	Comments document the use of variables and statements in a program. They are ignored by the compiler.

Quick-Check Exercises

1. What value is assigned to X by the following statement?

   ```
   X = 25.0 * 3.0 / 2.5
   ```

2. What value is assigned to X by the following statement, assuming X is 10.0?

   ```
   X = X - 20 / 3
   ```

3. When does the operator / mean real division and when does it mean integer division?

4. Evaluate the following when X is 22.0 and Y is 3.0.

   ```
   X + Y / SQRT(X + Y)
   ```

5. Complete the formula below for integers N and M:

   ```
   N = (N / M) * _____ + MOD(_____, _____)
   ```

6. Write a Fortran expression to compute the real average of N items whose sum is stored in variable SUM where N and SUM are type INTEGER.

7. Show the output line displayed when X is 3.456.

   ```
   PRINT *, 'The value of X is ', X
   ```

8. What data type would you use to represent the following items: (a) number of children at school, (b) a letter grade on an exam, (c) the average number of school days absent each year?

9. What is the purpose of the PRINT statement used with a READ from the keyboard? Which statement executes first: READ or PRINT?

10. If a READ statement is reading two numbers, what character separates the two numbers? What key is pressed after the second number is entered?

11. If a READ statement is reading a student's letter grade, what character does the program user type first?

12. How does the computer determine how many data values to enter when a READ statement executes?

13. How does the program user determine how many data values to enter when a READ statement executes?

14. Does the compiler listing show syntax or run-time errors?

Answers to Quick-check Exercises

1. 30.0
2. 3.0
3. The operator / means real division if one or both of its operands is type REAL; it means integer division when both of its operands are type INTEGER.
4. 22.0 + (3.0 / SQRT(25.0)) is 22.0 + (3.0 / 5.0) is 22.6
5. N = (N / M) * M + MOD(N, M)
6. REAL(SUM) / REAL(N)
7. The value of X is 3.45600.
8. INTEGER, CHARACTER *1, REAL
9. PRINT displays a prompt; PRINT is first.

10. A blank; the Return or Enter key
11. An apostrophe
12. It depends on the number of variables in the input list.
13. From reading the prompt
14. Syntax errors

Review Questions

1. Does a compiler translate comments?
2. What are two ways to denote comments?
3. What are three characteristics of structured programs?
4. Check the variables that are syntactically correct:

```
INCOME  _____      TWO FOLD  _____
1TIME   _____      C3PO       _____
CONST   _____      MYINCOME  _____
TOM'S   _____      R2DTWO    _____
```

5. What action is required by the statement below?

```
REAL CELL1
```

6. What is illegal about the following statements?

```
REAL PI, C, R
PARAMETER (PI = 3.14159)
PI = C / (2 * R ** 2)
```

7. Write a program to read a five-character name and print the name out following the string 'Hello '.
8. If the average size of a family is 2.8 and this value is stored in the variable FAMSIZ, provide the Fortran statement to display this fact in a readable way.
9. List three data types of Fortran.
10. What are the advantages of data type INTEGER over data type REAL?
11. What is the result of the expression (3 + 5.0 / 2) + 8 − 15 / 4?
12. Given the following declarations, indicate the data type and value of each expression below when X is 7.0, Y is 2.0, A is 2, B is 7.

```
REAL X, Y
INTEGER A, B
```

	Type	Value
X * Y	_____	_____
A * B	_____	_____
B / Y	_____	_____
B / A	_____	_____
X / Y	_____	_____
MOD(A, B)	_____	_____
MOD(X, Y)	_____	_____

13. Indicate the answer to the operations presented below.

    MOD(11, 2)   _____   ABS(-37.5 + 20)   _____
    INT(-3.5)   _____   SQRT(12.0 + 13.0) _____
    MAXO(-27, 50, 4)   _____   INT(-25.7)   _____
    MINO(-27, 50, 4)   _____   NINT(-18.7)   _____

14. Write an assignment statement that rounds a real variable NUM1 to two digits after the decimal point leaving the result in NUM1.
15. List and explain three computational errors that may occur in type REAL expressions.
16. Consider the following mathematical formula:

$$\frac{2}{3Y} \sqrt{\frac{4Z^2 - Y}{2A - B}}$$

Which of the following expressions correctly represents the above formula? Assume all variables are type REAL.

a. 2 / 3 / Y * SQRT((4 * Z ** 2 - Y) / (2 * A - B))
b. 2 / (3 * Y) * SQRT((4 * Z * Z - Y) / (2 * A - B))
c. 2 / 3Y * SQRT((4Z ** 2 - Y) / (2A - B))
d. 0.667 / Y * SQRT((4 * Z ** 2 - Y) / (2 * A - B))
e. 2 / 3 * Y * SQRT((4 * Z * Z - Y) / (2 * A - B))

Fortran 90 Features: Program Format

Many features of Fortran 90 affect the style and appearance of Fortran programs. Some of these are described in this section.

Identifiers

Fortran 90 rules for forming identifiers allow you to choose more meaningful names for variables and parameters. For example, you can use longer identifiers (up to thirty-one characters) and include in them lowercase and uppercase letters and the underscore character. This means that long variable names such as circumference can be written without abbreviation. Also, two or more words can be joined to form a single identifier by using the underscore character between words, as in hours_worked. However, because Fortran does not distinguish between uppercase and lowercase letters in an identifier, the identifiers Hours_Worked, HOURS_WORKED, and hours_worked would all refer to the same variable, not to three different variables. Therefore we recommend using all lowercase for identifiers, which will distinguish them from the all uppercase Fortran keywords such as READ, PRINT, STOP, and END.

Free-form Statements

When writing a Fortran 90 program, you can either follow the rules for positioning Fortran statements as described in Section 2.4 or write it free-form. In a *free-form program,* a Fortran line can have up to 132 characters and you can begin a Fortran statement anywhere in the line. You can also place more than one statement on a line (although this is not recommended), provided you separate them with the symbol ;.

Because column positions have no significance in free-form programs, you cannot use a c or * in column 1 to indicate a comment. Instead, use the symbol! anywhere in a line to indicate that the rest of the line is a comment. Also, you cannot use column 6 to indicate statement continuation. Instead, you do this by typing one of the following:

- the symbol & as the last non-blank character on the current line or
- the symbol & as the last non-blank character before !.

Figure 2.21 shows a free-form version of a program that computes and displays the area and circumference (outputs) of a circle with radius r (input). The program identifiers are all in lowercase. The declarations for parameter pi are on a single line, and the REAL type declaration statement is written over three lines, with each line having a comment at the end that describes the purpose of the identifier being declared.

Figure 2.21. *Free-form Program*

```
PROGRAM circle_area_circumference
! Finds and displays the area and circumference of a circle.
! The program user enters the circle radius and units of
! measurement.

! Declarations
REAL pi ; PARAMETER (pi = 3.141593)    ! multiple statements

REAL r,                 &  ! input - radius of circle
     area,              &  ! output - area of circle
     circumference         ! output - circumference of circle
CHARACTER *12 units        ! input - units of measurement

! Read the value of radius and units.
PRINT *, 'Enter units (enclosed in apostrophes)' ; READ *, units
PRINT *, 'Enter radius (in ', units, ')'          ; READ *, r

! Find the area.
area = pi * r ** 2

! Find the circumference.
circumference = 2.0 * pi * r
```

```
! Print the values of area and circumference.
PRINT *, 'The area is ', area, ' square ', units
PRINT *, 'The circumference is ', circumference, ' ', units

STOP
END
```

```
Enter units (enclosed in apostrophes)
'centimeters'
Enter radius (in centimeters)
5.0
The area is        78.53976 square centimeters
The circumference is       31.41593 centimeters
```

Programming Projects

1. Write a program that converts a temperature in degrees Fahrenheit to degrees Celsius. Be careful in converting the formula below into Fortran.

Data Requirements and Formulas

Problem Input

temperature in degrees Fahrenheit (FAHREN : INTEGER)

Problem Output

temperature in degrees Celsius (CELSUS : REAL)

Relevant formula

$$\text{CELSUS} = \frac{5}{9} \times (\text{FAHREN} - 32)$$

2. Write a program that reads two data items and prints their sum, difference, product, and quotient.

Data Requirements

Problem Inputs

two data items (X, Y : INTEGER)

Problem Outputs

sum of X and Y	(SUM : INTEGER)
difference of X and Y	(DIFRNC : INTEGER)
product of X and Y	(PRODCT : INTEGER)
quotient of X divided by Y	(QUOTNT : REAL)

3. Write a program to read in the weight (in pounds) of an object, and compute and print its weight in kilograms and grams. (*Hint:* One pound is equal to 0.453592 kilograms or 453.59237 grams.)

4. Write a program that computes the current and power through a resistor given the voltage and the resistance value. Use the formulas

$$I = V/R,$$
$$P = I^2R,$$

where V is voltage, R is resistance, I is current, and P is power.

5. Write a program that determines how many times a human heart beats in a lifetime. Your program should work for any pulse-rate (for example, 72 beats per minute) and any lifetime (example, 75 years). Use 365.25 for days in a year.

6. Write a program that computes the duration of a projectile's flight and its height above ground when it reaches the target. The program inputs are the initial angle of elevation for the projectile, its initial velocity, and the distance to the target.

   ### Problem Parameter

   Gravitational constant (in feet/sec^2) (G = 32.17)

   ### Problem Input

angle (in radians) of elevation	(THETA : REAL)
distance (in feet) to target	(DISTNC : REAL)
projectile velocity (in feet/sec)	(VELOCY : REAL)

   ### Problem Output

time (in seconds) of flight	(TIME : REAL)
height at impact (in feet)	(HEIGHT : REAL)

   ### Relevant Formulas

   time = distance/(velocity × cos Theta)
   height = velocity × time − (g × time^2)/2

7. Write a program that reads in the length and width (in meters) of a rectangular yard and the length and width of a rectangular house situated in the yard. Your program should compute the time required to cut the grass at the rate of 2 m^2/sec.

8. Write a program that reads in the numerators and denominators of two fractions. Your program should print the numerator and denominator of the fraction that represents the product of the two fractions. Also, print the percent equivalent of the resulting product.

9. Redo project 8, this time computing the sum of the two fractions.

10. Eight track stars entered the mile race at the Penn Relays. Write a program that will read in the race time in minutes (MINUTE) and seconds (SECOND) for each runner, then compute and print the speed in feet per second (FPS) and in meters per second (MPS). (*Hint:* There are 5280 feet in one mile, and one kilometer equals 3282 feet.)

Test your program on each of the times below:

Minutes	Seconds
3	52.83
3	59.83
4	00.03
4	16.22

11. You are planning to rent a car to drive from Boston to Philadelphia. You want to be certain you can make the trip on one tankful of gas. Write a program to read in the miles per gallon (MPG) and tank size (TNKSIZ) in gallons for a particular rental car, then print out the distance that can be traveled on one tank. Test your program for the following data:

Miles per Gallon	Tank Size (Gallons)
10.0	15.0
40.5	20.0
22.5	12.0
10.0	9.0

12. A cyclist coasting on a level road slows from a speed of 10 mi per hour to 2.5 mi per hour in 1 minute. Write a computer program that calculates the cyclist's constant rate of acceleration and determines how long it will take the cyclist to come to rest, given an initial speed of 10 mi per hour. (*Hint:* Use the equation

$$a = (v_f - v_i)/t,$$

where a is acceleration, t is time interval, v_i is initial velocity, and v_f is the final velocity.)

13. The diagram below shows two airline routes from Philadelphia to Dallas. Read each distance shown into a type INTEGER variable and then find the distance from Philadelphia to Dallas for each route.

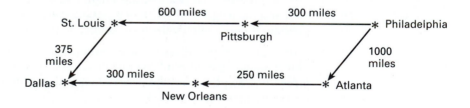

14. In shopping for a new house, you must consider several factors. In this problem, the initial cost of the house, estimated annual fuel costs, and annual tax rate are available. Write a program that will determine the total cost after a five-year period for each set of house data below. You should be able to inspect your program output to determine the "best buy."

Initial House Cost	Annual Fuel Cost	Tax Rate
$67,000	$2,300	0.025
$62,000	$2,500	0.025
$75,000	$1,850	0.020

To calculate the house cost, add the initial cost to the fuel cost for 5 years, then add the taxes for 5 years. Taxes for 1 year are computed by multiplying the tax rate by the initial cost.

15. Write a program that reads in the values of three resistors and calculates their total combined resistance. The three resistors are arranged in parallel as shown below:

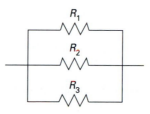

The formula for calculating the total resistance in this circuit is:

$$\frac{1}{\dfrac{1}{R_1} + \dfrac{1}{R_2} + \dfrac{1}{R_3}}$$

16. The Pythagorean theorem says that the sum of the squares of the sides of a right triangle is equal to the square of the hypotenuse. For example, if two sides of a right triangle are of lengths 3 and 4, then the hypotenuse is of length 5 ($3^2 + 4^2 = 5^2$). The three integers, 3, 4, and 5, together form a *pythagorean triple*. There is an infinite number of such triples. Given two positive integers, m and n, where $m > n$, a pythagorean triple can be generated by the following formulas:

$$side\ 1 = m^2 - n^2$$
$$side\ 2 = 2mn$$
$$hypotenuse = m^2 + n^2$$

Write a program that reads in values for m and n and calculates the pythagorean triple generated according to the formulas above.

17. A manufacturer wishes to determine the cost of producing the top for a cylindrical container. The cost of each top will be COST dollars per square inch of the material needed to produce the top. The amount of material needed for each top is the area of the top, which is circular. Recall that the area of a circle is *pi* times the radius squared. Write a program to read in the radius (RADIUS) of a top, the cost per square inch of the top (COST), and the number of tops to be produced (QUANT). Calculate the final cost of producing all the tops.

18. The diagram below shows an insulated pipe carrying a hot fluid. We need to calculate the heat loss through the insulation, the thermal resistance of the insulation, and the temperature at the midpoint radius of the insulation. The relevant equations are:

R = thermal resistance of insulation
r_1 = inner radius of insulation
Ts_1 = insulation temperature at r_1
T = insulation temperature at r
Q = heat loss through the insulation
L = length of pipe
r_2 = outer radius of insulation
Ts_2 = insulation temperature at r_2
k = thermal conductivity of insulation
$r = 1/2(r_1 + r_2)$

For calcium silicate insulation:

k = .0364 Btu/hr ft °F
Ts_1 = 327°F
r_1 = 10.75 in.
Ts_2 = 90°F
r_2 = 12.75 in.
L = 1 ft

CHAPTER 3
Decisions and the IF Statement

WE BEGIN THIS chapter by discussing structured programming and the need for control structures, which enable a program to make decisions or to repeat sequences of steps. We then introduce the LOGICAL data type and show how to use it to write expressions that evaluate to true or false. We also show how to use logical expressions in IF statements, which are statements that can make decisions, and demonstrate writing algorithms with decision steps.

We continue our study of problem solving and introduce another problem-solving strategy: solution by analogy. And finally, we show how to hand-check, or trace, the execution of an algorithm or a program to ensure that it does what we expect it to.

3.1 Structured Programming and Control Structures

Structured programming is a disciplined approach to programming that results in programs that are easy to read and understand and less likely to contain errors. It emphasizes following accepted program style guidelines, such as using meaningful names for identifiers, to write code that is adequately documented with comments and that is clear and readable. Obscure tricks and programming shortcuts are strongly discouraged.

Further, structured programs are easier to maintain than are unstructured programs, which makes them strong favorites with government and industry. This maintenance will usually involve removing previously undetected bugs and updating the program as government regulations or company policies change. It is common for a structured program to be maintained long after the programmers who originally coded it have moved on to other positions. In fact, many Fortran programs currently in use in industry have been around for 10 years or more.

Structured programming also involves organizing a program as a sequence of separate steps using control structures and modules. We discuss control structures in the next section and demonstrate how to write modules in Chapter 6.

Control Structures

Structured programming uses control structures to control the flow of statement execution in a program. A *control structure* is a group of related statements with one entry point and one exit point. There are three categories of control structures: sequence, selection, and iteration.

Sequence Control Structures   We can use sequence control structures to organize statements in a particular group so they are always executed in the order in which they are listed. For example, if a Fortran program consists of the following group of statements:

$statement_1$
$statement_2$
· · ·
$statement_n$

then $statement_1$ must execute before $statement_2$, $statement_2$ must execute before $statement_3$, and so on.

We can use different control structures to implement each step of an algorithm. Figure 3.1 shows a program as a sequence of control structures, one for each of three subproblems.

A program that consists of a few control structures will be much easier to understand than one that consists of a large number of unrelated statements.

Selection Control Structures   Often, an algorithm must select one of several alternatives depending on the input data. A selection control structure can be set up to ensure the correct alternative is selected for the given circumstances.

For example, suppose hourly employees are to earn a higher rate of pay for overtime hours they work, where overtime hours are the number of hours in

Figure 3.1. *A Program as a Sequence of Three Control Structures*

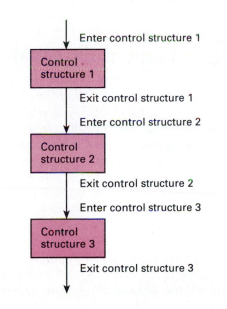

Enter control structure 1

Control structure 1

Exit control structure 1

Enter control structure 2

Control structure 2

Exit control structure 2

Enter control structure 3

Control structure 3

Exit control structure 3

excess of 40 hours per week. Therefore an employee who works 60 hours a week would be paid the regular rate for the first 40 hours and the overtime rate for the last 20 hours. Given this, a payroll program that computes the employee's pay should use the formula

pay = hours × rate

when an employee works 40 hours or less and the following formula

pay = 40.0 × rate + 1.5 × rate × (hours − 40.0)

when an employee works more than 40 hours and is paid 1.5 times the regular rate for the overtime hours (hours − 40.0).

Iteration Control Structures   The third category of control structure, iteration, causes a section of a program to execute more than one time, a useful function when we want to perform the same computation for many different sets of data.

For example, suppose we want a payroll program to compute the weekly pay for a group of employees instead of just one. We can use an iteration control structure to do this. We discuss iteration in greater detail in Chapter 4.

3.2 Logical Expressions

Suppose a payroll program must be able to determine the answer to the question "Did the employee work more than 40 hours?" where the answer could be only true or false. In Fortran, this determination is accomplished by having the program evaluate a logical expression, or condition. A *logical expression*, or *condition*, is an expression for which there are only two possible values: true or false.

For example, in our payroll program, let's assume the number of hours worked is stored in the variable HOURS; therefore the logical expression corresponding to the above question would be

HOURS .GT. 40

where the symbol .GT. means greater than. If HOURS is greater than 40, the logical expression would evaluate to true; if HOURS is less than or equal to 40, the expression would evaluate to false.

Most logical expressions we use will be in one of the following forms:

variable   relational operator   variable

or

variable   relational operator   constant

as in our example, where HOURS is the *variable*, .GT. the *relational operator*, and 40 the *constant*.

Relational operators will be one of the following:

- .LT.   (less than)
- .LE.   (less than or equal to)
- .GT.   (greater than)
- .GE.   (greater than or equal to)
- .EQ.   (equal to)
- .NE.   (not equal to)

The two operands of a relational operator must be either (1) the same data type or (2) one type REAL and the other type INTEGER. A constant may be a literal constant (for example, 3, 4.5, 'X') or a parameter.

EXAMPLE 3.1   Table 3.1 shows the relational operators and some sample conditions. Each condition is evaluated assuming the following variable values:

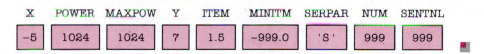

Table 3.1. *Fortran Relational Operators and Sample Conditions*

OPERATOR	CONDITION	ENGLISH MEANING	LOGICAL VALUE
.LE.	X .LE. 0	X less than or equal to 0	true
.LT.	POWER .LT. MAXPOW	POWER less than MAXPOW	false
.GE.	X .GE. Y	X greater than or equal to Y	false
.GT.	ITEM .GT. MINITM	ITEM greater than MINITM	true
.EQ.	SERPAR .EQ. 'S'	SERPAR equal to 'S'	true
.NE.	NUM .NE. SENTNL	NUM not equal to SENTNL	false

Type LOGICAL Variables and Values

The simplest logical expression is a type LOGICAL variable or constant. A *LOGICAL variable* can be set to either of the LOGICAL constants: .TRUE. or .FALSE.. The declaration statements

```
LOGICAL DEBUG
PARAMETER (DEBUG = .TRUE.)
LOGICAL FLAG, SWITCH
```

declare SWITCH and FLAG to be LOGICAL variables, i.e., variables that may be assigned only the values .TRUE. and .FALSE.. DEBUG, on the other hand, is a LOGICAL parameter with the value .TRUE..

The expression parts of the assignment statements

```
SWITCH = .FALSE.
FLAG = SWITCH
```

are a LOGICAL value (.FALSE.) and a LOGICAL variable (SWITCH). After executing these statements, both SWITCH and FLAG will have the value .FALSE..

LOGICAL Operators

As mentioned in the previous section, the simplest form of a logical expression is a LOGICAL variable or constant (for example, SWITCH). We also found that we can use the relational operators—.LT., .EQ., etc.—to form simple logical expressions or conditions.

In this section, we discuss five LOGICAL operators: .AND., .OR., .NOT., .EQV., .NEQV.. These operators are used with operands that are logical expressions to form other logical expressions; for example:

```
(PAY .LT. MINPAY) .OR. (DEPEND .GT. 5)
```

which determines whether an employee needs to pay income tax. It evaluates to true if either condition is true (pay < minimum pay or dependents > 5).

```
(TEMP .GT. 90) .AND. (HUMID .GT. 0.90)
```

which can be used to describe an unbearable summer day (temperature over 90 degrees and humidity over 90%). The expression evaluates to true only when both conditions are true.

```
(TEMP .GT. 90) .OR. (HUMID .GT. 0.90)
```

which is similar to the second expression except it describes a day that is uncomfortable because of high temperature or high humidity or both.

```
WINREC .AND. (.NOT. PROBAT)
```

which manipulates two LOGICAL variables (WINREC and PROBAT). A college team for which this expression is true (winning record and not on probation) would be eligible for the postseason tournament. As we will see, this condition is true if WINREC has the value .TRUE. and PROBAT has the value .FALSE..

LOGICAL operators can be used only with logical expressions. The .AND., .OR., and .NOT. operators are described in Tables 3.2, 3.3, and 3.4.

Table 3.2 shows that the .AND. operator yields a true result only when both its operands are true; Table 3.3 shows that the .OR. operator yields a false result only when both its operands are false. The .NOT. operator has a single operand; from Table 3.4, we see that the .NOT. operator yields the logical complement, or negation, of its operand.

Table 3.2. *.AND. Operator*

OPERAND1	OPERAND2	OPERAND1 .AND. OPERAND2
.TRUE.	.TRUE.	.TRUE.
.TRUE.	.FALSE.	.FALSE.
.FALSE.	.TRUE.	.FALSE.
.FALSE.	.FALSE.	.FALSE.

Table 3.3. *.OR. Operator*

OPERAND1	OPERAND2	OPERAND1 .OR. OPERAND2
.TRUE.	.TRUE.	.TRUE.
.TRUE.	.FALSE.	.TRUE.
.FALSE.	.TRUE.	.TRUE.
.FALSE.	.FALSE.	.FALSE.

Table 3.4. *.NOT. Operator*

OPERAND1	.NOT. OPERAND1
.TRUE.	.FALSE.
.FALSE.	.TRUE.

Table 3.5. *.EQV. Operator*

OPERAND1	OPERAND2	OPERAND1 .EQV. OPERAND2
.TRUE.	.TRUE.	.TRUE.
.TRUE.	.FALSE.	.FALSE.
.FALSE.	.TRUE.	.FALSE.
.FALSE.	.FALSE.	.TRUE.

Table 3.6. *.NEQV. Operator*

OPERAND1	OPERAND2	OPERAND1 .NEQV. OPERAND2
.TRUE.	.TRUE.	.FALSE.
.TRUE.	.FALSE.	.TRUE.
.FALSE.	.TRUE.	.TRUE.
.FALSE.	.FALSE.	.FALSE.

The operators .EQV. (equivalent) and .NEQV. (not equivalent) are used instead of the relational operators .EQ. and .NE. to compare two logical expressions. They are described in Tables 3.5 and 3.6.

EXAMPLE 3.2   If SWITCH and FLAG are type LOGICAL, the expression

SWITCH .EQV. FLAG

is correct and true if SWITCH and FLAG have the same LOGICAL value (both .TRUE. or both .FALSE.). The expression

SWITCH .EQ. FLAG

causes a syntax error because the relational operator .EQ. cannot have type LOGICAL operands. ■

Operator Precedence

The precedence of an operator determines its order of evaluation. Table 3.7 shows the precedence of all operators discussed so far, including the relational operators.

As Table 3.7 shows, arithmetic operators have the highest precedence, followed by the relational operators and, lastly, the LOGICAL operators. When in doubt, use parentheses to specify the order of operator evaluation.

Table 3.7. *Operator Precedence*

OPERATOR	PRECEDENCE
Arithmetic Operators	
`**`	highest
`*, /`	
`+, −`	
Relational Operators	
`.EQ., .NE., .LT., .LE., .GT., .GE.`	
LOGICAL Operators	
`.NOT.`	
`.AND.`	
`.OR.`	
`.EQV., .NEQV.`	lowest

EXAMPLE 3.3

The expression

`X .LT. Y + Z`

involving the real variables X, Y, and Z is interpreted correctly as

`X .LT. (Y + Z)`

because + has higher precedence than `.LT.`.
  The expression

`MIN .LE. X .AND. X .LE. MAX`

is interpreted as

`(MIN .LE. X) .AND. (X .LE. MAX)`

because `.LE.` has higher precedence than `.AND.`. In this case, the use of parentheses helps clarify the meaning of the expression. This expression implements the familiar algebraic relationship, $MIN \leq X \leq MAX$, which is true if the value of X lies within the range of values MIN to MAX, inclusive. ■

EXAMPLE 3.4

The expressions in Table 3.8 are all valid if X, Y, and Z are type REAL and FLAG is type LOGICAL. The value of each expression is shown on the right, assuming that X is 3.0, Y is 4.0, Z is 2.0, and FLAG is `.FALSE.`.

Table 3.8. *Expressions with X = 3.0, Y = 4.0, Z = 2.0, FLAG = .FALSE.*

EXPRESSION	VALUE
1. (X .GT. Z) .AND. (Y .GT. Z)	.TRUE.
2. (X + Y / Z) .LE. 3.5	.FALSE.
3. (Z .GT. X) .OR. (Z .GT. Y)	.FALSE.
4. .NOT. FLAG	.TRUE.
5. (X .EQ. 1.0) .OR. (X .EQ. 3.0)	.TRUE.
6. (0.0 .LT. X) .AND. (X .LT. 3.5)	.TRUE.
7. (X .LT. Z) .OR. (X .GT. Y)	.FALSE.
8. .NOT. FLAG .OR. ((Y + Z) .GE. (X − Z))	.TRUE.
9. .NOT. (FLAG .OR. ((Y + Z) .GE. (X − Z)))	.FALSE.

Expression 1 gives the Fortran form of the relationship "x and y are greater than z." Avoid the temptation to write this as

X .AND. Y .GT. Z

which is invalid because the real variable x cannot be an operand of the LOGICAL operator .AND..

In Expression 2, the arithmetic expression (X + Y / Z) evaluates to 5.0 (not 3.5), so the logical expression is false.

Expression 5 shows the correct way to express the relationship "x is equal to 1.0 or to 3.0."

Expression 6 is the Fortran form of the relationship 0.0 < x < 3.5, i.e., "x is in the range 0.0 to 3.5."

Figure 3.2. *Evaluation Tree for .NOT. FLAG .OR. ((Y + Z) .GE. (X − Z))*

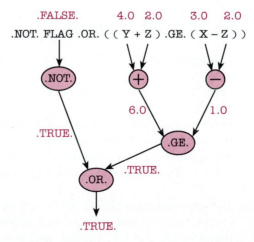

Expression 7 is true if the value of X is less than Z (the smallest number) or greater than Y (the largest number). This means this expression is true if X is outside the range Z through Y, inclusive.

Expression 8 is evaluated in Fig. 3.2; the values given at the beginning of Example 3.4 are shown above the expression. ∎

LOGICAL Assignment

We can write assignment statements that assign the value of a logical expression to a LOGICAL variable, as shown in Example 3.5.

EXAMPLE 3.5

If SAME is type LOGICAL, the statement

```
SAME = .TRUE.
```

assigns the value .TRUE. to SAME. Because assignment statements have the general form

> *variable = expression*

we can use the statement

```
SAME = (X .EQ. Y)
```

to assign the value of the logical expression (X .EQ. Y) to SAME. The value of SAME will be .TRUE. when X and Y are equal; otherwise, SAME will be .FALSE..

EXAMPLE 3.6

The assignment statements below assign values to two logical variables, INRANG and ISLETR. INRANG gets .TRUE. if the value of N is in the range -10 through 10, inclusive. Assuming CH is type CHARACTER *1, ISLETR gets .TRUE. if CH is an uppercase or lowercase letter.

```
INRANG = (-10 .LE. N) .AND. (N .LE. 10)
ISLETR = (('A' .LE. CH) .AND. (CH .LE. 'Z') .OR.
+        ('a' .LE. CH) .AND. (CH .LE. 'z'))
```

The expression in the first assignment statement is true if N satisfies both of the conditions listed ($-10 \le N$ and $N \le 10$); otherwise, the expression is false. The expression in the second assignment statement uses the logical operators .AND., .OR.. The subexpression on the first line is true if CH is an uppercase letter; the subexpression on the second line is true if CH is a lowercase letter. Consequently, ISLETR gets .TRUE. if CH is a letter; otherwise, ISLETR gets .FALSE.. ∎

EXAMPLE 3.7   The assignment statement below assigns the value .TRUE. to EVEN (type LOGICAL) if N is an even number.

```
EVEN = (MOD(N, 2) .EQ. 0)
```

The MOD function returns 0 when N is an even number (divisible by 2). If the function result is 0, EVEN gets .TRUE.; otherwise, EVEN gets .FALSE.. ■

Complementing a Condition

The logical operator .NOT. is used to form the complement, or opposite, of a condition. If a logical expression is true, then its complement must be false and vice versa, as shown in Example 3.8.

EXAMPLE 3.8   Two forms of the complement of the condition

```
(ITEM .EQ. SENVAL)
```

are

```
(ITEM .NE. SENVAL)    |    (.NOT. (ITEM .EQ. SENVAL))
```

The form on the left is obtained by changing the relational operator from .EQ. to .NE.; the complement on the right is obtained by applying the .NOT. operator to the original condition.

To complement a condition, change the relational operator when you are dealing with simple conditions like the one shown in Example 3.8. The relational operator .LE. should be changed to .GT., .LT. to .GE., etc. To complement more complicated conditions, place the .NOT. operator in front of the entire condition (see Example 3.9). ■

EXAMPLE 3.9   The condition

```
(AGE .GT. 25) .AND. (STATUS .EQ. 'Single')
```

is true for a single person over age 25. The complement of this condition is written below.

```
.NOT. ((AGE .GT. 25) .AND. (STATUS .EQ. 'Single'))
```
■

DeMorgan's Theorem

We also can form complements of a logical expression using DeMorgan's theorem, which we state below:

■ The complement of *expr*$_1$ .AND. *expr*$_2$ is written as *comp*$_1$ .OR. *comp*$_2$, where *comp*$_1$ is the complement of *expr*$_1$ and *comp*$_2$ is the complement of *expr*$_2$.
■ The complement of *expr*$_1$ .OR. *expr*$_2$ is written as *comp*$_1$ .AND. *comp*$_2$, where *comp*$_1$ is the complement of *expr*$_1$ and *comp*$_2$ is the complement of *expr*$_2$.

See Example 3.10.

EXAMPLE 3.10

Using DeMorgan's theorem, we find that the complement of

```
(AGE .GT. 25) .AND. (STATUS .EQ. 'Single' .OR. STATUS .EQ. 'Divorced')
```

may be written as

```
(AGE .LE. 25) .OR. (STATUS .NE. 'Single' .AND. STATUS .NE. 'Divorced')
```

The original condition is true for anyone over age 25 and either single or divorced. The complement would be true for anyone who is age 25 or younger or anyone who is currently married. ■

Reading and Writing LOGICAL Values

As we will see in the next section, logical expressions appear primarily in control structures, where they are used to determine the sequence in which Fortran statements are executed. We usually do not process LOGICAL data in the same way that we process numerical data. Consequently, we seldom read LOGICAL values as input data or display LOGICAL values as program results. If necessary, we can display the value of a LOGICAL variable (T for .TRUE., F for .FALSE.) using the PRINT statement. Similarly, we can read a LOGICAL constant (.TRUE., .FALSE.) into a LOGICAL variable using the READ statement. If SWITCH is .FALSE., the statement

```
PRINT *, 'Value of SWITCH is ', SWITCH
```

displays the line

```
Value of SWITCH is F
```

EXERCISES FOR SECTION 3.2

Self-check
1. Assuming X is 15.0 and Y is 25.0, what are the values of the following conditions?

```
X .NE. Y    X .LT. X    X .GE. (Y - X)    X .EQ. (Y + X - Y)
```

2. Evaluate each expression below if A is 5, B is 10, C is 15, and FLAG is .TRUE..

    a. (C .EQ. (A + B)) .OR. .NOT. FLAG
    b. (A .NE. 7) .AND. (C .GE. 6) .OR. FLAG
    c. .NOT. (B .LE. 12) .AND. (MOD(A, 2) .EQ. 0)
    d. .NOT. ((A .GT. 5) .OR. (C .LT. (A + B)))

3. Draw the evaluation tree for expression 9 in Table 3.8 in Example 3.4.

Programming

1. Write a logical expression for each relationship described below.

    a. X is in the range −1.5 to 3.2.
    b. A is in the range 17 to 23, inclusive.
    c. Y is greater than X and less than Z.
    d. W is equal to 6 or not greater than 3.

2. Write the following logical assignment statements:

    a. Assign a value of .TRUE. to BETWEN if N is in the range −K through +K, inclusive; otherwise assign a value of .FALSE..
    b. Assign a value of .TRUE. to UPCASE if CH is an uppercase letter; otherwise assign a value of .FALSE..
    c. Assign a value of .TRUE. to DIVISR if M is a divisor of N; otherwise assign a value of .FALSE..

3.3 Comparing Character Data

We can use the relational operators to compare character data. For example, the conditions

```
MOMDAD .EQ. 'M'
STATUS .EQ. 'SINGLE'
```

test whether a CHARACTER variable contains a particular string value. Order comparisons also can be performed on CHARACTER variables and strings using other relational operators (e.g., .LT., .GE.).

To compare two strings of equal length, the computer simply compares the binary numbers representing each string. If the strings are not the same length, the shorter string is first padded with blanks until it contains as many characters as the longer string. The binary numbers representing each of these equal-length strings are then compared.

Obviously, the result of comparing two strings depends on the numeric codes for the characters in these strings. The code values assigned unfortunately are not the same for every computer, so the internal representation for a string may vary from computer to computer. However, Fortran requires the following *collating sequence*, or relative ordering of certain characters, regardless of their actual numeric codes:

- The blank character precedes (is less than) all the digit characters and all the letters.
- The letters follow the normal alphabetic sequence (i.e., the letter A precedes the letter B, the letter B precedes the letter C, etc.).
- The digit characters follow the normal numeric sequence (i.e., digit 0 precedes digit 1, digit 1 precedes digit 2, etc.).
- The digits and letters cannot be intermixed in the collating sequence.

The Fortran collating sequence ensures that two strings consisting of letters only will follow their normal dictionary sequence. This results in the string ordering 'ACE' < 'BAT' < 'CAT', since A precedes B and B precedes C. Similarly, the string 'BAT' is less than the string 'BIGGER' because A is less than I. To compare the strings 'BAT' and 'BATTY', Fortran compares the binary numbers representing the two equal-length strings 'BAT□□' and 'BATTY'. The string 'BAT□□' is less than the string 'BATTY' because the blank character precedes the letter T in the collating sequence.

The collating sequence also ensures that two equal-length numeric strings will follow their normal numeric sequence (e.g., '123' is less than '345'). However, unexpected results may occur when numeric strings of different lengths are compared. For example, to compare the strings '12345' and '345', Fortran compares the binary numbers representing the equal-length strings '12345' and '345□□'. The string '12345' is less than '345' because the digit 1 precedes the digit 3 in the collating sequence. To avoid this kind of error, use leading or trailing zeros in numeric strings as required. The string '12345' is greater than the string '00345' but less than the string '34500'.

EXERCISES FOR SECTION 3.3

Self-check

1. What is the value of each of the conditions shown below?

   a. 'SMITH' .LE. 'SMYTH'
   b. '120' .GE. '34'
   c. '34' .EQ. '34 '
   d. 'JONES' .LT. 'JONES '
   e. 'FREE' .LT. 'BUSY'
   f. '120' .GE. '034'
   g. '34 ' .EQ. '340'
   h. 'JO' .LT. 'JOSEPH'
   i. '*/+' .NE. ' */+'
   j. '*/+' .NE. '*/+ '

3.4 IF Statement

We can select among several alternatives by using the IF statement, which always contains a logical expression. For example, the IF statement

```
IF (GROSS .GT. 100.00) THEN
   NET = GROSS - TAX
ELSE
   NET = GROSS
END IF
```

selects one of the two assignment statements listed. It selects the statement following THEN if the logical expression is true (i.e., GROSS is greater than 100.00); it selects the statement following ELSE if the logical expression is false (i.e., GROSS is not greater than 100.00).

Figure 3.3 is a graphical description, called a *flow diagram,* of the IF statement above. It shows that the condition (GROSS > 100.00) enclosed in the diamond-shaped box is evaluated first. If the condition is true, the arrow labeled true is followed and the assignment statement in the rectangle on the right is executed; if the condition is false, the arrow labeled false is followed and the assignment statement in the rectangle on the left is executed. The IF statement shown earlier has two alternatives, but only one will be executed for a given value of GROSS. An IF statement can also have a single alternative that is executed only when the condition is true, as shown in the next several examples.

Figure 3.3. *Flow Diagram of IF Statement with Two Alternatives*

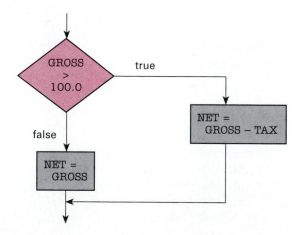

EXAMPLE 3.11

The following IF statement has one alternative that is executed only when X is not equal to zero. It causes PRODCT to be multiplied by X; the new value is saved in PRODCT and printed. If X is equal to zero, these steps are not performed.

```
C Multiply PRODCT by a nonzero X only
      IF (X .NE. 0) THEN
          PRODCT = PRODCT * X
          PRINT *, 'New product is ', PRODCT
      END IF
```

EXAMPLE 3.12

The following IF statement could be used by a biologist to compute the percentage growth in population (PCTGRO) when POPNEW is larger than POPOLD. Nothing is done if POPNEW is not larger than POPOLD.

```
IF (POPNEW .GT. POPOLD) THEN
    GROWTH = POPNEW - POPOLD
    PCTGRO = 100.0 * GROWTH / POPOLD
END IF
```

EXAMPLE 3.13

The following IF statement has two alternatives. Assuming that R1 and R2 represent two resistor values, the statement will compute their combined resistance when they are connected in series (SERIES is .TRUE.) or parallel (SERIES is .FALSE.). The formula used for serial resistors is R1 + R2; the formula used for parallel resistors is

$$\frac{R1 \times R2}{R1 + R2}.$$

```
C Compute combined resistance for R1, R2 in series or parallel.
      IF (SERIES) THEN
          COMBRES = R1 + R2
      ELSE
          COMBRES = R1 * R2 / (R1 + R2)
      END IF
```

Syntax of IF Statements

The syntax of Fortran IF statements is described in the next displays. Remember that an IF statement must always end with the words END IF and that ELSE (if present) and END IF must always be on lines by themselves. Later, we will see that IF statements with several (more than two) alternatives are also possible in Fortran.

IF Statement (Two Alternatives)

SYNTAX: IF (*condition*) THEN
$\qquad$ *task*$_T$
$\quad$ ELSE
$\qquad$ *task*$_F$
$\quad$ END IF

EXAMPLE: IF (X .GE. 0) THEN
$\qquad$ PRINT *, X, ' is positive'
$\quad$ ELSE
$\qquad$ PRINT *, X, ' is negative'
$\qquad$ X = −X
$\quad$ END IF

INTERPRETATION: If the *condition* evaluates to true, then *task*$_T$ (the true alternative) is executed and *task*$_F$ (the false alternative) is skipped; otherwise, *task*$_T$ is skipped and *task*$_F$ is executed. *task*$_T$ or *task*$_F$ can be one or more Fortran statements.

IF Statement (One Alternative)

SYNTAX: IF (*condition*) THEN
$\qquad$ *task*$_T$
$\quad$ END IF

EXAMPLE: IF (X .GT. 0) THEN
$\qquad$ POSSUM = POSSUM + X
$\qquad$ COUNT = COUNT + 1
$\quad$ END IF

INTERPRETATION: If the *condition* evaluates to true, then *task*$_T$ (the true alternative) is executed; otherwise, it is skipped. *task*$_F$ can be one or more Fortran statements.

Program Style: *Structuring the IF Statement*

In all our IF statement examples, the true and false alternatives are indented. If the word ELSE appears, you should type it on a separate line and align it under the word IF. Finally, type the words END IF on a separate line at the end of the IF statement and align END IF with IF and ELSE.

Indenting *task*$_T$ and *task*$_F$ makes the IF statement easier to read and its meaning more apparent. This is done solely to improve program readability; the indentation used makes no difference to the compiler.

Self-check

1. What do the following statements display?

a.
```
IF (X .LT. X) THEN
    PRINT *, 'Always'
ELSE
    PRINT *, 'Never'
END IF
```
b.
```
VAR1 = 15.0
VAR2 = 25.12
IF (VAR2 .LE. 2.0 * VAR1) THEN
    PRINT *, 'O.K.'
ELSE
    PRINT *, 'NOT O.K.'
END IF
```
2. What do the following IF statements do?

a.
```
IF (NUM1 .LT. 0) THEN
    PRODUC = NUM1 * NUM2 * NUM3
    PRINT *, 'Result is ', PRODUC
ELSE
    SUM = NUM1 + NUM2 + NUM3
    PRINT *, 'Result is ', SUM
END IF
```
b.
```
IF (X .GT. Y) THEN
    T = X
    X = Y
    Y = T
ELSE
    X = Y
    Y = X
END IF
```

Programming

1. Write Fortran statements to carry out the steps below.
   a. If ITEM is nonzero, then multiply PRODCT by ITEM and save the result in PRODCT; otherwise, skip the multiplication. In either case, print the value of PRODCT.
   b. Store the absolute difference of X and Y in Z, where the absolute difference is X − Y or Y − X, whichever is positive.
   c. If X is zero, then add 1 to ZROCNT; if X is negative, add X to MINSUM; if X is positive, add X to PLUSUM.
2. Write an IF statement that computes the average of a set of N numbers whose sum is TOTAL. Instead of computing the average, your IF statement should print an error message when N is negative or zero.
3. Write a program that computes the area of a rectangle (*area = base × height*) or triangle (*area = 1/2 × base × height*) after prompting the user to enter the first character of the figure name ('R' or 'T') and its base and height.

3.5 Solving Problems with Decision Steps

This section contains three problems that use decision steps in their solutions.

Case Study: Payroll Problem

PROBLEM STATEMENT

Write a payroll program that computes an employee's gross pay and net pay. An employee who works more than 40 hours per week should be paid at the overtime rate (1.5 × *regular rate*) for all hours over 40. Compute net pay by deducting 10% of gross pay only if an employee earns more than $100.00.

ANALYSIS

The problem inputs are not described in the problem statement; however, we know from experience that the number of hours worked and the hourly wage rate must be data items. The problem outputs are the employee's gross pay, the tax amount deducted, and the net pay. The data requirements below describe four program parameters in addition to the problem inputs and outputs. Note that the tax rate of 10% (value of TAXRAT) is represented in Fortran as the decimal fraction 0.10.

Data Requirements and Formulas

Problem Parameters

maximum hours without overtime pay (MAXREG = 40.0)
overtime rate (OVRRAT = 1.5)
maximum salary without a tax deduction (TXBRAK = 100.00)
tax rate percentage as a fraction (TAXRAT = 0.10)

Problem Inputs

hours worked (REAL HOURS)
hourly rate (REAL RATE)

Problem Outputs

gross pay (REAL GROSS)
net pay (REAL NET)
tax amount (REAL TAXAMT)

Relevant Formulas

gross pay = *hours worked* × *hourly rate*
gross pay = 40 × *hourly rate* + 1.5 × *hourly rate* × *overtime hours*
tax amount = *tax rate* × *gross pay*
net pay = *gross pay* − *tax amount*

Two formulas are listed for gross pay. The first is used when the employee does not receive overtime pay; the second, when the employee does receive overtime pay. The formula introduces an additional variable—overtime hours—which is described next.

Additional Program Variable

overtime hours (REAL OVHOUR)

DESIGN

The algorithm below shows three computation steps to be performed, which must be done in the order listed: compute gross pay, compute tax amount, and compute net pay.

Algorithm

1. Enter hours worked and hourly rate.
2. Compute gross pay.
3. Compute tax amount.
4. Compute net pay.
5. Print gross pay, tax amount, and net pay.

Algorithm Refinement

Next, we refine algorithm steps 2 through 4. We describe each step in *pseudocode,* an informal mixture of English and Fortran. The condition in each IF statement is written as an English phrase that must be translated into Fortran when we write the program.

Step 2 Refinement

```
2.1 IF there is no overtime pay THEN
        2.2 GROSS = HOURS * RATE
    ELSE
        2.3 OVHOUR = HOURS - MAXREG
        2.4 GROSS = MAXREG * RATE + OVRRAT * RATE * OVHOUR
    END IF
```

Step 3 Refinement

```
3.1 IF there is no tax deduction THEN
        TAXAMT = 0.0
    ELSE
        TAXAMT = TAXRAT * GROSS
    END IF
```

Step 4 Refinement

```
4.1 NET = GROSS - TAXAMT
```

IMPLEMENTATION

Figure 3.4 shows the program, in which the logical expression

```
(HOURS .LE. MAXREG)
```

implements the pseudocode expression "there is no overtime pay" and

```
(GROSS .LE. TXBRAK)
```

implements the pseudocode expression "there is no tax deduction."

TESTING AND VERIFICATION

To test this program, run it with several different sets of data. To verify that the gross pay computation is correct, ensure that one data set has HOURS < 40.0, one has HOURS > 40.0, and one has HOURS = 40.0. To verify that the tax computation is correct, ensure that one data set yields a gross pay > $100.00, one yields a gross pay < $100.00, and one yields a gross pay = $100.00. You can combine some of these tests in the same run (for example, HOURS > 40.0 and GROSS < $100.00).

Figure 3.4. *Program for Payroll Problem*

```
      PROGRAM PAYROLL

C Compute and print gross pay, tax amount, and net pay given
C hourly rate and number of hours worked. Overtime pay is earned
C when more than 40 hours are worked. Deduct a tax of 10%
C when gross pay exceeds $100; otherwise, deduct no tax.

C Declarations
      REAL MAXREG, OVRRAT, TXBRAK, TAXRAT
      PARAMETER (MAXREG = 40.0)
      PARAMETER (OVRRAT = 1.5)
      PARAMETER (TXBRAK = 100.00)
      PARAMETER (TAXRAT = 0.10)
      REAL HOURS, RATE, GROSS, TAXAMT, NET, OVHOUR

C Enter HOURS and RATE
      PRINT *, 'Enter hours worked:'
      READ *, HOURS
      PRINT *, 'Enter hourly rate:'
      READ *, RATE
```

```
C Compute gross pay
      IF (HOURS .LE. MAXREG) THEN
         GROSS = HOURS * RATE
      ELSE
         OVHOUR = HOURS - MAXREG
         GROSS = MAXREG * RATE + OVRRAT * RATE * OVHOUR
      END IF

C Compute tax amount
      IF (GROSS .LE. TAXBRAK) THEN
         TAXAMT = 0.0
      ELSE
         TAXAMT = TAXRAT * GROSS
      END IF

C Compute net pay
      NET = GROSS - TAXAMT

C Print GROSS, TAXAMT, and NET
      PRINT *, 'Gross pay is $', GROSS
      PRINT *, 'Tax amount is $', TAXAMT
      PRINT *, 'NET pay is $', NET

      STOP
      END

Enter hours worked:
40.0
Enter hourly rate:
5.00
Gross pay is $ 200.00000
Tax amount is $ 20.00000
NET pay is $ 180.00000
```

Case Study: Finding the Smallest of Three Numbers

PROBLEM STATEMENT

Read three integer values and find and print the smallest one.

ANALYSIS

From our prior experience with conditions and decision steps, we know how to use the relational operator .LT. to compare two items to determine which is smaller. To compare three items, we will need a sequence of comparisons. The problem inputs and outputs are listed next, followed by the algorithm.

Data Requirements

Problem Inputs

three numbers (INTEGER NUM1, NUM2, NUM3)

Problem Output

the smallest number (INTEGER MINNUM)

DESIGN

The algorithm follows:

Algorithm

1. Read three numbers into NUM1, NUM2, and NUM3.
2. Save the smallest of NUM1, NUM2, and NUM3 in MINNUM.
3. Print the smallest number.

Algorithm Refinements

Step 2 can be performed by first comparing NUM1 and NUM2 and saving the smaller number in MINNUM; this result can then be compared to NUM3. The refinement of step 2 follows.

Step 2 Refinement

2.1 Save the smaller of NUM1 and NUM2 in MINNUM.
2.2 Save the smaller of NUM3 and MINNUM in MINNUM.

Steps 2.1 and 2.2 require further refinement as shown next.

Step 2.1 Refinement

2.1.1 IF NUM1 is less than NUM2 THEN
      2.1.2 Store NUM1 in MINNUM
  ELSE
      2.1.3 Store NUM2 in MINNUM
  END IF

Step 2.2 Refinement

2.2.1 IF NUM3 is less than MINNUM THEN
      2.2.2 Store NUM3 in MINNUM
  END IF

IMPLEMENTATION

Figure 3.5 shows the program, in which the IF statement with two alternatives saves either NUM1 or NUM2 in MINNUM and the IF statement with one alternative stores NUM3 in MINNUM if NUM3 is less than the value already in MINNUM.

Figure 3.5. *Finding the Smallest Number*

```
      PROGRAM SMALL3
C Finds and prints the smallest number.

C Declarations
      INTEGER NUM1, NUM2, NUM3, MINNUM

C Read three numbers
      PRINT *, 'Enter three integers separated by blanks:'
      READ *, NUM1, NUM2, NUM3

C Store the smaller of NUM1 and NUM2 in MINNUM
      IF (NUM1 .LT. NUM2) THEN
         MINNUM = NUM1
      ELSE
         MINNUM = NUM2
      END IF

C Store the smaller of NUM3 and MINNUM in MINNUM
      IF (NUM3 .LT. MINNUM) THEN
         MINNUM = NUM3
      END IF

C Print result
      PRINT *, MINNUM, ' is the smallest number.'
      STOP
      END

Enter three integers separated by blanks:
2 3 1
1 is the smallest number.
```

TESTING AND VERIFICATION

To test this program, ensure it works when the smallest number is in any of the three positions. You also should see what happens when two or more of the numbers are the same and when one or more of the numbers is negative. Section 3.6 describes the cases that should be tested.

Case Study: Testing Column Safety

PROBLEM STATEMENT

Acme Construction needs a program that computes the stress on a rectangular column and displays a message indicating whether the column is safe or unsafe. Assume the column is safe if the stress is less than or equal to 2000 pounds per square inch (psi).

ANALYSIS

The stress on a short column is calculated by dividing the force (or weight) on the column by the cross-sectional area (*width × depth*) of the rectangular column. If force, depth, and width are provided as data, the program can calculate the stress and compare it to the maximum allowed stress. The data requirements and algorithm follow.

Data Requirements

Problem Parameter

the maximum stress allowed (REAL MXSTRS = 2000.0)

Problem Inputs

the force applied in pounds (REAL FORCE)
the width of the column in inches (REAL WIDTH)
the depth of the column in inches (REAL DEPTH)

Problem Outputs

the computed stress (REAL STRESS)
a message indicating whether the column is safe or unsafe

Additional Program Variable

the cross-sectional area of the column (REAL AREA)

DESIGN

The algorithm follows:

Algorithm

1. Enter the force on the column and its width and depth.
2. Compute the stress on the column.
3. Display the stress value.
4. Display a message indicating whether the column is safe or unsafe.

Algorithm Requirements

Steps 2 and 4 need refinement. For step 2, we can use the equations

area = depth × width
stress = force/area

to compute the stress. We need an additional program variable to store the cross-sectional area.

Step 2 Refinement

2.1 AREA = DEPTH * WIDTH
2.2 STRESS = FORCE / AREA

We can refine step 4 using the following decision step:

Step 4 Refinement

4.1 IF STRESS is less than or equal to the maximum allowed THEN
     4.2 Print that the column is safe
ELSE
     4.3 Print that the column is unsafe
END IF

IMPLEMENTATION

The program appears in Fig. 3.6.

Figure 3.6. *Computing Column Stress and Safety*

```
      PROGRAM COLUMN

C Determines whether a short column is safe or unsafe.
C The user enters the depth and width of a column along with
C the force on it. The area and stress are computed.

C Declarations
      REAL MXSTRS
      PARAMETER (MXSTRS = 2000.0)
      REAL DEPTH, WIDTH, FORCE, STRESS

C Enter data
      PRINT *, 'Enter force on the column (in pounds)'
      READ *, FORCE
      PRINT *, 'Enter column width (in inches)'
      READ *, WIDTH
      PRINT *, 'Enter column depth (in inches)'
      READ *, DEPTH

C Compute area and stress
      AREA = WIDTH * DEPTH
      STRESS = FORCE / AREA

C Display stress
      PRINT *, 'The stress on the column is ', STRESS, ' psi'

C Determine whether column is safe or unsafe
      IF (STRESS .LE. MXSTRS) THEN
         PRINT *, 'The column is within safety limits.'
      ELSE
         PRINT *, 'Warning the column is UNSAFE!!!!!'
      END IF

C Exit the program
      STOP
      END
```

```
Enter force on the column (in pounds)
20000.0
Enter column width (in inches)
8.0
Enter column depth (in inches)
12.0
The stress on the column is 208.3333 psi
The column is within safety limits.
```

TESTING AND VERIFICATION

To test the program, try values of stress that are less than, equal to, and greater than MXSTRS (2000 psi). One easy way to obtain a stress value equal to MXSTRS is to use a force of 20,000 pounds and a cross-sectional area of 10.

EXERCISES FOR SECTION 3.5

Self-check

1. What value is assigned to X for each of the following segments given that Y is 15.0? What if Y is 10.0?

   a. ```
   X = 25.0
   IF (Y .NE. (X - 10.00)) THEN
      X = X - 10.0
   ELSE
      X = X / 2.0
   END IF
   ```
   b. ```
   IF (Y .LT. 15.0) THEN
      X = 5.0 * Y
   ELSE
      X = 2.0 * Y
   END IF
   ```

Programming

1. Modify the algorithm and program in Fig. 3.5 to find the largest of three numbers.
2. Modify the algorithm and program in Fig. 3.5 to find the smallest of four numbers.

3.6 Tracing an Algorithm or Program

It is critical when designing an algorithm or program to verify that the algorithm is correct before extensive time is spent translating it into Fortran, typing in the Fortran program, and testing and debugging the program. Obviously, you shouldn't proceed with these latter steps if the algorithm is incorrect.

Often, a few extra minutes spent verifying the correctness of an algorithm will save hours of testing later.

An important technique for checking the correctness of an algorithm or program is a *hand trace* or *desk check*, a careful, step-by-step simulation on paper of how the algorithm or program would be executed by the computer. The results of the simulation should show the effect of each step as it is executed on data that are relatively easy to manipulate by hand.

For example, the refined algorithm for the smallest of three numbers problem appears next.

Refined Algorithm

1. Read three numbers into NUM1, NUM2, and NUM3.
2. Save the smallest of NUM1, NUM2, and NUM3 in MINNUM.
    2.1.1 IF NUM1 is less than NUM2 THEN
          2.1.2 Store NUM1 in MINNUM
      ELSE
          2.1.3 Store NUM2 in MINNUM
      END IF
    2.2.1 IF NUM3 is less than MINNUM THEN
          2.2.2 Store NUM3 in MINNUM
      END IF
3. Print the smallest number.

Table 3.9 shows a trace of the algorithm for the data values 12, 10, and 5. Each step is listed at the left in order of its execution. If an algorithm step changes the value of a variable, then the new value is shown; the effect of each step is described at the far right. For example, the table shows that step 1 (read, three numbers) stores the numbers 12, 10, and 5 in the variables NUM1, NUM2, and NUM3, respectively.

Table 3.9. *Trace of Smallest Number Algorithm*

STEP	NUM1	NUM2	NUM3	MINNUM	EFFECT
	?	?	?	?	
1.	12	10	5		Reads the data.
2.1.1					12 < 10 is false —
2.1.3				10	Store 10 in MINNUM.
2.2.1					5 < 10 is true —
2.2.2				5	Store 5 in MINNUM.
3.					Display 5.

The trace in Table 3.9 shows that the algorithm is correct when NUM2 is smaller than NUM1 (step 2.1.1 is false) and NUM3 is the smallest of all three numbers (step 2.2.1 is true). To completely verify that the algorithm is correct, you should select data that test all possible combinations. Because steps 2.1.1 and 2.2.1 each have two possible outcomes (true or false), you should try at least 2×2, or 4, different sets of data.

Also check that an algorithm works correctly for unusual data. For example, what would happen if all three numbers or a pair of numbers were the same?

FORTRAN in Focus

Simulations Save Time and Money

TRIANGLE PACKAGE MACHINERY COMPANY

Triangle Package Machinery Company manufactures machines that weigh food product, form a bag, and deliver the product into the bag. The machines are designed to package product so that the end customer gets exactly what is expected and the company that makes the product doesn't waste it with inaccurate measurements. Triangle's current packaging machines are computer-driven devices with a ten-level bill of materials. Every machine they produce is customized for the product to be handled. Parts on the machine may vary by product, and the computer programming also varies according to customer needs and specifications. Triangle packaging machines are designed to be easy to clean, to deliver an accurate weight to the bag, and to run at the very fast speeds needed to meet production schedules. Triangle prides itself on making top-of-the-line packaging machinery.

The first machines Triangle manufactured were cam-driven, with a strictly mechanical movement. Weights produced with these machines were fairly accurate. The next generation of machines incorporated resistors, a change that increased accuracy and reduced the complexity of the mechanics, but introduced greater complexity in the electronics. Both of these generations of machinery were tested by prototype; that is, the company had to build a machine to find out if the design would work properly. Today, Triangle builds machines with a computerized machine scaling system. These machines are more versatile than previous generations because they can be customized to support more than one food product simply by varying the programming. Just as important is the fact that their performance can also be tested before any manufacturing takes place. When the computerized

Would the algorithm still provide the correct result? To complete the desk check, you should verify that the algorithm does indeed handle special situations properly.

After verifying the algorithm is correct, you next should convert it to a Fortran program. Even though you have checked the algorithm, you still should trace the final program before you type it into the computer. For example, Table 3.10 traces the program in Fig. 3.6 for the same data values (12, 10, and 5).

scaling system was introduced, the engineering group realized that a computer model could help them test concepts being considered in the design and development of new machines. Using a computerized scaling system, a programming change alone may be enough to satisfy a variety of customers who all package different products. In other instances, a single machine can be programmed to handle a variety of products for one company. In either case, before production starts on a new machine, the concept is fully tested by means of a simulation.

When Triangle's data processing group began testing designs in this way in the early 1980s, they selected Fortran for the simulation. Because the application was of a scientific nature, Fortran was the obvious choice. (The packaging machines themselves are programmed in assembly language to accommodate their high-speed

operation.) Fortran's suitability for handling complicated formulas and providing accurate results made it a good match for the application. The data processing group, using specifications and product information provided by engineering, create and maintain the simulation on a Bull HN mainframe computer.

The simulation application incorporates a particular machine's features and the computerized algorithm for the weighing and delivery of a particular product. When parameters for a given product are entered (for example, the

physical characteristics of the product, and variations in weight from one piece to the next), the simulation provides data on the package weight that the machine and algorithm would generate for that product. Before a machine is developed, engineering has a good idea of whether the algorithm as written will meet company standards or whether the concept needs revision. The result is a savings in time and money to Triangle and, ultimately, to their customer.

We are grateful to Jerry Dusinski, Manager of the Data Processing Group at Triangle, for providing information about their use of Fortran. In addition to the simulation described here, the data processing group also supports COBOL on the mainframe for its business applications, such as materials requirements planning and accounting. Triangle Package Machinery is located in Chicago, Illinois.

Table 3.10. *Trace of Program in Fig. 3.6*

PROGRAM STATEMENT	NUM1	NUM2	NUM3	MINNUM	EFFECT
	?	?	?	?	
PRINT *, 'Enter three...'					Prints a prompt.
READ *, NUM1, NUM2, NUM3	12	10	5		Reads the data.
IF (NUM1 .LT. NUM2) THEN					12 < 10 is false —
MINNUM = NUM2				10	10 is smallest so far.
IF (NUM3 .LT. MINNUM)...					5 < 10 is true —
MINNUM = NUM3				5	5 is smallest.
PRINT *, MINNUM...					Displays 5 is the smallest number.

In performing each trace, be very careful to execute the program exactly as it would be executed by the computer. It is easy to carry out the operations you expect to be performed without explicitly testing each condition and tracing each program step. A trace performed in this way is of little value.

EXERCISES FOR SECTION 3.6

Self-check

1. Provide sample data and traces for the remaining three cases of the smallest number problem. Also, test the case where all three numbers are the same. Trace the algorithm and program.
2. Trace the program in Fig. 3.4 when HOURS is 30.0 and RATE is 5.00. Perform the trace when HOURS is 20.0 and RATE is 3.00.

3.7 Solution by Analogy

Sometimes a new problem is simply an old one presented in a new guise. When presented with what appears to be a new problem, first try to determine if you have solved a similar problem before and, if so, adapt the earlier solution to the current situation. To do this effectively requires careful reading of the problem statement to detect requirements that actually are similar to an earlier situation but which may be worded differently in the current problem.

Case Study: Computing the Price of Concrete

PROBLEM STATEMENT

You work for a building supply company that charges $44.75/cu yd for concrete. For quantities over 30 cu yd, a 5% discount is given. Your boss has asked you to write a program to calculate the price of any amount of concrete.

ANALYSIS

This problem is very similar to the payroll problem presented earlier in this chapter. You can determine the initial price of the concrete by first multiplying the amount purchased by the unit cost; this step is analogous to computing gross pay in the payroll program. If a discount applies, then compute the discount amount and subtract it from the initial price; this step is analogous to computing the tax deduction and subtracting it to obtain net pay in the payroll problem.

Data Requirements and Formulas

Problem Parameters

the cost per cubic yard (REAL COST = 44.75)
the minimum amount for a discount (REAL DISAMT = 30.0)
the discount rate of 5% (REAL DISRAT = 0.05)

Problem Input

the amount of concrete sold (REAL AMOUNT)

Problem Outputs

the price of the concrete (REAL PRICE)
the discount when applicable (REAL DISCNT)
the discounted price (REAL DISPRC)

Relevant Formulas

initial price = amount × cost
discount = 0.05 × initial price
discounted price = initial price − discount

DESIGN

The algorithm follows:

Algorithm

1. Enter amount sold.
2. Compute the initial price.
3. Compute the discount.
4. Compute the discounted price.
5. Display the initial price, the discount, and the discounted price.

Algorithm Refinements

The refinements of steps 2 and 3 follow.

Step 2 Refinement

2.1 PRICE = AMOUNT * COST

Step 3 Refinement

3.1 IF there is no discount THEN
      3.2 DISCNT = 0.0
  ELSE
      3.3 Compute the discount amount
  END IF

Step 3.3 Refinement

3.3.1 DISCNT = DISRAT * PRICE

IMPLEMENTATION

The complete program is shown in Fig. 3.7. One PARAMETER statement defines all three program parameters; the parameter definitions are separated by commas.

Figure 3.7. *Computing the Price of Concrete*

```
      PROGRAM CONCRT

C Calculates the price of any amount of concrete.

C Declarations
      REAL COST, DISAMT, DISRAT
      PARAMETER (COST = 44.75, DISAMT = 30.0, DISRAT = 0.05)
      REAL AMOUNT, PRICE, DISCNT, DISPRC

C Enter amount sold.
      PRINT *, 'Enter concrete amount (in cubic yards)'
      READ *, AMOUNT

C Compute the initial price.
      PRICE = AMOUNT * COST

C Compute the discount.
      IF (AMOUNT .LE. DISAMT) THEN
         DISCNT = 0.0
      ELSE
         DISCNT = DISRAT * PRICE
      END IF

C Compute the discounted price.
      DISPRC = PRICE - DISCNT

C Display the initial price, discount, and discounted price.
      PRINT *, 'The initial price is $', PRICE
      PRINT *, 'The discount is $', DISCNT
      PRINT *, 'The final price is $', DISPRC
```

```
      STOP
      END

Enter concrete amount (in cubic yards)
40.0
The initial price is $    1790.00
The discount is $     89.5000
The final price is $    1700.50
```

TESTING AND VERIFICATION

To test the price computation, run the program with values of AMOUNT that are less than DISAMT, equal to DISAMT, and greater than DISAMT.

3.8 Other IF Statement Forms

So far we have discussed IF statements with one and two alternatives. In this section, we describe more IF statement forms. The first such form is used to implement the conditional execution of a single Fortran statement; the other forms are used to implement conditions with multiple (more than two) alternatives.

Logical IF Statement

If a single alternative decision has only one statement in its true task, we can implement the decision using a simpler Fortran statement called the *logical IF statement*. An example of a logical IF statement and an equivalent IF structure follows. The logical IF is described in the syntax display.

```
IF (X .GT. LARGE) LARGE = X     |  IF (X .GT. LARGE) THEN
                                 |        LARGE = X
                                 |  END IF
```

SYNTAX DISPLAY

Logical IF Statement

SYNTAX: IF (*condition*) *dependent statement*

EXAMPLE: IF (X .EQ. 0.0) PRINT *, 'ZERO'

INTERPRETATION: The *condition* is evaluated. If it is true, the *dependent statement* is executed; otherwise, the *dependent statement* is not executed.

NOTES: Only one Fortran statement may follow the *condition*. The *dependent statement* may be any single executable statement such as assignment, STOP, READ, or PRINT. It may not be another logical IF statement or a control structure.

In this section, we examine how IF statements can be nested to implement decisions involving several alternatives. A nested IF structure occurs when the true or false task of an IF statement contains another IF statement.

EXAMPLE 3.14

In the nested IF structure

```
IF (AGE .GT. 25) THEN
   IF (STATUS .EQ. 'SINGLE') THEN
      IF (SEX .EQ. 'FEMALE') THEN
         PRINT *, NAME
      END IF
   END IF
END IF
```

the true task of the first two IF statements is itself an IF statement. Notice that each IF is terminated with its own END IF line; we could use this structure to print the names of all single females over age 25. The PRINT statement executes only when all three conditions evaluate to true. In the next display, we have used the .AND. operator to implement this decision structure without nesting.

```
IF ((AGE .GT. 25) .AND. (STATUS .EQ. 'SINGLE') .AND.
+    (SEX .EQ. 'FEMALE')) THEN
   PRINT *, NAME
END IF
```

The symbol + in column six of the second line indicates that the first line is continued. ∎

EXAMPLE 3.15

The Fortran code fragment given in the next display illustrates a nested IF structure with three alternatives. In this case, an IF statement is nested inside the false task of the outer IF statement. This nested IF structure causes one of three variables—NUMPOS, NUMNEG, or NUMZER—to be increased by one, depending on whether X is greater than zero, less than zero, or equal to zero, respectively. Both END IF lines at the end of this structure are required. As before, we have used indentation to make the nested IF structure more readable. The indentation is ignored by the compiler.

```
C Increment NUMPOS, NUMNEG, or NUMZER depending on X
      IF (X .GT. 0) THEN
         NUMPOS = NUMPOS + 1
      ELSE
         IF (X .LT. 0) THEN
            NUMNEG = NUMNEG + 1
         ELSE
            NUMZER = NUMZER + 1
         END IF
      END IF
```

Table 3.11. *Trace of IF Statement in Example 3.15 for X = −7*

STATEMENT	EFFECT
IF (X .GT. 0) THEN	−7 > 0 is false —
IF (X .LT. 0) THEN	
NUMNEG − NUMNEG + 1	−7 < 0 is true — adds 1 to NUMNEG.

The execution of this IF structure proceeds as follows: The first condition (X .GT. 0) is tested. If it is true, NUMPOS is incremented and the rest of the IF statement is skipped; if it is false, the second condition (X .LT. 0) is tested. If the second condition is true, NUMNEG is incremented; otherwise, NUMZER is incremented. Note that the second condition is tested only when the first condition is false. A trace of this statement is shown in Table 3.11, assuming X is −7.

You may find it helpful to understanding nested IF structures if you draw a flow diagram of the decision-making process. Figure 3.8 shows a flow diagram of the decision step from Example 3.15. Each condition is shown in a diamond-shaped box, and the true and false tasks are enclosed in rectangular boxes. Two paths lead from each condition: The path labeled true indicates the true task for that condition; the path labeled false indicates the false task for that condition. ◼

Figure 3.8. *Flow Diagram of a Nested IF Structure*

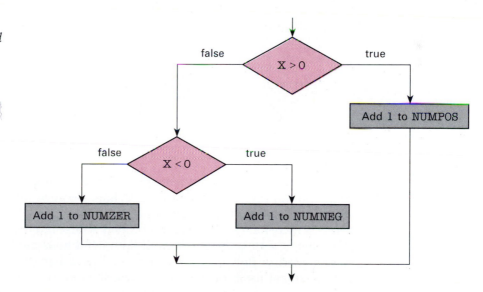

EXAMPLE 3.16   A traffic engineer uses the flow diagram in Fig. 3.9 to display warning messages on the electronic message boards on the New Jersey Turnpike. The messages are based on the road status (STATUS is 'C' when clear, STATUS is 'S' when slippery) and the temperature (TEMP). The following IF statement implements this decision step:

```
IF (STATUS .EQ. 'S') THEN
    IF (TEMP .GT. 32) THEN
        PRINT *, 'Wet roads'
    ELSE
        PRINT *, 'Icy roads'
    END IF
ELSE
    PRINT *, 'Drive carefully'
END IF
```

Multiple Alternative Decisions   Nested IF structures can become quite complex. If there are more than three alternatives and indentation is not done consistently, you may not be able to determine to which IF line a given ELSE line belongs. Often, you can use one general IF statement instead of a nest of IF structures, as shown in Example 3.17.

EXAMPLE 3.17   In the program that follows, we have implemented the nested IF structure of Example 3.15 using a general IF statement.

```
C Increment NUMPOS, NUMNEG, or NUMZER depending on X
      IF (X .GT. 0) THEN
          NUMPOS = NUMPOS + 1
      ELSE IF (X .LT. 0) THEN
          NUMNEG = NUMNEG + 1
      ELSE
          NUMZER = NUMZER + 1
      END IF
```

In this form, the first condition appears on the IF header line and the second condition appears on the first ELSE IF line. Because this is a single control structure, only one END IF line is needed. If the first condition is true, then NUMPOS is incremented; if the first condition is false but the second condition is true, then NUMNEG is incremented; if both conditions are false, then NUMZER is incremented. A flow diagram of a general IF statement is given in Fig. 3.10. The statement itself, or Block IF, is described in the next syntax display. ◼

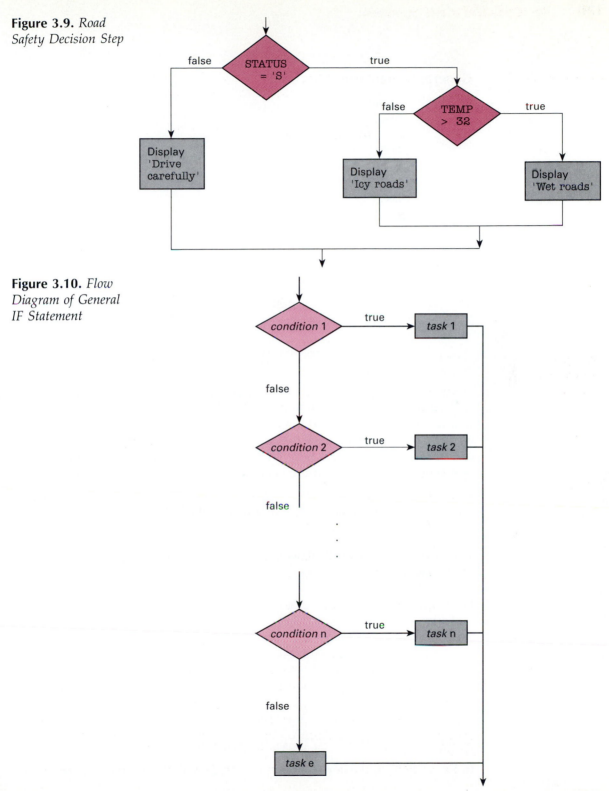

Figure 3.9. *Road Safety Decision Step*

Figure 3.10. *Flow Diagram of General IF Statement*

SYNTAX
DISPLAY

General IF Statement (Block IF)

SYNTAX: IF ($condition_1$) THEN
$\quad$ $task_1$
ELSE IF ($condition_2$) THEN
$\quad$ $task_2$
. . .
ELSE IF ($condition_n$) THEN
$\quad$ $task_n$
ELSE
$\quad$ $task_e$
END IF

EXAMPLE: IF (N .LT. O) THEN
$\quad$ PRINT *, 'N is negative'
ELSE IF (N .EQ. O) THEN
$\quad$ PRINT *, 'N is zero'
ELSE
$\quad$ PRINT *, 'N is positive'
END IF

INTERPRETATION: The conditions in a general IF statement are evaluated in sequence until a true condition is reached. If a condition is true, the task following it is executed and the rest of the general IF statement is skipped; if a condition is false, the task following it is skipped and the next condition is tested; if all conditions are false, then $task_e$ (between the lines ELSE and END IF) is executed. Exactly one of the tasks $task_1$, $task_2$, . . . , $task_e$ is executed.

NOTE: If there is no $task_e$, then ELSE may be omitted. In this case, no task within the general IF statement is executed when all conditions are false.

EXAMPLE 3.18

The next IF statement displays the "smallest" of the strings stored in NAME1, NAME2, NAME3 (type CHARACTER *10).

```
IF (NAME1 .LE. NAME2 .AND. NAME1 .LE. NAME3) THEN
   PRINT *, NAME1, ' is smallest'
ELSE IF (NAME2 .LE. NAME1 .AND. NAME2 .LE. NAME3) THEN
   PRINT *, NAME2, ' is smallest'
ELSE IF (NAME3 .LE. NAME1 .AND. NAME3 .LE. NAME2) THEN
   PRINT *, NAME3, ' is smallest'
END IF
```

Program Style: *Writing the General IF Statement*

In Example 3.18, the key words IF, END IF, and all the words ELSE are aligned and each dependent task is indented under the condition that controls its execution. This is done to make the general IF statement more readable; indentation is ignored by the Fortran compiler.

Order of Conditions

Very often, the conditions in a multiple-alternative decision are not mutually exclusive. This means that it may be possible for more than one condition to be true for given data values. In such a case, the order of the conditions becomes very important because only the statement following the first true condition will be executed (see Example 3.19).

EXAMPLE 3.19

Table 3.12 describes the assignment of grades based on exam scores.

The next multiple-alternative decision displays the letter grade assigned according to this table. The last three conditions are true for an exam score of 85; however, a grade of B is assigned because the first true condition is SCORE .GE. 80.

```
C Correct grade assignment
      IF (SCORE .GE. 90) THEN
          PRINT *, 'A'
      ELSE IF (SCORE .GE. 80) THEN
          PRINT *, 'B'
      ELSE IF (SCORE .GE. 70) THEN
          PRINT *, 'C'
      ELSE IF (SCORE .GE. 60) THEN
          PRINT *, 'D'
      ELSE
          PRINT *, 'F'
      END IF
```

Be careful not to write the decision as it is shown on the following page. Because the first condition would be true and the rest would be skipped, all passing exam scores (60 or above) would be incorrectly categorized as a grade of D.

Table 3.12. *Assignment of Grades*

EXAM SCORE	GRADE ASSIGNED
90 and above	A
80–89	B
70–79	C
60–69	D
below 60	F

```
C Incorrect grade assignment
      IF (SCORE .GE. 60) THEN
         PRINT *, 'D'
      ELSE IF (SCORE .GE. 70) THEN
         PRINT *, 'C'
      ELSE IF (SCORE .GE. 80) THEN
         PRINT *, 'B'
      ELSE IF (SCORE .GE. 90) THEN
         PRINT *, 'A'
      ELSE
         PRINT *, 'F'
      END IF
```

EXAMPLE 3.20

In Example 2.21, we showed how to compute the roots of a quadratic equation

$$Ax^2 + Bx + C = 0$$

when the roots were type REAL. The program in Fig. 3.11 first reads the coefficients A, B, and C. Next, it determines the number of roots (1 or 2) and computes and displays the root(s). The value of the discriminant, $B^2 - 4AC$, of the quadratic formula determines whether the equation has real or complex roots. If the discriminant is negative, the roots are complex; otherwise, they are real. The program in Fig. 3.11 prints the root value(s) or, if the roots are complex, an appropriate message.

Figure 3.11. *Finding the Roots of a Quadratic Equation*

```
      PROGRAM QUADEQ

C Program to compute the roots of a quadratic equation
      REAL A, B, C, ROOT1, ROOT2, DISC

      PRINT *, 'Enter the three coefficients A, B, C'
      PRINT *, 'Leave spaces between the three values:'
      READ *, A, B, C

C Find and print the roots or print a message
      DISC = B ** 2 - 4.0 * A * C
      IF (A .EQ. 0) THEN
         ROOT1 = -C / B
         PRINT *, 'Equation is not quadratic'
         PRINT *, 'The single real root is: ', ROOT1
      ELSE IF (DISC .GT. 0) THEN
         ROOT1 = (-B + SQRT(DISC)) / (2.0 * A)
         ROOT2 = (-B - SQRT(DISC)) / (2.0 * A)
         PRINT *, 'The two real roots are: ', ROOT1, ROOT2
```

```
        ELSE IF (DISC .EQ. 0) THEN
            ROOT1 = -B / (2.0 * A)
            PRINT *, 'There is only one real root'
            PRINT *, 'The root is: ', ROOT1
        ELSE
            PRINT *, ' There are two complex roots'
        END IF

        STOP
        END
```

```
Enter the three coefficients A, B, C
Leave spaces between the three values:
1 -1 -2
The two real roots are: 2.000000 -1.000000
```

EXAMPLE 3.21

Prince Valiant is trying to rescue Rapunzel by shooting an arrow with a rope attached through her tower window, which is 100 ft off the ground. Assume the arrow travels at a constant velocity toward the tower. The laws of physics tell us that the time (t) of flight of the arrow is given by the formula

$$t = \frac{d}{v\,(\cos\theta)},$$

where d is the distance the prince is standing from the tower, v is the velocity of the arrow, and θ is its angle of elevation (see Fig. 3.12).

To help him perfect his aim, Prince Valiant needs a computer program that will compute the height of the arrow when it reaches the tower. For him to be able to rescue Rapunzel, the arrow's height (h) must be between 100 and 110 ft, as given by the formula

$$h = v \cdot t \cdot \sin\theta - \frac{g \cdot t^2}{2},$$

where g is the gravitational constant and t is the value computed by the first formula.

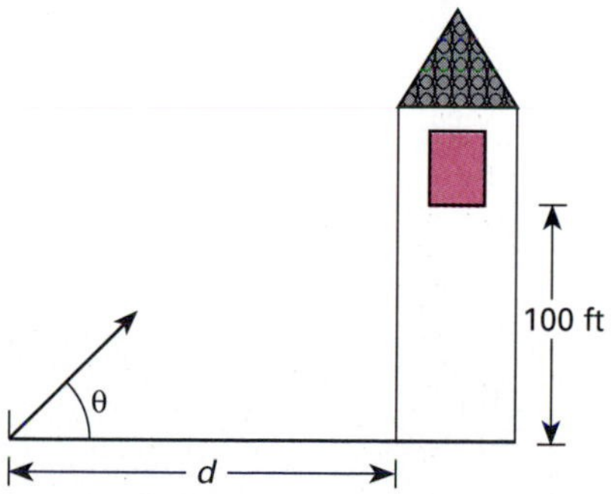

Figure 3.12. *Prince Valiant Aims at Rapunzel's Tower Window.*

The required program is shown in Fig. 3.13. The assignment statement

```
RADIAN = THETA * (PI / 180.0)
```

is used to convert the angle THETA from degrees to radians as required for input to the Fortran SIN and COS functions.

Figure 3.13. *Program RESCUE*

```
      PROGRAM RESCUE

C Prince Valiant attempts to rescue Rapunzel from a tower.

C Declarations
      REAL PI, G, BOTTOM, TOP
      PARAMETER (PI = 3.14159, G = 32.17, BOTTOM = 100.0, TOP = 110.0)
      REAL HEIGHT, TIME, VEL, THETA, DIST, RADIAN

C Read and print input data
      PRINT *, 'Distance from tower in feet:'
      READ *, DIST
      PRINT *, 'Velocity of arrow in feet per second:'
      READ *, VEL
      PRINT *, 'Angle of elevation in degrees:'
      READ *, THETA

C The Fortran trig functions require input angles in radians.
C Convert THETA from degrees to radians
      RADIAN = THETA * (PI / 180.0)
C Compute travel time of arrow
      TIME = DIST / (VEL * COS(RADIAN))
C Compute arrow height
      HEIGHT = VEL * TIME * SIN(RADIAN) - G * TIME ** 2 / 2.0

C Print message to correct Prince's aim
      IF (HEIGHT .LT. 0.0) THEN
         PRINT *, 'Arrow did not reach the tower'
      ELSE IF (HEIGHT .LT. BOTTOM) THEN
         PRINT *, 'Arrow was too low, height was ', HEIGHT
      ELSE IF (HEIGHT .LE. TOP) THEN
         PRINT *, 'Good shot, Prince!'
      ELSE
         PRINT *, 'Arrow was too high, height was ', HEIGHT
      END IF

      STOP
      END
```

```
Distance from tower in feet:
100.0
Velocity of arrow in feet per second:
500.0
Angle of elevation in degrees:
47.0
Good shot, Prince!
```

Case Study: Computing Compass Bearings

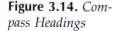

PROBLEM STATEMENT

While spending the summer as a surveyor's assistant, you decide to write a program that transforms compass headings in degrees (0–360 degrees) to compass bearings. The program enters a compass heading such as 110 degrees and displays the corresponding bearing (south 70 degrees east).

ANALYSIS

The compass bearing indicates a direction of travel corresponding to a compass heading. In this example, if you have a compass heading of 110 degrees, you should first face due south and then turn 70 degrees toward east (see Fig. 3.14). Each compass bearing consists of three items: the direction you face (north or south), an angle between 0 and 90 degrees, and the direction you turn (east or west) before walking. Table 3.13 shows how to transform compass headings to compass bearings. From the second line of this table, we can see that a heading of 110 degrees corresponds to a bearing of south (180.0–110.0) east, or south 70 degrees east.

Figure 3.14. *Compass Headings*

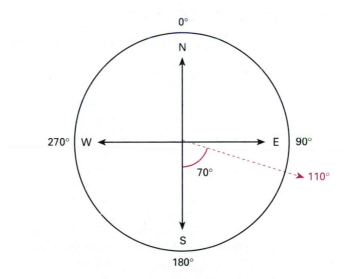

Table 3.13. *Computing Compass Bearings*

HEADING IN DEGREES	BEARING COMPUTATION
0– 89.999	north (heading) east
90–179.999	south (180.0 − heading) east
180–269.999	south (heading − 180.0) west
270–360	north (360.0 − heading) west

Data Requirements

Problem Input

the compass heading in degrees (REAL HEAD)

Problem Outputs

the direction to face (CHARACTER *5 FACE)
the compass bearing in degrees (REAL BEAR)
the direction to turn (CHARACTER *4 TURN)

DESIGN

The algorithm follows:

Algorithm

1. Enter the compass heading.
2. Compute the compass bearing.
3. Display the compass bearing.

Algorithm Refinements

To refine step 2, we specify Table 3.13 as a multiple-alternative decision step.

Step 2 Refinement

2.1 IF heading is less than zero THEN
    2.2 Bearing is undefined.
  ELSE IF heading is less than 90.0 THEN
    2.3 Use north (HEAD) east as the bearing.
  ELSE IF heading is less than 180.0 THEN
    2.4 Use south (180.0 − HEAD) east as the bearing.
  ELSE IF heading is less than 270.0 THEN
    2.5 Use south (HEAD − 180.0) west as the bearing.
  ELSE IF heading is less than 360.0 THEN
    2.6 Use north (360.0 − HEAD) west as the bearing.
  ELSE IF heading is greater than 360.0 THEN
    2.7 Bearing is undefined.
  END IF

IMPLEMENTATION

The program appears in Fig. 3.15. In the general IF statement, the assignment statement

```
FACE = '?????'
```

executes when the value of HEAD is out of range (less than zero or greater than 360), indicating that the bearing is undefined. Three assignment statements implement each of the algorithm steps 2.3 through 2.6, assigning values to

Figure 3.15. *Computing Compass Bearings*

```
      PROGRAM COMPASS

C Transforms a compass heading to a compass bearing

C Type declarations
      REAL HEAD, BEAR
      CHARACTER *5 FACE
      CHARACTER *4 TURN

C Enter compass heading
      PRINT *, 'Enter a compass heading (0 - 360 degrees)'
      READ *, HEAD

C Compute compass bearing
      IF (HEAD .LT. 0.0) THEN
         FACE = '?????'
      ELSE IF (HEAD .LT. 90.0) THEN
         FACE = 'north'
         BEAR = HEAD
         TURN = 'east'
      ELSE IF (HEAD .LT. 180.0) THEN
         FACE = 'south'
         BEAR = 180.0 - HEAD
         TURN = 'east'
      ELSE IF (HEAD .LT. 270.0) THEN
         FACE = 'south'
         BEAR = HEAD - 180.0
         TURN = 'west'
      ELSE IF (HEAD .LE. 360.0) THEN
         FACE = 'north'
         BEAR = 360.0 - HEAD
         TURN = 'west'
      ELSE
         FACE = '?????'
      END IF
```

```
C Display compass bearing
      IF (FACE .EQ. '?????') THEN
          PRINT *, 'Error - - heading must be between 0 and 360'
      ELSE
          PRINT *, 'The bearing is ', FACE, BEAR,
     +              'degrees ', TURN
      END IF

      STOP
      END

Enter a compass heading (0 - 360 degrees)
110.0
The bearing is south 70.00000 degrees east
```

FACE, BEAR, and TURN. The IF statement at the end of the program displays either an error message (when FACE is '?????') or the values assigned to FACE, BEAR, and TURN.

TESTING AND VERIFICATION

To test this program, try compass headings in each of the four quadrants. Also, try compass headings at the quadrant boundaries: 0, 90, 180, 270, and 360 degrees. Finally, see what happens when the heading value is out of range.

EXERCISES FOR SECTION 3.8

Self-check

1. Explain what is wrong with the nested IF structure below.

```
IF (GPA .GE. 3.0) THEN
   PRINT *, 'Dean's list'
ELSE
   IF (GPA .LT. 2.0) THEN
      PRINT *, 'On probation'
   ELSE IF (GPA .LT. 1.0) THEN
      PRINT *, 'Flunked out'
   END IF
END IF
```

2. Trace the execution of the general IF statement in Fig. 3.11 for $A = 1$, $B = 4$, and $C = 4$.
3. What value is assigned to X when Y is 15.0? When Y is 10.0? When Y is -10.0?

```
IF (Y .LT. 15.0) THEN
    IF (Y .GE. 0.0) THEN
        X = 5.0 * Y
    ELSE
        X = 2.0 * Y
    END IF
ELSE
    X = 3.0 * Y
END IF
```

Programming

1. Rewrite the IF statement for Example 3.19 using only the relational operator .LT. in all conditions.
2. Write an IF statement that assigns the larger of X and Y to LARGER and the smaller to SMALLR. Your statement should display 'X larger' or 'Y larger' depending on the situation.
3. Implement the decision table given in Table 3.14 using a general IF statement. Assume the grade point average is within the range 0.0 through 4.0.
4. Implement the Road Safety Decision Step shown in Fig. 3.9 as a multiple-alternative decision. You will need to use the LOGICAL operator .AND. to combine the two conditions that must be true in order to display the message 'Wet roads'.

Table 3.14. *Decision Table for Grade Point Averages*

GRADE POINT AVERAGE	TRANSCRIPT MESSAGE
0.0–0.99	Failed semester—registration suspended
1.0–1.99	On probation for next semester
2.0–2.99	(No message)
3.0–3.49	Dean's list for semester
3.5–4.0	Highest honors for semester

3.9 Common Programming Errors

1. When writing IF statements, remember that the words ELSE and END IF must always appear on lines by themselves unless ELSE is followed by IF.
2. To improve program readability, we recommend that you indent the true and false tasks.

3. Be careful to write the conditions in a multiple-alternative decision in the correct order. If the conditions are not mutually exclusive (i.e., more than one condition may be true), the most restrictive condition should come first.

Chapter Review

In this chapter, you learned about the six Fortran relational operators—.LT., .LE., .GT., .GE., .EQ., .NE.—and the LOGICAL data type and its operators—.NOT., .AND., .OR., .EQV., and .NEQV.. You also learned how to write logical expressions using the relational operators to specify conditions and how to combine these conditions using the LOGICAL operators. Conditions written in pseudocode (a mixture of English and Fortran) can be used to form decision steps in algorithms and these decision steps can be implemented using the Fortran IF statement. The Fortran IF statement contains a logical expression which is evaluated; the result of this evaluation determines which task is executed.

Decisions with one or two alternatives can be implemented using the Fortran IF statement, while nested IF statements and the general IF structure (Block IF) can be used to implement decisions with several alternatives. The one-line logical IF can be used for conditional execution of a single statement.

Desk checks or hand traces are used to verify that an algorithm or program is correct. Careful tracing can help you find errors in logic that if discovered before you enter the program into the computer, can save considerable time and effort. Remember to carefully "execute" each step just as the computer would; the trace is meaningless if you assume that a step does what it is supposed to do without checking that it actually does so.

Fortran Statements

The Fortran statements introduced in this chapter are described in Table 3.15.

Table 3.15. *Summary of Fortran Statements for Chapter 3*

STATEMENT	EFFECT
IF Statement (One Alternative)	

`IF (X .NE. 0.0) THEN`
`    PRODCT = PRODCT * X`
`END IF`
	Multiplies PRODCT by X only if X is nonzero.

IF Statement (Two Alternatives)	

`IF (X .GE. 0.0) THEN`
`    PRINT *, X, ' is positive'`
`ELSE`
`    PRINT *, X, ' is negative'`
`END IF`
	If X is greater than or equal to 0.0, the message ' is positive' is displayed; otherwise, the message ' is negative' is displayed.

STATEMENT	EFFECT

Multiple Alternative Decision

```
IF (SCORE .GE. 90) THEN
    PRINT *, 'A'
    COUNTA = COUNTA + 1
ELSE IF (SCORE .GE. 80) THEN
    PRINT *, 'B'
    COUNTB = COUNTB + 1
ELSE
    PRINT *, 'C'
    COUNTC = COUNTC + 1
END IF
```

If SCORE is greater than or equal to 90, increment COUNTA; otherwise, if SCORE is greater than or equal to 80, increment COUNTB; otherwise, increment COUNTC. Also, display score category (A, B, or C).

Logical IF Statement

```
IF (NUMRET .GT. 0) PRINT *, NUMRET
```

Displays the value of NUMRET only when NUMRET is greater than zero.

Quick-check Exercises

1. An IF statement implements a(n) _____ step.
2. What is pseudocode?
3. What values can a conditional expression have?
4. The relational operator .NE. means _____ .
5. A(n) _____ is used to verify that an algorithm is correct.
6. What value is assigned to FEE by the following IF statement when SPEED is 75?

```
IF (SPEED .GT. 35) THEN
    FEE = 20.00
ELSE IF (SPEED .GT. 50) THEN
    FEE = 40.00
ELSE IF (SPEED .GT. 75) THEN
    FEE = 60.00
END IF
```

7. Answer exercise 6 for the IF statement below. Which IF statement is correct?

```
IF (SPEED .GT. 75) THEN
    FEE = 60.0
ELSE IF (SPEED .GT. 50) THEN
    FEE = 40.00
ELSE IF (SPEED .GT. 35) THEN
    FEE = 20.00
END IF
```

8. What output line(s) are displayed by the following statements when X is 5.53? When X is 9.95?

```
IF (X .GT. 7.5) THEN
    X = 90.0
    PRINT *, 'X is ', X
ELSE
    X = 25.0
END IF
PRINT *, 'X is ', X
```

9. For the three fragments below, what is the final value of X if the initial value of X is 1?

```
a. IF (X .GE. 0) THEN
       X = X + 1
   ELSE IF (X .GE. 1) THEN
       X = X = 2
   END IF
b. IF (X .GE. 0) THEN
       X = X + 1
   END IF
   IF (X .GE. 1) THEN
       X = X + 2
   END IF
c. IF (X .GE. 1) THEN
       X = X + 2
   ELSE IF (X .GE. 0) THEN
       X = X + 1
   END IF
```

10. What is the effect of the following fragment when GRADE is 'I'? When GRADE is 'B'? When GRADE is 'b'?

```
IF (GRADE .EQ. 'A') THEN
    POINTS = 4 * CREDIT
ELSE IF (GRADE .EQ. 'B') THEN
    POINTS = 3 * CREDIT
ELSE IF (GRADE .EQ. 'C') THEN
    POINTS = 2 * CREDIT
ELSE IF (GRADE .EQ. 'D') THEN
    POINTS = CREDIT
ELSE IF ((GRADE .EQ. 'P') .OR. (GRADE .EQ. 'F') .OR.
+          (GRADE .EQ. 'I') .OR. (GRADE .EQ. 'W')) THEN
    POINTS = 0
ELSE
    PRINT *, 'Invalid grade'
END IF
```

Answers to Quick-check Exercises

1. decision
2. a mixture of English and Fortran used to describe algorithm steps
3. true or false
4. not equal
5. hand-trace or desk-check
6. 20.00
7. 40.00; the statement in question 7
8. X is 25.0; X is 90.0 printed twice.
9. (a) X = 2; (b) X = 4; (c) X = 3
10. POINTS = 0, POINTS = 3 * CREDIT, Displays Invalid grade

Review Questions

1. Briefly describe the steps to derive an algorithm for a given problem.
2. A decision in Fortran is actually an evaluation of a(n) _____ expression.
3. List the six relational operators discussed in this chapter.
4. What should be done by the programmer after the algorithm is written but before the program is entered (typed) into the computer?
5. Write the appropriate IF statement to compute GROSS, given that the hourly rate is stored in the variable RATE and the total hours worked is stored in the variable HOURS. Pay time and a half for more than 40 hours worked.
6. Implement the flow diagram in Fig. 3.16 using a nested IF structure.

Figure 3.16.

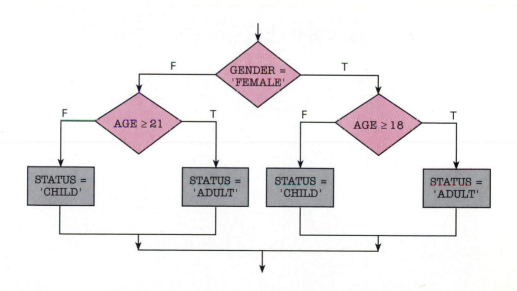

7. Trace the following program fragment and indicate what will be done if a data value of 27.34 is entered.

```
PRINT *, 'Enter a temperature:'
READ *, TEMP
IF (TEMP .GT. 32.0) THEN
    PRINT *, 'NOT FREEZING'
ELSE
    PRINT *, 'ICE FORMING'
END IF
```

8. Use a general IF statement to display whether a student is in elementary school ($0 \leq$ GRADE ≤ 5), middle school ($6 \leq$ GRADE ≤ 8), high school ($9 \leq$ GRADE ≤ 12), or college (GRADE > 12).

9. Which of the following answers gives a correct trace for the program on the right?

a.

X	Y
5.0	7.0
	3.0

b.

X	Y
5.0	7.0

c.

X	Y
5.0	7.0
3.0	

d.

X	Y
7.0	5.0
	3.0

e.

X	Y
7.0	5.0

```
PROGRAM QUIZ
REAL X, Y
X = 5.0
Y = X + 2.0
IF ((Y + 2.0) .GT. X) THEN
    Y = 3.0
ELSE
    X = 3.0
END IF
STOP
END
```

10. What will be the value of I after the Fortran statements on the right execute?

a. 5
b. 20
c. 23
d. 50
e. 53

```
I = 5
J = 10
IF ((I + 4) .LT. (J - I)) THEN
    I = J * I
ELSE
    I = 2 * J
END IF
I = I + 3
```

11. What will be the value of I after the Fortran statements on the right execute?

    a. 6   `I = 5`
    b. 8   `J = 10`
    c. 9   `IF ((3 * I) .LT. J) I = I + 1`
    d. 10   `I = I + 3`
    e. 15

Fortran 90 Features: CASE Control Structure

Relational Operators   Fortran 90 provides additional readable relational operators. The familiar symbols <=, <, >, >= can be used as well as the traditional operators .LE., .LT., .GT., .GE.. The symbols == and /= mean the same as the symbols .EQ. and .NE..

CASE Control Structure   The CASE control structure provides another way to specify selection. Given the following price structure for concert tickets:

Section	Ticket Price
50	50.00
100–140	25.00
200–240	25.00
300–340	20.00
400–440	15.00

the CASE structure below assigns the desired value to tixprice or displays an error message if the section is not listed in the table.

```
SELECT CASE (section)
CASE (50)
   tixprice = 50.00
CASE (100:140, 200:240)
   tixprice = 25.00
CASE (300:340)
   tixprice = 20.00
CASE (400:440)
   tixprice = 15.00
CASE DEFAULT
   PRINT *, 'Invalid section number'
END SELECT
```

The line beginning with SELECT contains a variable (section) whose value determines which of the alternatives that follow is executed. Each alternative begins with the word CASE and a list of possible values. If the expression value matches a value listed in a particular selector, the lines following that selector are executed and control is transferred to the line following END SELECT. For example, if the value of section is 105, tixprice gets 25.00.

The CASE structure is more readable and easier to code than a general IF statement whose conditions all involve a test of a single variable. The CASE structure is implemented next as a general IF statement using the new relational operators provided in Fortran 90. The syntax display follows the IF statement.

```
IF (section == 50) THEN
    tixprice = 50.00
ELSE IF ((100 <= section) .AND. (section <= 140) .OR.
         (200 <= section) .AND. (section <= 240)) THEN
    tixprice = 25.00
ELSE IF ((300 <= section) .AND. (section <= 340)) THEN
    tixprice = 20.00
ELSE IF ((400 <= section) .AND. (section <= 440)) THEN
    tixprice = 15.00
ELSE
    PRINT *, 'Invalid section number'
END IF
```

SYNTAX DISPLAY

CASE Statement

SYNTAX: SELECT CASE (*expression*)
      CASE (*selector$_1$*)
        statement$_1$
      CASE (*selector$_2$*)
        statement$_2$

      . . .

      CASE DEFAULT
        statement$_E$
      END SELECT

EXAMPLE: SELECT CASE (n)
      CASE (1 : 2)
        PRINT *, 'Buckle my shoe'
      CASE (3 : 4)
        PRINT *, 'Shut the door'
      CASE (5 : 6)
        PRINT *, 'Pick up sticks'
      CASE DEFAULT
        PRINT *, 'Incorrect value for n'
      END SELECT

INTERPRETATION: The *expression* is evaluated and compared to each *selector*, where each *selector* is a list of possible values of the *expression*. Only one *statement*$_i$ will be executed. If the *expression* value is included in *selector*$_i$, *statement*$_i$ is executed. Control is then passed to the first statement following the END SELECT. Each *statement*$_i$ may be one or more Fortran statements.

NOTE 1: CASE DEFAULT and *statement*$_E$ are optional. If present, *statement*$_E$ executes when the CASE *expression* does not match any *selector*$_i$. Otherwise, nothing is done when there is no match.

NOTE 2: A range of consecutive values in a *selector* may be written as *low* : *high* where *low* is the first value in the range and *high* is the last value in the range and *low* ≤ *high*.

NOTE 3: The values in a particular *selector* may not overlap, and a value cannot be present in more than one *selector*.

NOTE 4: The data type of each value in a *selector* must be the same as the type of the CASE *expression*. Data types CHARACTER and INTEGER are permitted, but not types REAL and LOGICAL.

Programming Projects

1. a. Write a program to display the "message" XXOXOX in block letters. Each block letter should be displayed using six columns and six rows. Display the block letters down the page.
   b. Modify your program so that any six-letter message consisting of Xs and Os will be displayed in block-letter form. The message to be displayed should be entered and displayed one character at a time. (*Hint:* Use a decision.)

2. Write a program to simulate a state police radar gun. The program should read an automobile speed and display the message "speeding" if the speed exceeds 55 mph.

3. A program is needed that will read a character value and a number. Depending on what is read, certain information will be displayed. The character should be either an 'S' or a 'T'. If an 'S' is read and the number is 100.50, the program will display

   ```
   Send money! I need $100.50
   ```

   If a 'T' is read instead of 'S', the program will display

   ```
   The temperature last night was 100.50 degrees
   ```

4. Write a program that reads in three numbers and finds and displays the smallest and the largest numbers.

5. Write a conversion program that displays a three-line prompting message and then performs the operation indicated by the first data value entered in response to the prompt (see the prompt below). If the first data value is 1, a pair of data values for feet and inches should be read and converted to a single real value (for example, 5 ft 6 in. would be converted to 5.5). If the first data value is 2, a single value should be read and converted to two output values representing the equivalent amount of feet and inches.

```
Conversion program: Select one operation below
1—Convert feet and inches to decimal feet
2—Convert decimal feet to feet and inches
```

6. A chemist uses the decision table in Table 3.16 to determine whether a solution is very acidic, acidic, neutral, alkaline, or very alkaline. Implement it using a multiple-alternative IF statement.

Table 3.16. *Decision Table for Chemical Solution*

PH RANGE	SOLUTION TYPE
>= 12	very alkaline
8–11	alkaline
7	neutral
3–6	acidic
<= 2	very acidic

Write a program that will read in the value of PH for a solution and display its type.

7. Modify the program in Fig. 3.11 so that it also displays complex roots of a quadratic equation. If the equation discriminant is negative, the two roots are:

$$R_1 = \frac{-B}{2A} + \frac{\sqrt{|D|}}{2A}i$$

$$R_2 = \frac{-B}{2A} - \frac{\sqrt{|D|}}{2A}i$$

where D is the discriminant. For example, if $A = 1$, $B = 2$, and $C = 3$, your program should display the roots as:

```
-1.0000 + 1.414i,    -1.0000 - 1.414i
```

You will need to allocate separate variables for storing the real part (e.g., -1.0) and imaginary part (e.g., 1.414) of each complex root. Then display the roots in the form shown above.

Table 3.17. *Decision Table for an Earthquake*

RICHTER SCALE NUMBER (N)	CHARACTERIZATION
N < 5.0	little or no damage
5.0 <= N < 5.5	moderate damage
5.5 <= N < 6.5	serious damage
6.5 <= N < 7.5	disaster
>= 7.5	catastrophic damage

8. The National Earthquake Information Center has asked you to write a program implementing the decision table shown in Table 3.17 to characterize an earthquake based on a Richter scale number. Your program should read the Richter number, N, and display an appropriate message.

9. Write a program that will determine the additional state tax owed by an employee. The state charges a 4% tax on net income. Net income is determined by subtracting a $500 allowance for each dependent from gross income. Your program will read gross income, number of dependents, and tax amount already deducted. It will then compute the actual tax owed and display the difference between tax owed and tax deducted, followed by the message 'SEND CHECK' or 'REFUND' depending on whether the difference is positive or negative.

10. A monthly magazine wants a program that will print out renewal notices to its subscribers and cancellation notices when appropriate. Your program first should read in the current month number (1–12) and year. For each subscription processed, read in four data items: the account number, the month the subscription started, the year the subscription started, and the number of years of subscription paid for.

    Read in a set of subscription information and display a renewal notice if the current month is either the month prior to expiration or the month of expiration. A cancellation notice should be displayed if the current month comes after the expiration month.
    Sample input might be:

10 93	for a current month of October 1993
1364 4 92 3	for account 1364 whose three-year subscription began in April 1992

11. Write a program that will read in the number of credit hours (HOURS) completed by a student at a university. Based on the number of credit hours completed, classify the student as a freshman, sophomore, junior, or senior. Each student should be classified according to the following rules:

Classification	Credit Hours
Freshman	HOURS < 32
Sophomore	32 <= HOURS < 64
Junior	64 <= HOURS < 96
Senior	96 <= HOURS

After reading in a student's number of credit hours completed, display the appropriate classification for that student.

12. Modify project 7 of Chapter 2 to allow a rectangular or a triangular house inside a rectangular yard. Your program should read in a letter representing the kind of house and then its dimensions. Instead of calculating the time required to cut the grass, your program should display an error message if the house is too big to fit inside the yard (house length or width larger than yard length or width). (*Hint:* The area of a triangle is 0.5 × *base* × *height*.)

13. The New Long Distance Company has the following rate structure for long-distance calls:

   ■ Any call started after 6:00 P.M. (1800 hours) but before 8:00 A.M. (0800 hours) is discounted 50%.
   ■ Any call started after 8:00 A.M. (0800 hours) but before 6:00 P.M. (1800 hours) is charged full price.
   ■ All calls are subject to a 4% federal tax.
   ■ The regular rate for a call is $0.40 per minute.
   ■ Any call longer than 60 min receives a 15% discount on its cost (after any other discount is subtracted and before tax is added).

   Write a program that reads the start time for a call based on a 24-hr clock and the length of the call. The gross cost (before any discounts or tax) should be displayed followed by the net cost (after discounts are deducted and tax is added).

14. Modify the program in Fig. 3.6 to read in the maximum allowable stress as a data value. Also, compute and display the safety factor when the column is judged to be safe. The safety factor is defined as the ratio of the maximum stress to the computed stress and should always be greater than 1.

15. Concrete weighs about 150 lb/cu ft. Have a user enter a pipe thickness (in inches), outside diameter (in inches), and the length of the pipe (in feet). Then calculate the weight of the pipe. (*Hint:* To find the volume of concrete in the pipe, subtract the volume of a cylinder of the inside diameter from the volume of a cylinder with the outside diameter.) An example run would be

```
Please enter the pipe thickness in inches
3
Enter the outside diameter in inches
36
Enter the pipe length in feet
10
The weight of the pipe is 3239.768 pounds
```

16. Modify project 18 of Chapter 2 so that your program tests to see whether the heat loss, Q, is greater than 260. If so, display a message to the user that more insulation is needed around the pipe. Display a new test value for r_2 which is 0.5 in. larger than the old one. The user should continue to run the program with the values suggested for r_2 until the message is no longer displayed. Use the initial values: $Ts_1 = 327$, $Ts_2 = 90$, $L = 1$, $k = .0364$, $r_1 = 10.75$, and $r_2 = 11.75$.

17. Write a program that will calculate and print out bills for the city water company. The water rates vary depending on whether the bill is for home, commercial, or industrial use.

    A code H means home use, a code C means commercial use, and a code I means industrial use. Any other code should be treated as an error.

    The water rates are computed as follows:

    code H: $5.00 plus $0.0005 per gallon used
    code C: $1000.00 for the first four million gallons used and $0.00025 for each additional gallon
    code I: $1000.00 if usage does not exceed four million gallons; $2000.00 if usage is more than four million gallons but does not exceed 10 million gallons; and $3000.00 if usage exceeds 10 million gallons

    Your program should prompt the user to enter an integer account number, using code character, and the gallons of water used expressed as a real number and should display the amount due from the user.

CHAPTER 4
Repetition and Loops

Control structures of a programming language enable the programmer to control the sequence and the frequency of execution of program segments. In the last chapter, we introduced the IF statement for implementing decision steps; in this chapter, we show you how to specify the repetition of a group of program statements, called a loop, and explain how to use two kinds of Fortran looping structures. We also discuss what happens when we nest control structures, that is, place one control structure inside another, and we present several case studies to demonstrate repetition and nested control structures.

4.1 Repetition in Programs

Just as the ability to instruct the computer to make decisions is an important programming tool, so is the ability to specify that a group of operations is to be repeated. For example, we might like to carry out the gross pay and net pay computations shown in Fig. 3.4 once for each employee in a company. This could be expressed in pseudocode as follows:

```
DO for each employee
    Read hours worked and hourly rate
    Compute gross pay
    Compute tax amount
    Compute net pay
    Display gross pay, tax amount, and net pay
END DO
```

This pseudocode indicates that a group of operations is to be performed repeatedly. The operations to be repeated are listed between the line that begins with DO and the line END DO and include reading an employee's data; computing an employee's gross pay, tax, and net pay; and displaying the results for that employee.

We describe in this text two control statements for specifying repetition: The first one, the DO loop, is introduced next and the second, the WHILE loop, is introduced in Section 4.6.

The DO Loop   We can use the Fortran DO loop to specify quite easily certain forms of repetition, as shown in the next examples.

EXAMPLE 4.1   The following two program fragments have the same effect:

```
PRINT *, 'Hi Mom'                    DO 10 LINE = 1, 5, 1
PRINT *, 'Hi Mom'                        PRINT *, 'Hi Mom'
PRINT *, 'Hi Mom'                10 CONTINUE
PRINT *, 'Hi Mom'
PRINT *, 'Hi Mom'
```

If LINE is declared as an integer variable, the DO loop causes the message 'Hi Mom' to be printed five times. We can cause more lines to be printed simply by changing the integer 5 to some larger value. The *loop header* is the first statement of the loop. The loop header

```
DO 10 LINE = 1, 5, 1
```

specifies that the statement(s) that follow should be repeated five times, once each for values of LINE equal to 1, 2, 3, 4, and 5. (It may help you understand the Fortran syntax if you read the header above as "DO through label 10 for values of LINE from 1 to 5, increasing LINE in steps of 1.") The *loop terminator*

```
10 CONTINUE
```

marks the end of the loop and follows the last statement that is to be repeated.

We call LINE the *loop-control variable* because its value controls the loop repetition. The loop-control variable is initialized to 1 when the DO loop is first reached; after each execution of the loop body, the loop-control variable is incremented by 1 and tested to see whether loop repetition should continue. Loop repetition continues as long as LINE is less than or equal to 5, which means that the value of LINE is 1 during the first loop repetition, 2 during the second loop repetition, and 5 during the last loop repetition.

The integer 10 appearing in both the loop header and the loop terminator is a *label*. You can use any integer up to 5 digits as a label; however, you must use the same label in both the header and the terminator statements of a loop and in the terminator statement, the label must appear somewhere in the label field (columns 1 through 5). In pseudocode, we use END DO as the loop terminator instead of *label* CONTINUE.

The loop header

```
DO 10 LINE = 1, 5
```

is equivalent to the one just discussed. The increment value is assumed to be 1 if it is not explicitly listed. However, we must always list the initial value of the loop control variable (1) and its final value (5). Most programmers prefer to use this form, which omits the increment when it is 1.

The loop-control variable also may be referenced in the loop body, but you cannot change its value. The next example shows a DO loop whose loop-control variable is referenced in the loop body. ■

EXAMPLE 4.2

The program in Fig. 4.1 uses a DO loop to print a table that shows a list of integer values from 1 to 4 in the first column and the square, square root, and exponential function value for each integer in subsequent columns. The first PRINT statement displays the table heading (a long string) before the DO loop is entered. During each repetition of the loop, the assignment statements define new values for variables SQUARE, ROOT, and IPOWER. The expression part of the statement

```
ROOT = SQRT(REAL(I))
```

contains a *nested function reference*, which means the innermost function reference—in this case, REAL(I)—is evaluated first. The function REAL converts the integer I to a real number before the SQRT function is called. The PRINT statement displays the next value of the loop-control variable I and the variable's square, square root, and exponential function (e^I). ■

Figure 4.1. *Displaying a Table of Integers and Function Values*

```
      PROGRAM INTFUN
C For each integer in the range 1 to MAXINT, prints each integer,
C its square, square root, and its exponential function value.

C Declarations
      INTEGER MAXINT
      PARAMETER (MAXINT = 4)
      INTEGER SQUARE
      REAL ROOT, IPOWER

C Display a heading.
      PRINT *, '         I      I ** 2  Square root   Exponential'

C Display each integer, its square, square root, exponential.
      DO 20 I = 1, MAXINT
         SQUARE = I ** 2
         ROOT = SQRT(REAL(I))
         IPOWER = EXP(REAL(I))
         PRINT *, I, SQUARE, ROOT, IPOWER
   20 CONTINUE

      STOP
      END
```

```
I        I ** 2   Square root   Exponential
1            1    1.000000      2.718282
2            4    1.414214      7.389056
3            9    1.732051      20.08554
4           16    2.000000      54.59815
```

A trace of this program is shown in Table 4.1. Only variables I and SQUARE are shown in the trace.

Table 4.1. *Trace of Program in Fig. 4.1*

STATEMENT	I	SQUARE	EFFECT
DO 20 I = 1, MAXINT	1		Initializes I to 1; 1 <= 4 is true—
SQUARE = I ** 2		1	assigns 1 to SQUARE
. . .			. . .
PRINT *, I, SQUARE, . . .			prints 1, 1, and function values.
Increment and test I	2		Increments I to 2; 2 <= 4 is true—
SQUARE = I ** 2		4	assigns 4 to SQUARE
. . .			. . .
PRINT *, I, SQUARE, . . .			prints 2, 4, and function values.
Increment and test I	3		Increments I to 3; 3 <= 4 is true—
SQUARE = I ** 2		9	assigns 9 to SQUARE
. . .			. . .
PRINT *, I, SQUARE, . . .			prints 3, 9, and function values.
Increment and test I	4		Increments I to 4; 4 <= 4 is true—
SQUARE = I ** 2		16	assigns 16 to SQUARE
. . .			. . .
PRINT *, I, SQUARE, . . .			prints 4, 16, and function values.
Increment and test I	5		Increments I to 5; 5 <= 4 is false— exits loop.

The trace in Table 4.1 shows that the loop-control variable I is initialized to 1 when the DO loop is reached. The DO loop causes the assignment statements and the PRINT statement to be repeated. Before each repetition, I is incremented by 1 and tested to see whether its value is still less than or equal to MAXINT (4). If the test result is true, the loop body is executed again and the next values of SQUARE, ROOT, and IPOWER are computed and displayed. I is equal to 4 during the last loop repetition.

Program Style: *Printing a Table*

The statement

```
PRINT *, '              I      I ** 2  Square root   Exponential'
```

before the loop causes a single string to be displayed that serves as a table heading with four column labels: I, I ** 2, and so on. This line is printed once, just before the loop is entered and executed.

Inside the loop, the statement

```
PRINT *, I, SQUARE, ROOT, IPOWER
```

prints four numbers each time it is executed. The actual position of these numbers will differ depending on the compiler used. If your compiler aligns these numbers in columns, you can reposition the column labels in the heading string so that each label appears over its respective column of numbers.

Unfortunately, some compilers will not align these numbers in columns. In Chapter 5, we discuss another method of printing a table that will produce the same output for all compilers.

Case Study: Physics of Falling Bodies

PROBLEM STATEMENT

Your skydiving club wants a program that will compute and display the distance a skydiver falls from a plane at 1-sec intervals from *time* = 1 sec until some predetermined maximum time.

ANALYSIS

From physics, we know that the distance an object falls from an airplane (ignoring air resistance) is given by the equation

$$distance = 1/2 \; acceleration \times time^2,$$

where the acceleration due to gravity is approximately 9.81 m/sec^2. We can use this equation in a loop to compute distance for each value of time from 1 through 10 sec. We can make the program more general by reading in the maximum time in seconds.

Data Requirements and Relevant Formula

Problem Parameter

the acceleration due to gravity in m/sec^2 (REAL GACCEL = 9.80665)

Problem Input

the maximum time in seconds (INTEGER MXTIME)

Problem Output

the distance fallen at the end of each second (REAL DISTNC)

Additional Program Variable

the elapsed time since the parachutist left the plane (INTEGER TIME)

Relevant Formula

$distance = 1/2\ acceleration \times time^2$

DESIGN

The algorithm follows:

Algorithm

1. Enter the maximum time (in seconds) for the fall.
2. Compute and display the distance fallen at the end of each second in the time interval from 1 second to the maximum.

Algorithm Refinement

Next, we refine algorithm step 2 by using a loop that is repeated for values of TIME between 1 and MXTIME.

Step 2 Refinement

    2.1 DO for values of TIME between 1 and MXTIME
          2.2 Compute distance fallen.
          2.3 Display distance fallen.
    END DO

IMPLEMENTATION

The program appears in Fig. 4.2. The assignment statement

```
DISTNC = 0.5 * GACCEL * TIME ** 2
```

implements the equation

$$distance = 1/2\ acceleration \times time^2$$

that describes the relationship among distance, acceleration, and elapsed time.

Figure 4.2. *Computing a Skydiver's Flight*

```
      PROGRAM SKYDIV
C Computes and displays the distance fallen by a skydiver in one-
C second intervals. The maximum time is entered as data.

C Declarations
      REAL GACCEL
      PARAMETER (GACCEL = 9.80665)
      INTEGER TIME, MXTIME, DISTNC

C Enter maximum time of fall
      PRINT *, 'Enter maximum freefall time (in seconds)'
      READ *, MXTIME

C Compute and display distance fallen after each second
      PRINT *
      PRINT *, '  Time (secs)     Distance (meters)'
      DO 10 TIME = 1, MXTIME
         DISTNC = 0.5 * GACCEL * TIME ** 2
         PRINT *, 'Time (secs) = ', TIME,
     +              ' Distance (meters) = ', DISTNC
   10 CONTINUE

C Exit program
      STOP
      END

Enter maximum freefall time (in seconds)
10

   Time (secs)     Distance (meters)
       1             4.903325
       2            19.613300
       3            44.129920
       4            78.453200
       5           122.583100
       6           176.519700
       7           240.262900
       8           313.812800
       9           397.169300
      10           490.332500
```

TESTING AND VERIFICATION

To test this program, run it for several increasing values of MXTIME. As MXTIME increases, the table size should grow, but the beginning lines of each succeeding table should be the same as for the previous table. Also check certain values of DISTNC that are relatively easy to calculate; for example, line 1 of each table (TIME is 1) should contain a value of GACCEL / 2 (DISTNC is 4.903325), line 2 of each table (TIME is 2) should contain a value of 2 * GACCEL (DISTNC is 19.6133), and line 10 of each table (TIME is 10) should contain a value of 50 * GACCEL (DISTNC is 490.3325).

EXERCISES FOR SECTION 4.1

Self-check

1. List the values of the loop control variable for each valid loop header below. Which are invalid?

   a. DO 20 I = 1, N
   b. DO 10I = 1, 10
   c. DO I10 = 1, 50
   d. DO I = 1, 5
   e. DO 10 I10 = 1, 10, 1
   f. DO 30 I = 5, 5
   g. DO 40 I = 1.2.3
   h. DO 10 I = 1, 4 * 5, 1
   i. DO 10 I = 5
   j. DO10I = 5

2. Trace the execution of the following DO loop. What is printed?

```
      N = 5
      DO 10 COUNT = 1, N
         PRINT *, '*****'
10    CONTINUE
```

3. Trace the execution of the following DO loop. What is printed?

```
      PROD = 1
      DO 20 I = 1, 5
      PROD = PROD * I
      PRINT *, I, PROD
20    CONTINUE
```

Programming

1. Write a DO loop that computes the first 10 powers of 2. Display a table showing each integer from 1 through 10 and 2 raised to that power.
2. Write a DO loop that reads in 20 test scores and "scales" each test score by adding 15 points to it. Display each initial score and the corresponding scaled score.

4.2   The General DO Loop

In the previous section, we used the DO loop to implement *counting loops,* which are executed once for each integer value between 1 and a specified final value. In a counting loop, the loop-control variable is increased by 1 each time the loop is repeated. In this section, we discuss other forms of the DO loop.

The DO Loop Step Parameter

It is possible to specify any positive or negative change to the value of a DO loop-control variable in the loop header. Thus the value of the DO loop-control variable may increase or decrease after each loop repetition, as illustrated in the next examples.

EXAMPLE 4.3

The program in Fig. 4.3 "counts down" from a specified starting value (an input variable) to "blast-off." Because INTERV is –1, the value of the loop-control variable, TIME, decreases by 1 each time the loop is repeated.   ■

Figure 4.3. *Counting Down to Blast-off*

```
        PROGRAM BLAST
C Counting down to blast-off

C Declarations
        INTEGER INTERV
        PARAMETER (INTERV = -1)
        INTEGER TIME, START

        PRINT *, 'Enter starting time (an integer) in seconds:'
        READ *, START

C Begin count down
        PRINT *, 'Begin count down'
        DO 10 TIME = START, 1, INTERV
            PRINT *, 'T -', TIME
    10 CONTINUE
        PRINT *, 'Blast-off!'

        STOP
        END

Enter starting time (an integer) in seconds:
5
Begin count down
T - 5
T - 4
T - 3
T - 2
T - 1
Blast-off!
```

DO Loop Syntax

In addition to integer constants or variables as DO loop parameters, we also can use expressions. For example, the DO loop header

```
DO 100 I = J + 3, 2 * JMAX
```

is valid. In this header, the initial parameter is the value of the expression J + 3 and the limit parameter is the value of the expression 2 * JMAX. These expression values are computed once when the loop header is first reached and are used to fix the minimum and maximum values of loop-control variable I during loop repetition. Even if the value of JMAX later is changed during loop execution, the number of loop repetitions will not be affected.

Although Fortran 77 permits type REAL expressions as DO loop parameters, we strongly discourage this practice because DO loops with type REAL parameters will not always execute the same number of times on different computers. The reason for this is discussed in Section 2.5 under "Numerical Inaccuracies."

SYNTAX DISPLAY

DO Loop Structure

SYNTAX: DO *label lcv = initial, limit, step*
                 loop body
       label CONTINUE

EXAMPLE: DO 10 I = 99, 0, −3
                PRINT *, I
    10 CONTINUE

INTERPRETATION: The loop parameters *initial*, *limit*, and *step* are expressions that represent the *initial* value, *limit* value, and *step* value for the loop-control variable, *lcv*. The *lcv* is set to the value of *initial* when the loop header is first reached. Before each repetition of the *loop body* (including the first), the value of *lcv* is tested to see whether it has "passed" the value of *limit*. If so, control passes to the first statement following the loop terminator, causing loop exit; otherwise, the *loop body* is executed. After the *loop body* is executed, the value of *lcv* is incremented by *step* and retested as explained next.

If *step* is positive, repetition will continue as long as *lcv* is less than or equal to *limit*; the loop will be exited when *lcv* becomes greater than *limit*. If *step* is negative, repetition will continue as long as *lcv* is greater than or equal to *limit*; the loop will be exited when *lcv* becomes less than *limit*. Upon exit, *lcv* retains the last value assigned to it, i.e., the value that caused the exit.

NOTES: The loop parameters may be arithmetic expressions. Each expression is evaluated only once—when the loop is first entered. It is permissible for the values of variables in these expressions (but not *lcv*) to be changed in the loop body; however, this will not affect the values of *initial, limit,* or *step,* nor will it change the number of loop repetitions.

A *step* value of zero is not allowed. If *step* is omitted, it is assumed to be one. The same statement *label* must be used in the DO loop header and terminator lines.

Number of Loop Repetitions

The loop parameters may be constants, variables, or arithmetic expressions. The *step* parameter determines the magnitude and direction of change in the loop-control variable after each loop repetition. The number of repetitions is determined by evaluating the formula

$$(final - initial + step) / (step)$$

when the loop header is first reached. For the DO loop header

```
DO 20 I = 1, 10, 1
```

this formula evaluates to `(10 - 1 + 1) / 1` `or` `10`. For the DO loop header

```
DO 20 I = 10, 4, -2
```

this formula evaluates to `(4 - 10 - 2) / -2` `or` `4` and the loop executes for `I = 10, 8, 6,` and `4`.

If this formula evaluates to `0` or a negative number, the loop body will not be executed at all. This can happen in either of the two following situations:

- If *step* is negative ($step < 0$), the loop will not be executed if *initial* is less than *limit* (e.g., `DO 20 I = 4, 10, -2`).
- If *step* is positive ($step > 0$), the loop will not be executed if *initial* is greater than *limit* (e.g., `DO 20 I = 10, 4, 1`).

If the loop body is not executed, the value of the loop-control variable is set equal to the value of *initial* and the first statement following the loop terminator is executed.

EXAMPLE 4.4

The program in Fig. 4.4 prints a table for converting temperatures from Celsius to Fahrenheit. Because of the values of CBEGIN and CLIMIT, the table runs from 20° Celsius to –20° Celsius. Because CSTEP is –5, the DO loop header

```
DO 10 CELSUS = CBEGIN, CLIMIT, CSTEP
```

causes the value of CELSUS to decrease by 5 after each loop repetition. Loop exit occurs when CELSUS becomes less than CLIMIT, i.e., when CELSUS is –25. ■

Figure 4.4. *Printing a Table for Temperature Conversions*

```
      PROGRAM TEMPER
C Conversion of Celsius to Fahrenheit temperature

C Declarations
      INTEGER CBEGIN, CLIMIT, CSTEP
      PARAMETER (CBEGIN = 20, CLIMIT = -20, CSTEP = -5)
      INTEGER CELSUS
      REAL FAHREN

C Print the table heading
      PRINT *, 'Celsius    Fahrenheit'

C Print table
      DO 10 CELSUS = CBEGIN, CLIMIT, CSTEP
         FAHREN = 1.8 * CELSUS + 32.0
         PRINT *, CELSUS,  FAHREN
   10 CONTINUE

      STOP
      END


Celsius    Fahrenheit
   20      68.00000
   15      59.00000
   10      50.00000
    5      41.00000
    0      32.00000
   -5      23.00000
  -10      14.00000
  -15      5.000000
  -20      -4.000000
```

**EXERCISES FOR
SECTION 4.2**

Self-check

1. Given the parameter values in Fig. 4.4 and repeated below

   `PARAMETER (CBEGIN = 20, CLIMIT = -20, CSTEP = -5)`

   use the formula in this section to compute how many times each DO loop would execute if the DO loop header were rewritten as follows. Also, list the values of CELSUS that would appear in the table display.
   a. `DO 10 CELSUS = CLIMIT, CBEGIN, CSTEP`
   b. `DO 10 CELSUS = CLIMIT, CBEGIN, -CSTEP`
   c. `DO 10 CELSUS = CLIMIT, CSTEP, CBEGIN`
   d. `DO 10 CELSUS = CSTEP, CBEGIN, CLIMIT`

2. How many times will the following PRINT statements be executed? What values will be displayed?
   a.   `DO 10 I = 2, 7, 2`
   `         PRINT *, I`
   `   10 CONTINUE`

b.
```
    DO 10 N = 5, 1, -2
        PRINT *, N
10 CONTINUE
```
c.
```
    DO 10 N = -3, 3
        PRINT *, N
10 CONTINUE
```

3. List the values that will be assigned to each loop variable in the following fragments. What values of K are displayed by each fragment?

a.
```
   K = 0
   DO 5 J = 3, 1
       K = K + J
 5 CONTINUE
   PRINT *, K
```
b.
```
   K = 3
   DO 5 L = 1, K
       K = 2
       PRINT *, K
 5 CONTINUE
```

Programming

1. Write a DO loop that displays each odd number from 1 to N (a data value) along with its square root.
2. Write a DO loop that displays the first 10 even powers of 2 (i.e., 2^0, 2^2, 2^4, and so on).

4.3 Accumulating a Sum

We can use a DO loop to accumulate the sum of a collection of data values, as shown in the following case study.

Case Study: Sum of Integers

PROBLEM STATEMENT

Write a program that finds the sum of all integers from 1 to N.

ANALYSIS

To solve this problem, we must find some way to form the sum of the first N integers. The data requirements and algorithm follow.

Data Requirements

Problem Input

the last integer in the sum (INTEGER N)

Problem Output

the sum of integers from 1 to N (INTEGER SUM)

DESIGN

The algorithm follows:

Algorithm

1. Read the last integer (N).
2. Find the sum (SUM) of all the integers from 1 to N inclusive.
3. Print the sum.

Algorithm Refinements

Step 2 is the only step needing refinement. One possible refinement is shown next.

Step 2 Refinement

2.0 Store 0 in SUM
2.1 Add 1 to SUM
2.2 Add 2 to SUM
2.3 Add 3 to SUM

   .
   .
   .

2.N Add N to SUM

For a large value of N, it would be time-consuming to write steps 2.1 through 2.N. We also would need to know the value of N before we could write the list of steps; consequently, the program would not be general because it would work for only one value of N.

However, steps 2.1 through 2.N are all similar and can be represented in the general form

2.i Add i to SUM

To accomplish the same task as steps 2.1 through 2.N, the general step must be executed for all values of i from 1 to N, inclusive. This suggests the use of a counting loop with I as the loop-control variable. Another possible refinement of step 2 follows:

Step 2 Refinement

2.0 Store 0 in SUM
2.1 DO for each integer I from 1 to N
      Add I to SUM
  END DO

In this refinement, the variable I would take on the successive values 1, 2, 3, . . . , N. Each time the loop repeated, the current value of I would be added to SUM. The description of variable I follows.

Additional Program Variable

loop-control variable—represents each integer from 1 through N to be included in the sum (INTEGER I)

IMPLEMENTATION

The complete program is shown in Fig. 4.5. The statements

```
    SUM = 0
    DO 10 I = 1, N
        SUM = SUM + I
10 CONTINUE
```

are used to perform step 2. To ensure the final sum is correct, you must initialize the value of SUM to zero before the first addition operation.

Figure 4.5. *Program for Sum of Integers from 1 to N*

```
        PROGRAM SUMINT
C Finds and prints the sum of all integers from 1 to N.

C Declarations
        INTEGER N, SUM, I

C Read the last integer (N)
        PRINT *, 'Enter the last integer in the sum'
        READ *,  N

C Find the sum (SUM) of all the integers from 1 to N inclusive
        SUM = 0
        DO 10 I = 1, N
            SUM = SUM + I
    10 CONTINUE
```

```
C Print the sum
      PRINT *, 'The sum is ', SUM
      END
```

```
Enter the last integer in the sum
6
The sum is 21
```

The DO loop causes the assignment statement

```
SUM = SUM + I
```

to be repeated N times. Each time, the current value of I is added to the sum being accumulated and the result is saved back in SUM. This is illustrated in Fig. 4.6 for the first two loop repetitions.

TESTING AND VERIFICATION

A trace of the program for a data value of 3 is shown in Table 4.2. The trace verifies that the program performs as desired because the final value stored in SUM is 6 (1 + 2 + 3). The loop exit occurs when the value of the loop-control variable I becomes greater than N. As shown in the table, the statement

```
SUM = SUM + I
```

is executed exactly three times.

Figure 4.6. *Effect of First Two Loop Repetitions*

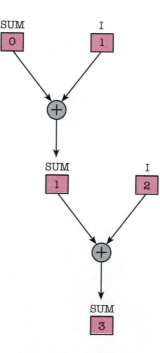

Table 4.2. *Trace of Program in Fig. 4.5*

STATEMENT	N	I	SUM	EFFECT
	?	?	?	
PRINT *, 'Enter the...'				Prints a prompt.
READ *, N	3			Reads 3 into N.
SUM = 0			0	Initializes SUM.
DO 10 I = 1, N		1		Initializes I to 1; 1 <= 1 is true—
SUM = SUM + I			1	adds 1 to SUM.
Increment and test I		2		2 <= 3 is true—
SUM = SUM + I			3	adds 2 to SUM.
Increment and test I		3		3 <= 3 is true—
SUM = SUM + I			6	adds 3 to SUM.
Increment and test I		4		4 <= 3 is false— exits loop.
PRINT *, 'The sum...'				Prints the sum, 6.

You should run this program for several different values of N. Use the formula

$$SUM = \frac{N(N + 1)}{2}$$

to check your results.

EXERCISES FOR SECTION 4.3

Self-check

1. Trace the execution of the following DO loop for the data 5, 3, −5, 7, 0, and −9. What value is read into N? What values are read into NEXT? What is printed?

```
READ *, N
SUM = 0
DO 30 I = 1, N
    READ *, NEXT
    IF (NEXT .GE. 0) THEN
        SUM = SUM + NEXT
    ELSE
        SUM = SUM - NEXT
    END IF
30 CONTINUE
    PRINT *, SUM
```

Programming

1. There is generally more than one way to solve a problem. It so happens that the formula

$$SUM = \frac{N(N + 1)}{2}$$

may be used to compute the sum of the integers from 1 to N inclusive. Write a program that compares the results of both methods and prints an appropriate message indicating whether the results are the same.
2. Write a program that finds the product of the integers from 1 to N inclusive.
3. Write a program that finds the sum of the odd integers from 1 to N inclusive.

4.4 Generalizing a Solution

It's not uncommon that after finishing a program, someone wants to know if the program would still work if some of the restrictions implied by the problem statement were removed. If the answer is no, modification of the program may be in order. It will usually be to your advantage if you try to anticipate these questions in advance and make your programs as general as possible from the beginning. Sometimes this can be accomplished easily by making a problem input from either a problem parameter or a constant.

One question comes to mind regarding the sum of N integers problem: What if we wanted to find the sum of any list of numbers, not just the first N integers? Would the program still work? Clearly, the answer to this question is no. However, it would not be too difficult to modify the program to solve this more general problem. In fact, we could extend our solution to compute the average value as well as the sum.

Case Study: Average of a Set of Measurements

PROBLEM STATEMENT

The control engineers at ACME Hydraulics need a program that will compute the average value for a set of measurements taken during the day. They would like to use the same program to calculate the average temperature, pressure, and so on.

ANALYSIS

Besides computing the average measurement value, the program must read the units of measurement—for example, degrees or pounds per square inch (p.s.i.)—and the total number of measurement values (NUMMES). Each measurement value can be temporarily stored in the same memory cell (ITEM) and added to an accumulating sum (SUM). The average can be obtained using the equation

```
AVERGE = SUM / NUMMES
```

Data Requirements

Problem Inputs

units of measurement (CHARACTER *15 UNITS)
number of measurements to be averaged (INTEGER NUMMES)
each observed value (REAL ITEM)

Problem Output

average of the data items (AVERGE)

Program Variable

sum of the observed values (SUM)

DESIGN

The algorithm follows:

Algorithm

1. Read the units of measurement.
2. Read the number of observed values.
3. Read each measurement and add it to the sum.
4. Compute the average value.
5. Print the average value.

Algorithm Refinements

Step 3 is similar to step 2 of the algorithm in the preceding sum-of-integers case study; its refinement follows.

Step 3 Refinement

3.1 Initialize SUM to zero.
3.2 DO for each data item.
     3.3 Read the next data item into ITEM.
     3.4 Add ITEM to SUM.
  END DO

In this refinement, the variable ITEM is used to store each number to be summed and each new value read into ITEM replaces the previous value. After each number is read into ITEM, the number will be added to SUM. This process will be repeated until all the data items have been read in and added to SUM.

In step 2, the number of data items to be summed is read into NUMMES. This value determines the number of loop repetitions required. We need a loop-control variable to count the data items as they are processed and ensure that all data are summed.

Additional Program Variable

loop-control variable—the number of data items added so far (INTEGER COUNT)

The refinement of step 4 (compute the average value) is shown below.

Step 4 Refinement

4.1 IF the number of items is positive THEN
    Divide SUM by the number of items.
    END IF

IMPLEMENTATION

Figure 4.7 shows the program. The DO loop in this figure begins with the header

```
DO 10 COUNT = 1, NUMMES
```

Because the initial value and step value are both 1, the value of NUMMES determines how many times the loop is repeated. If this value is not correctly defined prior to loop execution, the loop will not work properly. By using a READ statement to enter this value, we have made the program as general as possible. However, invalid data values can cause serious problems, as described in the program style subsection that follows the program.

Figure 4.7. *Computing the Average of a Set of Measurements*

```
      PROGRAM MEASUR
C Finds and prints the average value of a set of measurements.
C The units of measurement, the number of values, and the values
C themselves are provided as data.

C Declarations
      INTEGER NUMMES, COUNT
      REAL ITEM, SUM, AVERGE
      CHARACTER *15 UNITS

C Read the units of measurement and number of measurements.
      PRINT *, 'Enter units (enclosed in apostrophes)'
      READ *, UNITS
      PRINT *, 'Enter number of observed values'
      READ *, NUMMES
```

```
C Read each measurement and add it to the sum.
      SUM = 0
      DO 10 COUNT = 1, NUMMES
         PRINT *, 'Enter next value (in ', UNITS, ')'
         READ *, ITEM
         SUM = SUM + ITEM
   10 CONTINUE

C Compute the average value.
         IF (NUMMES .GT. 0) THEN
            AVERGE = SUM / NUMMES
         END IF

C Print the average value.
      PRINT *
      IF (NUMMES .GT. 0) THEN
         PRINT *, 'The average value is ', AVERGE, ' ', UNITS
      ELSE
         PRINT *, 'Average value is undefined'
      END IF

      STOP
      END

Enter units (enclosed in apostrophes)
'degrees Celsius'
Enter number of observed values
3
Enter next value in (degrees Celsius)
45.0
Enter next value in (degrees Celsius)
54.6
Enter next value in (degrees Celsius)
100.4

The average value is 66.66667 degrees Celsius
```

TESTING AND VERIFICATION

Test this program using a varying number of data values. Ensure the average computed is correct for negative measurement values as well as for positive ones. You will find that the program does not work properly when NUMMES is zero or negative. The next program style display discusses the reason for this and a way to correct the problem.

Program Style: *Defensive Programming*

In Fig. 4.7, the assignment statement

```
AVERGE = SUM / NUMMES
```

cannot be executed if the divisor is zero. Instead, the computer will print an error message such as "attempted division by zero" and then will stop program execution.

You may think that no reasonable person would enter a data value of zero for NUMMES; however, program users often do not know what is reasonable. Also, it is possible for anyone to make a typing error. Therefore experienced programmers often practice "defensive programming" to ensure a program operates properly even for invalid data. That is why we enclose the assignment

```
AVERGE = SUM / NUMMES
```

in an IF statement. A second IF statement displays either the program result or, if NUMMES is not positive, an error message, which is preferable to having the computer stop the program because of an error.

Programming
1. Write a DO loop that reads N items and accumulates the sum of all positive data items in one variable and the sum of all negative data items in another variable. Print both sums when done. Assume N is the first data value to be read.

4.5 Problem Solving Illustrated

When we began the discussion of repetition in programs, we mentioned that we would like to be able to execute the payroll program (see Fig. 3.4) for several employees in a single run. We see how to do this next.

Case Study: Computing the Payroll for Several Employees

PROBLEM STATEMENT

Modify the payroll program to compute the gross pay, tax amount, and net pay for a group of employees. Also, compute and display the total payroll amount.

ANALYSIS

The number of employees must be provided as input data followed by the hourly rate and the hours worked for each employee. The same variables (HOURS, RATE, GROSS, NET, TAXAMT) will be used to hold the data and computational results for each employee. The computations will be performed in the same way as before except that we will assume that overtime pay is not provided. The total payroll will be the sum of all employees' net pay.

Data Requirements

Problem Parameters

minimum salary without a tax deduction (TXBRAK = 100.00)
tax rate percentage as a fraction (TAXRAT = 0.10)

Problem Inputs

number of employees (INTEGER NUMEMP)
hours worked by each employee (REAL HOURS)
hourly rate for each employee (REAL RATE)

Problem Outputs

gross pay for each employee (REAL GROSS)
net pay for each employee (REAL NET)
total payroll amount (REAL PAYROL)

DESIGN

The initial algorithm follows:

Initial Algorithm

1. Enter the number of employees (NUMEMP).
2. For each employee, read the payroll data; compute and display the gross pay, tax amount, and net pay; and add net pay to the total payroll amount.
3. Display the total payroll amount.

Algorithm Refinements

We need an additional variable (shown next) to count the number of employees processed and to control the DO loop in step 2.

Additional Program Variable

loop-control variable—counts the employees that are processed (INTEGER CNTEMP)

Step 2 Refinement

2.1 PAYROL = 0.0
2.2 DO for each employee
       2.3 Enter employee data.
       2.4 Compute gross pay.
       2.5 Compute tax amount.
       2.6 Compute net pay.
       2.7 Display gross pay, tax amount, and net pay.
       2.8 Add net pay to PAYROL.
    END DO

IMPLEMENTATION

Figure 4.8 shows the payroll program. The DO loop header

```
DO 10 CNTEMP = 1, NUMEMP
```

implements step 2.2.

Figure 4.8. *Payroll Program*

```
      PROGRAM PAYER
C Computes and prints each employee's gross pay, tax amount,
C and net pay given hourly
C rate and number of hours worked. Deducts a tax of $25 if
C gross pay exceeds $100; otherwise, deducts no tax.
C Also computes total payroll

C Declarations
      REAL TXBRAK, TAXRAT
      PARAMETER (TXBRAK = 100.00)
      PARAMETER (TAXRAT = 0.10)
      REAL HOURS, RATE, GROSS, TAXAMT, NET, PAYROL
      INTEGER NUMEMP, CNTEMP

C Enter total number of employees
      PRINT *, 'Enter number of employees:'
      READ *, NUMEMP

C Compute and print gross pay and net pay for NUMEMP employees
C and total payroll amount
      PAYROL = 0.0
      DO 10 CNTEMP = 1, NUMEMP
         PRINT *, 'Enter hours worked:'
         READ *, HOURS
         PRINT *, 'Enter hourly rate:'
         READ *, RATE

         GROSS = HOURS * RATE

C        Compute tax amount
         IF (GROSS .LT. TXBRAK) THEN
            TAXAMT = 0.0
         ELSE
            TAXAMT = TAXRAT * GROSS
         END IF

         NET = GROSS - TAXAMT

         PRINT *, 'Gross pay is $', GROSS
         PRINT *, 'Tax amount due is $', TAXAMT
         PRINT *, 'Net pay is $', NET
         PRINT *
```

```
C          Add NET to PAYROL
           PAYROL = PAYROL + NET
     10 CONTINUE

C Display total payroll
           PRINT *, 'Total payroll is $', PAYROL
           STOP
           END
```

```
Enter number of employees:
2
Enter hours worked:
25
Enter hourly rate:
3.50
Gross pay is $ 87.50000
Tax amount due is $ 0.0
Net pay is $ 87.50000

Enter hours worked:
40
Enter hourly rate:
4.80
Gross pay is $ 192.0000
Tax amount due is $ 19.2000
Net pay is $ 172.8000

Total payroll is $ 260.30
```

TESTING AND VERIFICATION

Run the payroll program for 10 employees where some of the employees pay a tax amount and some do not. Also, ensure the program runs properly for the simple case of just one employee.

Using a DO Loop to Evaluate a Series (Optional)

A number of mathematical quantities can be represented using a series approximation, where a series is the summation of an infinite number of terms. The next case study shows how we can improve the accuracy of an approximate solution to a series by repeatedly computing and adding new terms. This is called the method of *iterative approximations*.

Case Study: Approximating the Value of e

PROBLEM STATEMENT

The base of the natural logarithms, $e = 2.71828 \ldots$, may be represented by the series

$$1 + 1/1! + 1/2! + 1/3! + \cdots + 1/n!$$

where $n!$ represents the factorial of n, as defined next:

$$n! = n \times (n - 1)! \text{ for } n > 1$$
$$n! = 1 \qquad\qquad \text{ for } n = 0 \text{ or } 1$$

(For example, 5! is $5 \times 4 \times 3 \times 2 \times 1$.) Use the method of iterative approximations to compute the value of e.

ANALYSIS

The above series may also be represented as

$$\sum_{i=0}^{n} 1/i!$$

using *summation notation*, where the first term is obtained by substituting 0 for i (1/0! is 1), the second term is obtained by substituting 1 for i (1/1!), and so on. The larger the value of n, the more terms that will be included in the series, resulting in increased accuracy. The value of n will be a problem input (N).

Data Requirements

> *Problem Input*
> the number of terms in the series (INTEGER N)
>
> *Problem Output*
> the approximate value of e (REAL E)
>
> *Program Variables*
> the ith term in the series (REAL TERM)
> the loop control variable (INTEGER I)

DESIGN

We can use a counting loop to implement the summation formula above in the following algorithm.

Algorithm

1. Read in the value of N.
2. Initialize the ith term to 1.0.
3. Initialize E to 1.0.
4. DO for each I from 1 to N.
> 5. Compute the ith term in the series.
> 6. Add the ith term to E.
> END DO
7. Print the value of E.

Figure 4.9. *Finding the Value of e*

```
      PROGRAM FINDE
C Computing the value of e using a DO loop

C Declarations
      REAL E, TERM
      INTEGER N, I

      PRINT *, 'Enter the number of terms to be summed'
      READ *, N

C Compute the next value of TERM and add it to the approximation for e
      TERM = 1.0
      E = 1.0
      DO 10 I = 1, N
         TERM = TERM / I
         E = E + TERM
   10 CONTINUE

C Print the result
      PRINT *, 'The value of e is ', E
      STOP
      END

Enter the number of terms to be summed
10
The value of e is 2.718282
```

IMPLEMENTATION

The program is shown in Fig. 4.9. Inside the DO loop, the statement

```
TERM = TERM / I
```

computes the value of the *i*th term in the series by dividing the previous term by the loop-control variable I. The following formula shows that this division does indeed produce the next term in the series:

$$(1 / (I - 1)!) / I = 1 / (I \times (I - 1)!) = 1 / I!$$

Because 0! is 1, TERM must be initialized to 1.0. The statement

```
E = E + TERM
```

adds the new value of TERM to the sum being accumulated in E.

The values of NEXT, TERM, and E are traced in Table 4.3 for three loop iterations. This trace shows that TERM does indeed take on the values 1/1!, 1/2!, 1/3!, etc., during successive loop iterations and that the value of E gets closer to *e*.

Table 4.3. *Trace of Program in Fig. 4.9*

STATEMENT	I	TERM	E	EFFECT
`TERM = 1.0`		1.0		
`E = 1.0`			1.0	
`DO 10 I = 1, N`	1			Initializes I;
`    TERM = TERM / I`		1.0/1		TERM is 1.0.
`    E = E + TERM`			2.0	
`DO 10 I = 1, N`	2			Increments I;
`    TERM = TERM / I`		1.0/2		TERM is 1/2! or 0.5.
`    E = E + TERM`			2.5	
`DO 10 I = 1, N`	3			Increments I;
`    TERM = TERM / I`		0.5/3		TERM is 1/3!
`    E = E + TERM`			2.6666...	or 0.1666....

EXERCISES FOR SECTION 4.5

Programming

1. The value of e^x is represented by the series

$$1 + x + x^2/2! + x^3/3! + x^4/4! + \cdots .$$

Write a program to compute and print the value of this series. (*Hint:* x and the number of terms to be summed should be input variables.)

4.6 The WHILE Loop

Whenever we use a DO loop, the exact number of loop repetitions to be performed is determined when the loop header is first reached. Even if we changed the loop-parameter values in the loop body, the number of loop repetitions would not be affected.

In many programming situations, the exact number of loop repetitions cannot be determined before loop execution begins. This number may depend on some aspect of the data that is not known beforehand, but it usually can be stated by a condition. A *conditional loop* is a loop whose repetition is controlled by evaluating a condition. For example, we may wish to continue writing checks as long as our bank balance is positive, as indicated by the following pseudocode description:

```
DO WHILE the balance is still positive
    Read in the next transaction.
    Update and print the balance.
END DO
```

The actual number of loop repetitions performed depends on the type of each transaction (deposit or withdrawal) and the amount. In this text, we use the WHILE loop to implement such a conditional loop.

EXAMPLE 4.5

The program in Fig. 4.10 traces the progress of a hungry worm approaching an apple. Each time it moves, the worm reduces the distance between itself and the apple by its own length until the worm is close enough to reach the apple. Because we have no idea beforehand how many moves will be required, a WHILE loop is the correct looping structure to use.

Figure 4.10. *Printing Distances between a Worm and an Apple*

```
      PROGRAM WORM
C Prints the distances between a worm and an apple
C until the worm is close enough to reach the apple.

C Declarations
      REAL START, DISTNC, WRMLEN

C Enter initial distance and worm length.
      PRINT *, 'Enter initial distance between the worm'
      PRINT *, 'and the apple (in inches)'
      READ *, START
      PRINT *, 'Enter the worm length (in inches)'
      READ *, WRMLEN

C Reduce the distance until worm is close enough to reach it.
      DISTNC = START
      DO WHILE (DISTNC .GT. WRMLEN)
         PRINT *, 'The distance is ', DISTNC
         DISTNC = DISTNC - WRMLEN
      END DO

C Display result.
      PRINT *, 'The distance is ', DISTNC
      PRINT *, 'The worm will reach the apple on its next move.'

      STOP
      END
```

```
Enter initial distance between the worm
and the apple (in inches)
12.5
Enter the worm length (in inches)
3.5
The distance is 12.500000
The distance is 9.000000
The distance is 5.500000
The distance is 2.000000
The worm will reach the apple on its next move.
```

The variable `DISTNC` is the loop-control variable in Fig. 4.10. Just before loop entry, the assignment statement

```
DISTNC = START
```

initializes the variable `DISTNC` to the starting distance that was previously read into variable `START`. The loop header

```
DO WHILE (DISTNC .GT. WRMLEN)
```

FORTRAN in Focus

Dehumidifying with Fortran

SOMERSET TECHNOLOGIES, INC.

When a hospital, factory, or other large facility needs equipment to control the humidity on site, they turn to Kathabar Systems, one of three divisions of Somerset Technologies, Inc. Kathabar manufactures and customizes dehumidification systems to suit the needs of their clients. Fortran is an active player in the process.

When designing a system for a particular site, the engineers use Microsoft's Fortran on 386-based PC workstations to determine the characteristics of the equipment required. Data on the temperature, moisture load, and amount of air in the space to be controlled are fed into a computer model that includes the operating parameters of the humidity control system. Because the systems work with a liquid desiccant, the engineers must calculate the concentra-

tion and temperature of the desiccant needed to achieve a desired result. The physical and chemical properties of the desiccant are built into the simulation model, and the computer calculates the amount of water to be removed from (or added to, in the case of a humidification system) the air space, the amount of desiccant needed, and the other operating parameters for the site.

Fortran was chosen for this application because it handles such calculation-intensive applications well. Many of the calculations are iterative, using a lot of computer time, and a compiled Fortran program offers speed that an interpreted language, such as BASIC, cannot provide. Most of the equations used to model the system's behavior also involve logarithms and exponents that are harder to program in other languages. Jeff Jelicks, a

tests the value of DISTNC before each loop repetition. If the current value of DISTNC is greater than the worm's length (WRMLEN), the loop is repeated; otherwise, the loop is exited and the first statement after END DO is executed. Within the loop, the statement

```
DISTNC = DISTNC - WRMLEN
```

reduces the value of DISTNC each time the loop is repeated.

Kathabar engineer with responsibility for the computing facilities, also points to Fortran's run-time formatting as an important feature for their application. When they measure the environmental factors for a given site, they will analyze data on the average temperature and humidity for that location that have been gathered every hour for a year. Because the range of temperatures can be very large (as in Alaska) or very small (as in Puerto Rico), the matrix size varies accordingly. Fortran will vary the formatting based on the data, and produce more usable output with less effort on the programmer's part.

Fortran's popularity with the engineers, who write and maintain the programs they use, made it the logical choice for the bill-of-materials system running on a Honeywell mainframe, too. Since 1981, the more than 400 stan-

dard bills of materials (lists of components used to manufacture and assemble a given system) have been organized and maintained in a program originally written by Jelicks to manage their product. Because it is a very user-friendly program, it is still in service and updated by the standards department as new products are created.

Jelicks points to the power of Fortran's character manipulations and its lexical intrinsic functions, too, as strengths of the program that frequently go unrecognized. He personally looks forward to the standardization of screen-interface enhancements that some versions of Fortran now support. As more engineers work interactively at the screen, these enhancements will preserve Fortran's status as the engineers' language of choice.

Sincere thanks to Jeff Jelicks, of Somerset Technologies, Inc., in Somerset, New Jersey, for talking with us about the ways in which Fortran is used in the Kathabar Systems Division. Jelicks, an unabashed Fortran aficionado, has yet to encounter a problem he could not solve with Fortran. His advice to students studying Fortran is, "Use it! After you use it for a couple of years, you start thinking in Fortran—which is nice."

The following three steps must be performed in every program that uses a WHILE loop:

1. Initialize the loop-control variable before the loop is reached.
2. Test the loop-control variable before each loop repetition.
3. Update the loop-control variable in the loop body.

If the first step is omitted, the initial test of the loop-control variable will be meaningless. If the last step is omitted, the loop-control variable value cannot change and the loop will execute "forever"; i.e., it will not terminate.

These steps are summarized in the following general form of a WHILE loop:

Initialize the loop control variable
DO WHILE (loop control variable test is true)
    Perform the loop body
    Update the loop-control variable
END DO

The step that initializes the loop-control variable is executed only once. The steps that test and update the loop-control variable are executed repeatedly until the condition evaluates to false and control is transferred to the first statement following the END DO (*loop exit*).

Figure 4.11. *Flow-chart of WHILE Loop.*

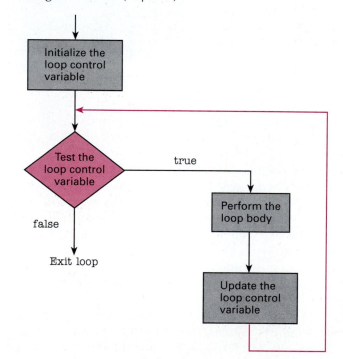

Figure 4.11 is a flowchart that demonstrates the general form of the WHILE loop. The arrow in color indicates that the condition is reevaluated before each repetition of the loop body. If the condition is true, the loop body is repeated; if the condition is false, the loop is exited. Although the step that updates the loop-control variable is actually part of the loop body, we show it as a separate step to emphasize its importance. In some situations, this statement may appear earlier in the loop body.

WHILE Loop Syntax

The WHILE loop is not part of standard Fortran 77; however, many versions of Fortran 77 support the WHILE loop and it is standard in Fortran 90. Although this loop is nonstandard, we include it in this text because we feel it is important to facilitating structured programming. Here, we will use the Fortran 90 syntax for the WHILE loop; your computer may use a different syntax. Appendix D discusses how to implement the WHILE loop in standard Fortran 77.

SYNTAX DISPLAY

WHILE Loop

SYNTAX: DO WHILE (*condition*)
            loop body
        END DO

EXAMPLE: DO WHILE (N .NE. 0)
            PRINT *, 'Enter N:'
            READ *, N
        END DO

INTERPRETATION: The *condition* is tested. If it is true, the *loop body* is executed and the condition is retested; the *loop body* is repeated as long as the *condition* is true. When the *condition* is tested and found to be false, loop exit occurs and the next program statement after END DO is executed.

NOTES: If the *condition* evaluates to false the first time it is tested, the *loop body* will not be executed. Because the WHILE loop is nonstandard in Fortran 77, it may not be implemented on your computer or may be implemented differently.

More WHILE Loop Examples

Several examples of programs with WHILE loops follow.

EXAMPLE 4.6

The following WHILE loop could be used in Fig. 4.7 to ensure a valid value is read into NUMMES. The loop body is repeated as long as the value of NUMMES is less than or equal to zero. The loop body will not be executed if the first value read is positive.

```
PRINT *, 'Enter number of observed values'
READ *, NUMMES
DO WHILE (NUMMES .LE. 0)
   PRINT *, 'Number not positive — try again:'
   READ *, NUMMES
END DO
```

The interaction that would result for the data –3, 0, 7 follows:

```
Enter number of observed values
–3
Number not positive — try again:
0
Number not positive — try again:
7
```

In this example, the READ statement appears twice, once before the WHILE loop and again at the end of the loop body. The first READ (called a priming read) reads the first data value (–3) into NUMMES; the second READ statement reads any additional values of NUMMES (0 and 7). The term *priming read* is an analogy to the process of priming a pump, which is done by pouring a cup of water into the pump chamber before the pump can be used to draw water out of a well. The priming read initializes the loop-control variable and is needed whenever the initial value of the loop-control variable is an input data item.

EXAMPLE 4.7

The program in Fig. 4.12 displays each power, POWER, of an input integer N that is less than 1000 (MAXPOW). The WHILE loop is exited when the value of NEXPOW becomes greater than or equal to 1000. The assignment statement

```
NEXPOW = 1
```

initializes NEXPOW to the zero power. The loop-repetition condition

```
(NEXPOW .LT. MAXPOW)
```

ensures that loop exit will occur at the proper time.
   Within the loop body, the statement

```
NEXPOW = NEXPOW * N
```

computes the next power of N by multiplying the previous power by N. If the

Figure 4.12. *Program POWERS*

```
      PROGRAM POWERS
C Prints all powers of N less than 1000.

C Declarations
      INTEGER MAXPOW
      PARAMETER (MAXPOW = 1000)
      INTEGER N, NEXPOW

C Read an integer N
      PRINT *, 'This program prints all powers < 1000 of an integer'
      PRINT *, 'Enter an integer:'
      READ *, N
      PRINT *, 'Powers of ', N

C Print each power of N less than MAXPOW
      NEXPOW = 1
      DO WHILE (NEXPOW .LT. MAXPOW)              9 IF C(...) THEN
         PRINT *, NEXPOW
         NEXPOW = NEXPOW * N
      END DO                                     GOTO 9
                                                 END IF
      STOP
      END

This program prints all powers < 1000 of an integer
Enter an integer:
2
Powers of            2
         1
         2
         4
         8
        16
        32
        64
       128
       256
       512
```

new value is less than MAXPOW, the loop is repeated, causing the current value of NEXPOW to be printed and the next one to be computed.

In the sample run shown in Fig. 4.12, the last value printed is 512; however, the last value assigned to NEXPOW in the loop body is 1024. Because 1024 is greater than 1000, the loop-repetition test fails the next time it is evaluated and the loop is exited. ■

It is important to realize that loop exit does not occur at the exact instant NEXPOW is assigned the value 1024. If there were more statements following the assignment statement in the loop body, they would be executed; loop exit does not occur until the loop-repetition test is reevaluated at the top of the loop.

Fortran 77
WHILE Loop

The grey text appearing in three lines of Fig. 4.12 shows the changes required to write the WHILE loop in standard Fortran 77 (see Appendix D). For the Fortran 77 code shown on the right of the line below

```
DO WHILE (NEXPOW .LT. MAXPOW)                          9 IF (...) THEN
```

the integer 9 should appear in the label field (columns 1 through 5) and the IF condition should be the same as the WHILE condition. We will continue to provide Fortran 77 and Fortran 90 forms of the WHILE loop in all complete programs.

EXAMPLE 4.8

The distance traveled by a body dropped from a tower in t seconds is represented by the formula

$$distance = 1/2 \times gt^2,$$

where g is the gravitational constant. The program in Fig. 4.13 prints a table showing the height of an object at fixed time intervals after it has been dropped from a tower and while the object is still above the ground. The object height is given by the formula

$$height = tower\ height - distance.$$

The number of lines in the table shown in Fig. 4.13 depends on the time interval between displays (INTERV) and the tower height (TOWER). During each loop repetition, the current time (starting at 0.0) and the current object height, HEIGHT, are printed. Next, the elapsed time is increased by INTERV and the object height is recomputed. HEIGHT is the loop-control variable, and the loop is repeated as long as the object height is positive. The messge following the table is printed when the object hits the ground.

Compare this program with the one in Fig. 4.2 that uses a DO loop to control loop repetition. Why would a DO loop be inappropriate here?   ■

Figure 4.13. *Table of Heights for an Object Dropped from a Tower*

```
      PROGRAM DROPIT
C Shows the height of an object until it hits the ground

C Declarations
      REAL G
      PARAMETER (G = 9.80665)
      REAL HEIGHT, TIME, INTERV, TOWER
```

```
C Enter tower height and time interval between data points
      PRINT *, 'Enter the tower height in meters:'
      READ *, TOWER
      PRINT *, 'Enter the time in seconds between height displays:'
      READ *, INTERV

C Initialize TIME
      TIME = 0.0

C Print the object height until it hits the ground
      PRINT *
      PRINT *, '   Time    Height'
      HEIGHT = TOWER
      DO WHILE (HEIGHT .GT. 0.0)                          9 IF (...) THEN
         PRINT *, TIME, HEIGHT
         TIME = TIME + INTERV
         HEIGHT = TOWER - 0.5 * G * TIME ** 2
      END DO                                               GOTO 9
                                                           END IF
      PRINT *
      PRINT *, 'SPLAT!!!'
      STOP
      END

Enter the tower height in meters:
100
Enter the time in seconds between height displays:
1.0

     Time    Height
  0.000000   100.0000
  1.000000    95.09667
  2.000000    80.38670
  3.000000    55.87008
  4.000000    21.54680

SPLAT!!!
```

EXAMPLE 4.9

The program in Fig. 4.14 determines the number of years required to double your money if you purchase a certificate of deposit that returns a fixed interest rate (RATE) each year. Before the loop is reached, the statements

```
YEAR = 0
BALANC = DEPOS
DOUBLE = 2.0 * DEPOS
```

initialize YEAR to zero, BALANC to the deposit amount, and DOUBLE to twice the deposit amount. The loop-repetition condition

```
(BALANC .LT. DOUBLE)
```

Figure 4.14. *Doubling Your Money*

```
      PROGRAM BANKER
C Finds and prints the time required to double your money

C Declarations
      REAL DEPOS, BALANC, RATE, INTRST, DOUBLE
      INTEGER YEAR

      PRINT *, 'Enter the deposit amount in dollars:'
      READ *, DEPOS
      PRINT *, 'Enter the interest rate as a decimal fraction:'
      READ *, RATE

C Initialize YEAR, BALANC, and DOUBLE
      YEAR = 0
      BALANC = DEPOS
      DOUBLE = 2.0 * DEPOS

C Recompute BALANC until the initial deposit amount is doubled
      DO WHILE (BALANC .LT. DOUBLE)                    9 IF (...) THEN
         YEAR = YEAR + 1
         INTRST = BALANC * RATE
         BALANC = BALANC + INTRST
      END DO                                           GOTO 9
                                                       END IF
      PRINT *, 'Deposit amount is doubled after ', YEAR, ' years'
      PRINT *, 'New balance is $', BALANC

      STOP
      END

Enter the deposit amount in dollars:
100.00
Enter the interest rate as a decimal fraction:
0.075
Deposit amount is doubled after 10 years
New balance is $   206.1032
```

causes the loop to be repeated until the current balance is twice the deposit amount. Within the loop, the statements

```
INTRST = BALANC * RATE
BALANC = BALANC + INTRST
```

recompute the balance at the end of each year by adding the interest earned (INTRST) during the year to the current balance. Note that BALANC, not YEAR, is the loop-control variable. (Why?)

Comparison of WHILE and DO Loops

As shown in the next example, a WHILE loop also can be used to implement a counting loop.

EXAMPLE 4.10

We could use the following WHILE loop to find the sum of the first N integers. The loop body is the pair of statements between the line beginning with DO WHILE and that beginning with END DO. The loop body is repeated as long as (that is, WHILE) the value of NXTINT is less than or equal to N. In the loop body, each value of NXTINT (starting with 1) is added to SUM and NXTINT is incremented by 1. Loop execution stops when NXTINT is equal to N + 1. The equivalent DO loop is provided for comparison. ■

```
         WHILE Loop                        DO Loop

      SUM = 0                          SUM = 0
      NXTINT = 1                       DO 10 NXTINT = 1, N
      DO WHILE (NXTINT .LE. N)            SUM = SUM + NXTINT
         SUM = SUM + NXTINT          10 CONTINUE
         NXTINT = NXTINT + 1
      END DO
```

The most obvious difference between these loops is that the WHILE loop is longer, a fact that illustrates why the WHILE loop should not be used to implement a counting loop. The DO loop is easier to write and should be used when the number of loop repetitions needed can be determined before loop entry.

The main reason for the extra length of the WHILE loop involves the manner in which the loop-control variable NXTINT is manipulated:

- NXTINT is set to an initial value of 1 (NXTINT = 1).
- NXTINT is tested before each loop repetition (NXTINT .LE. N).
- NXTINT is updated during each loop repetition (NXTINT = NXTINT + 1).

Although these three steps are implicit in the DO loop, they must be specified explicitly when the WHILE loop is used. If the loop-control variable is not initialized properly before the WHILE statement is reached, the loop-repetition test will be meaningless. If the loop-control variable is not updated, the loop-repetition test will always be true and the loop will not be exited (infinite loop).

Sentinel-controlled Loops

Frequently, you will not know exactly how many data items there will be when a program begins execution. This may happen because there are too many data items to count beforehand or because the number of data items provided depends on how the computation proceeds.

One way to handle this situation is to instruct the user to enter a unique

Figure 4.15. *Program to Multiply Nonzero Data*

```
      PROGRAM NONZERO
C Finds the product of all nonzero data items -- stops at
C first 0.0

C Declarations
      REAL SNTNEL
      PARAMETER (SNTNEL = 0.0)
      REAL ITEM, PRODCT
      PRODCT = 1.0

C Multiply PRODCT by each nonzero data item
      PRINT *, 'Enter first number or 0 to stop:'
      READ *, ITEM
      DO WHILE (ITEM .NE. SNTNEL)          9 IF (...) THEN
         PRODCT = PRODCT * ITEM
         PRINT *, 'Next number or 0:'
         READ *, ITEM
      END DO                               GOTO 9
                                           END IF
C Print result
      PRINT *, 'The product is ', PRODCT
      STOP
      END


Enter first number or 0 to stop:
10
Next number or 0:
12
Next number or 0:
22
Next number or 0:
0
The product is 2640.000
```

data value, called a *sentinel value,* as the last data item. The program then will test each data item and terminate when the sentinel value is read. Note, this value must be carefully chosen and must be a value that would not normally occur as data.

EXAMPLE 4.11   The program in Fig. 4.15 finds the product of a collection of data values. It stops reading data after a value of zero is entered. ∎

   The program in Fig. 4.15 illustrates the proper use of a sentinel value. To determine whether data entry is complete, you must compare each data item to the value stored in SNTNEL (0.0). For this test to make sense in the beginning, the first number must be read before the WHILE loop is reached. The last step in the WHILE loop must read the next number so that it can be tested to determine whether the loop body should be repeated. This general pattern is illustrated next.

Sentinel-controlled Loop Form

Read the first value of input variable
DO WHILE input variable is not the sentinel value
   Process current value of input variable
   Read the next value of input variable
END DO

Remember, proper use of a sentinel value requires that the READ statement appear twice. The initial READ statement enters the first data value and occurs before the WHILE loop.

Using LOGICAL Variables as Program Flags

LOGICAL variables are often used as *program flags,* which signal whether a particular event occurs. The flag's value should be .FALSE. if the event has not occurred and .TRUE. if it has occurred. A flag-controlled loop executes until the event being monitored occurs.

EXAMPLE 4.12

Program GUESS (see Fig. 4.16) prompts the user to guess a number in its "secret interval." The WHILE loop continues to read integer values into N until an integer between NMIN and NMAX is entered. The program flag BETWEN is described next.

Program Variable

program flag which controls loop repetition—its value is .TRUE. only after a valid data value is read (LOGICAL BETWEN)

Figure 4.16. *Using a Program Flag*

```
      PROGRAM GUESS
C Displays the first data value in the interval defined by
C parameters NMIN and NMAX

C Declarations
      INTEGER NMIN, NMAX
      PARAMETER (NMIN = 1, NMAX = 10)
      INTEGER N
      LOGICAL BETWEN

C Initially assume an integer between NMIN and NMAX is not
C entered
      BETWEN = .FALSE.
```

```
C Keep reading until an integer between NMIN and NMAX is entered
      DO WHILE (.NOT. BETWEN)                              9 IF (...) THEN
         PRINT *, 'Guess an integer in my secret interval:'
         READ *, N
         BETWEN = (NMIN .LE. N) .AND. (N .LE. NMAX)
      END DO                                               GOTO 9
                                                           END IF
C Display result
      PRINT *, N, ' is the first guess in the interval ', NMIN,
     +                ' to ', NMAX

C Exit program
      STOP
      END


Guess an integer in my secret interval:
15
Guess an integer in my secret interval:
3
3 is the first guess in the interval 1 to 10
```

Because no data value has been read before the loop executes, we initialize BETWEN to .FALSE.. The WHILE loop must continue to execute as long as BETWEN is .FALSE. because as long as BETWEN is .FALSE., the event "guessed a data value between NMIN and NMAX" has not yet occurred. Therefore the loop-repetition condition should be (.NOT. BETWEN) because this condition is .TRUE. when BETWEN is .FALSE..

Inside the loop, the LOGICAL assignment statement

BETWEN = (NMIN .LE. N) .AND. (N .LE. NMAX)

resets BETWEN to .TRUE. when an integer between NMIN and NMAX is entered; otherwise, BETWEN remains .FALSE.. If BETWEN becomes .TRUE., loop exit occurs right after the next test of the loop-repetition condition; if BETWEN remains .FALSE., the loop continues to execute until a valid number is guessed.   ■

Flag-controlled Loop Form

Initialize *flag* to .FALSE.
DO WHILE (.NOT. *flag*)
    Perform loop body
    Reset *flag* to .TRUE. if event being monitored occurs
END DO

EXERCISES FOR
SECTION 4.6

Self-check

1. What values would be printed if the order of the statements in the loop body of Fig. 4.12 were reversed?

2. What does the following segment do? Rewrite it using a DO loop.

```
VAL = 100
DO WHILE (VAL .GE. -100)
    VAL = VAL - 5
    PRINT *, VAL
END DO
```

3. The following DO loop accumulates the sum of a collection of 50 exam scores and then computes the average. Rewrite it as a sentinel-controlled loop. Assume we do not know beforehand how many students took the exam. Your fragment should count the number of scores read as well as computing their sum. (*Hint:* Assume parameter SENVAL has a value of -1.)

```
    SUM = 0
    DO 10 I = 1, 50
        READ *, SCORE
        SUM = SUM + SCORE
10 CONTINUE
```

4. Given that SENVAL is -1, what will be the values of SUM and COUNT after the following fragment executes, assuming the data values are 50, 75, 80, 90, -1? What statement after the loop could be used to compute the average of all the actual data values read?

```
SUM = 0
COUNT = 0
READ *, SCORE
DO WHILE (SCORE .GT. SENVAL)
    SUM = SUM + SCORE
    COUNT = COUNT + 1
    READ *, SCORE
END DO
```

5. For the loops shown in (a)–(e), list the value of I during each loop repetition and the value of I after loop exit. Which loop executes "forever"?

a.
```
I = 5
DO WHILE (I .GT. 0)
    I = I - 1
END DO
```
b.
```
I = 5
DO WHILE (I .GT. 0)
    I = I - 2
END DO
```
c.
```
I = 5
DO WHILE (I .NE. 0)
    I = I - 1
END DO
```
d.
```
I = 5
DO WHILE (I .NE. 0)
    I = I - 2
END DO
```

```
e. I = 5
   DO WHILE (I .GT. 0)
      I = I / 2
   END DO
```

Programming

1. Modify the program in Fig. 4.12 to print both the power and its value. For the example shown, the table printed should begin

Power	Value
0	1
1	2
2	4

2. Rewrite the fragment in self-check exercise 4 as a DO loop. What additional data item will need to be provided before you can begin reading in each value of SCORE?
3. Write a program that prints the cumulative product of all numbers entered as long as that product is less than a specified maximum. Your procedure should ignore zero data values.
4. Modify the program that computes the value of *e* (see Fig. 4.9) to use a WHILE loop. The new program should continue to add terms until the value of $1/n!$ becomes less than 0.0005. Print the final value of *e*.
5. Write a flag-controlled loop that continues to read pairs of integers and displays the integer remainder of the first number divided by the second until it reads a pair with the property that the first integer is divisible by the second.

4.7 Nested Control Structures

In Chapter 3, we discussed nested IF statements. Any Fortran control structure can be nested within another. It is fairly common to nest an IF structure inside a loop-control structure. In this case, the IF statement performs the selection process each time the loop is repeated. We give an example of this next.

EXAMPLE 4.13

The program in Fig. 4.17 contains a logical IF statement nested within a WHILE loop. This statement finds the product (PRODUC) of all data items that are nonzero. Each data value is read into DATITM and tested; the nonzero values are included in the product being accumulated in PRODUC. The loop is exited after the sentinel value (SNTNEL) is read into DATITM. ■

Nested DO Loops

The last category of nested structures we consider is nested DO loops. These loops are the most difficult of all nested structures to deal with. For each

Figure 4.17. *Finding the Product of Nonzero Data Items*

```
      PROGRAM NONZER
C Finds product of nonzero data

C Declarations
      REAL SNTNEL
      PARAMETER (SNTNEL = -1000.0)
      REAL PRODUC, DATITM

C Initialize product and read first data value
      PRODUC = 1.0
      PRINT *, 'Enter first data item or -1000:'
      READ *, DATITM

C Multiply only nonzero data values
      DO WHILE (DATITM .NE. SNTNEL)                      9 IF (...) THEN
         IF (DATITM .NE. 0.0) PRODUC = PRODUC * DATITM
         PRINT *, 'Enter next data item or -1000:'
         READ *, DATITM
      END DO                                             GOTO 9
                                                         END IF
C Print the result
      PRINT *, 'The product of nonzero data is ', PRODUC
      STOP
      END

Enter first data item or -1000:
3.0
Enter next data item or -1000:
0.0
Enter next data item or -1000:
-1.0
Enter next data item or -1000:
-1000.0
The product of nonzero data is -3.000000
```

iteration of the outer loop in a nest, the control structure that is the inner loop is entered and repeated until done.

EXAMPLE 4.14

Figure 4.18 shows a program with a pair of nested loops. The outer loop executes M times and, for each repetition of the outer loop, the inner loop executes N times. Therefore, the statement

```
PRINT *, 'OUTER ', I
```

in the outer loop executes M times, and the statement

```
PRINT *, '  INNER', I, J
```

Figure 4.18. *Nested Loops*

```
      PROGRAM NESTED
C Illustrates nested loops.

C Declarations
      INTEGER M, N
      PARAMETER (M = 3, N = 2)
      INTEGER I, J

C Display table of values for I and J
      PRINT *, '                I       J
      DO 10 I = 1, M
         PRINT *, 'OUTER ', I
         DO 20 J = 1, N
            PRINT *, '  INNER', I, J
 20      CONTINUE
 10 CONTINUE

      STOP
      END

              I       J
OUTER         1
    INNER     1       1
    INNER     1       2
OUTER         2
    INNER     2       1
    INNER     2       2
OUTER         3
    INNER     3       1
    INNER     3       2
```

in the inner loop executes M × N times. For the sample run shown in Fig. 4.18, M is 3 and N is 2, so the PRINT statement in the inner loop displays 6 pairs of values for I and J; each pair is preceded by the word INNER.

Note that the inner loop and the outer loop must have different loop-control variables and labels. Also, the inner-loop terminator must always come before the outer-loop terminator (i.e., 20 CONTINUE must precede 10 CONTINUE). ■

EXAMPLE 4.15   The program in Fig. 4.19 uses nested DO loops to display the divisors of several integer values read into ITEM. The program begins by reading the number of integers to be tested into NUMITM. The outer loop

```
DO 10 COUNT = 1, NUMITM
```

is a counting loop that executes NUMITM times. Within this loop, the statements

```
PRINT *, 'You want the divisors for which integer?'
READ *, ITEM
PRINT *, 'List of divisors:'
```

enter an integer value to be tested and display a heading for a list of divisors that are printed by the inner loop. The inner DO loop

```
DO 20 DIV = 1, ITEM
```

is a counting loop that executes for all values of DIV between 1 and ITEM, inclusive. The IF statement tests whether DIV is a divisor of ITEM and displays DIV if it is a divisor.

Figure 4.19. *Finding Divisors*

```
      PROGRAM DIVISR
C Displays all divisors of a set of integer values.

C Declarations
      INTEGER ITEM, NUMITM, DIV, COUNT

C Determine number of integers to test.
      PRINT *, 'How many numbers will you test?'
      READ *, NUMITM

C Process each integer.
      DO 10 COUNT = 1, NUMITM
         PRINT *, 'You want the divisors for which integer?'
         READ *, ITEM
         PRINT *, 'List of divisors:'

C        Display all divisors of ITEM.
         DO 20 DIV = 1, ITEM
            IF (MOD(ITEM, DIV) .EQ. 0) THEN
               PRINT *, DIV
            END IF
  20     CONTINUE
         PRINT *
  10  CONTINUE
      STOP
      END

How many numbers will you test?
2
You want the divisors for which integer?
12
```

```
List of divisors:
1
2
3
4
6
12

You want the divisors for which integer?
101
List of divisors:
1
101
```

Self-check

1. What is displayed by the following program segments, assuming N is 5?

```
a.      DO 10 I = 1, N
            DO 20 J = 1, I
                PRINT *, I, J
    20      CONTINUE
            PRINT *
    10 CONTINUE
b.      DO 10 I = 1, N
            DO 20 J = N, I, -1
                PRINT *, I, J
    20      CONTINUE
            PRINT *
    10 CONTINUE
c.      DO 10 I = 1, N
            PRINT *, 'I = ', I
            DO 20 J = I, 0, -1
                PRINT *, I + J
    20      CONTINUE
    10 CONTINUE
```

Programming

1. Write a nest of loops that causes the following output to be displayed.

```
1
1
2
1
2
3
```

4.8 Problem Solving Illustrated

In this section, we examine a programming problem that illustrates most of the concepts discussed in this chapter. Its solution contains an IF statement nested within a WHILE loop.

We demonstrate the *top-down design process* in solving this problem. Using this process, we will implement the program in a stepwise manner, starting with a list of major algorithm steps and continuing to add detail through refinement until the program can be written.

Case Study: Computing Radiation Levels

PROBLEM STATEMENT

In a certain building at a top secret research lab, some Yttrium-90 has leaked into the computer programmers' coffee room. It currently would expose personnel to 150 millirems of radiation a day. The half-life of the substance is about three days, which means that the radiation level is only half of what it was three days previously. The programmers want to know how long it will be before the radiation is reduced to a safe level of 0.466 millirem a day so they can get back to their "hot" coffee. They would like a chart that displays the radiation level for every three days and includes a message UNSAFE or SAFE after every line. The chart should stop just before the radiation level is one tenth of the safe level because the more cautious programmers will require a safety factor of 10.

ANALYSIS

The chart can be printed by a WHILE loop whose loop-control variable is the current radiation level. Because the radiation level is cut in half every three days, we can use the formulas

day = day + 3
radiation level = radiation level / 2.0

inside the loop. The data requirements and algorithm follow.

Data Requirements

Program Parameters

the safe radiation level in millirems (REAL SAFRAD = 0.466)
the safety factor (REAL SAFFAC = 10.0)

Problem Outputs

the day number (INTEGER DAY)
the radiation level in millirems (REAL RADLEV)

DESIGN

The algorithm follows:

Algorithm

1. Initialize DAY to zero and read the initial radiation level into RADLEV.
2. Compute and display the day number and the radiation level every three days that the radiation level exceeds the safe level divided by the safety factor. Also, indicate whether each level is safe or unsafe.

Algorithm Refinements

We can use a WHILE loop to implement step 2. For reasons of efficiency that we discuss after we present the program, we introduce a new variable to hold the stopping level of radiation, which is the safe level divided by the safety factor.

Additional Program Variable

the stopping level of radiation (REAL RADMIN)

Step 2 Refinements

2.1 Compute RADMIN.
2.2 DO WHILE RADLEV exceeds RADMIN
    2.3 Display the value of DAY, RADLEV, and the string 'UNSAFE' or 'SAFE'.
    2.4 Add 3 to the value of DAY.
    2.5 Compute RADLEV for the next period.
END DO

The refinement of step 2.3 is the following decision step:

Step 2.3 Refinement

2.3.1 IF RADLEV exceeds SAFRAD THEN
    Display DAY, RADLEV, and 'UNSAFE'.
ELSE
    Display DAY, RADLEV, and 'SAFE'.
END IF

IMPLEMENTATION

The program appears in Fig. 4.20.

Figure 4.20. *Computing Radiation Levels*

```
      PROGRAM NUKE
C Calculates safe zone of a coffee room

C Type declarations
      REAL SAFRAD, SAFFAC
      PARAMETER (SAFRAD = 0.466, SAFFAC = 10.0)
      INTEGER DAY
      REAL RADLEV, RADMIN

C Initialize DAY and RADLEV
      DAY = 0
      PRINT *, 'Enter the radiation level (in millirems)'
      READ *, RADLEV

C Display table
      PRINT *, 'DAY      Radiation       Status'
      PRINT *, '         (millirems)'
      RADMIN = SAFRAD / SAFFAC
      DO WHILE (RADLEV .GT. RADMIN)                    9 IF ( ... ) THEN
         IF (RADLEV .GT. SAFRAD) THEN
            PRINT *, DAY, RADLEV, '      UNSAFE'
         ELSE
            PRINT *, DAY, RADLEV, '      SAFE'
         END IF
         DAY = DAY + 3
         RADLEV = RADLEV / 2.0
      END DO                                           GOTO 9
                                                       END IF
C Exit program
      STOP
      END


Enter the radiation level (in millirems)
150.0

Day      Radiation         Status
         (millirems)
 0       150.0000          UNSAFE
 3       75.00000          UNSAFE
 6       37.50000          UNSAFE
 9       18.75000          UNSAFE
12       9.375000          UNSAFE
15       4.687500          UNSAFE
18       2.343750          UNSAFE
21       1.171875          UNSAFE
24       0.5859375         UNSAFE
27       0.2929688         SAFE
30       0.1464844         SAFE
33       7.3242188E-02     SAFE
```

TESTING AND VERIFICATION

The only data item for this program is the initial radiation level of 150 millirems, so one run should suffice. Ensure that each radiation value is one half the previous value and that the number of days always increases by 3. Also, ensure that the first safe value is less than 0.466 millirem. If you divide the last radiation value displayed by 2.0, you must obtain a value that is less than or equal to 0.0466 (*Safe radiation level / Safety factor* = 0.466/10.0 = 0.0466).

Program Style: *Removing Redundant Computations from Loops*

In Fig. 4.20, we introduced an additional program variable, RADMIN, and used the following statements to define RADMIN prior to loop entry and to test RADLEV:

```
RADMIN = SAFRAD / SAFFAC
DO WHILE (RADLEV .GT. RADMIN)
```

Instead of doing this, however, we could combine these two statements, as follows:

```
DO WHILE (RADLEV .GT. (SAFRAD / SAFFAC))
```

This loop header is less efficient because it recomputes the quotient SAFRAD / SAFFAC each time the loop is repeated. Because both variables involved in the computation are parameters, and thus the value of the quotient cannot change, it makes no sense to recompute it. You should look for redundant computations like this in loops and remove them. Some Fortran compilers will optimize a program by removing redundant computations for you.

EXERCISES FOR SECTION 4.8

Self-check

1. How would you get the program in Fig. 4.20 to stop the table display after, instead of before, the radiation level becomes less than or equal to the safe level of radiation divided by the safety factor?

4.9 Debugging and Testing Programs

In Section 2.8, we described the general categories of error messages you are likely to see: syntax errors and run-time errors. It is also possible for a program to execute without generating any error messages, yet still produce incorrect results. Sometimes the cause of a run-time error or the origin of incorrect results is apparent and the problem can be easily fixed; however, very often the error is not obvious and so may require considerable effort to locate.

The best approach to debugging is to prevent errors from occurring in the first place (called *antibugging*). If you carefully desk check the refined algorithm using one or more data samples, you may be able to determine that a logic error exists (and correct it) before you implement the incorrect algorithm as a buggy program.

The first step in debugging is to determine what part of the program is generating incorrect results. For example, if the final answer does not match your hand-computed result, an earlier partial result that was also incorrect may be the cause. Check all prior displayed values to determine where the first error occurred. If no partial results are displayed, then add extra diagnostic PRINT statements to display partial results. If one partial result is correct, but the next one is incorrect, the statements that lie between these two diagnostic PRINT statements must contain the source of the error. Once you have located the buggy section of the program, you should zero in on the computations performed in that section.

As an example of this process, refer to the program in Fig. 4.7, which computed the average value (AVERGE) of a set of measurements whose sum is accumulated in SUM. If the value of AVERGE displayed in Fig. 4.7 is incorrect, you would want to insert a diagnostic PRINT statement that displays the value of SUM. If SUM is correct, then the assignment statement used to compute AVERGE from SUM must be wrong. However, if SUM is also incorrect, focus on the DO loop used to compute SUM. Trace the loop's execution by inserting the following diagnostic PRINT statement as the last statement in the loop body:

```
   DO 10 COUNT = 1, NUMMES
       PRINT *, 'Enter next value (in ', UNITS, ')'
       READ *, ITEM
       SUM = SUM + ITEM
       PRINT *, '****** COUNT = ', COUNT, ' ITEM = ', ITEM,
  +              ' SUM = ', SUM
10 CONTINUE
```

Each time the loop executes, this diagnostic PRINT statement will display the current values of COUNT and ITEM and each partial sum that is accumulated. The PRINT statement will display a string of asterisks at the beginning of its output line, thus making it easier to identify diagnostic output in the debugging runs and to locate the diagnostic PRINT statements in the source program.

Once you have located the error, you will want to take out the extra diagnostic statements. As a temporary measure, you might want to turn these diagnostic statements into comments by placing a c or an * in column 1; then if errors crop up again in later testing, you'll find it easier to remove the c or * than to retype the diagnostic statements.

Using Debugger Programs

Many computer systems have debugger programs to help you debug a program. This type of program lets you execute your program one statement at a time so you can see the effect of each statement. You also can instruct the program to display the values of selected variables after each statement executes, thus enabling you to trace those variables. However, if you don't want your program to pause after each statement, you can set breakpoints at certain key statements; then you can instruct the debugger to execute all statements from one breakpoint to the next.

Testing a Program

After all errors have been corrected and the program appears to execute as expected, you should test the program thoroughly to ensure it works. In Section 3.6, we discussed tracing an algorithm and suggested that enough sets of test data be provided to ensure that all possible paths are traced. The same is true for the completed program. Make enough test runs to verify the program works properly for representative samples of all possible data combinations. Further, always investigate how your program reacts to zero and negative numbers entered as data.

4.10 Common Programming Errors

1. Students sometimes confuse decision steps with conditional loops because the header statement for both structures contains a condition. Ensure you use an IF statement to implement a decision step and a WHILE loop for a conditional loop.
2. The first words in the header statement of a control structure (IF, DO, or DO WHILE) indicate the type of the control structure. Use the corresponding structure terminator—END IF, CONTINUE, or END DO—to mark the end of the control structure.
3. The syntax of the DO loop header is repeated as follows:

    DO *label lcv* = *initial, limit, step*

    Remember to use an integer of five digits or fewer as a label between the keyword DO and the variable *lcv*. Also, place this same integer in the label field (columns 1 through 5) of the loop terminator (CONTINUE) statement.
4. A comma is required as a separator between the *initial* and the *limit* parameters. If this comma is omitted, Fortran will attempt to translate the DO loop header as an assignment statement. For example, DO 10 I = 1 5 assigns the

value 15 to the variable DO10I. The reason for this is that Fortran ignores spaces after column 7 (except in strings), so the characters to the left and to the right of the equal sign are treated as a variable (DO10I) and an integer (15), respectively.

5. Another common mistake is placing the last digit of the label for a CONTINUE statement in column 6 instead of column 5. Because the last digit appears in the continuation column (column 6), Fortran will not include it as part of the label, thus possibly causing a missing-label syntax error.

6. Be careful not to mistype the letter O as the digit 0, or vice versa. For example, ending the reserved word DO with a zero will lead to syntax errors. Similarly, mistyping a zero in a label as the letter "O" may cause a missing-label syntax error.

7. Missing terminator statements can be detected easily by the Fortran compiler, which will print a diagnostic message indicating that the terminator is missing. When control structures are nested, the terminator for the innermost structure must come first because if the terminator statements are in the wrong order, the structures will overlap and the compiler will be unable to translate these structures (see Fig. 4.21). The compiler will print a diagnostic message indicating that the structures overlap or are terminated improperly.

8. Be very careful when using tests for inequality to control the repetition of a WHILE loop. The following loop is intended to process all transactions for a bank account while the balance is positive.

```
DO WHILE (BALANC .NE. 0.0)
      . . .
END DO
```

Figure 4.21. *Over-lapping Structures*

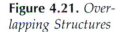

```
DO WHILE ( . . . )
      - - - - - - -
      - - - - - - -
            IF ( . . . ) THEN
                  - - - - - - -
                  - - - - - - -
            ENDDO
      - - - - - - -
      - - - - - - -
ENDIF
```

If the bank balance goes from a positive to a negative amount without being exactly `0.0`, the loop will not terminate. The next loop would be safer.

```
DO WHILE (BALANC .GT. 0.0)
      . . .
END DO
```

You should verify that the repetition condition for a WHILE loop will eventually become false; otherwise, an infinite (non-terminating) loop may result. If a sentinel value is used to control loop repetition, make sure that the program user is told what value to enter to stop loop repetition.

Chapter Review

In this chapter, we described how to repeat steps in a program. You learned how to implement counting loops using DO statements. For example, a counting loop with the header

DO *label counter* = 1, N

performs N iterations. You also learned how to use the general DO statement, such as the DO loop with the header

DO *label lcv* = *initial, limit, step*

which executes for values of *lcv* equal to *initial, initial* + *step, initial* + 2 × *step,* and so on, until the value of *lcv* passes *limit*.

A conditional looping structure, the WHILE loop, is used to implement loops whose repetition is controlled by a condition. The WHILE loop is useful when the exact number of repetitions required is not known before the loop begins. Separate Fortran statements are needed for initializing, updating, and testing the value of the loop-control variable associated with a WHILE loop.

One common technique for controlling the repetition of a WHILE loop involves using a special sentinel value to indicate that all required data have been processed. In this case, the loop-control variable is a problem input. Its initial value (the first data value) is read prior to loop entry; its value is updated at the end of the loop when the next data value is read. Loop repetition terminates after the sentinel value is read into the loop-control variable.

New Fortran Statements

The Fortran statements introduced in this chapter are described in Table 4.4.

Table 4.4. *Fortran Statements for Chapter 4*

STATEMENT	EFFECT
Counting Loop	

```
      DO 10 NUM = 1, 25
         PRINT *, NUM, NUM ** 2
   10 CONTINUE
```
Prints 25 lines, each containing an integer from 1 to 25 and its square.

General DO Loop

```
      DO 30 VOLTS = 20, -20, -10
         CURENT = VOLTS / RESIST
         PRINT *, VOLTS, CURENT
   30 CONTINUE
```
For values of VOLTS equal to 20, 10, 0, -10, -20, computes the value of CURENT and displays VOLTS and CURENT.

WHILE Loop (Not part of standard Fortran 77)

```
SUM = 0.0
PRINT *, 'Enter first number'
READ *, NEXT
DO WHILE (NEXT .NE. SENVAL)
   SUM = SUM + NEXT
   PRINT *, 'Next number'
   READ *, NEXT
END DO
```
Accumulates the sum (SUM) of a group of numbers entered as data. The sum is complete when the sentinel value (SENVAL) is read into NEXT.

Quick-check Exercises

1. A(n) _____ loop is used to implement a counting loop.
2. A(n) _____ loop is called a conditional loop.
3. A sentinel value is used to terminate the execution of a(n) _____ loop.
4. If we change the *limit* parameter of a DO loop during loop execution, we can change the number of iterations performed. True or false?
5. The *lcv* for a DO loop can decrease in value. True or false?
6. The priming step for a sentinel-controlled loop is what kind of statement? Where must this statement appear in the program?
7. The sentinel value is the last value added to a sum being accumulated in a sentinel-controlled loop. True or false?
8. For the following loop headers, how many times will each loop execute? What will be the value of I after loop exit?

   a. DO 10 I = 1, 15
   b. DO 20 I = -10, 5, 10
   c. DO WHILE (I .LE. 10)

9. What does the following program segment display? What can you say about X after loop exit?

```
PRODUC = 1
READ *, X
DO WHILE (X .GT. 0)
    PRODUC = PRODUC * X
    READ *, X
END DO
PRINT *, PRODUC
```

10. How many times does the PRINT statement below execute? What are the output lines?

```
DO 10    I = 1, 3
    DO 20 J = I, 2
        PRINT *, I, J
20      CONTINUE
10  CONTINUE
```

11. How many times does the following PRINT statement execute? What are the output lines?

```
DO 10 I = 1, 2
    DO 20 J = I, 3
        PRINT *, I, J
20      CONTINUE
10  CONTINUE
```

Answers to Quick-check Exercises

1. DO
2. WHILE
3. sentinel-controlled WHILE loop
4. false
5. true
6. A READ statement. It appears twice, just before the loop and at the end of the loop body.
7. False. The sentinel should not be processed with the normal data.
8. a. fifteen; 16
   b. two; 10
   c. unknown; I is greater than 10
9. It displays the product of an initial sequence of positive data values. X is less than or equal to zero after loop exit.
10. three times

```
1 1
1 2
2 2
```

11. five times

```
1 1
1 2
1 3
2 2
2 3
```

Review Questions

1. Explain the difference between the following two control structures.

   ```
   IF (X .GT. 0.0) THEN
       X = X - 2.0
       PRINT *, X
   END IF
   ```

   ```
   DO WHILE (X .GT. 0.0)
       X = X - 2.0
       PRINT *, X
   END DO
   ```

2. For Review Question 1, indicate what would be printed by each control structure for the following values of X: 8.0, 7.0, 0.0, ⁻7.0, ⁻8.0.

3. Which control structure—IF, DO, or WHILE—would you use for each of the following situations?

   a. Print a message indicating whether a person is old enough to vote.
   b. Compute the gross pay for five employees.
   c. Select one of five tax rates to use for a particular employee based on gross pay.
   d. Count the number of zeros in a data collection of unknown size.
   e. Find the product of all odd integers from 1 through 99.
   f. Determine the letter grade corresponding to a particular exam score.
   g. Keep dividing a data value in half until it is smaller than 0.5 and print all quotients.

4. Provide sample control structures for each situation in Review Question 3. Don't bother to declare variables.

5. Explain the difference between a WHILE loop and a DO loop.

6. Define a sentinel value.

7. For a sentinel value to be used properly when reading in data, where should the READ statements appear?

8. Write a WHILE loop to sum a collection of payroll amounts entered at the keyboard until a sentinel value of ⁻1.0 is entered.

9. Hand trace the program below given the following data:

   ```
   4.0    2.0    8.0    4.0
   9.0    3.0    3.0    1.0
   0.0    0.0    0.0    0.0
   ```

```
PROGRAM ENTER4
REAL SENVAL, SLOPE, Y2, Y1, X2, X1
PARAMETER (SENVAL = 0.0)
PRINT *, 'Enter four real numbers:'
READ *, Y2, Y1, X2, X1
SLOPE = (Y2 - Y1) / (X2 - X1)
DO WHILE (SLOPE .NE. SENVAL)
    PRINT *, 'Slope is ', SLOPE
    PRINT *
    PRINT *, 'Enter four real numbers:'
    READ *, Y2, Y1, X2, X1
    SLOPE = (Y2 - Y1) / (X2 - X1)
END DO
STOP
END
```

10. What is printed by the following program fragment for the data values 3, 5, 1, 2, 0, −1, −2, 0?

```
READ *, X
DO WHILE (X .GE. 0)
    IF (X .GE. 3) THEN
        PRINT *, 'GOOD'
    ELSE IF (X .GE. 2) THEN
        PRINT *, 'FAIR'
    ELSE
        PRINT *, 'POOR'
    END IF
    READ *, X
END DO
```

11. Explain the effect of deleting the second READ statement in Review Question 10.
12. What will be the value of SUM after the Fortran fragment on the right executes?

a.	3	`SUM = 0`
b.	5	`DO 10 I = 1, 5`
c.	12	`    IF (I .GE. 3) THEN`
d.	15	`        SUM = SUM + I`
e.	120	`    ELSE`
		`        SUM = SUM * I`
		`    END IF`
		`10 CONTINUE`

13. How many times will the PRINT * statement be executed in the Fortran fragment on the right?

a.	5	`DO 10 K = 9, 1, -3`
b.	6	`    DO 20 L = 4, K, 2`
c.	7	`        PRINT *, L`
d.	9	`20      CONTINUE`
e.	10	`10 CONTINUE`

Fortran 90 Features: DO Loops, EXIT, and CYCLE

There are several significant differences between loop structures in Fortran 77 and those in Fortran 90. As we mentioned earlier, the WHILE loop is part of standard Fortran 90, but not of Fortran 77. Also in Fortran 90, only type INTEGER variables and expressions may be used as DO loop control variables and loop parameters, whereas in Fortran 77, type REAL DO loop control variables and parameters are allowed, although their use is discouraged.

DO Loops without Labels

Fortran 90 also supports alternate syntactical forms of the DO loop. In Fortran 90, we may delete the label from the DO loop header. If we do this, the matching loop terminator is END DO (same as for WHILE loop) instead of a labeled CONTINUE statement. DO loops without labels can be nested like other loops. The following DO loop forms the product of 10 data values entered as data:

```
product = 1
DO I = 1, 10
    PRINT *, 'Enter a data value'
    READ *, item
    product = product * item
END DO
```

EXIT and CYCLE Statements

Fortran 90 also provides loop EXIT (exit a loop) and CYCLE (repeat a loop) statements. The following loop forms the product of up to 10 positive data items:

```
product = 1
DO I = 1, 10
    PRINT *, 'Enter a data value'
    READ *, item
    IF (item = 0) EXIT      ! Exit early if 0 is read
    IF (item < 0) CYCLE     ! Ignore negative data
    product = product * item
END DO
```

Loop exit occurs in the normal way after the tenth data value is read and processed. If a data value of 0 is read, the EXIT statement executes, causing early loop exit. If a negative data value is read, the CYCLE statement executes, causing the rest of the loop body (the assignment statement) to be skipped and the next loop iteration to begin immediately. Although negative values are not included in the product, they are included in the count of data values processed.

DO Loop without Parameters

Finally, Fortran 90 enables us to omit the loop-control variable and loop parameters from a DO loop, thereby forming a loop that can execute indefinitely (a potentially infinite loop). The following loop forms the product of an unlimited number of positive data values. Loop exit occurs when a data value of 0 is read; negative data values are ignored.

```
product = 1
DO
    PRINT *, 'Enter a data value'
    READ *, item
    IF (item = 0) EXIT     ! Exit if 0 is read
    IF (item < 0) CYCLE    ! Ignore negative data
    product = product * item
END DO
```

The DO loop without parameters also can be used effectively when we want to read a data file until the end of the file is reached. For example, the following DO loop reads and echoes each line of a data file associated with unit number 1 and transfers control to label 99 when the end-of-file record is read:

```
    DO
        READ (1, *, END = 99) X, Y
        PRINT *, 'X = ', X, ' Y = ', Y
    END DO

99 CONTINUE
```

SYNTAX DISPLAY

DO Loop without Parameters and EXIT Statement

SYNTAX: DO

    . . .

    IF (condition) EXIT

    . . .

END DO

EXAMPLE:
```
product = 1
DO
    PRINT *, 'Product so far is ', product
    IF (product > 10000) EXIT
    PRINT *, 'Enter next factor'
    READ *, factor
    product = product * factor
END DO
```

INTERPRETATION: The DO loop repeats until the EXIT statement is executed. The EXIT statement then transfers control to the first statement following the END DO.

SYNTAX DISPLAY

CYCLE Statement

SYNTAX: CYCLE

INTERPRETATION: The CYCLE statement initiates the next repetition of a loop by causing an immediate transfer to the END DO, thus skipping over the rest of the loop body.

Programming Projects

1. Write a program that will find the smallest, largest, and average values in a collection of N numbers, where the value of N is the first data item read.

 2. Modify Programming Project 1 to compute and display both the range of values in the data collection and the variance of the data collection. To compute the variance, accumulate the sum of the squares of the data values in the main loop. After loop exit, use the formula

$$variance = sum\text{-}of\text{-}squares - (sum\text{-}of\text{-}data)^2 / N.$$

Finally, compute the standard deviation, s, which is a measure of how much the data values deviate from the average value. Use the formula

$$s^2 = variance / (N - 1).$$

3. Write a program that estimates the value of the following infinite series:

$$\cos(X) = 1 - \frac{X^2}{2!} + \frac{X^4}{4!} - \frac{X^6}{6!} + \frac{X^8}{8!} \cdots$$

The relationship between successive terms is

$$term_N = term_{N-1} \times \frac{-X^2}{(2N)(2N - 1)}$$

where the first term (which is equal to 1) is term number 0. Determine how changing the number of terms affects the accuracy of your results.

4. Write a program to read in a collection of exam scores ranging in value from 1 to 100. Your program should count and print the number of outstanding scores (90–100), the number of satisfactory scores (60–89), and the number of unsatisfactory scores (1–59). Test your program on the following data:

```
63  75  72  72  78  67  80   63  75
90  89  43  59  99  82  12  100
```

In addition, print each exam score and its category.

5. Write a program to process weekly employee time cards for all employees of an organization. Each employee will have three data items: an identification number, the hourly wage rate, and the number of hours worked during a given week. Each employee is to be paid time and a half for all hours worked over 40. A tax amount of 3.625% of gross salary will be deducted. The program output should show the employee's number and net pay.

6. Write a program that finds the equivalent series and parallel resistance for a collection of resistor values. Your program should first read in the number of resistors and then compute the equivalent series resistance for all resistors in the collection and the equivalent parallel resistance. For example, if there are 3 resistors of 100, 200, and 300 Ohms, respectively, their equivalent series resistance is 100 + 200 + 300 and their equivalent parallel resistance is 1/(1/100 + 1/200 + 1/300). Your program should read each resistance value (R), add R to the series sum (RS) and add 1/R to the parallel sum (RP). After loop exit, display RS and 1/RP.

After your program works for a single collection of resistors, modify it so it will process several collections of resistors in a single run. Use a sentinel value of 0 (zero resistors in the collection) to signal the end of the program data.

7. A major manufacturer of engines wants to identify engines whose efficiency is greater than a specified target value. The manufacturer has tested a large quantity of engines (less than 100) and recorded each engine's identification number (an integer) and measured its torque, T, engine speed, N, and fuel consumption, M. Write a program that reads the data for each engine and computes its power, BHP, and efficiency (EFF) using the formulas

$$BHP = \frac{T \times N}{5252}$$

$$EFF = \frac{BHP}{414 \times M}.$$

Display the results for each engine. Write a message after each output line indicating whether the engine's efficiency exceeds the target value (a data item).

8. a. Write a program to process a collection of savings account transactions (deposits or withdrawals). Your program should begin by reading in the previous account balance and then read and process each transaction. Enter a positive value for a deposit and a negative value for a withdrawal. For each transaction, print the message 'Withdrawal' or 'Deposit' and the new balance. Print an error message if a withdrawal would result in a negative balance and do not change the balance.

    b. Compute and print the number of deposits, the number of withdrawals, the number of invalid withdrawals, and the total dollar amount for each type of transaction.

9. a. Write a program that computes and prints the fractional powers of two (1/2, 1/4, 1/8, etc.). The program should also print the decimal value of each fraction as shown next:

Power	Fraction	Decimal Value
1	1/2	0.5
2	1/4	0.25
3	1/8	0.125

    Print all values through power equal to 10.

    b. Add an extra output column that shows the sum of all decimal values so far. The first three sums are 0.5, 0.75, and 0.875.

10. a. The trustees of a small college are considering voting a pay raise for the twelve faculty. They want to grant a 5.5% pay raise; however, before doing so, they want to know how much this will cost. Write a program that will print the pay raise for each faculty member and the total amount of the raises. Also, print the total faculty payroll before and after the raise. Test your program for the following salaries:

$22500	$24029.50	$26000	$23250
$25500	$22800	$30000.50	$28900
$23780	$27300	$24120.25	$24100

    b. Redo Programming Project 10(a) assuming that faculty members earning less than $24,000 receive a 4% raise, faculty earning more than $26,500 receive a 7% raise, and all others receive a 5.5% raise. For each faculty member, print the raise percentage as well as the amount.

11. The assessor in your town has estimated the market value of 14 properties and would like a program that determines the tax owed on each property and the total tax to be collected. The tax rate is 125 mil/dollar of assessed value. (A mil = 0.1 cent.) The assessed value of each property is 28% of its estimated market value. The market values are as follows:

$150000	$148000	$145500	$167000
$137600	$147100	$165000	
$153350	$128000	$158000	$152250
$148000	$156500	$143700	

12. Patients required to take many kinds of medication often have difficulty remembering when to take their medicine. Given the following set of medications, write a program that prints an hourly table indicating what medication to take at any given hour. Use a counter variable CLOCK to go through a 24-hr day. Print the table based upon the following prescriptions:

Medication	Frequency
Iron pill	0800, 1200, 1800
Antibiotic	Every 4 hr starting at 0400
Vitamin	0800, 2100
Calcium	1100, 2000

13. The square root of a number N can be approximated by repeated calculation using the formula

    $$NG = .5(LG + N/LG),$$

    where NG stands for "next guess" and LG stands for "last guess." Write a program that calculates the square root of a number using this method.

    The initial guess will be the starting value of LG. The program should compute a value for NG using the formula given immediately above. The difference between NG and LG is checked to see whether these two guesses are almost identical. If so, NG is the square root; otherwise, the new guess (NG) becomes the last guess (LG) and the process is repeated (another value is computed for NG, the difference is checked, etc.).

    For this program, the loop should be repeated until the difference is less than 0.005 (DELTA). Use an initial guess of 1.0 and test the program for the numbers 4, 120.5, 88, 36.01, and 10000.

14. (nested loops) Write a program to read in a collection of integers and determine whether each integer is a prime number. A prime number is a number that has no divisors except for 1 and itself.

15. You are a quality control engineer in a manufacturing plant. Your job is to ensure that lots of widgets conform with company standards for quality. To do this, you inspect samples from a lot for the precision with which threaded holes are drilled into them. The holes are measured in hundredths of an inch. Tolerances for defects are ±0.01 in.

    Write a Fortran program that will prompt the user for the required size of each hole in the sample lot. The program then should continuously prompt the user to enter a series of hole measurements until 0.0 is entered, thus signalling the end of input.

    The program should maintain a count of the number of widgets whose hole sizes were entered and for each hole size, determine whether the size falls within the tolerance level. If the size does not, the program should increment a counter of defective widgets. When the program ends, it then should determine whether the lot should be passed or rejected. The threshold for passing a lot is 95% accepted.

16. One branch of Civil Engineering deals with the study of automobile traffic patterns, road and highway design, and traffic signal timing and coordination. Traffic studies are conducted to determine current roadway usage. Often, counts of cars are

obtained by mechanical means. However, at times, an engineer may use a counting board. Counting boards resemble a clipboard, but with counters on each of the four sides, representing the four approaches to an intersection. Each counter has a series of three buttons that, when pressed, will increment a counter. The left button represents cars making a left turn; the right button represents cars making right turns; and the middle button represents cars going straight through an intersection.

Write a Fortran program to simulate one of these counters. You may use keys on the keyboard to represent the three different buttons on a counter: R for right, L for left, and S for straight. When one of these keys is depressed, an associated counter within the program should be incremented. The program should continue to allow for keys to be depressed until the E key is hit, signalling the end of the count. At this point, the program should display the number of cars that turned right and left and that went straight.

17. Write a Fortran program to simulate the operation of a drill press found in a manufacturing plant. The key elements for this simulation are the processing rate of the drill press and the arrival rate of sheets of metal into the hopper that feeds the press. Assume the processing rate of the press is 3 sec for each sheet of metal and the arrival rate of the sheets of metal at the press will be one sheet every 3 sec.

You will need to track the clock time, starting with a time of zero. You also must maintain a count of the number of sheets of metal in the processing queue and a count of the number of sheets of metal processed so far.

You can represent the clock by a DO loop counter variable, with each repetition of the DO loop representing another second of clock time. At any clock time, an event, either the arrival of a sheet of metal or the ejection of one from the press, may occur. Update the appropriate counters based upon the event.

Run the simulation for 1 hr of simulated time (3600 sec), and print a status report of the number of sheets processed and the current queue size every 5 min (300 sec). Try adjusting the arrival and processing rates and see what happens.

18. A thermostat is a device that continuously measures temperature and, depending on the setting of the thermostat and the current temperature reading, turns a heater either on or off. Write a Fortran program to simulate a thermostat. The initial temperature and the setting of the thermostat should be obtained from the program user.

The program body should be a loop. During each iteration of the loop, the temperature should be incremented or decremented by 1 degree, depending upon the current setting of the thermostat. If the current temperature is less than the thermostat reading, add 1 to the temperature; otherwise subtract 1. Once the temperature and thermostat setting are equal, make no further changes to the temperature unless the thermostat setting is changed by the user.

Also, during each iteration of the loop, prompt the user for a change to the thermostat setting. If a small positive or negative value is entered, adjust the thermostat setting by this amount and continue with the program. If the value entered is zero, make no change to the thermostat setting and continue. Enter a change of 99° to exit the loop.

When loop exit occurs, print (a) the current temperature and thermostat settings and (b) the maximum and minimum temperatures reached during the simulation.

CHAPTER 5
FORMAT Statements and Introduction to Files

I N YOUR programming so far, you have been able to exercise very little control over the appearance of an output line. It was difficult to align table values under table headings and the compiler determined how many decimal places to use in printing a real value and the number of spaces to leave between consecutive values on the same output line. In this chapter, we discuss how to specify the exact form of program output by using formatted PRINT statements and how to use formatted READ statements to read input data.

We also discuss using files for input and output: how to enter program data from data input files and save program output on output files. Using data files frees you from having to continually re-enter the same data while debugging a program; using output files enables you to save program output in a semipermanent form on disk rather than simply viewing it on the screen.

5.1 Formatted Output

In our programs so far, we have used PRINT * to display output values. The * following the word PRINT indicates *list-directed output,* which means that the data type of each output list item determines the form of the value printed.

In a formatted PRINT statement, a statement label replaces the symbol * following the word PRINT. The label references a FORMAT statement, as shown next.

EXAMPLE 5.1

When N is 5347, the statements

```
    PRINT 15, 'N has the value ', N
15 FORMAT (1X, A, I5)
```

display the line

```
N has the value  5347
```

The label 15 in the PRINT statement specifies that FORMAT statement 15 determines how the two output list items will be displayed. The FORMAT statement consists of a list of three *edit descriptors* enclosed in parentheses. The first edit descriptor, 1X, controls the line spacing between this output line and the preceding one. In this case, single-line spacing is specified. The edit descriptor A causes the first output list item, a string, to be displayed exactly as it appears in the PRINT statement. The edit descriptor I5 causes the value of N to be displayed *right-justified* in an output *field* of five columns, that is, the last digit of N will appear in the rightmost column of the output field. If N has fewer than five digits, leading blanks will precede the number.

EXAMPLE 5.2   If X has the value 96.63825, the statements

```
    PRINT 25, 'X has the value ', X
25 FORMAT (1X, A, F5.2)
```

display the line

```
X has the value 96.64
```

The edit descriptor F5.2 specifies that the value of X is to be displayed in a field width of five columns (including the decimal point), accurate to two decimal places. As shown in the output line, the fractional part is rounded to two decimal places before it is displayed.   ■

EXAMPLE 5.3   The formatted PRINT and FORMAT statements

```
    PRINT 35,    NAME,    GROSS,    DEPEND
35 FORMAT (1X, A10, 3X, F7.2, 2X, I2)
```

specify how the values of NAME, GROSS, and DEPEND should be printed. Some of the edit descriptors—A10, F7.2, and I2—describe how a value is to be printed; others—3X and 2X—specify how many spaces are to be left between values. Each edit descriptor is explained in Table 5.1.

FORMAT statement 35 is a *template* that specifies the exact appearance (as described in Table 5.1) of any output line that is printed using it. In the following form, the A's indicate where the string value will be printed, the F's where the real value will be printed, and the I's where the integer will be printed. The symbol □ indicates which columns will be left blank. The first character in the template controls the spacing between output lines and should not be displayed.

```
□AAAAAAAAAA□□FFFF.FF□□II
```

Table 5.1. *Edit Descriptors in FORMAT Statement 35*

DESCRIPTOR	EFFECT
1X	Specifies single-line spacing.
A10	Prints a string value (NAME) right-justified in 10 columns.
3X	Leaves three spaces (between the first and second values).
F7.2	Prints a real value (GROSS) right-justified in seven columns with two decimal places.
2X	Leaves two spaces (between the second and third values).
I2	Prints an integer value (DEPEND) right-justified in two columns.

The position of the decimal point in the real value is also shown in the sketch. Recall from Table 5.1 that the edit descriptor F7.2 specifies that there are two decimal places in the real value and a total of seven print columns, including the decimal point itself. Counting characters from the left, we can determine that the decimal point must appear in column 19.

In this example, the formatted PRINT statement has three output list items: NAME, GROSS, and DEPEND. Each is paired with an edit descriptor that begins with the letter A, F, or I, respectively—NAME with A10, GROSS with F7.2, and DEPEND with I2. To illustrate this pairing, each output list item appears directly above its corresponding edit descriptor.

Once this pairing is determined, the output values are printed according to the template shown earlier. Given the variable values

```
   NAME           GROSS      DEPEND
JOHNNY□JONES     346.9763      3
```

the line that would be printed is shown next under its template.

```
□AAAAAAAAAA□□FFFF.FF□□II
 JOHNNY JON    346.98    3
```

Note that the value of NAME is truncated to 10 characters, the value of GROSS is rounded to two decimal places, and the numeric values are each printed right-justified (with a leading blank) in their output fields.

Each edit descriptor must be associated with an output list item of the correct data type. The type of data item required for each edit descriptor and the general form of the edit descriptors are described in Table 5.2. In this table, n, w, and d represent integer constants (parameters may not be used).

Table 5.2. *General Form of Edit Descriptors*

DESCRIPTOR	EFFECT
Aw	Exactly w characters are printed. If there are more than w characters in the associated string value, the extra characters on the right are not printed; if there are fewer than w characters, the string value is padded with blanks on the left (right-justified).
A	The number of characters printed exactly matches the length of the output list item.
Fw.d	A real number is printed right-justified in w columns. The fractional part is rounded to d decimal places.
Iw	An integer is printed right-justified in w columns.
nX	There are n blanks or spaces "printed."

As shown in Table 5.2, the edit descriptor A by itself instructs the compiler to use as many output columns as there are characters in the string value being printed. If the output list item is a CHARACTER variable, its declared length determines the number of columns used.

The FORMAT statement is nonexecutable, must have a unique label, and may be placed anywhere in a program; generally, it follows the first PRINT statement that references it. There may be more than one formatted PRINT statement that references a particular FORMAT statement. The FORMAT statement is described in the next display.

SYNTAX DISPLAY

FORMAT Statement

SYNTAX: *label* FORMAT (*edit descriptors*)

EXAMPLE: 15 FORMAT (1X, A, 2X, I3)

INTERPRETATION: The *edit descriptors* provide a template describing the form of an output line. This template applies to any line printed by each formatted PRINT statement that references the FORMAT statement *label*. The first edit descriptor beginning with A, F, or I is paired with the first output list item in the formatted PRINT, the second edit descriptor beginning with A, F, or I is paired with the second output list item, and so on.

NOTE: The *label* is an integer and is typed in the label field (columns 1–5).

Review of Edit Descriptors

In this section, we provide more examples of using Fortran edit descriptors.

EXAMPLE 5.4

Table 5.3 shows some integer values printed using different edit descriptors. Each edit descriptor must begin with the letter I. The symbol □ represents a blank space. ■

Table 5.3. *Printing Integer Values Using Edit Descriptors*

VALUE	DESCRIPTOR	PRINTED OUTPUT
234	I4	□234
234	I5	□□234
234	I6	□□□234
234	I2	compiler-dependent
−234	I4	−234
−234	I5	□−234
−234	I6	□□−234
−234	I3	compiler-dependent

As shown in Table 5.3, an integer value is always printed right-justified in its field. There should be enough columns specified to print the integer value and its sign. If there are insufficient columns specified, the value displayed is compiler-dependent; however, many compilers display a string of asterisks.

EXAMPLE 5.5   Table 5.4 shows some real values printed using different edit descriptors. Each edit descriptor must begin with the letter F.   ■

Table 5.4. *Printing Real Values Using Edit Descriptors*

VALUE	DESCRIPTOR	PRINTED OUTPUT
3.14159	F5.2	□3.14
3.14159	F5.1	□□3.1
3.14159	F6.3	□3.142
3.14159	F4.0	□□3.
3.14159	F3.2	compiler-dependent
−5.678	F4.1	−5.7
−5.678	F6.2	□−5.68
−5.678	F4.0	□−6.
−5.678	F9.5	□−5.67800
−5.678	F7.5	compiler-dependent

As shown in this table, a real value is always rounded before it is printed. You can even specify that a real value should be rounded to zero decimal places. In this case, the real value is rounded to the nearest whole number. Ensure you leave enough columns for all the digits required, the decimal point, and the sign of the number. If insufficient columns are specified, the value displayed is compiler-dependent; however, many compilers display a string of asterisks.

EXAMPLE 5.6   Table 5.5 shows some string values printed using different edit descriptors. Each edit descriptor must begin with the letter A.   ■

Table 5.5. *Printing String Values Using Edit Descriptors*

VALUE	DESCRIPTOR	PRINTED OUTPUT	VALUE	DESCRIPTOR	PRINTED OUTPUT
'*'	A	*	'ACES'	A	ACES
'*'	A1	*	'ACES'	A1	A
'*'	A2	□*	'ACES'	A2	AC
'*'	A3	□□*	'ACES'	A3	ACE
'*'	A4	□□□*	'ACES'	A4	ACES
'*'	A5	□□□□*	'ACES'	A5	□ACES

As this table shows, a string value is always printed right-justified in its output field. If insufficient columns are specified to print the complete string, then only the part of the string that fits in the output field will be printed.

Table 5.5 assumes the string values '*' and 'ACES' are inserted directly in an output list. The situation is a bit different when we store a string in a CHARACTER variable first and then display the CHARACTER variable; for example, if CARD is type CHARACTER *10, the assignment

```
CARD = 'ACES'
```

stores the string ACES followed by six blanks in variable CARD. Consequently, if we print CARD using format specification A or A10, Fortran displays the string ACES followed by six blanks (the value of CARD). If we print CARD using format specification A15, Fortran displays the value of CARD right-justified, so we see five blanks before the string ACES and six blanks after the string.

Line-control Characters

The first edit descriptor in FORMAT statement 35 of Example 5.3 is 1X. This descriptor causes the template to begin with a blank and is required on some terminals (and all line printers) that use the first character in a formatted output line to determine spacing between lines. On such terminals, the first blank would not be printed but instead would cause the current output line to be printed on the line following the previous line (single-line spacing).

The line-control character also can be specified using a string value as the edit descriptor. The FORMAT statement

```
35 FORMAT (' ', A10, 3X, F7.2, 2X, I2)
```

is equivalent to the one given in Example 5.3.

If the output list for a formatted PRINT statement begins with a string, we can prefix the string with the line-control character. In the following PRINT statement (see Example 5.1), the initial blank character in the string is used as the line-control character and is not displayed.

```
  PRINT 15, ' N has the value ', N
15 FORMAT (A, I5)
```

Table 5.6 shows the line-control characters.

Failure to specify the line-control character when one is expected prompts Fortran to use the first output character for line control instead of printing it. This can lead to some very undesirable results.

Table 5.6. *Line-control Characters*

DESCRIPTOR	EFFECT
`' '` or 1X	Prints the current line on the line following the previous line (single-line spacing).
`'0'`	Leaves one blank line between the current line and the previous line (double-line spacing).
`'1'`	Prints the current line at the top of the next page.
`'+'`	Prints the current line over the previous line.

If your terminal does not process the line-control character, you may prefer to omit it. Should the line-control character 1X or `' '` not be processed, an initial blank is displayed, which can easily be ignored. However, if the line-control character `'1'` is not processed, a 1 will appear in the first output column.

Output Tables

We can use formatted PRINT statements to simplify the process of setting up output tables.

EXAMPLE 5.7

The formatted PRINT statement

```
   PRINT 25, 'EMPLOYEE', 'RATE', 'DEPENDENTS'
25 FORMAT ('1', A15, 5X, A10, 5X, A15)
```

prints a table heading line at the top of the next output page. This statement should precede a loop that prints the table values. The template described by FORMAT statement 25 and the table heading are shown next.

```
1AAAAAAAAAAAAAAA□□□□□AAAAAAAAAA□□□□□AAAAAAAAAAAAAAA
        EMPLOYEE              RATE            DEPENDENTS
```

Within the loop body, the formatted PRINT statement

```
   PRINT 35, NAME, RATE, DEPEND
35 FORMAT (' ', A15, 5X, F10.2, 5X, I15)
```

could be used to print an output value under each column heading. Because the output field widths specified in FORMAT statements 25 and 35 are the same—15, 10, and 15—each output value would right-align with its respective column heading. The template for FORMAT statement 35 is shown next under the template for FORMAT statement 25.

```
1AAAAAAAAAAAAAAA□□□□AAAAAAAAAAA□□□□AAAAAAAAAAAAAAA
□AAAAAAAAAAAAAAA□□□□FFFFFFF.FF□□□□□IIIIIIIIIIIIIII
```

The table heading and two sample output lines are as follows:

```
        EMPLOYEE              RATE        DEPENDENTS
SMITH, JOHN                   55.95               10
WILEY, WILLIAMS              123.00                3
```

Notice that the strings stored in variable NAME (type CHARACTER * 15) appear to be left-aligned rather than right-aligned. This occurs because a string that is too short is padded with blanks when it is stored in NAME. All characters stored, including the blank padding, are displayed when the value of NAME is printed. ■

Format Specifications in PRINT Statements

Generally when debugging programs, we need to insert debugging statements that print key variable values. We can use a shorter version of formatted PRINT statements for this purpose.

Fortran permits us to insert a format specification string directly in a PRINT statement. In the following statement, the string '(1X, A, I2)' appears after the word PRINT (instead of a statement label) and eliminates the need for a separate FORMAT statement. Don't forget the comma after this string.

```
PRINT '(1X, A, I2)', 'Value of COUNT is ', COUNT
```

This form is particularly convenient when the format specification is relatively short, as it would be in PRINT statements used for debugging. Assuming COUNT has the integer value 37, this formatted PRINT statement above would display the output line

```
Value of COUNT is 37
```

The edit descriptor A causes the string value to be printed in an output field that matches the string length.

In the format specification string '(1X, A, I2)', the symbols 1X denote a blank line-control character. You also can use a string to denote the line-control character, as follows:

```
PRINT '(''0'', A, I2)', 'Value of COUNT is ', COUNT
```

In this case, the line-control character is the symbol 0, which specifies double line spacing, therefore Fortran would insert a blank line before displaying the output list. Ensure you place two consecutive apostrophes on each side of the line-control character (''0'') inside a format specification string used with a PRINT statement.

EXERCISES FOR SECTION 5.1

Self-check

1. Which of the following format specifications are correct? Which contain syntax errors? Correct any syntax errors you find.

   a. (A, 3X, I4, F12.2)
   b. (A, 4I, 2X, F12.1)
   c. (A, F16.35X)
   d. (A, 2A, F3.3, X6)
   e. (A, I4, 4X, F4.2)

2. Let K contain the value 1234 and ALPHA contain the value 555.4567. What would be printed by each of the following statements?

   a. PRINT '(1X, I4, F12.4)', K, ALPHA
   b. PRINT '(1X, I4, 4X, F8.4)', K, ALPHA
   c. PRINT '(1X, A, I4)', 'K = ', K
   d. PRINT '(1X, A, F8.2)', 'ALPHA = ', ALPHA
   e. PRINT '(1X, A, I5, 10X, A, F10.3)', 'K = ', K, 'ALPHA = ', ALPHA

Programming

1. Consider these variable values:

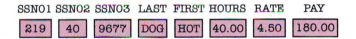

SSNO1	SSNO2	SSNO3	LAST	FIRST	HOURS	RATE	PAY
219	40	9677	DOG	HOT	40.00	4.50	180.00

Write a segment of a Fortran program (including declarations) to produce the following output:

```
Line 1      SOCIAL SECURITY NUMBER 219-40-9677
Line 2
Line 3      DOG, HOT
Line 4
Line 5      HOURS RATE PAY
Line 6      40.00 4.50 180.00
```

5.2 Problem Solving Illustrated

In the next case study, we perform a sequence of computations and use formatted output to display the results in a table.

Case Study: Computing Maximum Tensile Loads

PROBLEM STATEMENT

Joe Bob's steel company produces steel reinforcing bars (*rebars*). The size of a rebar is designated by a number. That number divided by 8 gives the diameter of the bar in inches; for example, a number 5 rebar is $\frac{5}{8}$ of an inch in diameter. The company needs to produce a chart showing the maximum tensile load of the bars when they are made from certain grades of steel. Joe Bob makes number 2 to number 11 rebars. Each chart should have the form shown next.

```
              Joe Bob's Steel Company
                 Rebar load chart
For bars with a steel strength of  8000.00 psi


Bar                 Cross-sectional           Max. Load
Number               Area (sq. in.)            (lbs.)
                    ───────────────           ─────────
    2                    0.05                    393.
    3                    0.11                    884.
    4                    0.20                   1571.
    5                    0.31                   2454.
    6                    0.44                   3534.
    7                    0.60                   4811.
    8                    0.79                   6283.
    9                    0.99                   7952.
   10                    1.23                   9817.
   11                    1.48                  11879.
```

ANALYSIS

The maximum tensile load on a bar is the amount of force the bar can hold in tension. It is calculated by multiplying the cross-sectional area of the bar by the tensile strength of the steel, as follows:

load = area × steel strength.

For a given tensile strength, we can display each line of the preceding table by first determining the cross-sectional area corresponding to that number rebar. We then can use the formula given above to compute the maximum load.

Data Requirements and Relevant Formula

Problem Parameters

first rebar number in the table (INTEGER FIRBAR)
last rebar number in the table (INTEGER LASBAR)

Problem Input

tensile strength of the steel (REAL STRNTH)

Problem Outputs

the rebar number (INTEGER BARNUM)
the cross-sectional area (REAL AREA)
the maximum tensile load (REAL LOAD)

Relevant Formula

$$load \ = \ area \ \times \ steel \ strength$$

DESIGN

The algorithm follows:

Algorithm

1. Read the steel strength.
2. Display the table heading.
3. Display a table showing the rebar number, cross-sectional area, and maximum load for each rebar from FIRBAR to LASBAR.

Algorithm Refinements

For Step 3, we need a loop to find and display the area and load for each rebar. Its refinements follow.

Step 3 Refinement

3.1 DO for each rebar from number FIRBAR through LASBAR
    3.2 Compute the cross-sectional area
    3.3 LOAD = AREA * STRNTH
    3.4 Display rebar number, area, and load
END DO

Additional Program Variable

the radius of the cross-section (REAL RADIUS)

Step 3.2 Refinement

3.2.1 *radius = rebar number*/16.0
3.2.2 Compute the area of a circle given its radius.

Figure 5.1. *Computing Table of Loads for Rebars*

```
      PROGRAM REBAR
C  Prints a table of maximum tensile load on rebars
C  Declarations
      INTEGER FIRBAR, LASBAR
      PARAMETER (FIRBAR = 2, LASBAR = 11)
      REAL PI
      PARAMETER (PI = 3.14159)
      REAL STRNTH, AREA, LOAD, RADIUS
      INTEGER BARNUM

C  Read steel strength
      PRINT *, 'Enter steel tensile strength (in psi)'
      READ *, STRNTH

C  Display table heading
      PRINT 1, 'Joe Bob''s Steel Company'
    1 FORMAT (11X, A)
      PRINT 2, 'Rebar load chart'
    2 FORMAT (15X, A)
      PRINT 3, 'For bars with a steel strength of ', STRNTH, ' psi'
    3 FORMAT (1X, A, F7.1, A)
      PRINT *
      PRINT 4, 'Bar   ', 'Cross-sectional', 'Max Load'
      PRINT 4, 'Number', 'Area (sq. in.) ', ' (lbs.) '
      PRINT 4, '_____', '_____', '_____'
    4 FORMAT (1X, A, 10X, A, 10X, A)

C  Perform calculations and print table.
      DO 10 BARNUM = FIRBAR, LASBAR
         RADIUS = REAL(BARNUM) / 16.0
         AREA = PI * RADIUS ** 2
         LOAD = AREA * STRNTH
         PRINT 5, BARNUM, AREA, LOAD

   10 CONTINUE

      STOP
      END
```

IMPLEMENTATION

Figure 5.1 shows the program.

TESTING AND VERIFICATION

A sample run would begin with the prompt

```
Enter steel tensile strength (in psi)
```

If a positive data value is entered, the program should display a meaningful table of values (see sample table at the beginning of the case study).

EXERCISE FOR SECTION 5.2

Programming

1. Add statements to compute the weight per linear foot of each rebar. Steel has a weight of 490 lb/cu ft.

5.3   Formatted Input

Partitioning a Data Line into Fields

The function of an input format is analogous to that of an output format. Output formats provide a line-by-line description of the external appearance of data that are to be printed. Input formats, on the other hand, are normally used to describe the line-by-line appearance of input data.

The format specification in a formatted READ statement partitions the data line (sometimes called a *record*) into fields. It may cause some columns to be skipped and enables strings to be typed without enclosing quotes. You should not include a line-control character in a format specification used for input.

As was the case with list-directed input, each execution of a READ statement causes at least one new data line to be read. The data items in these lines are placed into the memory cells designated by the input list.

EXAMPLE 5.8

An important benefit of using formatted input is that it allows us to type in a character data item without enclosing apostrophes. The formatted READ statement

```
PRINT *, 'Enter your first name:'
READ '(A)', NAME
```

reads character data into character variable NAME. The format specifier A tells Fortran that character data will be read, so type in only the letters starting in column 1; for example, enter Bill Jones instead of 'Bill Jones'.   ■

EXAMPLE 5.9   If the data 07–04–91 are typed in columns 1–8 of a data line, then the statements

```
    READ 62, MONTH, DAY, YEAR
62 FORMAT (I2, 1X, I2, 1X, I2)
```

will have the following effect.

MONTH	DAY	YEAR
7	4	91

FORMAT 62 partitions the data line into five fields, as shown next. Three of these fields contain integer data that are stored in memory, and two fields (columns 3 and 6) are skipped. The column numbers are shown under the data.

```
07 - 04 - 91
12 3 45 6 78 9 10 . . .
```

EXAMPLE 5.10   The list-directed READ statement

```
READ *, FIRST, LAST, IDEMPL, HOURS, RATE, OTHRS

'JOHN' 'CAGE'  37458   35.0   6.75   0.0
1 2 3 4 5 6 7 8910111213141516171819202122232425262728293031323334 35
```

will cause the data line that follows it to be read and its contents to be stored in memory, as shown next, where FIRST and LAST are type CHARACTER *4.

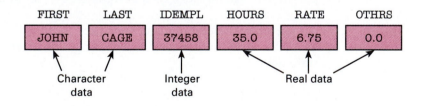

FIRST	LAST	IDEMPL	HOURS	RATE	OTHRS
JOHN	CAGE	37458	35.0	6.75	0.0

Character data   Integer data   Real data

Given a similar line without apostrophes, the statements

```
    READ 25, FIRST, LAST, IDEMPL, HOURS, RATE, OTHRS
25 FORMAT (1X, A4, 3X, A4, 2X, I5, 1X, F5.1, 1X, F4.2, 1X, F4.1)
```

will have the same effect. FORMAT 25 partitions the data line into the following fields.

JOHN		CAGE		37458		35.0	6.75		0.0
1	2 3 4 5	6 7 8	9 101112	1314	1516171819	20	2122232425	26	27282930	31	32333435

To see why the second set of statements has the same effect as the first statement, you need to understand the meaning of the edit descriptors listed in FORMAT 25. They are described in Table 5.7. ■

Table 5.7. *Meaning of Edit Descriptors in FORMAT 25*

EDIT DESCRIPTOR	CORRESPONDING INPUT LIST ITEM	MEANING
1X	None	Skip the first column in the line.
A4	FIRST	Treat the next four columns in the line (2–5, in this case) as a field containing a string (JOHN), which is to be stored in the variable FIRST.
3X	None	Skip the next three columns in the line (columns 6, 7, and 8).
A4	LAST	Treat the next four columns in the line (9–12) as a field containing a string (CAGE), which is to be stored in the variable LAST.
2X	None	Skip the next two columns in the line (columns 13, 14).
I5	IDEMPL	Treat the next five columns (15–19) as containing a five-digit integer (37458) to be stored in variable IDEMPL.
1X	None	Skip the next column in the line (column 20).
F5.1	HOURS	Treat the next five columns (21–25) as containing a real number (35.0) with one digit (0) to the right of the decimal point. This number is to be stored in variable HOURS.
1X	None	Skip the next column in the line (column 26).
F4.2	RATE	Treat the next four columns (27–30) as containing a real number (6.75) with two digits (75) to the right of the decimal point. This number is to be stored in variable RATE.
1X	None	Skip the next column in the line (column 31).
F4.1	OTHRS	Treat the next four columns (32–35) as containing a real number (0.0), with one digit to the right of the decimal point. This number is to be stored in the variable OTHRS.

The rules that must be followed when using formatted input are summarized next.

Rules for Formatted Input

1. The FORMAT statement determines which data columns are to be skipped and which are to be read. It also describes the type and width (number of columns) of the information contained in each field and the number of decimal places in each type real data item.
2. As is the case with output formats, all edit descriptors in an input format should be separated from one another with commas.
3. The data descriptors (A, F, or I) must be compatible with the corresponding variable type (character, real, or integer). Also, the type of data in the data field must be compatible with the data descriptor (i.e., digits and a sign for I; digits, a sign, and a decimal point for F).
4. The field width (w) information for each data descriptor, where w is an integer constant, immediately follows the type indication.

    Aw: The A indicates that a string of characters is to be read into a memory cell; the w indicates the total width (or number of characters) contained in the string. If the w is omitted, the field width is the same as the length of the corresponding input variable. Any legal Fortran character may appear in the string. If the length, w, of the data string is less than the length, n, of the variable, then the string will be stored with blank padding on the right. If the length, w, of the data string is greater than the length, n, of the variable, then only the rightmost n characters of the string will be stored.

    Iw: I indicates that a type integer value is to be read. The w indicates the width (the number of decimal digits) contained in the integer.

    F$w.d$: F indicates that a type real value is to be read. The w indicates the total width (including the sign and the decimal point); the d indicates the number of decimal places in the real number that are assumed to be to the right of the decimal point if no explicit decimal point appears.

5. The edit descriptor nX indicates that a field of n columns is to be skipped. These columns need not contain blanks; they will be skipped regardless of what they contain.
6. It is not necessary that the data occupying a character, integer, or real data field fill the entire field. However, the following guidelines should be followed:

    a. Integer values should appear in the rightmost portion of the field.

    b. Real values may appear anywhere in the field as long as the decimal point is included. If the decimal point is not typed, the number should appear in the rightmost portion of the field and the decimal point will be assumed to be placed as indicated by the d parameter of the edit descriptor. If the decimal point is typed, then it overrides the d parameter in the Fw.d edit descriptor.

This rule is concerned with the position of real and integer values in a data field. These values generally should be right-justified, since some systems may read any blanks in an integer or real data field as zeros. An I or F field with all blanks will be read as the number 0. Real values may be typed with or without a decimal point.

EXAMPLE 5.11   Given the READ statement

```
    READ 672, X, Y, Z
672 FORMAT (F4.1, F4.2, F4.2)
```

and the data line

```
 −25 6.3   .623
1 2 3 4 5 6 7 8 9 10 11 12
```

the real variables X, Y, and Z will be defined as

X	Y	Z
−2.5	6.3	.623

In the first field, the decimal point is assumed to be between the 2 and the 5, according to the edit descriptor F4.1. In the last two fields, the decimal point overrides the edit descriptor.

The general form of the edit descriptors used in input formats is summarized in Table 5.8.

Table 5.8. *Edit Descriptors for Formatted Input*

EDIT DESCRIPTOR	MEANING
nX	A field of n columns is to be skipped.
Iw	A field of width w (w columns) is to be treated as an integer.
Aw	A field of width w is to be treated as a character string. The w may be omitted.
Fw.d	A field of width w is to be treated as a real number with d digits to the right of the decimal point. If a decimal point is present, it overrides the d specification.

Often you may want to echo print data being read. In such cases, it is tempting to try the same FORMAT statement for both the READ and the PRINT statements. You should avoid this temptation because there is no guarantee that the first character read will be suitable for use as a carriage-control character for printing.

EXAMPLE 5.12

The program in Fig. 5.2 uses Manning's equation, shown next, to calculate the flow of water through a pipe:

$$Q = \frac{1.49}{N} AR^{2/3}S^{1/2},$$

where Q is the flow of water (cubic feet per sec), N is the roughness coefficient (unitless), A is the area (square feet), R is the hydraulic radius (feet), and S is the slope (feet/foot). For readability, the program uses the variables FLOW, RUFNES (for roughness coefficient), AREA, RADIUS, and SLOPE.

Figure 5.2. *Computing Flow Using Manning's Equation*

```
      PROGRAM MANING
C Computes the flow of water through a pipe
C in cubic feet per second (cfs)

C Declarations
      CHARACTER STREET *30
      REAL FLOW, RUFNES, AREA, RADIUS, SLOPE

C Enter data
      PRINT *, 'Enter street name'
      READ '(A)', STREET
      PRINT *, 'Enter each item under its units on the 3rd line below:
      PRINT 15, ' roughness,' , 'area,' ,
     +           'hydraulic radius,' , 'and slope'
      PRINT 15, '(unitless),' , '(sq. ft.),' ,
     +           '(feet),' , '(feet/foot)'
   15 FORMAT (1X, A11, A11, A18, A12)
      READ 25, RUFNES, AREA, RADIUS, SLOPE
   25 FORMAT (F11.4, F11.4, F18.4, F12.4)

C Perform calculations
      FLOW = (1.49/RUFNES) * AREA * (RADIUS ** (2.0/3.0)) *
     +          SQRT(SLOPE)
```

```
C Display the input values and display results
      PRINT '(''0'', A)', 'City of Byran Civil Engineering Report'
      PRINT '(1X, A, A)', 'Hydraulic data for ', STREET
      PRINT *
      PRINT '(1X, A, F6.4)', 'The roughness coefficient is ',
     +                       RUFNES
      PRINT '(1X, A, F6.2, A)', 'The area of the culvert is ',
     +                       AREA, ' square feet'
      PRINT '(1X, A, F5.2, A)', 'The hydraulic radius is ',
     +                       RADIUS, ' feet'
      PRINT '(1X, A, F7.5, A)', 'The slope is ', SLOPE,
     +                       ' feet/foot'
      PRINT *
      PRINT '(1X, A, F8.1, A)', 'The calculated flow is ', FLOW,
     +                       ' cfs'

      STOP
      END


Enter street name
Aggie Drive
Enter each item under its units on the 3rd line below:
 roughness,        area, hydraulic radius,    and slope
(unitless), (sq. ft.),             (feet), (feet/foot)
  .0130        28.27               1.5       .0015

City of Byran Civil Engineering Report
Hydraulic data for Aggie Drive

The roughness coefficient is .0130
The area of the culvert is  28.27 square feet
The hydraulic radius is  1.50 feet
The slope is .00150 feet/foot

The calculated flow is     164.4 cfs
```

In Fig. 5.2, formatted READ statements are used to enter all input data. Two PRINT statements use FORMAT statement 15 to align lines 4 and 5 of the program output. The READ statement uses FORMAT statement 25 to enter four data items that should be typed on line 6 under their units (e.g., 28.27 under (sq. ft.)). The remaining formats are inserted directly as strings in PRINT statements.

EXERCISES FOR SECTION 5.3

Self-check

1. For the READ statement

```
      READ 15, NAME, X, N
```

what data values are stored for the following FORMAT statements when NAME is type CHARACTER *8, X is type REAL, and N is type INTEGER? Assume the data line

```
Silly Me34567*/@ 23
```

starts in column 1.

a. 15 FORMAT (A, F5.2, 3X, I3)
b. 15 FORMAT (A10, 6X, F3.1)
c. 15 FORMAT (2X, A6, F3.1, I2)
d. 15 FORMAT (2X, A, F2.1, I1)
e. 15 FORMAT (A10, F3.2, 4X, I2)

2. You are given the following declarations and READ statement:

```
REAL ALPHA, BETA
INTEGER GAMMA, EPS
CHARACTER *4 DELTA
READ 30, ALPHA, GAMMA, DELTA, BETA, EPS
```

Write FORMAT 30 so that the information in the following three data lines shown on the left will be read in as indicated on the right.

```
   16.3
1 2 3 4 5 6 7 8 9 10 11

   12    DAWN
1 2 3 4 5 6 7 8 9 10 11

  -32.1 49
1 2 3 4 5 6 7 8 9 10 11
```

ALPHA	GAMMA	DELTA	BETA	EPS
16.3	12	DAWN	-32.1	49

3. How would you type the data shown in exercise 2 if FORMAT 30 appeared as shown below?

```
30 FORMAT (F3.1, I2, A4, F4.1, 3X, I3)
```

Programming

1. You are given a data line with the following format:

Columns	Contents	Sample Data
1–11	Social security number	552-63-0179
12–31	Last name	BROWN
32–44	First name	JERRY
45	Middle initial	L
46–48	Blanks	
49–50	Age	58
51–54	Blanks	

Columns	Contents	Sample Data
55–59	Total years of education	23
60–63	Blanks	
64–66	Occupation code	12
67–80	Blanks	

Assign variable names to the data in each of the nonblank fields. Give these names appropriate types and write a READ statement and appropriate FORMAT for reading such a line. Draw a picture of the line and show how the sample data would be arranged in each field (left-adjusted, right-adjusted, and so on).

2. Design a data line layout for an account records program. For each account, the following information must appear on a single line:

Information	Form
Account number	A 6-digit integer
Name of firm	Character string (maximum width of 25)
Previous account balance	A real number between -9999.99 and 9999.99
Charges for current month	A real number between 0.0 and 999.99
Credits for current month	A real number between 0.0 and 999.99
Total amount due	A real number between -999.99 and 999.99

Ensure there is at least one space between each of the six data items listed. Write the appropriate variable declarations, READ statement, and FORMAT statement for reading in the line you designed.

3. Suppose you decided you did not want to have to type the decimal points in the four real values in exercise 2 and you didn't want to bother typing zero entries (if any) for these four values. Will your Fortran statements for exercise 2 still work? Why? If not, change them.

5.4 More Edit Descriptors

In this section, we introduce three additional edit descriptors: T, /, and E.

The T Descriptor We discussed the alignment of output columns in Section 5.1. The x descriptor was used to position output data under column headings. This can be done more easily using the T descriptor, which is analogous to setting a tab position on a typewriter.

EXAMPLE 5.13   The following statements print a line of column labels at the top of a page followed by a line of output data:

```
    PRINT 35
35 FORMAT ('1', 'NAME', T15, 'SALARY', T25, 'DEPENDENTS')
    PRINT 45, NAME, GROSS, DEPEND
45 FORMAT (1X, A10, T15, F6.2, T25, I5)
```

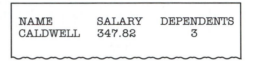

```
NAME        SALARY    DEPENDENTS
CALDWELL    347.82        3
```

The edit descriptors T15 and T25 cause an advance to positions 15 and 25 of the output line. You must be careful when specifying tab positions. For example, in FORMAT 35, if T20 was specified instead of T25, SALARDEPENDENTS would be printed as the second column heading.

Remember that the carriage control character may occupy position 1 of the output line even though it is not displayed. If it does this, the column label SALARY will begin in position 14 of the display screen, not position 15. ◼

The Slash Descriptor

We can use a single FORMAT statement to describe the appearance of more than one line of output. The slash, /, may be used in a format specification to separate the description of one output line from the next. When a slash is encountered, the current line is terminated and a new line is started.

A string of consecutive slashes has the effect of causing blank lines to appear on a page. If the slashes are in the middle of the format specification, the number of blank lines will be one less than the number of consecutive slashes. The number of blank lines will be equal to the number of slashes if the slashes appear at the very beginning or very end of the format specification. Commas are not required to separate consecutive slashes or to separate slashes from other edit descriptors. A large number of consecutive slashes may be indicated using the descriptor form $n(/)$, where n is a positive integer constant indicating the number of slashes to be used.

EXAMPLE 5.14   The statements

```
    PRINT 18, X, Y
18 FORMAT (1X, F8.2, 5(/), 1X, F8.2)
```

cause four blank lines to appear between the values of X and Y. The first slash in FORMAT 18 terminates the output line containing the value of X; the next four slashes terminate blank output lines.

The format specification begins with the edit descriptor 1X, which represents a blank space. This blank would be used for carriage control.   ■

EXAMPLE 5.15   The statements

```
   READ 15, MONTH, RATE, MINUTS, YEAR
15 FORMAT (A8 / F10.4 / I6, I4)
```

describe the appearance of 3 data lines. The first line is described as containing one field that is to be treated as a character string of width 8. The second line is described as having a field of width 10 containing a real number. If the decimal point is not typed in this number, it will be assumed to be between the digits in columns 6 and 7. The third line is described as containing two integer fields, the first of width 6 and the second of width 4.   ■

EXAMPLE 5.16   The Raisem Higher Home Loan Association maintains lists of home loan mortgage interest payments. A sample page of these lists is shown next.

```
RAISEM HIGHER HOME LOAN ASSOCIATION          07-04-91

HOME LOAN MORTGAGE INTEREST PAYMENT TABLES

AMOUNT = $30000.00   LOAN DURATION (MONTHS) = 300

RATE (PERCENT)  MONTHLY PAYMENT      TOTAL PAYMENT
     10.50            XXX.XX            XXXXXX.XX
     10.75            XXX.XX            XXXXXX.XX


     13.50            349.69            104908.04


     16.00            XXX.XX            XXXXXX.XX
```

The person who wrote the program to print this table used the following six variables:

1. The date the loan was made (CHARACTER *8 DATE)
2. The amount of the loan (REAL AMOUNT)
3. The period of time (in months) for loan repayment (INTEGER MONTHS)
4. The interest rate (percent) applied to the loan (REAL RATE)
5. The monthly payment required from the borrower (REAL MPAYMT)
6. Total amount to be paid over the entire loan period (REAL TPAYMT)

The program contains three PRINT statements:

a.   PRINT 26, DATE, AMOUNT, MONTHS
       26 FORMAT ('1', 'RAISEM HIGHER HOME LOAN ASSOCIATION', 9X, A8/
          + '0', 'HOME LOAN MORTGAGE INTEREST PAYMENT TABLES'/
          + '0', 'AMOUNT = $', F8.2, 6X, 'LOAN DURATION (MONTHS) = ', I3)

b.   PRINT 27
       27 FORMAT ('0', 'RATE (PERCENT)', 4X, 'MONTHLY PAYMENT', 4X,
          + 'TOTAL PAYMENT')

c.   PRINT 28, RATE, MPAYMT, TPAYMT
       28 FORMAT (1X, 5X, F5.2, 13X, F6.2, 10X, F9.2)

Together, these three statements produce the sample page of output just shown. Statement (a) prints the three lines of page-heading information that appear at the top of the page. The values of the variables DATE, AMOUNT, and MONTHS are included as part of the heading. Statement (b) prints the column heading labels, and statement (c) is used inside a loop in the program to print the numbers appearing in each output line, the values of RATE, MPAYMT, TPAYMT.

You should convince yourself that FORMATS 26, 27, and 28 do indeed produce the output shown in Example 5.16. To help you, Table 5.9 provides a detailed description of the formation of the three output lines defined in FORMAT 26.

Table 5.9. *FORMAT Statement 26*

EDIT DESCRIPTOR	CORRESPONDING OUTPUT LIST ITEM	MEANING
Line 1 of FORMAT 26		
'1', 'RAISEM ... ASSOCIATION'	None	The string 'RAISEM ... ASSOCIATION' is to be entered into the line being formed. (The 1 is not printed; it is used for carriage control.)
9X	None	A field of nine blanks is to be entered into the line being formed.
A8	DATE	A field of width 8 (eight print positions) is to be used to print the character string stored in DATE.
/	None	Indicates the end of the output line being formed.

(continued)

EDIT DESCRIPTOR	CORRESPONDING OUTPUT LIST ITEM	MEANING
First Continuation Line		
`'0'`, `'HOME ...` `TABLES'`	None	The string `'HOME ...` `TABLES'` is to be entered into the line being formed. (The 0 is not printed; it is used for carriage control.)
`/`	None	Indicates the end of an output line.
Second Continuation Line		
`'0'`, `'AMOUNT = $'`	None	The string `'AMOUNT = $'` is to be entered into the line being formed. (The 0 is not printed; it is used for carriage control.)
`F8.2`	AMOUNT	A field of width 8 is to be used to print the real number stored in AMOUNT (two digits will appear to the right of the decimal point).
`6X`	None	Indicates six spaces are to be skipped.
`'LOAN ...` `MONTHS) = '`	None	The string `'LOAN ...` `MONTHS) = '` is to be entered into the line being formed.
`I3`	MONTHS	A field of width 3 is to be used to print the integer stored in MONTHS.

The E Format Descriptor

Another method for reading (or displaying) real numbers is to use the E format descriptor (rather than F). A number to be read under E format must be typed in exponential notation, using the letter E. The E descriptor $Ew.d$ contains a total width specification, w, and a count of the number of decimal digits to the right of the decimal point, d. However, the width specification must include not only the sign and the decimal point (if present), but also the letter E and the sign and the value of the integer exponent. Thus, in the E format descriptor, w should normally be larger than $d + 5$.

For example, the number

$$-6.245E-6$$

could be read using a format descriptor of E9.3. Here again, if the decimal point appears in the data line, it overrides the *d* parameter of the E descriptor.

The E format descriptor also may be used for printing real data. Often, it is convenient to use the E descriptor when the magnitude of a real number is not known or it is so large that the use of the F format descriptor is impractical. Real data printed using the E format descriptor will usually appear in the form

$$\pm 0.X_1X_2 \ldots X_dE\pm exp$$

where the X_i are the *d* most significant digits of the number (after rounding) and *exp* is the base 10 exponent. When the E descriptor is used for output, *w* must include the zero (if present), the two signs, the decimal point, the E, and the width of the exponent, as well as the *d* digits to the right of the decimal point. Therefore *w* should always be greater than $d + 7$ when E*w.d* is used in output (the exponent should not exceed two digits in width).

EXAMPLE 5.17 The READ statement

```
    READ 37, INDEX, A, B, C
37 FORMAT (I5, E10.3, E10.3, E10.3)
```

will cause the information in the data line

36	6.107E+02	3.993E+4	−92.6E−3
1 2 3 4 5	6 7 8 9 10 11 12 13 14 15	16 17 18 19 20 21 22 23 24 25	26 27 28 29 30 31 32 33 34 35

to be placed in the named variables as follows.

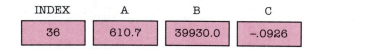

INDEX	A	B	C
36	610.7	39930.0	−.0926

Repeating Edit Descriptors

We can use a shorthand notation to indicate that we want to repeat one or more edit descriptors in a FORMAT statement. For example, the statements

```
    READ 15, X, Y, Z
15 FORMAT (3F3.2)
```

read data into three type REAL variables (X, Y, Z) from the first nine columns of a data line. The FORMAT statement is equivalent to the following:

```
15 FORMAT (F3.2, F3.2, F3.2)
```

We also can specify that we want to repeat a group of edit descriptors. For example, the statements

```
    PRINT 25, X, Y, Z
25 FORMAT (1X, 3(F6.2, 5X))
```

display three type REAL values on a single output line. The descriptor group—(F6.2, 5X)—is repeated three times, so each value is displayed in a field of six columns accurate to two decimal places; there are five spaces between values.

EXERCISES FOR SECTION 5.4

Self-check

1. Show the lines printed by the following fragment:

```
    FIRST = 20
    SECOND = 12225.0123
    PRINT 15, 'FIRST IS ', FIRST, 'SECOND IS ', SECOND
15 FORMAT (1X, A, T10, I2 // 1X, A, T15, E14.7)
```

Programming

1. Write the PRINT and FORMAT statements using the T edit descriptor that will display the following table form. Assume the label Month starts in the first output column, label Supplies starts in column 13, label Salaries starts in column 27, and label Miscellaneous starts in column 40.

```
Month      Supplies  Salaries  Miscellaneous
AAAAAAAAA  FFFFF.FF  FFFF.FF    FFFF.FF
```

The Fortran variables that will be displayed are MONTH (type CHARACTER *9), SUPPLY, SALARY, and MISC (all type REAL).

5.5 Files and Batch Processing

Interactive Mode and Batch Mode

There are two basic modes of computer operation: interactive and batch. The programs we have written so far are intended to be run in interactive mode. In *interactive mode*, the program user can interact with the program and enter data while the program is executing. In *batch mode*, the program user cannot interact with the program while it is executing. To use batch mode, you first must prepare a data file before you can execute your program. When a program executes in batch mode, the READ statements enter data from a data file instead of the keyboard.

You can use a system editor to create and save a *data file* just like you do a program file. Starting with an empty file, type in all data items in the sequence in which they will be read by the program when it executes. Press the RETURN or ENTER key after each line. After you have typed in all the data lines, you can edit any incorrect data values. Finally, you would need to name the file and save it as a file on disk.

Until now, we have displayed all program results on the screen. Doing this,

FORTRAN in Focus

Engineering Consulting with Fortran

HMF ASSOCIATES

HMF Associates is a small consulting firm founded by Howard Fishman, a practicing engineer who takes on engineering problems for a variety of clients. Companies go to Fishman for analytic and numerical solutions to their mechanical, dynamic, and structural engineering problems. He may develop a model to verify the adequacy of a structural system, such as a building's ability to withstand an earthquake's impact or a boiler's behavior under extreme pressure, or the software tools he creates may be used in the design of proprietary hardware.

One such hardware design assignment illustrates the role of Fortran in the consulting work done by HMF Associates. A client wished to design a bearing system that would meet an unusual set of performance characteristics. The cost of procuring hardware on a trial-and-error basis is prohibitive, so HMF Associates was retained to simulate and test the design of the bearing system before it was manufactured. The "on-paper" design required the solution of the nonlinear fluid-film lubrication problem for the special case of compliant bearing surfaces. HMF developed a software product that would solve this problem for a wide range of parameters.

HMF Associates used Fortran to implement the solution algorithm. When solving a problem of this complexity, a large number of iterations are necessary to converge to a valid solution. Howard Fishman works with Fortran-77 on an IBM-PC compatible 386-20 MHz computer, using a text editor and a simple batch file to compile and link his programs. Fortran was selected for this application because some of the matrix operations and mathematical subroutines had already been developed for other products and could be reused with little or no modifications. While developing

however, results in no permanent record of a program's output; the output disappears when it scrolls off the screen. To produce a permanent output record in Fortran, you can have the program write the results to an *output file*. An output file doesn't normally exist on the system disk before the program begins execution. During execution, however, the program writes program results to the output file, thereby saving this information as a file on the system disk.

and testing the algorithm, he has the program prompt him for input and write to the screen periodically so he can monitor the data being generated. Once an algorithm is tested and verified, he writes an input file and has the program create an output file without printing to the screen.

The bearing system design application was to be run primarily on the client's 486 system. Its different compiler was not limited to the memory constraints of the 386 machine, but transporting the Fortran code to the new compiler was easily achieved and revealed few inconsistencies. The PARAMETER and IN-CLUDE statements in Fortran also made it easy to modify the program to run the larger problems required by the client.

When HMF is asked to create a graphical user interface for a client, C and, less frequently, BASIC are used for the development of an interface that links to the Fortran

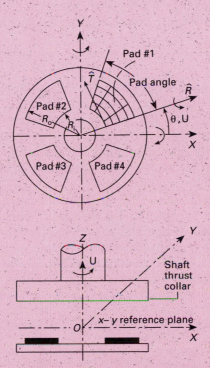

MATHEMATICAL MODEL OF THRUST BEARING. (COURTESY OF RBTS, INC.)

module. Sometimes less computationally intensive algorithms are developed with the use of spreadsheets.

Howard Fishman's 30 years of experience writing software in Fortran is his primary reason for using it. He points

to Fortran's long history of providing engineers with an analytic tool that is readable, accurate, and relatively easy to use. The various extensions of Fortran-77 have made Fortran a modern structured language, while maintaining compatibility with older versions. Given the work that he does, a standard hardware-independent screen interface would be an appealing way in which Fortran could continue to be improved. He personally finds Fortran to be a very intuitive language, requiring infrequent reference to documentation, and recommends that engineering students continue to learn Fortran so that they may use and expand the wealth of existing engineering software.

Our thanks to Howard Fishman, President of HMF Associates in Elkins Park, Pennsylvania, for talking with us about the engineering consulting he does using Fortran as a tool.

The Open Statement

Before it can read or write a file, the computer system must be provided with some basic information about the file. For example, it must know the name of the file being accessed and whether the file is a data file—a file previously created using an editor—or an output file—a file that will be created by the program's execution. The OPEN statements communicate this information. For example, the OPEN statement

```
OPEN (UNIT = 1, FILE = 'MEASURE', STATUS = 'OLD')
```

indicates that the file associated with UNIT number 1 is an existing (STATUS = 'OLD') data file saved on disk under the FILE name MEASURE. The OPEN statement

```
OPEN (UNIT = 2, FILE = 'RESULTS', STATUS = 'NEW')
```

indicates that the file associated with UNIT number 2 is a new (STATUS = 'NEW') output file that will be created and saved on disk under the FILE name RESULTS. The unit number will be used in subsequent program statements to identify which file is being processed (1 for file MEASURE, 2 for file RESULTS). The file name appears only in the OPEN statement and is the name under which the file would be listed on the system disk. Check with your instructor to see if your system has restrictions on file names.

On most systems, the unit numbers are chosen arbitrarily and you can use any integer except 5 and 6, which are preassigned. (See the section below, "Unit Numbers for the Keyboard and Display Screen," for further explanation of assigned numbers 5 and 6.) The unit number for each OPEN statement must be unique and must match the unit number appearing in all READ or WRITE statements that process that file. The OPEN statement for a particular unit number must precede the first READ or WRITE statement that references that unit number.

SYNTAX DISPLAY

OPEN Statement

SYNTAX: OPEN (UNIT = *unum*, FILE = *fname*, STATUS = *fstat*)

EXAMPLES: OPEN (UNIT = 1, FILE = 'MYDATA', STATUS = 'OLD')
 OPEN (UNIT = 2, FILE = 'MYOUT', STATUS = 'NEW')

INTERPRETATION: The OPEN statement prepares a file for processing. It specifies the unit number, *unum*, associated with file *fname*. It also tells Fortran the status, *fstat*, of the file to be processed. The file specifier *unum* must be an integer not associated with another file. The file specifier *fstat* must be the string 'NEW' (for an output file) or 'OLD' (for an existing data file).

Reading a Data File

To read information from a data file, you must use a modified form of the READ statement. If X and Y are two type REAL variables, the READ statement

```
READ (1, *) X, Y
```

reads a pair of real numbers from the next line of the data file associated with unit number 1 (file MEASURE). Each READ statement used with a data file must specify the unit number (in this case, 1) of the file being processed. The symbol * indicates that the read operation is list-directed. There is no comma between the close parenthesis and the output list X, Y.

We also can use FORMAT statements with data files. The READ statement

```
READ (1, 25) X, Y
```

reads a pair of real numbers from the data file associated with unit number 1 using FORMAT 25.

SYNTAX DISPLAY

READ Statement for a Data File

SYNTAX: READ (*unum, format*) *input list*

EXAMPLES: READ (3, 25) FIRNAM
　　　　　 READ (4, *) X, Y

INTERPRETATION: Data are entered into each variable specified in the input list. The data are taken from the next line of the file associated with unit number *unum*. This association is determined by an OPEN statement, which must execute before the READ statement does. The *format* indicates whether the read operation is list-directed (*format* is *) or formatted (*format* is an integer).

NOTES: Each time a READ statement executes, a new line of the data file is processed starting with the first data item on that line. For this reason, any data items at the end of the previous line that were not processed by the most recently executed READ statement will be skipped. If there are insufficient data values on the first line that is read, data will be taken from the next data line.

Writing to an Output File

The WRITE statements

```
WRITE (2, *) 'The value of X and Y follow:'
WRITE (2, 35) X, Y
```

write two output lines to the file associated with unit number 2 (file RESULTS).

The first WRITE statement writes the message shown using list-directed output; the second writes the values of X and Y using FORMAT 35. Note, normally a line-control character is not written to an output file.

SYNTAX
DISPLAY

WRITE Statement

SYNTAX: WRITE (*unum, format*) *output list*

EXAMPLES: WRITE (3, *) 'Hours is ', HOURS
　　　　　　WRITE (4, 15) X, Y, 'X is larger than Y'

INTERPRETATION: The value of each variable or constant in the *output list* is written to the file associated with unit number *unum*. A string is printed without the enclosing apostrophes. A new output line is started each time a WRITE statement executes. The *format* indicates whether the output operation is list-directed (*format* is *) or formatted (*format* is an integer).

Ensure you understand the differences between PRINT and WRITE. The output list for a PRINT statement appears after a comma; that for a WRITE statement appears after a close parenthesis. The PRINT statement always writes information on the default output device (usually the screen); the WRITE statement can write information not only on the screen but also to a file, with the unit number specified in the statement determining where the file's output values will be sent.

EXAMPLE 5.18

Figure 5.3 rewrites the summation program first shown in Fig. 4.7 as a batch program. All data values are read from file MEASURE. The output file, RESULTS, contains a copy of all the values and the final average. The following PRINT statement

```
PRINT '(I3, A)', NUMMES, ' items were processed'
```

displays a single line that appears on the screen; this line informs the program user that the program has successfully completed its task.

Figure 5.3. *Batch Version of Sum and Average Program*

```
      PROGRAM MEASUR
C Finds the average value of a set of measurements and writes
C each measurement and their average to an output file.
C The units of measurement, the number of values, and the values
C themselves are read from a data file.

C Declarations
      INTEGER NUMMES, COUNT
      REAL ITEM, SUM, AVERGE
      CHARACTER *15 UNITS
```

```
C Open the data file and output file.
      OPEN (UNIT = 1, FILE = 'MEASURE', STATUS = 'OLD')
      OPEN (UNIT = 2, FILE = 'RESULTS', STATUS = 'NEW')

C Read the units of measurement and number of measurements.
      READ (1, 15) UNITS
      READ (1, 25) NUMMES
   15 FORMAT (A)
   25 FORMAT (I3)

C Read each measurement, write it to the output file,
C and add it to the sum.
      WRITE (2, *) 'List of data:'
      SUM = 0
      DO 10 COUNT = 1, NUMMES
          READ (1, 35) ITEM
          WRITE (2, 35) ITEM
   35     FORMAT (F8.2)
          SUM = SUM + ITEM
   10 CONTINUE

C Compute the average value.
      AVERGE = SUM / NUMMES

C Write the average value to the output file.
      WRITE (2, 45) 'The average value is ', AVERGE, UNITS
   45 FORMAT (A, F8.5, 1X, A)

C Write a message to the screen.
      PRINT '(I3, A)', NUMMES, ' items were processed'

C Close files.
      CLOSE (UNIT = 1)
      END FILE (UNIT = 2)
      CLOSE (UNIT = 2)

      STOP
      END
```

```
3 items were processed
```

Table 5.10 shows one data file and its corresponding output file. The statements

```
READ (1, 15) UNITS
READ (1, 25) NUMMES
```

read the first two data lines into UNITS and NUMMES, respectively. Before the loop

Table 5.10. *Sample Data File and Output File*

DATA FILE MEASURE	OUTPUT FILE RESULTS
degrees Celsius	List of data:
3	45.0
45.0	54.6
54.6	100.4
100.4	The average value is 66.66667 degrees Celsius

begins, the statement

```
WRITE (2, *) 'List of data:'
```

writes a table heading as the first line of the output file. Inside the loop, the statements

```
READ (1, 35) ITEM
WRITE (2, 35) ITEM
```

read each data value into ITEM and write it to file RESULTS. Because there is no need to write a line-control character to an output file, FORMAT 35 can be used for both the read and write operations. After loop exit, the statement

```
WRITE (2, 45) 'The average value is ', AVERGE, UNITS
```

writes the computational result to file RESULTS. ■

Two important factors differentiate between the batch version of the program and earlier interactive programs. First, in batch programs no WRITE statements display prompting messages. This occurs because the program reads its data from a previously prepared data file, not from the keyboard. Second, the WRITE statement inside the loop writes a copy (called an *echo*) of each data value saved in ITEM to the output file; therefore the program output will contain a permanent record of the data processed. An interactive program doesn't use this WRITE statement because the data values appear on the screen as they are typed in by the program user.

In Fig. 5.3, a data file is used for program input and an output file is used for program output. You don't need to use an output file when you use a data file, and vice versa. A program that uses a data file can write its output to the screen. Similarly, a program that writes its results to an output file can read its data from the keyboard.

END FILE and CLOSE

The statement

```
END FILE (UNIT = 2)
```

at the bottom of Fig. 5.3 marks the end of the output file by appending a special *end-of-file record* after the last file line. This must be the last record written to every output file.

The statements

```
CLOSE (UNIT = 1)
CLOSE (UNIT = 2)
```

disconnect, or *close*, the files associated with unit numbers 1 and 2 from the program. Every file that is opened should be closed before a program stops execution.

SYNTAX DISPLAY

END FILE Statement

SYNTAX: END FILE (UNIT = *unum*)

INTERPRETATION: The END FILE statement writes a special end-of-file record onto the file specified by *unum*. No data may be written following the end-of-file record.

SYNTAX DISPLAY

CLOSE Statement

SYNTAX: CLOSE (UNIT = *unum*)

INTERPRETATION: The CLOSE statement disconnects the file specified by *unum* from the program. Unit number *unum* can be reconnected to another file.

Unit Numbers for the Keyboard and Display Screen

On most Fortran systems, unit numbers 5 and 6 are preassigned. Generally, unit number 5 is associated with the keyboard and unit number 6 is associated with the display screen. If this is the case on your system, the statements

```
WRITE (6, *) 'Enter hours worked'
READ (5, *) HOURS
```

will display a prompt on the screen (unit 6) and then read the next data value typed on the keyboard (unit 5) into variable HOURS. (On some systems, unit number 6 is associated with the line printer instead of the display screen.)

You also can use the symbol * as a unit number to denote the default input device or output device. Normally, the default input device is the keyboard and the default output device is the screen. If this is the case, the statements

```
WRITE (*, *) 'Enter hours worked'
READ (*, *) HOURS
```

are equivalent to the following simpler ones:

```
PRINT *, 'Enter hours worked'
READ *, HOURS
```

Both sets of statements specify list-directed input/output on the default device.

**The END
Control Specifier**

The END FILE statement in Fig. 5.3 writes a special end-of-file record following the last line in a file. When you use an editor program to create a data file, your computer system also inserts an end-of-file record following the last line of data that you type. Fortran provides an automatic test for this record. The END control specifier can be used with a READ statement to cause a transfer of control when the end-of-file record has been read. We can use this feature to exit out of a loop that is reading and processing a data file.

EXAMPLE 5.19

We can use the program fragment in Fig. 5.4 to replace the DO loop in Fig. 5.3. This loop reads one type REAL data item from each line of the file associated with unit number 1 and accumulates their sum in variable SUM.

The loop repetition condition in Fig. 5.4 is the LOGICAL constant .TRUE., so the loop could execute "forever." The READ statement

```
READ (1, 35, END = 99) ITEM
```

Figure 5.4. *Loop Exit After Reading End-of-file Record*

```
      SUM = 0
      DO WHILE (.TRUE.)
         READ (1, 35, END = 99) ITEM
         WRITE (2, 35) ITEM
35       FORMAT (F8.2)
         SUM = SUM + ITEM
      END DO

C End-of-file record was read.
   99 CONTINUE
```

causes a transfer of control to label 99 right after the end-of-file record is read. In this case, the CONTINUE statement with label 99 is a non-executable statement that marks the continuation point in the program after the transfer of control occurs. Because of the automatic test for the end-of-file record, there is no need to use a special sentinel value to signal the end of the data list. ■

SYNTAX DISPLAY

End-of-File Specifier

SYNTAX: READ (*unum, format,* END = *label*) *input list*

EXAMPLE: READ (1, *, END = 99) NAME, SALARY

INTERPRETATION: The READ statement attempts to satisfy its *input list* by reading data from the file associated with unit number *unum*. If the file contains insufficient data, control transfers to the statement denoted by *label*.

EXERCISES FOR SECTION 5.5

Self-check

1. A Fortran program contains the following OPEN statements:

```
OPEN (UNIT = 15, FILE = 'TEST', STATUS = 'OLD')
OPEN (UNIT = 16, FILE = 'STUFF', STATUS = 'NEW')
```

What would be the effect of each of the following valid statements, assuming X and Y are type REAL variables? Which statements are invalid and why?

a. READ (15, 15) X, Y
b. READ (15, *) X, Y
c. READ (*, 15) X, Y
d. READ (15, *, END = 15) X, Y
e. READ (*, 15, END = 15) X, Y
f. WRITE (15, *) X, Y
g. WRITE (*, 15) X, Y
h. WRITE (*, 20, END = 25) X, Y
i. WRITE (16, 20) X, Y
j. READ (16, 20) X, Y
k. CLOSE (UNIT = 16)
l. END FILE (UNIT = 15)
m. END FILE (UNIT = 16)

Programming

1. Write the OPEN statement needed to connect an existing file named 'TEXT' to unit number 10.
2. Write an OPEN statement for a data file and write a loop that reads a collection of integer values (one per line) from that data file and accumulates their sum in variable SUM. Loop exit should occur after the end-of-file record is reached.

5.6 Problem Solving Illustrated

In the next case study, we analyze a list of data values, looking for local maxima or peaks in the data. This kind of data analysis is quite common, and some relatively sophisticated programs have been designed for this purpose. The case study shows a straightforward approach to finding local peaks.

Case Study: Placement of Microwave Towers

PROBLEM STATEMENT

Your company wants to use microwave radio transmission for data communications between a computer in a rural branch office and the central computer in the main office. To accomplish this, your company must erect a series of microwave towers along the route from the branch office to the main office. Because microwave transmission is by line-of-sight, each tower must be placed on top of a hill. You have a data file that lists the altitude every 100 yd along the chosen route, starting with the altitude of the branch office and ending with the altitude of the main office. You need a program that will analyze these data and create an output file giving the altitude of only those points that are possible locations for microwave towers. Along with each point's altitude, your program also should write its distance from the previous point written to the output file.

ANALYSIS

To solve this problem, your program must identify the points that are local peaks or local maxima. A point is a local peak if it is higher than the point that precedes it and is also higher than the point that follows it. If your program creates an output file containing the altitude of each local peak and its distance from the previous local peak, you will have a much smaller list of candidate locations for towers. Later, you can examine this list to select appropriate locations for the towers, ensuring they are not too far apart.

Table 5.11 shows a sample input file and its corresponding output file. Besides the points representing the branch office altitude (100.0) and main office altitude (155.0), there are three local peaks included in the output file.

Data Requirements

Problem Parameter

the distance between data points in yards (REAL PNTDIS = 100.0)

Table 5.11. *Sample Input File and Output File*

DATA FILE POINTS	OUTPUT FILE PEAKS	
branch office altitude → 100.0	Altitude	Distance
200.0	of peak	from last peak
300.0	100.0	0.0
250.0	300.0	200.0
275.0	275.0	200.0
260.0	150.0	300.0
100.0	155.0	300.0
150.0		
140.0		
145.0		
main office altitude → 155.0		

Problem Inputs

a data file containing the altitude of each data point along the route (file POINTS)
the altitude of the branch office (REAL BRANCH)
the altitude of the main office (REAL MAIN)

Problem Outputs

an output file containing each peak's altitude and distance from the previous peak (file PEAKS)
the distance between the current peak and the last peak (REAL DISTNC)

DESIGN

The algorithm follows:

Algorithm

1. Read the altitude of the branch office and write it to the output file.
2. Find each local peak and write its altitude and distance from the last point displayed to the output file.
3. Write the altitude of the main office and its distance from the last local peak to the output file.

Step 1 writes the branch office altitude (the first data value) to the output file. Step 3 writes the main office altitude (the last data value) and its distance from the last peak to the output file. We do not need to refine these steps.

Step 2 is the main processing loop. Its primary task is to find each local peak. To find a local peak, we must compare the last three altitudes read as data and saved in BEFORE, MIDDLE, and AFTER, respectively. If the value in MIDDLE is the largest, point MIDDLE is a local peak. After checking whether MIDDLE is a local peak, we then would advance to the next point in the data file by resetting point BEFORE to old point MIDDLE, resetting point MIDDLE to old point AFTER, and reading in a new data value for point AFTER. If the last three data values read are 15.0, 45.0, and 30.0, the three altitudes being compared will have the values

BEFORE	MIDDLE	AFTER
15.0	45.0	30.0

Because MIDDLE is largest, we must write it to the output file. After resetting points BEFORE and MIDDLE and reading in the next altitude (say, 20.0), we compare the following three values:

BEFORE	MIDDLE	AFTER
45.0	30.0	20.0

In this case, MIDDLE is not a local peak, so we should not write it to the output file.

Additional Program Variable

the last three altitudes read (REAL BEFORE, MIDDLE, AFTER)

Step 2 Refinements

2.1 Initialize distance between peaks to PNTDIS.
2.2 Set BEFORE to BRANCH.
2.3 Read the next data value into MIDDLE.
2.4 DO WHILE there are more data points
    2.5 Read the next data value into AFTER.
    2.6 IF point MIDDLE is a local peak THEN
        2.7 Write its altitude and its distance from
            the last peak to the output file.
        2.8 Reset distance between peaks to PNTDIS.
    ELSE
        2.9 Increment distance between peaks by PNTDIS.
    END IF
  2.10 Reset BEFORE to MIDDLE and MIDDLE to AFTER.
  END DO
2.12 Set MAIN to MIDDLE.

Steps 2.1, 2.8, and 2.9 are used to track the distance between peaks. Each time a new peak is located, this distance is written to the output file and then reset to PNTDIS (step 2.8).

IMPLEMENTATION

Figure 5.5 shows the completed program along with a sample run. The main processing loop is exited right after the end-of-file record is read.

Figure 5.5. *Finding Local Peaks*

```
      PROGRAM TOWERS
C Finds and displays the altitude of each local peak and its
C distance from the last peak displayed. The altitude of each
C point along a path is provided as data. All data points are
C a fixed distance apart (value of PNTDIS).

C Declarations
      REAL PNTDIS
      PARAMETER (PNTDIS = 100.0)
      REAL BRANCH, MAIN, BEFORE, MIDDLE, AFTER, DISTNC

C Open the files and write the heading for the output file.
      OPEN (UNIT = 1, FILE = 'POINTS', STATUS = 'OLD')
      OPEN (UNIT = 2, FILE = 'PEAKS', STATUS = 'NEW')
      WRITE (2, 15) 'Altitude', 'Distance'
      WRITE (2, 15) ' of peak', 'from last peak'
   15 FORMAT (A10, T20, A)

C Read the altitude of the branch site and write it to the
C output file.
      READ (1, *) BRANCH
      WRITE (2, 25) BRANCH, 0.0
   25 FORMAT (F10.1, T20, F10.1)

C Find each local peak and display its altitude and
C distance from the last point displayed.
      DISTNC = PNTDIS
      BEFORE = BRANCH
      READ (1, *) MIDDLE
      DO WHILE (.TRUE.)                                9 IF (.TRUE.) THEN
         READ (1, *, END = 99) AFTER
         IF ((MIDDLE .GT. BEFORE) .AND.
     +       (MIDDLE .GT. AFTER)) THEN
            WRITE (2, 25) MIDDLE, DISTNC
            DISTNC = PNTDIS
         ELSE
            DISTNC = DISTNC + PNTDIS
         END IF
         BEFORE = MIDDLE
         MIDDLE = AFTER
      END DO                                           GOTO 9
                                                       END IF
C End-of-file record was read.
   99 CONTINUE
```

```
C Display the altitude of the main office and its distance
C from the last local peak.
      MAIN = MIDDLE
      WRITE (2, 25) MAIN, DISTNC

C Close files and stop.
      END FILE (UNIT = 2)
      CLOSE (UNIT = 1)
      CLOSE (UNIT = 2)
      PRINT *, 'File of local peaks created'
      STOP
      END
```

```
File of local peaks created
```

TESTING AND VERIFICATION

Before you can test the program, you must create a data file named POINTS that will contain at least two lines. If it contains exactly two lines, these values will represent the branch office and main office altitudes and they should be copied to the output file. Try running your program with the sample input file shown in Table 5.11.

EXERCISES FOR SECTION 5.6

Self-check

1. What would be the effect of reversing the order of the two assignment statements at the end of the loop that update BEFORE and MIDDLE?

Programming

1. Modify the program in Fig. 5.5 so it counts and displays the total number of data points that were read.

5.7 Common Programming Errors

Format Errors

Many very common errors can occur when you work with formatted input and output. Some are described in the following list. Note that the errors discussed in numbers 3, 5, and 6 are not unique to formatted input and output and can just as easily be made in working with list-directed input and output.

1. Type mismatches in the correspondence between variable names and edit descriptors will result in execution-time errors. This type of error can result from providing an insufficient number of descriptors to accommodate an input or output list. When this error occurs, a diagnostic message might be printed and many Fortran compilers will immediately terminate execution of your program.

2. An integer that is not right-justified in its field might cause the blanks on

the right to be interpreted as trailing zeros during input. This action could change the value of the input data. Similarly, embedded blanks in an integer field can be read as zeros. These comments also apply to real numbers that are typed without a decimal point.

3. If apostrophes in character strings are not carefully paired, the format specification will be interpreted incorrectly and a compile-time syntax error will occur.

4. Attempting to print a number in a field that is too small can result in an execution-time error on some systems. However, many compilers will print only part of the number along with one or more asterisks; in this case, no explicit diagnostic would be printed.

5. Providing insufficient data to satisfy the input variable list will result in an execution-time error. A diagnostic message will indicate either that there were insufficient input data or that the end of the input file was reached.

6. Failure to provide a line-control character (1, +, 0, or blank) in an output format for the line printer will produce unpredictable program output. This failure might be noted by a warning diagnostic, but usually it will go undetected during compilation.

File Errors

1. When working with files, be sure to use an OPEN statement to connect each file before it is processed. Check with your instructor to determine any local restrictions on file names and unit numbers. If the file is formatted, ensure you use the same format to read it as was used to create it.

2. Ensure you use the correct STATUS string with each file you open. Use STATUS = 'NEW' with each new output file your program is creating and STATUS = 'OLD' with each data file your program is reading.

3. You must write an end-of-file record, using the END FILE statement, at the end of each output file. Also, use the CLOSE statement to disconnect each opened file before your program terminates.

4. You can use the END = *label* control specifier in a READ statement associated with a data file. Generally, doing this is the only way to determine when all the file records have been processed; otherwise, an "attempt to read beyond end of file" error might occur.

Chapter Review

Formatted output permits you to have direct control over the use of every print position of every line printed on a page or displayed on the screen. We discussed how to use format statements to provide all details of spacing, data types, and data widths.

We discussed various edit descriptors. Those beginning with A, F, and I are used for printing character, real, and integer data, respectively. The X descriptor is used for horizontal spacing in a line. On many computer systems, each output line should begin with one of the characters blank, 0, 1, or +; this character is used for vertical spacing, that is, line control. The T descriptor advances you to a particular column,

Table 5.12. *Fortran Statements for Chapter 5*

STATEMENT	EFFECT
Formatted PRINT	
``` PRINT 25, MONTH, DAY 25 FORMAT ('1', A, 1X, I2)```	Displays a character value MONTH, a blank, and a two-digit integer value (DAY) on a new page.
Formatted READ	
`READ '(A)', DATE`	Enters a string of characters into DATE.
OPEN **Statement**	
``` OPEN (UNIT = 1, FILE = 'EZRA', + STATUS = 'OLD')```	Connects an existing file named EZRA to the program. The file is associated with unit number 1.
END FILE **Statement**	
`END FILE (UNIT = 1)`	Appends an end-of-file record to the file associated with unit number 1.
CLOSE **Statement**	
`CLOSE (UNIT = 1)`	Disconnects the file associated with unit number 1.
General READ	
`READ (1, 10, END = 11) N, A`	Reads two data values from the file with unit number 1 using FORMAT 10. If the end-of-file record is read, a transfer to label 11 occurs.
General WRITE	
``` WRITE (2, 26) MONTH, DAY 26 FORMAT (A, I2)```	Writes the values of MONTH (a string) and DAY (a two-digit integer) to unit 2.

the / descriptor advances you to a new line, and the E descriptor reads or displays data values in scientific notation.

We also provided an introduction to file processing in Fortran. We described the OPEN, CLOSE, and END FILE statements and the file parameters that must be specified in the OPEN statement. We discussed the general READ/WRITE in Fortran and showed how to use the END = control specifier in a READ statement. The statements introduced in this chapter are described in Table 5.12.

Quick-check Exercises

1. A group of data items accessed by a single READ or WRITE statement is called a(n) _____ .

2. A(n) _____ is used to connect a file to a program that references it.
3. The _____ descriptor may be used when a single format specification describes the appearance of several output lines.
4. The END FILE statement is used to write a(n) _____ to a(n) _____ file.
5. Which format descriptor is used for entering (or displaying) the following?

   a. An integer
   b. A real number
   c. A character string

6. How is the X format descriptor used?
7. Why is it not always possible to reuse an input format specification as an output format specification?
8. Write an OPEN statement for a pre-existing data file named YOURFILE.
9. Assume X is 5.9456, Y is 6.1234, and Z is 'DONALD DUCK'. Show the output displayed by the following statements:

```
    PRINT 15, '+', X, Y, Z
15 FORMAT (1X, A, F5.2, F8.5, 1X, A6)
    PRINT '(''0'', A, F4.1, A12, F6.3)', '+', X, Z, Y
```

Answers to Quick-check Exercises

1. record
2. OPEN statement
3. slash
4. end-of-file record; output
5. a. I
   b. F or E
   c. A
6. to enter blank characters into a line of output; to skip over columns of an input line
7. An input format does not specify a carriage-control character, which may be required for each output line.
8. OPEN (UNIT = 3, FILE = 'YOURFILE', STATUS = 'OLD')
9. + 5.95 6.12340 Donald

   + 5.9 Donald Duck 6.123

Review Questions

1. Write statements that print the values of NAME, HOURS, RATE, and PAY in the following table form. Show one PRINT and FORMAT pair for the heading and one for the table values. Leave five spaces between the values shown in the table.

NAME	HOURS	RATE	PAY
AAAAAAAAAA	XXX.X	XXX.XX	XXXXX.XX

2. Write a READ and a FORMAT statement to enter the following input line into the variables listed.

Columns	Contents	Variable	Type
1–14	Name	NAME	CHARACTER *15
15–19	Weekly salary (2 decimal places)	WKSAL	REAL
20–21	Age	AGE	INTEGER
22–27	Favorite author	AUTHOR	CHARACTER *10
28	Number of children	NCHILD	INTEGER

3. Assume the READ statement written for question 2 has been used to enter the following input line, which begins with two blanks:

```
   BOB SOLOMON 1476384ARTHUR8
```

Show the output displayed by the following statements:

```
    PRINT 15, NAME, AGE, WKSAL
15 FORMAT ('1', A, 'IS ', I2, ' YEARS OLD' / ' HE EARNS ',
   + F6.2, ' DOLLARS PER WEEK')
    PRINT 19, ' HIS FAVORITE AUTHOR IS ', AUTHOR,
   + ' AND HE HAS ', NCHILD, ' CHILDREN'
19 FORMAT (A, A6, A, I1, A)
```

4. What is wrong with each of the following statements?

```
a. OPEN (FILE = 'AFILE', STATUS = 'OLD')
b. PRINT '(3X, Z10, A10, 5X, A4)', A, B, C
c. FORMAT ('+', I4, 5X, A10)
```

5. Rewrite the following loop using a test for the end-of-file record to terminate loop repetition rather than reading a sentinel value. Write a complete program, including OPEN statements.

```
    PRINT (2, *) 'List of names'
    READ (1, 5) NAME
5 FORMAT (A)
    DO WHILE (NAME .NE. '****')
       PRINT (2, 5) NAME
       READ (1, 5) NAME
    END DO
```

6. For the Fortran fragment

```
CHARACTER *6 SEASON
INTEGER K
REAL X
SEASON = 'Spring'
K = 17
X = 87.65
PRINT 123, SEASON, K, X
```

what is printed for each of the following FORMAT statements?

a. 123 FORMAT (1X, A8, 1X, I2, 3X, F5.2)
b. 123 FORMAT (A8, I3, F8.2)
c. 123 FORMAT ('1', A8, I3, F8.2)
d. 123 FORMAT ('1', A8, I2, 2X, F5.2)

7. For the data item 23456, what value will X (type REAL) have after the READ statement below executes

READ 100, X

for each of the FORMAT statements listed? Assume that the data item begins in column 1.

a. 100 FORMAT (F4.2)
b. 100 FORMAT (F5.1)
c. 100 FORMAT (F5.0)
d. 100 FORMAT (F3.2)

8. For the data lines 12.345678 and ABCDEFGHIJ, what is read by the following READ statement (X type REAL, I type INTEGER, and TEXT type CHARACTER *6) for each of the following FORMAT statements? Assume that the data items begin in column 1.

READ 10, X, I, TEXT

a. 10 FORMAT (1X, F5.2, I2 / A4)
b. 10 FORMAT (F3.0, I1 / A8)
c. 10 FORMAT (F6.3, 1X, I2 / A6)
d. 10 FORMAT (F6.2, I2, A)

9. What value will SUM have after the Fortran fragment on the right executes?

a. 46.5
b. 46.6
c. 57.9
d. 357.6
e. 469.0

```
      REAL X1, X2, SUM
      READ 100, X1, X2
100   FORMAT (F3.1, F3.1)
      SUM = X1 + X2
12.345678   ← data
```

Programming Projects

1. Write a program to read in the addresses of all the students in the class and print each address on an envelope. You may assume that a "skip to the top of the next page" operation implies that the next envelope is put in position for the first line of an address.

   Each address will be printed on three lines. The information to be printed on the first line is in columns 1–20 of each input line. The second line of information is in columns 21–40, and the third line is contained in columns 41–80. A sample data line follows:

```
MR. JOHN JONES      325 CEDAR ST.      PHILADELPHIA      PA. 19122
1                   21                 41                61
```

2. Especially during the colder months of the year, weather forecasters frequently inform us not only of the Fahrenheit-degree temperature (TEMP) reading at a given hour, but also of the wind-chill factor (WCF) at that time. This factor is used to indicate the relative degree of coldness that we are likely to experience if we are outside. Its calculation is based on the thermometer reading (TEMP) and the velocity (V) of the wind at the time. Write a program to compute the wind-chill factor for temperatures ranging from −50° to +50° in increments of 5° and for wind velocities of from 5 to 60 mph, in increments of 5 mph. Your output should appear similar to the following table:

```
WIND-CHILL FACTOR TABLE (DEGREES F)
TEMPERATURE                 WIND VELOCITY (MILES PER HOUR)
READING (DEG F)       5 10 15 20 25 30 35 . . .
     −50
     −45
     −40                             .

      .                              .

      .                              .

      .

      0
      5

      .

      .

      .

     20         . . .             −16

      .

      .

      .

     50
```

The formula for computing the wind-chill factor is

$$WCF = 91.4 - (.486 + .305\sqrt{V} - .020V) \times (91.4 - temp)$$

Your answers should be rounded to the nearest whole degree. The WCF of −16 has been given as a test value. It is the WCF when TEMP is 20° and V is 25 mph.

3. Write a program that, given the size of an angle in degrees, computes the size in radians and then computes the sine, cosine, and tangent of the angle. The program should print a neatly arranged, appropriately labeled five-column table for degrees, radians, sine, cosine, and tangent of angles from −90° to +90° in steps of 1°. Note that the SIN, COS, and TAN functions all require real arguments in radians and that tan 90° and tan −90° are not mathematically defined. You should note undefined computations in a meaningful way in your table. Keep your answers accurate to five decimal places. Use the following formula for degrees-to-radians

conversion:

$$number\ of\ radians = 0.01745 \times number\ of\ degrees.$$

4. Write a program that reads a student name and a list of three exam scores from a data file and writes the information for each student as a single file record in an output file. Each output record should contain the student's name, three exam scores, and the average score. For example, the output record corresponding to the input record

        IVORY   47 82 93

   would be

        IVORY   47 82 93 74

5. The following equations are used to determine the solar reflectance of transparent materials where θ represents the angle of incident radiation, β the angle of transmitted radiation, and r the single surface reflectance of the transparent material. Create a data file that contains pairs of data values for θ and β. Your program should read each data pair and calculate the three r-values indicated below (perpendicular, parallel, and combined). Create an output file with five columns, one each for the two angles and the three r-values. Use formatted input and output. Don't forget to convert degrees to radians.

$$r_\perp = \frac{\sin^2(\theta - \beta)}{\sin^2(\theta + \beta)}$$

$$r_\parallel = \frac{\tan^2(\theta - \beta)}{\tan^2(\theta + \beta)}$$

$$r = 0.5(r_\perp + r_\parallel)$$

6. Data communications often requires a large message to be broken down into small chunks called *packets* for transmission to another site. Each packet consists of a three-character address to which the packet will be sent. The next four characters of a packet represent its sequence number. Each packet has a unique sequence number, and the sequence numbers are assigned in order, e.g., packet number 1 should have sequence number 1, and so on. This allows the packets to be reassembled on the receiving end. Finally, each message chunk will be 10 characters in length.

   We need a program that will assemble the packets. The program's data file should contain a sequence of messages and each message should be preceded by a three-character address. We will assume that all messages fit on a single line of 80 characters. The packets corresponding to each message should be written to an output file.

   A sample data file is shown next. The corresponding output file follows the data file. Notice that the sequence number is not reset to 1 when the packets for a new message are built. (*Hint:* Use a formatted READ to split the message into separate fields.)

```
Data File

EBKThe message is not too long, but it is confusing.
ACEPlease send programming help!


Output File

EBK0001The messag
EBK0002e is not t
EBK0003oo long, b
EBK0004ut it is c
EBK0005onfusing.
ACE0006Please sen
ACE0007d programm
ACE0008ing help!
```

7. Each month a bank customer deposits $50 in a savings account. The account earns 6.5% interest calculated on a quarterly basis (one fourth of 6.5% each quarter). Write a program to compute the following for each of 120 mo of a 10-yr period: the total investment, the total amount in the account, and the interest accrued. You may assume that the rate is applied to all funds in the account at the end of a quarter regardless of when the deposits were made.

    Print all values accurate to two decimal places. A table of the form shown next should be written to an output file.

MONTH	INVESTMENT	NEW AMOUNT	INTEREST	TOTAL SAVINGS
1	50.00	50.00	0.00	50.00
2	100.00	100.00	0.00	100.00
3	150.00	150.00	2.44	152.44
4	200.00	202.44	0.00	202.44
5	250.00	252.44	0.00	252.44
6	300.00	302.44	4.91	307.35
7	350.00	357.35	0.00	357.35

8. Compute the monthly payment and the total payment for a bank loan, given

    a. the amount of the loan,
    b. the duration of the loan in months, and
    c. the interest rate for the loan.

    Your program should (a) read in one record at a time (each containing a loan value, a months value, and a rate value), (b) perform the required computation, and (c) print the values of the loan, month, rate; the monthly payment; and the total payment. Test your program with at least the following data (and more if you want):

Loan	Months	Rate
16000	300	12.50
24000	360	13.50
30000	300	15.50
42000	360	14.50
22000	300	15.50
300000	240	15.25

Note: The formula for computing monthly payment is

$$monthly = \left[\frac{rate}{1200} \times \left(1 + \frac{rate}{1200}\right)^{months} \times loan\right] / \left[\left(1 + \frac{rate}{1200}\right)^{months} - 1\right]$$

The formula for computing the total payment is

$$total = monthly \times months.$$

To simplify the computation of the monthly payment, you also may find it helpful to introduce the following additional variables. You can print the values of *ratem* and *expm* to see if your program's computations are accurate.

$$ratem = rate/1200$$
$$expm = (1 + ratem)$$

(*Hint:* You will need a loop to multiply *expm* by itself *months* times.)

9. An employee time card is represented as one long line of data items. Write a program that processes a collection of these lines. Assume the data items follow the sequence given next.

Positions	Data
1–10	Employee's last name enclosed in apostrophes
12–20	Employee's first name enclosed in apostrophes
22–24	Contains 'C' for city office or 'S' for suburban office
26–28	Contains 'U' (union) or 'N' (non-union)
30–35	Employee's identification number in apostrophes
37–38	Number of regular hours (a whole number)
40–45	Hourly rate (dollars and cents)
47–48	Number of dependents
50–54	Number of overtime hours (a real number)

a. Compute gross pay using the formula:

$$gross = regular\ hours \times rate + overtime\ hours \times 1.5 \times rate$$

b. Compute net pay by subtracting the following deductions:

federal tax = .14 × (*gross* − 13 × *dependents*)
social security = 0.052 × *gross*
city tax = .04 × *gross* (if employee works in the city)
union dues = 6.75 × *gross* (if employee is a union member)

10. A concrete channel is being designed to bring water to Mono Lake. It will have vertical walls and a width of 15 ft. It will be 10 ft deep, have a slope of .0015 feet/foot, and a roughness coefficient of .014. How deep will the water be when 5,000 cu ft/sec is flowing through it?
   To solve this problem, we can use Manning's equation

$$Q = \frac{1.49}{N} AR^{2/3}S^{1/2},$$

where Q is the flow of water (cubic feet per second), N is the roughness coefficient (unitless), A is the area (square feet), S is the slope (feet/foot), and R is the hydraulic radius (feet).
   The hydraulic radius is the cross-sectional area divided by the wetted perimeter. For square channels, like the one in this example,

   hydraulic radius = *depth* × *width*/(2.0 × *depth* + *width*).

To solve this problem, we guess a depth and then calculate the corresponding flow. If the flow is too little, then we guess a little higher depth; if it is too high, then we guess a little lower depth. We repeat this process until we are within .1% of the flow desired.
   For the initial guess, try half the channel depth, as in the following example run:

trial depth	trial flow	target flow	difference
5.217247	643.0518	1000.000	−356.9482
5.406021	682.4061	1000.000	−317.5939
5.570860	716.9747	1000.000	−283.0253
5.715399	747.4297	1000.000	−252.5703
.	.	.	.
.	.	.	.
.	.	.	.
6.888953	998.6530	1000.000	−1.346985
6.889561	998.7847	1000.000	−1.215332
6.890110	998.9034	1000.000	−1.096558
6.890604	999.0106	1000.000	−0.989380

The depth will be 6.890604 ft.

11. Write a program to create a table showing the underwater pressure (in pounds per square inch) from 1 ft to 30 ft. Water weighs 62.4 lb/cu ft, which means that a column 1 ft high and 1 in. square will weigh 0.433 lb. Have the table resemble the following:

```
Underwater    Pressure Table
   Depth          Pressure
   (ft)           (p.s.i.)


    1             0.433333
    2             0.866667
    3             1.300000
    .                 .
    .                 .
    .                 .
   29            12.56667
   30            13.00000
```

12. Bunyan Lumber Co. needs to create a table of the engineering properties of its lumber. The dimensions of the wood are given as base and height in inches. Engineers need to know the following information about lumber:

   - Cross-sectional area (*base* × *height*)
   - Moment of inertia [(*base* × *height*^{3})/12]
   - Section modulus [(*base* × *height*^{2})/6]

   The owner, Paul, makes lumber with base sizes 2, 4, 6, 8, 10, and 12 in. and height sizes of 2, 4, 6, 8, and 10 in. Use nested DO loops to produce a table to show these values. In the chart, do not duplicate a 2-by-6 with a 6-by-2 board. The table should resemble the following:

```
                  Bunyan Lumber Company
                   882 Blue Ox Drive
              Engineering Properties of Our Lumber


                                   Moment of    Section
   Base    Height     Area          Inertia     Modulus
   (in.)   (in.)     (sq in.)       (in. 4)     (in. 3)
     2       2        4.000          1.333        1.333
     2       4        8.000         10.667        5.333
     2       6       12.000         36.000       12.000
    . . .
     4       4       16.000         21.333       10.667
     4       6       24.000         72.000       24.000
     4       8       32.000        170.667       42.667
    . . .
```

CHAPTER 6
Top-down Design with Subprograms

I N CHAPTER 2, we discussed how to use library functions to simplify computations. In this chapter, we illustrate how to write functions to implement computational steps in an algorithm, how to define functions, and how to reference these functions in expressions.

A *function* is an independent program module, or *subprogram*, that always returns a single result. In this chapter, we discuss another type of subprogram, a *subroutine*, that can return any number of results. The use of functions and subroutines will enable you to implement each major program step as an independent program module. You can implement and test each subprogram individually. Then you can combine these subprograms as "building blocks" to form a complete program. You can also reuse a subprogram when the operation it performs is required again in the same program or another program.

We demonstrate how to use subprograms to facilitate the top-down design process and introduce the structure chart as a means of documenting the flow of information between a program and its subprograms. Finally, we discuss how to debug and test a program system containing several subprograms.

6.1 User-defined Functions

In Section 2.7, we introduced functions and discussed how functions return a single result to the program that calls them. We also showed how to call a function by referencing its name in an expression. For example, the expression part of the assignment statement

```
K = MOD(N, M)
```

calls the library function MOD, which computes the remainder of its first argument, N, divided by its second argument, M. Variable K gets the function result after function exit occurs.

In this section, we learn how to write our own functions. Our first example discusses two functions that could be used in many different engineering design programs.

- Function DOAREA(R)—Returns the area of a circle with radius R
- Function DOCIRC(R)—Returns the circumference of a circle with radius R

EXAMPLE 6.1   Figure 6.1 demonstrates how to write functions DOAREA and DOCIRC.

Figure 6.1. *Functions DOAREA and DOCIRC*

```
      REAL FUNCTION DOAREA (R)
C Computes the area of a circle with radius R.
C Precondition : R is defined.
C Postcondition: Function result is the circle area.

C Argument declaration
      REAL R

C Local declaration
      REAL PI
      PARAMETER (PI = 3.14159)

C Define function result
      DOAREA = PI * R ** 2

C Exit function
      RETURN
      END

C _____

      REAL FUNCTION DOCIRC (R)
C Computes the circumference of a circle with radius R.
C Precondition : R is defined.
C Postcondition: Function result is the circle circumference.

C Argument declaration
      REAL R

C Local declaration
      REAL PI
      PARAMETER (PI = 3.14159)

C Define function result
      DOCIRC = 2.0 * PI * R

C Exit function
      RETURN
      END
```

As you can see, the functions in Fig. 6.1 resemble a program. However, they differ from a program as follows:

- A function begins with a special header statement of the form

  ftype FUNCTION *fname* (*dummy argument list*)

  where *ftype* specifies the data type of the result returned by function *fname*.

- A function does not normally print its result; instead, the result is assigned to the function name by a statement of the form

fname = expression

The last value assigned to the function name, *fname,* is "returned" as the function result.
- The last statement executed in a function is RETURN instead of STOP. Although more than one RETURN statement is permitted, generally it's best to have only a single one. Execution of a RETURN statement causes a transfer of control to the statement that called the function. The RETURN statement can be omitted; if there is no RETURN statement, the function return will occur when the END statement is reached.

The function headings in Fig. 6.1 indicate that functions DOAREA and DOCIRC return a type REAL result. Each function has a single *dummy argument*, R, that represents the *actual argument* in the function body. Each function begins by declaring the data type (REAL) of its argument and the data type of a local parameter, PI. A *local parameter* can be referenced only within the function that declares it, not within the main program.

In function DOAREA, the assignment statement

```
DOAREA = PI * R ** 2
```

defines the function result as the value of the expression PI * R ** 2. This value is returned to the calling program. Similarly, in function DOCIRC, the assignment statement

```
DOCIRC = 2.0 * PI * R
```

defines the function result.

SYNTAX DISPLAY

Function Definition

SYNTAX: *ftype* FUNCTION *fname (dummy argument list)*
         function interface
         dummy argument declarations
         local declarations
         function body

(continued)

```
EXAMPLE:        INTEGER FUNCTION SQUARE (N)
         C Computes the square of N
         C Precondition : N is defined
         C Postcondition: Function result is N ** 2
         C Argument declarations
               Integer N
         C Define function result
               SQUARE = N * N
               RETURN
               END
```

INTERPRETATION: The FUNCTION header statement specifies the function name, *fname,* and the type of the result returned, *ftype* (INTEGER, REAL, LOGICAL, CHARACTER * *n*). The *dummy argument list* provides a list of identifiers that are used as function dummy arguments. The type of each *dummy argument* must be declared. Also, the type of any local variable manipulated by the function should be declared in the *local declarations.* The next program style subsection describes the *function interface.*

The *function body* describes the data manipulation performed on the function arguments and local variables. The function name, *fname,* must be defined in the *function body.* The last value stored in *fname* is returned as the function value when a RETURN statement is executed or the END statement is reached. The END statement is used to mark the end of the function definition.

NOTE: If the function does not have any arguments, an empty pair of parentheses () must appear in the FUNCTION header statement following *fname.* If *ftype* is missing, the function type (INTEGER or REAL) is determined from *fname* using implicit typing.

Program Style: *Function Interface*

The first few lines at the beginning of functions DOAREA and DOCIRC contain all the information anyone needs to know in order to use the function. The initial comment describes what the function does. The comment line

```
C Precondition : R is defined.
```

describes the condition that must be true before the function is called; this condition is known as the *precondition.* The line in DOCIRC

```
C Postcondition: Function result is the circle circumference.
```

describes the condition that must be true after the function execution is completed; this condition is called the *postcondition*. Next, the lines

```
C Argument declaration
      REAL R
```

identify and declare the function argument(s).

Using preconditions and postconditions provides valuable documentation to other programmers who might want to use the function. For example, the precondition tells a programmer what must be done before the function is called; in this case, a single data value must be assigned or read into the actual function argument prior to calling DOAREA or DOCIRC. The postcondition tells a programmer the effect of the function's execution.

We can say that the preconditions and postconditions serve as an informal contract between the function and any program that uses it. The precondition indicates any expectations the function might have regarding its arguments; the postcondition tells what the function does and what will happen if the precondition is met. However, all bets are off if the precondition is not met; therefore the calling program must check to ensure that all actual arguments satisfy the function preconditions before each call.

We recommend you begin all function declarations in this way. These comments and dummy argument declarations provide valuable documentation to other programmers who might want to reuse your functions in a new program. If you list explicit preconditions and postconditions, other programmers can determine what your function does and how to call it without having to read the code.

More Function Examples

The next function we discuss has two arguments and contains an IF structure in the function body. It is followed by a function with a WHILE loop and a function with a DO loop in the function body.

EXAMPLE 6.2

Function ROUND in Fig. 6.2 rounds its first argument to the number of decimal places indicated by its second argument. This means that the function reference

```
ROUND(2.51863, 3)
```

returns the real number 2.519.

Figure 6.2. *Function ROUND*

```
      REAL FUNCTION ROUND (X, PLACES)
C Rounds the value of X
C Precondition : X is defined and PLACES >= 0.
C Postcondition: Function result is X rounded to PLACES decimal points.

C Argument Declarations
      REAL X
      INTEGER PLACES

C Local Declarations
      REAL TEMPX, POWER

C Perform rounding operation
      IF (PLACES .GE. 0) THEN
         POWER = 10.0 ** PLACES
         TEMPX = X * POWER
         ROUND = NINT(TEMPX) / POWER
      ELSE
         PRINT *, '**** Negative argument for PLACES — no rounding done'
         ROUND = X
      END IF

C Exit function
      RETURN
      END
```

If PLACES is greater than or equal to zero, the rounding operation is performed. Table 6.1 traces the execution of the function when dummy argument
X is 2.51863 and PLACES is 3. The function result is 2519/1000.0, or 2.519, as
desired.

Table 6.1. *Trace for X = 2.51863 and PLACES = 3*

STATEMENT	X	PLACES	POWER	TEMPX	EFFECT
	2.51863	3	?	?	
IF (PLACES .GE. 0)					True–does True task
POWER = 10.0 ** PLACES			1000.0		
TEMPX = X * POWER				2518.63	
ROUND = NINT(TEMPX) / POWER					Assigns 2519/1000.0 to ROUND

Function ROUND illustrates that a user-defined function can call a Fortran library function; ROUND calls NINT. It also is possible for one user-defined function to call another; however, a function cannot call itself (although this is allowed in Fortran 90).

Program Style: *Graceful Degradation*

The IF structure in Fig. 6.2 displays an error message if its second argument (PLACES) is negative. The precondition states that PLACES should not be negative. Rather than compute an answer that makes no sense or perform a computation that results in a run-time error, the function prints an error message and returns its first argument as the function result. In this way, the function user is warned that the computation did not take place; however, the program is able to continue execution because a reasonable value is returned as the function result.

EXAMPLE 6.3   Function ENTER (see Fig. 6.3) returns the first data value read that lies between its arguments, NMIN and NMAX. The body of function ENTER is based on the body of program GUESS, shown in Fig. 4.16. The WHILE loop continues to execute until a valid data value is read into local variable N, thereby causing the program flag BETWEN to be set to .TRUE.. After loop exit, the statement

```
ENTER = N
```

defines the function result as the last value read into N. The function reference

```
ENTER(1, 10)
```

would call function ENTER to read a data value between 1 and 10.

Figure 6.3. *Function ENTER*

```
        INTEGER FUNCTION ENTER (NMIN, NMAX)
C Returns the first data value read between NMIN and NMAX
C Preconditions : NMIN is less than or equal to NMAX.
C Postconditions: Function result lies between NMIN and NMAX.

C Argument Declarations
        INTEGER NMIN, NMAX

C Local Declarations
        INTEGER N
        LOGICAL BETWEN
```

```
C Initially assume an integer between NMIN and NMAX is not entered
      BETWEN = .FALSE.

C Keep reading until an integer between NMIN and NMAX is entered
      DO WHILE (.NOT. BETWEN)                              9 IF (...) THEN
         PRINT *, 'Enter an integer between ',
     +             NMIN, ' and ', NMAX
         READ *, N
         BETWEN = (N .GE. NMIN) .AND. (N .LE. NMAX)
      END DO
                                                           GOTO 9
C Define result                                            END IF
      ENTER = N


C Exit function
      RETURN
      END
```

EXAMPLE 6.4

The function FACTRL in Fig. 6.4 computes the factorial of an integer argument. The integer whose factorial (N!) will be computed is represented by the dummy argument N in the function description; its value is passed into the function when it is called. ■

Figure 6.4. *Function to Compute Factorial*

```
      INTEGER FUNCTION FACTRL (N)
C Computes the factorial of N
C Precondition : N is greater than or equal to zero.
C Postcondition: Function result is N!

C Argument Declarations
      INTEGER N

C Local Declarations
      INTEGER I, PRODUC

C Accumulate partial products in PRODUC
      PRODUC = 1
      DO 10 I = N, 2, -1
         PRODUC = PRODUC * I
   10 CONTINUE

C Define function result
      FACTRL = PRODUC

C Exit function
      RETURN
      END
```

The variables PRODUC and I are called local variables because they are declared in the function and, therefore, can be manipulated only within the function body. Except for special COMMON data (to be discussed in Chapter 8), a function can reference only its own local variables and dummy arguments.

EXERCISES FOR SECTION 6.1

Self-check

1. Trace the execution of function ROUND when its argument X is 3.14159 and its argument PLACES is 2.
2. Trace the execution of function FACTRL when its argument N is 5.

Programming

1. Write a function that returns the larger of two type REAL values. Show how to use this function to find the largest of three values.
2. Write a function POWER(N, K) that computes N^K by repeated multiplication (i.e., don't use the operator **). Assume that N and K are type INTEGER and that K is positive. The function should be type INTEGER.
3. Write a function that calls POWER from exercise 2 to compute N^K for any integer K (positive, negative, or zero). The function should be type REAL.

6.2 Calling User-defined Functions

The functions in Section 6.1 are subprograms. A subprogram cannot be executed by itself; it must be called into execution by a main program or another subprogram. We call a user-defined function in the same way that we call a library function, by referencing it in an expression.

EXAMPLE 6.5

Figure 6.5 shows a main program CIRCLE that uses functions DOAREA and DOCIRC (see Fig. 6.1) to compute the area and circumference of a circle. The data type (REAL) of each function is declared in the main program, so the compiler knows what type of result will be returned by the function. The function definitions should be inserted after the main program END as indicated by the comments at the end of the figure.

Figure 6.5. *Flow of Control from CIRCLE to its Functions*

```
      PROGRAM CIRCLE
C Finds and prints the area and circumference of a circle.
C The program user enters the circle radius and units of
C measurement.

C Declarations
      REAL RADIUS, AREA, CIRCUM
      CHARACTER *12 UNITS
      REAL DOAREA, DOCIRC
```

```
C Read the value of RADIUS and UNITS
      Print *, 'Enter units (enclosed in apostrophes)'
      READ *, UNITS
      PRINT *, 'Enter radius (in ', UNITS, ')'
      READ *, RADIUS

C Find the area
      AREA = DOAREA(RADIUS) ──────────→ control flows to DOAREA
           ↑────────────────────────── control returns to CIRCLE

C Find the circumference
      CIRCUM = DOCIRC(RADIUS) ─────────→ control flows to DOCIRC
             ↑──────────────────────── control returns to CIRCLE

C Print the values of AREA and CIRCUM
      PRINT *, 'The area is ', AREA, ' square ', UNITS
      PRINT *, 'The circumference is ', CIRCUM, ' ', UNITS

      STOP
      END

C ─────────────────────────────────────────────────────────

C Insert function DOAREA here (see Fig. 6.1).

C ─────────────────────────────────────────────────────────

C Insert function DOCIRC here (see Fig. 6.1).
```

The assignment statement

```
AREA = DOAREA(RADIUS)
```

calls function DOAREA, causing a transfer of control to the statements in the body of function DOAREA. The main program variable RADIUS is the actual argument in the function reference above, so the value of RADIUS is passed to dummy argument R and is used in the function computation. After the function execution is completed, control returns to the assignment statement above in the main program (program CIRCLE). The assignment statement saves the function result in the main program variable AREA.

Next, the assignment statement

```
CIRCUM = DOCIRC(RADIUS)
```

calls function DOCIRC, causing a transfer of control to the statements in the body of function DOCIRC. After function execution is completed, control returns to the assignment statement and the function result is saved in the main program variable CIRCUM. After the values of AREA and CIRCUM are displayed, the STOP statement is reached and program execution terminates.

The arrows drawn in Fig. 6.5 show the flow of control, which we summarize as follows:

- Controls flows from the main program to function DOAREA.
- Control flows from DOAREA back to the function reference in the main program.
- Control flows from the main program to function DOCIRC.
- Control flows from DOCIRC back to the function reference in the main program.

EXAMPLE 6.6 Figure 6.6 shows a main program that reads in an integer value, calls function FACTRL to compute its factorial, and prints the result returned by FACTRL.

Figure 6.6. *Main Program with Call to Function FACTRL*

```
        PROGRAM FUNCAL
C Illustrates a function call

C Declarations
        INTEGER NUM, FACT
        INTEGER FACTRL

C Read an integer and compute its factorial.
        PRINT *, 'Enter an integer between 0 and 10'
        READ *, NUM
        IF (NUM .GE. 0) THEN
           FACT = FACTRL(NUM)
           PRINT *, 'The factorial of ', NUM, ' is ', FACT
        ELSE
           PRINT *, 'The factorial of a negative number is undefined.'
        END IF

        STOP
        END

C  ─────────────────────────────────────────────────

        INTEGER FUNCTION FACTRL (N)
C Computes the factorial of N
C Precondition : N is greater than or equal to zero.
C Postcondition: Function result is N!

C Argument Declarations
        INTEGER N

C Local Declarations
        INTEGER I, PRODUC
```

```
C Accumulate partial products in PRODUC
      PRODUC = 1
      DO 10 I = N, 2, -1
         PRODUC = PRODUC * I
   10 CONTINUE

C Define function result
      FACTRL = PRODUC

C Exit function
      RETURN
      END


Enter an integer between 0 and 10
6
The factorial of 6 is 720
```

The top part of Fig. 6.6 (through the first END) is the main program; the bottom part is the function FACTRL. The main program declares the type of the input variable NUM whose factorial is to be computed. The type of function FACTRL (type INTEGER) is also declared.

Figure 6.7. *Effect of Execution of FACTRL When NUM is 6*

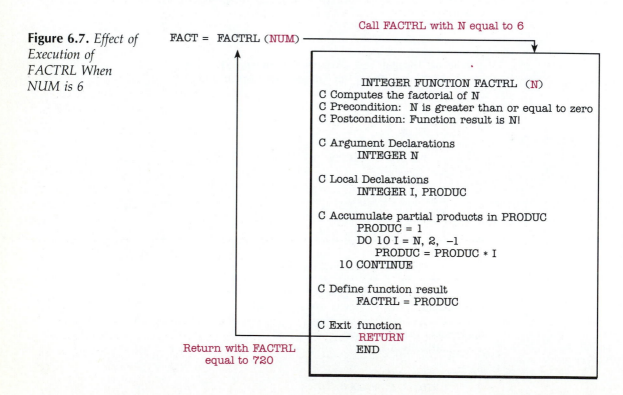

If a nonnegative integer is read into NUM, the statement

```
FACT = FACTRL(NUM)
```

in the main program is executed. The expression references function FACTRL, so function FACTRL is called into execution and the assignment statement waits for the function result. The value of NUM is passed into FACTRL as its actual argument (i.e., the actual value to be used in the factorial computation), and the function body is executed. The result of the function execution is returned to the main program, assigned to variable FACT, and printed. Program execution terminates when STOP is reached.

A trace of the execution of the function call and return is shown in Fig. 6.7 when NUM (the actual argument) is 6. The top arrow shows that 6 is passed into the function as the value of N (the dummy argument). After the function is executed, the value 720 is returned to the main program and stored in FACT. ■

EXAMPLE 6.7   We can use a formula from probability theory to compute the number of different ways in which r items can be selected from a collection of n items without regard to order. This formula is written as follows:

$$C\,(n,\,r) = \frac{n!}{r!(n\,-\,r)!}\,.$$

This formula represents the number of different combinations of n items taken r at a time. For example, if we have a class of five students and we want to know the number of different pairs of students that can be selected, we perform the computation

$$C(5,\,2) = \frac{5!}{2!(5\,-\,2)!} = \frac{5!}{2!3!} = \frac{120}{2\,\times\,6} = 10.$$

The answer is 10 different pairs of students.

The program in Fig. 6.8 uses function FACTRL to perform this computation. First N and R are read. If R is not greater than N, the statement

```
C = FACTRL(N) / (FACTRL(R) * FACTRL(N-R))
```

calls function FACTRL with three different actual arguments: N, R, and $N - R$ (an expression). The results of these calls are manipulated, as specified above, and the number of different combinations of N items taken R at a time is saved in variable C. ■

Figure 6.8 *Finding Combinations of N Items Taken R at a Time*

```
      PROGRAM COMBIN
C Computes the number of combinations of N items taken R at a time

      INTEGER N, R, C
      INTEGER FACTRL

      PRINT *, 'Enter number of items in the collection:'
      READ *, N
      PRINT *, 'Enter number of items to be selected:'
      READ *, R
      IF ((R .GE. 0) .AND. (R .LE. N)) THEN
         C = FACTRL(N) / (FACTRL(R) * FACTRL(N-R))
         PRINT *, 'The number of combinations is ', C
      ELSE
         PRINT *, 'Items to be selected must be >= 0 and <= total items'
      END IF

C Exit program
      STOP
      END


C  ────────────────────────────────────────────────


      INTEGER FUNCTION FACTRL (N)
C Computes the factorial of N
C Precondition : N is greater than or equal to zero.
C Postcondition: Function result is N!

C Argument declarations
      INTEGER N

C Local Declarations
      INTEGER I, PRODUC

C Accumulate partial products in PRODUC
      PRODUC = 1
      DO 10 I = N, 2, -1
         PRODUC = PRODUC * I
  10  CONTINUE

C Define function result
      FACTRL = PRODUC

C Exit function
      RETURN
      END


Enter number of items in the collection:
5
Enter number of items to be selected:
2
The number of combinations is 10
```

Table 6.2. *Effect of Each Call to FACTRL*

CALL	ACTUAL ARGUMENT	ARGUMENT VALUE	FUNCTION RESULT
1	N	5	120
2	R	2	2
3	N − R	3	6

In the main program of Fig. 6.8, a different actual argument is passed in each call to function FACTRL; consequently, a different result is computed each time. The effect of each call to function FACTRL is summarized in Table 6.2.

Table 6.2 illustrates one of the most important reasons for using functions. A function may be called several times in a program, each time with a different actual argument. Each call to the function causes the program statements associated with the function definition to be executed. If functions were not used, these program statements would have to be listed several times in the main program. As you can see, it is easier to insert a function reference in a program instead of inserting the entire function body.

Name Independence

Figure 6.9 shows the data storage area for the main program and function FACTRL just after the data values for N and R are read into the main program and before the function is called. There is a memory cell for variable N (value 5) in the main program and a memory cell for dummy argument N (initially undefined) in the function data area. Although they have the same names, dummy argument N and variable N in the main program are unrelated. Consequently, when the value 5 is read into main program variable N, the value of dummy argument N is unaffected. Each call to function FACTRL redefines the value of dummy argument N, and this value may be different from that of main program variable N (value is 5). This is perfectly natural when you consider that their values are stored in different memory cells.

By the same reasoning, local variables I and PRODUC in FACTRL are unrelated to any other use of these names in either the main program or any other function. A similar statement may be made regarding the use of label 10 in function FACTRL: This use of label 10 is unrelated to any other use of label 10 in the main program. Although label 10 may be associated with only one state-

Figure 6.9. *Data Areas for Main Program and Function FACTRL*

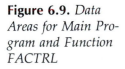

Main program data area

N	R	C
5	2	?

Function FACTRL data area

N	I	PRODUC
?	?	?

ment in FACTRL, this label also may appear in the main program or another subprogram.

Finally, variables C and R are declared in the main program and may be manipulated only in the main program. The function cannot directly access either C or R.

Type and Order Correspondence

The type of each actual argument used in a function call must be the same as the type of its corresponding dummy argument. If this is not the case, an error diagnostic such as "illegal argument type" may be printed. If your compiler does not detect this error, the function will be called and might return an incorrect result.

When using multiple-argument functions, ensure you use the correct number of actual arguments in the function reference. Also ensure that the order of actual arguments used in the function reference corresponds to the order of dummy arguments listed in the function definition. Corresponding actual and dummy argument lists must agree in Number, Order, and Type (NOT).

EXAMPLE 6.8

Assume that main program variable Y is declared as type REAL and that Y is 2.51863. Table 6.1 in Section 6.1 traces the effect of the function reference

ROUND(Y, 3)

which rounds Y to 3 decimal places (new value of Y is 2.519). If we were to transpose the arguments, the function call

ROUND(3, Y)

would be incorrect. The first actual argument, 3, cannot correspond to the first dummy argument, X, because dummy argument X (the number to be rounded) is supposed to be type REAL. Your compiler might not detect this error. Consequently, you must carefully follow the rules for argument correspondence summarized next.

Argument Correspondence Rules

- The number of actual arguments used in each call to a function must be the same as the number of dummy arguments listed in the function definition.
- Each actual argument must be the same type and in the same order as its corresponding dummy argument. The first actual argument corresponds to the first dummy argument, the second actual argument corresponds to the second dummy argument, and so on.

A Reminder about Declarations

Remember to declare the type of each user-defined function in the program unit that references it. This type should match the type specified in the FUNCTION header statement and is determined by the type of the result returned by the function.

Also, remember to declare the type of each dummy argument listed in a function header and the types of any local variables. As we mentioned earlier, it does not matter whether a name was used elsewhere in the program; its type must still be declared in the function definition. Its use in the function is independent of any other use of that name elsewhere.

Program Style: *Side Effects of Functions*

Function dummy arguments are used to store values passed into a function. Although Fortran allows you to change the value of a dummy argument inside a function, this is a bad programming practice and should not be done. Changing the value of a dummy argument might modify the value of the corresponding actual argument in the calling program. This undesirable change is called a *function side effect* and is a violation of the rule that a function should return only a single value. In Section 6.4, when we introduce subroutines, we will see that it is acceptable, and even desirable, for a subroutine to modify its dummy arguments.

EXERCISES FOR SECTION 6.2

Self-check

1. Assuming the main program declarations

```
INTEGER MAXINT
PARAMETER (MAXINT = 32767)
REAL X, Y, Z, MASSAG
INTEGER M, N
```

and function MASSAG, declared as follows,

```
REAL FUNCTION MASSAG (A, B, X)
REAL A, B
INTEGER X
```

which of the following references to function MASSAG are incorrect in the main program and why?

a. MASSAG(A, B, X)
b. MASSAG(MASSAG, Y, M)
c. MASSAG(Y, Z, N)
d. MASSAG(3.5, 4.5, 6)
e. MASSAG(X, Y, M)
f. MASSAG(X, Y)
g. MASSAG(Z, X, MAXINT)
h. MASSAG(3.5, 4.5, 6.7)

6.3 Single-statement Functions

Sometimes a function definition can be written in a single line. Fortran provides the single-statement function to implement such functions.

EXAMPLE 6.9   The following single-statement function RAISE can be used to raise a number (represented by X) to the power N:

```
REAL X, Z
INTEGER N
REAL RAISE
RAISE(X, N) = X ** N
```

Although it has the appearance of an executable statement, a single-statement function definition is actually a declaration; therefore it should come directly after all other declarations and before the executable statements of a program. The type of the single-statement function and its arguments also should be declared before the function, as shown in Example 6.9. The dummy argument names (X and N for RAISE) may be reused for other purposes in the program.

A single-statement function is called just like any other function. For example, the assignment statement

```
Z = RAISE(1.5, 10)
```

calls function RAISE to raise the value of 1.5 to the power 10; the result is stored in Z. The single-statement function is described next.

SYNTAX DISPLAY

Definition of the Single-statement Function

SYNTAX: *fname* (*dummy argument list*) = *expression*

EXAMPLE: SQUARE(X) = X * X

INTERPRETATION: *fname* is defined as a single-statement function whose value is determined by evaluating the *expression*. The *expression* may reference variables, constants, and other functions as well as the *dummy arguments*. When the function *fname* is called, each actual argument value is substituted for its corresponding *dummy argument* in the *expression* and the *expression* is evaluated.

NOTE: *fname* and *expression* either must be the same data type or one may be type REAL and the other type INTEGER. In the latter case, the compiler will convert the *expression* value to match the type of *fname*.

EXAMPLE 6.10   A common operation is finding the square root of a sum of squares, for example,

$$\sqrt{x^2 + y^2}.$$

The single-statement functions HYPOT and SQUARE defined next can be used for this purpose.

```
REAL X, Y, C
REAL HYPOT, SQUARE
SQUARE(X) = X * X
HYPOT(X, Y) = SQRT(SQUARE(X) + SQUARE(Y))
```

The statement

```
C = HYPOT(X, 2.0)
```

uses HYPOT to assign the square root of $x^2 + 4.0$ to C.   ■

LOGICAL Functions   Functions can return LOGICAL results. A LOGICAL function is often used to make a condition more readable.

EXAMPLE 6.11   The following function POSTIV returns .TRUE. when its REAL argument, NUM, is positive (greater than zero) and returns .FALSE. when its argument is zero or negative:

```
REAL NUM
LOGICAL POSTIV
POSTIV = (NUM .GT. 0.0)
```

Function POSTIV is used in the IF structure below, which prints the square root of X.

```
IF (X .EQ. 0.0) THEN
    PRINT *, 'Square root is 0.0'
ELSE IF (POSTIV(X)) THEN
    PRINT *, 'Square root is ', SQRT(X)
ELSE
    PRINT *, 'Square root is imaginary'
END IF
```
■

Finding the Roots of an Equation (Optional)

In Section 12.1, we discuss how to find the roots of an equation of the form

$$y = f(x)$$

where the roots are the values of x for which $f(x)$ is zero. In the next case study, we illustrate a technique that uses two single-statement functions: $f(x)$ and $f'(x)$, the derivative of $f(x)$. If you are not familiar with calculus, you may prefer to skip this case study.

Case Study: Newton's Method for Finding Roots (Optional)

PROBLEM STATEMENT

Your calculus instructor would like you to write a program that uses Newton's method for finding a root of an equation, $y = f(x)$, where k is a root if $f(k)$ equals zero. Newton's method starts with an initial guess for a root, x_0, and then generates successive approximate roots $x_1, x_2, \ldots, x_j, x_{j+1}, \ldots$ using the iterative formula

$$x_{j+1} = x_j - \frac{f(x_j)}{f'(x_j)},$$

where $f'(x_j)$ is the derivative of function f evaluated at $x = x_j$. The formula above generates a new guess, x_{j+1}, from a previous one, x_j. Newton's method terminates when successive guesses are sufficiently close in value, that is, when

$$|x_{j+1} - x_j| < \varepsilon$$

where ε (*epsilon*) is a very small constant (for example, 0.00001).

Sometimes Newton's method will fail to converge to a root. In this case, the program should terminate after a large number of trials (say 100).

ANALYSIS

Figure 6.10 shows the geometric interpretation of Newton's method where x_0, x_1, and x_2 represent successive guesses for the root. At each point x_j, the derivative, $f'(x_j)$, is the tangent to the curve, $f(x)$. The next guess for the root, x_{j+1}, is the point where the tangent crosses the x-axis.

From geometry, we get the equation

$$\frac{y_{j+1} - y_j}{x_{j+1} - x_j} = m,$$

Figure 6.10. *Geo-metric Interpreta-tion of Newton's Method*

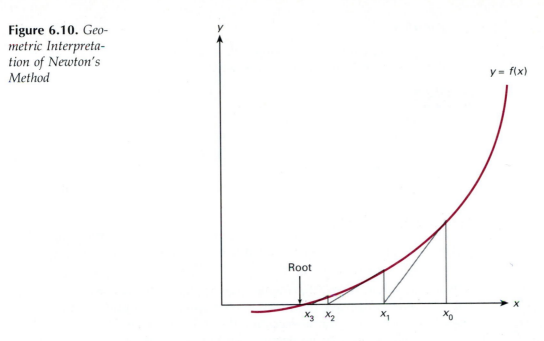

where m is the slope of the line between points (x_{j+1}, y_{j+1}) and (x_j, y_j). From Fig. 6.10, if (x_j, y_j) is a point on the curve and (x_{j+1}, y_{j+1}) is the next point on the x-axis, then y_{j+1} is zero, y_j is $f(x_j)$, and m is $f'(x_j)$, so by substituting and rearranging terms, we get

$$-f(x_j) = f'(x_j) \times (x_{j+1} - x_j),$$

which leads to the formula shown at the beginning of this case study. In the data requirements that follow, XLAST corresponds to x_j and XNEXT corresponds to x_{j+1}.

Data Requirements

Problem Parameters

the minimum distance between successive guesses (EPSLON = 0.00001)
the maximum number of guesses (MAXGES = 100)

Program Outputs

the next guess for a root (REAL XNEXT)
the count of guesses (INTEGER NUMGES)

Program Variables

the last guess for a root (REAL XLAST)

Functions

the function whose root is sought (REAL F(X))
the function's derivative (REAL FPRIME(X))

DESIGN

The initial guess for the root is read into XNEXT. Inside a loop, we compute the next guess for the root value, XNEXT, from the last guess, XLAST. The loop must continue to execute until the difference between successive guesses is less than EPSLON. The algorithm follows.

Algorithm

1. Read the initial guess into XNEXT.
2. Generate up to MAXGES values for XNEXT and XLAST. If XNEXT and XLAST differ by less than EPSLON, display the value of XNEXT and F(XNEXT) and exit from the loop.

The refinement of step 2 that follows uses a DO loop with loop-control variable NUMGES. Step 2.5 displays the function root when it is found. At this point, there is no need to continue executing the DO loop, so step 2.7 causes a loop exit. We will see how to implement the loop exit step when we study the program.

Step 2 Refinement

2.1 DO NUMGES = 1, MAXGES
      2.2 Set XLAST to the last guess which is stored in XNEXT.
      2.3 Compute the next guess, XNEXT, from XLAST by evaluating f(XLAST) and f'(XLAST).
      2.4 IF (ABS(XNEXT − XLAST) < EPSLON) THEN
          2.5 Display the root and the function value at the root.
          2.6 Display the number of guesses.
          2.7 Exit from the loop.
          END IF
    END DO

IMPLEMENTATION

The program must contain declarations for function $f(x)$, the function whose root is being computed, and function FPRIME(X), the derivative of $f(x)$. The program in Fig. 6.11 computes the root for the function

$$f(x) = 5x^3 - 2x^2 + 3$$

with derivative

$$f'(x) = 15x^2 - 4x.$$

Figure 6.11 *Newton's Method*

```
        PROGRAM NEWTON
C Finds a root of an equation using Newton's method.

C Declarations
        REAL EPSLON
        INTEGER MAXGES
        PARAMETER (EPSLON = 0.00001, MAXGES = 100)
        REAL XLAST, XNEXT
        INTEGER NUMGES

C Functions
        REAL F, FPRIME, X
        F(X) = 5 * X * X * X - 2 * X * X + 3
        FPRIME(X) = 15 * X * X - 4 * X

C Read the initial guess into XNEXT.
        PRINT *, 'Enter the initial guess for a root:'
        READ *, XNEXT

C Compute successive guesses.
        DO 20 NUMGES = 1, MAXGES
           XLAST = XNEXT
           XNEXT = XLAST - F(XLAST) / FPRIME(XLAST)
           IF (ABS(XNEXT - XLAST) .LT. EPSLON) THEN
              PRINT 5, 'The approximate root is ', XNEXT
              PRINT 5, 'The function value is ', F(XNEXT)
    5         FORMAT (1X, A, E17.11)
              PRINT 15, NUMGES, ' guesses were made'
   15         FORMAT (1X, I3, A)
C             Exit from the loop
              GOTO 99
           END IF
   20 CONTINUE

C Normal exit — display a message that a root was not found.
        PRINT 25, 'Root not found before ', MAXGES, ' guesses.'
   25 FORMAT (1X, A, I3, A)

C Continuation point after loop exit
   99 CONTINUE

        STOP
        END


Enter the initial guess for a root:
1.0
The approximate root is -.72900142869E-01
The function value is -3.6379788071E-12
  9 guesses were made
```

The statement

```
GOTO 99
```

causes an immediate transfer of control to the statement with label 99. Because label 99 comes after the loop terminator (20 CONTINUE), the loop is exited. The GOTO statement is executed only if a root is found. However, if no root is found, the DO loop executes MAXGES times and loop exit occurs in the normal way. After loop exit, the statement

```
PRINT 25, 'Root not found before ', MAXGES, ' guesses.'
```

displays a message indicating that no root was found.

TESTING AND VERIFICATION

Because the function value in Fig. 6.11 is sufficiently close to zero, we can feel confident we have found a root. To test Newton's method, run the program on several mathematical functions and with several different starting points for each function. In most cases, Newton's method should find a solution relatively quickly.

You may find there are situations in which Newton's method will not work, but will cycle until MAXGES guesses are made. At other times, Newton's method will fail because FPRIME(XLAST) becomes zero and a division by zero run-time error occurs. In these cases, you must try a different technique for finding function roots. One such technique (the bisection method) is described in Section 12.1.

GOTO Statement

We feature the syntax display for the GOTO statement next. The program style subsection discusses why the GOTO statement should be used with care.

SYNTAX DISPLAY

GOTO Statement

SYNTAX: GOTO *label*

EXAMPLE: GOTO 99

INTERPRETATION: Control is transferred immediately to the statement specified by *label*. The *label* must appear in columns 1 through 5 of exactly one executable Fortran statement.

Program Style: *GOTO Considered Harmful*

Earlier versions of Fortran did not support the IF and WHILE control structures, so programmers often used the GOTO statement to implement decision steps and loops. Programs written this way were called *spaghetti code* to indicate that they were difficult to follow. While it is perfectly reasonable to use a GOTO to exit early from a DO loop, as is done in Fig. 6.11, you should avoid overuse of this statement.

EXERCISES FOR SECTION 6.3

Self-check

1. Determine the output from program Newton shown in Fig. 6.10 if the initial guess for the root is 0.0, the value used for constant EPSLON is 0.1, and

$$f(x) = x^2 - 2x + 1$$
$$f'(x) = 2x - 2.$$

Programming

1. Write a single-statement function ROUND(X, N) to round a real number (represented by X) to N decimal digits (N is a nonnegative integer).
2. a. Write a single-statement function CONVRT(C) that converts temperatures given in degrees Celsius (C) to temperatures in degrees Fahrenheit (F), where

$$F = 1.8 \times C + 32.0.$$

   b. Using the function CONVRT defined in part (a), write a Fortran program segment (a DO loop) to generate a table for Celsius to Fahrenheit conversion for degrees C = 0, 1, 2, . . . , 99, 100.
3. The coordinates of two points on the x-y plane are represented by (X1, Y1) and (X2, Y2), respectively. Write a Fortran statement that uses the single-statement functions HYPOT and SQUARE to find the distance between these points.

6.4   Defining a Subroutine

A *subroutine* is a separate program module whose execution can return any number of results (including zero) to the calling program. The subroutine in the next example simply displays a table heading and does not return any results back to the calling program.

EXAMPLE 6.12

Subroutine TABHED in Fig. 6.12 displays the table heading for the rebar strength program shown in Fig. 5.1. When called, the subroutine displays each of the messages in the PRINT statements.

Figure 6.12. *A Subroutine with Zero Results*

```
      SUBROUTINE TABHED (STRNTH)
C Displays the heading for the rebar table.
C Precondition : STRNTH is defined.
C Postcondition: Table heading is displayed.

C Argument Declarations
      REAL STRNTH

C Display heading
      PRINT *, '            Joe Bob''s Steel Company'
      PRINT *, '              Rebar load chart'
      PRINT *, 'For bars with a steel strength of ', STRNTH, ' psi'
      PRINT *
      PRINT *, 'Bar            Cross-sectional          Max. Load'
      PRINT *, 'Number         Area (sq. in.)           (lbs.)'
      PRINT *, '_____         _____           _____   '

C Exit subroutine
      RETURN
      END
```

The definition of subroutine TABHED is very similar to that of a function except that it begins with the word SUBROUTINE. There is one argument, STRNTH. After the subroutine body executes, the statement

RETURN

returns control back to the calling program, while the statement

END

marks the end of the subroutine definition.

We stated earlier that a subroutine can return any number of results, or even zero results, as does TABHED. A result is returned when a dummy argument is changed in the subroutine body. The arguments of a subroutine can be used both to pass data into the subroutine and to return results back to the calling program.

EXAMPLE 6.13   Subroutine BREAK in Fig. 6.13 returns the whole and fractional parts of its first argument. This argument value is passed into dummy argument X and is used to determine the values assigned to dummy arguments WHOLE and FRAC. The statements

```
WHOLE = INT(X)
FRAC = X - REAL(WHOLE)
```

Figure 6.13. *Subroutine BREAK*

```
      SUBROUTINE BREAK (X, WHOLE, FRAC)
C Breaks a real number into its whole and fractional parts
C Precondition : X is defined.
C Postcondition: WHOLE is integral part of X;
                 FRAC is fractional part of X.

C Input Argument
C   X — The value to be split (REAL)
C Output Arguments
C   WHOLE — The whole part of X (INTEGER)
C   FRAC — The fractional part of X (REAL)

C Argument Declarations
      REAL X, FRAC
      INTEGER WHOLE
C Define results
      WHOLE = INT(X)
      FRAC = X — REAL(WHOLE)

C Exit subroutine
      RETURN
      END
```

reference the type conversion functions INT and REAL (see Table 2.4). These statements assign values to the output arguments WHOLE and FRAC. Because the value passed into X is not modified by the subroutine execution, X is called an input argument.

Because all values are returned through the output arguments, no value is assigned to the subroutine name in Fig. 6.13. It is, in fact, illegal to reference the subroutine name within the subroutine body. It also is illegal to declare the type of a subroutine in the calling program or in the subroutine header. ∎

SYNTAX DISPLAY

Subroutine Definition

SYNTAX: SUBROUTINE *sname* (*dummy argument list*)
       interface section
       local declaration section
       subroutine body
       RETURN
       END

EXAMPLE: SUBROUTINE STUB
       PRINT *, 'STUB entered'
       RETURN
       END

(continued)

INTERPRETATION: The SUBROUTINE statement specifies the subroutine name, *sname;* the *dummy argument list* is a list of identifiers. The dummy arguments are used either to receive data (as *input arguments*) from the calling program or to return results to the calling program (as *output arguments*). Occasionally a dummy argument will be used for both purposes. We refer to such arguments as *input/output arguments.* The *interface section* contains descriptions and declarations for all the *dummy arguments.*

Other identifiers not appearing in the *dummy argument list* but required for writing the subroutine should be declared in the separate local declaration section.

The *subroutine body* describes the data manipulation performed by the subroutine. The RETURN statement transfers control back to the calling statement. The END statement terminates the subroutine definition.

Program Style: *Documentation of Subroutines*

Subroutine BREAK illustrates some conventions for writing subroutines that will be used throughout this text. Each subroutine begins with an interface section that describes the purpose of the subroutine, its preconditions and postconditions, and its arguments. The interface section consists of comments describing the subroutine and its arguments followed by the dummy argument declarations. This is all the documentation that a potential user of the subroutine needs to determine whether the subroutine can be used for a specific purpose and, if so, how to call it. There is no need to look beyond the interface section.

EXERCISES FOR SECTION 6.4

Self-check

1. What does the following subroutine do? If its argument value is 3 when the subroutine is called, what value is returned through its argument?

```
SUBROUTINE CUBE (N)
INTEGER N
N = N * N * N
RETURN
END
```

2. What would be the effect of the statement

```
CALL BREAK (2.16589, X, Y)
```

What data types are required for actual arguments X and Y? What would be the effect of transposing X and Y in the subroutine call statement?

Programming

1. Write a subroutine that returns both the square and the square root of the absolute value of its first argument. The subroutine also should return a

LOGICAL flag indicating whether its argument is positive (flag value is .TRUE.) or negative (flag value is .FALSE.). (*Hint:* There should be one input argument and three output arguments.)

2. Write a subroutine RECNGL, with arguments LENGTH and WIDTH, that displays a rectangle of WIDTH lines, each of which has LENGTH asterisks. (*Hint:* Use PRINT *, ('*', I = 1, WIDTH) to display each line.)

6.5 Calling a Subroutine

Because a function returns a single value, it is called by simply referencing it in an expression; however, a special Fortran statement, the CALL statement, is used to call a subroutine. Assuming X (type REAL), I1 (type INTEGER), and R1 (type Real) are declared in a program, the statement

```
CALL BREAK (X, I1, R1)
```

can be used to call subroutine BREAK. The argument correspondence would be as follows:

Actual Argument		*Dummy Argument*
X	$\longleftrightarrow$	X
I1	$\longleftrightarrow$	WHOLE
R1	$\longleftrightarrow$	FRAC

Within the body of the subroutine, each reference to a dummy argument causes its corresponding actual argument to be manipulated. This situation is depicted in Fig. 6.14, assuming the variable X in the main program has the value 7.234 and main-program variables I1 and R1 are initially undefined.

Figure 6.14. *Argument Correspondence for CALL BREAK(X, I1, R1)*

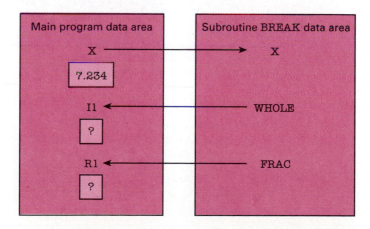

Figure 6.15. *Effect of CALL BREAK (X, I1, R1)*

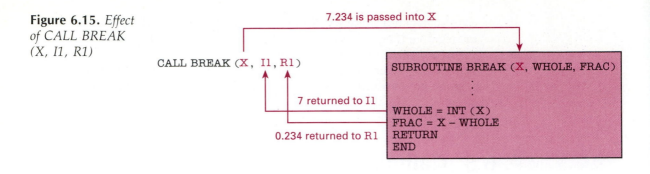

The statement

```
WHOLE = INT(X)
```

causes the integral part (7) of X to be stored in I1; the statement

```
FRAC = X - REAL(WHOLE)
```

causes the fractional part (0.234) of X to be stored in R1. After BREAK executes, control returns to the statement following the subroutine CALL statement. The effect of the subroutine call is illustrated in Fig. 6.15.

Each dummy argument for subroutine BREAK is used either for input (X) or for output (WHOLE, FRAC). An argument whose initial value is passed into the subroutine and then modified is called an *input/output argument*.

EXAMPLE 6.14   Subroutine ORDER in Fig. 6.16 places its arguments in numerical order. After execution of ORDER, the smaller value is in S and the larger value is in L. It may be necessary to switch the original values passed into S and L to accomplish this.

Figure 6.16. *Subroutine ORDER*

```
      SUBROUTINE ORDER (S, L)
C Arranges its arguments in numerical order
C Precondition : S and L are defined.
C Postcondition: S < L

C Input/Output Argument
C   S - Smaller number after execution of ORDER
C   L - Larger number after execution of ORDER

C Argument Declarations
      REAL S, L
```

```
C Local Declarations
      REAL TEMP

C Compare S and L and switch if necessary
      IF (S .GT. L) THEN
         TEMP = S
         S = L
         L = TEMP
      END IF

C Exit subroutine
      RETURN
      END
```

The argument correspondence specified by the statement

```
CALL ORDER (NUM1, NUM2)
```

is shown next.

Actual Argument		Dummy Argument
NUM1	⟷	S
NUM2	⟷	L

If before the call the value of NUM1 is 8.0 and the value of NUM2 is 6.0, then after the execution of subroutine ORDER, the value of NUM1 would be 6.0 and the value of NUM2 would be 8.0. The effect of the subroutine call is illustrated in Fig. 6.17.

Figure 6.17. *Effect of CALL ORDER (NUM1, NUM2)*

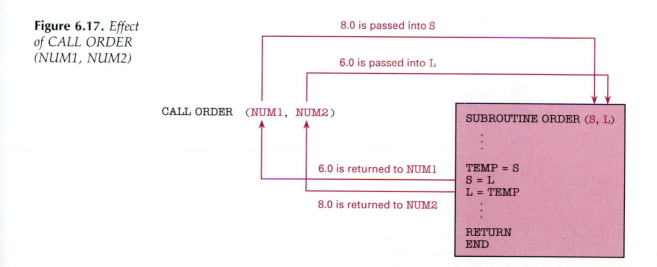

Table 6.3. *Trace of CALL ORDER (NUM1, NUM2) for NUM1 = 8.0, NUM2 = 6.0*

STATEMENT	S(NUM1)	L(NUM2)	TEMP	EFFECT
	8.0	6.0	?	
IF (S .GT. L) THEN				8.0 > 6.0 is true
TEMP = S			8.0	Saves 8.0 in TEMP
S = L	6.0			Saves 6.0 in NUM1
L = TEMP		8.0		Saves 8.0 in NUM2

This execution of the subroutine is traced in Table 6.3. The actual argument represented by each dummy argument is shown in parentheses in the table heading. The statement

S = L

stores the value (6.0) passed into dummy argument L in the actual argument (NUM1) that corresponds to dummy argument S. The statement

L = TEMP

stores the value (8.0) that was passed into dummy argument S and saved in local variable TEMP in the actual argument (NUM2) that corresponds to dummy argument L. The subroutine execution switches the values stored in the actual arguments NUM1 and NUM2 as desired. ▪

SYNTAX DISPLAY

Subroutine Call

SYNTAX: CALL *sname* (*actual argument list*)

EXAMPLE: CALL ORDER (A, B)

INTERPRETATION: Subroutine calls begin with the word CALL, followed by the name of the subroutine to be referenced, *sname*, and the *actual argument list*. The actual arguments may be variable names, expressions, or constants. Expressions and constants may be used only to pass data into the subroutine and must correspond to dummy input arguments. The parentheses should be omitted if there are no subroutine arguments.

Summary of Rules for Using Subroutines

- A CALL statement must be used to call each subroutine.
- There should be the same number of actual arguments as there are dummy arguments in the subroutine definition.

■ Each actual argument must have the same type and be in the same order as its corresponding dummy argument.

Because your Fortran compiler might not check to see whether each actual argument list appearing in a subroutine call satisfies these rules, violating one of them may lead to errors that are difficult to track down.

EXERCISES FOR SECTION 6.5

Self-check

1. What would be the effect of the following three call statements:

```
CALL ORDER (A, B)
CALL ORDER (A, C)
CALL ORDER (B, C)
```

2. Show the correspondence between the actual arguments and dummy arguments just before the first call to subroutine ORDER in Exercise 1 and just after the first return. Assume A is 5.0 and B is 3.0 before the first call.
3. Show the output displayed by the following program in the form of a table of values for X, Y, and Z.

```
      PROGRAM SHOW
      INTEGER X, Y, Z
      X = 5
      Y = 3
      PRINT *, ' X Y Z'
      CALL SUM (X, Y, Z)
      PRINT 5, X, Y, Z
    5 FORMAT (1X, I4, I4, I4)
      CALL SUM (Y, X, Z)
      PRINT 5, X, Y, Z
      CALL SUM (Z, Y, X)
      PRINT 5, X, Y, Z
      CALL SUM (Z, Z, X)
      PRINT 5, X, Y, Z
      CALL SUM (Y, Y, Y)
      PRINT 5, X, Y, Z
      STOP
      END

      SUBROUTINE SUM (A, B, C)
      INTEGER A, B, C
      C = A + B
      RETURN
      END
```

Programming
1. Rewrite SUM as a function and replace the CALL statements in the main program with assignment statements that reference the function.
2. Write a program fragment that reads in a data value and finds its square and square root by calling the subroutine from Programming exercise 1 at the end of Section 6.4. Your fragment should print the values returned and a message indicating that the square root is imaginary if the flag value returned is .FALSE..

6.6 Top-down Design and Structure Charts

With the introduction of the subroutine, you now have the capability of writing subprogram modules that return any number of values. You should use functions for modules that return a single value and subroutines for all other modules.

Top-down Design

By using subprograms, you should be able to implement programs in a top-down or stepwise manner. To begin the design phase, write the initial algorithm as a list of steps (or subproblems). Next, decide whether to implement the solution to each subproblem in-line (as part of the main program) or using a separate subprogram. If you decide to use a separate subprogram, implement the subproblem solution as a function if it returns a single value; otherwise, implement it as a subroutine.

When you start the implementation phase, write the main program as a sequence of calls to its subprogram modules without worrying about the details of the individual subprograms. Next, concentrate on each subprogram and implement it separately without being distracted by concerns about the other subprograms. If the algorithm for a particular subprogram requires substantial refinement, you might decide to implement certain refinement steps using separate subprograms as well. When you are finished, you will have a program system consisting of a single main program and a collection of independent subprograms.

You can view the final result as a program system constructed from a set of "building blocks," that is, the systems' subprograms. As you continue to program, you will begin to assemble a personal library of subprograms that have been tested and proved effective. If you write subprograms in a general manner, you might be able to reuse them when the operations they perform are required in another program system. Reusing tried and tested subprograms is a common software engineering practice as it saves considerable time and effort by keeping you from having to continually "reinvent the wheel."

Structure Chart   In the next case study, we practice the top-down design technique described above. We revisit the problem solved in Section 5.2 that was concerned with displaying a table of maximum tensile loads for different-sized steel reinforcing bars (rebars). We also introduce the *structure chart* and use it to illustrate the flow of control and data between the main program and its subprograms.

Case Study: Computing Maximum Tensile Loads with Subprograms

PROBLEM STATEMENT

Joe Bob's steel company produces steel reinforcing bars (rebars). The size of a rebar is designated by a number. That number divided by 8 gives the diameter of the bar in inches (e.g., a number 5 rebar is $\frac{5}{8}$ of an inch in diameter). The company needs to produce a chart showing the maximum tensile load of the bars when they are made from certain grades of steel. Joe Bob makes number 2 to number 11 rebars. Each chart should have the form shown in Section 5.2.

ANALYSIS

See Section 5.2 for the problem analysis. The data requirements and initial algorithm for this problem are given next.

Data Requirements

Problem Parameters

first rebar number in the table (FIRBAR = 2)
last rebar number in the table (LASBAR = 11)

Problem Input

tensile strength of the steel (REAL STRNTH)

Problem Output

a table of rebar numbers, areas, and maximum tensile loads

DESIGN

The algorithm follows.

Algorithm

1. Read the steel strength.
2. Display the table heading.
3. Display a table showing the rebar number, cross-sectional area, and maximum load for each rebar from FIRBAR to LASBAR.

Structure Chart

We write step 1 in the main program and implement steps 2 and 3 using subprograms. Both steps will be implemented as subroutines because they don't satisfy the definition of a function, that is, a subprogram that returns a single result. The structure chart is shown in Fig. 6.18.

The structure chart shows each of the major subproblems in the algorithm. The name of a subprogram (TABHED or TABBOD) appears under its subproblem description.

The labeled arrows in the structure chart show the data flow between subproblems. Only variables that are passed between subproblems or between the main program and a subproblem should appear in the initial structure chart; variables that are processed totally within a given subproblem are local variables and should not appear.

In the data requirements, we list the variable STRNTH as a problem input, which means that its value must be read as a data item by the program. The structure chart shows that STRNTH is passed between the main program and its three subproblems. The direction of the arrow indicates whether a variable is an input or an output for a particular subproblem. STRNTH is an output of the subproblem "Read steel strength"; STRNTH is an input to the subproblems "Display table heading" and "Display table body."

The fact that the same variable may be an input to one module and an output of another may be confusing initially. However, you should realize that the determination of whether a variable is a module input or output depends solely on the usage of the variable in that particular module. The

Figure 6.18. *Structure Chart for Tensile Load Problem*

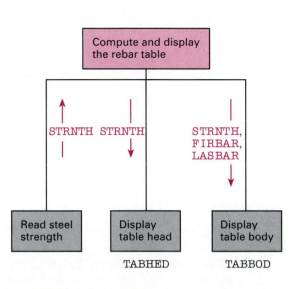

subproblem "Read steel strength" defines the value of the variable STRNTH; hence, STRNTH is an output of this subproblem. Subroutine TABHED displays the value of STRNTH in the table heading, so STRNTH must be passed as an input to subroutine TABHED. Subroutine TABBOD uses the value of STRNTH to compute the maximum tensile load for a rebar, so STRNTH must also be passed as an input to subroutine TABBOD.

IMPLEMENTATION

Main Program

With the structure chart in mind, we can write the main program (see REBAR2 in Fig. 6.19). Program REBAR2 is much more concise and readable than program REBAR shown in Fig. 5.1. Only variable STRNTH and parameters FIRBAR and LASBAR are declared in the main program. The statement

```
CALL TABHED (STRNTH)
```

Figure 6.19. *Main Program for Computing Tensile Loads Using Subprograms*

```
      PROGRAM REBAR2
C Prints a table of maximum tensile load on rebars
C using subprograms

C Declarations
      INTEGER FIRBAR, LASBAR
      PARAMETER (FIRBAR = 2, LASBAR = 11)
      REAL STRNTH

C Read steel strength
      PRINT *, 'Enter steel tensile strength (in psi)'
      READ *, STRNTH

C Display table heading.
      CALL TABHED (STRNTH)

C Display table body.
      CALL TABBOD (STRNTH, FIRBAR, LASBAR)

      STOP
      END


C  ─────────────────────────────────────────────────

C Insert subroutines TABHED and TABBOD here.
```

calls subroutine TABHED to display the table heading. The statement

```
CALL TABBOD (STRNTH, FIRBAR, LASBAR)
```

calls subroutine TABBOD to display the table for rebar numbers FIRBAR through LASBAR. If we change the values of parameters FIRBAR and LASBAR, then a different-sized table would be displayed.

It may look strange to see a main program that consists only of a READ

FORTRAN in Focus

Research Code Development

NATIONAL AERONAUTICS AND SPACE ADMINISTRATION

NASA Lewis Research Center's Icing and Cryogenic Technology branch actively investigates the aeronautics of aircraft icing and uses computer simulations both as a tool for performing their basic research and as a means of applying it. To study the effects of icing on aircraft performance, they develop models to predict ice growth on the aircraft and the change in performance resulting from the ice.

The engineers who work in the group are both scientists and programmers. They develop models from the physics and chemistry underlying the icing phenomenon, and then write their own computer programs to simulate the behavior of the aircraft flying through a given set of atmospheric conditions. These programs may be small pieces of code for a one-of-a-kind application, or may be multi-thousand line applications that are in development for years.

One of these large-scale simulations allows a user to input the geometry of a particular aircraft and the atmospheric conditions through which it will fly. The simulation models the behavior of the aircraft and predicts the shape of the ice that forms, the extent of the ice formation, and the changes in lift and drag that result. The application itself may be implemented on a variety of platforms. Several versions of a simulation may exist, making the hardware choice a function of the computing resources required. The quantity of atmospheric data to be processed may dictate that the simulation run on a supercomputer. In other instances, the data may be such that running on a PC is fast enough.

Such a large-scale application is frequently distributed to aerospace companies for their use in aircraft design and certification. Unlike commercial code, which is routinely upgraded, customized,

statement, a PRINT statement, and two subprogram calls. However, this situation is very desirable because we have left the details to the two subprograms, TABHED and TABBOD, which are discussed after Fig. 6.19. This practice of providing the solution details in the subprograms is called *information hiding*.

Subroutine TABHED

Subroutine TABHED appears in Fig. 6.12.

and fully supported for the end user, the code written by the Icing and Cryogenic Technology group is considered "research" code. It contains the basic scientific models, and the aerospace companies are free to incorporate them into the applications they develop for their engineers and designers, perhaps adding a graphical interface, or customizing the I/O to work with the database of aircraft specifications created in another application.

Given the nature of the scientific programming being done in this branch of NASA, it is no surprise that 90% of the programming is done in Fortran. Mark Potapczuk, scientist, engineer, and programmer, highlights the universality of Fortran among the organizations they work with as its most important advantage—they can be certain that a potential user will be able to work with the code they create. He and his colleagues also enjoy the ability to use parts of pre-existing

COURTESY OF NATIONAL AERO-
NAUTICS AND SPACE ADMINISTRA-
TION, NASA LEWIS RESEARCH
CENTER.

code in the programs they write to solve new problems. The engineers are constantly updating the programs they work with and extending their capability. In addition, the group funds some outside contractors to do development that will benefit their

work, but that is beyond the manpower limits of the group. One such project currently under way is the implementation of some of their Fortran code on massively parallel computers.

The remaining 10% of the group's programming consists of shell programs available within UNIX and on certain workstations. These shells organize the Fortran code and provide command-line or graphical interfaces to the end user. The current generation of compilers and debuggers are a noticeable improvement to the language, according to Mark Potapczuk, and make the code development his group performs that much easier.

Our many thanks to Mark Potapczuk, Engineer in Icing and Cryogenic Technology at the NASA Lewis Research Center in Cleveland, Ohio, for giving us this insight into the aircraft icing research done at NASA.

Subroutine TABBOD

Subroutine TABBOD implements the initial algorithm's step 3, which is repeated below. The data requirements and algorithm for TABBOD follow.

Step 3. Display a table showing the rebar number, cross-sectional area, and maximum load for each rebar from FIRBAR to LASBAR.

Data Requirements for TABBOD

Subroutine Inputs

tensile strength of the steel (REAL STRNTH)
first rebar number in the table (INTEGER FIRBAR)
last rebar number in the table (INTEGER LASBAR)

Local Variables

the rebar number (INTEGER BARNUM)
the radius of the cross section (REAL RADIUS)
the cross-sectional area (REAL AREA)
the maximum tensile load (REAL LOAD)

Algorithm for TABBOD

1. DO for each rebar from number FIRBAR through LASBAR
    2. Compute the cross-sectional area.
    3. LOAD = AREA * STRNTH
    4. Display rebar number, area, and load.
   END DO

Step 2 is the only step that needs refinement. We could write another subprogram to implement this step; however, we already have a function, DOAREA (see Fig. 6.1), that computes the area of a circle. We mentioned earlier that it is very desirable to reuse subprograms, so all we need to do is determine how to call DOAREA. From Section 5.2, we obtain the refinement for step 2 as follows:

2.1 *radius = rebar number*/16.0
2.2 Compute the area of a circle given its radius.

We can use the statements

```
RADIUS = BARNUM / 16.0
AREA = DOAREA(RADIUS)
```

to implement step 2. The function result is returned to subroutine TABBOD and stored in local variable AREA.

Figure 6.20. *Subroutine TABBOD*

```
      SUBROUTINE TABBOD (STRNTH, FIRBAR, LASBAR)
C Displays a table showing the rebar number, cross-sectional
C area, and maximum load for each rebar.
C Precondition : STRNTH, FIRBAR, and LASBAR are defined and
C               FIRBAR <= LASBAR.
C Postcondition: Table body is displayed.

C Input Arguments
C   STRNTH — steel tensile strength
C   FIRBAR — first rebar number
C   LASBAR — last rebar number

C Argument Declarations
      REAL STRNTH
      INTEGER FIRBAR, LASBAR

C Local Declarations
      INTEGER BARNUM
      REAL AREA, LOAD, RADIUS, DOAREA

C Display table body
      DO 10 BARNUM = FIRBAR, LASBAR
         RADIUS = REAL(BARNUM) / 16.0
         AREA = DOAREA(RADIUS)
         LOAD = AREA * STRNTH
         PRINT 5, BARNUM, AREA, LOAD
    5    FORMAT (1X, I6, 10X, F15.2, 10X, F8.0)
   10 CONTINUE

C Exit subroutine
      RETURN
      END


C ───────────────────────────────────────────────

C Insert function DOAREA here.
```

The remaining steps are written in-line in subroutine TABBOD because they are relatively straightforward and involve a single line of code. Figure 6.20 shows subroutine TABBOD.

TESTING AND VERIFICATION

Insert subroutines TABBOD and TABHED and function DOAREA in the source program file that contains program REBAR2 (the order of the subprograms is immaterial). Once the complete source file is ready, the program can be run and tested. We discuss other aspects of testing a program system in the next section.

Locality of Declarations

In the original program shown in Fig. 5.1, all parameter and variable declarations occurred in one place. However, when we use subprograms, some declarations appear in the main program (STRNTH, FIRBAR, LASBAR) and some appear in the subprograms (BARNUM, AREA, LOAD, RADIUS in TABBOD; PI in DOAREA). This happens because a variable or parameter declared in the main program cannot be referenced in a subprogram unless it is passed as an argument to that subprogram. Therefore, a variable that is passed from the main program to one or more subprograms (for example, STRNTH), must be declared in the main program. However, if a variable or parameter is used in only one subprogram, it should be declared as a local variable in that subprogram.

6.7 Debugging and Testing a Program System

As the number of modules and statements in a program grows, the possibility of error also increases. If each module or subprogram is kept to a manageable size, then the likelihood of error will increase much more slowly. Short subprograms also are easier to read and understand, particularly if they are carefully documented, as illustrated in this text.

When possible, test each subprogram separately before including it in the program system. This can be done by writing a *driver program*, a short program written for the sole purpose of testing a single subprogram. The driver program should define all subprogram inputs, call the subprogram, and display the subprogram result(s).

EXAMPLE 6.15

The main program in Fig. 6.21 is a driver program that tests subroutine BREAK (see Fig. 6.13). The driver program repeats the following steps:

- Read a data value for X.
- Call subroutine BREAK with X as an argument.
- Display the subroutine results (saved in variables N and Y).

Figure 6.21. *Driver Program for Subroutine BREAK*

```
      PROGRAM DRIVER
C Driver program to test BREAK

C Declarations
      REAL X, Y
      INTEGER N
```

```
C Call BREAK until test is completed
      PRINT *, 'Enter a value to be split — enter 0.0 when done:'
      READ *, X
      DO WHILE (X .NE. 0.0)                           9 IF (...) THEN
         CALL BREAK (X, N, Y)
         PRINT *, 'N = ', N, ' Y = ', Y
         PRINT *, 'Enter a value to be split — enter 0.0 when done:'
         READ *, X
      END DO                                          GOTO 9
                                                      END IF
      STOP
      END

C ————————————————————————————————————————————————

C Insert subroutine BREAK (see Fig. 6.13) here.

C ————————————————————————————————————————————————


Enter a value to be split — enter 0.0 when done:
2.5
N = 2      Y = 0.5000000
Enter a value to be split — enter 0.0 when done:
—3.7
N = —3     Y = —0.7000000
Enter a value to be split — enter 0.0 when done:
25.
N = 25     Y = 0.0000000
Enter a value to be split — enter 0.0 when done:
1.25678E3
N = 1256   Y = 0.7800000
Enter a value to be split — enter 0.0 when done:
0.0
```

To use the driver program, enter a varied collection of data values for X (a very small number, a very large number, a negative number, and so on) and examine the corresponding values of N and Y displayed by the program. When you are satisfied that the subroutine works properly, enter the sentinel value (0.0).

Bottom-up Testing

You can write a separate driver program to test each subprogram in a program system. When you are confident that all subprograms work properly, you can include them in the source file following the main program. Because the subprograms have been tested and debugged, it should be significantly easier to debug the final program system. The process of separately testing each subprogram before testing the program system as a whole is called *bottom-up testing*.

Top-down Testing

Sometimes programmers choose to test the main program before completing all subprograms. To do this, you must insert a dummy subprogram called a *stub* in place of any subprograms that have not yet been written. The stub will simply display a message indicating that the subprogram has been called and then display the values of any input arguments. It also will assign some easily recognizable values (often zero) to any subprogram output arguments. Using stubs in this way enables you to test the flow of control through the main program and to verify that all subprogram calls are correct.

EXAMPLE 6.16

Figure 6.22 contains a main program that reads a data value representing the tensile strength of steel rebars and calls subroutines TABHED and TABBOD to display the heading and body of a table. It's very likely that TABHED will be completed before TABBOD is because it is so much simpler. If this is the case, then it would be desirable to write a stub for TABBOD so that you can compile, execute, and debug the main program and subroutine TABHED while waiting for TABBOD to be completed. Figure 6.22 shows one possible stub. ■

Figure 6.22. *Stub for Subroutine TABBOD*

```
      SUBROUTINE TABBOD (STRNTH, FIRBAR, LASBAR)
C Stub for a subroutine that displays a table showing the rebar
C number, cross-sectional area, and maximum load for each rebar.
C Precondition : STRNTH, FIRBAR, and LASBAR are defined and
C                FIRBAR <= LASBAR.
C Postcondition: Table body is displayed.

C Input Arguments
C   STRNTH - steel tensile strength
C   FIRBAR - first rebar number
C   LASBAR - last rebar number

C Argument Declarations
      REAL STRNTH
      INTEGER FIRBAR, LASBAR

C Display message and input arguments
      PRINT *, 'Entering stub for subroutine TABBOD'
      PRINT *, 'Value of STRNTH is ', STRNTH
      PRINT *, 'Value of FIRBAR is ', FIRBAR
      PRINT *, 'Value of LASBAR is ', LASBAR

C Exit stub
      RETURN
      END
```

The stub has the same interface section as the final subroutine; however, it has no local declarations and does not contain the actual subprogram body. If we insert the stub in the source file and execute the main program, the four PRINT statements in the stub body will display the table limits (FIRBAR and LASBAR) and the value of STRNTH. By examining these values, the program user can determine whether the call to TABBOD in the main program is correct. The user also can determine whether subroutine TABHED displays the table heading correctly and whether the main program calls the subprograms in the right order.

After the real subroutine TABBOD has been written, you should substitute it for its stub in the source file and complete the debugging and testing process. The use of stubs as described here is called *top-down testing*. Most programmers use a combination of top-down and bottom-up testing to debug a program system.

A list of suggestions for debugging complete program systems follows.

Debugging Tips for Program Systems

1. Carefully document each subprogram argument with comments. Also describe the subprogram operation with comments.
2. Before inserting the subprogram in the system, separately test each subprogram on a variety of input data using a short driver program.
3. When debugging the system, leave a trace of execution by printing each subprogram name as it is entered.
4. To test the flow of control and completed segments of an incomplete program system, use stubs for all subprograms that are not yet written.
5. When debugging, insert statements in a subprogram that print the values of all input arguments upon entry to a subprogram. Ensure these values make sense.
6. When debugging, insert statements in the calling program that print the values of all output arguments upon returning from a subprogram.

6.8 Common Programming Errors

1. When writing functions, ensure the function name is always defined (given a value) before the function RETURN is executed. Failure to do this may result in a syntax error such as "return function value not set." Within a function body, the function's name should appear only on the left side of an assignment statement and not at all in an expression. You also should declare the data type of a function in every program module that uses it.

2. The local variables declared inside a subprogram cannot be referenced outside the subprogram body. If you attempt to do this, the compiler will allocate another memory cell (contents undefined) and use that cell instead. The same thing will happen if you attempt to reference inside the subprogram body a variable or parameter that is declared in the main program. Only subprogram arguments and local variables and parameters may be referenced inside the subprogram.

3. To call a subroutine, use a CALL statement; to call a function, reference its name in an expression. Ensure the number of actual arguments in a subprogram call is the same as the number of dummy arguments for that subprogram and that each argument appears in its correct position. The order and data type of each actual argument must be the same as its corresponding dummy argument or an "argument type mismatch" syntax error may occur.

4. Finally, ensure that you spell each subprogram name consistently and that you include in the source program file the main program together with all subprograms called. If a subprogram is missing or if its name is misspelled, an "undefined external reference" error will occur when you attempt to link and run your program.

Chapter Review

In this chapter, we introduced the concept of modular programming using subprograms. A subprogram can be called repeatedly in a program to perform a particular operation. By changing the actual arguments listed in the subprogram call, we can get it to perform this operation on different data. A subprogram written for one program system also can be reused in another. This capability enables you to create your own library of subprograms and to use these subprograms as building blocks, or modules, to facilitate the design of larger program systems.

Table 6.4 shows the two types of subprograms discussed in this chapter: functions and subroutines. You can write your own functions, which are used in the same way as library functions. A user-defined function must always return a single result. The function result is the last value assigned to the function name during its execution. A function is called when an expression is evaluated that contains the function name followed by its actual arguments. Each actual argument is substituted for a dummy argument listed in the function header statement; the correspondence between actual arguments and dummy arguments is determined by position in the argument list, that is, the first actual argument corresponds to the first dummy argument, and so on.

Subroutines are subprograms that can return either any number of results or zero results. A subroutine returns a value by modifying one or more of its arguments. The correspondence between a subroutine's actual arguments and dummy arguments is also determined by position. A subroutine is called when a CALL statement is executed.

Finally, we showed how to use a structure chart to summarize the control flow and

Table 6.4. *Summary of Fortran Statements in Chapter 6*

STATEMENT	EFFECT

Function Definition

```
LOGICAL FUNCTION POSTIV (N)
INTEGER N
POSTIV = (N .GT. 0)
RETURN
END
```

Function POSTIV returns the value .TRUE. if the value of N is greater than zero; otherwise, the function returns .FALSE..

Single-Statement Function

```
REAL X, Y
REAL SUMSQ
SUMSQ(X, Y) = X ** 2 + Y ** 2
```

Function SUMSQ (type REAL) returns the sum of the squares of its two arguments.

Subroutine Definition

```
SUBROUTINE SWITCH (X, Y)
REAL X, Y
REAL TEMP
TEMP = X
X = Y
Y = TEMP
RETURN
END
```

Switches the values stored in the actual arguments corresponding to dummy arguments X and Y. The actual arguments must be two type REAL variables.

Subroutine Call

```
CALL SWITCH (A, B)
```

Calls subroutine SWITCH to exchange the data stored in variables A and B.

data flow between the main program and its subprograms. We recommend you use structure charts for this purpose in your own programming. A structure chart provides valuable documentation for the program system. It also helps you determine which variables must be declared in the main program and which arguments are needed for each subprogram call.

Quick-check Exercises

1. The _____*actual*_____ arguments appear in the subprogram call and the _____*dummy*_____ arguments appear in the subprogram definition.
2. The correspondence between dummy arguments and actual arguments is by _____*position*_____.
3. Functions return _____*1*_____ result(s); subroutines may return _____*many*_____ result(s).

4. A(n) _____ returns results by assigning a value to the _____ name; a(n) _____ returns results by assigning a value to a(n) _____

5. Which arguments can be expressions—actual or dummy?

6. Which kind of subprogram requires a special statement to call it? Which kind of subprogram should have its type declared in the calling program?

7. For the subroutine that begins

```
SUBROUTINE CONFUS (X, Y, N)
INTEGER X
REAL Y, N
```

indicate the argument correspondence for the call statement

```
CALL CONFUS (N, Y, X)
```

8. What are the requirements for the CALL statement in exercise 7 to be valid?

9. Which of the following subprogram headers are valid and which are invalid? Explain your answers.

   a. REAL FUNCTION (X, N)
   b. SUBROUTINE CHOP (X, N, RESULT)
   c. INTEGER FUNCTION ROUND (SQRT(I))
   d. SUBROUTINE FIXIT (W, 4.0)
   e. FUNCTION ROUND (X, N)

10. Functions may not return character or logical results. True or false?

11. Character-type variables may not be used as dummy arguments in subroutines. True or false?

12. Which of the following is not always an advantage of subprograms: more readable programs, separation of tasks, reduction in lines of code, easier debugging, reusability of modules? Explain your answer.

13. What is the value of main program variable X after the following program executes?

```
PROGRAM MAIN
REAL X
CALL SILLY (X)
STOP
END

SUBROUTINE SILLY (Y)
REAL Y
REAL X
X = 25.0
Y = 2.0 * X
RETURN
END
```

Answers to Quick-check Exercises

1. actual, dummy
2. position
3. one, any number including zero
4. function, function, subroutine, argument
5. actual
6. subroutine, function
7. actual N to dummy X, actual Y to dummy Y, actual X to dummy N
8. In the calling program, N must be type INTEGER, and X and Y must be type REAL.
9. a. invalid—function name is missing
   b. valid
   c. invalid—dummy argument is an expression
   d. invalid—dummy argument is a constant
   e. valid—implicit type REAL is assumed for function
10. false
11. false
12. reduction in lines of code. If a subprogram is called only once, there might be more lines of code due to the subprogram documentation.
13. Main program variable X corresponds to dummy argument Y and has the value 50.0.

Review Questions

1. Write a function that converts an amount in dollars and cents to pennies. Assume the function has two arguments: The first is the number of dollars and the second is the number of pennies. For example, the function reference CHANGE(3, 75) returns 375 as its result.
2. Write a subroutine that has one input parameter called SCORE and that displays the corresponding letter grade using a straight scale (90–100 is an A, 80–89 is a B, and so on).
3. Redo question 2 using a function that returns the letter grade instead of displaying it.
4. Explain the allocation of memory cells when a subprogram is called.
5. Explain the use of a stub.
6. Explain the use of a driver program.
7. Explain the use of a structure chart.
8. Which of the three items mentioned in questions 5, 6, and 7 is used during the design phase?
9. Argue against the following statements: It is silly to use subprograms because a program together with its subprograms has many more lines than a program written without subprograms. Also, the use of subprograms leads to more errors because of mistakes in using argument lists.

10. What will be printed when the program below executes?

```
INTEGER A, B, D, ALPHA          INTEGER FUNCTION ALPHA (D)
A = 2                           INTEGER D
D = 3                           ALPHA = D * D * D
B = ALPHA(A)                    RETURN
PRINT *, B                      END
STOP
END
```

11. What will be printed when the program below executes?

```
INTEGER A, B, D                 SUBROUTINE BETA (D, B, A)
A = 3                           INTEGER A, B, D
D = 2                           A = D ** B
CALL BETA (A, D, B)             D = D + 1
PRINT *, A, B, D                RETURN
STOP                            END
END
```

Fortran 90 Features: Recursion and Internal Subprograms

Recursive Subprograms

A *recursive subprogram* is a subprogram that calls itself. Recursion is a useful programming tool available in most modern programming languages, including Fortran 90. Figure 6.22 shows a recursive function that computes the factorial of N (N!).

The function header indicates that `factorial` is a recursive function that returns its result by assigning a value to the result name `res`. We can use any valid identifier as the result name. Because `factorial` is recursive, it's not possible to assign a value to the function name like we do in nonrecursive functions. Within the function, we declare the type of res as `INTEGER`.

The IF statement in the function body implements the following formulas, which form the recursive definition of $N!$:

$$N! = N \times (N - 1)! \quad \text{for } N > 1$$
$$N! = 1 \quad \text{for } N = 0 \text{ or } 1$$

When N is greater than 1, the statement

```
res = N * factorial(N - 1)
```

Figure 6.23. *Recursive Factorial Function*

```
RECURSIVE FUNCTION factorial (N) RESULT (res)
! Recursively computes N factorial (N!)
! Precondition : N is greater than or equal to 0
! Postcondition: res is N!

! Argument and Result Declarations
INTEGER N, res

IF (N <= 1) THEN
   res = 1
ELSE
   res = N * factorial(N-1)
END IF


RETURN
END
```

which is the Fortran form of the first formula given above, executes. The function reference `factorial(N-1)` calls function `factorial` with an argument that is one less than the current argument (called a *recursive call*). For example, if N is 3, the value of the expression 3 * `factorial(2)` is the function result.

Because the argument value decreases with each new recursive call, it will eventually reach 1. When N is less than or equal to 1, the statement

`res = 1`

executes, stopping the chain of recursive calls and returning a result of 1.

If the argument in the initial call to `factorial` is 3, the following chain of recursive calls occurs:

`factorial(3)` → 3 * `factorial(2)` → 3 * (2 * `factorial(1)`).

The last call in the chain evaluates to 1 and the value of 3 * 2 * 1 or 6 is returned as the result of the original call.

Internal Subprograms

In Fortran 77, all subprograms are compiled separately from the main program; consequently, they are considered *external* subprograms. An external subprogram cannot reference a variable declared in the main program unless that variable is passed as an argument to the subprogram. However, in Fortran 90, you can declare one or more *internal* subprograms before the main program END (usually between STOP and END). The first internal subprogram must be preceded by a CONTAINS statement. Because this type of subprogram is compiled as part of the main program, it may access any main program variable or parameter that is not re-declared in the subprogram.

Figure 6.24 shows a program that contains an internal subprogram order_two. This subprogram places in numerical order two data items that are read into main program variables x and y (smaller value in x, larger value in y). Because x and y are not passed as arguments, the subprogram cannot place any other pair of main program variables in numerical order.

Figure 6.24. *Internal Subprogram*

```
PROGRAM read_and_order_two
! Places two data items in order and displays them.

! Declarations
  REAL x, y

! Enter data
  PRINT *, 'Enter two numbers:'
  READ *, x, y

!Order the data
  CALL order_two

!Display the results
  PRINT *, 'Smaller data value is ', x
  PRINT *, 'Larger data value is ', y

  STOP


! _____

CONTAINS

  SUBROUTINE order_two
  ! Orders the values in x and y.

  ! Local declarations
    REAL temp            ! temporary cell for exchange

  ! Exchange values if necessary
    IF (x > y) THEN
       temp = x
       x = y
       y = temp
    END IF

    RETURN
  END SUBROUTINE order_two


! _____

END ! of read_and_order_two
```

Internal subprograms have the advantage of enabling a programmer to quickly implement some subproblems of an algorithm as separate modules without the need for lengthy argument lists. Their disadvantage is that they cannot be reused in other program systems.

**SYNTAX
DISPLAY**

Internal Subprogram

SYNTAX: CONTAINS
        SUBROUTINE *sub-name* (*arguments*)
          local declarations
          subroutine body
        END SUBROUTINE *sub-name*

        FUNCTION *fun-name* (*arguments*)
          local declarations
          function body
        END FUNCTION *fun-name*

EXAMPLE: CONTAINS
        SUBROUTINE hello (name)
          CHARACTER *10 name
          PRINT *, 'Hello ', name
          RETURN
        END SUBROUTINE hello

        FUNCTION area_rectangle (base, height)
          REAL base, height
          area_rectangle = base * height
          RETURN
        END FUNCTION area_rectangle

INTERPRETATION: The CONTAINS statement must precede the declaration of internal subprograms. The subprograms are declared in the normal way and may be declared with or without arguments. A subprogram may access any identifier declared in the program unit that contains it. Optionally, you can include the kind of subprogram (FUNCTION or SUBROUTINE) on the subprogram END line. All internal subprograms must be placed between the main program STOP and END.

Programming Projects

1. Two positive integers I and J are considered to be relatively prime if there exists no integer greater than 1 that divides them both. Write a logical function RELPRM that has two parameters, I and J, and returns a value of true if, and only if, I and J are relatively prime. Otherwise, RELPRM should return a value of false.

2. The greatest common divisor, GCD, of two positive integers I and J is an integer N with the property that N divides both I and J (with 0 remainder) and is the largest integer dividing them both. The following algorithm for determining N was devised by the famous mathematician Euclid:

   1. Let I be the smaller integer and J the larger.
   2. Let R be the remainder of I divided by J.
   3. DO WHILE R is nonzero
      4. Let I be J.
      5. Let J be R.
      6. Let R be the remainder of I divided by J.
      END DO
   7. Print the value of J as the greatest common divisor.

   Write a program to read in four positive integers N1, N2, N3, and N4 and to find the GCD of all four numbers. (*Hint:* The GCD of the four integers is the largest N that divides all four of them. Implement the above algorithm as an integer function and call it as many times as necessary to solve the problem. Note that GCD (N1, N2, N3, N4) = GCD (GCD(N1, N2), GCD(N3, N4)). Print N1, N2, N3, and N4 and the resulting GCD.)

3. Given the lengths a, b, c of the sides of a triangle, write a function to compute the area, A, of the triangle. The formula for computing A is given by

   $$A = \sqrt{s(s - a)(s - b)(s - c)},$$

   where s is the semiperimeter of the triangle:

   $$s = \frac{a + b + c}{2}.$$

   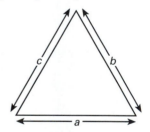

   Write a program to read in values for a, b, and c and call your function to compute A. Your program should print A, a, b, and c.

4. Write a function that converts a bearing measurement in degrees, minutes, and seconds (all integers) to degrees (a real number). Write a program to read several different sets of data, call this function, and display its result.

5. Write a subroutine that will convert either Fahrenheit to Celsius or Celsius to Fahrenheit. The subroutine header and precondition and postcondition follow:

```
      SUBROUTINE CONVRT (FTOC, FAHREN, CELSUS)
C Converts Fahrenheit to Celsius or Celsius to Fahrenheit
C Precondition : FTOC (type LOGICAL) is defined.
C Postcondition: If FTOC is .TRUE., the value returned through
C                CELSUS is the Celsius equivalent of the
C                temperature in FAHREN.  Otherwise, the value
C                returned through FAHREN is the Fahrenheit
C                equivalent of the temperature in CELSUS.
```

6. Write a subroutine that converts a distance measurement in yards, feet, and inches (all integer values) to a real value in yards and a real value in meters. The subroutine will have three inputs and two outputs.

7. Write a function that simulates a calculator. The inputs to the function will be two numbers and a character operator (either '∧', '*', '/', '+', or '−'). The function should return the result of applying its operand to its operators; for example, if the inputs are 6.0, '*', 5.0, the function result would be 30.0. Assume the operator symbol '∧' means exponentiation. Write a main program with a loop that reads a set of test data, calls the function to evaluate the test data, and displays the result. (*Hint:* The function body should contain a multiple-alternative IF that tests the character argument.)

8. The equation representing the displacement, d (in cm), of a damped oscillator, e.g., a shock absorber, is given as

$$d = Ae^{-(t/\tau)} \sin(\omega t + \phi),$$

where A = displacement amplitude (cm), t = time from initial displacement (sec), τ = oscillator time constant, ω = oscillator frequency, and ϕ = oscillator phase angle.

Write a function whose input arguments are A, T, TAU, OMEGA, and PHI, where OMEGA and PHI are expressed in degrees. Your function should convert OMEGA and PHI to radians and compute the displacement. Write a main program that reads in values of A, TAU, OMEGA, and PHI, and displays the displacement for values of T from 0 to 10 sec, with increments of 0.5 sec. Try A = 5 cm, TAU = 1.8 sec, OMEGA = 60°/sec, and PHI = 25°.

9. Write a subroutine that is passed values of voltage and resistance and returns the current flowing through the resistor and the power dissipated. Use the formulas

   current = *voltage/resistance*
   power = *current*² × *resistance*.

Write a main program that reads several sets of voltage and resistance, calls the subroutine, and displays the results.

10. Write a subroutine that computes the volume and surface area of either a right circular cylinder or a right circular cone. The subroutine inputs are the radius, height, and kind of figure (i.e., 'CYLINDER' or 'CONE'). The relevant formulas follow:

Right circular cylinder:

   volume = *height* × π × *radius*²
   area = *height* × 2.0 × π × *radius* + 2.0 × π × *radius*²

Right circular cone:

   volume = *height* × π × *radius*²/3.0
   area = π × *radius* × SQRT(*radius*² + *height*²) + π × *radius*²

11. Write a function LNAPRX that computes an approximation to the natural logarithm of a number between 1 and 2 by summing a given number of terms of the series

$$\ln(1 + x) = x - \frac{x^2}{2!} + \frac{x^3}{3!} - \frac{x^4}{4!} + \cdots .$$

Also write a driver program that calls LNAPRX twice with the same value, first requesting the sum of four terms of the series and then requesting the sum of seven terms. The program should display a message comparing the result of the two calls to the value returned by the library function ALOG.

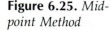

12. Write a program to help you determine the maximum number of traffic lights that can be purchased for $50,000. Assume the purchase cost of each light is $5000 and the installation cost is $1000. Each light uses 420 kWh of electricity a year; each kilowatt costs $0.047/kWh. Enter a guess as to how many lights can be purchased and keep re-running the program until the best answer is printed. Also write a function that computes the annual operating expense for a light and a function that computes the total cost, including purchase, installation, and operation for 1 yr.

13. We can approximate the area under the curve described by a function *f* by dividing the area into a number of rectangles and then accumulating the sum of all the rectangular areas. Figure 6.25 shows an example of the *midpoint method*, so named because the curve intersects each rectangle at its middle (as measured along the *x*-axis). The area of each rectangle is *w* (its width) times the function value at its midpoint. The area of the rectangle with left endpoint x_i is $w \times f(x_i + w/2)$. If the interval [*a, b*] is divided into *n* rectangles, the area under the curve is represented by the sum

$$Area = w \sum_{i=0}^{n-1} f(a + i \times w + w/2),$$

Figure 6.25. *Mid-point Method*

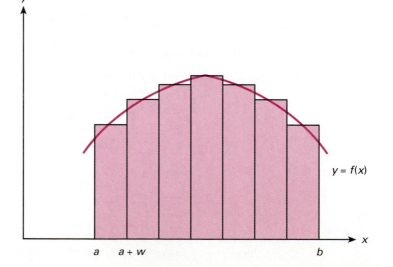

where w is $(b - a)/n$ and the first rectangle begins at $x = a$, the second at $x = a + w$, the third at $x = a + 2w$, and so on.

Write a program that uses the midpoint approximation to find the area under the curve (the value of the definite integral) for the function

$$f(x) = -3x^2 + 2x + 4$$

over the interval $[-2, 3]$. Test your program using several different values of n. The larger n is, the better the approximation should be.

14. For you to design a square timber column in a structure, the following three formulas must be satisfied:

Buckling load:

$$maximum\ load = \frac{(0.30 \times E \times area)}{(length/width)^2}$$

Compressive stress:

$$maximum\ load = \frac{area}{maximum\ compressive\ strength}$$

Slenderness limits:

$$\frac{length}{width} \quad \text{must be } \leq 50$$

In these formulas, E is the modulus of elasticity (1,700,000 psi), area is expressed in square inches, and maximum compressive strength = 445 psi (Douglas fir).

Write a program that uses these three formulas to give an initial design to a structural engineer. Assume the columns to be used are square and are available in intervals of 2 in. (i.e., 2 by 2, 4 by 4, . . .). Have the output look like the following:

```
Please enter the expected load in pounds
9000
Please enter the length of the column in inches
120
Testing a beam with width of     2.000000      inches
The current width has failed the tests.
Testing a beam with width of     4.000000      inches
The current width has failed the tests.
Testing a beam with width of     6.000000      inches

For a load of      9000.000      pounds
and a length of      120.0000      inches
recommend a square beam with sides of    6.000000 inches
```

15. It was a dark and stormy night. Our secret agent, Mr. Rogers, was behind enemy lines at a fuel depot. He walked over to a huge, upright cylindrical fuel tank that stood 20 ft tall and was 8 ft in diameter. He opened the 2-in.-diameter circular nozzle. Instinctively, he knew that the volume of fuel leaving the tank was

$$volume\ lost = velocity \times (area\ of\ the\ nozzle) \times time$$

and that

$$velocity = 8.02 \times \sqrt{(height\ of\ fluid)}.$$

How long will it take for the tank to empty? (*Hint:* Although this is really a calculus problem, we can simulate it with a computer and obtain a close answer. First, we assume the loss of fluid is constant and calculate the volume lost over a brief period of time, for instance, a minute. We then subtract the volume from the tank to arrive at the new height of fluid in the tank at the end of that minute. Next, we calculate the loss for the next minute. We can do this over and over until the tank is dry.)

Print a table showing the elapsed time, the volume lost, and the height of the fluid. At the very end, convert the total elapsed seconds to minutes. The fluid height can be negative on the last line. Have the table look like the following:

Time	Volume Lost	Fluid Height
(secs)	(cubic feet)	(feet)
60.	46.95	19.07
120.	45.84	18.15
180.	44.73	17.26
.	.	.
.	.	.
.	.	.
2340.	3.93	0.06
2400.	2.62	0.01
2460.	1.05	−0.01

```
Total time to drain is 41.00000      minutes
```

16. The electric company charges according to the following rate schedule:

- 8 cents a kWh for the first 300 kWh
- 6 cents a kWh for the next 300 kWh (up to 600 kWh)
- 5 cents a kWh for the next 400 kWh (up to 1000 kWh)
- 3 cents a kWh for all electricity used over 1000 kWh

Write a function to compute the total charge for each customer. Also write a program to call this function using the following data:

Customer Number	Kilowatt-hours Used
123	725
205	115
464	600
596	327

Customer Number	Kilowatt-hours Used
601	915
613	1011
722	47

The calling program should print a three-column table listing the customer number, hours used, and charge for each customer. It should also compute and print the number of customers, total hours used, and total charges.

17. Each week, the employees of a local manufacturing company turn in time cards containing the following information:

a. An identification number (a five-digit integer)
b. Hourly pay rate (a real number)
c. Time worked Monday, Tuesday, Wednesday, Thursday, and Friday (each a four-digit integer of the form HHMM, where HH is hours and MM is minutes)

For example, last week's time cards contained the following data:

Time Worked (*Hours, Minutes*)

Employee Number	Hourly Rate	Monday	Tuesday	Wednesday	Thursday	Friday
16025	4.00	0800	0730	0800	0800	0420
19122	4.50	0615	0800	0800	0800	0800
21061	4.25	0805	0800	0735	0515	0735
45387	3.50	1015	1030	0800	0945	0800
50177	6.15	0800	0415	0800	0545	0600
61111	5.00	0930	0800	0800	1025	0905
88128	4.50	0800	0900	0800	0800	0700

Write a program system that will read the above data and compute for each employee the total hours worked (in hours and minutes), the total hours worked (to the nearest quarter-hour), and the gross salary. Your system should print the data shown above with the total hours (both figures) and gross pay for each employee. Assume that overtime is paid at $1\frac{1}{2}$ the normal hourly rate and that it is computed on a weekly basis (only on the total hours in excess of 40), rather than on a daily basis. Your program system should contain the following subprograms:

a. A function for computing the sum (in hours and minutes) of two four-digit integers of the form HHMM; for example, 0745 + 0335 = 1120
b. A function for converting hours and minutes (represented as a four-digit integer) into hours rounded to the nearest quarter hour; for example, 1120 = 11.25
c. A function for computing gross salary, given total hours and hourly rate
d. A function for rounding gross salary accurate to two decimal places

Test your program using the time cards shown in the chart.

18. All college students are familiar with queueing problems. *Queues* are waiting lines (such as the drop/add lines for changing your registration). For this project, you will be working with queueing equations that predict waiting line performance (and you will begin to understand why drop/add doesn't work very well).

Queueing systems are modeled to have some type of arrival distribution, some type of service distribution, and one or more servers (e.g., registration clerks) available to provide service to the arriving customers. The measures of performance of a queueing system are the following:

RHO : The utilization of the service of the queueing system
L : The average number of customers in the system
LQ : The average number of customers waiting to be served
W : The average time in the system for a customer
WQ : The average waiting time for a customer
Pn : The probability of *n* customers in the system

Equations are provided for a particular kind of queueing system that uses a Poisson (exponential) distribution for service rates and arrival rates. This means that if we plotted the actual arrival rates, we would get a bell-shaped curve around a mean value (provided as data). The model also allows for multiple servers. The problem inputs are the following:

LAMBDA (mean arrival rate)
MU (mean service rate)
S (number of servers)

The formulas that describe the queueing system follow:

FOR S = 1:

$$RHO = LAMBDA/MU$$
$$P0 = 1 - RHO$$
$$Pn = P0 * RHO$$
$$L = LAMBDA/(MU - LAMBDA)$$
$$LQ = LAMBDA^2/(MU \times (MU - LAMBDA))$$
$$W = 1/(MU - LAMBDA)$$
$$WQ = LAMBDA/(MU \times (MU - LAMBDA))$$

FOR S > 1:

$$RHO = LAMBDA/(MU * S)$$

$$P0 = \cfrac{1}{\dfrac{(LAMBDA/MU)^S}{S!(1 - RHO)} + \displaystyle\sum_{N=0}^{S-1} \dfrac{(LAMBDA/MU)^N}{N!}}$$

$$Pn = \begin{cases} \dfrac{P0(LAMBDA/MU)^N}{N!} & \text{if } 1 \leq N \leq S \\[2ex] \dfrac{P0(LAMBDA/MU)^N}{S!S^{(N-S)}} & \text{if } N > S \end{cases}$$

$$LQ = \frac{P0(LAMBDA/MU)^S RHO}{S!(1 - RHO)^2}$$

$$WQ = LQ/LAMBDA$$
$$W = WQ + 1/MU$$
$$L = LQ + LAMBDA/MU$$

Your program output should show the results of each call to the simulation subroutine and should resemble the following:

```
Enter the number of servers, (S)
1
Enter the arrival rate, (LAMBDA)
8
Enter the service rate, MU (Must be greater than LAMBDA/S):
10
Results:
      Server utilization (RHO)                              =  0.8000
      Average number of customers in system (L)             =  4.0000
      Average number of customers waiting for service (LQ)  =  3.2000
      Average time in system for a customer (W)             =  0.5000
      Average waiting time for a customer (WQ)              =  0.4000
      _____

      Probability of finding n customers in system (Pn)
          P0 = 0.2000    P3 = 0.1024    P6 = 0.0524
          P1 = 0.1600    P4 = 0.0819    P7 = 0.0419
          P2 = 0.1280    P5 = 0.0655    P8 = 0.0336
      _____


Enter the number of servers, (S)
4
Enter the arrival rate, (LAMBDA)
8
Enter the service rate, MU (Must be greater than LAMBDA/S):
2.5
Results:
      Server utilization (RHO)                              =  0.8000
      Average number of customers in system (L)             =  5.5857
      Average number of customers waiting for service (LQ)  =  2.3857
      Average time in system for a customer (W)             =  0.6982
      Average waiting time for a customer (WQ)              =  0.2982
      _____

      Probability of finding n customers in system (Pn)
          P0 = 0.0273    P3 = 0.1491    P6 = 0.0763
          P1 = 0.0874    P4 = 0.1193    P7 = 0.0611
          P2 = 0.1398    P5 = 0.0954    P8 = 0.0489
      _____
```

CHAPTER 7
Arrays

IN ALL previous programs in this text, each variable was associated with a single memory cell. Such variables are called *simple variables*. In this chapter, we study a Fortran data structure. A *data structure* is a grouping of related data items in memory. The items in a data structure can be processed individually, although some operations may be performed on the structure as a whole.

An *array* is a data structure used for storage of a collection of data items that are all the same type (e.g., all the exam scores for a class). By using an array, we are able to associate a single variable name (e.g., SCORES) with a group of related data items (exam scores). The individual data items in an array are stored in adjacent cells of main memory (one item per memory cell). Because each item is saved in a separate memory cell, we can process the individual items more than once and in any order we wish.

In earlier programs, we reused the same memory cell to store each exam score. Each time a new item was read into the cell, its previous contents were lost. Consequently, we could no longer access the third score after the fourth score was read. By using an array to store each score in a separate memory cell, this no longer is a problem.

7.1 Declaring and Referencing Arrays

An array is a collection of two or more adjacent memory cells, called *array elements*, that are associated with a particular symbolic name. To set up an array in memory, we must declare both the name of the array and the number of cells associated with it.

The declaration

```
REAL X(8)
```

instructs the compiler to associate eight memory cells with the name X; these memory cells will be adjacent to each other in memory. Each element of array X may contain a single real value, so a total of eight real values may be stored and referenced using the array name X.

To process the data stored in an array, we must be able to reference each individual element. To reference a particular element, we need to specify the array name and identify the element desired (e.g., the third element of array X). The *subscripted variable* X(1) (read as X sub 1) may be used to reference the first element of the array X, X(2) the second element, X(3) the third element, and so on. The integer enclosed in parentheses is the *array subscript*.

EXAMPLE 7.1   If X is the array declared as

REAL X(8)

then we may refer to the elements of the array X as shown in Fig. 7.1. ◼

Figure 7.1. *The Eight Elements of the Array X*

Array X

X(1)	X(2)	X(3)	X(4)	X(5)	X(6)	X(7)	X(8)
16.0	12.0	6.0	8.0	2.5	12.0	14.0	−54.5

First element   Eighth element

EXAMPLE 7.2   Let X be the array shown in Fig. 7.1. A sequence of statements that manipulate this array is shown in Table 7.1.

Table 7.1. *Statements that Manipulate Array X*

STATEMENT	EXPLANATION
PRINT *, X(1)	Displays the value of X(1) or 16.0.
X(4) = 25.0	Stores the value 25.0 in X(4).
SUM = X(1) + X(2)	Stores the sum of X(1) and X(2) or 28.0 in the variable SUM.
SUM = SUM + X(3)	Adds X(3) to SUM. The new SUM is 34.0.
X(4) = X(4) + 1.0	Adds 1.0 to X(4). The new X(4) is 26.0.
X(3) = X(1) + X(2)	Stores the sum of X(1) and X(2) in X(3). The new X(3) is 28.0.

The contents of array X after execution of these statements are shown below. Only X(3) and X(4) are changed.

Array X

X(1)	X(2)	X(3)	X(4)	X(5)	X(6)	X(7)	X(8)
16.0	12.0	28.0	26.0	2.5	12.0	14.0	−54.5

First element   Eighth element ◼

EXAMPLE 7.3   Two arrays are declared as follows:

CHARACTER *20 NAMES(50)
INTEGER SCORES(50)

The arrays NAMES and SCORES each have fifty elements. Each element of array NAMES can be used to store a string of up to twenty characters; each element of array SCORES can be used to store a single integer value. If these declarations are used in the exam score problem, the first student's name can be stored in NAMES(1), and the first student's score can be stored in SCORES(1). Because the data stored in NAMES(I) and SCORES(I) relate to the Ith student ($1 \leq I \leq 50$), the two arrays are called *parallel arrays*. Samples of these arrays follow:

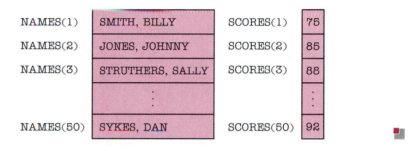

NAMES(1)	SMITH, BILLY	SCORES(1)	75
NAMES(2)	JONES, JOHNNY	SCORES(2)	85
NAMES(3)	STRUTHERS, SALLY	SCORES(3)	88
	⋮		⋮
NAMES(50)	SYKES, DAN	SCORES(50)	92

EXAMPLE 7.4   The type declaration

```
LOGICAL ANSWER(10)
```

declares an array ANSWER with ten elements; each element can store a LOGICAL value. This array could be used to store the ten answers for a true-false quiz (e.g., ANSWER(1) is .TRUE., ANSWER(2) is .FALSE.). A sample array follows:

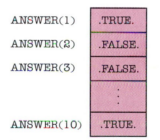

ANSWER(1)	.TRUE.
ANSWER(2)	.FALSE.
ANSWER(3)	.FALSE.
	⋮
ANSWER(10)	.TRUE.

EXAMPLE 7.5   More than one array may be declared in a single type declaration. The statements

```
REAL CACTUS(5), NEEDLE, PINS(6)
INTEGER FACTOR(12), N, INDEX
```

declare CACTUS and PINS to be arrays with five and six type REAL elements, respectively, and FACTOR to be an array with twelve type INTEGER elements. In addition, individual memory cells will be allocated for storage of the simple variables NEEDLE, N, and INDEX.

Often, we want to use a parameter to specify the number of array elements to allocate, which makes it easy to change the size of an array.

EXAMPLE 7.6   The statements

```
INTEGER MAX
PARAMETER (MAX = 20)
CHARACTER *10 FIRNAM(MAX), LASNAM(MAX)
```

allocate storage for two arrays of character strings. Each array can hold twenty strings consisting of ten characters each. Changing the value of MAX will change the array sizes but not the length of the strings.   ■

EXAMPLE 7.7   It's also possible to allocate storage for an array whose smallest subscript value is different from 1. The array VOLTS

```
INTEGER LOW, HIGH
PARAMETER (LOW = -2, HIGH = 2)
REAL VOLTS(LOW : HIGH)
```

has elements VOLTS(-2), VOLTS(-1), VOLTS(0), VOLTS(1), VOLTS(2). A sample array follows:

Volts(-2)	15.5
Volts(-1)	12.0
Volts(0)	16.1
Volts(1)	14.2
Volts(2)	15.0

All the points illustrated so far are summarized in the next display.

SYNTAX DISPLAY

Array Declaration

SYNTAX: *element-type aname*(*size*)
         element-type aname(*minval* : *maxval*)

EXAMPLE: REAL A(5), B(-2 : 2)

INTERPRETATION: The first form of the array declaration allocates storage space for array *aname* consisting of *size* memory cells. Each memory cell can store one data item whose data type is specified by *element-type* (i.e., REAL, INTEGER, CHARACTER, or LOGICAL). The individual array elements are referenced by the subscripted variables *aname*(1), *aname*(2), ..., *aname*(*size*). An INTEGER constant or parameter must be used to specify *size*.

In the second form of the array declaration, storage space is allocated for an array with subscripts *minval*, *minval* + 1, ..., *maxval* − 1, *maxval*. This form may be used to declare an array whose smallest subscript is different from 1. Both *minval* and *maxval* must be INTEGER constants or parameters, and *minval* must be less than or equal to *maxval*.

EXERCISES FOR
SECTION 7.1

Self-check

1. What is the difference between X3 and X(3)?
2. For the declaration

        CHARACTER *1 GRADES(−5 : 5)

   how many memory cells are allocated for data storage? What type of data can be stored there?

Programming

1. Allocate one array for storing the square roots of the integers from 1 through 10 and a second array for storing the cubes of the integers from −5 through 5.
2. Allocate an array for storing the 21 readings of a pressure gauge that are recorded at one-second intervals (from $t − 10$ seconds through $t + 10$ seconds) during a satellite launch.

7.2 Array Subscripts

A subscript is used to differentiate between the individual array elements and to allow us to specify which array element is to be manipulated. Any INTEGER expression may be used as an array subscript. However, the value of this subscript expression must lie between 1 and the declared size of the array (or between *minval* and *maxval* if *minval* is not 1); otherwise, an "out-of-range subscript" run-time error may occur.

It is essential to understand the distinction between an array subscript value and an array element value. The original array X from Fig. 7.1 is redrawn on the following page. The subscripted variable X(I) references a particular element of this array. If I has the value 1, the subscript value is 1, so X(1) is referenced. The value of X(I) in this case is 16.0. If I has the value 3, the subscript value is 3 and the value of X(I) is 6.0. If I has the value 9, the subscript value is 9 and the value of X(I) is undefined because the subscript value is out of the allowable range.

Array X

X(1)	X(2)	X(3)	X(4)	X(5)	X(6)	X(7)	X(8)
16.0	12.0	6.0	8.0	2.5	12.0	14.0	-54.5

EXAMPLE 7.8

Table 7.2 lists some sample statements involving the array X above. I is assumed to be an INTEGER variable with value 6. Make sure you understand each statement.

Table 7.2. *Some Sample Statements for Array X when I is 6*

STATEMENT	EFFECT
PRINT *, 5, X(5)	Displays 5 and 2.5 (value of X(5)).
PRINT *, I, X(I)	Displays 6 and 12.0 (value of X(6)).
PRINT *, X(I) + 1	Displays 13.0 (value of X(6) plus 1).
PRINT *, X(I) + I	Displays 18.0 (value of X(6) plus 6).
PRINT *, X(I+1)	Displays 14.0 (value of X(7)).
PRINT *, X(I+I)	Is an illegal attempt to display X(12).
PRINT *, X(2*I)	Is an illegal attempt to display X(12).
PRINT *, X(2*I-4)	Displays -54.5 (value of X(8)).
PRINT *, X(INT(X(5)))	Displays 12.0 (value of X(2)).
X(I-1) = X(I)	Assigns 12.0 (value of X(6)) to X(5).
X(I) = X(I+1)	Assigns 14.0 (value of X(7)) to X(6).
X(I) - 1 = X(I)	Is an illegal assignment statement.

Note that there are two illegal attempts to display element X(12), which is not in the array. These attempts may result in a *"subscript out of range"* run-time error.

The last PRINT statement uses INT(X(5)) as a subscript expression. Because this evaluates to 2, the value of X(2)—and not X(5)—is printed. If the value of INT(X(5)) is outside the range 1 through 8, it would be an illegal subscript expression. ■

SYNTAX DISPLAY

Array Subscripts

SYNTAX: *aname(subscript)*

EXAMPLE: B(I+1)

INTERPRETATION: The *subscript* may be any INTEGER expression. Each time a subscripted variable is encountered in a program, the subscript is evaluated and its value determines which element of array *aname* is referenced.

NOTE: If the value of *subscript* is not within the declared range, an "out-of-range subscript" run-time error may occur; however, some compilers do not check for subscript range errors.

EXERCISES FOR SECTION 7.2

Self-check

1. If an array is declared to have 10 elements, must the program use all 10?
2. The following sequence of statements changes the initial contents of array X displayed in this section. Describe what each statement does to the array and show the final contents of array X after all statements execute.

```
I = 3
X(I) = X(I) + 10.0
X(I - 1) = X(2 * I - 1)
X(I + 1) = X(2 * I) + X(2 * I + 1)
```

Programming

1. Write program statements that will do the following to array X shown in this section:

   a. Replace the third element with 7.0.
   b. Copy the fifth element into the first one.
   c. Subtract the first element from the fourth element and store the result in the fifth element.
   d. Increase the sixth element by 2.
   e. Find the sum of the first three elements.

7.3 Using DO Loops to Process Arrays

Very often, we wish to process the elements of an array in sequence, starting with the first; for example, we might want to enter data into the array or print its contents. In Fortran, we can accomplish this easily by using a DO loop with a loop-control variable (e.g., I) that is also used as the array subscript (e.g., X(I)). Increasing the value of the loop-control variable by 1 causes the next array element to be processed.

EXAMPLE 7.9

The array CUBE declared as follows will be used to store the cubes of the first ten integers (e.g., CUBE(1) is 1, CUBE(10) is 1000).

```
INTEGER CUBE(10), I
```

The DO loop

```
      DO 10 I = 1, 10
          CUBE(I) = I ** 3
10 CONTINUE
```

initializes this array, as shown next.

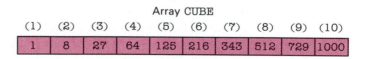

Statistical Computations Using Arrays

One common use of arrays is to store a collection of related data values. Once the values are stored, some simple statistical computations may be performed. The array X is used for this purpose in the program discussed next.

The program in Fig. 7.2 uses three DO loops to process the array X. The parameter MAXITM determines the size of the array. The variable I is used as the loop-control variable and array subscript in each loop.

The first DO loop,

```
      DO 10 I = 1, MAXITM
          READ *, X(I)
10 CONTINUE
```

reads one data value into each element of array X (the first item is stored in X(1), the second item in X(2), etc.). The READ statement is repeated for each value of I from 1 to 8; each repetition causes a new data value to be read and stored in X(I). The subscript I determines which array element receives the next data value. The data shown in the sample run cause the array to be initialized as in Fig. 7.1.

Figure 7.2. *Printing a Table of Differences*

```
          PROGRAM AVESTD
C Computes the average value and standard deviation of an array of
C data and prints the difference between each value and the average

          INTEGER MAXITM
          PARAMETER (MAXITM = 8)
          INTEGER I
          REAL X(MAXITM), AVERAG, STDEV, SUM, SUMSQR

C Enter the data
          PRINT *, 'Enter ', MAXITM, ' numbers, one per line:'
          DO 10 I = 1, MAXITM
              READ *, X(I)
   10     CONTINUE
```

```
C Compute the sum and sum of the squares of all elements
      SUM = 0.0
      SUMSQR = 0.0
      DO 20 I = 1, MAXITM
         SUM = SUM + X(I)
         SUMSQR = SUMSQR + X(I) ** 2
   20 CONTINUE

C Compute and print the average and standard deviation
      AVERAG = SUM / REAL(MAXITM)
      STDEV = SQRT(SUMSQR / REAL(MAXITM) - AVERAG ** 2)
      PRINT *
      PRINT 15, 'The average value is ', AVERAG
      PRINT 15, 'The standard deviation is ', STDEV
   15 FORMAT (1X, A, F8.1)

C Display the difference between each item and the average
      PRINT *
      PRINT *, 'Table of differences between X(I) and average'
      PRINT 25, 'I', 'X(I)', 'Difference'
   25 FORMAT (1X, A4, 3X, A8, 3X, A14)
      DO 30 I = 1, MAXITM
         PRINT 35, I, X(I), X(I)-AVERAG
   35    FORMAT (1X, I4, 3X, F8.1, 3X, F14.1)
   30 CONTINUE

C Exit program
      STOP
      END

Enter          8 numbers, one per line:
16
12
6
8
2.5
12
14
-54.5

The average value is     2.0
The standard deviation is    21.8

Table of differences between X(I) and average
    I       X(I)      Difference
    1       16.0          14.0
    2       12.0          10.0
    3        6.0           4.0
    4        8.0           6.0
    5        2.5           0.5
    6       12.0          10.0
    7       14.0          12.0
    8      -54.5         -56.5
```

We use the second DO loop (with label 20) to accumulate (in SUM) the sum of all values stored in the array and (in SUMSQR) the sum of the squares of all element values. The formulas implemented by this loop are

$$SUM = X(1) + X(2) + \cdots + X(7) + X(8) = \sum_{I=1}^{MAXITM} X(I)$$

$$SUMSQR = X(1)^2 + X(2)^2 + \cdots + X(7)^2 + X(8)^2 = \sum_{I=1}^{MAXITM} X(I)^2.$$

This loop will be discussed in more detail later.

The last DO loop

```
    DO 30 I = 1, MAXITM
        PRINT 35, I, X(I), X(I)-AVERAG
35      FORMAT (1X, I4, 3X, F8.1, 3X, F14.1)
30  CONTINUE
```

prints a table. Each line of the table displays an array subscript, an array element, and the difference between that element and the average value, X(I) – AVERAG. Note how the edit descriptors in FORMAT statements 25 and 35 cause each column of values in the output table to be right-aligned with its respective column heading.

Now that we have seen the entire program, let's take a closer look at the DO loop with label 20, which follows:

```
C Compute the sum and the sum of the squares of all elements
        SUM = 0.0
        SUMSQR = 0.0
        DO 20 I = 1, MAXITM
            SUM = SUM + X(I)
            SUMSQR = SUMSQR + X(I) ** 2
    20  CONTINUE
```

This loop accumulates the sum of all eight elements of array X in the variable SUM. Each time the DO loop is repeated, the next element of array X is added to SUM. Then this array element value is squared, and its square is added to the sum being accumulated in SUMSQR. The execution of this program fragment is traced in Table 7.3 for the first three repetitions of the loop.

The *standard deviation* of a set of data is a measure of the spread of the data values around the average value; for example, a small standard deviation means the data values are all relatively close to the average value. For MAXITM data items, the standard deviation is given by the formula

$$standard\ deviation = \sqrt{\frac{\sum_{I=1}^{MAXITM} X(I)^2}{MAXITM} - AVERAG^2}.$$

Table 7.3. *Partial Trace of DO Loop with Label 20*

STATEMENT	I	X(I)	SUM	SUMSQR	EFFECT
SUM = 0.0			0.0		Initializes SUM.
SUMSQR = 0.0				0.0	Initializes SUMSQR.
DO 20 I = 1, MAXITM	1	16.0			1 ≤ 8 is true;
SUM = SUM + X(I)			16.0		adds X(1) to SUM,
SUMSQR = SUMSQR + ...				256.0	adds 256.0 to SUMSQR.
increment and test I	2	12.0			2 ≤ 8 is true;
SUM = SUM + X(I)			28.0		adds X(2) to SUM,
SUMSQR = SUMSQR + ...				400.0	adds 144.0 to SUMSQR.
increment and test I	3	6.0			3 ≤ 8 is true;
SUM = SUM + X(I)			34.0		adds X(3) to SUM,
SUMSQR = SUMSQR + ...				436.0	adds 36.0 to SUMSQR.

In Fig. 7.2, this formula is implemented by the statement

```
STDEV = SQRT(SUMSQR / REAL(MAXITM) - AVERAG ** 2)
```

Program Style: *Using DO Loop-control Variables as Array Subscripts*

In Fig. 7.2, the DO loop-control variable I determines which array element is manipulated during each loop repetition. The use of the loop-control variable as an array subscript is common because it allows the programmer to specify easily the sequence in which the elements of an array are to be manipulated. Each time the loop-control variable is increased, the next array element is automatically selected. Note that the same loop-control variable is used in all three loops. This is not necessary but is permitted since the loop-control variable is always initialized at loop entry. Thus I is reset to 1 when each loop is entered.

EXERCISES FOR SECTION 7.3

Self-check

1. For an array X with eight type INTEGER elements, describe the result of executing each of the following DO loops. The sequence of numbers stored in array X by the DO loop in part (e) are called *Fibonacci numbers*. What is the eighth Fibonacci number?

    a.
```
    DO 5 I = 1, 8
        X(I) = I * I
        PRINT *, I, X(I)
    5 CONTINUE
```

b.
```
    DO   10 I = 1, 8
           X(I) = 0
           X(I) = X(I) + I
      10 CONTINUE
```
c.
```
      X(4) = 5
      DO 20 I = 4, 7
           X(I + 1) = X(I)
      20 CONTINUE
```
d.
```
      X(4) = 10
      DO 30 I = 3, 1, -1
           X(I) = X(I + 1)
      30 CONTINUE
```
e.
```
      X(1) = 1
      X(2) = 1
      DO 40 I = 3, 8
           X(I) = X(I - 1) + X(I - 2)
      40 CONTINUE
```

Programming

1. Write program statements that do the following to array x described in Self-check exercise 1.

   a. Find the sum of the first 5 elements using a loop.
   b. Multiply each of the first 6 elements by 2 and place each product in the corresponding element of the array ANSWER.
   c. Display all elements with even-numbered subscripts.

2. Write DO loops to fill with data the arrays described in Programming exercise 1 at the end of Section 7.1. Each array element should be assigned the value specified for it.

7.4 Input and Output of Arrays

In Fig. 7.2, a DO loop was used to read in the eight elements of array x. This program fragment is repeated next.

```
    PRINT *, 'Enter ', MAXITM, ' numbers, one per line:'
    DO 10 I = 1, MAXITM
       READ *, X(I)
10 CONTINUE
```

Each data item was entered by the program user on a separate line. Next, we discuss two other methods that may be used to read in an array of values.

Reading an Array of Data

The program fragment

```
PRINT *, 'Enter ', MAXITM, ' numbers:'
READ *, X
```

could also be used to read MAXITM values and store them in consecutive elements of the array X (i.e., the first data item in X(1), the second data item in X(2), etc.). The program user could enter one value on each of eight lines as before, all eight values on one line, or any other combination.

In the READ statement above, no subscripts are used to identify specific elements in array X. Whenever an array name appears without subscripts, the entire array is being referenced.

There are two advantages to using the program fragment above. First, it is simpler than using a DO loop. Second, it allows you to enter several data items on one line. The only disadvantage is that the number of data items needed is determined by the declared size of the array and you must always enter exactly that number of data items.

EXAMPLE 7.10

We could use the following program fragment to read data into the arrays NAMES and SCORES, assuming that MAXSTU students took the exam, where MAXSTU is the declared size of both arrays:

```
PRINT *, 'Enter the name of each student'
READ *, NAMES
PRINT *, 'Enter each score in the same order as the names'
READ *, SCORES
```

Enter all the student names first and then all the exam scores as directed by the prompting messages. However, there are two problems with this approach. First, the ith score in the list of scores must belong to the ith student in the list of names. Second, even if fewer than MAXSTU students sit for the exam, MAXSTU names and MAXSTU scores still must be entered. We discuss alternative techniques that do not have these problems next. ∎

Reading Data into Part of an Array

In many applications, we will not know beforehand exactly how many data items will need to be saved in an array. In fact, the number of data items will often change from one run of a program to another. For example, a grading program must be able to handle different-sized classes. For this reason, we need to declare an array that is large enough to hold the largest expected set of data; we then instruct the program to read in the actual number of data items processed in a given run.

EXAMPLE 7.11

The program fragment in Fig. 7.3 reads the number of students taking an exam into the variable NUMSTU and then reads the students' names and scores into the parallel arrays NAMES and SCORES (size MAXSTU).

Figure 7.3. *DO Loop to Read Data into Part of an Array*

```
      PRINT *, 'Enter number of students'
      READ *, NUMSTU

C Enter the exam data
      DO 10 I = 1, NUMSTU
         PRINT *, 'Enter next name and score pair'
         READ *, NAMES(I), SCORES(I)
   10 CONTINUE
```

The prompting message

```
Enter next name and score pair
```

is printed each time the loop is repeated and a new name and score are read into the next pair of array cells. If NUMSTU is less than MAXSTU, only part of the arrays NAMES and SCORES will be defined, as shown by the darker color in Fig. 7.4. The first data pair should be 'SMITH, BILLY' 75.

Because the data for NAMES(I) and SCORES(I) are entered together, it is less likely that student names and scores will not match. Note, you should use the variable NUMSTU as the upper limit in any later DO loop that processes the arrays to ensure that only elements with subscripts 1 through NUMSTU are manipulated. ■

Program Style: *Verifying Array Bounds*

The variable NUMSTU serves a very important role in the processing of arrays NAMES and SCORES because it denotes the portion of these arrays that is filled with meaningful data. If the value of NUMSTU does not lie within the range 1 to MAXSTU, inclusive, a "subscript out of range" diagnostic may occur during program execution. For this reason, it is a good idea to use a function that not only reads a value into NUMSTU but also verifies that this value is within the allowable range.

Figure 7.4. *A Partially Defined Array*

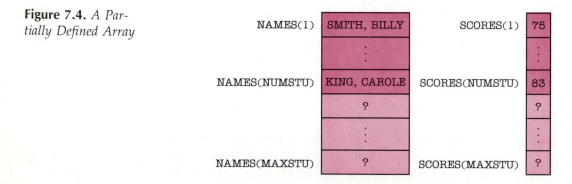

**Implied
DO Loop**

The need to read data into part of an array is so common that a special form of the DO loop, called the *implied DO loop,* is available for this purpose. An implied DO loop is inserted directly in the input list of a READ statement or the output list of a PRINT statement. The part of the input list or output list that makes up the implied DO loop is enclosed in parentheses. The DO loop variable and control parameters appear at the end of the implied DO loop.

EXAMPLE 7.12

The following input list contains an implied DO loop:

```
READ *, (NAMES(I), I = 1, 10)
```

The control portion (I = 1, 10) appears at the end of the implied DO loop and specifies that the data-entry operation is to be repeated for each integer value of I from 1 to 10. The input list specified by the implied DO loop is equivalent to NAMES(1), NAMES(2), ..., NAMES(10). ■

EXAMPLE 7.13

We can use an implied DO loop to replace the explicit DO loop shown in Fig. 7.3. If the following implied DO loop is used

```
C Enter the exam data
      PRINT *, 'Enter each name and score pair until done'
      READ *, (NAMES(I), SCORES(I), I = 1, NUMSTU)
```

the prompt

```
Enter each name and score pair until done
```

is displayed one time, after which you must enter exactly NUMSTU name and score pairs. In this example, the input list specified by the implied DO loop is equivalent to

```
NAMES(1),SCORES(1),NAMES(2),SCORES(2),...,NAMES(NUMSTU),SCORES(NUMSTU)
```
■

The implied DO loop is the most flexible means for reading data into an array. Unlike the explicit DO loop shown in Fig. 7.3, it enables you to enter more than one name and score pair on a data line. The implied DO loop is also shorter and simpler to write than the explicit DO loop, because there is no CONTINUE statement or label required. In most cases, you will find this the best technique to use for data entry.

**End-of-File
Specifier**

In the examples so far, we assumed that we knew beforehand the number of data items being read. Often, this is not the case. In Section 4.6, we showed how to use a sentinel value as an extra data item entered at the terminal to signal that all actual data were read. Although we could insert a sentinel value at the end of a data file, it's much easier to use an end-of-file specifier in a READ statement that enters data from a file (see Section 5.5).

EXAMPLE 7.14

The DO loop in Fig. 7.5 reads the student exam data from a data file. Each time the loop executes, the statement

```
READ (2, *, END = 99) NAMES(I), SCORES(I)
```

enters a new student name and score from the data file associated with unit 2 and stores the data in the next pair of array elements. A sample data file is shown in Fig. 7.6.

We would expect DO loop 20 to execute MAXSTU times, where MAXSTU is the declared size of the arrays. However, what happens if the data file contains fewer than MAXSTU pairs of data? In this case, we would like to exit the DO loop after the last pair of data items is stored. The file specifier END = 99 causes this to happen.

The end of the data file in Fig. 7.6 is reached after the last data pair is read into array elements NAMES(3) and SCORES(3). When the READ statement executes again, the file specifier END = 99 causes a transfer of control to the statement with label 99. Without this specifier, an "attempt to read beyond the end of file" run-time error would occur.

If the data file contains more than MAXSTU data pairs, the arrays will be filled with data before the end of the data file is reached. In this case, normal loop exit occurs after the last element in each array receives its data (I is MAXSTU + 1). The PRINT statement displays a message warning that there may be more data left on the file. Normal loop exit also occurs if the data file contains exactly MAXSTU data pairs. In this case, the warning message can be ignored.

After loop exit, the assignment statement with label 99

```
99 NUMSTU = I - 1
```

stores in NUMSTU the number of data pairs read. The value stored, I − 1, represents the value of I during the last successful READ operation.

Figure 7.5. *Loop to Read a Data File*

```
        DO 20 I = 1, MAXSTU
            READ (2, *, END = 99) NAMES(I), SCORES(I)
20      CONTINUE
        PRINT *, 'WARNING - ARRAY FILLED BEFORE END OF FILE REACHED'

C File read operation completed
C Store count of students in NUMSTU
    99 NUMSTU = I - 1
```

Figure 7.6. *Sample Data File*

```
'SMITH, BILLY'    75
'JONES, GORDY'    92
'KING, CAROLE'    83
```

End-of-File Specifier with Implied DO

We can also use an implied DO loop with a READ statement that has an end-of-file specifier. For example, the statement

```
READ (2, *, END = 99) (NAMES(I), SCORES(I), I = 1, MAXSTU)
```

reads data pairs into arrays NAMES and SCORES, transferring control to label 99 when there are no more data on the file associated with unit 2. If both arrays become filled with data, the statement following the READ statement executes next. Note, it is not necessary to list each data pair on a separate line of the data file.

Review of Array-input Methods

The properties of the five array-input methods discussed so far are summarized in Table 7.4, assuming that N represents the number of data pairs available. N must be less than or equal to the array size.

Table 7.4. *Five Array-input Methods*

EXAMPLE	DATA FORMAT	COMMENTS
READ *, NAMES, SCORES	'BILL' 'JILL' ...'JOE' 95 67 ... 85	Entire array must be filled (first NAMES, then SCORES). Many data items may be on each line.
DO 10 I = 1, N READ *, NAMES(I), + SCORES(I) 10 CONTINUE	'BILL' 95 'JILL' 67 'SUE' 98	Part of array may be filled. Only one data pair may be on a line.
READ *, (NAMES(I), + SCORES(I), I = 1, N)	'BILL' 95 'JILL' 67 'SUE' 98	Part of array may be filled. Many data items may be on each line.

(continued)

EXAMPLE	DATA FORMAT				COMMENTS

`DO 20 I = 1, MAXSTU`
`    READ (2, *, END = 99)`
`+        NAMES(I), SCORES(I)`
`20 CONTINUE`
	`'BILL'`
	`'JILL'`
	`'SUE'`
		`95`
		`67`
		`98`
					Part of array may be filled. Only one data pair may be on a line.

`    READ (2, *, END = 99)`
`+      (NAMES(I), SCORES(I),`
`+       I = 1,    MAXSTU)`
	`'BILL'`
	`'SUE'`
		`95`
		`98`
			`'JILL'`	`67`	Part of array may be filled. Many data items may be on each line.

Array Output

The techniques for array input may also be used for array output. However, because we generally prefer to have array data displayed in a table, the explicit DO loop is most commonly used. The other methods may display as many values as will fit across an output line.

EXAMPLE 7.15

Given the arrays NAMES and SCORES described in Fig. 7.4, the statement

```
PRINT *, NAMES, SCORES
```

causes a list of student names to be printed, followed by a list of student scores. Remember that when arrays are referred to by name only (no subscripts), the entire array is indicated. The number of values printed on a line depends on the field width used for each value and the line length. Exactly $2 \times$ MAXSTU values are printed, where MAXSTU is the declared size of each array. Because all names are printed first, followed by all scores, it is difficult to determine which score goes with which name, as in the output list

```
NAMES(1),NAMES(2),....,NAMES(MAXSTU),SCORES(1),SCORES(2),....,SCORES(MAXSTU)
```

EXAMPLE 7.16

The DO loop

```
DO 10 I = 1, NUMSTU
    PRINT *, NAMES(I), SCORES(I)
10 CONTINUE
```

prints one name and score pair on each output line. The number of pairs printed, NUMSTU, may be between 1 and MAXSTU. This configuration gives the most legible output and is the form commonly used for tables. ◼

EXAMPLE 7.17 The PRINT statement with implied DO loop

```
PRINT *, (NAMES(I), SCORES(I), I = 1, NUMSTU)
```

prints a name followed by a score. As many name and score pairs as will fit are displayed on each line. The number of pairs printed, NUMSTU, may be between 1 and MAXSTU. This output is equivalent to the output list NAMES(1), SCORES(1), NAMES(2), SCORES(2), ... , NAMES(NUMSTU), SCORES(NUMSTU).

The three array-output methods are summarized in Table 7.5, assuming that N represents the number of data pairs stored in the arrays. N must be less than or equal to the array size. ◼

Table 7.5. *Three Array-output Methods*

EXAMPLE	OUTPUT	COMMENTS
`PRINT *, NAMES, SCORES`	BILL JILL SUE ... JOE 95 67 98 ... 85	Both arrays are printed (NAMES and then SCORES). As many values as will fit appear on each line.

`DO 10 I = 1, N`
`    PRINT *, NAMES(I),`
`+           SCORES(I)`
`10 CONTINUE`
	BILL 95
	JILL 67
	SUE 98
		Part of array may be printed. Only one pair of values appears on a line.

`PRINT *, (NAMES(I),` `+ SCORES(I), I = 1, N)`	BILL 95 JILL 67 SUE 98	Part of array may be printed. As many values as will fit appear on each line.

The implied DO loop is described in the next display.

SYNTAX
DISPLAY

Implied DO Loop

SYNTAX: READ *, (*input list, lcv = initial, final, step*)
           PRINT *, (*output list, lcv = initial, final, step*)

EXAMPLE: READ *, (X(I), I = 1, N)

INTERPRETATION: The READ (or PRINT) statement is executed. The *input list* (or *output list*) is repeated once for each integer value of *lcv* from *initial* to *final* in increments of *step* (1 if *step* is unspecified). Thus the statement

PRINT *, (A(I), B(I), I = 1, 3)

has the same effect as the statement

PRINT *, A(1), B(1), A(2), B(2), A(3), B(3)

The rules for specifying the implied DO loop parameters are the same as for the explicit DO (see Section 4.2).

**EXERCISES FOR
SECTION 7.4**

Self-check

1. Assume array X can contain a maximum of 100 type REAL values. Indicate how many values will be read into array X by each statement below. Also, indicate whether there are any special requirements on the form of the data lines in the data file associated with unit number 1 for this to happen.

    a.   `READ (1, *) X`
    b.   `NUMX = 25`
            `DO 10 I = 1, NUMX`
                `READ (1, *) X(I)`
      `10 CONTINUE`
    c.   `NUMX = 25`
            `READ (1, *) (X(I), I = 1, NUMX)`
    d.   `READ (1, *, END = 25) (X(I), I = 1, 100)`

2. Answer Self-check question 1 if WRITE is used instead of READ and unit number 1 is associated with an output file.

Programming

1. Using the arrays in Programming exercise 1 at the end of Section 7.1, write a DO loop to print the square roots and cubes of the integers from 1 through 5. Each output line should show an integer value followed by its square root and cube.

2. Rewrite DO loop 30 in Fig. 7.2 as an implied DO loop. Will the output remain in table form?

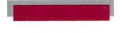

7.5   Using Formats with Arrays

When using formats with arrays, the compiler requires an edit descriptor for each array element read or printed. If the FORMAT statement does not have enough edit descriptors, it will be reused as explained below.

Using Implied DO Loop in a Formatted PRINT

One problem with using the implied DO loop to print data in parallel arrays is that more than one set of data may be printed on each line, so the data will not be printed in a table. FORMAT statements can be used to solve this problem. If a FORMAT statement is written to describe the appearance of one set of data, then that FORMAT statement can be reused when more than one set of data is printed. Each time a FORMAT statement is reused, a new line of output is automatically started.

EXAMPLE 7.18

The formatted PRINT statement

```
  PRINT 5, (I, NAMES(I), SCORES(I), I = 1, NUMSTU)
5 FORMAT (1X, I3, 2X, A, 5X, I3)
```

causes student number I (1 through NUMSTU) and a name and score pair to be displayed on each output line. FORMAT statement 5 describes how three output list items should be printed. If NUMSTU is greater than 1, there will be more items in the output list than there are edit descriptors in the FORMAT statement, so the format specification must be reused. Each time the specification is reused, a new output line is started. The student names and scores will be printed in a table similar to that produced by an explicit DO loop. ■

EXAMPLE 7.19

Given the declaration

```
INTEGER K(20)
```

and the PRINT statement

```
PRINT 10, K
```

FORMAT 10 should have one or more edit descriptors beginning with the letter I. They can be provided individually, as in

```
10 FORMAT (2X, I3, 2X, I3, 2X, I3, 2X, I3)
```

or by specifying the repetition of one or more edit descriptors, as in

```
10 FORMAT (4(2X, I3))
```

In FORMAT 10 above, the notation 4(2X, I3) indicates that the *descriptor group* (2X, I3) is to be repeated four times. The 20 elements of array K will be displayed with four values on each line. ■

EXAMPLE 7.20   Let W be a real array of up to 200 elements and N be an integer variable used to indicate the number of data items to be stored in W. If the value of N is typed on one line (in I3 format) and the N values to be read into W are typed on successive data lines (8 items per line in F10.3 format), then the statements

```
   READ 40, N
40 FORMAT (I3)
   READ 50, (W(I), I = 1, N)
50 FORMAT (8F10.3)
```

can be used to read in N, and the items to be stored in array W. FORMAT 50 will work regardless of the size of N (as long as N is in range). Each time the format specification is exhausted during the execution of the READ 50 statement, a new line will be read and the format specification will be reused automatically. The

FORTRAN in Focus

The Life Cycle of a Fortran Program

McDONNELL DOUGLAS
SPACE SYSTEMS COMPANY

It has been 20 years since a human first walked on the moon. When President Bush announced that the United States would once again go to the moon, and later to Mars, it prompted aerospace companies like McDonnell Douglas to revitalize their lunar mission planning operations. The engineers who plan these missions use Fortran to handle the large number of calculations needed to design spacecraft and launch vehicles and determine their earth–moon trajectories.

When engineers program in Fortran, they are creating the tools they need to get results. Warren W. James, Senior Engineer/Scientist in the Advanced Projects Area at McDonnell Douglas, distinguishes between two kinds of people who program computers. One type of programmer has the task of creating a running, debugged piece of software. When the program is written, the job is complete. For the other type of programmer, the job begins when the program is complete. The computer program is just a means to an end; in the engineer's case, the program is the tool that is needed to do the calculations required for the tasks at hand. Fortran is popular with the engineer/programmer because it does mathematics faster than other languages and because its code closely resembles conventional mathematics. Just as

format still describes the layout of a single line, but it will be repeated as often as necessary until all N elements of W have been filled with data.

The statements

```
    PRINT 60
60 FORMAT ('1', 'THE DATA IN W ARE:')
    PRINT 70, (W(I), I = 1, N)
70 FORMAT (1X, 12F10.3)
```

print a short heading at the top of a page and then print the data in the array W, 12 items per line. FORMAT 70 describes a single line of output, but the format specification will be reused as often as necessary until all N elements in W have been printed. Each time the format is reused, a new line is started, and a blank is used for carriage control.

The input or output list in a READ or PRINT statement completely determines the number of data items to be processed regardless of the number of data

important, its widespread usage has yielded a large collection of problem-solving programs.

Sharing Fortran programs and enhancing them is an integral part of the engineer's problem-solving process. The lunar mission planning that Warren James does at McDonnell Douglas illustrates the typical life cycle of a Fortran tool.

As a spacecraft moves from the earth to the moon, the influence of the gravitational forces of the earth, sun, and moon have varying effects on its trajectory. There is no analytical means of combining all three influences to determine a trajectory, so the trajectory for any set of launch/arrival dates

must be calculated numerically. A Fortran program, called Multiconic, was developed at McDonnell Douglas in the late 1960s as a tool for approximating the effect of these gravitational forces on a spacecraft's path. It was developed to be accurate enough to be useful, yet fast enough to feasibly evaluate multiple launch/arrival opportunities. Once the field of potential trajectories is narrowed, more accurate (and more time-consuming) flight mechanics programs are used to calculate the trajectory for the selected launch/arrival dates.

The Multiconic program originally ran on a CDC 6600 series mainframe computer.

(continued)

descriptors in the associated FORMAT statement. During processing, each item in the input or output list is matched with the corresponding data descriptor. If there are more data descriptors than items in the input or output list, any extra data descriptors are ignored (although leftover space descriptors, including strings, are processed up to the next data descriptor).

If there are more items than data descriptors, all or part of the format specification will be reused. If the format specification contains no internal parentheses, the entire format specification will be reused. If the format specification contains internal parentheses, format control reverts to the left parenthesis that matches the next-to-last right parenthesis. The re-scan of the format specification will begin with the repetition count, if any, preceding this left parenthesis.

Reading a Character Array

One way to read a line of text is to read it into a single character string. We can use the following statements to store a data line of up to 80 characters into

Twenty years later, that program was ported to a VAX by the engineers in the Advanced Projects Area. Without rewriting the core program, they modified it to suit the needs of today's mission-planning operations. For example, the program as written in the 1960s propagated a trajectory to the moon, but not an orbit around the Moon. Multiconic was modified to propagate the motion of a spacecraft following lunar orbit insertion so that the effects of various lunar orbit insertion strategies could be studied.

This revision process is typical of a Fortran tool. Designed by an engineer for a specific problem, it is made available to others with similar problems. As time goes on, other programmers add additional features to the program. Tools for commonly encountered problems become part of a company's resources, and are documented more thoroughly than tools developed for one-time use. Years later, or days later, the cycle may begin again, as new elements are added, debugged, and shared. Fortran's portability between platforms makes this kind of retooling readily achievable.

Warren James, a self-described "microrevolutionary," is currently involved in starting the cycle again by porting the Multiconic program to the personal computer. His goal is to integrate Multiconic with another tool, called an N-body integrator. After a launch opportunity is identified, the N-body integrator calculates the trajectory more accurately. By integrating the tools on a PC, James will make it easy to scope out a launch space, feed the calculations to the N-body integrator, and display the results of these calculations in one smooth operation. The resulting tool will allow engineers to design a lunar mission in much less time and at a lower cost than previously possible.

James's undertaking reveals not only the way in which tools can be enhanced

the character variable `LINE`

```
CHARACTER *80 LINE
READ '(A80)', LINE
```

Although doing this allows us to read and store the textual data, we cannot process individual characters stored in the string. (We will learn how to do this in Chapter 10.) However, if we read the line of text into an array of characters instead of into a character string, the individual data characters will be stored in separate array elements, ready for further processing.

EXAMPLE 7.21   We can use the following statements to read the contents of an 80-character line into an 80-element array of characters:

```
CHARACTER *1 BUFFER(80)
      READ 27, BUFFER
27 FORMAT (80A1)
```

and reused, but also the growing popularity of Fortran on the microcomputer. While CPU time may be somewhat longer when running a program on the PC, the delays involved in time-sharing systems often make the time to results with a PC shorter than that with a larger computer.

Because Fortran was designed for mathematical calculations, it is unsurpassed by other languages in this arena. However, James foresees a time when mixed language programming will allow programmers to use a variety of languages, each selected for their fit with a given task, and combine the parts into a problem-solving whole. He is using such an approach with the trajectory system he is preparing. The Fortran code for Multiconic and the N-body integrator are being compiled and made accessible to a different language being used for the graphical user interface. The user will continue to use the Fortran tools originally developed more than 20 years ago, but will access them through a user interface written in the 1990s using a computer language that provides the specific tools needed to create a graphical user interface.

From his engineering perspective, Warren James predicts that Fortran will keep doing what it does best— solving problems into the next century.

Sincere thanks to Warren W. James, Senior Engineer/Scientist, for sharing his insights into the role of Fortran in the Advanced Projects Area at McDonnell Douglas Space Systems Company in Huntington Beach, California. His affinity for computers extends to his avocation as well, as he regularly hosts a science and science fiction radio show in Southern California. It is the only radio show he knows of that broadcasts the orbital elements for the space shuttle so listeners can program the orbit on their personal computers and predict the shuttle's passage overhead.

FORMAT 27 specifies that the data line contains 80 individual character fields of width one. Consequently, each column will be stored separately in an element of the array BUFFER. We can then process any character on the data line by specifying its corresponding array subscript (e.g., BUFFER(1) represents the first column).

The statement

```
READ '(80A)', BUFFER
```

would have the same effect as the READ 27 statement. Each line contains 80 fields; the width of each field must be the same as the length of an element of BUFFER (length 1). For the data line

```
This is a string.
```

BUFFER(1) would contain the letter T, BUFFER(2) would contain the letter h, BUFFER(17) would contain the period, and BUFFER(18) through BUFFER(80) would contain blank characters.

EXERCISES FOR SECTION 7.5

Self-check

1. Assuming arrays X and Y each contain up to 20 type REAL elements, what would the following statements display?

   a.   `PRINT 10, X, Y`
       `10 FORMAT (1X, F10.2, 5X, F10.2)`
   b.   `PRINT 20, (X(I), Y(I), I = 1, 20)`
       `20 FORMAT (1X, F10.2, 5X, F10.2)`

2. For the array BUFFER described in Example 7.21, what would the following statements display?

   a.   `PRINT 5, BUFFER`
       `5 FORMAT (1X, 80A1)`
   b.   `PRINT 10, (BUFFER(I), I = 1, 80)`
       `10 FORMAT (1X, 80A1)`
   c.   `PRINT 10, BUFFER`
       `10 FORMAT (1X, A1)`
   d.   `PRINT 20, BUFFER`
       `20 FORMAT (1X, 80(A1, 1X))`
   e.   `PRINT 30, (BUFFER(I), I = 1, 80, 2)`
       `30 FORMAT (1X, 80A1)`

Programming

1. Assume array X can contain a maximum of 100 type REAL values. Write a formatted PRINT statement that displays five elements per line on every

other output line until all 100 elements are printed. The format statement should contain the line-control character and the edit descriptor (F10.2) for each array element value.

2. Let WCF be an integer array of size twelve containing values ranging from $-130°F$ to $+50°F$ and TEMP be an integer variable whose values range from $-50°$ to $+50°$. Write the PRINT and FORMAT statement to output the contents of TEMP and WCF in one row:

```
TEMP WCF(1) WCF(2) . . . WCF(12)
```

The value of TEMP should be separated from WCF(1) by at least five blanks, and the contents of the elements of WCF should be separated from one another by at least two blanks.

3. Write the PRINT and FORMAT statements needed to produce the output described in (a)–(d). Start each new line described by your format with the descriptor 1X, which indicates a blank for line control for these lines.

a. Let X be a real array of 20 elements, each containing positive real numbers ranging in value from 0 to 99999.99. Print the contents of X, accurate to two decimal places, four elements per line.

b. Do the same as for part (a), but print the contents of the variable N (containing an integer ranging in value from 1 to 20) on one line and then print the contents of the first N elements of the array X, four per line.

c. Let QUEUE be a 1000-element array of real numbers whose range of values is not easily determined but is known to be very large. Print the contents of QUEUE six elements per line, accurate to six decimal places.

d. Let ROOM and TEMP be 120-element arrays. ROOM contains the numbers of the rooms in a nine-story building (these range from 101 through 961). TEMP contains the temperatures of these rooms on a given day, accurate to one decimal place. Print two parallel columns of output, one containing all room numbers and the other containing the temperature of each room.

7.6 Array Arguments

Until now, all subprogram arguments were simple variables. In this section, we study how to use arrays as subprogram arguments. Each actual array must be declared in the main program. A subprogram that processes the array must be passed information that enables it to correctly access the array elements. Usually the array name and number of elements are passed as arguments.

Figure 7.7. *Function GETMAX*

```
      INTEGER FUNCTION GETMAX (LIST, N)

C Returns the largest of the first N values in array LIST
C Precondition : First N elements of array LIST are defined and N > 0.
C Postcondition: Function result is LIST(I) (1 <= I <= N) where
C                      LIST(I) is the largest of the first N elements.

C Argument Declarations
      INTEGER N, LIST(N)

C Local Declarations
      INTEGER I, CURLRG

C     Assume the first element is the largest so far
      CURLRG = LIST(1)

C Compare each element to the largest so far; save the larger value
      DO 10 I = 2, N
         IF (LIST(I) .GT. CURLRG) THEN
            CURLRG = LIST(I)
         END IF
   10 CONTINUE

C Define result and exit function
      GETMAX = CURLRG
      RETURN
      END
```

EXAMPLE 7.22   Function GETMAX in Fig. 7.7 returns the largest value that is stored in the array represented by dummy argument LIST. Within the DO loop, the current array element value, LIST(I), is compared to the largest value found so far, CURLRG. If the current element value is larger, it is stored in CURLRG. CURLRG is initialized to the first array element; its final value is returned as the function result.

The declaration statement

```
INTEGER N, LIST(N)
```

indicates to the compiler that dummy argument LIST represents an array with N elements. Dummy argument N is used as the limit value in the DO loop and determines how many array elements are processed. N may be passed any value from 1 to the size of the array as declared in the main program. ■

If X is an INTEGER array with five elements, the statement

```
XLARGE = GETMAX(X, 5)
```

calls function GETMAX to search array X and find its largest element; this value is returned and stored in variable XLARGE. If Y is an INTEGER array with 10 elements, the statement

```
YLARGE = GETMAX(Y, 10)
```

causes the largest value in array Y to be stored in YLARGE. The statement

```
YLARGE = GETMAX(Y, 5)
```

causes the largest value in the first half (subscripts 1 through 5) of array Y to be stored in YLARGE.

Argument Correspondence for Arrays

The argument correspondence for GETMAX(X, 5) is shown in Fig. 7.8 for a particular array X. There is no need to copy array X in the function data area; instead, the location in memory of the first array element is stored in the function data area, thus enabling the function to access array X. Consequently, each reference to dummy array element LIST(I) causes X(I) to be manipulated. The value returned by the function reference GETMAX(X, 5) is 37; the value returned by the function reference GETMAX(X, 3) is 15. In the latter case, only the first three elements of array X are examined.

Returning an Array of Values

A subroutine can return several values using different output arguments. It can also return an array of values using one output argument, as shown in the next example. In this example, we also show how an array declared in a subprogram can correspond to actual arrays declared with different sizes in the main program.

Figure 7.8. *Argument Correspondence for GETMAX(X, 5)*

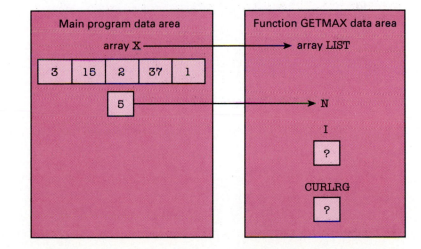

EXAMPLE 7.23 Subroutine ADDER in Fig. 7.9 adds two arrays. The sum of arrays A and B is defined as the array C such that C(I) is equal to A(I) + B(I) for each subscript I. The last argument, N, specifies how many array elements are summed.
The declaration

```
REAL A(*), B(*), C(*)
```

indicates that dummy arguments A, B, and C are type REAL arrays. The * specifies that each array size is the same as the declared size of its corresponding actual array, thus allowing us to use the subroutine with any size array. Arrays A, B, and C are called *assumed-size dummy arrays*.
The argument correspondence specified by

```
CALL ADDER(X, Y, Z, 5)
```

is shown in Fig. 7.10. The values stored in arrays X and Y in the main program are added together and saved in array Z. Dummy argument N (not shown) corresponds to the constant 5.

Figure 7.9. *Subroutine ADDER*

```
          SUBROUTINE ADDER (A, B, C, N)

C Stores element—by—element sum of arrays A and B in array C
C Preconditions : N > 0 and first N elements
C     of arrays A and B are defined.
C Postconditions: C(I) = A(I) + B(I) for 1 <= I <= N.

C Input Arguments
C    A, B — Arrays being summed
C    N — Number of elements summed
C Output Argument
C    C — Sum of arrays A and B

C Argument Declarations
      REAL A(*), B(*), C(*)
      INTEGER N

C Local Declarations
      INTEGER I

C Add elements of arrays A and B with the same subscript
      DO 10 I = 1, N
          C(I) = A(I) + B(I)
   10 CONTINUE

C Exit subroutine
      RETURN
      END
```

Figure 7.10. *Argument Correspondence for ADDER (X, Y, Z, 5)*

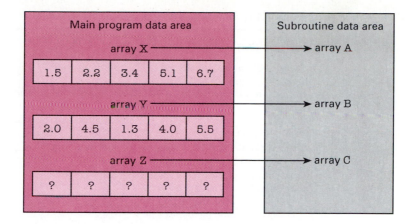

After the subroutine is executed, Z(1) will contain the sum of X(1) and Y(1), or 3.5; Z(2) will contain the sum of X(2) and Y(2), or 6.7; and so on; arrays X and Y will be unchanged. The new contents of array Z are as follows:

Array Z after subroutine execution

3.5	6.7	4.7	9.1	12.2

EXAMPLE 7.24

Subroutine ENTSTU in Fig. 7.11 reads data into a pair of parallel arrays. The first dummy argument (MAXSIZ) is an input argument that specifies the declared size of the arrays. The remaining arguments are input/output arguments used to store the array data (NAMES, SCORES) and the number of array elements (NUMSTU) that are currently filled with data. ENTSTU can be called more than once; each time it is called, additional data are entered and positioned after the data entered during the previous call.

NUMSTU is used to select the next pair of array elements that receive data. The value of NUMSTU passed into the subroutine is the subscript of the last pair of elements that currently contain data; it should be zero the first time ENTSTU is called. NUMSTU is increased by 1 before each data pair is stored. The value of NUMSTU returned to the calling program specifies the number of element pairs that contain data after the new data are entered.

Each name and score pair is temporarily saved in NXTNAM and NXTSCR before being stored in the arrays. The subroutine return occurs after the sentinel name is read or the arrays become filled (NUMSTU is MAXSIZ). The sentinel name ('*') and score (0) are not saved in the arrays.

Dummy arrays NAMES and SCORES are considered input/output arguments because they may be partially defined before each call to ENTSTU. Any new data entered during each call are returned to the calling program along with the original data.

Figure 7.11. *Subroutine ENTSTU*

```
          SUBROUTINE ENTSTU (MAXSIZ, NAMES, SCORES, NUMSTU)

C Returns data in the parallel arrays NAMES and SCORES
C and updates NUMSTU
C Precondition : NUMSTU <= MAXSIZ and first NUMSTU
C     elements of arrays NAMES and SCORES are defined.
C Postcondition: NUMSTU is incremented by the number of
C     data pairs read, NUMSTU <= MAXSIZ, and
C     first NUMSTU elements of arrays NAMES and SCORES are defined.

C Input Argument
C    MAXSIZ - The array size
C Input/Output Arguments
C    NAMES - Array of student names
C    SCORES - Array of exam scores
C    NUMSTU - Number of array elements currently filled with data

C Argument Declarations
          INTEGER MAXSIZ, NUMSTU, SCORES(MAXSIZ)
          CHARACTER *20 NAMES(MAXSIZ)
C Local Declarations
          INTEGER NXTSCR
          CHARACTER *20 NXTNAM

C Print instructions
          PRINT *, 'Enter a name (in quotes) and a score'
          PRINT *, 'Enter the sentinel pair ''*'' 0 when done'

C Read each name and score pair and store it in the arrays
          READ *, NXTNAM, NXTSCR
          DO WHILE ((NXTNAM .NE. '*') .AND.             9 IF (...) THEN
       +          (NUMSTU .LT. MAXSIZ))
             NUMSTU = NUMSTU + 1
             SCORES(NUMSTU) = NXTSCR
             NAMES(NUMSTU) = NXTNAM
             PRINT *, 'Enter next name and score'
             READ *, NXTNAM, NXTSCR
          END DO                                        GOTO 9
                                                        END IF
C Exit subroutine
          RETURN
          END
```

Figure 7.12. *Effect of Call to ENTSTU*

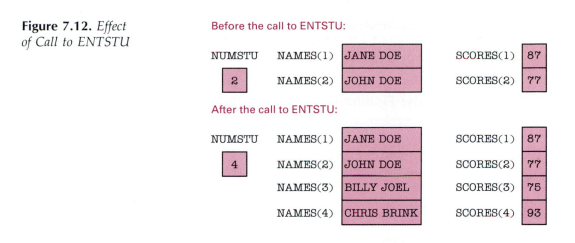

Before the call to ENTSTU:

NUMSTU		
	NAMES(1)	JANE DOE	SCORES(1)	87
2	NAMES(2)	JOHN DOE	SCORES(2)	77

After the call to ENTSTU:

NUMSTU		
	NAMES(1)	JANE DOE	SCORES(1)	87
4	NAMES(2)	JOHN DOE	SCORES(2)	77
	NAMES(3)	BILLY JOEL	SCORES(3)	75
	NAMES(4)	CHRIS BRINK	SCORES(4)	93

The main program data area is shown in Fig. 7.12 before and after the statement

```
CALL ENTSTU (MAXSIZ, NAMES, SCORES, NUMSTU)
```

is executed, assuming MAXSIZ is 100 and NUMSTU is 2 before the call. Only the array elements with defined values are shown. The new data are

```
'BILLY JOEL' 75
'CHRIS BRINK' 93
'*' 0
```

The value returned for NUMSTU is 4. ■

Using Individual Array Elements as Arguments

We also can use individual array elements as actual, but not dummy, arguments. An array element used as an actual argument must correspond to a dummy argument that is a simple variable of the same type as the array element. For example, the statement

```
CALL ORDER (X(1), X(2))
```

calls subroutine ORDER (see Fig. 6.16) to place the first two elements of actual array X in ascending order. The call statement establishes a correspondence between array element X(1) and the first dummy argument and between array element X(2) and the second dummy argument. Because both dummy arguments of subroutine ORDER are type REAL, the calling program must declare

X as a type REAL array with at least two elements. Remember, it is illegal for an array element to be listed as a dummy argument in either a function or a subroutine definition.

Case Study: Finding the Area of a Polygon

PROBLEM STATEMENT

Your math professor needs a program for computing the area of a polygon. The (X, Y) coordinates of each point of the polygon are stored on a data file in which each line contains the X and Y coordinates of a single point.

ANALYSIS

Assume the points of a polygon with n sides are numbered in sequence, as shown in Fig. 7.13, where point (X_1, Y_1) lies between points (X_n, Y_n) and (X_2, Y_2), and point (X_2, Y_2) lies between points (X_1, Y_1) and (X_3, Y_3). We can store the points of the polygon in a pair of parallel arrays, X and Y, of size NMAX and then find the area of the polygon. According to your math professor, you can use the formula

$$area = \tfrac{1}{2}|X_1Y_2 + X_2Y_3 + \cdots + X_{n-1}Y_n + X_nY_1$$
$$- Y_1X_2 + Y_2X_3 - \cdots - Y_{n-1}X_n - Y_nX_1|$$

to find the area.

Data Requirements

Problem Parameter

the maximum number of sides in a polygon (NMAX = 20)

Problem Inputs

the array of X coordinates (REAL X(NMAX))
the array of Y coordinates (REAL Y(NMAX))

Problem Output

the area of the polygon (REAL AREA)

Additional Program Variable

the actual number of sides in the polygon (INTEGER N)

DESIGN

The initial algorithm follows Fig. 7.13.

Figure 7.13. *Sample Polygon with Five Sides*

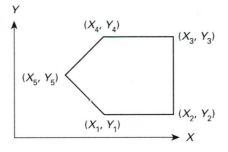

Algorithm

1. Read the coordinates into the arrays X and Y and define the number of sides in the polygon.
2. Display the coordinates.
3. Compute the area of the polygon.
4. Display the area.

Algorithm Refinements

Figure 7.14 shows the structure chart for finding the polygon's area. We can implement steps 1 and 2 using subroutines ENTCOR and SHOCOR, respectively, and step 3 using function SUMSID. Arrays X and Y and variable N are returned as outputs from ENTCOR and are passed as inputs to SHOCOR and SUMSID.

Figure 7.14. *Structure Chart for Finding the Area of a Polygon*

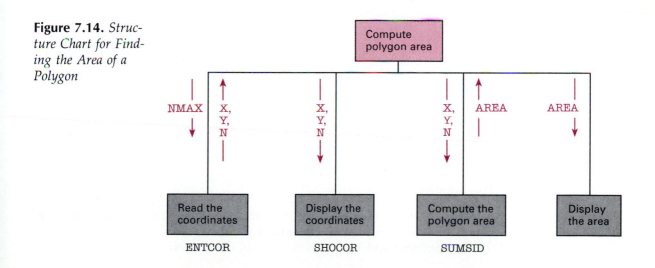

Figure 7.15. *Main Program for Computation of Polygon Area*

```
      PROGRAM POLGON
C Computes the area of a polygon whose coordinates are read from
C a data file

C Declarations
      INTEGER NMAX
      PARAMETER (NMAX = 20)
      REAL X(NMAX), Y(NMAX), AREA
      INTEGER N
      REAL SUMSID

C Read the array coordinates into arrays X and Y
      CALL ENTCOR (NMAX, X, Y, N)

C Display the coordinates
      CALL SHOCOR (X, Y, N)

C Compute area of polygon
      AREA = SUMSID(X, Y, N)

C Display area
      PRINT 5, 'Area is ', AREA
    5 FORMAT ('0', A, F10.2)

C Exit program
      STOP
      END
```

IMPLEMENTATION

The Main Program

Figure 7.15 shows the main program. The program begins by calling ENTCOR and SHOCOR to enter and display the coordinates. Next, the statement

```
AREA = SUMSID(X, Y, N)
```

calls function SUMSID, passing arrays X and Y as arguments along with N. The function result is stored in AREA and displayed by the PRINT statement in the main program.

The Subprograms

Subroutines ENTCOR and SHOCOR are relatively straightforward and are shown in Fig. 7.16. ENTCOR uses a READ statement with an end-of-file specifier to read the coordinates, and SHOCOR uses an implied DO loop to display them. The declaration

```
REAL X(NMAX), Y(NMAX)
```

identifies dummy arguments X and Y as type REAL arrays with NMAX elements. The variable I is used as a loop-control variable and array subscript in each subroutine. It is declared as a local variable in each subprogram.

Figure 7.16. *Subroutines ENTCOR and SHOCOR*

```
      SUBROUTINE ENTCOR (NMAX, X, Y, N)
C Reads up to NMAX coordinates into arrays X and Y
C Preconditions : NMAX is defined.
C Postconditions: N <= NMAX and X, Y coordinates are
C    read into first N elements of arrays X and Y.

C Input Arguments
C   NMAX - the maximum number of coordinates

C Output Arguments
C   X, Y - the coordinate points
C   N - the number of points read

C Argument Declarations
      INTEGER NMAX, N
      REAL X(NMAX), Y(NMAX)

C Local Declarations
      INTEGER I

C Prepare data file for input
      OPEN (UNIT = 1, FILE = 'POLY.DAT', STATUS = 'OLD')

C Read the coordinate pairs
      READ (1, *, END = 99) (X(I), Y(I), I = 1, NMAX)
      PRINT *, 'WARNING - ARRAY FILLED BEFORE END OF FILE'

C Store the number of points read in N
   99 N = I - 1

C Exit subroutine
      RETURN
      END

C ------------------------------------------------------

      SUBROUTINE SHOCOR (X, Y, N)
C Displays the first N values in parallel arrays X and Y
C Preconditions : N <= NMAX and first N elements of arrays X and Y
C    are defined.
C Postconditions: First N elements of arrays X and Y are displayed.
```

```
C Input Arguments
C    X, Y - the coordinate points
C    N - the number of points

C Argument Declarations
      INTEGER N
      REAL X(*), Y(*)

C Local Declarations
      INTEGER I

C Display the table heading
      PRINT 25, 'X', 'Y'
   25 FORMAT (1X, A10, 2X, A10)

C Display N pairs of points
      PRINT 35, (X(I), Y(I), I = 1, N)
   35 FORMAT (1X, F10.2, 2X, F10.2)

C Exit subroutine
      RETURN
      END
```

SUMSID must implement the formula for the area of a polygon given earlier. The number of product terms in this formula increases with N. We can use summation notation to write the following formula for any N:

$$area = \frac{1}{2} \left| \left(\sum_{i=1}^{N-1} X_i Y_{i+1} \right) + X_N Y_1 - \left(\sum_{i=1}^{N-1} Y_i X_{i+1} \right) - Y_N X_1 \right|.$$

Rearranging terms, we get

$$area = \frac{1}{2} \left| \sum_{i=1}^{N-1} (X_i Y_{i+1} - Y_i X_{i+1}) + X_N Y_1 - Y_N X_1 \right|.$$

We can use a single DO loop to compute the sum. The data requirements and algorithm for SUMSID follow. Figure 7.17 shows function SUMSID.

Data Requirements for SUMSID

Local Variables

the array subscript and loop-control variable (INTEGER I)
the sum of the XY products (REAL SUM)

Algorithm for SUMSID

1. Set SUM to zero
2. DO I = 1, N − 1
       SUM = SUM + X_iY_{i+1} − Y_iX_{i+1}
   END DO
3. SUM = SUM + X_NY_1 − Y_NX_1
4. SUMSID = ABS(SUM) / 2.0

Figure 7.17. *Function SUMSID*

```
      REAL FUNCTION SUMSID (X, Y, N)
C Computes the area of a polygon of N sides whose coordinates
C are stored in arrays X and Y
C Preconditions : Arrays X and Y contain N polygon coordinates and N lies
C                 between 3 and NMAX.
C Postconditions: Returns the polygon area

C Argument Declarations
      INTEGER N
      REAL X(*), Y(*)

C Local Declarations
      INTEGER I
      REAL SUM

C Compute SUM
      SUM = 0.0
      DO 20 I = 1, N − 1
         SUM = SUM + X(I) * Y(I + 1) − Y(I) * X(I + 1)
   20 CONTINUE
      SUM = SUM + X(N) * Y(1) − Y(N) * X(1)

C Define result
      SUMSID = ABS(SUM) / 2.0

C Exit function
      RETURN
      END
```


TESTING AND VERIFICATION

Figure 7.18 shows a sample run of the area-computation program for a square centered around the origin of the coordinate system. To test it, use simple polygons such as triangles and rectangles whose areas can be verified using well-known formulas. Make sure the program works for coordinates that are negative as well as positive.

Figure 7.18. *Sample Run of Area-Computation Program*

X	Y
−2.00	−2.00
2.00	−2.00
2.00	2.00
−2.00	2.00

Area is   16.00

Program Style: *Checking for Subscript-range Errors*

In function SUMSID, DO loop 20 adds together a collection of products of elements in arrays X and Y. The array subscripts used within the DO loop are I and I + 1. It is important to verify that these subscripts are in range during all loop iterations. We can do this by checking their values at the *loop boundaries;* i.e., when I is 1 and I is N − 1. When I is 1, the two subscript values are 1 and 2; when I is N − 1, the two subscript values are N − 1 and N. Because the subscript values are in range for the first and last loop iterations, we can be fairly certain they will be in range for all loop iterations.

EXERCISES FOR SECTION 7.6

Self-check

1. When is it better to pass an entire array of data, rather than individual elements, to a subroutine?
2. Assume a main program contains declarations for three arrays, C, D, and E, each with six elements. Explain the effect of each valid CALL statement to subroutine ADDER (see Fig. 7.9). Explain why each invalid CALL statement is invalid.

   a. CALL ADDER (A, B, C, 6)
   b. CALL ADDER (C(6), D(6), E(6), 6)
   c. CALL ADDER (C, D, E, 6)
   d. CALL ADDER (C, D, E, 7)
   e. CALL ADDER (C, D, E, 5)
   f. CALL ADDER (C, D, 6, E)
   g. CALL ADDER (E, D, C, 6)
   h. CALL ADDER (C, C, C, 6)
   i. CALL ADDER (C, D, E, C(1))
   j. CALL ADDER (C, D, E, INT(C(1)))
   k. CALL ADDER (C, D, E, INT(AMIN1(ABS(C(1)), 6.0)))

Programming

1. Write a subroutine that negates the values stored in an array. The first argument should be the array, and the second should be the number of elements being negated.

2. Write a subroutine that copies each value stored in one array to the corresponding element of another array. (For example, if the arrays are INARY and OUTARY then copy INARY(1) to OUTARY(1), next copy INARY(2) to OUTARY(2), and so on.)

3. Write a subroutine that reverses the values stored in an array. If array X has N elements, then X(1) will become X(N), X(2) will become X(N-1), and so forth. (*Hint:* Make a local copy of the array before starting to reverse the elements.)

4. Write a subroutine with two input array arguments (type INTEGER) and one output array argument (type LOGICAL). An additional input argument indicates how many elements are defined in both input arrays. The subroutine should assign a value of .TRUE. to element I of its output array if element I of one input array has the same value as element I of the other input array; otherwise it should assign a value of .FALSE..

7.7   The DATA Statement

The DATA statement provides a convenient method for initializing the values of simple variables and arrays.

EXAMPLE 7.25   The DATA statement

```
DATA A, B, C /2.5, 6.5, 9.0/
```

initializes the three variables listed as shown next.

A	B	C
2.5	6.5	9.0

The DATA statement

```
DATA A /2.5/, B /6.5/, C /9.0/
```

would have the same effect.

EXAMPLE 7.26   The statements

```
INTEGER CNTSIZ
PARAMETER (CNTSIZ = 20)
INTEGER COUNTR(CNTSIZ)
DATA COUNTR /CNTSIZ * 0/
```

initialize an array of counters (COUNTR) to all zeros. Because array COUNTR appears without a subscript in the DATA statement, the entire array is initialized. The notation CNTSIZ * 0 means that the value 0 is to be repeated twenty (value of CNTSIZ) times. ■

EXAMPLE 7.27   If LETTER is an array declared as

```
CHARACTER *1 LETTER(26)
```

the DATA statement

```
 DATA LETTER /'A','B','C','D','E','F','G','H','I','J','K','L','M',
+              'N','O','P','Q','R','S','T','U','V','W','X','Y','Z'/
```

initializes LETTER(1) to 'A', LETTER(2) to 'B', and so on. ■

When only part of an array is to be initialized, an implied DO loop may be used in the DATA statement.

EXAMPLE 7.28   If I is type INTEGER, the DATA statement

```
DATA (LETTER(I), I = 1, 5) /'A','B','C','D','E'/
```

initializes only the first five elements of array LETTER. The implied DO loop specifies that the string constants listed should be placed in elements LETTER(1) through LETTER(5), inclusive. ■

SYNTAX DISPLAY

The DATA Statement

SYNTAX: DATA *variable list* / *constant list* /
         DATA *variable₁*/*constant₁*/, *variable₂*/*constant₂*/, ...

EXAMPLE: DATA N, X /0, 0.0/
         DATA N/0/, X/0.0/

INTERPRETATION: The *variable list* may contain combinations of the following:

- Variable names
- Array element names (array names with subscripts)
- Array names (for initializing entire arrays)
- Implied loops (for initializing portions of arrays)

The *constant list* provides the corresponding initial values for the items in the *variable list*. There may be numeric, character, or logical constants or named constants previously declared in a PARAMETER statement.

The type of each constant and its corresponding variable should be the same. The correspondence is established in left-to-right order. There should be the same number of constants as there are memory cells being initialized. The notation $n * c$ can be used to specify n repetitions of the constant c. (n must be a positive integer constant or parameter, and c must be a constant.)
DATA statements must be placed after the type and parameter declarations.

NOTES: Any array subscripts must be integer constants or parameters or expressions involving integer constants and parameters. Any loop parameters should be integer constants or parameters or expressions involving integer constants and parameters.

The DATA statement must appear at the beginning of a program following the type and PARAMETER declarations. The DATA statement is a nonexecutable statement and is processed when the program is loaded into computer memory. Because it is not executable, the DATA statement has no effect once program execution begins. Consequently, a DATA statement cannot be reused in a program to reset an array after the array has already been processed.

Take care when using DATA statements to initialize local variables or arrays declared in a subprogram. The local variable will be initialized correctly the first time the subprogram is called. However, there is no guarantee that this initialization will occur in subsequent calls. If you wish the local variable to be reinitialized each time the subprogram is called, then you must use an assignment statement.

Plotting a Function

The next example illustrates how to use an array to store successive lines in a function plot. See Chapter 11 for additional discussion of function plots and graphs.

EXAMPLE 7.29

The program in Fig. 7.19 plots the value of the function $T^2 - 4T + 5$ for values of T between 0 and 10. It does this by storing an asterisk in the element of CHARACTER array PLOT corresponding to the function value, while all other elements contain the blank character. The first element of array PLOT has a subscript of zero; the array is initialized to all blanks using the DATA statement

```
DATA PLOT /' ', MAXVAL * ' ' /
```

Because MAXVAL is 65, 66 blanks are stored.

Within the DO loop, the assignment statement

```
FUNVAL = F(T)
```

calls the single-statement function F and saves the value returned in FUNVAL.

Figure 7.19. *Plot of Function $T^2 - 4T + 5$*

```
      PROGRAM PLOTIT
C Plots the function T ** 2 - 4 * T + 5 for T between 0 and 10

C Declarations
      INTEGER MAXVAL
      PARAMETER (MAXVAL = 65)
      INTEGER F, T, I, FUNVAL
      CHARACTER *1 PLOT(0 : MAXVAL)
      DATA PLOT /' ', MAXVAL * ' '/
      F(T) = T ** 2 - 4 * T + 5

C Display heading lines
      PRINT 5, (I, I = 0, MAXVAL, 5)
    5 FORMAT (1X, 14I5)
      PRINT 15, ('    !', I = 0, MAXVAL, 5)
   15 FORMAT (1X, 14A)

C Compute and print function value for each T between 0 and 10
      DO 10 T = 0, 10
         FUNVAL = F(T)
         PLOT(FUNVAL) = '*'
         PRINT 25, 'T=', T, PLOT
   25    FORMAT (1X, A2, I2, 66A1)
         PLOT(FUNVAL) = ' '
   10 CONTINUE

C Exit program
      STOP
      END


      0    5    10   15   20   25   30   35   40   45   50   55   60   65
      !    !    !    !    !    !    !    !    !    !    !    !    !    !
T= 0      *
T= 1    *
T= 2    *
T= 3      *
T= 4        *
T= 5           *
T= 6              *
T= 7                   *
T= 8                         *
T= 9                               *
T=10                                     *
```

The assignment

```
PLOT(FUNVAL) = '*'
```

places an asterisk in the element that corresponds to the function value. The formatted PRINT

```
    PRINT 25, 'T=', T, PLOT
25 FORMAT (1X, A2, I2, 66A1)
```

displays a line that begins with the value of T followed by array PLOT. The edit descriptor 66A1 is equivalent to the edit descriptor A1 repeated 66 times. Consequently, the array elements will be printed one after the other in adjacent columns across the output line. Because all but one of the elements contain blanks, a single asterisk will be displayed, with the position of the asterisk depending on the value of FUNVAL. After each line is printed, the assignment statement

```
PLOT(FUNVAL) = ' '
```

resets the nonblank element back to a blank.

There are three formatted PRINT statements in Fig. 7.19. The first one prints the heading line consisting of the integers 0, 5, 10, and so on, spaced five columns apart. The second one prints a line directly beneath the first consisting of fourteen occurrences of the symbol '!' spaced five columns apart. As mentioned above, the last formatted PRINT statement prints the current value of T and the corresponding function value (denoted by the symbol *). The first output line shows that F(0) is 5. ∎

General Function Plot

The function in Fig. 7.19 was relatively easy to plot because its values range from 1 (T = 0) to 65 (T = 10), and there is an array element corresponding to each integer value within this range. This approach can be generalized to plot any function. You first will need to change the definition of the single-statement function F. If the new function values do not lie within the range 0 to 65, you will have to scale them so that they do fall in this range.

As an example, consider a function with values between –30 and 250. A value of –30 should cause an asterisk to be placed in PLOT(0), and a value of 250 should cause an asterisk to be placed in PLOT(65). For such a function, the assignment statement

```
SCALED = 65 * (FUNVAL + 30) / 280
```

can be used to compute a scaled function value (SCALED) based on the actual

Table 7.6. *Computation of SCALED at Boundary Values*

FUNVAL	COMPUTATION OF SCALED	SCALED
−30	65 * (−30 + 30) / 280	
	65 * 0 / 280	0
250	65 * (250 + 30) / 280	
	65 * 280 / 280	65

function value (FUNVAL). The expression on p. 381 is derived from the formula

$$scaled\ value = 65 \times (FUNVAL - minval) / (maxval - minval)$$

where *minval* (−30) and *maxval* (250) are the smallest and largest function values to be plotted, respectively.

The assignment statements

```
PLOT(SCALED) = '*'
PLOT(SCALED) = ' '
```

can be used to insert and remove the asterisk in array PLOT. They should be used instead of

```
PLOT(FUNVAL) = '*'
PLOT(FUNVAL) = ' '
```

shown in Fig. 7.19.

Program Style: *Checking Boundary Values*

The discussion immediately above states that the value of SCALED ranges from 0 to 65 as the function value goes from −30 to 250. It is always a good idea to check the accuracy of these assumptions. This can be done by checking the boundaries of the range, as shown in Table 7.6. Because the value of SCALED is correct at the boundaries, it should be correct throughout the range.

EXERCISES FOR SECTION 7.7

Self-check

1. Assuming X and Y are type INTEGER arrays with 10 elements, explain the effect of the following DATA statements.

   a. DATA X /10 * 0/
   b. DATA X, Y /10 * 0, 10 * 1/
   c. DATA X /10 * 0/, Y /10 * 1/
   d. DATA (X(I), Y(I), I = 1, 10) /10 * 0, 10 * 1/

Programming

1. Declare an array PRIME for storing the first 10 prime numbers and write a DATA statement to initialize the array PRIME to those numbers.
2. Modify the program in Fig. 7.19 to plot the function $T^3 - 10T$ for values of T between -5 and 5. Determine the smallest and largest function values and write an assignment statement that scales these values into the range 0 to 70. Ensure you change the heading for the function plot as well.

7.8 Array Processing Illustrated

We have written programs that accumulate the sum of all input data items in a single variable. Often, we have different categories of data items, and we might want to accumulate a separate total for each category rather than lump all items together. The following problem uses an array to accomplish this.

This problem also illustrates two common ways of selecting array elements for processing. Sometimes we need to manipulate all elements of an array in some uniform manner (e.g., initialize them all to zero). In situations like this, it makes sense to process the array elements in sequence (*sequential access*), starting with the first and ending with the last.

At other times, the order in which the array elements are accessed is completely dependent on the order of the problem data. Because the order is not predictable beforehand, this method of selecting elements is called *random access*.

Case Study: Budget Problem

PROBLEM STATEMENT

Your consulting firm separates its monthly expenses into 10 categories (computer supplies, salaries, equipment, rent, etc.) You need a program that tracks monthly expenditures in each category. The program should read each expense amount, add it to the appropriate category total, and print the total expenditure by category. The input data consist of the category number and the amount of each purchase made during the past month.

ANALYSIS

There are 10 separate totals to be accumulated; each total can be associated with a different element of a 10-element array. The program must read each expenditure, determine to which category it belongs, and then add the expense amount to the appropriate array element. When done with all expenditures, the program can print a table showing each category and its accumulated total.

As in all programs that accumulate a sum, each total must be initialized to zero.

Data Requirements

Problem Parameter

the number of budget categories (NUMCAT = 10)

Problem Input

each expense category and amount

Problem Output

the array of budget totals (REAL BUDGET(NUMCAT))

DESIGN

The initial algorithm follows:

Algorithm

1. Initialize all budget totals to zero.
2. For each expenditure, read the category and expense amount and add the amount to the appropriate total.
3. Print the accumulated total for each category.

Algorithm Refinements

The structure chart in Fig. 7.20 shows the relationship among the three steps.

Figure 7.20. *Structure Chart for Budget Problem*

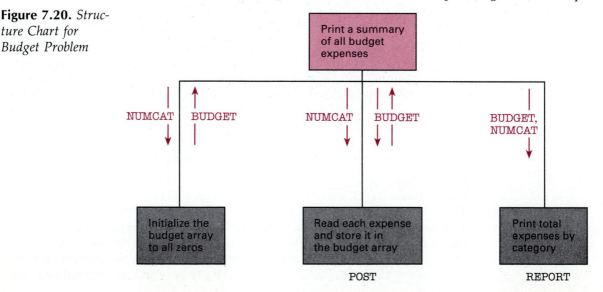

Figure 7.21. *Main Program for Budget Problem*

```
      PROGRAM DOBUDG
C Prints a summary of all expenses by budget category

C Declarations
      INTEGER NUMCAT
      PARAMETER (NUMCAT = 10)
      REAL BUDGET(NUMCAT)

C Initialize array BUDGET to all zeros
      DATA BUDGET /NUMCAT * 0.0/

C Read each expense amount and add it to the appropriate category
      CALL POST (BUDGET, NUMCAT)

C Print each category and its budget total
      CALL REPORT (BUDGET, NUMCAT)

C Exit program
      STOP
      END
```

The array BUDGET is an output of step 1 (performed in the main program), an input/output argument for step 2 (subroutine POST), and an input argument for step 3 (subroutine REPORT).

IMPLEMENTATION

Main Program

Figure 7.21 shows the main program. The statement

```
DATA BUDGET /NUMCAT * 0.0/
```

initializes all elements of array BUDGET to zero. Only parameter NUMCAT and array BUDGET are declared in the main program.

Subroutines REPORT and POST

Subroutine REPORT (Fig. 7.22) uses a formatted PRINT statement with an implied DO loop in its output list to display each budget category and expense amount on a separate line.

Subroutine POST (Fig. 7.23) must read each expense amount and add it to the appropriate budget category. A sentinel value for each category will be used to indicate the end of data. The data requirements and algorithm for POST follow Fig. 7.23.

Figure 7.22 *Subroutine REPORT*

```
      SUBROUTINE REPORT (BUDGET, NUMCAT)
C Prints each category and its expense total
C Preconditions : NUMCAT and BUDGET are defined.
C Postconditions: Array BUDGET is displayed.

C Input Arguments
C   BUDGET - array of expenses
C   NUMCAT - number of expense categories

C Argument Declarations
      INTEGER NUMCAT
      REAL BUDGET(NUMCAT)

C Local Declarations
      INTEGER NEXTCAT

C Display heading
      PRINT 15, 'Category', Expenses'
   15 FORMAT ('0', A10, 5X, A15)

C Display each category number and budget total
      PRINT 25, (NEXCAT, BUDGET(NEXCAT), NEXCAT = 1, NUMCAT)
   25 FORMAT (1X, I10, 5X, F15.2)

C Exit subroutine
      RETURN
      END
```

Figure 7.23. *Subroutine POST*

```
      SUBROUTINE POST (BUDGET, NUMCAT)
C Prints each category and its expense total
C Preconditions : BUDGET is initialized to all zeros.
C Postconditions: BUDGET(I) is the sum of expenses for category I.

C Input Arguments
C   NUMCAT - number of expense categories

C Input/Output Arguments
C   BUDGET - array of expenses

C Argument Declarations
      INTEGER NUMCAT
      REAL BUDGET(NUMCAT)

C Local Declarations
      INTEGER SENVAL
      PARAMETER (SENVAL = 0)
      INTEGER ENTER
      INTEGER NEXCAT, CATGRY
      REAL EXPENS
```

```
C Read each budget category, expense amount, and save it
      PRINT *, 'Enter the budget category or 0 to stop:'
      CATGRY = ENTER(SENVAL, NUMCAT)
      DO WHILE (CATGRY .NE. SENVAL)                    9 IF (...) THEN
          PRINT *, 'Enter the expenditure'
          READ *, EXPENS
          BUDGET(CATGRY) = BUDGET(CATGRY) + EXPENS
          PRINT *, 'Enter the budget category or 0 to stop:'
          CATGRY = ENTER(SENVAL, NUMCAT)
      END DO                                           GOTO 9
                                                       END IF

C Exit subroutine
      RETURN
      END


C-----------------------------------------------------------------


      INTEGER FUNCTION ENTER (NMIN, NMAX)
C Returns the first data value read between NMIN and NMAX
C Precondition : NMIN is less than or equal to NMAX.
C Postcondition: Function result lies between NMIN and NMAX.

C Argument Declarations
      INTEGER NMIN, NMAX

C Local Declarations
      INTEGER N
      LOGICAL BETWEN

C Initially assume an integer between NMIN and NMAX is not entered
      BETWEN = .FALSE.

C Keep reading until an integer between NMIN and NMAX is entered
      DO WHILE (.NOT. BETWEN)                          9 IF (...) THEN
          PRINT *, 'Enter an integer between ',
     +               NMIN, ' and ', NMAX
          READ *, N
          BETWEN = (N .GE. NMIN) .AND. (N .LE. NMAX)
      END DO                                           GOTO 9
                                                       END IF
C Define result
      ENTER = N

C Exit function
      RETURN
      END
```

Data Requirements for POST

Local Parameter

the sentinel category (SENVAL = 0)

Local Variables

the category of the current expenditure (INTEGER CATGRY)
the amount of the current expenditure (REAL EXPENS)

Algorithm for POST

1. Read in the budget category for each expenditure.
2. DO WHILE there are more expenditures
    3. Read in the expense amount.
    4. Add the amount to the appropriate budget total.
    5. Read in the category of the next expenditure.
   END DO

Subroutine POST calls function ENTER (see Figs. 6.3 and 7.23) to perform steps 1 and 5, so ENTER (type INTEGER) must be declared in POST. If the value returned to CATGRY by ENTER is a valid budget category, the statement

```
BUDGET(CATGRY) = BUDGET(CATGRY) + EXPENS
```

adds the expense amount (EXPENS) to the element of array BUDGET selected by the subscript CATGRY.

The WHILE loop in function ENTER executes until the READ statement enters a data value between its two arguments into local variable N. After loop exit, this data value is returned as the function result. The arguments in the function call

```
CATGRY = ENTER(SENVAL, NUMCAT)
```

ensure that CATGRY will be assigned a value between 0 (SENVAL) and 10 (NUMCAT).

TESTING AND VERIFICATION

Ensure you insert the main program, subroutines POST and REPORT, and function ENTER in the source file before attempting to compile and run the budget program. Figure 7.24 shows a sample run of the budget program. As shown in this run, the budget categories can be entered in arbitrary (random) order. Also, verify that all budget categories without purchases remain zero and that an out-of-range category value does not cause a run-time error.

Figure 7.24. *Sample Run of Budget Program*

```
Enter the budget category or 0 to stop:
Enter an integer between        0 and       10
4
Enter the expenditure
10.00
Enter the budget category or 0 to stop:
Enter an integer between        0 and       10
10
Enter the expenditure
15.00
Enter the budget category or 0 to stop:
Enter an integer between        0 and       10
4
Enter the expenditure
35.00
Enter the budget category or 0 to stop:
Enter an integer between        0 and       10
11
Enter an integer between        0 and       10
0


        Category         Expenses
               1             0.00
               2             0.00
               3             0.00
               4            45.00
               5             0.00
               6             0.00
               7             0.00
               8             0.00
               9             0.00
              10            15.00
```

Program Style: *Allowing for Array Expansion*

The constant NUMCAT is used throughout the Budget program to represent the number (10) of budget categories. Doing this enables us to easily extend the program to handle more budget categories by changing the value of a single constant, which is consistent with our prior use of program parameters to write general programs.

Program Style: *Avoiding Out-of-Range Errors*

Several measures are taken in Fig. 7.23 to prevent the occurrence of a "subscript out of range" execution error. Function ENTER ensures that only valid category values are assigned to the variable CATGRY. The WHILE loop is exited when CATGRY is 0 so there will be no attempt to increment the nonexistent array element BUDGET(0).

7.9 Common Programming Errors

1. It is very important that you declare each array used in a program and its size. You must also consistently spell the array name correctly. If you forget to declare an array or its size, the compiler will assume you are referencing a function, since both array and function names can be followed by a left parenthesis. For example, the statement

```
GRADES(I) = 0
```

is valid if GRADES is declared as an array; it is invalid and will be detected as an illegal function reference during program execution if array GRADES is not declared.

2. A subscript-range error is also common when using arrays. This occurs when the subscript value is outside the range specified in the array declaration. For the array VOLTS

```
REAL VOLTS(-5 : 5)
```

a subscript-range error occurs when VOLTS is used with a subscript that has a value less than –5 or greater than 5. If the value of I is 15, a reference to the subscripted variable VOLTS(I) may cause an error message such as

```
SUBSCRIPT RANGE ERROR AT LINE NO. 28 FOR ARRAY VOLTS, I = 15
```

Subscript-range errors are not syntax errors; consequently, they will not be detected until program execution begins. They most often are caused by an incorrect subscript expression or by a loop parameter error or nonterminating loop. Before considerable time is spent in debugging, you should carefully check all suspect subscript calculations for out-of-range errors. You can do this most easily by inserting diagnostic output statements in your program to print subscript values that might be out of range.

If a subscript range error occurs inside a DO loop, you should verify that the subscript is in range for both the initial and the final values of the loop-control variable. If these values are in range, it is likely that all other subscript references in the loop are in range as well.

If a subscript-range error occurs in a WHILE loop, verify that the loop-control variable is being updated as required. If it is not, the loop may be repeated more often than expected, causing the subscript-range error. This could happen if the control-variable update step was placed after the END DO statement or was inadvertently omitted.

3. As with all Fortran data types, ensure that there are no type inconsistencies. The type of each subscript expression must be type INTEGER; the type of

data stored in an array element must correspond to the type specified in the array declaration.

4. When using DATA statements, the size of the constant list must be the same as the size of the variable list. Any DATA statements should be placed right after the type declarations. Remember that a DATA statement is not an executable statement; consequently, if it is placed in a subprogram, the variables listed in the DATA statement will have the initial values specified only during the first execution of the subprogram. During subsequent executions, the DATA statement will have no effect.

Chapter Review

In this chapter, we introduced a special data structure called an array, which is a convenient facility for naming and referencing a collection of like items. We discussed how to declare an array and how to reference an individual array element by placing a subscript in parentheses, following the array name.

The DO loop enables us to easily reference the elements of an array in sequence and can be used to initialize arrays, read and print arrays, and control the manipulation of individual array elements. We studied several different ways to read data into an array and to display data stored in an array. These included the use of READ and PRINT statements which contained implied DO loops. We also introduced the DATA statement as a means of initializing arrays.

Fortran Statements

The Fortran statements introduced in this chapter are described in Table 7.7.

Table 7.7. *Summary of Fortran Statements for Chapter 7*

STATEMENT	EFFECT
Array Declaration	
`INTEGER CUBE(10), Y(0 : 5)`	Allocates storage for ten INTEGER items in array CUBE (CUBE(1), ... , CUBE(10)) and six INTEGER items in array Y (Y(0), ... , Y(5)).
Array References	

`DO 10 I = 1, 10`
`   CUBE(I) = I ** 3`
`10 CONTINUE`
	Saves I^3 in the ith element of array CUBE.

(continued)

STATEMENT	EFFECT
`IF (CUBE(5) .GT. 100) THEN`	Compares `CUBE(5)` to 100.
`PRINT *, CUBE(1), CUBE(2)`	Displays the first two cubes.

Array Initialization

`DATA Y /6 * 0/`	Initializes each element of `Y` to 0.
`DATA (CUBE(I), I = 1, 4)` `+       /1, 8, 27, 64/`	Initializes the first four cubes.

Array Read and Print

`READ *, Y` `PRINT *, Y`	Reads and prints the entire array. More than one value may appear on a line.

`DO 10 I = 2, 5`
`  PRINT *, 'Enter value ', I`
`  READ *, Y(I)         '`
`  PRINT *, Y(I)`
`10 CONTINUE`
	Reads and prints the values stored in `Y(2)` through `Y(5)`, one value per line.

`PRINT *, 'Enter Y(2) through Y(5)'`
`READ *, (Y(I), I = 2, 5)`
`PRINT *, (Y(I), I = 2, 5)`
	Reads and prints the values in `Y(2)` through `Y(5)`. More than one value may appear on a line.

`PRINT '(1X, I4, 2X, I4)', CUBES`	Displays all elements of array `CUBES`, two values per line.

Read with End-of-File Specifier

`DO 20 I = 1, 5`
`  READ (1, *, END = 99) Y(I)`
`20 CONTINUE`
	Reads up to 5 values into array `Y` from the data file on unit 1. Continues at label 99 if there are fewer than 5 data values.

Quick-check Exercises

1. What is a data structure?
2. Of the data types REAL, INTEGER, CHARACTER, and LOGICAL, which cannot be used to subscript an array?
3. Can values of different types be stored in an array?
4. If an array is declared to have 10 elements, must the program use all 10?

5. When can the assignment operator be used with an array as its operand? Answer the same question for the relational operators such as `.EQ.`, `.LE.`, `.GT.`.
6. The two methods of array access are _____ and _____ .
7. The _____ loop allows us to access the elements of an array in _____ order.
8. What is the difference between the following two declarations?

```
CHARACTER *10 NAME
```

and

```
CHARACTER NAME(18)
```

9. Let `SCORES(12)` be an array of 12 integers. Describe how each of the following two Fortran loops will work. Discuss any differences between the loops.

```
   READ (2, *, END = 99) (SCORES(I), I = 1, 12)
99 ...

   DO 10 I = 1, 12
      READ (2, *, END = 99) SCORES(I)
10 CONTINUE
99 ...
```

10. What is the total number of characters that can be stored in the following array?

```
CHARACTER *30 X(80)
```

Answers to Quick-check Exercises

1. A data structure is a grouping of related values in main memory.
2. `REAL`, `CHARACTER`, and `LOGICAL`
3. no
4. no
5. not allowed under any circumstances
6. random and sequential
7. DO, sequential
8. The first declares a simple variable to be used to store a string of 18 characters; the second declares an 18-element array in which each element is a character string of length 1.
9. Both loops behave the same. They read up to 12 integer values from the file associated with unit 2. Reading will terminate as soon as 12 values are read or the end of the file is reached, whichever comes first.

   The second loop reads each data item from a separate line. The first loop does not impose this requirement.
10. 2400

Review Questions

1. Identify the error in the following segment of Fortran statements:

   ```
   INTEGER X(1 : 8), I
   DO 10 I = 1, 9
       X(I) = I
   10 CONTINUE
   ```

   When will the error be detected?

2. Declare an array of real values called SALES that can be referenced by using any day of the week as a subscript, where 0 represents Sunday, 1 represents Monday, and so on.

3. Identify the error in the following segment:

   ```
   CHARACTER *10 NAMES(100)
   INTEGER I
   I = 1
   NAMES(I) = 8.384
   ```

4. The statement with label 5 in the following segment is a valid Fortran statement. True or false?

   ```
   INTEGER COUNTS(10), I
   REAL X(5)
   PRINT *, Enter a small integer'
   I = 1
   READ *, COUNTS(I)
   5 X(COUNTS(I)) = 8.384
   ```

5. What are the two common ways of selecting array elements for processing?

6. Write a Fortran program segment to print out the index of the smallest and the largest numbers in an array X of 20 integers. Array X has a range of values of 0 to 100. Assume array X already has values assigned to each element.

7. Declare arrays X and Y, each of which may store up to 100 REAL numbers. Let N represent the number of items currently stored in array X. Write a DO loop that copies the values in array X to array Y in reverse order (e.g., Y(1) gets X(N), Y(N) gets X(1)).

8. If a program contains the statements at the right, which one of the following statements contains a syntax error?

a. PRICE(N + 4) = 14.95	REAL PRICE(40)
b. PRICE(N) = PRICE(N) + PRICE(4)	INTEGER N
c. X = PRICE(N) * 3.0	REAL X
d. PRICE(N) + PRICE(4) = 3.59	N = 20
e. X = PRICE(N + 4) + PRICE(N − 4) ·	

9. What will be the values of K(2) and K(4) after the Fortran statements on the right execute with the data shown under the line?

a. K(2) = 1 K(4) = 4
b. K(2) = 6 K(4) = 0
c. K(2) = 3 K(4) = 3
d. K(2) = 4 K(4) = 0
e. K(2) - 6 K(4) - 2

```
INTEGER K(6), L, N
DATA K /6 * 0/
DO 10 L = 4, 6
    READ *, N
    K(N) = L
10 CONTINUE
```
_____

```
3
1
2
```

10. What will be the value of F(5) and F(10) after the statements at the right are executed?

a. F(5) = 3 F(10) = 34
b. F(5) = 5 F(10) = 34
c. F(5) = 5 F(10) = 55
d. F(5) = 8 F(10) = 89
e. F(5) = 34 F(10) = 3

```
INTEGER SIZE
PARAMETER (SIZE = 10)
INTEGER F(0 : SIZE)
F(0) = 1
F(1) = 1
DO 10 K = 2, SIZE
    F(K) = F(K-1) + F(K-2)
10 CONTINUE
```

11. At the right are declarations for a main program and a function. Which of the following calls to the function FUN would not violate any of the rules for function usage?

a. C = FUN(X, Z, CMU(K))
b. FUN(Y, Z, K) = CMU(K)
c. CALL FUN (Y, Z, K)
d. K = FUN(A, B, K)
e. CMU(K) = FUN(X, Y, Z)

```
REAL X(10), Y(20), Z(20)
REAL A, B, C, FUN
INTEGER CMU(5), K
```
_____

```
REAL FUNCTION FUN (R, S, N)
REAL R(*), S(*)
INTEGER N
```

Fortran 90 Features: Array Operations

Whole Array Operations

In Fortran 77, each operand of an arithmetic or relational operator must represent a single value; in Fortran 90, an operator can have an array as its operand, which means that operations on whole arrays are permitted. The following examples assume the declarations

```
INTEGER A(10), B(10), C(6:15)
LOGICAL T(10)
```

The assignment statements

```
A = B    ! Assign B(I) to A(I), I = 1,2, ... , 10
C = B    ! Assign B(I) to C(I+5), I = 1,2, ... , 10
```

show that one array can be assigned to another. In this case, each element of the array on the right is copied to the corresponding element of the array on the left. Arrays B and C have the same *shape* (both one-dimensional arrays with 10 elements), so the second assignment copies all 10 elements of array B to the corresponding elements of array C (C(6) gets B(1), C(7) gets B(2), and so on).

The following statements are carried out on all elements of the array operands:

```
A = 2 * B  ! Assign 2 * B(I) to A(I), I = 1,2, ... , 10
C = A + B  ! Assign A(I) + B(I) to C(I+5), I = 1, 2, ... , 10
C = A * B  ! Assign A(I) * B(I) to C(I+5), I = 1, 2, ... , 10
T = A > B  ! Assign A(I) > B(I) to T(I), I = 1, 2, ..., 10
```

The first assignment statement shows that an array can be multiplied by a scalar value; each element of array B is multiplied by 2. In the second and third assignment statements, the operators are applied in an *elementwise* manner to arrays A and B; each result is assigned to the corresponding element of array C (C(6) gets A(1) + B(1) or A(1) * B(1), C(7) gets A(2) + B(2) or A(2) * B(2)). In the last assignment, each element T(I) of array T gets .TRUE. or .FALSE. depending on the value of the condition A(I) > B(I).

Intrinsic functions with array arguments are also interpreted elementwise. Some examples follow:

```
A = SQRT(B)     ! Assign SQRT(B(I)) to A(I)
C = MOD(A, B)   ! Assign remainder of A(I) / B(I) to C(I+5)
```

Array Sections and Array Constructors

You can declare a subarray of array A, called an *array section,* using the notation A(3 : 6), which consists of elements A(3) through A(6). You can specify an array constant by using an *array constructor,* which is a parenthesized list of constant expressions enclosed by the symbol pairs (/ and /). These features are illustrated as follows.

```
A = (/1, 0, 1, 0, 1, 0, 1, 0, 1, 0/) ! A(I) = 1 for odd I
                                      ! A(I) = 0 for even I
A(3 : 6) = (/-1, 0, -1, 0/)           ! A(3), A(5) = -1
                                      ! A(4), A(6) = 0
```

If a triplet $(m : n : p)$ is used to denote an array section, the third parameter (p) is analogous to a DO loop step. The array section A(1 : 10 : 2) represents the elements of array A with odd subscripts; the array section A(2 : 10 : 2) represents the elements of array A with even subscripts. The first assignment statement immediately above could also be written as

```
A(1 : 10 : 2) = (/5 * 1/) ! A(1), A(3), ... , A(9) = 1
A(2 : 10 : 2) = (/5 * 0/) ! A(2), A(4), ... , A(10) = 0
```

where the notation (/5 * 1/) denotes a constant list consisting of 5 values of 1.

SYNTAX DISPLAY

Array Sections

SYNTAX: *array (lb : ub : step)*

EXAMPLE: A(1 : N)
        VOLTS(-5 : 5 : 2)
        X(5 : : 2)

INTERPRETATION: The array section contains the elements of the named *array* indicated by the bounds specified in parentheses where *lb* represents the lower bound, *ub* represents the upper bound, and *step* represents the increment in going from *lb* to *ub*. If the value of *lb* or *ub* is omitted, the value in the array declaration is used. If the value of *step* is omitted, it is assumed to be 1.

WHERE statement

The WHERE statement enables you to limit array assignment to only certain elements of an array. For example

```
WHERE (T) A = 0  ! A(I) gets 0 if T(I) is .TRUE.
```

The WHERE statement can be used with multiple array assignments and can have an ELSEWHERE clause:

```
WHERE  (A > B)
    C = A - B
ELSEWHERE
    C = B - A
END WHERE
```

This construct is equivalent to

```
C = ABS(A - B)   ! C(I+5) gets absolute value of A(I) - B(I),
                 ! for I = 1, 2, ... , 10
```

SYNTAX DISPLAY

WHERE construct

SYNTAX: WHERE *logical array expression*
           array assignment
     ELSEWHERE
         array assignment
     END WHERE

EXAMPLE: WHERE (A > 0.0)
        C = A
      ELSEWHERE
        C = -A
      END WHERE

INTERPRETATION: The *logical array expression* is evaluated for every possible subscript of the array(s) involved in the expression. The *array assignment* statements following WHERE are executed for all subscripts where the result is true; for all other subscripts, the *array assignment* statements following ELSE-WHERE are executed.

New Intrinsic Functions

There are several new functions in Fortran 90 that process array arguments and return a scalar (single value) as a result. We list some of these next.

```
MAXVAL(A)            ! Returns the largest value in A
MINVAL(A)            ! Returns the smallest value in A
DOT_PRODUCT(A, B)    ! Returns the dot product of arrays A and B
SUM(A)               ! Returns the sum of elements of A
PRODUCT(A)           ! Returns the product of elements of A
ALL(T)               ! Returns .TRUE. if all T(I) are .TRUE.
ANY(T)               ! Returns .TRUE. if any T(I) is .TRUE.
COUNT(T)             ! Returns count of elements of T that are .TRUE.
```

5. Consider the situation in which the pricing of official Baltimore Oriole banners is based upon the quantity purchased as illustrated in the following table.

Number Purchased	Price Per Hundred
0– 100	$ 32.50
101– 300	$ 32.00
301– 500	$ 31.50
501 800	$ 31.00
801–1200	$ 30.00
1201–1600	$ 29.00
1601–2000	$ 28.00
2001–2500	$ 26.00
2501–3000	$ 24.00
3001–4000	$ 21.00
4001–5000	$ 18.00
5001–7500	$ 15.00
7501–9999	$ 12.00
More than 10,000	$ 5.00

Write a program that, given a count, COUNT, of banners to be purchased, will determine the price for this number of banners. Use a pair of parallel arrays NUMPUR and PURPRI in which to store an appropriate value for each category of purchase quantity and the corresponding price per hundred respectively. Use a DATA statement to initialize both arrays.

6. Write a Fortran subroutine that converts a Julian date to the traditional form. A Julian date is a pair of integers of the form 1993 027 which represents the Gregorian date January 27, 1993. Your subroutine should return the month number (1 in this case), the day (27), and the year (1993). The main program should read a collection of Julian date pairs, convert each to Gregorian form, and then display the Gregorian form. Your program should declare and initialize two arrays: one to store the number of days in each month and one to store the names of each month. Use DATA statements to initialize the arrays. Ensure your subroutine accounts for leap years (DAYS(2) is 29 instead of 28).

7. The New Bunion Shoe Company is performing a quality-control check on its newest line of running shoes. They have weighed 10 shoes selected from their assembly line and need to determine the following statistics: the average weight of the shoes, the variance, and the standard deviation. They plan to use the formulas below where W_i represents the weight of the ith shoe. Write a Fortran program, with subprograms, that accomplishes this task.

$$average = \frac{1}{N} \sum_{i=1}^{N} W_i$$

$$variance = \frac{1}{N} \sum_{i=1}^{N} (W_i - \overline{W})^2$$

$$standard\ deviation = \sqrt{variance}$$

Programming Projects

1. Write a program to read N data items into two arrays X and Y of size 20. Store the product of corresponding elements of X and Y in a third array Z, also of size 20. Print a three-column table displaying the arrays X, Y, and Z. Then compute and print the square root of the sum of the items in Z. Make up your own data, with N less than 20.

2. Let A be an array containing 20 integers. Write a program that first reads up to 20 data items into A and then finds and prints the subscript of the largest item in A and that item.

3. The Department of Traffic Accidents each year receives accident-count reports from a number of cities and towns across the country. To summarize these reports, the department provides a frequency-distribution printout that gives the number of cities reporting accident counts in the following ranges: 0–99, 100–199, 200–299, 300–399, 400–499, and 500 or above. The department needs a computer program to read the number of accidents for each reporting city or town and to add one to the count for the appropriate accident range. After all the data have been processed, the resulting frequency counts are to be printed.

4. Assume for the moment that your computer has the very limited capability of being able to read and print only single decimal digits and to add together two integers consisting of one decimal digit each. Write a program to read in two integers of up to 10 digits each, add these numbers together, and print the result. Test your program on the following numbers:

```
X = 1487625        X = 60705202        X = 1234567890
Y =    12783        Y = 30760832        Y = 9876543210
```

(*Hints:* Store the numbers X and Y in two integer arrays X and Y of size 10, one decimal digit per element. If the number is fewer than 10 digits in length, enter enough leading zeros (to the left of the number) to make the number 10 digits long.)

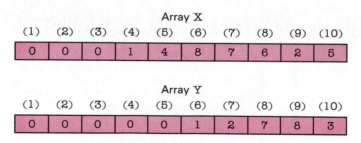

You will need a loop to add together the digits in corresponding array elements, starting with the element with subscript 10. Don't forget to handle the carry if there is one! Use a LOGICAL variable CARRY to indicate whether the sum of the last pair of digits is greater than 9.

8. You have recorded the serial number and outside diameter of a collection of 20 steel parts coming off the same assembly line. Write a subroutine that reads these data into a pair of arrays. Assume that each data line contains a serial number (an integer) followed by the diameter (a real number). Write a subroutine that displays the serial number of all parts whose diameters differ from the design diameter (provided as data) by more than 2%. This subroutine should also return a count of parts that satisfy the design specification (within 2% of the design diameter). Write a main program that reads the design diameter, calls both of these subroutines, and displays the count of parts that satisfy the design specification.

9. Write a program for the following problem. You are given a collection of scores for the last exam in your computer course. You are to compute the average of these scores and then assign grades to each student according to the following rule: If a student's score is within 10 points (above or below) of the average, assign the student a grade of SATISFACTORY. If the score is more than 10 points higher than the average, assign the student a grade of OUTSTANDING. If the score is more than 10 points below the average, assign the student a grade of UNSATISFACTORY. Test your program on the following data:

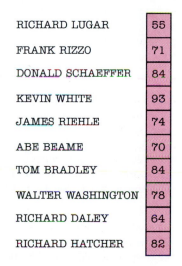

RICHARD LUGAR	55
FRANK RIZZO	71
DONALD SCHAEFFER	84
KEVIN WHITE	93
JAMES RIEHLE	74
ABE BEAME	70
TOM BRADLEY	84
WALTER WASHINGTON	78
RICHARD DALEY	64
RICHARD HATCHER	82

(*Hint:* The output from your program should consist of a labeled three-column list containing the name, exam score, and grade of each student.)

10. Write a program to read N data items into each of two arrays X and Y of size 20. Compare each of the elements of X to the corresponding element of Y. In the corresponding element of a third array Z, store

```
+ 1    if X is larger than Y
  0    if X is equal to Y
- 1    if X is less than Y
```

Then print a three-column table displaying the contents of the arrays X, Y, and Z, followed by a count of the number of elements of X that exceed Y and a count of the number of elements of X that are less than Y. Make up your own test data with N less than 20.

11. It can be shown that a number is prime if there is no smaller prime number that divides it. Consequently, to determine whether N is prime, it is sufficient to check only the prime numbers less than or equal to N as possible divisors. Use this information to write a program that stores the first 100 prime numbers in an array. Have your program print the array after it is done.

12. Modify the area-computation program in Fig. 7.15 to find the area of a piece of land that is shaped like a polygon. The X and Y coordinates (in feet) at the edges of the property are available in a data file. Compute and display the acreage where 1 acre = 43,560 sq ft. Use the following sample data file:

```
12.342   34.476
19.564   43.556
34.451   55.026
46.735   77.323
50.034   70.432
43.958   65.361
30.985   59.207
22.894   38.976
15.347   36.890
```

13. Generate a table indicating the rainfall for the city of Bedrock that can be used to compare the average rainfall for the city with the previous year's rainfall. Print some summary statistics that will indicate (1) annual rainfall for each year and (2) average monthly rainfall for each year. The input data will consist of 12 pairs of numbers. The first number in each pair will be this year's rainfall for a month, and the second number, the rainfall for the previous year. The first data pair will represent January, the second February, and so forth. Assuming the data begin

```
3.2  4   (for January)
2.2 1.6 (for February)
```

the output should resemble the following:

```
              Table of monthly rainfall

              January  February  March ...
This year       3.2       2.2
Last year       4.0       1.6

Total rainfall this year: 35.7
Total rainfall last year: 42.8

Average monthly rainfall for this year: 3.6
Average monthly rainfall for last year: 4.0
```

14. The results of a survey of the households in your township have been made available. Each record contains data for one household, including a four-digit integer identification number, the annual income for the household, and the number of members of the household. Write a program to read the survey results into three arrays and perform the following analyses:

   a. Count the number of households included in the survey and print a three-column table displaying the data read in. (You may assume that no more than 25 households were surveyed.)
   b. Calculate the average household income and list the identification number and income of each household that exceeds the average.
   c. Determine the percentage of households having incomes below the poverty level. The poverty level income may be computed using the formula

   $$P = \$6500.00 + \$750.00 \times (m - 2),$$

   where m is the number of members of each household. This formula shows that the poverty level depends on the number of family members, m, and the poverty level increases as m gets larger.

   Test your program on the following data:

Identification Number	Annual Income	Household Members
1041	$12,180	4
1062	13,240	3
1327	19,800	2
1483	22,458	8
1900	17,000	2
2112	18,125	7
2345	15,623	2
3210	3,200	6
3600	6,500	5
3601	11,970	2
4725	8,900	3
6217	10,000	2
9280	6,200	1

15. Write an interactive program that plays the game of HANGMAN. Read the word to be guessed into successive elements of an array (WORD) of individual characters. The player must guess the letters belonging to WORD. The program should terminate when either all letters have been guessed correctly (player wins) or a specified number of incorrect guesses has been made (computer wins). (*Hint:* Use another array, GUESSD, to keep track of the solution so far. Initialize array GUESSD to symbols '*'. Each time a letter in WORD is guessed, replace the corresponding '*' in GUESSD with that letter.)

16. An operation consists of transporting items of industrial equipment on small river barges. Because it is important that the load on each barge is properly balanced, the loading plan is developed by a technician and the center of gravity is checked by a computer program. A loading plan consists of the name of the barge (up to 60 alphanumeric characters), the number of items (N), the weight (W_i) for each

item, and the coordinates (X_i and Y_i) for each item. The coordinate system is illustrated in the following figure:

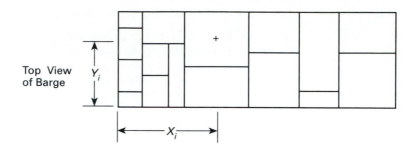

The coordinates for the center of gravity (X_w and Y_w) are computed using the following formulas:

$$X_w = \frac{\sum\limits_{i=1}^{N} X_i W_i}{S_w} \quad \text{and} \quad Y_w = \frac{\sum\limits_{i=1}^{N} Y_i W_i}{S_w}$$

where

$$S_w = \sum\limits_{i=1}^{N} W_i.$$

Write a Fortran program that will calculate the center of gravity for a particular loading plan. Two data samples follow the problem statement. Use separate functions to compute S_w, X_w, and Y_w.

Mississippi Zephyr			Michigan-Superior		
X	Y	W	X	Y	W
3.2	6.4	1239	25.6	13.4	10064
7.8	5.4	2346	45.7	10.2	15386
10.3	7.2	684	64.9	12.6	20009
16.6	3.4	324	34.7	18.4	12863
22.1	6.8	794	54.9	15.8	9039
34.2	9.4	10340			
46.8	12.2	1283			
55.7	10.6	3348			
20.4	16.9	10978			
40.9	17.4	13649			

17. For a given set of observations, it is often more desirable to plot a straight line that approximates the data, rather than plot a curve that passes through each data point. To do this, we use the method of least squares (see Section 12.4).

To obtain a function of the form $y = mx + b$ from a set of n observations for x and y, m and b are computed using the following:

$$m = \frac{n\Sigma x_i y_i - \Sigma x_i \Sigma y_i}{n\Sigma(x_i^2) - (\Sigma x_i)^2} \qquad b = \frac{\Sigma(x_i^2)\Sigma y_i - \Sigma x_i \Sigma x_i y_i}{n\Sigma(x_i^2) - (\Sigma x_i)^2}$$

To see if $y = mx + b$ is a good approximation to our data, we use the correlation coefficient r:

$$r = \frac{\Sigma x_i y_i}{\sqrt{\Sigma(x_i^2)\Sigma(y_i^2)}}$$

If $|r|$ is close to 1, then there is a high degree of linear association (i.e., $y = mx + b$ is a good approximation to the data). If r is close to 0, then the linear fit is not a very good one.

Design a Fortran program to perform the following steps for each data set:

a. Read and print n and the problem description.
b. Read x_i and y_i for $i = 1, 2, \ldots, n$.
c. Compute Σx_i, Σy_i, $\Sigma(x_i^2)$, $\Sigma(y_i^2)$, and $\Sigma x_i y_i$.
d. Compute and print m, b, and r. If $|r| > 0.9$, print HIGH DEGREE OF LINEAR ASSOCIATION BETWEEN X AND Y. If $|r| < 0.1$, print SMALL DEGREE OF LINEAR AS-SOCIATION BETWEEN X AND Y.
e. If $|r| > 0.2$, compute $y_i^* = mx_i + b$ and print x_i, y_i, and y_i^* for $i = 1, 2, \ldots,$ n. If $|r| < 0.2$, print only x_i and y_i for $i = 1, 2, \ldots, n$. (If there is no linear association, there is little use in calculating the linear results.)

Use the following data sets to test your program:

(1) *Description:* Concentration of Reactant vs. Time
   x_i is the time and y_i is the concentration

x_i	y_i	x_i	y_i
0.0	3.00	6.0	0.15
1.0	1.82	7.0	0.09
2.0	1.10	8.0	0.06
3.0	0.67	9.0	0.03
4.0	0.41	10.0	0.02
5.0	0.25		

(2) *Description:* Velocity Profile of a Fluid in a Pipe
   x_i is the distance from the center and y_i is the velocity.

x_i	y_i	x_i	y_i
-1.75	0.00	0.50	2.75
-1.50	0.75	1.00	2.00
-1.00	2.00	1.50	0.75
-0.50	2.75	1.75	0.00
0.00	3.00		

CHAPTER 8
More Arrays and Subprograms

IN THIS chapter, we cover additional features of arrays and subprograms and introduce multidimensional arrays, that is, arrays with two or more dimensions. We will use two-dimensional arrays to represent tables of data, matrices, and other two-dimensional objects.

We also discuss two common operations performed on arrays—searching and sorting—and describe techniques for searching and sorting arrays. We will write subprograms for implementing these operations and show how to reuse these subprograms in other applications.

The chapter includes two case studies that involve multiple subprograms. We focus on the reusability of subprograms and introduce COMMON blocks for data communication between subprograms. We also describe the SAVE statement and show how to use it to write a random-number function. Finally, we show how to use a random-number function in the simulation of an experiment.

8.1 Multidimensional Arrays

In this section, we discuss how to store tables of data and how to represent multidimensional objects using arrays. A two-dimensional object we are all familiar with is a tic-tac-toe board. The array declaration

```
CHARACTER *1 TICTAC(3, 3)
```

allocates storage for a two-dimensional array (TICTAC) with three rows and three columns.

This array has nine elements, each of which must be referenced by specifying a row subscript (1, 2, or 3) and a column subscript (1, 2, or 3). Each array element contains a character value. The array element TICTAC(2,3) pointed to in Fig. 8.1 is in row 2, column 3 of the array; it contains the character 0. The diagonal line consisting of array elements TICTAC(1,1), TICTAC(2,2), and TICTAC(3,3) represents a win for player X, because each cell contains the character X.

Figure 8.1. *A Tic-tac-toe Board Stored as Array TICTAC*

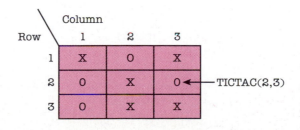

SYNTAX DISPLAY

Array Declaration (for Multidimensional Arrays)

SYNTAX: *element-type aname*($size_1$, $size_2$, ... , $size_n$)

element-type aname($minval_1$: $maxval_1$, $minval_2$: $maxval_2$, ... ,
$minval_n$: $maxval_n$)

EXAMPLE: REAL TABLE(10, 0 : 6)

INTERPRETATION: The first form allocates storage space for an array *aname* consisting of $size_1 \times size_2 \times \cdots \times size_n$ memory cells. Each memory cell can store one data item whose data type is specified by *element-type* (i.e., REAL, INTEGER, CHARACTER, LOGICAL). The individual array elements are referenced by the subscripted variables *aname*(1, 1, ..., 1) through *aname*($size_1$, $size_2$, ... , $size_n$). An INTEGER constant or parameter must be used to specify $size_i$.

In the second form of the array declaration, the minimum value for the subscript associated with dimension *i* is $minval_i$ and the maximum value is $maxval_i$. Both $minval_i$ and $maxval_i$ must be INTEGER constants or parameters, and $minval_i$ must be less than or equal to $maxval_i$.

NOTE: A multidimensional array can have a maximum of seven dimensions.

EXAMPLE 8.1

The array TABLE

```
REAL TABLE(7, 5, 6)
```

consists of three dimensions: The first subscript may take on values from 1 to 7; the second from 1 to 5; and the third from 1 to 6. A total of $7 \times 5 \times 6$, or 210, real numbers may be stored in the array TABLE. All three subscripts must be specified in each reference to array TABLE (e.g., TABLE(2, 3, 4)). ∎

Manipulation of Two-dimensional Arrays

A row and a column subscript must be specified to reference an element of a two-dimensional array. If I is type INTEGER, the statement

```
PRINT *, (TICTAC(1,I), I = 1, 3)
```

displays the first row of array TICTAC (TICTAC(1,1), TICTAC(1,2), and TIC-TAC(1,3)) on the next output line. The indexed DO loop

```
    DO 10 I = 1, 3
        PRINT *, TICTAC(I,2)
10 CONTINUE
```

displays the second column of TICTAC (TICTAC(1,2), TICTAC(2,2), and TIC-TAC(3,2)) in a vertical line.

Nested loops are used to access all elements of a multidimensional array in a predetermined order. In the next examples, the outer loop determines the row being accessed and the inner loop is used to select each element in that row.

EXAMPLE 8.2 The program fragment in Fig. 8.2 displays the current status of a tic-tac-toe board. A sample output of this fragment is also shown in Fig. 8.2.

Figure 8.2. *Printing a Tic-tac-toe Board*

```
C Display the status of a tic-tac-toe board (array TICTAC)
      PRINT *, '————'
      DO 10 ROW = 1, 3
C         Print all columns of current row
         PRINT 15, (TICTAC(ROW,COLUMN), COLUMN = 1, 3)
   15    FORMAT (1X, 3('!', A1), '!')
         PRINT *, '————'
   10 CONTINUE
```

```
————
!X!O! !
————
!O!X!O!
————
!X! !X!
————
```

In Fig. 8.2, the formatted PRINT statement

```
PRINT 15, (TICTAC(ROW,COLUMN), COLUMN = 1, 3)
```

is used to display each row of the tic-tac-toe board. The implied DO loop causes the three columns across a row to be printed. The FORMAT specification 3('!', A1) causes each X or O to be preceded by the symbol !. A final '!' is printed at the end of each row. ■

EXAMPLE 8.3 The following program fragment assigns a value of .TRUE. to FILLED if a tic-tac-toe board is all filled up; it assigns a value of .FALSE. if there is at least one empty cell (contains a blank).

```
C Assign a value of .TRUE. to FILLED if TICTAC is filled
C Assign a value of .FALSE. to FILLED if TICTAC is not filled
```

```
C Assume the board is filled
      FILLED = .TRUE.

C Reset FILLED to .FALSE. if an empty cell is found
      DO 10 ROW = 1, 3
         DO 20 COLUMN = 1, 3
            IF (TICTAC(ROW,COLUMN) .EQ. ' ') THEN
               FILLED = .FALSE.
            END IF
20       CONTINUE
10    CONTINUE
```

Row-major vs. Column-major Order

The programs shown for examples 8.2 and 8.3 process the array TICTAC one row at a time. This is because the row subscript is the loop-control variable for the outer loop of each pair of nested loops. An array that is processed one row at a time is processed in *row-major* order.

If we make the column subscript the loop-control variable for the outer loop, the arrays will be processed one column at a time. This is called *column-major* order.

EXAMPLE 8.4

The following program fragment enters array data one column at a time. There are five rows in the array; therefore, five data values should be entered after each prompt. Because there are three columns, the prompt will be displayed three times.

```
      INTEGER TABLE(5, 3), ROW, COLUMN

C Enter one column of data at a time
      DO 10 COLUMN = 1, 3
         PRINT *, 'Enter the data for column ', COLUMN
         READ *, (TABLE(ROW, COLUMN), ROW = 1, 5)
10    CONTINUE
```

Column-major order is not as natural for people as row-major order; we generally process array data one row at a time. However, Fortran uses column-major order to store arrays in memory. Consequently, the following statements also will cause 15 data values to be stored in the same array elements as the nested DO loop above.

```
PRINT *, 'Enter the 15 array values starting with column one'
READ *, TABLE
```

When you use a two-dimensional array name without subscripts in a READ, PRINT, or DATA statement, the entire array will be processed in column-major order. If you do not want to process the entire array or if you prefer row-major order, then you must use subscripts.

DATA Statements with Multidimensional Arrays

The DATA statement also can be used to initialize multidimensional arrays. The statement

```
DATA TABLE /15 * 0.0/
```

initializes array TABLE to all zeros. The DATA statement

```
 DATA ((TABLE(I, J), J = 1, 3), I = 1, 5)
+      /1, 2, 3,  4, 5, 6,  7, 8, 9,  10, 11, 12,  13, 14, 15/
```

stores 1, 2, 3 in the first row of TABLE, 4, 5, 6 in the second row of TABLE, and so on. The implied-DO list in the DATA statement references the array elements in row-major order.

Arrays with Several Dimensions

So far, we have concentrated on arrays with two dimensions. In standard Fortran, you can declare arrays with up to seven dimensions, although it is difficult to visualize arrays with more than three.

The array ENROLL declared below

```
INTEGER MAXCRS, MAXCAM, MAXYR
PARAMETER (MAXCRS = 100, MAXCAM = 5, MAXYR = 4)
INTEGER ENROLL (MAXCRS, MAXCAM, MAXYR)
```

and pictured in Fig. 8.3 is a three-dimensional array that may be used to store the enrollment data for an undergraduate college. We will assume that the college offers 100 (MAXCRS) courses at five different campuses. ENROLL(1, 3, 4) represents the number of seniors taking course 1 at campus 3. The range of values for the subscript denoting YEAR is 1 (for first year) through 4 (for senior).

There are a total of 2000 ($100 \times 5 \times 4$) elements in array ENROLL. This points out a potential pitfall when you are dealing with multidimensional arrays. Memory space can be used up rapidly if several multidimensional arrays are declared in the same program. You should be aware of the amount of memory space required by each large array in a program.

Figure 8.3. *Three-dimensional Array ENROLL*

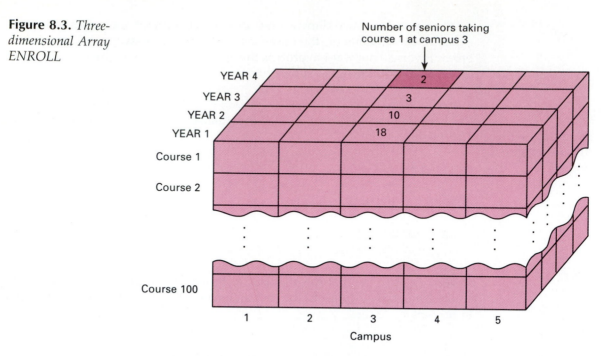

There are many different ways to process the data in Fig. 8.3. We could determine the total number of students taking courses at a particular campus, the total number of students taking a particular course, the number of juniors in course 2 at all campuses, and so on. The type of information desired determines the order in which we must reference the array elements.

EXAMPLE 8.5   The following program fragment finds and prints the total number of students in each course.

```
C Find and print number of students in each course
      DO 10 COURSE = 1, MAXCRS
         CRSSUM = 0
         DO 20 CAMPUS = 1, 5
            DO 30 YEAR = 1, 4
               CRSSUM = CRSSUM + ENROLL(COURSE, CAMPUS, YEAR)
30          CONTINUE
20       CONTINUE
         PRINT *, 'Number of students in course', COURSE, ' is', CRSSUM
10 CONTINUE
```

Because we are printing the number of students in each course, the loop-control variable for the outermost DO loop is the subscript that denotes the course.

The following program fragment prints the number of students at each campus. This time the loop-control variable for the outermost DO loop is the subscript that denotes the campus.

```
C Find and print number of students at each campus
      DO 10 CAMPUS = 1, 5
         CMPSUM = 0
         DO 20 COURSE = 1, MAXCRS
            DO 30 YEAR = 1, 4
               CMPSUM = CMPSUM + ENROLL(COURSE, CAMPUS, YEAR)
30          CONTINUE
20       CONTINUE
         PRINT *, 'Number of students in campus', CAMPUS, ' is', CMPSUM
10 CONTINUE
```

EXERCISES FOR SECTION 8.1

Self-check

1. How many elements are in the following two declared arrays?

   ```
   INTEGER MATRIX(5, 5),    TABLE(-5 : 4, 10, 3)
   ```

2. What is the effect of the following DATA statement?

   ```
   DATA MATRIX /10 * 0, 15 * 1/
   ```

3. Explain the effect of each of the following statements. Which would you use to display the array MATRIX one row per output line, starting with the first row? Which statements provide the same output? Format statement 10 follows.

   ```
       10 FORMAT (1X, 5I10)

   a.    PRINT 10, MATRIX
   b.    PRINT 10, ((MATRIX(I, J), J = 1, 5), I = 1, 5)
   c.    PRINT 10, ((MATRIX(I, J), I = 1, 5), J = 1, 5)
   ```

Programming

1. Write a DATA statement that initializes the first two rows of array MATRIX in Self-check exercise 1 to all zeros and the last three rows to all ones.
2. Redefine MAXCRS as 5 and write and test program segments that perform the following operations:

   a. Enter the enrollment data.
   b. Find the number of juniors in all classes at all campuses. Students will be counted once for each course in which they are enrolled.

    c. Find the number of sophomores on all campuses who are enrolled in course 2.

    d. Compute and print the number of students at campus 3 enrolled in each course and the total number of students at campus 3 in all courses. Count students once for each course in which they are enrolled.

    e. Compute and print the number of upperclass students in all courses at each campus, as well as the total number of upperclass students enrolled. (Upperclass students are juniors and seniors.) Again, count students once for each course in which they are enrolled.

8.2 Multidimensional Array Arguments

Multidimensional arrays may be used as subroutine arguments. In Chapter 11, we will discuss some matrix operations involving two-dimensional arrays. A short example is provided next.

EXAMPLE 8.6

Subroutine ADDER can be easily modified to form the sum of two matrixes. If matrixes A and B have the same number of rows (M) and columns (N), they can be added together to form a new M × N matrix. If their sum is stored in matrix C, then each element $C(i,j)$ must equal $A(i,j) + B(i,j)$. Subroutine ADDMAT in Fig. 8.4 performs this operation.

The declaration

```
REAL A(M,N), B(M,N), C(M,N)
```

indicates that A, B, and C are matrixes. The number of rows is determined by dummy argument M, and the number of columns is determined by dummy argument N. ∎

When a multidimensional array is used as an argument, the size of the last dimension may be left unspecified. The argument declaration

```
REAL A(M,*), B(M,*), C(M,*)
```

indicates that A, B, and C are assumed-size dummy arrays with M rows. The number of columns in each array is determined by the actual argument declaration.

The next case study illustrates the processing of a two-dimensional array as a rectangular grid of integer values. In this problem, we need to reference the individual elements of the grid in sequence and also need to access the eight neighbors of each element.

Figure 8.4. *Subroutine ADDMAT*

```
      SUBROUTINE ADDMAT (A, B, C, M, N)

C Stores element–by–element sum of matrixes A and B in matrix C
C Preconditions : M, N and arrays A, B are defined.
C Postconditions: C(i,j) = A(i,j) + B(i,j), for 1 <= i <= M
C                     and 1 <= j <= N

C Input Arguments
C   A, B — Matrixes being summed
C   M — Number of rows in the matrixes
C   N — Number of columns in the matrixes
C Output Argument
C   C — Sum of matrixes A and B

C Argument Declarations
      INTEGER M, N
      REAL A(M,N), B(M,N), C(M,N)

C Local Declarations
      INTEGER ROW, COL

C Add corresponding elements of matrixes A and B
      DO 10 ROW = 1, M
         DO 20 COL = 1, N
            C(ROW,COL) = A(ROW,COL) + B(ROW,COL)
  20     CONTINUE
  10  CONTINUE

C Exit subroutine
      RETURN
      END
```

Case Study: Image Enhancement

PROBLEM STATEMENT

A secret military satellite has taken a digital image of a foreign military base. The information from the satellite is in an array of integers with each element having a value from 0 through 9. Each number in the array is a *pixel* (picture element). However, because the transmission was jammed, random noise has entered into the image. This noise can be detected when the value of a pixel is very different from its neighbors. For example, in the image section

24456
34187
48899

the pixel with the value of 1 can be assumed to be noise since its value is so different from its neighbors. If a pixel has a value that is different from its eight neighbors by 3 or more, it can be assumed to be noise. We will ignore the pixels on the edge of the picture. A noisy value should be replaced with the rounded average of all those neighbors. In the example, the 1 should be replaced with a 6:

$$value = (4 + 4 + 4 + 5 + 8 + 8 + 8 + 9)/8 = 6$$

Another problem with digital images is that detail is often blurred by the many numbers. Because humans discern shapes better with fewer symbols, in our image we lump the numbers 0 to 3 into one category and set them to 0. We also set 4, 5, and 6 to 1 and 7, 8, and 9 to 4. Doing this will increase the contrast and allow our photo interpreters to see the message in the image. Figure 8.5 shows an image before and after this enhancement.

ANALYSIS

Our task is to write a program to remove the noise and increase the contrast in a digital image.

We will read the digital image from a data file into a two-dimensional array IMAGE that is 24 rows by 78 columns. Next, we will check for noise, as described earlier, and then reduce the number of different symbols in the image to render it more readable. Finally, we will display the resulting image.

Data Requirements

Problem Parameters

the number of rows in the array (MAXROW = 24)
the number of columns in the array (MAXCOL = 78)

Problem Input

the original digital image (INTEGER IMAGE(MAXROW, MAXCOL))

Problem Output

the enhanced digital image (array IMAGE)

DESIGN

The algorithm follows:

Algorithm

1. Read the digital image into array IMAGE.

2. Check each element (except the edges) for noise and redefine any noisy elements.
3. Reduce the number of distinct symbols in IMAGE.
4. Display the reduced image.

Figure 8.5. *Digital Image Before (top) and After (bottom) Enhancement*

```
211111122221211111221212222112121112112221111111133311111111111221121211111211111
121100013233221110033130322201322212322221020002123320000101223200202000032011
128808870021322117778999219888779979799997898911128899958770113232177787888220
101464447221211284554549166655404546165656544920246546465659122221366456445833
114564545822300946460468024555455444651661540712366516554493120222264165655821
236140414582228460454258224464604146545455458000656461544712332135556466490
126452565159186664546458326504445450566446464700254545654580092122652454569222
135514466464965646565154832122201444556932119333115661464647013213156545544732
126554745646651565146649032221125650568233333330156665465481226220464245549101
105504814646566652146569202021104664649232333331116551651547011236545645481233
104646700465454511165467323231104450659349333331346666456591192256561544711
125404721255664020264149101822105544418222333323266514551492121264565656811
116464800011222140145458133108024044657332333300065466554471233256166146912
236645912211111121540482328100045455592113333390914541551557013564655447222
216565702211111110165658121123815404553333333333326644646447031450525406100
226654710213333311144067203823126565533333333333160651414571116544646471231
224555711113333311146459222121114406467222333332111255066454471545604447212213
124464200113333312146540128328144456623263333322131266645656456655666710190
623200102111111112020000210202220110003233333333333333333333003333023221231113
122002011111111110101101122800808080828161333331001323231100023232232210119210
222331121333132322201000113421101010121220333330002202121101101132232110011112
```

```
00000000000000000000000000000000000000000000000000000000000000000000000000000000
00000000000000000000000000000000000000000000000000000000000000000000000000000000
00440444000000000444444400444444444444444444440000444441444000000000044444444000
00011111400000004111111140111111111111411111111400011111111400000000111111114000
00111111400000041111011400111111111111111111111400011111111400000000111111114000
00111011114000411111101400111111111111111111111400011111111400000000111111114000
00111011114041111111101400110111111111111111111400011111111400000000110111114000
00110111111411111111114000000000111111400000000001111111114000000000111111114000
00111141111111111101111400000000011111140000000000011111111140000000011101111400
00111140111111111100111140000000001111114000000000001111111114000001111111140000
00111140011111110001111400000000011111140100000000011111111114000001111111140000
00111140001111100001111400000000011111140000000000011111111114000001111111140000
00111140000000000100111140000000001111114000000000001111111114000001111111140000
00111140000000000001111400000000011111140000000000001111111114000111111111400000
00111140000000000001111400000000011111100000000000001111111114000111101111100000
00111140000000000001111400000000011110000000000000010110111114000111111111400000
00111140000000000001111400000000011111400000000000011011111140111111111140000000
00111100000000000001110000000000011111100000000000001111111111111111140000000
10000000000000000000000000000000000000000000000000000000000000000000000000000000
00000000000000000000000000000000000000000000000000000000000000000000000000000000
00000000000000000000000000000000000000000000000000000000000000000000000000000000
```

Figure 8.6. *Structure Chart for Image Enhancement*

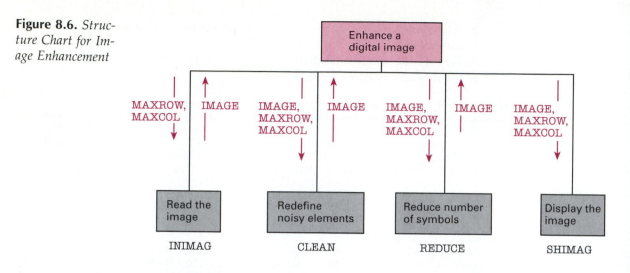

Structure Chart and Algorithm Refinements

As shown in the structure chart in Fig. 8.6, we use separate subroutines to perform each algorithm step. The data passed between the main program and its subprograms consist of the array IMAGE and the two parameters representing its dimensions (MAXROW and MAXCOL).

IMPLEMENTATION

Main Program

The main program declares the three subroutine parameters and then calls the subroutines. Figure 8.7 shows the main program.

Figure 8.7. *Main Program for Image Enhancement*

```
      PROGRAM ENHANC
C Enhances digital images in two steps:
C    1. Reduces noise fluctuations. If a pixel is different from all its
C       neighbors by 3 or more, it is set to their average value.
C    2. Reduces the number of symbols by setting each pixel to
C       one of three standard values.

C Declarations
      INTEGER MAXROW, MAXCOL
      PARAMETER (MAXROW = 24, MAXCOL = 78)
      INTEGER IMAGE(MAXROW, MAXCOL)

C Read the digital image
      CALL INIMAG (IMAGE, MAXROW, MAXCOL)
```

```
C Replace each noisy pixel
      CALL CLEAN (IMAGE, MAXROW, MAXCOL)

C Reduce the number of symbols
      CALL REDUCE (IMAGE, MAXROW, MAXCOL)

C Display the reduced image
      CALL SHIMAG (IMAGE, MAXROW, MAXCOL)

      STOP
      END
```

Subroutine INIMAG

Subroutine INIMAG (Fig. 8.8) reads the digital image from file DIGITAL.DAT using a READ statement with an implied DO loop in its input list. Each line of the data file is read into a row of array IMAGE. The FORMAT statement referenced in the

Figure 8.8. *Subroutine INIMAG*

```
      SUBROUTINE INIMAG (IMAGE, MAXROW, MAXCOL)
C Reads the image
C Preconditions : MAXROW and MAXCOL are defined.
C Postconditions: MAXROW × MAXCOL data values are read into array IMAGE.

C Input Arguments
C   MAXROW — number of rows in IMAGE
C   MAXCOL — number of columns in IMAGE
C Output Arguments
C   IMAGE — the array of pixels

C Argument Declarations
      INTEGER MAXROW, MAXCOL
      INTEGER IMAGE(MAXROW, MAXCOL)

C Local Declarations
      INTEGER I,J

C Read each row of data until done
      OPEN (UNIT = 2, FILE = 'DIGITAL.DAT', STATUS = 'OLD')
      DO 10 I = 1, MAXROW
         READ (2, 15) (IMAGE(I, J), J = 1, MAXCOL)
   15    FORMAT (78I1)
   10 CONTINUE

C Exit subroutine
      RETURN
      END
```

READ statement

```
15 FORMAT (78I1)
```

specifies that each line of the data file contains 78 single-digit integer values.

Subroutine CLEAN

Subroutine CLEAN must check each element to see whether its value is noisy. If it is, we should replace it with the average value of its neighbors. We do not check elements on the edge of the image (rows 1 and 24 and columns 1 and 78).

Local Parameter

the noise level threshold (NOSLEV = 3)

Local Variables

the row subscript (INTEGER I)
the column subscript (INTEGER J)
a flag indicating whether an element contains noise (LOGICAL NOISY)
the value of the current element of IMAGE (INTEGER CELL)

Algorithm for CLEAN

1. DO for each row I not on the edge
2.   DO for each column J not on the edge
3.   Set NOISY to .TRUE. if IMAGE(I,J) is noisy.
4.   IF (NOISY) THEN
5.   Replace IMAGE(I,J) with the average
               of its neighbors.
           END IF
       END DO
   END DO

In step 3, we must compare the value in IMAGE(I,J) with the values stored in its eight neighbors. To facilitate this comparison, we can store the value of IMAGE(I,J) in local variable CELL. The neighbors are the eight elements with row subscripts I−1, I, or I+1 and column subscripts J−1, J, or J+1. The eight neighbors of IMAGE(I,J) are listed in the LOGICAL assignment statement shown in the subroutine (see Fig. 8.9). The first subexpression in the LOGICAL assignment

```
(IABS(CELL − IMAGE(I−1,J−1)) .GE. NOSLEV)
```

compares the value of CELL with its neighbor in row I−1, column J−1. If the absolute difference of these values is greater than or equal to the noise threshold, the subexpression is .TRUE.. NOISY is set to .TRUE. only if all eight subexpressions are .TRUE..

Figure 8.9. *Subroutine CLEAN*

```
        SUBROUTINE CLEAN (IMAGE, MAXROW, MAXCOL)
C Finds noisy pixels and substitutes their neighbors' average value
C Preconditions : IMAGE(MAXROW, MAXCOL) is defined.
C Postconditions: Each cell containing noise has been cleaned up.


C Input Arguments
C    MAXROW — number of rows in IMAGE
C    MAXCOL — number of columns in IMAGE
C Input/Output Arguments
C    IMAGE — the array of pixels


C Argument Declarations
        INTEGER MAXROW, MAXCOL
        INTEGER IMAGE(MAXROW, MAXCOL)


C Local Declarations
        INTEGER NOSLEV
        PARAMETER (NOSLEV = 3)
        INTEGER CELL, I, J
        LOGICAL NOISY


C Check for noise and replace noisy pixels
        DO 10 I = 2, MAXROW-1
          DO 20 J = 2, MAXCOL-1
            CELL = IMAGE(I,J)
            NOISY =    (IABS(CELL — IMAGE(I-1,J-1)) .GE. NOSLEV)  .AND.
     +                 (IABS(CELL — IMAGE(I-1,J  )) .GE. NOSLEV)  .AND.
     +                 (IABS(CELL — IMAGE(I-1,J+1)) .GE. NOSLEV)  .AND.
     +                 (IABS(CELL — IMAGE(I  ,J-1)) .GE. NOSLEV)  .AND.
     +                 (IABS(CELL — IMAGE(I  ,J+1)) .GE. NOSLEV)  .AND.
     +                 (IABS(CELL — IMAGE(I+1,J-1)) .GE. NOSLEV)  .AND.
     +                 (IABS(CELL — IMAGE(I+1,J  )) .GE. NOSLEV)  .AND.
     +                 (IABS(CELL — IMAGE(I+1,J+1)) .GE. NOSLEV)
C            Redefine IMAGE(I,J) if noisy
            IF (NOISY) THEN
              IMAGE(I,J) = NINT(REAL(IMAGE(I-1,J-1) + IMAGE(I-1,J)
     +                          + IMAGE(I-1,J+1) + IMAGE(I,J-1)
     +                          + IMAGE(I,J+1) + IMAGE(I+1,J-1)
     +                          + IMAGE(I+1,J)
     +                          + IMAGE(I+1,J+1)) / 8.0)
            END IF
  20      CONTINUE
  10 CONTINUE

C Exit subroutine
        RETURN
        END
```

The IF statement replaces a noisy value with the average value of its eight neighbors. Function REAL converts the sum of these eight values to a real number, and function NINT returns the nearest integer value after the sum is divided by eight.

Subroutine REDUCE

Subroutine REDUCE (Fig. 8.10) simply replaces each value in IMAGE with one of three standard symbols. SYMBL1 replaces values 0–3, SYMBL2 replaces values 4–6, and SYMBL3 replaces values 7–9. A pair of nested DO loops is used to access the array elements in sequence. The IF statement selects the appropriate standard symbol.

Figure 8.10. *Subroutine REDUCE*

```
      SUBROUTINE REDUCE (IMAGE, MAXROW, MAXCOL)
C Replaces each of the symbols in IMAGE with a standard symbol
C Preconditions : Array IMAGE(MAXROW, MAXCOL) is defined.
C Postconditions: For all I,J: if 0 <= IMAGE(I,J) <= 3,
C    IMAGE(I,J) is 0; if 4 <= IMAGE(I,J) <= 6, IMAGE(I,J) is 1;
C    if 7 <= IMAGE(I,J) <= 9, IMAGE(I,J) is 4

C Input Arguments
C    MAXROW — number of rows in IMAGE
C    MAXCOL — number of columns in IMAGE
C Input/Output Arguments
C    IMAGE — the array of pixels

C Argument Declarations
      INTEGER MAXROW, MAXCOL
      INTEGER IMAGE(MAXROW, MAXCOL)

C Local Declarations
      INTEGER SYMBL1, SYMBL2, SYMBL3
      PARAMETER (SYMBL1 = 0, SYMBL2 = 1, SYMBL3 = 4)
      INTEGER I, J

C Perform the replacement
      DO 10 I = 1, MAXROW
         DO 20 J = 1, MAXCOL
            IF (IMAGE(I,J) .LE. 3) THEN
               IMAGE(I,J) = SYMBL1
            ELSE IF (IMAGE(I,J) .LE. 6) THEN
               IMAGE(I,J) = SYMBL2
            ELSE
               IMAGE(I,J) = SYMBL3
            END IF
20       CONTINUE
10 CONTINUE
```

```
C Exit subroutine
      RETURN
      END
```

Subroutine SHIMAG

Subroutine SHIMAG (Fig. 8.11) displays the enhanced image. The FORMAT statement

```
15 FORMAT (1X, 78I1)
```

causes the value of each array element to be displayed as a single-digit integer.

TESTING AND VERIFICATION

You can construct your own test file by drawing a "stick figure" and then "encoding" it as a set of digits that all reduce to the same value. Pick "random" values outside this range for all other points in your image. Write each row of

Figure 8.11. *Subroutine SHIMAG*

```
      SUBROUTINE SHIMAG (IMAGE, MAXROW, MAXCOL)
C Displays the enhanced image
C Preconditions : Array IMAGE is defined.
C Postconditions: Each element of IMAGE is displayed.

C Input Arguments
C   IMAGE — the array of pixels
C   MAXROW — number of rows in IMAGE
C   MAXCOL — number of columns in IMAGE

C Argument Declarations
      INTEGER MAXROW, MAXCOL
      INTEGER IMAGE(MAXROW, MAXCOL)

C Local Declarations
      INTEGER I, J

C Display each row of the image
      DO 10 I = 1, MAXROW
         PRINT 15, (IMAGE(I,J), J = 1, MAXCOL)
   15    FORMAT (1X, 78I1)
   10 CONTINUE

C Exit subroutine
      RETURN
      END
```

values to data file DIGITAL.DAT and see what happens. For test purposes, you probably will want to redefine MAXROW and MAXCOL to smaller values. Programming Project 9 at the end of this chapter discusses how to construct a noisy image.

Self-check

1. Assume MAXROW and MAXCOL are 4. Show the contents of the following array IMAGE after the return from subroutine CLEAN and then after the return from subroutine REDUCE.

```
1231
2222
2434
5429
```

8.3 Searching an Array

A common problem is searching an array to determine the location of a desired value. For example, we might wish to search an array of student names to locate a particular student name (called the *target*). This can be accomplished by examining each array element in a loop and testing to see whether it matches the target name. The search loop should be exited when the target name is found. A search algorithm follows.

Algorithm

1. Assume the target has not been found.
2. Start with the first array element.
3. DO WHILE the target is not found and there are more elements
    4. IF the current element matches the target THEN
        5. Set a flag to indicate that the target is found.
        6. Set the search result to the target index.
    ELSE
        7. Advance to the next array element.
    END IF
END DO

A function that implements this algorithm is shown in Fig. 8.12. This function returns the target index (subscript) if the target is present in the array; otherwise, it returns zero. The local variable I (initial value 1) selects the array element that is compared to the target value.

The LOGICAL flag FOUND is used for loop control in Fig. 8.12. The value of FOUND indicates whether the target has been found. It is initially set to .FALSE. (target

Figure 8.12. *Function SEARCH*

```
      INTEGER FUNCTION SEARCH (NAMES, TARGET, N)

C Searches for TARGET item in first N elements of array NAMES
C Returns TARGET index or 0 if not found
C Preconditions : TARGET and first N elements of array NAMES are
C                 defined and N > 0.
C Postconditions. Function result is subscript of first occurrence
C                 of TARGET or 0 if TARGET is not found.

C Argument Declarations
      INTEGER N
      CHARACTER *20 NAMES(*), TARGET

C Local Declarations
      INTEGER I
      LOGICAL FOUND

C Assume TARGET is not yet found
      FOUND = .FALSE.
      SEARCH = 0

C Compare each element to TARGET starting with the first element
      I = 1
      DO WHILE (.NOT. FOUND .AND. I .LE. N)          9 IF (...) THEN
         IF (NAMES(I) .EQ. TARGET) THEN
            FOUND = .TRUE.
            SEARCH = I
         ELSE
            I = I + 1
         END IF
      END DO                                         GOTO 9
                                                     END IF
C Exit function
      RETURN
      END
```

is not found prior to search) and is reset to .TRUE. only if the target is found. If FOUND becomes .TRUE., the function result is set to I and the search loop is exited.

If array NAMES is defined in the calling program, the assignment statement

```
INDEX = SEARCH(NAMES, 'JANE DOE', 20)
```

calls function SEARCH to search the first 20 elements of array NAMES for the target name 'JANE DOE'. The subscript of the first occurrence of 'JANE DOE' is saved in INDEX. If 'JANE DOE' is not found, then INDEX is set to zero.

Self-check

1. What value is returned by function SEARCH if the first, third, and fifth array elements all contain the target?

Programming

1. Modify SEARCH so that the index of the last occurrence of the target is always returned.

8.4 Sorting an Array

There are many times when we would like an array to contain either an increasing sequence or a decreasing sequence of values. For example, your Fortran instructor might want to store the names of all students in your class in alphabetical order (alphabetically first name in element 1) to make it easier to print the final semester grade report. At other times, your instructor might want the exam scores to be stored in decreasing order (largest score in element 1), so that they could be printed out with the highest score first. If the array values are not entered in any particular order initially, they must be rearranged to form an increasing or a decreasing sequence. This process is called *sorting*.

In this section, we discuss a fairly simple (but not very efficient) algorithm called the *bubble sort*. The bubble sort compares adjacent array elements and exchanges their values if they are out of order. In this way, the smaller values ''bubble'' to the top of the array (toward the first element), while the larger values sink to the bottom of the array. The data requirements and algorithm for a bubble sort subroutine follow.

Data Requirements

Subroutine Inputs

the array being sorted (INTEGER LIST(*))
the number of array elements (INTEGER N)

Subroutine Output

the sorted array (INTEGER LIST(*))

Algorithm for Bubble Sort Subroutine

0. Assume the array is not sorted.
1. DO WHILE the array is not sorted
    2. Examine every pair of adjacent array elements and exchange any values that are out of order.

   END DO

Figure 8.13. *One
Pass of Bubble Sort
of Array M*

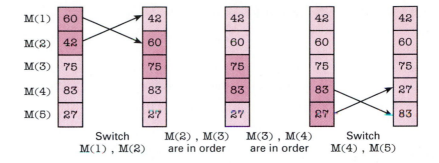

As an example, we will trace through one execution of step 2 above, that
is, one *pass* through an array being sorted. By scanning the diagrams in Fig.
8.13 from left to right, we see the effect of each comparison. The pair of array
elements being compared is shown in a darker color in each diagram. The
first pair of values—M(1) is 60, M(2) is 42—is out of order, so the values are
exchanged. The next pair of values—M(2) is now 60, M(3) is 75—is compared
in the second array shown in Fig. 8.13; this pair is in order, as is the next
pair—M(3) is 75, M(4) is 83. The last pair—M(4) is 83, M(5) is 27—is out of
order, so the values are exchanged, as shown in the last diagram.

The last array shown in Fig. 8.13 is closer to being sorted than is the original.
The only value that is out of order is the number 27 in M(4). Unfortunately,
three more passes through the entire array will be required before this value
bubbles to the top of the array. In each of these passes, only one pair of values
will be out of order, so only one exchange will be made. The contents of array
M after the completion of each pass are shown in Fig. 8.14.

We can tell by looking at the contents of the array at the end of pass 4 that
the array is now sorted; however, the computer can recognize this only by
making one additional pass without doing any exchanges. If no exchanges are
made, then all pairs must be in order, hence the reason for the extra pass
shown in Fig. 8.14 and for the LOGICAL flag SORTED described next.

Figure 8.14. *Array
M after Completion
of Each Pass*

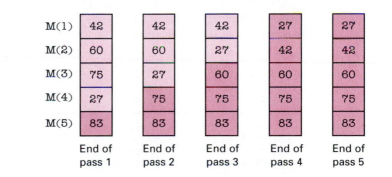

Local Variables for Bubble Sort

flag to indicate whether the array is assumed to be sorted (LOGICAL SORTED)
loop-control variable and subscript (INTEGER FIRST)
number of the current pass starting with 1 (INTEGER PASS)

Refinement of Step 2 of Bubble Sort

2.1 Initialize SORTED to .TRUE..
2.2 DO for each pair of adjacent array elements
    2.3 IF the values in a pair are out of order THEN
        2.4 Exchange the values.
        2.5 Set SORTED to .FALSE..
    END IF
END DO

Step 2 will be implemented using a DO loop. The DO loop-control variable, FIRST, also will be the subscript of the first element in each pair; consequently, FIRST+1 will be the subscript of the second element in each pair. During each pass, the initial value of FIRST is 1. The final value of FIRST must be less than the number of array elements so that FIRST+1 will be in range.

For an array of n elements, the final value of FIRST can be n–PASS, where PASS is the number of the current pass, starting with 1 for the first pass. The reason for this is that at the end of pass 1, the last array element must be in its correct place; at the end of pass 2, the last two array elements must be in their correct places; at the end of pass 3, the last three array elements must be in their correct places, and so on. There is no need to examine array elements that are already in place. The section of the array that is already sorted is shown in a darker color in Fig. 8.14.

Subroutine BUBBLE in Fig. 8.15 performs a bubble sort on the array represented by LIST. If the pair of elements represented by LIST(FIRST) and LIST (FIRST+1) is out of order, their values are exchanged and SORTED is set to .FALSE.. When BUBBLE is done, the array elements will be in order.

Subroutine BUBBLE begins by setting SORTED to .FALSE. (step 0 in the algorithm shown earlier in this section). This is done to ensure that the WHILE loop will be executed at least one time.

Figure 8.15. *Bubble Sort Subroutine*

```
      SUBROUTINE BUBBLE (LIST, N)
C Sorts the data in array LIST
C Preconditions : N >= 1 and LIST(1) through LIST(N) are defined.
C Postconditions: LIST(I) <= LIST(I+1) for all I < N.
```

```
C Input Argument
C   N — Number of array elements to be sorted
C Input/Output Argument
C   LIST — Array being sorted

C Argument Declarations
      INTEGER LIST(*), N

C Local Declarations
      INTEGER FIRST, PASS, TEMP
      LOGICAL SORTED

C Start with pass 1
      PASS = 1
C Exchange out of order pairs while array is not sorted
      SORTED = .FALSE.
      DO WHILE (.NOT. SORTED)                    9 IF (...) THEN
          SORTED = .TRUE.
          DO 10 FIRST = 1, N—PASS
              IF (LIST (FIRST) .GT. LIST(FIRST+1)) THEN
C                 Exchange pair
                  TEMP = LIST(FIRST)
                  LIST(FIRST) = LIST(FIRST+1)
                  LIST(FIRST+1) = TEMP
                  SORTED = .FALSE.
              END IF
   10     CONTINUE
          PASS = PASS + 1
      END DO                                     GOTO 9
                                                 END IF
C Exit subroutine
      RETURN
      END
```

**EXERCISE FOR
SECTION 8.4**

Self-check

1. Modify BUBBLE to place the array values in descending order (largest value first).

8.5   Using Subprograms in a Large-scale Problem

In this section, we use many of the subprograms developed in the last two chapters to solve a rather large programming problem. The problem solution demonstrates the advantage of using subprograms to split a large problem into manageable modules. Because many of these subprograms are general and were not written specifically for this problem, they can be reused in other programs.

Case Study: Grading Problem

PROBLEM STATEMENT

The instructors at your college would like a grading program to help them assign grades for an examination. They would like to use this program to display data for either all students or a particular student, to calculate exam statistics, to assign letter grades, and even to chart the distribution of grades. Because each instructor will have a different use for the program, the program should be *menu driven*. The program user can request a display of the following menu either before the first task or after completing each task; the number entered by the program user determines which task will be performed next.

FORTRAN *in Focus*

Supercomputing with Fortran

NORTH CAROLINA
SUPERCOMPUTING CENTER

The North Carolina Supercomputing Center (NCSC) is a division of MCNC, a private nonprofit corporation, located in Research Triangle Park, North Carolina. This company introduces high-performance computing into the research and development activities of corporations, and provides opportunities for scientists and engineers in academia to use its resources to tackle challenging problems. The scientific support staff at NCSC is comprised of scientists and engineers who assist a large user community in optimizing the use of available computing resources. Their knowledge and use of Fortran is extensive, since most

of the supercomputing applications are done in Fortran.

Several departments within NCSC use Fortran daily. The first such department is the technology group. They evaluate new systems and integrate the many computing environments at NCSC to provide a seamless operation between networking, computing, and data storage. They use Fortran to write test modules and benchmarks for acceptance tests of new or proposed computers.

Another department using Fortran daily is the visualization group. They assist NCSC users in making sense out of the billions of numbers that may result from a single computer simulation by turning

```
Select one of the operations below by number.

 0.   Display the menu
 1.   Enter exam data
 2.   Find the score of a particular student
 3.   Change a score and grade
 4.   Sort the student data by name
 5.   Sort the student data by score
 6.   Find the low score
 7.   Find the high score
 8.   Find the mean and standard deviation
 9.   Find the median
10.   Assign a letter grade
11.   Plot a histogram of grades
12.   Display the student exam data
13.   Exit the program
```

the vast quantity of data into visual representations that can be studied further. This group uses Fortran to interface with user applications, and uses modules written in Fortran to build visualization applications.

Lastly, the education group uses Fortran to introduce computational science (the correct match of application, algorithm, and architecture to do science on a computer) into all education levels including K–12, community colleges, undergraduate, graduate, and postdoctoral programs. Fortran is used to code computational science modules that are incorporated into existing classes in science, engineering, and

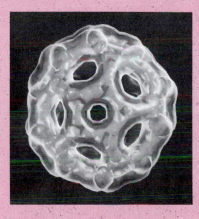

IMAGE OF C-60 OR BUCKMINSTER-FULLERENE, ALSO CALLED BUCKEY-BALLS, GENERATED BY TOM PALMER OF CRAY RESEARCH INC., AT THE N. C. SUPERCOMPUTING CENTER FOR WORK BY J. BERN-HOLC, Q.-M. ZHANG, J.-Y. YI, AND C. BRABEC OF THE DEPARTMENT OF PHYSICS AT N. C. STATE UNIVERSITY.

mathematics as examples or student projects. These modules also form the core of new computational science courses.

One of the most important uses of supercomputing resources at NCSC is the predictive computation of the properties of atoms, molecules, and the compound systems they form. Quantum Monte Carlo is a powerful technique that permits ground state properties, such as the average energy per atom or the average distance between atoms, of strongly interacting quantum fluids to be studied accurately and efficiently. These systems can be described by

(continued)

ANALYSIS

We will write a separate subprogram to accomplish each of the tasks listed above. In fact, we already have subprogram solutions to several of them. The input data for the new grading program consist of the name and score of each student. Also, each menu selection will be read as data. The outputs consist of the letter grades assigned and the exam statistics. The student names, scores, and grades will be stored in a set of parallel arrays. The problem data requirements follow.

Data Requirements

Problem Parameters
the maximum array sizes (MAXSIZ = 100)
the number of the exit option (EXITCH = 13)

Problem Inputs
the number of students taking the exam (INTEGER NUMSTU)
the name of each student (CHARACTER *20 NAMES(MAXSIZ))
the score of each student (INTEGER SCORES(MAXSIZ))
the operation to be performed (INTEGER CHOICE)

Problem Outputs
the lowest score (INTEGER MINSCR)
the highest score (INTEGER MAXSCR)
the mean score (REAL MEAN)

using both classical physics or chemistry and quantum mechanics.

Drs. Panoff and Schmidt at the NCSC developed the computer code NLII (pronounced "analyze"), which is used in conjunction with Quantum Monte Carlo. This code is designed so that many processors in parallel can divide the analysis of thousands of configurations of hundreds of atoms. These configurations are stored on disk and are then reanalyzed with changing parameters.

The output is thousands of configurations recording the coordinates of each atom in the system.

The code has been run on many systems, from the earliest VAX computers, to IBM 3090s, to the Cray YMP. Because the code is written entirely in Fortran and uses only one specialized library routine to invert matrices, the code is completely portable across systems. Only by using Fortran were the scientists/engineers able to achieve an extremely high

level of performance and portability. Code and results were easily shared with colleagues.

Dr. Robert M. Panoff, computational scientist at NCSC and a developer of NLII, believes that the use of Fortran on supercomputers has allowed scientists at NCSC to accomplish work sooner and to get more work done. In his opinion, they have also performed better calculations since the larger number of atoms results in more realistic quantum simulations.

the standard deviation (REAL STDEV)
the median score (REAL MEDIAN)
the assigned letter grades (CHARACTER *1 GRADES(MAXSIZ))

DESIGN

The algorithm follows.

Algorithm

1. DO WHILE the user is not done
    2. Read and validate the user's choice.
    3. Perform the option selected.
   END DO

Structure Chart and Algorithm Refinements

The structure chart corresponding to this algorithm is shown in Fig. 8.16. Subroutine OPRATE will contain the code required to perform each option selected by the program user. It is in color in the structure chart to indicate that it has subordinate subprograms, which will be shown later.

Only variable CHOICE and parameter EXITCH are shown as arguments in Fig. 8.16. None of the other problem inputs or outputs appears because these variables are manipulated by subroutine OPRATE and its subordinate subprograms. For this reason, only CHOICE and EXITCH should be declared in the main program; the other problem inputs and outputs will be declared in OPRATE.

Dr. Panoff believes that the most important change in Fortran has been the way in which scientists have adopted a structured programming style, eliminating the GOTO constructs that used to make Fortran look like spaghetti code. Fortran programming style now closely resembles Pascal and C, and the movement toward vector processing and parallel programming is reflected in the way in which Fortran compilers identify loop dependencies. As programming needs have changed over the years, so have Fortran and its implementation on various computer architectures.

His advice to students learning Fortran is, "Keep in mind that Fortran, and all of scientific computing, is a means and not an end. If a particular application can be coded easier in another language, great. There is no need to use Fortran just to prove that you can, but there is every reason to be sure that Fortran will be the working language of productive scientists and engineers for many years to come, as Fortran adapts to the needs of every generation."

Sincere thanks to Dr. Robert M. Panoff, computational scientist at the Research Institute of the North Carolina Supercomputing Center, located in Research Triangle Park, North Carolina, for sharing his knowledge and use of Fortran as well as his extensive supercomputing expertise.

Figure 8.16. *Structure Chart for New Grading Program*

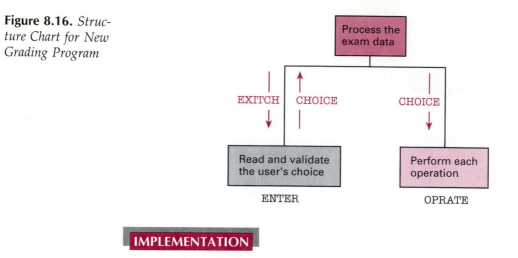

IMPLEMENTATION

Main Program

The main program (Fig. 8.17) begins by setting CHOICE to 0 to ensure that the main loop is entered and executed at least once. Function ENTER (see Fig. 6.3) is used to read the user's choice into CHOICE. The first-time user should select option 0 to see the menu. After CHOICE is read, subroutine OPRATE is called.

Figure 8.17. *Main Program for New Grading Program*

```
      PROGRAM GRADER
C Grades student exams
C Performs a set of operations on student exam data

C Declarations
      INTEGER CHOICE, EXITCH, ENTER
      PARAMETER (EXITCH = 13)

C Read and process each option until user is done
      CHOICE = 0
      DO WHILE (CHOICE .NE. EXITCH)          9 IF (...) THEN
         PRINT *
         PRINT *, 'Enter your choice -- enter 0 to see the menu'
         CHOICE = ENTER(0, EXITCH)
         CALL OPRATE (CHOICE, EXITCH)
      END DO                                  GOTO 9
                                              END IF
      STOP
      END

C ─────────────────────────────────────────────────
C Insert function ENTER (see Fig. 6.3) here.
```

Subroutine OPRATE

Each time it is called, OPRATE must perform the operation selected by its first input argument, CHOICE. Consequently, the algorithm for OPRATE consists of a multiple-alternative decision structure.

Certain preconditions must be satisfied before some of the operations can be performed. For example, the student exam data must be read before any of the other operations can be performed (i.e., NUMSTU must be nonzero). The exam data must be sorted by score before the median score can be determined. Also, the letter grades must be assigned before a histogram can be drawn. The two program flags below will be used to signal whether the last two preconditions are satisfied.

Local Variables for OPRATE

program flag to indicate whether data is sorted by score (LOGICAL SORTED)
program flag to indicate whether grades are assigned (LOGICAL GRADED)
the mean or average score (REAL MEAN)
the standard deviation of the scores (REAL STDEV)
the median score (REAL MEDIAN)
the lowest and highest score (INTEGER MINSCR, MAXSCR)

Algorithm for OPRATE

1. IF CHOICE is 0 THEN
     2. Print the menu.
   ELSE IF CHOICE is not 1 and NUMSTU is 0 THEN
     3. Print a message to read in student data first.
   ELSE IF CHOICE is 1 THEN
     4. Read the student data and set flags to .FALSE..
   ELSE IF CHOICE is 2 THEN
     5. Read a student's name and display the score.
   ELSE IF CHOICE is 3 THEN
     6. Read a student's name and change that score and grade.
   ELSE IF CHOICE is 4 THEN
     7. Sort the student data by name and set SORTED to .FALSE..
   ELSE IF CHOICE is 5 THEN
     8. Sort the student data by score and set SORTED to .TRUE..
   ELSE IF CHOICE is 6 THEN
     9. Find the low score and display it.
   ELSE IF CHOICE is 7 THEN
     10. Find the high score and display it.
   ELSE IF CHOICE is 8 THEN
     11. Find the mean score and standard deviation and display them.
   ELSE IF CHOICE is 9 and scores are sorted THEN
     12. Find the median score and display it.

```
ELSE IF CHOICE is 9 THEN
    13. Print a message that scores must be sorted first.
ELSE IF CHOICE is 10 THEN
    14. Assign letter grades and set GRADED to .TRUE..
ELSE IF CHOICE is 11 and grades are assigned THEN
    15. Plot the histogram of grades.
ELSE IF CHOICE is 11 THEN
    16. Print a message that letter grades must be assigned.
ELSE IF CHOICE is 12 THEN
    17. Display all student data.
ELSE IF CHOICE is EXITCH THEN
    18. Exit from the grading program.
ELSE
    19. Print a message that CHOICE is invalid.
END IF
```

Figure 8.18. *Structure Chart for OPRATE*

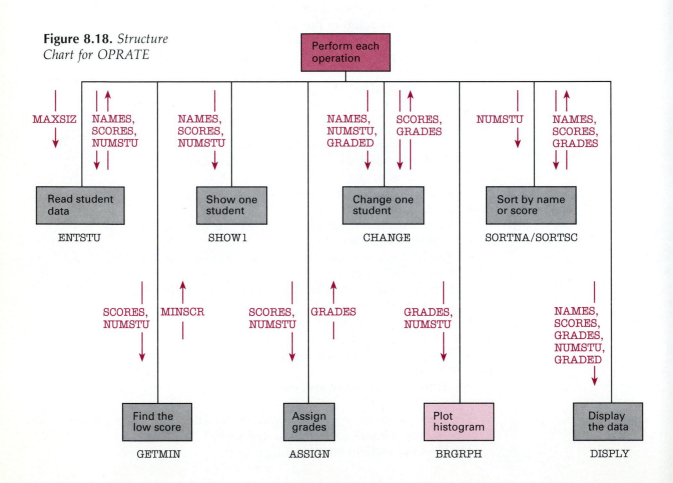

Steps 2, 3, 13, 16, 18, and 19 consist of simple PRINT statements. Of the rest, only steps 14 and 15 require subprograms that are unfamiliar to us. The structure chart for subroutine OPRATE is shown in Fig. 8.18.

Because of space limitations, subroutine PRMENU is omitted from the structure chart. All the subprograms shown in Fig. 8.18 are subroutines with the exception of GETMIN, which, because it returns a single result, should be implemented as a function. The functions GETMAX (returns the high score—see Fig. 7 7) and GETMED (returns the median value) are not shown in the structure chart; however, they have the same input arguments as GETMIN. Subroutine AVESTD, which returns both the average value and the standard deviation, also is not shown. Subroutine OPRATE is shown in Fig. 8.19.

The statement

```
SAVE NAMES, SCORES, GRADES, GRADED, SORTED, NUMSTU
```

is used in Fig. 8.19 to instruct the compiler to retain the values of the local

Figure 8.19. *Subroutine OPRATE*

```
        SUBROUTINE OPRATE (CHOICE, EXITCH)
C Performs the option selected by CHOICE
C Preconditions : 0 <= CHOICE <= EXITCH
C Postconditions: A subroutine is selected based on the value of CHOICE.

C Input Arguments
C    CHOICE - The number of the option selected (0 to EXITCH)
C    EXITCH - The number of the exit option

C Argument Declarations
        INTEGER CHOICE, EXITCH

C Local Declarations
        INTEGER MAXSIZ
        PARAMETER (MAXSIZ = 100)
        INTEGER SCORES(MAXSIZ), NUMSTU
        INTEGER MINSCR, MAXSCR
        CHARACTER *20 NAMES(MAXSIZ)
        CHARACTER *1 GRADES(MAXSIZ)
        REAL MEAN, STDEV, MEDIAN
        LOGICAL SORTED, GRADED

        INTEGER GETMIN, GETMAX
        REAL GETMED

C Save all local data between calls
        SAVE NAMES, SCORES, GRADES, GRADED, SORTED, NUMSTU
        DATA NUMSTU /0/
```

```
C Perform option selected
      IF (CHOICE .EQ. 0) THEN
         CALL PRMENU
      ELSE IF ((CHOICE .NE. 1) .AND. (NUMSTU .EQ. 0)) THEN
         PRINT *, 'Read student data first'
      ELSE IF (CHOICE .EQ. 1) THEN
         CALL ENTSTU (MAXSIZ, NAMES, SCORES, NUMSTU)
         GRADED = .FALSE.
         SORTED = .FALSE.
      ELSE IF (CHOICE .EQ. 2) THEN
         CALL SHOW1 (NAMES, SCORES, NUMSTU)
      ELSE IF (CHOICE .EQ. 3) THEN
         CALL CHANGE (GRADED, NUMSTU, NAMES, SCORES, GRADES)
      ELSE IF (CHOICE .EQ. 4) THEN
         CALL SORTNA (NUMSTU, NAMES, SCORES, GRADES)
         SORTED = .FALSE.
      ELSE IF (CHOICE .EQ. 5) THEN
         CALL SORTSC (NUMSTU, NAMES, SCORES, GRADES)
         SORTED = .TRUE.
      ELSE IF (CHOICE .EQ. 6) THEN
         MINSCR = GETMIN(SCORES, NUMSTU)
         PRINT *, 'The lowest score is ', MINSCR
      ELSE IF (CHOICE .EQ. 7) THEN
         MAXSCR = GETMAX(SCORES, NUMSTU)
         PRINT *, 'The highest score is ', MAXSCR
      ELSE IF (CHOICE .EQ. 8) THEN
         CALL AVESTD (SCORES, NUMSTU, MEAN, STDEV)
         PRINT *, 'The mean score is ', MEAN
         PRINT *, 'with a standard deviation of ', STDEV
      ELSE IF ((CHOICE .EQ. 9) .AND. SORTED) THEN
         MEDIAN = GETMED(SCORES, NUMSTU)
         PRINT *, 'The median score is ', MEDIAN
      ELSE IF (CHOICE .EQ. 9) THEN
         PRINT *, 'Scores must first be sorted'
      ELSE IF (CHOICE .EQ. 10) THEN
         CALL ASSIGN (SCORES, NUMSTU, GRADES)
         GRADED = .TRUE.
      ELSE IF (CHOICE .EQ. 11 .AND. GRADED) THEN
         CALL BRGRPH (GRADES, NUMSTU)
      ELSE IF (CHOICE .EQ. 11) THEN
         PRINT *, 'Assign grades first'
      ELSE IF (CHOICE .EQ. 12) THEN
         CALL DISPLY (NAMES, SCORES, GRADES, NUMSTU, GRADED)
      ELSE IF (CHOICE .EQ. EXITCH) THEN
         PRINT *, 'Exiting from the grading program'
      ELSE
         PRINT *, 'Choice must be between 0 and ', EXITCH
      END IF

C Exit subroutine
      RETURN
      END
```

variables that are listed after SAVE between successive calls to OPRATE. The SAVE statement is described in detail in Section 8.6.

The statement

```
DATA NUMSTU /0/
```

initializes the value of NUMSTU to 0 when the subroutine is first loaded into memory. Consequently, NUMSTU will be zero the first time ENTSTU is called to enter student data. The DATA statement has no effect during subsequent calls to OPRATE, so NUMSTU will not be reset to zero.

The top-down approach has been utilized in designing the grading program. We have progressed fairly far in writing the program and have an overall design that is clear, readable, and well documented. However, we still have not explored the details of many subprograms that actually perform the grading operations. Most of these will be left as exercises. Functions GETMED and PLOT are discussed next.

Function GETMED

Function GETMED in Fig. 8.20 returns the median score. The median item in a list is defined as the item that occupies the middle position when the list is sorted. Function GETMED is called only when the scores are in order, thus making it easier to determine the median score, as explained next.

Figure 8.20. *Function GETMED*

```
      REAL FUNCTION GETMED (SCORES, NUMSTU)
C Returns the median value in the sorted array SCORES
C Preconditions : The first NUMSTU elements of array SCORES are in
C                 ascending order and NUMSTU > 0.
C Postconditions: The function result is the median of
C                 the first NUMSTU values in score.

C Argument Declarations
      INTEGER SCORES(*), NUMSTU

C Define median value
      IF (MOD(NUMSTU, 2) .EQ. 1) THEN
C         Median is the middle item of an odd item count
          GETMED = REAL(SCORES(NUMSTU/2 + 1))
      ELSE
C         Median is the average of two middle items of an even item count
          GETMED = REAL(SCORES(NUMSTU/2) + SCORES(NUMSTU/2 + 1)) / 2.0
      END IF

C Exit function
      RETURN
      END
```

Figure 8.21. *The Median of a Sorted Array*

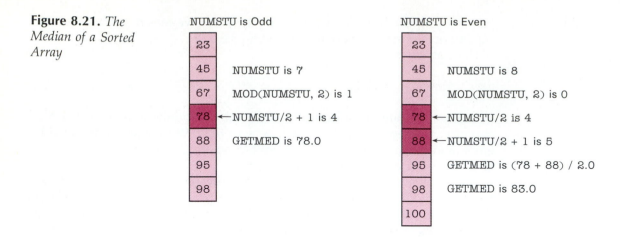

If the items are in order and there are an odd number of items, then the median is the middle item. If the items are in order but there are an even number of items, then the median is the average of the two middle items.

Both cases are illustrated in Fig. 8.21. The value of NUMSTU is 7 for the diagram on the left and 8 for the diagram on the right. In the diagram on the left, the median, 78, is in the darker color. In the diagram on the right, the median, 83, is the average of the two items in the darker color.

Subroutine BRGRPH

Choice 11 of the grading program requests a histogram of the grade distribution. A numerical value is represented in a histogram, or bar graph, by a bar whose length is proportional to the value.

Before the grade distribution can be plotted, the number of scores in each letter grade category (the number of A's, B's, etc.) must first be determined. Two local arrays, CATGRY and COUNTS, will be used to store the five letter grades and a counter for each grade category. The local data requirements and algorithm for subroutine BRGRPH follow.

Data Requirements

Local Parameters

the number of grade categories (NUMCAT = 5)
the character plotted (STAR = '*')

Local Variables

the array of grade categories (CHARACTER *1 CATGRY(NUMCAT))
the array of category counters (INTEGER COUNTS(NUMCAT))

subscript for array of assigned grades (INTEGER NXTGRD)
subscript for array of grade categories (INTEGER NXTCAT)
loop-control variable (INTEGER NSTAR)

Algorithm for BRGRPH

1. Count the number of assigned grades in each of the five letter-grade categories.
2. Plot the array of counters as a bar graph.

   Subroutine CNTGRD will be called by subroutine BRGRPH to determine the number of grades in each of the five grade categories. The structure chart segment in Fig. 8.22 shows the data flow between BRGRPH and CNTGRD. The subroutines are shown in Fig. 8.23, and a sample histogram appears in Fig. 8.24. This histogram shows 2 grades of A, 3 grades of B, and so on.

Figure 8.22. *Structure Chart for BRGRPH and CNTGRD*

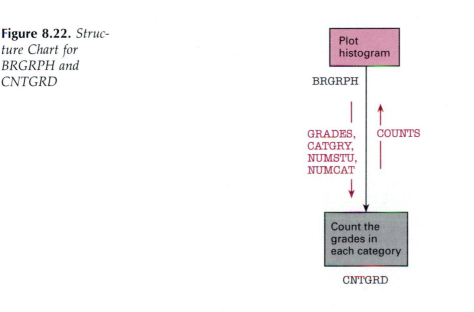

Figure 8.23. *Subroutines BRGRPH and CNTGRD*

```
      SUBROUTINE BRGRPH (GRADES, NUMSTU)
C Plots the distribution of GRADES as a bar graph (histogram)
C Preconditions : GRADES(1) through GRADES(NUMSTU) are defined.
C Postconditions: Displays each element of GRADES as a bar of *'s.

C Input Arguments
C    GRADES - The array of grades
C    NUMSTU - The number of elements in GRADES
```

```
C Argument Declarations
      CHARACTER *1 GRADES(*)
      INTEGER NUMSTU

C Local Declarations
      CHARACTER *1 STAR
      PARAMETER (STAR = '*')
      INTEGER NUMCAT
      PARAMETER (NUMCAT = 5)
      INTEGER NXTCAT, NSTAR
      INTEGER NUMGRD, NXTGRD
      INTEGER COUNTS(NUMCAT)
      CHARACTER *1 CATGRY(NUMCAT)
      DATA CATGRY /'A', 'B', 'C', 'D', 'F'/

C Print the title
      PRINT 5, 'HISTOGRAM OF GRADE DISTRIBUTION'
    5 FORMAT ('1', A)
      PRINT *

C Count the number of occurrences of each grade
      CALL CNTGRD (GRADES, CATGRY, NUMSTU, NUMCAT, COUNTS)

C Plot a bar for the count associated with each grade category
      DO 10 NXTCAT = 1, NUMCAT
         PRINT 15, CATGRY(NXTCAT), ' I',
     +            (STAR, NSTAR = 1, COUNTS(NXTCAT))
   15    FORMAT (1X, A, A, 50A1)
   10 CONTINUE

C Print a legend at the bottom
      PRINT *, '   I—-I—-I—-I—-I—-I—-I—-I—-I—-I—-I'
      PRINT *, '   0   5  10  15  20  25  30  35  40  45  50'

C Exit subroutine
      RETURN
      END


C————————————————————————————————————————————————————————


      SUBROUTINE CNTGRD (GRADES, CATGRY, NUMSTU, NUMCAT, COUNTS)
C Count the number of grades in each category
C Preconditions : CATGRY(1) through CATGRY(NUMCAT) are defined;
C     GRADES(1) through GRADES(NUMSTU) are defined.
C Postconditions: COUNTS(I) is the number of elements in
C     array GRADES that match CATGRY(I), for 1 <= I <= NUMCAT.

C INPUT ARGUMENTS
C    GRADES — The array of grades
C    CATGRY — The array of categories
C    NUMSTU — The number of GRADES
C    NUMCAT — The number of categories
```

```
C OUTPUT ARGUMENTS
C    COUNTS — The array of counters

C Argument Declarations
      CHARACTER *1 GRADES(*), CATGRY(*)
      INTEGER COUNTS(*), NUMSTU, NUMCAT

C Local Declarations
      INTEGER NXTCAT, NXTGRD

C Initialize all counters to zero
      DO 10 NXTCAT = 1, NUMCAT
         COUNTS(NXTCAT) = 0
   10 CONTINUE

C Categorize each grade
      DO 20 NXTGRD = 1, NUMSTU
C        Compare the current grade to each grade category
C        and increment the counter for the matched category
         IF (GRADES(NXTGRD) .EQ. CATGRY(1)) THEN
            COUNTS(1) = COUNTS(1) + 1
         ELSE IF (GRADES(NXTGRD) .EQ. CATGRY(2)) THEN
            COUNTS(2) = COUNTS(2) + 1
         ELSE IF (GRADES(NXTGRD) .EQ. CATGRY(3)) THEN
            COUNTS(3) = COUNTS(3) + 1
         ELSE IF (GRADES(NXTGRD) .EQ. CATGRY(4)) THEN
            COUNTS(4) = COUNTS(4) + 1
         ELSE IF (GRADES(NXTGRD) .EQ. CATGRY(5)) THEN
            COUNTS(5) = COUNTS(5) + 1
         ELSE
            PRINT *, 'Invalid grade ', GRADES(NXTGRD)
         END IF
   20 CONTINUE

C Exit subroutine
      RETURN
      END
```

Figure 8.24. *Sample Histogram Printed by BRGRPH*

```
HISTOGRAM OF GRADE DISTRIBUTION

A I**
B I***
C I***
D I*
F I*
  I—I—I—I—I—I—I—I—I—I—I
  0   5  10  15  20  25  30  35  40  45  50
```

Subroutine BRGRPH begins by calling subroutine CNTGRD

```
CALL CNTGRD (GRADES, CATGRY, NUMSTU, NUMCAT, COUNTS)
```

to define the array of counters (COUNTS). The IF structure in subroutine CNTGRD attempts to match each element of array GRADES to one of the five grade categories and increments the counter for the matched category.

In subroutine BRGRPH, the formatted PRINT statement

```
      PRINT 15, CATGRY(NXTCAT), ' I',
     +          (STAR, NSTAR = 1, COUNTS(NXTCAT))
15    FORMAT (1X, A, A, 50A1)
```

is executed once for each of the letter grade categories. It displays a letter grade label for a bar, the string ' I', and then the bar itself as a string of adjacent STAR characters. The implied DO loop (second line) uses the value of COUNTS(NXTCAT) to determine how many asterisks are to be printed in each bar.

TESTING AND VERIFICATION

Before you can test the grading program completely, you must supply the missing subprograms. Or, you can perform a partial test by using a dummy subprogram or stub in place of each subprogram that is not yet completed (see Section 6.7); doing this will allow you to compile the grading program. Ensure you don't select an option that calls a missing subroutine.

Complete subroutine DISPLY before you begin testing so that you can view the letter grade assignments and verify that all data items were stored properly.

EXERCISES FOR SECTION 8.5

Self-check

1. Subroutine ASSIGN assigns a letter grade corresponding to each exam score. Show the first five elements of array GRADES if the first five elements of array SCORES are 80 65 70 60 50 and the lowest A is 90, the lowest B is 80, the lowest C is 70, and the lowest D is 60.

Programming

1. Write a DO loop containing a LOGICAL IF statement that can be used to replace the IF structure in subroutine CNTGRD of Fig. 8.23.
2. Write the remaining subroutines and functions that are called by subroutine OPRATE.

8.6 The SAVE Statement and Simulation

The SAVE statement was used in subroutine OPRATE (see Fig. 8.19) to save the values of several local variables declared in that subroutine. Otherwise, the local variables could become undefined when we exit from OPRATE and could be lost.

This situation has not been a problem before because either each subprogram was called just once or if a subprogram was called multiple times, there was no need to retain local variable values between calls. Also in earlier programs, any data that needed to be saved between subprogram calls were stored in main program variables instead of in local variables. The SAVE statement is summarized in the next display.

SYNTAX DISPLAY

SAVE Statement

SYNTAX: SAVE
       SAVE *list*

EXAMPLE: SAVE A, B, C

INTERPRETATION: The *list* contains the names of local variables or arrays whose values are to be saved following the execution of a subprogram RETURN. Otherwise, the values of these local variables may be lost. If the SAVE statement appears without a *list*, all local variable values will be saved. The SAVE statement is nonexecutable and must appear in the declaration section of a subprogram before any executable statements. A SAVE statement in the main program has no effect.

NOTE: The SAVE statement must appear with the declarations and before any executable statements. The *list* must not contain the names of subprograms or dummy arguments. Items defined by a DATA statement and not redefined do not have to be included in the SAVE statement.

Random-number Generation

The SAVE statement can be used within a function that generates random numbers. Although a computer cannot generate a truly random number, it can generate what is called a *pseudorandom number*. Pseudorandom numbers are not really random, but they are close. Random numbers are used in many computer applications, for example, for simulation of ship arrivals at a port or of traffic flow through a city.

EXAMPLE 8.7

Function RANDOM (see Fig. 8.25) generates pseudorandom numbers. Its argument, SEED, is the initial *seed* of the random-number generator and should be

Figure 8.25. *Function RANDOM*

```
      REAL FUNCTION RANDOM (SEED)
C Generates a random number using SEED as the initial seed for the
C random-number generator
C Preconditions : SEED is defined and OLDSED contains the previous
C                 seed value.
C Postconditions: Returns a value between 0.0 and 1.0 and OLDSED contains
C                 the next seed value.

C Argument Declarations
      INTEGER SEED

C Local Declarations
      INTEGER C1, C2
      PARAMETER (C1 = 19423, C2 = 811)
      INTEGER OLDSED
      SAVE OLDSED
      DATA OLDSED /0/

C Set OLDSED to SEED if this is the first call
      IF (OLDSED .EQ. 0) THEN
          OLDSED = SEED
      END IF

C Generate a new value of OLDSED
      OLDSED = MOD(C1 * OLDSED, C2)

C Define the result
      RANDOM = REAL(OLDSED) / REAL(C2)

C Exit function
      RETURN
      END
```

a large prime number. The idea behind random-number generation is to multiply the seed value by a very large number and then perform a division operation, thereby returning a "random" result.

The local variable OLDSED represents the current seed value. The DATA statement initializes OLDSED to 0 when the function is loaded into memory. OLDSED is set to SEED the first time function RANDOM executes. Thereafter, the statement

```
OLDSED = MOD(C1 * OLDSED, C2)
```

computes a new value for OLDSED by first multiplying it by a very large prime number (parameter C1) and then finding the remainder after division by another prime number (parameter C2). The statement

```
RANDOM = REAL(OLDSED) / REAL(C2)
```

divides OLDSED by C2 to get a pseudorandom number between 0.0 and 1.0. The SAVE statement is used to ensure OLDSED retains its value during successive calls to function RANDOM.

EXAMPLE 8.8   The following DO loop calls function RANDOM 10 times in succession and displays the values returned for an initial seed of 20029 (value of ISEED).

```
   ISEED = 20029
   DO 20 I = 1, 10
      X = RANDOM(ISEED)
      PRINT *, X
20 CONTINUE
```

As another example of the use of function RANDOM, the statement

```
N = 1 + INT(10 * RANDOM(ISEED))
```

assigns to N a random integer between 1 and 10, inclusive. In general, the expression

```
A + INT((B − A + 1) * RANDOM(ISEED))
```

yields a random integer in the range A to B, inclusive.   ■

In Example 8.8, we used a large prime number, 20029, as the initial seed value. The theory behind random-number generation is beyond the scope of this text; refer to other texts for more information.†

Simulation Using Random Numbers

Interestingly enough, we can estimate the values of π using random numbers, as follows. We divide the first quadrant of a graph into two regions by drawing the arc of a circle with radius 1 (see Fig. 8.26). The area of region 1 is $\pi r^2/4$ or simply $\pi/4$ when r is 1. The area of the entire quadrant (region 1 and region 2) is 1. Therefore the ratio of region 1 to the entire quadrant area is $\pi/4$.

If we "throw darts" into the quadrant, the number of darts landing in region 1 should be proportional to the area of region 1. We can simulate throwing a dart by generating a pair of random numbers that represent the X- and Y-

---

† See, for example, Donald Knuth, *The Art of Computer Programming, Seminumerical Algorithms*, vol. 1 (Reading, Mass.: Addison-Wesley, 1981).

Figure 8.26. *Regions of a Unit Circle*

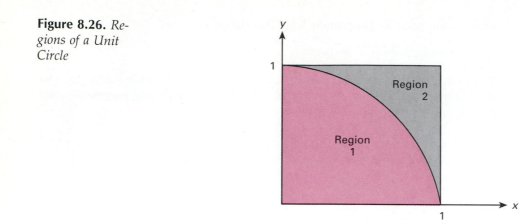

coordinates of the point where the dart lands. If we divide the number of darts landing in region 1 by the total number of darts thrown, we should get an estimate of $\pi/4$.

How do we know whether a dart lands in region 1? If the distance of the dart from the origin is less than 1, the dart must lie within region 1. The distance formula is

$$distance = \sqrt{X^2 + Y^2}.$$

If we throw a large number of darts (say, 1000 or more), we should come pretty close to an accurate estimate of $\pi/4$. Multiplying this value by 4 gives us an estimate of π. Figure 8.27 shows a sample run of a program that estimates the value of π using function RANDOM.

Figure 8.27. *Estimating Pi*

```
      PROGRAM PIEST
C Estimates the value of pi using random numbers

C Declarations
      INTEGER SEED
      PARAMETER (SEED = 20029)
      INTEGER DART, TRIES, HITS
      REAL X, Y, PI, RANDOM

C Enter number of darts to throw
      PRINT *, 'How many tries?'
      READ *, TRIES
```

```
C Throw each dart and count the number of hits inside the circle
      HITS = 0
      DO 10 DART = 1, TRIES
          X = RANDOM(SEED)
          Y = RANDOM(SEED)
          IF (SQRT(X ** 2 + Y ** 2) .LT. 1.0) THEN
              HITS = HITS + 1
          END IF
   10 CONTINUE

C Estimate pi
      PI = (REAL(HITS) / REAL(TRIES)) * 4.0
      PRINT '(1X, A, F10.7)', 'Pi is ', PI

      STOP
      END

How many tries?
1000
Pi is 3.1640000
```

**EXERCISE FOR
SECTION 8.6**

Self-check

1. Display the first 50 random numbers generated by a call to function RANDOM with a seed of 20029. Count the number between 0.0 and 0.1, between 0.1 and 0.2, and so on.

8.7 COMMON Blocks

The only data communication between main programs and subprograms discussed so far is through argument lists. Fortran also provides the capability of data communication through a storage area called a *COMMON block.* For example, we could use the declarations

```
INTEGER MAXSIZ
PARAMETER (MAXSIZ = 100)
COMMON SCORES(MAXSIZ)
INTEGER SCORES
```

in OPRATE (see Fig. 8.19) to allocate a COMMON block for storage of an integer array (SCORES) with MAXSIZ elements. The statement beginning with COMMON is called a COMMON statement; it lists the names of variables in the COMMON block. The type of each variable in the COMMON block must be declared either before or after the

Figure 8.28. *Interface Section for Subroutine GETMED*

```
      REAL FUNCTION GETMED (NUMSTU)
C Returns the median value in the sorted array SCORES
C Preconditions : The first NUMSTU elements of array SCORES are in
C                 ascending order and NUMSTU > 0.
C Postconditions: The function result is the median of
C                 the first NUMSTU values in score.

C Argument Declarations
      INTEGER NUMSTU

C Common Declarations
      INTEGER MAXSIZ
      PARAMETER (MAXSIZ = 100)
      COMMON SCORES(MAXSIZ)
      INTEGER SCORES
```

COMMON statement. If the variable is an array, its size may be declared in the COMMON statement or in the type declaration.

Placing the array SCORES in the COMMON block enables other subprograms called by OPRATE to reference the data in SCORES without the need to pass SCORES as an argument. The interface section for function GETMED (see Fig. 8.20) is rewritten in Fig. 8.28 to include the COMMON statement given above. The array SCORES must be deleted from the dummy argument list for GETMED. The assignment statement

```
MEDIAN = GETMED(NUMSTU)
```

can be used in subroutine OPRATE to call GETMED.

COMMON statements enable us to shorten the argument lists used in subprogram definitions and calls by not passing as arguments items in COMMON storage. Their disadvantage, however, is that when some external data are passed as arguments and some are not, it becomes less clear exactly what external data are being referenced by a subprogram. This problem is exacerbated when a team of programmers is working together on a large project.

A COMMON statement also may be used in a main program to enable easy reference to data that are manipulated by many of the main program's subprograms. When the COMMON statement appears in the main program, the data in the COMMON block are called *global data*. Each subprogram that references the global data must contain a COMMON statement similar to the one in the main program.

There are some restrictions on the use of COMMON storage, however, which we list next.

Restrictions on the Use of COMMON Storage

- A parameter cannot be stored in a COMMON block.
- A variable listed in a COMMON statement in a subprogram cannot also be a dummy argument for that subprogram.
- Variables of type CHARACTER cannot be combined with variables of other types in a COMMON block.
- Items in a COMMON block cannot appear in a SAVE or DATA statement.

These restrictions prevent us from placing MAXSIZ (a parameter) and NUMSTU (initialized by a DATA statement) in the COMMON block declared for subroutine OPRATE. They also prevent our placing the array NAMES (type CHARACTER *20) and the array SCORES together in a COMMON block.

The data in the COMMON block declared at the beginning of this section are automatically saved between calls to subroutine OPRATE. Therefore it's unnecessary (and illegal) to include SCORES in the variable list associated with the SAVE statement in OPRATE. The SAVE statement from Fig. 8.19,

```
SAVE NAMES, SCORES, GRADES, GRADED, SORTED, NUMSTU
```

should be rewritten as

```
SAVE NAMES, GRADES, GRADED, SORTED, NUMSTU
```

Name Independence of COMMON Data

The COMMON block declared in the previous section contains an array of 100 type INTEGER values. A different array name may be used to reference these INTEGER data in another subprogram. In fact, there is no requirement that the structure of the data be the same in all subprograms that reference the same COMMON block.

EXAMPLE 8.9

We could use the declarations

```
COMMON FIRST, MIDDLE(98), LAST
INTEGER FIRST, MIDDLE, LAST
```

in another subprogram to reference the 100 type INTEGER values in the COMMON block shown at the beginning of this section. In this case, the COMMON data would have the correspondence shown in Fig. 8.29. In the subprogram containing the COMMON statement given immediately above, the variable FIRST references the first cell of the COMMON block and the variable LAST references the last cell of the COMMON block. In subroutine OPRATE, the names of these cells are SCORES(1) and SCORES(100), respectively. ∎

Figure 8.29. *Correspondence of COMMON Data*

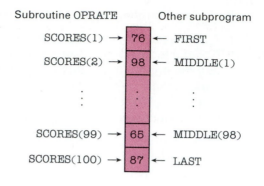

Even though this flexibility exists, we strongly recommend consistency in naming items in a COMMON block and duplicating the COMMON statement in each subprogram that contains it. Remember to declare the structure of each item in the COMMON block as well as its data type.

Named COMMON Blocks

In some cases, there may be variables that are shared by a group of subprograms in a program system but not by all the subprograms. Rather than include these variables in the general common storage area, one or more additional *named COMMON blocks* may be declared. The COMMON block described earlier is called the *blank COMMON block* because it has no name.

EXAMPLE 8.10

Several subprograms in Fig. 8.19 reference data stored in the character arrays NAMES and GRADES. These variables are not included in the blank COMMON block because there are many subprograms that don't reference them and because it's not possible to combine character data with noncharacter data in a COMMON block.

The declaration

```
COMMON /STUDAT/ NAMES(MAXSIZ), GRADES(MAXSIZ)
```

identifies NAMES and GRADES as belonging to the named COMMON block STUDAT. This named COMMON statement must appear in OPRATE and any subprogram that references these data without the use of argument lists. The type and structure of variables in named COMMON blocks also must be declared. The declarations for subroutine OPRATE shown in Fig. 8.30 include the blank COMMON block and the COMMON block named STUDAT. The new SAVE statement is explained in the next subsection, "The SAVE Statement and Named COMMON Blocks." ▪

Figure 8.30. *Declarations for Subroutine OPRATE*

```
      SUBROUTINE OPRATE (CHOICE, EXITCH)
C Performs the option selected by CHOICE
C Preconditions : 0 <= CHOICE <= EXITCH
C Postconditions: A subroutine is selected based on the value of CHOICE.

C Input Arguments
C    CHOICE — The number of the option selected (0 through EXITCH)
C    EXITCH — The number of the exit option

C Common Data
C    SCORES — Array of scores in blank COMMON
C    NAMES — Array of names in COMMON block STUDAT
C    GRADES — Array of grades in COMMON block STUDAT

C Argument Declarations
      INTEGER CHOICE, EXITCH

C Common Declarations
      INTEGER MAXSIZ
      PARAMETER (MAXSIZ = 100)
      COMMON SCORES(MAXSIZ)
      INTEGER SCORES
      COMMON /STUDAT/ NAMES(MAXSIZ), GRADES(MAXSIZ)
      CHARACTER *20 NAMES
      CHARACTER *1 GRADES

C Local Declarations
      INTEGER NUMSTU
      INTEGER MINSCR, MAXSCR
      REAL MEAN, STDEV, MEDIAN
      LOGICAL SORTED, GRADED
      INTEGER GETMIN, GETMAX
      REAL GETMED

C Save all local data between calls
      SAVE GRADED, SORTED, NUMSTU, /STUDAT/
      DATA NUMSTU /0/
```

EXAMPLE 8.11 The interface section for subroutine SORTNA ("sort by name") is shown in Fig. 8.31. The blank COMMON block and named COMMON block are both declared in SORTNA. The argument list for SORTNA contains only the dummy argument NUMSTU. The statement

```
CALL SORTNA (NUMSTU)
```

must be used in OPRATE to call subroutine SORTNA.

Figure 8.31. *Interface Section for SORTNA*

```
      SUBROUTINE SORTNA (NUMSTU)
C Rearranges the data in arrays NAMES, SCORES, and GRADES. When done,
C the data will be in alphabetical order by student name.
C Preconditions : 1 <= NUMSTU <= MAXSIZ
C Postconditions: NAMES(i) <= NAMES(i+1) for 1 <= i < NUMSTU.

C Input Argument
C    NUMSTU — The number of students in the arrays

C Common Data
C    SCORES — Array of scores in blank COMMON
C    NAMES — Array of names in COMMON block STUDAT
C    GRADES — Array of grades in COMMON block STUDAT

C Argument Declarations
      INTEGER NUMSTU

C Common Declarations
      INTEGER MAXSIZ
      PARAMETER (MAXSIZ = 100)
      COMMON SCORES(MAXSIZ)
      INTEGER SCORES
      COMMON /STUDAT/ NAMES(MAXSIZ), GRADES(MAXSIZ)
      CHARACTER *20 NAMES
      CHARACTER *1 GRADES
```

The COMMON statement for declaring blank and named COMMON blocks is described in the next display.

SYNTAX
DISPLAY

COMMON Declaration

SYNTAX: COMMON *list*
         COMMON */name/ list*

EXAMPLE: COMMON A, B(10)
          COMMON /HAT/ C, D

INTERPRETATION: The defined COMMON block is treated as one large array of consecutive memory cells containing data in the order indicated by the variables and arrays appearing in *list*. The statement

COMMON */name/ list*

defines a COMMON block called *name*. The declaration

COMMON *list*

defines a COMMON block with a blank name (the blank COMMON block). The COMMON declarations must precede the executable statements.

NOTE: Character data may not be placed in a COMMON block containing data of any other type (REAL, INTEGER, or LOGICAL).

Program Style: *Type Declarations for COMMON Data*

Each COMMON statement used in a module should be preceded or followed by one or more type declarations defining the type of each of the items listed in the COMMON statement. If arrays are included in a COMMON block, it is good practice to define the array sizes in the COMMON statement and not in the type declarations. Doing this can help provide a clear indication of the organization and structure of the COMMON block. All COMMON declarations should precede any executable statements. We recommend placing COMMON declarations at the very beginning of a main program and immediately following the argument descriptions in a subprogram.

The SAVE Statement and Named COMMON Blocks

Unlike data in the blank COMMON block, data in a named COMMON block can become undefined when a subprogram RETURN is executed. The contents of a named COMMON block are automatically saved upon return from a subprogram only if that block is declared in the main program or the subprogram that has called the current one. In all other cases, the COMMON block name must be listed in a SAVE statement to ensure its contents are saved.

Because COMMON block STUDAT is declared in OPRATE, its contents are automatically saved upon return from any subprogram called by OPRATE. However, the SAVE statement

SAVE GRADED, SORTED, NUMSTU, /STUDAT/

is needed in OPRATE to ensure the data in STUDAT are also saved upon return to the main program. The COMMON block name preceded and followed by a slash must be used in the SAVE list; the names of individual variables stored in blank COMMON or a named COMMON block cannot appear in a SAVE statement.

Warnings about COMMON

COMMON blocks appear to be a panacea to beginning programmers because they lead to shorter argument lists and in some cases, to the elimination of argument lists altogether. Unfortunately, improper use of COMMON blocks can cause program errors that are difficult to detect.

Passing data through argument lists has the advantage that the variables being used to pass and receive data are clearly listed in the subprogram call, thus providing valuable program documentation. Conversely, there is no indication of which variables in a COMMON block are likely to be modified by a subprogram. For this reason, extensive use of COMMON blocks can lead to programs that are difficult to read, understand, and maintain.

Another problem with using COMMON blocks is that as they grow, it becomes easier to make an error in the COMMON statement and to omit a variable name or to transpose two names. In these cases, because the correspondence between COMMON data items is based on relative position in the COMMON declaration, the wrong correspondence will be established. This type of error often is not detected by the compiler and can be extremely difficult to find. The best way to avoid it is to use your system editor to duplicate the COMMON statement wherever it is needed.

Another error that is difficult to detect and correct results from choosing a name for a local variable that happens to be a name listed in a COMMON statement. In this case, references to this "local variable" in the subprogram can cause the corresponding data item in COMMON to be modified as a *side effect* of the subprogram execution. This type of error is more likely to occur as the number of variables in the COMMON block increases.

The use of named COMMON blocks enables you to shorten individual COMMON statements, because only data items that are manipulated together are declared in the same named block. Also, only those named COMMON blocks that are needed by a particular subprogram are declared in that subprogram. For these reasons, using several named COMMON blocks instead of a single blank COMMON block is preferable.

Program Style: *What to Put in COMMON Storage*

The discussion in this subsection has focused on potential problems associated with the use of COMMON blocks. That there are potential problems with using these blocks doesn't mean they should be avoided altogether; rather, they should be used with discretion. We recommend you place in the blank COMMON block only data that are referenced by almost all the subprograms in a program system. You should assume that these data can be manipulated by every subprogram and would be included in almost every argument list anyway.

You can place data that are referenced by a smaller group of subprograms in a named COMMON block. Only subprograms containing the declaration of this named COMMON block will be able to manipulate these data directly. Individual variables in a named COMMON block may be passed as arguments to other subprograms that do not declare the named COMMON block.

Finally, it is reasonable to have more than one named COMMON block declared in a program. One group of subprograms may reference certain data, and another may reference a different collection of data. By setting up several named COMMON blocks, you can restrict access to the named COMMON block(s) needed in each subprogram.

EXERCISES FOR SECTION 8.7

Self-check

1. What printed values result from the execution of the following program and subroutine?

```
PROGRAM TSTCOM
COMMON A, B
REAL A, B
REAL C
CALL JUMBLE (C)
PRINT *, A, B, C
STOP
END
```

```
SUBROUTINE JUMBLE (X)
REAL X
COMMON A, B
REAL A, B
A = 1.0
B = 2.0
X = 4.0
RETURN
END
```

2. What printed values result from the execution of the following program and subroutines?

```
PROGRAM TEST2
COMMON /WHAT/ NEXT(5)
INTEGER NEXT
INTEGER I
CALL DEFINE (NEXT, 5)
CALL EXCH (1, 4)
I = 2
CALL EXCH (I, I+1)
PRINT *, NEXT
STOP
END
```

```
SUBROUTINE DEFINE (ARRAY, SIZE)
INTEGER SIZE, ARRAY(*)
INTEGER I
DO 40 I = 1, SIZE
    ARRAY(I) = 2 * I - 1
40 CONTINUE
RETURN
END
```

```
SUBROUTINE EXCH (S1, S2)
INTEGER S1, S2
COMMON /WHAT/ NEXT(5)
INTEGER NEXT
INTEGER TEMP
TEMP = NEXT(S1)
NEXT(S1) = NEXT(S2)
NEXT(S2) = TEMP
RETURN
END
```

What is the relationship between the variable I in the main program and the variable I in subroutine DEFINE? Why is it unnecessary to declare the COMMON block WHAT in subroutine DEFINE?

8.8 Common Programming Errors

1. When you use multidimensional arrays, ensure the subscript for each dimension is always in range; otherwise, a run-time error may occur.
2. If you declare a multidimensional array as a subprogram dummy argument, you must specify the correct sizes for all dimensions except the last one. The symbol * may be used to represent the size of the last dimension only.
3. If you use nested DO loops to process the elements of a multidimensional array, ensure the loop-control variables used as array subscripts are in the correct order. The order of the loop-control variables determines the sequence in which the array elements are processed.
4. Algorithms for searching and sorting arrays can sometimes cause subscript-range errors. Ensure each array reference is in range at the boundary values of the loop-control variable.
5. Argument list errors are the major source of difficulty in using subroutines. The actual argument list must have the same number of arguments as does the dummy argument list. Also, the data type and structure (variable or array) of each actual argument must match the data type and structure of its corresponding dummy argument.
6. Passing some data through COMMON blocks may help to reduce the length of the argument list; however, COMMON blocks can cause problems of their own. Changing the value of a "local" variable that also happens to be declared in a COMMON block can cause a side-effect error. These errors are extremely difficult to detect, since there may be no documentation in a subroutine indicating what COMMON block data should be manipulated by the subroutine. When all data are communicated through argument lists, this documentation is automatically provided by the argument list itself. Ensure you don't attempt to list either a dummy argument or a parameter in a COMMON block.

Chapter Review

In this chapter, we showed how to use multidimensional arrays to represent tables of information and game boards. A nested loop structure is needed to manipulate the elements of a multidimensional array in a systematic way. The correspondence between the loop-control variables and the array subscripts determines the order in which the array elements are processed.

Techniques for searching and sorting an array were introduced along with several examples of subprograms with array arguments.

We also wrote a function that generates random numbers and showed how to use this function in a simulation program. We described how to use COMMON storage to pass information between a main program and its subprograms.

Fortran
Statements

The Fortran statements introduced in this chapter are described in Table 8.1.

Table 8.1. *Summary of Fortran Statements for Chapter 8*

STATEMENT	EFFECT
Multidimensional Array Declaration	
`REAL SALES (52, 7)`	Allocates storage for 52 × 7, or 364, REAL numbers. The first subscript may represent the week (1 to 52) and the second subscript the day (1 to 7).
Array References	
`PRINT *, SALES(3, 5)`	Displays the sales amount for week 3 and day 5.

`DO 10 WEEK = 1, 52`
`   DO 20 DAY = 1, 7`
`      SALES(WEEK, DAY) = 0.0`
`20   CONTINUE`
`10 CONTINUE`
	Initializes each element of SALES to zero.

Array Initialization	
`DATA SALES /364 * 0.0/`	Initializes each element of SALES to zero.
Blank COMMON Declaration	

`COMMON X(100), N`
`REAL X`
`INTEGER N`
	Declares a blank COMMON block consisting of an array X with 100 type REAL elements and an INTEGER variable N.

Named COMMON Declaration	
`COMMON /INBLOK/ Y(100), Z(5)` `REAL Y, Z`	Declares a COMMON block named INBLOK consisting of an array Y with 100 REAL elements and an array Z with five REAL elements.
SAVE Statement	
`SAVE COUNT, FLAT, /INBLOK/`	Specifies that the values of local variables COUNT and FLAG and COMMON block INBLOK are to be saved between subprogram calls.

Quick-check Exercises

1. How many subscripts can a Fortran array have?
2. What is the difference between row-major and column-major order? Which does Fortran use for array storage?
3. How many elements does array MULTI(5, −5:5, 10) have? List the first six elements and the last element in the array storage area.
4. Which control structure is used to process all elements in a multidimensional array?
5. If array LIST is an array with six REAL elements, what does the following program fragment do?

```
      DO 10 I = 1, 5
         LIST(I + 1) = LIST(1)
   10 CONTINUE
```

6. Answer exercise 5 for the program fragment

```
      DO 20 I = 2, 6
         LIST(I − 1) = LIST(I)
   20 CONTINUE
```

7. Subroutine SWITCH has two type REAL arguments, and SWITCH exchanges the values of its arguments. Write a statement that calls SWITCH to exchange the first and last elements in array LIST.
8. Are type and structure correspondence for the items in two COMMON block lists as important as for argument lists? Is this correspondence required for COMMON block lists?
9. List one advantage and two disadvantages of using COMMON blocks.
10. Are all local variable values automatically saved with a SAVE statement between calls of a subprogram? Explain your answer.

Answers to Quick-check Exercises

1. seven
2. Row-major order means the elements are processed one row at a time; column-major order means they are processed one column at a time. Fortran uses column-major order.
3. 5 × 11 × 10, or 550, elements. The first six elements are MULTI(1, −5, 1), MULTI(2, −5, 1), MULTI(3, −5, 1), MULTI(4, −5, 1), MULTI(5, −5, 1), MULTI(1, −4, 1). The last element is MULTI(5, 5, 10).
4. nested DO loops
5. It copies the value of LIST(1) into all elements of array LIST.
6. It shifts all array elements up by one position (i.e., LIST(2) moves up to LIST(1), LIST(3) moves up to LIST(2), and so on.)
7. CALL SWITCH (LIST(1), LIST(6))
8. Yes, they are just as important to prevent misalignment of COMMON list elements. Type and structure correspondence of individual items are not required.

9. An advantage is shorter argument lists. One disadvantage is lack of documentation regarding the COMMON list elements that are being manipulated in a subprogram. Another disadvantage is the possibility of inadvertent side effects caused by misalignment of COMMON list items.
10. Only the local variables listed in the SAVE statement are saved. If there is no list of variables, all local variables are saved.

Review Questions

1. Declare an array that can be used to store each title of the top 10 hits for each week of the year. Each title can be up to 20 characters.
2. Declare an array HOURS to store the hours that each of five employees works each day of the week, each week of the year. Write a nest of DO loops that initializes this array to all zeros. Also, provide a DATA statement that does the same task.
3. Write a program segment to display the sum of the REAL values in each row of array TABLE (5, 3). How many row sums will be displayed? How many elements are included in each sum?
4. Answer question 3 for the column sums.
5. Trace the operation of a bubble sort on the array

   20 30 25 80 40 60

   Show the array after each pass is completed. Assume we are sorting in increasing order.
6. Write a DO loop that shifts all elements of the array LIST(6) down one position (i.e., move LIST(1) down to LIST(2), LIST(2) down to LIST(3), and so on).
7. What is the reason for using both named COMMON and blank COMMON blocks?
8. The subroutine PSUM computes the sum of elements I through J of an array. PSUM has six arguments:

   - The name of the array of items to be summed (real, input)
   - The size of the array (integer, input)
   - The index of the first array element included in the sum (integer, input)
   - The index of the last array element included in the sum (integer, input)
   - A flag used to indicate whether an illegal array index occurred (an array index is illegal if it is out of bounds or if the index of the first element to be summed exceeds the index of the last element to be summed) (logical, output)
   - The sum of the selected elements (sum is zero if an index is illegal) (real, output)

   Write a CALL statement for each of the following circumstances. Assume A is a real array of MAXSIZ elements and FIRST and LAST are integer variables. Use the actual output arguments VALID (logical) and SUM (real) for each reference to PSUM.

   a. Compute the sum of all the elements of A.
   b. Compute the sum of the FIRST through LAST elements of A.
   c. Compute the sum of the FIRST + 4 through LAST elements of A.
   d. Compute the sum of the second through seventh elements of A.
   e. Compute the sum of the FIRST through 2 * LAST elements of A.

9. Assume that A, MAXSIZ, FIRST, and LAST contain the following values:

A(1) A(2) A(3) A(4) A(5) A(6) A(7) A(8) A(9) A(10)

4.2	1.1	0.0	3.0	7.1	2.2	0.0	8.1	3.7	6.8

MAXSIZ   FIRST   LAST

10	3	6

What are the values of SUM and VALID after execution of each of the CALL statements you wrote for question 8?

10. Write the COMMON declaration and type declarations needed to define a COMMON block named EMPBLK, which contains the following items in the order listed:

- An integer array NUMDEP of size 50
- A real array SALARY of size 100
- An integer variable N
- An integer variable COUNT
- A real variable X
- A real variable Y

Could you include a CHARACTER *30 array NAME in this COMMON block?

11. Write the subroutine PSUM described in question 8.

Fortran 90 Features: Matrix Operations and Modules

Array Declarations

Fortran 90 provides an alternate form for declarations. Identifiers M, N, and P declared below represent two-dimensional arrays. Arrays M and N have 5 rows and 10 columns, and array P has 10 rows and 5 columns. Array N has row subscripts 1 through 5 and column subscripts 6 through 15. Array P has row subscripts 1 through 10 and column subscripts 1 through 5.

```
REAL, DIMENSION (5, 10) :: M
REAL, DIMENSION (5, 6 : 15) :: N
REAL, DIMENSION (10, 5) :: P
```

Rank, Shape, and Size of Multidimensional Arrays

The *rank* of an array is the number of dimensions of the array. The rank of a scalar (simple variable or value) is 0; the rank of a one-dimensional array, or *vector*, is 1; the rank of a two-dimensional array, or *matrix*, is 2; and so on. Arrays M, N, and P have a rank of 2.

The *shape* of array M is an array of rank 1 with one element for each dimension of array M. The value of each element in the shape of an array represents the number of elements in that dimension. Arrays M and N declared above have 5 rows and 10 columns, so their shape is the vector with 2 elements denoted as /5, 10/. The *size* of an array is the total number of elements in the array; for example, the size of arrays M and N are 50 (5 × 10).

Two arrays are *conformable* if they have the same shape, so M and N are conformable arrays. Conformable arrays can be used as operands of the Fortran operators. The following statements are all valid and assign new values to all 50 elements of array M.

```
M = N          ! M(I, J) gets N(I, J+5)
M = M + N      ! M(I, J) gets M(I, J) + N(I, J+5)
M = MAX(M, N)  ! M(I, J) gets larger of M(I, J) and N(I, J+5)
```

The MAX function returns the maximum value of its arguments.

Array Sections

Array sections for a multidimensional array can have the same number of dimensions as the original array or fewer dimensions. Several sections of array M are shown next.

```
M(3:5, 8:10) ! a two-dimensional array with row subscript
             ! 3 through 5 and column subscript 8 through 10
M( : ,  : 5) ! a two-dimensional array with row subscript
             ! 1 through 5 and column subscript 1 through 5
M(2,  : )    ! a one-dimensional array consisting of all
             ! elements in row 2
M( : , 5)    ! a one-dimensional array consisting of all
             ! elements in column 5
M(3:5, 10)   ! a one-dimensional array consisting of the
             ! third, fourth, and fifth elements of column 10
```

The notation $l : u$ for a particular dimension specifies the lower bound (l) and upper bound (u) of that dimension. If l is missing, the lower bound in the array declaration is assumed; if u is missing, the upper bound in the array declaration is assumed. If a single integer value is used for a particular dimension, the subscript for that dimension is fixed at the indicated value and the rank of the array section is reduced by one.

Intrinsic Functions and the DIM Parameter

All intrinsic functions described on p. 398 can be used with multidimensional array arguments with the exception of the function DOT_PRODUCT. For example, the function reference SUM(M) returns the sum of all elements in matrix M.

Each function can be used with an optional DIM parameter to return a result array whose rank is one less than the array argument. The value of DIM indicates which dimension is being eliminated. For example, the function reference SUM(M, DIM = 2) returns a one-dimensional array with 5 elements: The first element is the sum of elements in array section M(1, :) or row 1; the second element is the sum of elements in array section M(2, :) or row 2; and so on. The function reference SUM(M, DIM = 1) returns a one-dimensional array with 10 elements: The first element is the sum of elements in array section M(: , 1) or column 1; the second element is the sum of elements in array section M(: , 2) or column 2; and so on.

New Intrinsic Functions

The following two intrinsic functions require matrix arguments:

```
MATMUL(M, P) ! Multiplies matrix M by matrix P
TRANSPOSE(N) ! Transposes matrix N
```

The result of MATMUL(M, P) is a square matrix with 5 rows and 5 columns.

Other intrinsic functions also can perform operations on arrays with one or more dimensions, as follows:

```
LBOUND(M) ! Returns a rank 1 array whose elements represent
          ! the lower subscript bound for each dimension
SHAPE(M)  ! Returns a rank 1 array whose elements represent
          ! the number of elements in each dimension
SIZE(M)   ! Returns an integer representing the number of
          ! elements in array M
UBOUND(M) ! Returns a rank 1 array whose elements represent
          ! the upper subscript bound for each dimension
```

Modules

Fortran 90 provides a module feature that enables the programmer to group together, that is, *encapsulate*, a set of declarations for data objects (variables and arrays) and subprograms that operate on those data objects. The full use of modules is beyond the scope of this text, but we will show how modules can be used to simplify the specification of COMMON data.

Module blank_common contains declarations for an integer array (scores) and a parameter (max_size). In addition to these data, module stu_data contains declarations for two character arrays.

```
MODULE blank_common
    INTEGER max_size
    PARAMETER (max_size = 100)
    INTEGER scores(max_size)
END MODULE blank_common
```

```
MODULE stu_data
   USE blank_common

   CHARACTER *20 names(max_size)
   CHARACTER *1 grades(max_size)
END MODULE stu_data
```

Each module should be saved in its own source file and compiled separately. The statement

```
USE blank_common
```

appearing in module stu_data indicates that stu_data has access to all the declarations in module blank_common. This frees us from having to declare parameter max_size in both modules. Module stu_data is called a *client* of blank_common. Module blank_common must be compiled before module stu_data or any other client module is compiled.

If a program or another module uses both modules, the client's declarations must be preceded by the statement

```
USE blank_common, stu_data
```

and both modules must be compiled before their client. (If only module blank_common or stu_data is needed, then only that module name should appear in the USE statement.) Using modules in this way is simpler than using COMMON declarations to accomplish the same purpose.

Programming Projects

1. Use a two-dimensional array of individual characters to store a collection of five words where each word is up to 20 characters in length. Enter each word one character at a time. For each word read, your program should do the following:

   a. Print the actual length of the word.
   b. Count the number of occurrences of four-letter words.

2. The results from the mayor's race have been reported by each precinct as follows:

Precinct	Candidate A	Candidate B	Candidate C	Candidate D
1	192	48	206	37
2	147	90	312	21
3	186	12	121	38
4	114	21	408	39
5	267	13	382	29

Write a program to do the following:

a. Print the table with appropriate headings for the rows and columns.
b. Compute and print the total number of votes received by each candidate and the percentage of the total votes cast.
c. If any one candidate received over 50 percent of the votes, the program should print a message declaring that candidate the winner.
d. If no candidate received at least 50 percent of the votes, the program should print a message declaring a run-off between the two candidates receiving the highest number of votes; the two candidates should be identified by their letter names.
e. Run the program once with the above data and once with candidate C receiving only 108 votes in precinct 4.

3. Write a subroutine, MERGE, that will merge together the contents of two sorted (ascending order) real arrays A and B, storing the result (still in ascending order) in the real array C.

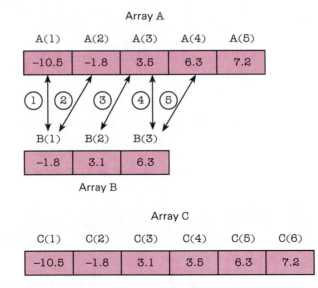

Array A

	A(1)	A(2)	A(3)	A(4)	A(5)
	−10.5	−1.8	3.5	6.3	7.2

	B(1)	B(2)	B(3)
	−1.8	3.1	6.3

Array B

Array C

	C(1)	C(2)	C(3)	C(4)	C(5)	C(6)
	−10.5	−1.8	3.1	3.5	6.3	7.2

(*Hint:* When one of the input arrays has been exhausted, don't forget to copy the remaining data in the other array into the array C.) Test your subroutine using a representative set of unsorted data in the arrays A and B. Sort both arrays before calling your MERGE subroutine. Use either COMMON blocks or subprogram arguments for data communication among the various modules you write.

4. The following binary search algorithm may be used to search an array when the elements are in order.

Algorithm for Binary Search

1. Let BOTTOM be the subscript of the first array element.
2. Let TOP be N.

3. Let FOUND be false.
4. DO WHILE BOTTOM is less than TOP and FOUND is false
    5. Let MIDDLE be the subscript of the element halfway between BOTTOM and TOP.
    6. IF the element at MIDDLE is the target THEN
        Set FOUND to true and INDEX to MIDDLE.
    ELSE IF the element at MIDDLE is larger than the target THEN
        Let TOP be MIDDLE-1.
    ELSE
        Let BOTTOM be MIDDLE+1.
    END IF
  END DO

Write and test subroutine BNSRCH. Which of the subroutines SEARCH and BNSRCH do you think is faster when N is a large number?

5. The selection sort is another technique for sorting an array. In the selection sort, the first pass through the array finds the largest value in the array and the subscript of the largest value. The largest value is then switched with the value in the last position of the array, which places the largest value in the last position, where it belongs, much like the bubble sort. The process is then repeated (the second pass) but the last position is not included in the search for the largest value. After the second pass, the second-largest value is now known and can be switched with the value currently in the second position from the end of the array. This process continues until each item is in its correct location and requires N-1 passes to sort an array of N elements (why?). Write and test a subroutine that implements this method to sort an array.

6. Write a subroutine that will determine the dot product of two square (N × N) arrays. The dot product, array C, of some elements of arrays A and B is defined as follows:

```
C(1,1) = A(1,1) * B(1,1) + A(1,2) * B(2,1) + A(1,3) * B(3,1)
C(2,3) = A(2,1) * B(1,3) + A(2,2) * B(2,3) + A(2,3) * B(3,3)
C(i,j) = A(i,1) * B(1,j) + A(i,2) * B(2,j) + A(i,3) * B(3,j)
```

The dot product of arrays A and B is as follows:

```
N = 3
A =  |4 5 1|        |2  1 10|
     |0 2 5|  B  =  |5 20  0|
     |1 6 1|        |4  0  5|

     |37 104 45|
C =  |30  40 25|
     |36 121 15|
```

7. Write a program to test the uniform nature of function RANDOM in Fig. 8.25. Use this function to generate 500 integer values between 1 and 10, save the occurrence

counts in an array, and then draw a bar graph of the occurrence counts. We would expect to see approximately the same number of occurrences of each integer.

8. Suppose the melting points of a series of samples have been measured during several trials. The results have been stored in the NMAT by NTRIAL real array MELT so that MELT(I,J) is the melting point of the ith sample on the jth trial. Because of the probability of experimental error, the lowest measured melting point for each sample is to be eliminated from the data. In addition, any sample whose melting point on the last trial was recorded as negative is to be eliminated. Write a Fortran subroutine that will take the array MELT and calculate a singly subscripted array AVGMEL containing the average (after dropping the lowest) melting points of each sample not eliminated. AVGMEL and the number of samples not dropped (NREM) should be returned to the calling program. In addition, the subroutine should write the number of samples at the beginning (NMAT) and the number that have been dropped in the following format at the top of a new page:

```
We started the experiments with XXX samples.
YYY have been eliminated.
```

You must use formatted output. The values of NMAT, NTRIAL, and MELT will be supplied from the calling program. Your subroutine should not contain any READs. All parameters should be passed through the argument list. You may assume $1 \leq$ NMAT ≤ 300 and $1 \leq$ NTRIAL ≤ 10.

9. Write a program that simulates the movement of radioactive particles in a two-dimensional shield around a reactor. A particle in the shield can move in one of four directions. The direction for the next second of travel is determined by generation of a random number between 1 and 4 (forward, backward, left, right). A change in direction is interpreted as a collision with another particle, which results in a dissipation of energy. Each particle can have only a limited number of collisions before it dies.

   For each particle that enters the shield, determine whether that particle exits the shield before it dies. A particle exits the shield if its net forward travel time is N seconds before K collisions occur (i.e., it takes N more forward steps than backward steps). Determine the percentage of particles that exit the shield where N, K, and the number of particles are data items.

10. For the case study in Section 8.2, we wrote a program that removed noise from a picture. We can generate a noisy image from a nonnoisy one by adding random noise. Write a program that randomly selects the coordinates of several points (say 10 percent of the total) in a two-dimensional image and then randomly selects an integer value for that pixel. Next, for each pixel that is not on the edge of the image, select one of three values $(-1, 0,$ or $1)$ at random and add it to the pixel value. Ensure you change any negative pixel values back to zero. After perturbing your image in this way, run it through the image enhancement program to see what you get.

11. Mahogany Airlines stores its reservation information in a file RESERV. For each flight, there are up to 100 lines of information, one for each row in the plane. Each line consists of up to 10 values, one for each seat in a row. For any seat, a value of 0 indicates the seat is empty and a value of 1 indicates the seat is full.

Write a Fortran program to read the reservation information on file RESERV into a two-dimensional integer array SEATS and then find and print all pairs of adjacent empty seats. You may ignore the aisles in the plane and assume that seats on either side of an aisle are adjacent; thus the location of the aisle(s) is irrelevant to the problem. If more than two adjacent seats are empty, all adjacent empty pairs should still be printed (for example, if four adjacent seats are empty, three pairs should be printed)

Use PARAMETER statements wherever possible, in case larger planes are ever built (of course, they already exist).

Your output should appear as follows:

```
     MAHOGANY AIRLINES
ADJACENT PAIRS OF SEATS ANALYSIS


      Available Seat Pairs


  Row Number        Seat Number
  _____        _____


      xxx              xx-xx
      xxx              xx-xx
       .                .
       .                .
       .                .
```

12. Statistical analysis of data makes heavy use of arrays. One such analysis, called *cross-tabulation*, is used to help decide whether a relationship exists between two or more variables. For example, the following data might represent opinions from a survey taken concerning an amendment to the U.S. Constitution making it illegal to destroy or damage the U.S. flag in any way:

	Sex		*Row*
Opinion	*Male*	*Female*	*Total*
In Favor	63	27	90
Opposed	19	42	61
No Opinion	6	39	45
Column Total	88	108	196

Write a Fortran program that will read in the following pairs of male/female response totals (one pair per line)

```
63   27
19   42
 6   39
```

and print out the above cross-tabulation matrix including the row totals and the column totals.

The program should also print out the percentage in each category. For example, we would want to know that the 39 females with no opinion represent 36 percent of the total females interviewed and 87 percent of those with no opinion. Present all output as attractively as possible.

13. The game of Life, invented by John H. Conway, is supposed to model the genetic laws for birth, survival, and death (see *Scientific American*, October 1970, p. 120). We will play it on a board consisting of 25 squares in the horizontal and vertical directions. Each square can be empty or contain an X indicating the presence of an organism. Each square (except the border squares) has eight neighbors. The small square shown in the segment of the board drawn below connects the neighbors of the organism in row three, column three:

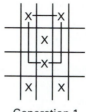

Generation 1

The next generation of organisms is determined according to the following criteria:

a. Birth: An organism will be born in each empty location that has exactly three neighbors.
b. Death: An organism with four or more organisms as neighbors will die from overcrowding. An organism with fewer than two neighbors will die from loneliness.
c. Survival: An organism with two or three neighbors will survive to the next generation. Generations 2 and 3 for the sample follow:

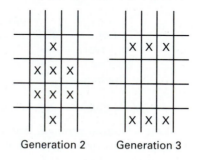

Generation 2   Generation 3

Read in an initial configuration of organisms. Print the original game array, calculate the next generation of organisms in a new array, copy the new array into the original game array, and repeat the cycle for as many generations as you wish. (*Hint:* Assume that the borders of the game array are infertile regions where organisms can neither survive nor be born; you will not have to process the border squares.)

14. A mail order house with the physical facilities for stocking up to 200 circuit boards decides it wants to maintain inventory control records on a small computer. For each stock item, the following data are to be stored on the computer:

    1. The stock number (a five-digit integer)
    2. A count of the number of items on hand
    3. The total year-to-date sales count
    4. The price
    5. The date (month and day) of the last order for restocking an item (a four-digit integer of the form MMDD)
    6. The number of items ordered

    Both items 5 and 6 will be zero if there is no outstanding order for an item.

    Design and implement a program system to keep track of the data listed in 1 through 6. You will need six arrays, each of size 200. Your system should contain subprograms to perform the following tasks:

    a. Change the price of an item (given the item stock number and the new price).
    b. Add a new item to the inventory list (given the item number, the price, and the initial stock on hand).
    c. Enter information about the date and size of a restock order.
    d. Reset items 5 and 6 to zero and update the amount on hand when a restock order is received.
    e. Increase the total sales and decrease the count on hand each time a purchase order is received (if the order cannot be filled, print a message to that effect and reset the counts).
    f. Search for the array element that contains a given stock number.

    The following information should be initially stored in memory (using data initialization (DATA) statements). This information should be printed at the start of execution of your program system.

Stock Numbers	On-hand Count	Price
02421	12	100.00
00801	24	32.49
63921	50	4.99
47447	100	6.99
47448	48	2.25
19012	42	18.18
86932	3	67.20

    Write a menu-driven program that can be used to keep the inventory up-to-date. Your program should handle options (a) through (f) by reading in the required data and calling the appropriate subprogram. Each subprogram should print an appropriate informative message for each transaction, indicating whether the transaction was processed and giving other pertinent information about changes in the stored data that were affected by the processing of the transaction.

15. A program to calculate grades should have flexibility unless the instructor using it is inflexible. Assume that Dr. Prof is a flexible person and sometimes lets his students skip tests, quizzes, or projects as rewards for exemplary performance.

The first five lines of a grade file are assumed to look like the following:

```
Max Grades              10   10   10   10   20  100
Weights                 1.0  1.0  1.0  2.0  1.0  1.0
Angel, Angelia  568475675   9    8   10   10   17   83
Babuska, Bambino 432434321   8    9    9    9   18   82
Carmen, Carlotta 123434234  10   10   10   10        99
```

The first record indicates the maximum grade for each entry; the second indicates the weight to be applied to the entry. The records indicated here are worth a total of 170 points, since the fourth column of grades has a weight of 2.0. Dr. Prof does not include grades for tests skipped in calculating averages, so Ms. Carmen's grade is to be based upon a total of 150 points. Write this program to read such a file, output the grades and averages for each person, and output the averages for each grade column. This program should include a function that calculates the averages for each student. (*Hint:* This function should have at least three arguments that are arrays.)

16. Write a program to simulate a game of tic-tac-toe. The input is the initial position of the first 'X'. The program then should simulate subsequent moves by selecting squares at random among those remaining until someone wins the game or it ends in a "draw." The output should be the final configuration and a message indicating the outcome. For each initial move, five simulations should be done. The tic-tac-toe "board" may be represented by a 3×3 integer array.

Initially all entries should be zero, corresponding to "blank." Use a '1' to represent an 'X' and a '2' to represent a '0'. To identify the individual squares, we arbitrarily number them beginning at the "upper left": $(1, 1) \rightarrow 1$; $(1, 2) \rightarrow 2$; $(1, 3) \rightarrow 3$; $(2, 1) \rightarrow 4$; $(2, 2) \rightarrow 5$; $(2, 3) \rightarrow 6$; $(3, 1) \rightarrow 7$; $(3, 2) \rightarrow 8$; $(3, 3) \rightarrow 9$. Thus if the initial position is read as a 6, the game would start with the following:

0	0	0
0	0	1
0	0	0

We then have 8 remaining squares: $\{1, 2, 3, 4, 5, 7, 8, 9\}$. Choosing a random number between 1 and 8, suppose we get 7. The seventh entry in our list of remaining squares is 8, so we put a 2 in the eighth square

0	0	0
0	0	1
0	2	0

and check to see if the game is over. In this case it is not. Our list of remaining squares now has 7 numbers—{1, 2, 3, 4, 5, 7, 9}—so we select a random number between 1 and 7, say 3. The third entry is 3 so we put a 1 in square three

0	0	1
0	0	1
0	2	0

and again check to see if the game is over. Because it is not, we choose a random number from 1 to 6 in order to select one of the six remaining squares {1, 2, 4, 5, 7, 9}, and so forth.

Your program should call a function to generate a random number between 1 and N; a function CHECK that will examine a board to determine whether 'X' has won, 'O' has won, the game ends in a draw, or the game is not over; and a subroutine UPDATE that will update the board by making one move as described.

17. Matrixes and simple matrix operations often are utilized to conveniently organize, display, and manipulate data. As a simple example, suppose an electronics company begins with the raw materials copper, zinc, glass, and plastic and from them produces transistors, resistors, buttons, cases, and computer chips. These latter five products are then combined to produce three types of hand calculators—T-1, T-2, and T-3. We form the following array showing the amount of each raw material used in the intermediate products:

		Transistors	Resistors	Buttons	Cases	Chips
A =	copper	2	2	0	0	3
	zinc	1	1	0	0	2
	glass	1	2	0	1	1
	plastic	0	0	1	3	0

For example, the first entry tells us that 2 units of copper are used in each transistor.

The next array shows the number of intermediate products used in each calculator:

		T-1	T-2	T-3
B =	transistors	5	6	10
	resistors	7	8	16
	buttons	20	25	45
	cases	1	1	1
	chips	4	6	10

For example, there are 5 transistors in each T-1 calculator.

Additional information also may be formulated as arrays as follows:

- D = demand array, indicating the demand for each type of calculator
- C = cost array, indicating the cost per unit of each raw material
- L = labor array, indicating the labor cost involved in each type of calculator
- P = price array, indicating the selling price of each calculator

Then, matrix operations can be used to find the following:

- X = array showing amount of raw materials used in each calculator, e.g., $X(1, 2)$ = amount of copper used in T-2; $X = AB$
- Y = array showing profit to be made per unit on each type of calculator; $Y = P - (CX + L)$
- Z = array showing total profit if calculators are made and sold according to the demand array; $Z = YP$

Write a program that will input the arrays A, B, D, C, L, and P as well as suitable character arrays containing the names of the various raw materials, products, and calculators. As each array is input, it should be written out and clearly labeled in a format similar to that given above. Your program then should use matrix operations as appropriate to calculate X, Y, and Z and write them out, suitably labeled. Your program must include subroutines as follows:

1. Subroutine for matrix multiplication: MATMPY(NRA, NCA, A, NRB, NCB, B, NRC, NCC, C, IERROR), which is a general subroutine to multiply the NRA × NCA matrix A by the NRB × NCB matrix B to obtain the NRC × NCC matrix C. The subroutine should contain a test to determine that C = A × B is defined, using IERROR as a signal (IERROR = 1 if OK, IERROR = 0 if not).
2. Subroutine for matrix addition/subtraction: MATAD(NRA, NCA, A, NRB, NCB, B, NRC, NCC, C, ISIGN, IERROR), which is a general subroutine to add/subtract the NRA × NCA matrix A and the NRB × NCB matrix B to obtain the NRC × NCC matrix C with ISIGN used to indicate addition or subtraction (ISIGN = 1 for A + B, ISIGN = −1 for A − B) and IERROR as a signal for the operation being defined (IERROR = 1 if OK, IERROR = 0 if not).

Design your program to handle situations involving different numbers of raw materials, intermediate products, and finished goods and to process variable numbers of data sets. Run your program for the following:

a. A and B as in the previous discussion
b. Demand = 25 of T-1, 20 of T-2, and 35 of T-3
c. Cost = $.05 per unit copper, $.03 per unit zinc, $.01 per unit glass, $.025 per unit plastic
d. Labor = $2.50 for T-1, $3.00 for T-2, and $3.50 for T-3
e. Price = $15 for T-1, $12 for T-2, and $25 for T-3.

(*Note:* You may assume the various data are to be input in consistent order; i.e., if glass is the first row of A, then glass is the first component of the cost vector, etc.)

18. Suppose each of the four edges of a thin square metal plate is maintained at a constant temperature and we want to determine the temperature at each interior

point of the plate. To model the plate, we can use a two-dimensional array with each array element representing the temperature at a point on the plate.

Write a Fortran program that reads the four constant temperatures along the edges of the plate and then uses these values to initialize the outer rows and columns of the array and initialize the other elements of the array to zero. For the four corner points, use the average of the corresponding two edge temperatures. Then determine the equilibrium temperature at each interior point by repeatedly averaging the temperatures at each of its four "neighbors"; that is, replace each array element by the average of the elements immediately left and right of it and above and below it. Repeat this procedure until the new temperature at each interior point differs from the old temperature at that point by no more than EPSLON. Then print the array and the number of iterations used to produce the final result. Design your program to test the case of "immediate" updating (begin with the first interior row and proceed across each row, changing the interior elements immediately so that the latest value is used in the calculation of the next element). It also should test the case where all the elements are calculated using the previous values. Compare the number of iterations required for both of these approaches. Run your program for EPSLON = .01 and the following data:

Array Size	Top Temp	Bottom Temp	Left Temp	Right Temp
5 × 7	100	90	75	75
10 × 10	60	60	60	60
8 × 5	112.3	81.4	93.7	98.6

Sample output for the first array follows:

```
ARRAY

87.5   100.0   100.0   100.0   100.0   100.0   87.5
75.0    87.9    92.5    93.8    92.5    87.9   75.0
75.0    83.9    88.6    90.0    88.6    83.9   75.0
75.0    84.2    87.9    89.0    87.9    84.2   75.0
82.5    90.0    90.0    90.0    90.0    90.0   82.5


ITERATION COUNT =  35 (without immediate updating)

ARRAY

87.5   100.0   100.0   100.0   100.0   100.0   87.5
75.0    87.9    92.6    93.8    92.6    87.9   75.0
75.0    83.9    88.6    90.0    88.6    83.9   75.0
75.0    84.2    87.9    89.0    87.9    84.2   75.0
82.5    90.0    90.0    90.0    90.0    90.0   82.5


ITERATION COUNT =  20 (with immediate updating)
```

19. Baggage's, a software retailer, is considering setting up a new distribution center in Florida. They have come to you for help in locating their warehouse. They want the distribution center to serve the cities listed in the following table.

LOC. #	CITY	X–Y LOCATION	DEMAND
1	BOCA RATON	137, −218	280
2	GAINESVILLE	0, 0	315
3	JACKSONVILLE	36, 48	290
4	MIAMI	129, −259	350
5	ORLANDO	56, −73	400
6	PENSACOLA	−340, 48	280
7	TAMPA	−16, −113	360

The optimal location of the distribution center can be found by solving the Single Facility Squared Euclidean-Distance Location Problem. The solution to this problem identifies the optimal X–Y-coordinates for the warehouse. The solution follows:

$$X^* = \frac{\sum_{I=1}^{M} W(I) \times X(I)}{\sum_{I=1}^{M} W(I)}$$

and

$$Y^* = \frac{\sum_{I=1}^{M} W(I) \times Y(I)}{\sum_{I=1}^{M} W(I)}$$

where X^* = the optimal X location for the warehouse, Y^* = the optimal Y location for the warehouse, M = the number of service locations, $X(I)$, $Y(I)$ = the location of service location I, and $W(I)$ = the relative weight of demand of service location I. Implement a program to do the following:

1. Read in the data file. Each line of the data file should contain the name, the X–Y location, and the demand of a location to be serviced.
2. Display the values of the input file.
3. Calculate and print the optimal X–Y location for the warehouse.
4. Calculate and print the distance between each service location and the optimal warehouse location.

A sample data file follows:

```
'BOCA RATON', 137, −218, 280
'GAINESVILLE', 0, 0, 315
'JACKSONVILLE', 36, 48, 290
'MIAMI', 129, −259, 350
'ORLANDO', 56, −73, 400
'PENSACOLA', −340, 48, 280
'TAMPA', −16, −113, 360
```

The optimal location for the distribution center in this example is DADE CITY, North East of Tampa on US Highway 98, 9 mi off Highway I-75. A sample run follows:

```
THE SINGLE FACILITY EUCLIDEAN DISTANCE LOCATION PROBLEM

Input data:
SEQ #    Name              X           Y      Weight
  1      BOCA RATON      137.00    -218.00    280.00
  2      GAINESVILLE       0.00       0.00    315.00
  3      JACKSONVILLE     36.00      48.00    290.00
  4      MIAMI           129.00    -259.00    350.00
  5      ORLANDO          56.00     -73.00    400.00
  6      PENSACOLA      -340.00      48.00    280.00
  7      TAMPA           -16.00    -113.00    360.00


Optimal location is:  X =      6.76, Y =   -85.37

                 B    G    J    M    O    P    T    *
                 O    A    A    I    R    E    A    *
                 C    I    C    M    L    N    M    O
                 A    N    K    A    A    S    P    P
                      E    S    I    N    A    A    T
                 R    S    O         D    C         I
                 A    V    N         O    O         M
                 T    I    V              L         A
                 O    L    I              A         L
                 N    L    L                        *
                      E    L                        *
                           E                        *
          _____
BOCA RATON    :   0. 257. 285.  42. 166. 546. 186. 186.
GAINESVILLE   : 257.   0.  60. 289.  92. 343. 114.  86.
JACKSONVILLE  : 285.  60.   0. 321. 123. 376. 169. 137.
MIAMI         :  42. 289. 321.   0. 200. 561. 206. 212.
ORLANDO       : 166.  92. 123. 200.   0. 414.  82.  51.
PENSACOLA     : 546. 343. 376. 561. 414.   0. 362. 372.
TAMPA         : 186. 114. 169. 206.  82. 362.   0.  36.
**OPTIMAL**   : 186.  86. 137. 212.  51. 372.  36.   0.
```

CHAPTER 9
Sequential and Direct Access Files

Most program examples in this text prompt the program user to type in all data at the keyboard while the program is running. Some of the programs also read data from a previously prepared data file. In this chapter, we focus on the use of input data files and output files.

In many computer applications, it is important to be able to share data among programs, enabling data generated by one program to be processed by another. Also, it is often desirable to read data from more than one input data file or to combine these data to form a new output file. For example, a bank that has a file of accounts and a file of daily transactions might want to update the file of accounts based on today's transactions. This new file of accounts could become an input file to be processed later with tomorrow's transactions.

Because files are physically located in secondary memory, they can be extremely large. Normally, only one component of a file, called a *record*, will be stored in main memory and processed at a given time.

Fortran has two kinds of files: sequential and direct access. We introduced batch processing and sequential files in Section 5.5. A *sequential file* consists of records that must always be processed serially, starting with the first one. At any point, the next record to be processed is the record following the last one processed. In a *direct access file*, on the other hand, it's possible to reference any record at any time; hence, we say that the access order is *random*. However, to facilitate random access to a direct access file, all records must be of uniform length, a requirement that does not apply to sequential files. In this chapter, we study both file types, starting with sequential.

9.1 Sequential Files

A Fortran program is stored in secondary memory as a source file; each program line is a record in this source file. Similarly, each line printed by a program is a record in the program output file. Both are sequential files because they are processed in serial order (e.g., the first five program lines must be read before the sixth line).

Creating a Sequential File

To create a file for later use, we must read or generate data under program control and write those data onto a file. In the example, we show how to do this.

EXAMPLE 9.1

The program in Fig. 9.1 creates a file of the odd numbers from 1 to 999. Each odd number becomes an individual record of the newly created file named ODDNUM, as shown next.

file ODDNUM

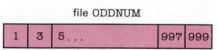

The OPEN statement is used to *connect* a file so it can be read or written to. The OPEN statement in Fig. 9.1 specifies a number of properties of the file, including its unit number (UNIT = 3), its name (FILE = 'ODDNUM'), that it is written using formatted output (FORM = 'FORMATTED'), that it is a sequential file (ACCESS = 'SEQUENTIAL'), and that the file is newly created by this program (STATUS = 'NEW').

These file properties are all quite straightforward given our knowledge so far. Files are either sequential (ACCESS = 'SEQUENTIAL') or direct access (ACCESS = 'DIRECT'). A file may be processed using list-directed or formatted input/output (FORM = 'FORMATTED'); otherwise, the file is considered unformatted (FORM = 'UNFORMATTED').

The file specifier STATUS = 'NEW' is used when a new file is being created; the file specifier STATUS = 'OLD' is used when a previously created file is being read. If we do not wish to retain a file that is being created, we use the file specifier STATUS = 'SCRATCH'.

Figure 9.1. *Creating a File of Odd Numbers*

```
      PROGRAM DOODD
C Create a sequential file of odd numbers

C Declarations
      INTEGER ODDMAX
      PARAMETER (ODDMAX = 999)
      INTEGER NEXODD

C Open file ODDNUM for output
      OPEN (UNIT = 3, FILE = 'ODDNUM', FORM = 'FORMATTED',
     +      ACCESS = 'SEQUENTIAL', STATUS = 'NEW')

C Write each odd number to file ODDNUM
      DO 10 NEXODD = 1, ODDMAX, 2
         WRITE (UNIT = 3, FMT = 19) NEXODD
   19    FORMAT (I3)
   10 CONTINUE

C Terminate and close file
      END FILE (UNIT = 3)
      CLOSE (UNIT = 3)

C Exit program
      STOP
      END
```

The file name is used to locate and identify each file that is in secondary memory. On some systems, the file name must follow a prescribed form. However, files with a STATUS parameter of 'SCRATCH' should not be given names, since they are not retained after the execution of the program.

The unit number is an integer value associated with the file. Usually, restrictions unique to each computer system determine what integers may be specified as unit numbers. On most systems, the integers 5 and 6 are reserved for the primary input and output devices being used by the system (job-control stream and line printer for a batch program; the keyboard and screen for an interactive program). The unit number must appear in all subsequent program statements that manipulate the file.

In Fig. 9.1, the statement

```
WRITE (UNIT = 3, FMT = 19) NEXODD
```

is used to write the output list (NEXODD) to the file designated by unit number 3 using FORMAT statement 19. You also can use the shorter version

```
WRITE (3, 19) NEXODD
```

Note that a carriage-control character is not specified in FORMAT 19; carriage control is needed only when writing to a unit that represents the line printer. The statement

```
END FILE (UNIT = 3)
```

is used to mark the end of a file by appending a special end-of-file record to the newly created file. You should include this statement whenever you create or write a new sequential file. The statement

```
CLOSE (UNIT = 3)
```

disconnects the file associated with unit number 3 from the program. Always ensure that before the program terminates, you close every open file. ◼

The OPEN statement is described in the next display. CLOSE and END FILE were described in Section 5.5.

SYNTAX DISPLAY

OPEN Statement

SYNTAX: OPEN (*speclist*)

INTERPRETATION: The OPEN statement connects a file to the program. *Speclist* is a list of file specifiers separated by commas. The file specifiers describe the properties of the file being connected.

(continued)

Required specifiers

UNIT = *unum:*   *unum* is the unit number (a positive integer expression).

Optional specifiers

FILE = *name:*   *name* is a string giving the file name (not required for 'SCRATCH' files).

ACCESS = *acc:*   The value of *acc* must be 'SEQUENTIAL' or 'DIRECT'. If omitted, 'SEQUENTIAL' is assumed.

FORM = *format:*   The value of *format* must be 'FORMATTED' or 'UNFORMATTED'. If omitted, 'FORMATTED' is assumed for sequential files; 'UNFOR-MATTED' for direct access.

STATUS = *stat:*   The value of *stat* must be 'NEW', 'OLD', 'SCRATCH', or 'UN-KNOWN'. If omitted, 'UNKNOWN' is assumed.

Other specifiers

RECL = *len:*   *len* is an integer expression indicating the length of each record in a direct access file (used only when ACCESS = 'DIRECT').

NOTES: The values allowed for *unum* and *name* may depend on your computer system. If STATUS = 'SCRATCH', then omit the specifier FILE = *name*.

The internal binary forms of data are stored directly in an unformatted file. In a formatted file, however, each data item is represented as a string of characters, so consequently, formatted files are easier to move from one computer to another. On the other hand, the particular computer system used to create an unformatted file determines the form of each record of that file. Although they are less portable, unformatted files can generally be processed more quickly.

On some systems, file properties may be specified using special control statements as well as the OPEN statement. You should find out what special statements, if any, are required on your system. Many systems write an end-of-file record automatically when the file is closed or the program terminates.

Reading an Existing File

We mentioned that one motivation for using files was to enable the output generated by one program to be used as data by another program. This process is illustrated next.

EXAMPLE 9.2

The program in Fig. 9.2 reads the file 'ODDNUM' created by the execution of the program in Fig. 9.1 and echo prints each file record. Note that the OPEN statement is the same as before except that the value of STATUS is now 'OLD'. The END FILE statement is no longer needed because the file is being read, not written to. The unit number for file 'ODDNUM' is still specified as 3, although another unit number could be used instead.

Figure 9.2. *Echo Printing the File ODDNUM*

```
      PROGRAM ODDFIL
C Read the file ODDNUM

C Declarations
      INTEGER NEXNUM

C Open file ODDNUM for input
      OPEN (UNIT = 3, FILE = 'ODDNUM', FORM = 'FORMATTED',
     +        ACCESS = 'SEQUENTIAL', STATUS = 'OLD')

C Read and print each record
      PRINT *, 'List of file data'
      DO  WHILE (.TRUE.)
          READ (UNIT = 3, FMT = 25, END = 35) NEXNUM
  25      FORMAT (I3)
          PRINT *, NEXNUM
      END DO

C End of file reached
   35 CONTINUE
      CLOSE (UNIT = 3)
      PRINT *, 'File read completed'

C Exit program
      STOP
      END
```

    9 IF (...) THEN

    GOTO 9
    END IF

Within the WHILE loop, each record of file 'ODDNUM' is read (using FORMAT 25) into the variable NEXNUM. A list-directed output statement prints each value of NEXNUM. Because the loop-repetition condition is always true, the loop could execute "forever." However, we want the loop to terminate either when all file records have been read or the end of the file is reached. The optional *control specifier* END = 35 causes a transfer to label 35 when the end-of-file record is read. Because the repeat condition is always true, this is the only method provided for loop exit. ■

The general READ and WRITE statements are described next.

SYNTAX DISPLAY

General READ/WRITE Statements

SYNTAX: READ (UNIT = *unum, control list*) *input list*
    WRITE (UNIT = *unum, control list*) *output list*

INTERPRETATION: The READ or WRITE operation is performed on the file associated with unit *unum*. The variables receiving data (for READ) are provided in *input*

(*continued*)

list; the variables and values to be written (for WRITE) are provided in *output list*.

Control list

FMT = *flab:* Specifies the label of the FORMAT statement to be used with a formatted file (omitted if the file is unformatted). FMT = * specifies list-directed input/output.

END = *endlab:* Specifies the label to transfer to when the end-of-file record is read. This specifier may not appear in a WRITE statement or with a direct access file.

REC = *recnum:* Specifies the record number (a positive integer) of a direct access file (omitted if the file is sequential).

NOTE: There are additional control specifiers that are beyond the scope of this discussion. The symbols UNIT = and FMT = may be omitted from a READ or WRITE statement. When this is done, Fortran assumes the first item in the control list is the unit number and the second item is the format label for formatted files.

Creating a File from Keyboard Data

The program in Fig. 9.1 generated data to be stored in a sequential file. You also could read or enter data from the keyboard and save these data in a file for later use. This process is illustrated in the next example.

EXAMPLE 9.3

The inventory for a bookstore is read from a keyboard by the program in Fig. 9.3. Each input record consists of the stock number, author's name, title, cost, and quantity on hand. GETREC is called to reach each data record. The statement

```
WRITE (UNIT = 1) STOCK, AUTHOR, TITLE, PRICE, QUANT
```

writes this record to the file (INVEN) associated with unit number 1; because the file is unformatted, there is no format specified.

Figure 9.3. *Main Program for Creating the Inventory File INVEN*

```
      PROGRAM BOOKST
C Writes the book store inventory to a file

C Declarations
      INTEGER SENVAL
      PARAMETER (SENVAL = 0)
      INTEGER STOCK, QUANT, TOTAL
      REAL PRICE
      CHARACTER *20 AUTHOR, TITLE
      CHARACTER *8 DATE

C Open file INVEN for output
      OPEN (UNIT = 1, FILE = 'INVEN', FORM = 'UNFORMATTED',
     +     ACCESS = 'SEQUENTIAL', STATUS = 'NEW')
```

```
C Get date and initialize TOTAL
      PRINT *, 'Enter the date in the form ''MM/DD/YY'' :'
      READ *, DATE
      PRINT *, 'Enter each book record as of ', DATE
      TOTAL = 0

C Read each book record, write it to file INVEN,
C and accumulate the total number of books in TOTAL.
      CALL GETREC (STOCK, AUTHOR, TITLE, PRICE, QUANT)
      DO WHILE (STOCK .NE. SENVAL)                           9 IF (...) THEN
         WRITE (UNIT = 1) STOCK, AUTHOR, TITLE, PRICE, QUANT
         TOTAL = TOTAL + QUANT
         CALL GETREC (STOCK, AUTHOR, TITLE, PRICE, QUANT)
      END DO                                                 GOTO 9
                                                             END IF
C Print final TOTAL and terminate and close file INVEN
      PRINT *
      PRINT *, 'Total number of books in stock = ', TOTAL
      PRINT *, 'File INVEN created'
      END FILE (UNIT = 1)
      CLOSE (UNIT = 1)

C Exit program
      STOP
      END
```

The WHILE loop in Fig. 9.3 terminates when the sentinel record (stock number is 0) is read. The total number of books is counted and displayed after loop exit. A sample of the output for this program is shown in Fig. 9.4. (See Self-check exercise 2 at the end of this section for a description of subroutine GETREC.)

Figure 9.4. *Sample Run of File Creation Program*

```
Enter the date in the form 'MM/DD/YY' :
'12/25/93'
Enter each book record as of 12/25/93

Stock Number (enter 0 when done):
1
Author in quotes:
'Ty Cobb'
Title in quotes:
'No Place Like Home'
Price:
5.95
Quantity:
18
```

```
Stock Number (enter 0 when done):
15
Author in quotes:
'Pete Rose'
Title in quotes:
'My Greatest Hits'
Price:
9.95
Quantity:
500

Stock Number (enter 0 when done):
0

Total number of books in stock =      518
File INVEN created
```

EXAMPLE 9.4   We could use the program in Fig. 9.5 to update file INVEN by adding additional data records to the end of this file. The first WHILE loop advances to the current end of the file by reading each record until the end-of-file record is read. After loop exit, the statement

```
BACKSPACE (UNIT = 1)
```

repositions the file to the start of the last record read (the current end-of-file record). The additional data records are then written onto the file INVEN, erasing the original end-of-file record, and a new end-of-file record is written following the last data record added to the file.   ■

Figure 9.5. *Adding More Records to File INVEN*

```
      PROGRAM FEXTEN
C Extends existing inventory file

C Declarations
      INTEGER STOCK, QUANT, TOTAL
      REAL PRICE
      CHARACTER *20 AUTHOR, TITLE

C Open file INVEN for extension
      OPEN (UNIT = 1, FILE = 'INVEN', FORM = 'UNFORMATTED',
     +      ACCESS = 'SEQUENTIAL', STATUS = 'OLD')

C Find current end of file
      DO WHILE (.TRUE.)                              9  IF (...) THEN
         READ (UNIT = 1, END = 25) STOCK, AUTHOR,
     +      TITLE, PRICE, QUANT
         PRINT *, STOCK, AUTHOR, TITLE, PRICE, QUANT
      END DO                                         GOTO 9
                                                     END IF
```

```
C Add new data starting at the end of the current file
   25 CONTINUE
         BACKSPACE (UNIT = 1)
         CALL GETREC (STOCK, AUTHOR, TITLE, PRICE, QUANT)
         DO WHILE (STOCK .NE. 0)                              29 IF ( ... ) THEN
            WRITE (UNIT = 1) STOCK, AUTHOR,
      +        TITLE, PRICE, QUANT
            CALL GETREC (STOCK, AUTHOR, TITLE, PRICE, QUANT)
         END DO                                               GOTO 9
                                                              END IF
C Terminate and close file
         PRINT *, 'Extension of INVEN complete'
         END FILE (UNIT = 1)
         CLOSE (UNIT = 1)

C Exit program
         STOP
         END
```

Another command

```
REWIND (UNIT = unum)
```

may be used to reposition a sequential file to its first record. This enables the data in a sequential file to be processed more than once during the execution of a program.

SYNTAX
DISPLAY

BACKSPACE Statement

SYNTAX: BACKSPACE (UNIT = *unum*)

INTERPRETATION: The file position pointer for the file connected to unit number *unum* is repositioned before the record last processed. If the file position pointer is past the end-of-file record, it is repositioned just before the end-of-file record.

SYNTAX
DISPLAY

REWIND Statement

SYNTAX: REWIND (UNIT = *unum*)

INTERPRETATION: The file position pointer for the file connected to unit number *unum* is positioned just before the first file record.

**EXERCISES FOR
SECTION 9.1**

Self-check

1. Explain the difference between the STATUS specifiers: 'NEW', 'OLD', and 'SCRATCH'. With which one would you not expect to use a file name?

2. Explain the difference between a formatted file and an unformatted file. Which type is more portable? Which type provides for faster input/output? With which type can you specify FMT = *?
3. Indicate whether each of the specifiers below should appear in an OPEN statement, a READ statement, or both.

a. ACCESS   c. UNIT   e. STATUS   g. REC
b. FMT   d. FILE   f. END   h. RECL

Programming
1. Write the OPEN statement needed to connect an existing, sequential, unformatted file named 'TEXT' to unit number 3.
2. Write subroutine GETREC consisting of the prompt and the READ statements needed to enter one book record.

9.2 Problem Solving Illustrated

We present two case studies in this section. The first shows how to *merge,* or combine, the data in two existing files into a third file. The first file is considered the *master file* because it contains the current status of all file records. The second file, called the *update file* or *transaction file,* contains new information about the file records that has not yet been entered in the master file. The file merge modifies the master file by incorporating the information in the update file, thereby creating an up-to-date file, called the *new master file.*

Case Study: Merging Files

PROBLEM STATEMENT

The Junk Mail Company has recently received a new mailing list (file UPDATE) that it wishes to merge with its master file (file OLDMST). Each of the files is in alphabetical order by name. The name field is considered the record *key,* which serves as a unique ID for the record. The company wants to produce a new master file (NEWMST) that is also in alphabetical order. Each client name and address on either mailing list is represented by four character strings, as follows:

```
'CLAUS, SANTA'
'1 STAR LANE'
'NORTH POLE'
'ALASKA, 99999'
```

A sentinel name and address are at the end of each of the files UPDATE and OLDMST. The sentinel is the same for both files; one copy should be written at the end of the NEWMST file. The sentinel entry consists of four character strings containing all z's (the alphabetically largest character). We shall assume there are no names that appear on both files OLDMST and UPDATE.

In addition to the two input files (OLDMST and UPDATE), we will need an output file (NEWMST) that will contain the merged data from OLDMST and UPDATE. NEWMST will then serve as the new master file of mailing labels.

Figure 9.6 illustrates the result of merging two small sample files. For simplicity, only the name portion of each record is shown. The original mailing list and the update list each contain four records (including the sentinel); the new mailing list contains seven records. The records on all three files are in alphabetical order by name.

Data Requirements

Input Files

the original mailing list in alphabetical order by name (OLDMST)
the additions to be made to OLDMST, also in alphabetical order by name (UPDATE)

Figure 9.6. *Sample File Merge*

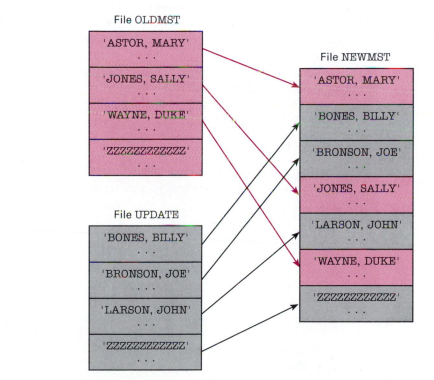

Output Files

the final mailing list, formed by merging OLDMST and UPDATE (NEWMST)

DESIGN

The algorithm follows:

Algorithm

1. Read first records from OLDMST and UPDATE.
2. Compare names of current records. Copy the record with the alphabetically first name into NEWMST. Read the next record from the file containing the record that was just copied. Continue to merge until the ends of both files are reached.

Algorithm Refinements

The program must read one name and address entry at a time from each input file. These two entries are compared, and the one that comes first alphabetically is copied to the output file (NEWMST). Another entry is then read from the file containing the entry just copied, and the comparison process is repeated.

When the sentinel record is read from one of the input files (OLDMST or UPDATE), the program should copy the remaining information from the other input file to NEWMST. After the other sentinel record is read, the program should write it to NEWMST.

To simplify the implementation of the algorithm, we will use two string arrays, OLDATA and UPDATA, to hold the current records from OLDMST and UPDATE, respectively. Each array provides storage for four strings of length 20.

Figure 9.7 shows the program.

Input Variables

string array to hold current record from OLDMST (CHARACTER *20 OLDATA(4))
string array to hold current record from UPDATE (CHARACTER *20 UPDATA(4))

Step 2 Refinement

```
2.1 DO WHILE (.TRUE.)
        IF OLDATA(1) is less than UPDATA(1) THEN
```
    2.2 Copy OLDATA to NEWMST. Read next record from OLDMST to OLDATA. Exit loop when the end-of-file record is read.
```
        ELSE
```
    2.3 Copy UPDATA to NEWMST. Read next record from UPDATE to UPDATA. Exit loop when the end-of-file record is read.
```
        END IF
    END DO
```

Figure 9.7. *Merging Two Sequential Files*

```fortran
        PROGRAM MERGE
C Merges OLDMST and UPDATE to NEWMST
C Records in all 3 files are in alphabetical order by name
C Uses OLDATA and UPDATA to store file data

C Declarations
        CHARACTER *20 OLDATA(4), UPDATA(4)

C Open three sequential files
        OPEN (UNIT = 1, FILE = 'OLDMST', FORM = 'UNFORMATTED',
     +        ACCESS = 'SEQUENTIAL', STATUS = 'OLD')
        OPEN (UNIT = 2, FILE = 'UPDATE', FORM = 'UNFORMATTED',
     +        ACCESS = 'SEQUENTIAL', STATUS = 'OLD')
        OPEN (UNIT = 3, FILE = 'NEWMST', FORM = 'UNFORMATTED',
     +        ACCESS = 'SEQUENTIAL', STATUS = 'NEW')

C Read first data entries from each input file
        READ (UNIT = 1, END = 94) OLDATA
        READ (UNIT = 2, END = 95) UPDATA

C Merge alphabetically smaller data to NEWMST and
C get next record from input file with smaller
C data.  Continue until end of either file is read
        DO WHILE (.TRUE.)
C          Copy record with smaller name
           IF (OLDATA(1) .LT. UPDATA(1)) THEN
              WRITE (UNIT = 3) OLDATA
              READ (UNIT = 1, END = 40) OLDATA
           ELSE
              WRITE (UNIT = 3) UPDATA
              READ (UNIT = 2, END = 40) UPDATA
           END IF
        END DO

C Close files and exit program
  40    CONTINUE
        PRINT *, 'Merge completed'
        END FILE (UNIT = 3)
        CLOSE (UNIT = 1)
        CLOSE (UNIT = 2)
        CLOSE (UNIT = 3)
        STOP

C Error section
C Print error message if either input file is empty
  94    CONTINUE
        PRINT *, 'File OLDMST is empty'
        STOP
  95    CONTINUE
        PRINT *, 'File UPDATE is empty'
        STOP
        END
```

9 IF(...) THEN

GOTO 9
END IF

491

IMPLEMENTATION

We must verify that all remaining data on one file are copied into NEWMST when the end-of-file record on the other file has been read. Just before reaching the end-of-file record on UPDATE (or OLDMST), the sentinel record should be read into UPDATA (or OLDATA). Because the sentinel name (all z's) alphabetically follows any other client name, the remaining client data on the unfinished file should be copied to NEWMST, as desired. During the last repetition of the loop, both OLDATA and UPDATA should contain the sentinel record, which is copied to NEWMST just before loop exit.

In the program shown in Fig. 9.7, a transfer to label 94 or 95 occurs if either UPDATE or OLDMST is empty (a file consisting of an end-of-file record only). In this case, there is no need to perform the merge operation since the other file contains the required alphabetical list.

TESTING AND VERIFICATION

Test the merge program by providing files that contain only the sentinel record as well as files with one or more actual records. Ensure the merge program works properly regardless of which of the two input files has all of its data processed first. Also, ensure there is exactly one sentinel record on the merged file.

Case Study: Land Boundary Survey

PROBLEM STATEMENT

The surveying firm of Harris, Neilson, and Gallop has completed a land boundary survey. The result consists of the *X*- and *Y*-coordinates of points defining the edges of a piece of property. These coordinates are stored in a data file named SURVIN.DAT, one pair per line. The firm needs to know the distance between adjacent points and the total length of the boundary. For error correction purposes, the firm also would like to know the percentage of the total length of each line and the cumulative percentage, starting with the first line. The output results will be written to an output file and also displayed in tabular form, as shown in Fig. 9.8.

ANALYSIS

The program first reads the survey data into a pair of arrays, X and Y. The distance between adjacent points, (X_i, Y_i), and (X_j, Y_j), is given by the formula

$$distance = \sqrt{(X_i - X_j)^2 + (Y_i - Y_j)^2}.$$

The total length of the land boundary is the sum of the individual lengths. After computing the total length, we can determine the percentage of each

Figure 9.8. *Land Survey Table*

```
             Harris, Neilson, and Gallop, Surveyors

The number of points read was  6
Total boundary length is    1365.685 feet
```

Line Number	Start Point X	Y	Line Length (in feet)	% of Boundary	Cumulative %
1	100.000	100.000	141.421	10.355	10.355
2	200.000	200.000	141.421	10.355	20.711
3	300.000	300.000	141.421	10.355	31.066
4	400.000	400.000	400.000	29.289	60.355
5	.000	400.000	400.000	29.289	89.645
6	.000	.000	141.421	10.355	100.000

individual length, add it to the cumulative percentage, and write the required output file and table.

The problem data requirements and algorithm follow. Note that the first element in array CUMPCT, a problem output, has a subscript of 0. The reason for this will be discussed later.

Data Requirements

Input File

the coordinate file (SURVIN.DAT)

Output File

the line lengths and percentages (SURVOUT.DAT)

Problem Parameters

the size of the arrays (MAX = 100)

Problem Inputs

the X-coordinates of edge points (REAL X(MAX))
the Y-coordinates of edge points (REAL Y(MAX))

Problem Outputs

the coordinates of edge points (arrays X and Y)
the distance between adjacent points (REAL LENGTH(MAX))
the percentage of total boundary length (REAL PERCNT(MAX))
the cumulative percentage so far (REAL CUMPCT(0 : MAX))
the number of points on the boundary (INTEGER N)
the total boundary length (REAL PERIM)

Figure 9.9. *Structure Chart for Surveying Problem*

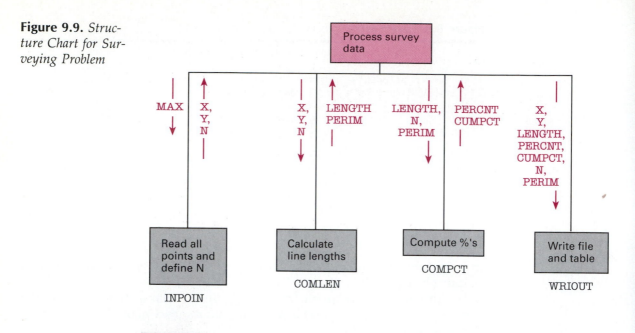

DESIGN

The initial algorithm follows:

Algorithm

1. Read all coordinate points and count the number of points read.
2. Calculate the length of each line and the total boundary length.
3. Compute percentages of individual line lengths and cumulative percentages.
4. Write the output file and table.

Algorithm Refinements

We will use subroutines to perform each step of the algorithm. Figure 9.9 shows the structure chart.

IMPLEMENTATION

Main Program

The main program, shown in Fig. 9.10, contains declarations for all arrays and simple variables listed in the data requirements section and calls to the four subroutines.

Figure 9.10. *Main Survey Program*

```
      PROGRAM SURVEY
C This program reads the X, Y coordinates of a collection
C of edge points around the boundary of a plot of land and
C computes the distances between adjacent points. The
C coordinates of the individual lines, their lengths, the
C percentages of total length, and the cumulative percentages
C are written to an output file and displayed in a table.

C Declarations
      INTEGER MAX
      PARAMETER (MAX = 100)
      REAL X(MAX), Y(MAX), LENGTH(MAX)
      REAL PERCNT(MAX), CUMPCT(0 : MAX), PERIM
      INTEGER N

C Read all coordinate points
      CALL INPOIN (MAX, X, Y, N)

C Calculate the length of each line and the total boundary
      CALL COMLEN (X, Y, N, LENGTH, PERIM)

C Compute individual line percentages
      CALL COMPCT (LENGTH, N, PERIM, PERCNT, CUMPCT)

C Write output file and table
      CALL WRIOUT (X, Y, LENGTH, PERCNT, CUMPCT, N, PERIM)

C Exit program
      STOP
      END
```

Subroutine INPOIN

Subroutine INPOIN (see Fig. 9.11) begins by connecting the data file SURVIN.DAT to unit number 1. It uses a READ statement with an end-of-file specifier to read coordinates into arrays X and Y. The value of N is defined after loop exit.

Figure 9.11. *Subroutine INPOIN*

```
      SUBROUTINE INPOIN (MAX, X, Y, N)
C Enters survey data from file SURVIN.DAT and defines N
C Preconditions : MAX is defined.
C Postconditions: 1 <= N <= MAX and N data pairs
C   are read into array elements X(1) through X(N) and
C   Y(1) through Y(N)
```

```
C Input Arguments
C    MAX — The maximum number of points

C Output Arguments
C    X — the X coordinate of each point
C    Y — the Y coordinate of each point
C    N — the number of points read (0 <= N <= MAX)

C Argument Declarations
      INTEGER MAX, N
      REAL X(MAX), Y(MAX)

C Local Declarations
      INTEGER I

C Open data file
      OPEN (UNIT = 1, FILE = 'SURVIN.DAT', FORM = 'FORMATTED',
     +      ACCESS = 'SEQUENTIAL', STATUS = 'OLD')

C Read coordinate points
      DO 10 I = 1, MAX
         READ (UNIT = 1, FMT = *, END = 99) X(I), Y(I)
   10 CONTINUE
      PRINT *, 'Warning — array filled before end of file read'

C Store number of points in N
   99 N = I - 1

C Close file and exit subroutine
      CLOSE (UNIT = 1)
      RETURN
      END
```

Subroutine COMLEN

Subroutine COMLEN (see Fig. 9.12) computes the length of each line on the boundary. The first line connects points 1 and 2, the second line connects points 2 and 3, and so on. The last line connects points N and 1. The algorithm follows Fig. 9.12.

Figure 9.12. *Subroutine COMLEN and Function DISTNC*

```
      SUBROUTINE COMLEN (X, Y, N, LENGTH, PERIM)
C Calculates the length of each line and the total boundary
C Preconditions : 1 <= N <= MAX and first N elements of
C    arrays X and Y are defined.
C Postconditions: (LENGTH(I) is the length of the line between
C    points (X(I), Y(I)) and (X(I + 1), Y(I + 1)) and PERIM is
C    the sum of all values in array LENGTH
```

```
C Input Arguments
C    X — the X coordinate of each point
C    Y — the Y coordinate of each point
C    N — the number of points read

C Output Arguments
C    LENGTH — the length of each line
C    PERIM — the total boundary length

C Argument Declarations
      INTEGER N
      REAL X(*), Y(*), LENGTH(*), PERIM

C Local Declarations
      INTEGER I
      REAL DISTNC

C Define each individual line length and add it to the total
      PERIM = 0.0
      DO 10 I = 1, N - 1
          LENGTH(I) = DISTNC(X(I), Y(I), X(I + 1), Y(I + 1))
          PERIM = PERIM + LENGTH(I)
   10 CONTINUE
      LENGTH(N) = DISTNC(X(N), Y(N), X(1), Y(1))
      PERIM = PERIM + LENGTH(N)

C Exit subroutine
      RETURN
      END

C  _____

      REAL FUNCTION DISTNC (XSTART, YSTART, XEND, YEND)
C Computes the distance of the line between points
C (XSTART, YSTART) and (XEND, YEND)
C Preconditions : The X, Y coordinates of 2 points
C                 are defined.
C Postconditions: The function result is the length of the line
C                 between these coordinates.

C Argument Declarations
      REAL XSTART, YSTART, XEND, YEND

C Define function result
      DISTNC = SQRT((XEND - XSTART) ** 2 +
     +              (YEND - YSTART) ** 2)

C Exit function
      RETURN
      END
```

Algorithm for COMLEN

1. Set PERIM to zero.
2. DO I = 1, N - 1
   3. Set LENGTH(I) to the length of the line from point I to point I + 1.
   4. Add the new line length to PERIM.
   END DO
5. Set LENGTH(N) to the length of the line from point N to point 1.
6. Add the new line length to PERIM.

Figure 9.12 shows subroutine COMLEN along with function DISTNC. Function DISTNC calculates the distance of the line whose end points are passed as the function arguments.

Subroutine COMPCT

Subroutine COMPCT performs the percentage calculations for each line, defining arrays PERCNT and CUMPCT. Figure 9.13 shows subroutine COMPCT. In the DO loop, the statements

```
PERCNT(I) = (LENGTH(I) / PERIM) * 100.00
CUMPCT(I) = CUMPCT(I - 1) + PERCNT(I)
```

Figure 9.13. *Subroutine COMPCT*

```
      SUBROUTINE COMPCT (LENGTH, N, PERIM, PERCNT, COMPCT)
C Calculates the percentage length of each line and the cumulative
C    percentage
C Preconditions : 1 <= N <= MAX and first N elements of
C    array LENGTH are defined and PERIM contains their sum.
C Postconditions: PERCNT(I) is the relative percentage of
C    LENGTH(I) compared to PERIM and CUMPCT(I) is the
C    sum of PERCNT(1) through PERCNT(I).

C Input Arguments
C    LENGTH - the length of each line
C    N - the number of points read
C    PERIM - the total boundary length

C Output Arguments
C    PERCNT - the percentage length of each line
C    CUMPCT - the cumulative percentage so far

C Dummy Argument Declarations
      INTEGER N
      REAL PERIM, LENGTH(*), PERCNT(*)
      REAL CUMPCT(0 : *)
```

```
C Local Declarations
      INTEGER I

C Compute the percentage of each line and the
C cumulative percentage so far
      CUMPCT(0) = 0.0
      DO 10 I = 1, N
          PERCNT(I) = (LENGTH(I) / PERIM) * 100.00
          CUMPCT(I) = CUMPCT(I - 1) + PERCNT(I)
   10 CONTINUE

C Exit subroutine
      RETURN
      END
```

define the percentage of the current line, PERCNT(I), and the cumulative percentage so far, CUMPCT(I). The latter is obtained by adding PERCNT(I) to the previous cumulative percentage, CUMPCT(I - 1). When I is 1, the value of PERCNT(1) is added to CUMPCT(0) (value is zero), hence the reason for the extra element in array CUMPCT. The declaration

```
REAL CUMPCT(0 : *)
```

identifies CUMPCT as an assumed-size dummy array with a smallest subscript of zero.

Subroutine WRIOUT

Subroutine WRIOUT writes the output file, SURVOUT.DAT, as an unformatted file. This file contains one record for each boundary line. The record for each line consists of the coordinates of its endpoints, its length, the percentage of the total length, and the cumulative percentage so far.

After file SURVOUT.DAT is completed, we can verify its correctness by reading each record and echo printing it on the screen in the body of the display table. Because of screen width limitations, we display only the starting point of each line. (The ending point of line i is the same as the starting point of line i + 1.)

Figure 9.14 shows subroutine WRIOUT. DO loop 10 creates the output file, and DO loop 20 displays the output table. Just before DO loop 20 begins, the statement

```
REWIND (UNIT = 2)
```

rewinds file SURVOUT.DAT so its records can be read and echo printed in the body of the table. DO loop 20 reads the file data into local variables instead of back into the arrays.

Figure 9.14. *Subroutine WRIOUT*

```
            SUBROUTINE WRIOUT (X, Y, LENGTH, PERCNT, CUMPCT, N, PERIM)
C Writes the output file, SURVOUT.DAT, and
C echo prints it in a display table.
C Preconditions : 1 <= N <= MAX and first N elements of all array
C     arguments are defined.
C Postconditions: A table of results is written to the output file and to
C     the screen.

C Input Arguments
C   X — the X coordinate of each point
C   Y — the Y coordinate of each point
C   LENGTH — the length of the ith line
C   PERCNT — the percentage length of each line
C   CUMPCT — the cumulative percentage so far
C   N — the number of points read
C   PERIM — the total boundary length

C Argument Declarations
      INTEGER N
      REAL X(*), Y(*), LENGTH(*), PERCNT(*), PERIM
      REAL CUMPCT(0 : *)

C Local Declarations
      INTEGER I
      REAL XSTART, YSTART, XEND, YEND, TEMLEN, TEMPER, TEMCUM

C Open output file and write records 1 through N — 1
      OPEN (UNIT = 2, FILE = 'SURVOUT.DAT',
     +      FORM = 'UNFORMATTED', ACCESS = 'SEQUENTIAL',
     +      STATUS = 'NEW')

      DO 10 I = 1, N — 1
         WRITE (UNIT = 2) X(I), Y(I), X(I + 1), Y(I + 1),
     +                 LENGTH(I), PERCNT(I), CUMPCT(I)
   10 CONTINUE

C Write record N and end of file
      IF (N .GT. 0) THEN
         WRITE (UNIT = 2) X(N), Y(N), X(1), Y(1),
     +           LENGTH(N), PERCNT(N), CUMPCT(N)
      END IF
      END FILE (UNIT = 2)

C Write table heading
      WRITE (6, *) '              Harris, Neilson, and ',
     +            'Gallop, Surveyors'
      WRITE (6, 11) N
   11 FORMAT ('0', 'The number of points read was ', I3)
      WRITE (6, 12) PERIM
   12 FORMAT (1X, 'Total boundary length is ', F12.3, ' feet')
      WRITE (6, *)
      WRITE (6, *) 'Line          Start Point ',
     +          '           Line Length      % of        Cumulative'
      WRITE (6, *) 'Number           X          Y',
     +          '           (in feet)      Boundary         %'
```

```
C Read and echo print all records of file SURVOUT.DAT
      REWIND (UNIT = 2)
      DO 20 I = 1, N
         READ (UNIT = 2) XSTART, YSTART, XEND, YEND,
     +                    TEMLEN, TEMPER, TEMCUM
         WRITE (UNIT = 6, FMT = 13) I, XSTART, YSTART,
     +                              TEMLEN, TEMPER, TEMCUM
   13    FORMAT (1X, I3, 5F12.3)
   20 CONTINUE

C Close file and exit subroutine
      CLOSE (UNIT = 2)
      RETURN
      END
```

TESTING AND VERIFICATION

Perform a sample run of the survey program, which will produce a table similar to the one shown in the problem statement. Ensure all values printed are positive and the final cumulative percentage is 100. To verify the correctness of the table, try some adjacent points with the same X-coordinates but different Y-coordinates (or same Y but different X). In this case, the line length should be the absolute value of the difference between the Y-coordinates. Also, see what happens to the display table when point 1 is placed at the end of the data file instead of the beginning. The table lines should all move up one position, and the last line displayed should be the same as the old first line.

EXERCISES FOR SECTION 9.2

Self-check

1. Which of the two data files being merged, OLDMST and UPDATE, must be in sequence by key? Show the effect of merging the two files whose record keys are the following:

   file OLDMST: 3, 5, 7, 12, 15
   file UPDATE: 1, 2, 4, 14, 16

2. What would program MERGE do if a particular key value was present in both files being merged (for example, replace key 16 in the second file above with key 15)? Would both records be copied to file NEWMST or just one? If the answer is one, which one?
3. What would be the effect of running program SURVEY with an empty data file? Would there be a run-time error? What would be displayed on the screen if subroutine WRIOUT were executed?

Programming

1. Modify the program in Fig. 9.7 to handle the situation in which the UPDATE file may contain some of the same names as the OLDMST file. In this case,

only one address should appear on the NEWMST file; the address in file UPDATE should be used since it is more recent. Also, print a count of the number of file entries in each of the three files.

9.3 Direct Access Files

A direct access file is analogous to an array that is stored in secondary memory rather than main memory. Like an array, the records of a direct access file may be accessed in arbitrary, or random, order.

Each record of a direct access file is assigned a unique record number, starting with 1. Because each record is a fixed size, Fortran can determine where on disk a particular record is stored and access it. For example, if all

FORTRAN in Focus

The Language of Science

GLAXO PHARMACEUTICALS

A pharmaceuticals firm based in the United Kingdom, Glaxo develops and markets prescription pharmaceuticals worldwide. "Glaxo babies" in India, Australia, and the Far East grew up on its infant food products since the turn of the century, but now prescription drugs are its only products.

Staff chemists call on Glaxo's Chemical Systems Group to help them develop the computer applications they need to design new pharmaceutical products. The members of the Chemical Systems Group are often trained in both computer science and chemistry and use a wide array of chemical analysis tools to solve the problems brought to them.

Many of the tools used to design and analyze chemical structures have been designed by academic researchers in the course of their basic research. Studies of the physical properties of a chemical structure, for example, often result in simulations and analytical programs that can then be used by others who wish to apply the basic science to the development of commercial products. These tools are marketed by the academic institution, or licensed to a third-party developer for distribution and support. In either case, they are available to the chemists at Glaxo, and they are most frequently written in Fortran, the language of choice for many science applications.

When a chemist wants to understand the physical properties of a given structure, the group develops a meth-

records are 20 characters in length, record 1 occupies the first 20 characters allocated to the file, record 2 occupies the next 20 characters, and so on.

The length of a record, its *record length,* must be declared by a file specifier in the OPEN statement (i.e., RECL = *len*, where *len* is an integer). The length of a formatted record is equal to the number of characters specified by the associated FORMAT statement. For an unformatted record, the length depends on the computer system.

The OPEN statement

```
OPEN (UNIT = 2, FILE = 'DIRINV', FORM = 'FORMATTED',
+      ACCESS = 'DIRECT', RECL = 54, STATUS = 'NEW')
```

declares file DIRINV as a new direct access file with formatted records consisting of 54 characters each.

odology for doing so, pulling together the tools and data needed and giving the chemist the results in an understandable form. Data transfer routines and input/output formats may need to be written to make a particular tool work with another. For example, some large Fortran applications are written to accept only the I/O formats needed by the original developer. The Chemical Systems Group will write an I/O superstructure (generally in C) to make the application accept and produce a wider range of formats.

A walk-through of this method development process reveals the nature of much of the Chemical Systems Group's activities, and illustrates the role of Fortran in scientific applications. A chemist initiates the process

LEO LUCISANO (LEFT) AND ALLEN MOSS (IN MIRROR) PROGRAMMING THE SPECTRUM MICROWAVE PROCESSOR PRIOR TO MANUFACTURING A DEVELOPMENT BATCH OF ZANTAC EFFERVESCENT IN THE PILOT PLANT.

by explaining, for example, that she would like to modify a particular chemical structure in three or four places, see what the resulting structure would look like, and analyze its structural and physical properties. The Group would first generate a 2-D database of the resulting

structures, typically using a tool like Molecular Design Limited's MACCS database (much of which is written in Fortran) on a VAX cluster. This database serves as a notebook, providing everyone on the project with a standard list of the structures to be investigated. The next step is to use these 2-D structures to generate 3-D models. A tool such as MacroModel (a Fortran application created and distributed by Columbia University) is used to generate the models, optimize their geometries, and output files suitable for the computational tools to be used to analyze their properties and generate structural data.

The computational analysis is likely to be the most time- and computation-intensive

(continued)

Figure 9.15. *Subroutine INTLIZ*

```
      SUBROUTINE INTLIZ (UNUM)
C Writes blank records to the direct access file on unit number UNUM.
C Preconditions : The direct access file with unit number
C     UNUM is open.
C Postconditions: All file records contain a blank string.

C Input Argument
C   UNUM - the unit number of the file being initialized

C Dummy argument declaration
      INTEGER UNUM

C Local declarations
      INTEGER MAXSTK
      PARAMETER(MAXSTK = 1000)
      INTEGER RECNUM

C Write all blank records.
      DO 10 RECNUM = 1, MAXSTK
C        Write next blank record
         WRITE (UNIT = UNUM, FMT = 11, REC = RECNUM)
   11    FORMAT(A54)
   10 CONTINUE

C Exit subroutine.
      RETURN
      END
```

step of the process and, depending on the size of the project, may be run on the Cray supercomputer available to the Group at the nearby North Carolina Supercomputing Center. The tools for the numerically intensive applications used in this step, such as the Gaussian-80 program from the University of California, San Francisco, are most frequently written in Fortran. After the analysis is complete, the final step is to process the data from the various analytical tools to make it accessible to the chemists. The Chemical Systems Group may generate tables for further analysis in a statistical package, spreadsheet files, and files for graphical display and analysis on the chemist's Macintosh personal computer.

Making computer tools work for the chemists requires the Chemical Systems Group to perform two other types of activities as well. Writing specialized applications for mathematical and statistical analysis, generally in Fortran, and supporting the applications on the many different hardware platforms available to Glaxo—from UNIX machines, to a VAX network, to the supercomputer—keep the group busy. Sal Profeta, Chemical Systems Group Manager, points to the relative ease with which a Fortran application can be ported from one machine to another as an important improvement in the language over the years. Because Fortran has standardized many of the extensions

EXAMPLE 9.5 Before writing data to a direct access file, you should initialize each record of the file to a string of blank characters. Doing this enables you to determine at a later time whether a particular record exists. Subroutine INTLIZ in Fig. 9.15 may be called to initialize a direct access file. The DO loop-control variable RECNUM is used to access each file record in sequence. The WRITE statement

```
      WRITE (UNIT = UNUM, FMT - 11, REC = RECNUM)
11 FORMAT (A54)
```

initializes the record selected by RECNUM to all blank characters. The unit number, UNUM, is an input argument. ■

A direct access file may be created from a sequential file or by reading in data from the terminal. The program in Fig. 9.3 may be modified to create a direct access file instead of a sequential file.

EXAMPLE 9.6 We can use the program in Fig. 9.16 to write the book store inventory discussed in Example 9.3 as a direct access file instead of a sequential file. It uses subroutine GETREC (not shown) to enter each book record and subroutine INTLIZ to initialize the direct access file. Each stock number (STOCK) entered by GETREC is used as a record number, provided it is between 1 and MAXSTK (1000). Only the records specified by the program user will be changed. The program output will be similar to that shown in Fig. 9.4. If the call to INTLIZ is omitted, this program could be used to modify or insert new records in an existing file (STATUS = 'OLD').

that were at one time idiosyncratic to a particular computer, converting a large pre-existing application (such as the Gaussian-80 program and its 150,000 lines of code) may take only days instead of months.

Maintaining portability may be the most significant change Fortran will make in the future, too, according to Profeta. Fortran is the language of choice for numerically intensive applications. As the users of these computing-intensive applications look to enjoy the speed that data sharing, distributed processing, and massively parallel systems can provide, the ability of Fortran to adapt to these environments will have a large impact on its continued popularity.

We are grateful to Sal Profeta, Manager of the Chemical Systems Group at Glaxo in Research Triangle Park, North Carolina, for giving us such a clear view of the way in which chemists and programmers work together in the design of new pharmaceutical products. *When asked what he would recommend to a student of Fortran today, he replied, "Practice, practice, practice! When you are very fluent in Fortran, then the spectrum of problems you can address is limited only by your imagination. My colleagues who learned the language in an organized way, practiced, and stuck with it are the people who have made the greatest impact on the computational chemistry arena."*

Figure 9.16. *Creating the Inventory File DIRINV*

```
      PROGRAM CREATE
C Write the book store inventory to a direct access file.
C The file data are read from the keyboard.

C Declarations
      INTEGER SENVAL, MAXSTK
      PARAMETER (SENVAL = 0, MAXSTK = 1000)
      INTEGER STOCK, QUANT, TOTAL
      REAL PRICE
      CHARACTER *20 AUTHOR, TITLE
      CHARACTER *8 DATE

C Open file INVEN for output.
      OPEN (UNIT = 2, FILE = 'DIRINV', FORM = 'FORMATTED',
     +      ACCESS = 'DIRECT', RECL = 54, STATUS = 'NEW')

C Get date, initialize TOTAL, and initialize file DIRINV to blanks.
      PRINT *, 'Enter the date in the form ''MM/DD/YY'' :'
      READ *, DATE
      PRINT *, 'Enter each book record as of ', DATE
      PRINT *, 'Stock (record) numbers must be between 1 and ', MAXSTK
      TOTAL = 0
      CALL INTLIZ (2)

C Read each book record, write it to file DIRINV,
C and accumulate the total number of books in TOTAL.
      CALL GETREC (STOCK, AUTHOR, TITLE, PRICE, QUANT)
      DO WHILE ((STOCK .GT. SENVAL) .AND. (STOCK .LE. MAXSTK))   9 IF (...) THEN
         WRITE (UNIT = 2, FMT = 21, REC = STOCK)
     +        STOCK, AUTHOR, TITLE, PRICE, QUANT
   21    FORMAT (I4, A20, A20, F6.2, I4)
         TOTAL = TOTAL + QUANT
         CALL GETREC (STOCK, AUTHOR, TITLE, PRICE, QUANT)
      END DO                                                      GOTO 9
                                                                  END IF
C Print final TOTAL and terminate and close file DIRINV.
      IF (STOCK .GT. MAXSTK) PRINT *, 'Record number out-of-range'
      PRINT *
      PRINT *, 'Total number of books in stock = ', TOTAL
      PRINT *, 'File DIRINV created'
      CLOSE (UNIT = 2)

C Exit program
      STOP
      END
```

Note that the WRITE statement in Fig. 9.16 uses FORMAT 21 to control the layout of the record being written. Adding up the number of "print positions" described by this format gives us a record length of exactly 54 characters. This is the same as the record length specified in the OPEN statement for file DIRINV.

We also could use the sequential file INVEN that was created earlier as an input file and create a new direct access file from it. To accomplish this, we would need to open both files using the statements

```
OPEN (UNIT = 1, FILE = 'INVEN', FORM = 'UNFORMATTED',
+      ACCESS = 'SEQUENTIAL', STATUS = 'OLD')
OPEN (UNIT = 2, FILE = 'DIRINV', FORM = 'FORMATTED',
+      ACCESS = 'DIRECT', RECL = 54, STATUS = 'NEW')
```

The loop in Fig. 9.16 would be rewritten as follows:

```
C Read each book record from file INVEN, write it to file DIRINV,
C and accumulate the total number of books in TOTAL.
      DO WHILE (.TRUE.)
         READ (UNIT = 1, END = 99)
+          STOCK, AUTHOR, TITLE, PRICE, QUANT
         WRITE (UNIT = 2, FMT = 21, REC = STOCK)
+          STOCK, AUTHOR, TITLE, PRICE, QUANT
   21    FORMAT (I4, A20, A20, F6.2, I4)
         TOTAL = TOTAL + QUANT
      END DO
C
   99 CONTINUE
```

Records are read from file INVEN and then written to file DIRINV in the order in which they are read. Even though the corresponding record in INVEN was unformatted, each record of file DIRINV would be formatted. The control specifier REC = STOCK uses the stock number of each record read to determine where it will be stored in DIRINV.

EXERCISES FOR SECTION 9.3

Self-check

1. Can you process the records in a direct access file in sequence, starting with the first file record? If so, how?

Programming

1. Write a program fragment that reads in a record number from the keyboard and a data string representing an author's name. Next, read the selected record from the book store inventory file (on unit number 2). Then rewrite this record to the inventory file, replacing the AUTHOR field with new data string. All other fields of this record should remain the same. Show the declarations that must precede this fragment.

9.4 Updating a Direct Access File

A direct access file has the property that any record may be read or written without disturbing the rest of the file. For this reason, direct access files are used when a relatively small number of randomly selected records of a file are likely to be modified during a file update. Sequential files are used when most, or all, of the records are likely to be changed during a file update and the records are modified in serial order.

Case Study: Direct Access File Update

PROBLEM STATEMENT

A program is needed to update a bookstore inventory file. The input data for the program consist of the record number (RECNUM) and amount sold (ORDER) for each book that is purchased. These data are not arranged in any special order.

ANALYSIS

Considering the random nature of the input data, a direct access file (DIRINV) should be used. We will assume that all inventory records contain the same information about a book as the records shown in Example 9.6 (stock number, title, author, price, quantity). This information must be read from each inventory record that is to be modified; the inventory amount (QUANT) should then be updated and the new inventory record written to the file.

Data Requirements

Program Parameter

maximum record number for file DIRINV (MAXSTK = 1000)

Input/Output Files

direct access inventory file (DIRINV)

Problem Inputs

the stock number of book ordered (INTEGER RECNUM)
the quantity purchased (INTEGER ORDER)
the current inventory file record is read from INVEN and saved in the following variables:

```
(INTEGER STOCK)
(CHARACTER *20 AUTHOR)
(CHARACTER *20 TITLE)
(REAL PRICE)
(INTEGER QUANT)
```

Problem Output

each updated inventory file record is written to file DIRINV

DESIGN

The algorithm follows:

Algorithm

1. For each order, read the record number (RECNUM) and order amount (ORDER) from the keyboard and update the corresponding record of the inventory file (DIRINV).

Step 1 Refinement

1.1 Read the order stock number.
1.2 DO WHILE the order stock number is in range.
    1.3 Read the order amount.
    1.4 Read the inventory record from DIRINV.
    1.5 IF the order is valid THEN
        Update the inventory record and write it to DIRINV.
        ELSE
        Print an error message.
        END IF
    1.6 Read the order stock number.
    END DO

Algorithm Refinements

Step 1.5 updates the inventory record selected by the order stock number (RECNUM), provided the order is valid. The order is considered valid if the stock number of the inventory record (STOCK) matches the order stock number and the inventory quantity is sufficient to fill the order. Otherwise, an appropriate error message is printed.

IMPLEMENTATION

Figure 9.17 shows program UPDATE. The program user enters the stock number, RECNUM, and quantity of each book sold. The corresponding record is retrieved from file DIRINV. The error message Error – record does not exist is displayed when the inventory record has a stock number of 0. This should happen when a blank record is read from file DIRINV. (This is the reason DIRINV was initialized to all blanks.) The error message Error – record and stock number don't match is displayed if the stock number field of the record read is different from its record number; however, this should never happen.

Figure 9.17. *Updating the Inventory File DIRINV*

```
      PROGRAM UPDATE
C Updates a direct access inventory file
C Reads the record number and quantity ordered
C from the keyboard. Updates the inventory amount for each record
C selected.

C Declarations
      INTEGER SENVAL, MAXSTK
      PARAMETER (SENVAL = 0, MAXSTK = 1000)
      INTEGER STOCK, QUANT, TOTAL, ORDER, RECNUM
      REAL PRICE
      CHARACTER *20 AUTHOR, TITLE

C Open file INVEN for update
      OPEN (UNIT = 2, FILE = 'DIRINV', FORM = 'FORMATTED',
     +     ACCESS = 'DIRECT', RECL = 54, STATUS = 'OLD')

C Read the record number and quantity of each book sold
C Update the inventory record if order is valid
      PRINT *, 'Enter record number of book sold (or 0 to stop):'
      READ *, RECNUM
      DO WHILE ((RECNUM .GT. SENVAL) .AND. (RECNUM .LE. MAXSTK))
         PRINT *, 'Enter quantity sold:'
         READ *, ORDER
C        Get record RECNUM
         READ (UNIT = 2, FMT = 21, REC = RECNUM)
     +      STOCK, AUTHOR, TITLE, PRICE, QUANT

C        If order is valid, update the inventory quantity
         IF ((STOCK .EQ. RECNUM) .AND. (QUANT .GE. ORDER)) THEN
            QUANT = QUANT - ORDER
            PRINT *, 'New inventory amount = ', QUANT
            WRITE (UNIT = 2, FMT = 21, REC = RECNUM)
     +         STOCK, AUTHOR, TITLE, PRICE, QUANT
21          FORMAT (I4, A20, A20, F6.2, I4)
         ELSE IF (STOCK .EQ. 0) THEN
            PRINT *, 'Error - record does not exist'
         ELSE IF (STOCK .NE. RECNUM) THEN
            PRINT *, 'Error - record and stock number don''t match'
         ELSE
            PRINT *, 'Inventory insufficient to fill order'
         END IF

         PRINT *, 'Enter record number of book sold (or 0 to stop):'
         READ *, RECNUM
      END DO
      IF (RECNUM .GT. MAXSTK) PRINT *, 'Record number out-of-range'
      CLOSE (UNIT = 2)

C Exit program
      STOP
      END
```

Figure 9.18. *Sample Run of Update Program*

```
Enter record number of book sold (or 0 to stop):
5
Enter quantity sold:
300
New inventory amount =      200

Enter record number of book sold (or 0 to stop):
3
Error - record does not exist

Enter record number of book sold (or 0 to stop):
1
Enter quantity sold:
30
Inventory insufficient to fill order

Enter record number of book sold (or 0 to stop):
0
```

TESTING AND VERIFICATION

Figure 9.18 shows a sample run of the update program for a direct access file. This run assumes there are two inventory records (record 1, quantity 18 and record 5, quantity 500). As shown in this sample, ensure your test data cause all the normal warning messages to be displayed. The error message

```
Error - record and stock number don't match
```

should not be displayed unless your computer system accesses the file incorrectly. After completing the file update, run a program with a DO loop that reads and echos each of the records in file DIRINV in sequence (see exercise 1 below). You should examine the output of this program to ensure the file update was performed correctly.

EXERCISES FOR SECTION 9.4

Programming

1. Write a DO loop that echo prints the records in file DIRINV in sequence. Use the loop-control variable as the record number in the READ statement.
2. Modify the program in Fig. 9.17 so that it deletes a record in file DIRINV if the ORDER for that record exceeds the quantity, QUANT. (*Hint:* To delete a record, replace it with a blank record.)

9.5 Common Programming Errors

1. When working with files, use the OPEN statement to connect each file before it is processed. Check with your instructor to determine the local restrictions

on file names and unit numbers. If the file is formatted, you must be careful to use the same format to read it as was used to create it.

2. Ensure an END = *lab* control specifier is used in each READ statement associated with a sequential file. Doing this is generally the only way to determine when all the file records have been processed; otherwise, an "attempt to read beyond end of file" error may occur. When writing a sequential file, ensure you always append an end-of-file record before disconnecting the file. When performing a READ/WRITE operation with a direct access file, the record number of the file being accessed must always be specified via a REC = *recnum* control specifier. You also should verify that the integer expression for *recnum* is within range for the file being processed; otherwise, a file access error will occur.

Chapter Review

We introduced you to file processing in Fortran and to the two types of Fortran files: sequential and direct access. These files differ in that the records of sequential files are always processed in a fixed, serial order, whereas the records of a direct access file may be processed in random order. In two case study solutions, we showed how to update both kinds of files.

The OPEN, CLOSE, REWIND, BACKSPACE, and END FILE statements were described as were the file parameters that must be specified in the OPEN statement. We also discussed the general READ/WRITE in Fortran and the control specifiers needed for file input/output operations. The statements introduced in this chapter are described in Table 9.1.

Table 9.1. *Fortran Statements for Chapter 9*

STATEMENT	EFFECT
OPEN Statement	

`OPEN (UNIT = 1, FILE = 'ERZA',`
`+      STATUS = 'OLD',`
`+      FORM = 'UNFORMATTED',`
`+      ACCESS = 'SEQUENTIAL')`
	Connects an existing sequential file named ERZA to the program. The file is associated with unit number 1.

REWIND Statement	
`REWIND (UNIT = 1)`	Resets the file position pointer for the file associated with unit number 1 to precede the first record.
BACKSPACE Statement	
`BACKSPACE (UNIT = 1)`	Moves the file position pointer to precede the record just processed.

STATEMENT	EFFECT
END FILE Statement	
END FILE (UNIT = 1)	Appends an end-of-file record to the file associated with unit number 1.
CLOSE Statement	
CLOSE (UNIT = 1)	Disconnects the file associated with unit number 1.
General READ	
READ (UNIT = 1, FMT = 10, + END = 11) N, A	Reads two data values from the file with unit number 1 using FORMAT 10. If the end-of-file record is read, a transfer to label 11 occurs.
General WRITE	
WRITE (UNIT = 2, + REC = I) N, A	Writes the value of N and A as the Ith record on the file with unit number 2.

Quick-check Exercises

1. A group of data items accessed by a single READ or WRITE statement is called a _____ .
2. The records of a _____ file may be accessed _____ , but the records of a _____ file must be accessed in order, beginning with the first record.
3. A(n) _____ is used to connect a file to a program that references it.
4. The END FILE statement is used to write a(n) _____ to a(n) _____ file.
5. Write an OPEN statement for a preexisting, direct access file named YRFILE, with records of length 100.
6. Provide a READ and FORMAT statement to read record I of the file in Quick-check exercise 5 into variables NAME, ADRESS, CITY, STATE, ZIP. Assume the first 3 data fields are type A30, the fourth is type A2, and the fifth is type I8. Provide appropriate declarations for the variables listed above.
7. Provide a WRITE statement that could be used to store your own name and address in record number 1 of this file.
8. Provide an OPEN statement for connecting an unformatted scratch file that will be used for output to unit number 2.
9. Provide a WRITE statement that writes the data read in Quick-check question 6 to the scratch file if the value of STATE is PA.

Answers to Quick-check Exercises

1. record
2. direct access; randomly; sequential

3. OPEN statement
4. end-of-file record; sequential
5. OPEN (UNIT = 3, FILE = 'YRFILE', FORM = 'FORMATTED',
       ACCESS = 'DIRECT', RECL = 100, STATUS = 'OLD')
6.   CHARACTER NAME *30, ADRESS *30, CITY *30, STATE *2
      INTEGER ZIP

       READ (UNIT = 3, FORM = 25, REC = I) NAME, ADRESS, CITY,
      +   STATE, ZIP
    25 FORMAT (3A30, A2, I8)
7. WRITE (UNIT = 3, FORM = 5, REC = 1) 'Your name',
       'Your address', 'Your city', 'ST', 19122
8.   OPEN (UNIT = 2, FORM = 'UNFORMATTED',
      +   ACCESS = 'SEQUENTIAL', STATUS = 'NEW')
9.   IF (STATE .EQ. 'PA') WRITE (UNIT = 2) NAME, ADRESS,
      +   CITY, STATE, ZIP

Review Questions

1. What is wrong with each of the following statements?

   a. OPEN (FILE = 'AFILE', FORM = 'FORMATTED', ACCESS = 'DIRECT',
        +   RECL = 100, STATUS = 'OLD')
   b. PRINT '(3X, 2Z10, 3A10, 5X, A4)', A,B,C,D,E,F
   c. FORMAT (' ', 2I4, 5X, A10)

2. Write a READ statement to read the Nth record of a direct access file into the variable INREC. Assume the direct access file is unformatted, contains MAXNUM records, and is associated with unit 2. Be sure to verify that N is in range.

3. Provide a loop that reads records 10, 20, 30, 40, 50 from the file described in Quick-check exercises 5 and 6 and copies those records to a sequential connected to unit number 2.

4. Provide a loop that adds two zeros to the end of each zip code stored in the file described in Quick-check exercises 5 and 6 (e.g., change 19117 to 1911700). Assume the file has 100 records.

5. Identify the kind(s) of input/output statements in which the following specifiers can appear:

   a. REC
   b. FMT
   c. UNIT
   d. STATUS
   e. END

6. If a Fortran OPEN statement contains the specifier STATUS = 'SCRATCH', then it usually will not contain which of the following specifiers:

   a. ACCESS = 'DIRECT'
   b. ACCESS = 'SEQUENTIAL'
   c. FILE = *file-name*
   d. FORM = 'FORMATTED'
   e. RECL = *record-length*

7. If a Fortran program contains the following OPEN statement:

   ```
   OPEN (UNIT = 13, FILE = 'TEST', ACCESS = 'SEQUENTIAL',
   +      FORM = 'FORMATTED', STATUS = 'UNKNOWN')
   ```

   then it should not contain which one of the following statements:

   a. READ (UNIT = 13, END = 99)
   b. READ (UNIT = 13, FMT = 100)
   c. READ (UNIT = 13, FMT = 100, END = 99)
   d. READ (UNIT = 13, FMT = *)
   e. READ (UNIT = 13, FMT = *, END = 99)

8. Which one of the following is not true about direct access files?

   a. The file should be initialized before it is used.
   b. A record cannot be deleted from the file.
   c. Records cannot be inserted between two consecutive integer record numbers by using a real record number.
   d. Each record has a unique record number beginning with 0.
   e. All records in a file are the same length.

9. Which one of the following statements is not valid?

   a. READ (UNIT = 13, FMT = 100, END = 99)
   b. READ (UNIT = 13, FMT = 100, REC = 37)
   c. READ (UNIT = 13, END = 99, REC = 37)
   d. READ (UNIT = 13, END = 99)
   e. READ (UNIT = 13, REC = 37)

Programming Projects

1. Especially during the colder months of the year, weather forecasters frequently inform us not only of the Fahrenheit-degree temperature (TEMP) reading at a given hour, but also of the wind-chill factor (WCF) at that time. This factor is used to indicate the relative degree of coldness that we are likely to experience if we are outside. Its calculation is based on the thermometer reading (TEMP) and the velocity (V) of the wind at the time. Write a program to compute the wind-chill factor for

temperatures ranging from $-50°$ to $+50°$ in increments of 5° and for wind velocities of from 5 to 60 mph, also in increments of 5°. Your output should appear similar to the following table and should be written to an output file. When you are done, rewind this file and read and echo each record to the screen.

```
WIND-CHILL FACTOR TABLE (DEGREES F)
TEMPERATURE                 WIND VELOCITY (MILES PER HOUR)
READING (DEG F)         5 10 15 20 25 30 35 . . .
        -50
        -45
        -40                              .
          .                              .
          .                              .
          .
          0
          5
          .
          .
          .
         20          . . .                    -16
          .
          .
          .
         50
```

The formula for computing the wind-chill factor is

$$WCF = 91.4 - (.486 + .305\sqrt{V} - .020V) \times (91.4 - temp).$$

Your answers should be rounded to the nearest whole degree. The WCF of -16 has been given as a test value. It is the WCF when TEMP is 20° and V is 25.

2. *Base 2 addition.* Write a program to read two 15-digit binary numbers (strings of 0s and 1s) into the arrays I and J (both of size 15) using the 15I1 format. Then compute the decimal (base 10) representation of these numbers and print both the binary and decimal representations.

Next, compute the column-by-column sum of these two numbers, moving *right to left*. Use the variable CARRY to indicate whether a previous addition contained a CARRY. A value of 0 for CARRY should indicate that the previous addition had no carry; a value of 1 should be used when a carry occurs. (Initially, CARRY is 0.) Store the column-by-column sum in the array SUMIJ of size 16. The value of each element SUMIJ(L+1) and the next value of CARRY is determined by adding the values of elements I(L),J(L), and CARRY, as shown next.

For all L from 15 to 1:

If only one of I(L),J(L), or CARRY is 1, then

SUMIJ(L+1) is 1, and CARRY must be set to 0.

If all three of I(L),J(L), and CARRY are 1, then

SUMIJ(L+1) is 1 and CARRY must be set to 1.

If any two of I(L),J(L), or CARRY are 1, then

SUMIJ(L+1) is 0 and CARRY must be set to 1.

Otherwise, SUMIJ(L+1) is 0 and CARRY must be set to 0.

This will define the values of SUMIJ(16) through SUMIJ(2), from I(15),J(15) through I(1) and J(1), respectively. Once the other "additions" are done, SUMIJ(1) can be defined directly from CARRY. Compute the decimal representation of the SUM and print the binary and decimal representations.

Test your program on the following strings:

```
I = 00000 00010 11011
J = 00000 01010 11110
I = 00000 00010 00110
J = 00000 00001 11101
I = 10001 00010 00100
J = 11100 11101 11001
```

Your output, for example, for the second set of data might appear as follows:

```
    I =   00000 00010 00110
    J =   00000 00001 11101
SUMIJ = 000000 00100 00011
```

Use functions and subroutines as needed and draw a structure chart.

3. We can consider a single sheet of printer paper as a piece of graph paper containing a grid of 50 × 100—50 rows and 100 columns (with space left over). We can use this grid to plot a function *f* on *x,y*-axes, in much the same way as we would plot *f* on a piece of graph paper. To do this, we set up two 100-element real arrays, Y and XLIST, and a CHARACTER *1 array LINE of size 100. LINE will be used to define 50 lines of 100 print positions each. Initially, LINE is to contain all blanks. Y will be used to store 100 values of *f* (one for each of 100 values of *x* along the *x*-axis). XLIST will be used to define the index of each *x* in the 100-item list used to compute *f(x)*. Thus, initially, XLIST (*i*) = *i* for all values of *i* between 1 and 100. These indices will be used to indicate which of the 100 horizontal grids corresponds to each value of *x* for which *f(x)* was computed.

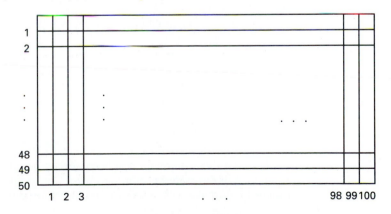

Now proceed as shown in the following algorithm.

Algorithm

1. Let XMIN be the smallest value of X and XMAX the largest value of X.
2. Define a subinterval length, SUBINT, equal to (XMAX − XMIN) / 99.0.
3. Initialize X to XMIN.
4. DO for each value of LV from 1 to 100
    5. Compute f(X) and store it in Y(LV).
    6. Increment X by SUBINT.
   END DO

This will compute a value of f for each of the 100 values of X used. Each x index and the corresponding value f(x) will be stored in corresponding elements of XLIST and Y, respectively.

Next we sort, in descending order, the array Y, exchanging the contents of the elements in XLIST in parallel with the exchanges in Y.

Then we determine 50 y-axis values (one for each line of output) as follows: Compute YINT as

$$YINT = \frac{Y(1) - Y(100)}{49.0}$$

where Y(1) now contains the largest value of f and Y(100) contains the smallest value. We must print each of the 50 lines of the grid. The first line corresponds to the value Y(1), the second to Y(1) − YINT, the third to Y(1) − 2 * YINT, . . . , and the 50th to Y(1) − 49 * YINT, or Y(100). For example, if Y(1) = 1000.0 and Y(100) = 100.0, then the lines would correspond to

   1000.00, 981.63, 963.26, . . . , 136.74, 118.37, 100.00.

(Note that 900.0/49.0 = 18.37.)
We do this as follows:

Algorithm

1. Initialize array LINE to all blanks.
2. Initialize LINVAL to Y(1).
3. DO WHILE LINVAL is greater than or equal to Y(100)
    4. For each K such that Y(K) is closer to LINVAL than to LINVAL − YINT, place a '$' in LINE(XLIST(K)).
    5. Display LINE.
    6. Replace each '$' in LINE with ' '.
    7. Reset LINVAL to LINVAL − YINT.
   END DO

Because the data in array Y has been sorted, the implementation of step 4 is simplified. We illustrate by example, using the y-axis values computed earlier. Suppose the first few elements in Y and XLIST are defined as follows:

XLIST(1)	XLIST(2)	XLIST(3)	XLIST(4)	XLIST(5)
37	53	36	54	35

Y(1)	Y(2)	Y(3)	Y(4)	Y(5)
996.3	992.2	987.3	980.1	970.5

The first time through loop 3, LINVAL will be equal to 1000. Because both 996.3 and 992.2 are closer in value to 1000 than to 981.63, a $ will be entered into LINE(37) and LINE(53). The next time through loop 2, LINVAL will be 981.63. Because 987.3 and 980.1 are closer to 981.63 than to 963.26, a $ will be placed in LINE(36) and LINE(54). Therefore the test for the condition

ABS(Y(K) – LINVAL) < ABS(Y(K)–(LINVAL – YINT))

must be made only for consecutive elements in Y, starting where the previous test failed and continuing until the test fails again.

Write a program to implement the above algorithms. Use subroutines whenever possible. Test your program on the function

$$f(x) = (x - 1)^4/(x - 6),$$

where x ranges from -1 to $+6$ ($[-1, 6]$). Provide a structure chart to describe the components of your system. Write your output to a file.

4. Let FILEA and FILEB be two files containing the name and identification number of the students in two different programming classes. Assume that these files are arranged in ascending order by student number and that no student is in both classes. Write a program to read the information on FILEA and FILEB and merge them onto a third file (FILEC), retaining the ascending order.

5. Write a program that reads a name and a list of three exam scores for each student in a class and copies this information onto a sequential file called GRADES. Test your program on the following data:

```
IVORY     47 82 93
CLARK     86 42 77
MENACE    99 88 92
BUMSTEAD  88 74 81
```

Provide a subroutine that reads and echo prints the file GRADES. Then write a program that adds a fourth exam score to each component of the file GRADES. Assume each student's name and fourth exam score are provided as input data.

6. Write a program to read the sequential file created in Example 9.3, sort the file in ascending order according to stock number, and write the results on a new file. You may assume that the entire sequential file will fit in memory at once.

7. Create a sequential file SALMEN containing the salaries of 10 men, and a second sequential file SALWOM containing the salaries of 10 women. For each employee on these files, there is an employee number (four digits), an employee name (a string), and an employee salary. Each file is arranged in ascending order by employee number. Write a program that will read each of these files and merge the contents onto a third file, SALARY, retaining the ascending order of employee numbers. For each employee written to the file SALARY, write an M (for male) or an F (for female) following the employee number.

8. Write a program to read and print the file SALARY and compute the average salary for all employees.

9. Assume you have a file of records, each containing a person's last name, first name, birth date, and sex. Create a new file containing only first names and sex. Also, print out the complete name of every person whose last name begins with the letter A, C, F, or P through Z and who was born in a month that begins with the letter J.

10. Write a program that prints every record of a direct access file whose record number ends with a zero.

11. Write a menu-driven program that will update an electronic parts inventory file. The menu options should include

   a. creating an initial blank file,
   b. inserting records in a file,
   c. updating selected records,
   d. displaying selected records, and
   e. displaying all nonblank records.

   If option (b) or (c) is chosen, the new record data should be entered at the terminal. The program user should be able to verify that the record is correct before it is written to the file.

12. The description of a truss (and many other engineering structures or concepts) could be described by a data file like the following:

```
node     1   0.0 0.0
node     2  10.0 0.0
node     3   5.0 8.3333
member 1  1    2
member 2  1    3
member 3  2    3
```

This small data set has described a simple truss that is an equilateral triangle. The first three records give the labels (numbers in this case) of the nodes and their x and y values, which specify the position of the node. The next three records label the members and state the beginning and ending nodes of the members. A real truss would have many similar triangles to make up a structure. Write a program that will input such a data set and create a possible description of the truss. For these purposes, the program should check the following:

1. Members should begin and end with nodes in the list of defined nodes.
2. Each node must have at least two members connected to it. (It does not matter if it is a beginning or ending node for a member.)

13. A generalization of the previous truss problem is to do almost any kind of layout. Electrical circuits can be placed on "boards" with a similar data structure. The node definitions would be geometric as in the truss problem. The member definitions would need another field that would indicate the type of element: wire, capacitor, resistor, ... Write a program to input these data and create a description of the circuit parts.

CHAPTER 10
String Manipulation

So FAR, we have seen limited use of character data. Character variables have appeared in the list portion of data initialization and READ and PRINT statements, and they have been used for storing character strings that were later displayed to identify program output. Strings also have been used in PRINT statements to annotate program output and for format specification.

Many computer applications are concerned with the manipulation of textual data rather than numerical data. Computer-based word processing systems enable a user to compose letters, term papers, newspaper articles, and even books at a computer terminal instead of using a typewriter. The advantage of using such a system is that words and sentences can be modified, whole paragraphs can be moved, and then a fresh copy can be printed without mistakes or erasures.

Additional applications include computerized typesetting equipment in the publishing industry; text editors to update telephone directories and annual reports on a regular basis; programs to analyze great works of literature.

In the sections that follow, we introduce some fundamental operations that can be performed on character data. We also describe how to reference a character substring and how to concatenate (or join) two strings. Finally, we discuss how to search for a substring in a larger string and how to delete a substring or replace it with another.

10.1   Character String Declaration

We have already used the CHARACTER statement to declare character strings and string arrays. For example, the declaration

```
CHARACTER *10 A(20), FLOWER, ANIMAL
```

allocates storage space for 22 character strings consisting of 10 characters each. (Twenty of these strings are elements of the array A.)

The concept of the length of a character string is important to the discussion of character-type data. We introduce this concept by defining what is meant by the length of a character string constant or variable. The definition of the length of other character entities will be given as they are introduced in later sections.

Length of Character String Constants and Variables

1. The length of a character string constant is equal to the number of characters in the constant (excluding the apostrophes used to delimit the constant) except that a pair of adjacent apostrophes within the constant is counted as a single character.
2. The length of a character variable is defined as the length given to the variable when it is declared.

Note that the length of any character entity is a positive number and may not change. Zero-length character strings are not permitted in Fortran.

Although the length of a character variable remains unchanged, character data of different lengths may be assigned to the variable. Any character string shorter than the declared length of a variable will be padded on the right with blanks when assigned to that variable; a string that is too long can't be stored in its entirety and is truncated.

Fortran provides a library function LEN that can be used to determine the length of its character string argument. We describe this function and provide examples of its use in Section 10.6.

Internal Representation of Character Data

All information stored in a computer must be represented as a string of binary digits; character data are no exception. Each individual character has a unique binary code, and a character string is represented by joining the individual codes together. This means that the internal representation for 'ABC' is the binary number formed by joining the codes for the letters A, B, and C.

There are several different sets of binary codes for characters. Most prevalent is the American Standard Code for Information Interchange, or ASCII (pronounced "askey"). In ASCII, 8 binary digits (bits) are used to encode 127 different characters.

EXAMPLE 10.1

The ASCII binary codes for the letters A, B, and C follow:

```
A 01000001
B 01000010
C 01000011
```

Therefore the string 'ABC' is represented by the binary number

```
01000001 01000010 01000011
    A        B        C
```

in ASCII.

Table 10.1 shows the ASCII code for 12 characters. The numbers listed under the columns labeled CODE are the decimal values corresponding to the actual eight-bit strings (e.g., decimal 65 corresponds to 01000001, the code for A). Some features of Table 10.1 are listed next; Appendix B shows the complete ASCII code and two other less common codes.

- The blank character has a code value of 32.
- The digit characters 0 through 9 have the code values 48 through 57.
- The uppercase letters have smaller code values than the lowercase letters.
- The difference between the code values for each lowercase letter and its corresponding uppercase letter is always 32.

Table 10.1. *Examples of ASCII Codes (in decimal)*

CHARACTER	CODE	CHARACTER	CODE	CHARACTER	CODE
blank	32	+	43	−	45
0	48	A	65	a	97
1	49	B	66	b	98
9	57	Z	90	z	122

**EXERCISES FOR
SECTION 10.1**

Self-check

1. How would the digit string '123' be represented in the ASCII code?

10.2   Substrings

We often need to reference substrings of a longer character string. For example, we might want to examine the day, '25', in the string 'JUNE 25, 1990' or remove the substring 'Machinery' from the string 'Association for Computing Machinery'. In this section, we discuss how to use special features of Fortran to segment a character string into substrings or to extract part of a longer string.

To specify a substring of a character variable or character array element, we write the substring name in the form shown next.

**SYNTAX
DISPLAY**

Substring Reference

SYNTAX: *cname* ($exp_1 : exp_2$)

EXAMPLE: FLOWER(4 : 8)

INTERPRETATION: *Cname* is a character variable or character array element, and exp_1, exp_2 are substring expressions. The values of exp_1 and exp_2 should be type integer. exp_1 and exp_2 are used to specify which substring of *cname* should be referenced. The value of exp_1 indicates the position in *cname* of the first character of the substring; the value of exp_2 indicates the position in *cname* of the last character of the substring.

NOTE: The reference *cname*($exp_1 : exp_2$) is called the *substring name*. The integer values of exp_1 and exp_2 must satisfy the following constraints:

$$1 \leq exp_1 \leq exp_2 \leq \text{length of } cname$$

If exp_1 is omitted, it is considered to be 1; if exp_2 is omitted, it is considered to be the same as the length of *cname*. The substring length is defined as $exp_2 - exp_1 + 1$.

EXAMPLE 10.2   The names of three substrings of the character variable PRES are as follows:

```
CHARACTER *18 PRES
DATA PRES /'ADAMS, JOHN QUINCY'/
```

```
          PRES(1 : 5)          PRES(13 : )

                    PRES(8 : 11)
```

EXAMPLE 10.3   The program segment

```
CHARACTER *11 SOSSEC
CHARACTER *3 SSN1
CHARACTER *2 SSN2
CHARACTER *4 SSN3
PRINT *, 'Enter a social security number in apostrophes'
READ *, SOSSEC
SSN1 = SOSSEC(1 : 3)
SSN2 = SOSSEC(5 : 6)
SSN3 = SOSSEC(8 : 11)
```

reads a character string representing a social security number. If the string '042–30–0786' is read, this program segment breaks the social security number into substrings, as shown next:

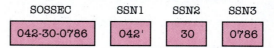

SOSSEC	SSN1	SSN2	SSN3
042-30-0786	042'	30	0786

The assignment statements in this program are *character assignment statements;* they each assign a character string to a character variable. We discuss character assignments in more detail later in this chapter.

EXAMPLE 10.4   The program in Fig. 10.1 prints each word of the sentence SENTNC on a separate line. It assumes that a single blank occurs between words.
    The statement

```
CHARACTER *(LENGTH) SENTNC
```

declares a character variable whose length is determined by the parameter LENGTH. Any expression involving integer constants and parameters may be used to specify the length of a character variable. The expression must be enclosed in parentheses.

Figure 10.1. *Program to Print Words in a Sentence*

```
      PROGRAM WORDS
C Print each word in a sentence

C Declarations
      INTEGER LENGTH
      CHARACTER *1 BLANK
      PARAMETER (LENGTH = 80, BLANK = ' ')
      CHARACTER *(LENGTH) SENTNC
      INTEGER FIRST, NEXT

C Enter data string
      PRINT *, 'Enter a string:'
      READ '(A)', SENTNC

C Print each word (the characters between the blanks)
      FIRST = 1
      DO 10 NEXT = 1, LENGTH
         IF (SENTNC(NEXT : NEXT) .EQ. BLANK) THEN
            PRINT *, SENTNC(FIRST : NEXT)
            FIRST = NEXT + 1
         END IF
   10 CONTINUE

C Print the last word if it is not yet printed
      IF (SENTNC(LENGTH : LENGTH) .NE. BLANK) THEN
         PRINT *, SENTNC(FIRST : LENGTH)
      END IF

C Exit program
      STOP
      END

Enter a string:
THE QUICK BROWN FOX JUMPED
THE
QUICK
BROWN
FOX
JUMPED
```

The program variable FIRST always points to the start of the current word and is initialized to 1. During each execution of the loop, the condition

```
(SENTNC(NEXT : NEXT) .EQ. BLANK)
```

tests to see whether the next character is a blank. If it is, the statements

```
PRINT *, SENTNC(FIRST : NEXT)
FIRST = NEXT + 1
```

cause all characters in the current word (from FIRST through the blank) to be printed and FIRST to be reset to point to the first character following the blank.

The statement

```
PRINT *, SENTNC(FIRST : LENGTH)
```

following the loop is used to print the last word. This statement is necessary only when the last character (SENTNC(LENGTH : LENGTH)) is not a blank.

The formatted READ statement

```
READ '(A)', SENTNC
```

is used to enter the data line as one long string (length 80) into SENTNC. The data string should not be enclosed in quotes.   ■

EXERCISES FOR SECTION 10.2

Self-check

1. Given the character variables SSN1 and PRES (defined in examples 10.2 and 10.3), list the characters that would be printed by the statements

```
PRINT *, SSN1(1 : 3)
PRINT *, PRES(6 : )
PRINT *, PRES( : 6)
PRINT *, PRES( : )
```

Programming

1. Indicate how you could modify the program in Fig. 10.1 to convert a sentence to "pig latin," in which the first letter of each word is moved to the end of the word, followed by the letters AY. The string 'THE QUICK BROWN FOX JUMPED' would become 'HETAY UICKQAY ROWNBAY OXFAY UMPEDJAY'. (*Hint:* You need to change only the two PRINT statements.)
2. Modify Example 10.4 so that the restriction of a single blank between words is removed. Your program will have to skip over a group of consecutive blanks.

10.3 Character Expressions

Until now, character expressions have consisted of individual character variables, substrings, or character string constants. In Fortran, we can join strings using the *concatenation operator* // (two consecutive slashes). The concatenation operator comes between the arithmetic operators and the relational operators in the precedence table shown in Section 3.2 (Table 3.7).

SYNTAX
DISPLAY

The Concatenation Operator

SYNTAX: S_1 // S_2

INTERPRETATION: The character string S_1 is concatenated with the character string S_2. This means the string S_2 is joined to the right end of the string S_1. The length of the resulting string is equal to the sum of the lengths of S_1 and S_2.

EXAMPLE 10.5

1. The expression

   ```
   'ABC' // 'DE'
   ```

   concatenates the string `'ABC'` and `'DE'` together to form one string of length 5, `'ABCDE'`.
2. Given a string MESSAG with 11 or more characters, the expression

   ```
   MESSAG (1 : 5) // '*****' // MESSAG (11 : )
   ```

   creates a new string that differs from MESSAG only in character positions 6 through 10 (which have been replaced with asterisks).
3. Given the string

   ```
   'ADAMS, JOHN QUINCY'
   ```

   stored in the character variable PRES (length 18), the expression

   ```
   PRES(8 : 12) // PRES(13 : 13) // '. ' // PRES( : 5)
   ```

   forms the string

   ```
   'JOHN Q. ADAMS'
   ```

   of length 13 (5 + 1 + 2 + 5). ■

Use of Character Expressions

In Fortran, we can use character expressions in character assignment statements, as operands of relational operators in logical expressions, in PRINT statements, and as arguments in subprogram calls. We describe the rules for using the first two in this section, and discuss character string arguments later in this chapter.

The character assignment statement is described next.

SYNTAX
DISPLAY

Character Assignment Statement

SYNTAX: *cname = expression*

INTERPRETATION: *Cname* may be a character variable, an array element, or a substring name. A character *expression* consists of a sequence of character string constants, character variables, character array elements, substrings, or character-valued functions connected by the concatenation operator //.

NOTES: If the length of *cname* exceeds the length of *expression*, *expression* will be padded on the right with blanks before being stored.

If the length of *cname* is less than the length of *expression*, the extra characters at the right of *expression* will be discarded.

If *cname* is a substring name, only the specified substring is defined by the assignment; all other characters in the string are unchanged, for example, NAME(2 : 4) = *expression* changes only characters 2 through 4 of NAME.

No character position being defined in *cname* may be part of *expression*. For example, NAME(1 : 2) = NAME(1 : 1) // 'A' is illegal because NAME(1 : 1) is being defined (NAME(2 : 2) = NAME(1 : 1) would be legal).

EXAMPLE 10.6   Consider the following sample program segment:

```
CHARACTER BIGGER *17, SMALLR *8, SAME *12
BIGGER = 'EXTRASENSORY'
SMALLR = BIGGER
SAME = BIGGER
```

The CHARACTER declaration allocates storage for three strings of different lengths. The result of executing the assignment statements is shown next.

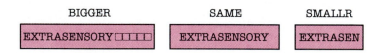

The assignment statement

```
BIGGER(6 : ) = SAME
```

would change BIGGER as follows:

BIGGER

EXTRAEXTRASENSORY

This result could also be obtained using the assignment statement

```
BIGGER = SMALLR(1 : 5) // SAME
```

EXAMPLE 10.7   Consider the following sample program segment:

```
CHARACTER *8 NAME, HERS, HIS
CHARACTER *4 FIRST, FIRSTA, FIRSTB, INITLS
CHARACTER *9 LSTFST
NAME = 'JOHN DOE'
FIRST = 'JIM'
FIRSTA = NAME(1 : 2)
FIRSTB = NAME
HIS = FIRST // NAME(6 : )
LSTFST = NAME(6 : ) // ', ' // NAME( : 4)
INITLS = NAME(1 : 1) // '.' // NAME(6 : 6) // '.'
HERS = NAME
HERS(3 : 3) = 'A'
```

The execution of the assignment statements in this segment will result in the following string assignments:

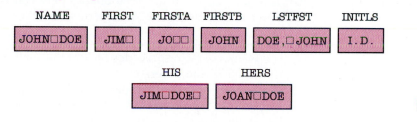

**EXERCISES FOR
SECTION 10.3**

Self-check

1. Given the string PRES

```
'ADAMS, JOHN QUINCY'
```

write the strings formed by the following expressions:

```
PRES(8 : 11) // ' ' // PRES( : 5)
PRES(1 : 5) // PRES(7 : 8) // '.' // PRES(13 : 13) // '.'
```

2. Let `HIPPO`, `QUOTE`, `QUOTE1`, `QUOTE2`, and `BIGGER` be declared and initialized as

```
CHARACTER *12 HIPPO, BIGGER
CHARACTER *30 QUOTE1
CHARACTER *24 QUOTE2, QUOTE
DATA HIPPO, BIGGER / 'HIPPOPOTAMUS', 'SMALL' /
DATA QUOTE1 / 'STRUCTURED PROGRAMS ARE BETTER' /
```

Carry out each of the following assignment statements in sequence. Indicate if any are illegal.

a. `QUOTE( : 24) = QUOTE1(21 : 24) // QUOTE( : 20)`
b. `QUOTE2 = QUOTE(21 : 24) // QUOTE( : 20)`
c. `QUOTE(1 : 24) = QUOTE2`
d. `HIPPO(4 : ) = 'S'`
e. `BIGGER = 'LARGE'`
f. `BIGGER(1 : 6) = BIGGER(7 : 12)`
g. `BIGGER(6 : 7) = 'ST'`

10.4 String Comparisons

We first discussed the comparison of character strings in Section 3.3, where we learned that the order relationship between two strings is based on the Fortran collating sequence, as described next.

Collating Sequence

1. The blank character precedes (is less than) all of the digits (`0`, `1`, `2`, . . . , `9`) and all of the letters (`A`, `B`, `C`, . . . , `Z`).
2. The letters are ordered lexigraphically (in dictionary sequence), that is, `A` precedes `B`, `B` precedes `C`, . . . , `Y` precedes `Z`.
3. The digits follow their normal numeric sequence, that is, the character `0` precedes `1`, `1` precedes `2`, . . . , `8` precedes `9`.

It also is important to note what is not specified by the collating sequence. In particular, the following:

■ The relationship between the special characters (punctuation symbols, arithmetic operators, etc.) and `A–Z`, `0–9`, and blank depend on the character code used.
■ The relationship between the letters `A–Z` and the characters `0–9` depend on the character code used.

As we mentioned in Chapter 3, the collating sequence ensures that order comparisons between strings of letters will follow their dictionary sequence; however, little else is guaranteed.

EXAMPLE 10.8 The relationships between the pairs of character strings shown next are not specified by the Fortran collating sequence.

`'ALLEN, R.'` and `'ALLEN, RICHARD'`	Depends on relative order of period and `I`.
`'X123'` and `'XYZ'`	Depends on relative order of `1` and `Y`.
`'./*'` and `'.*//*='`	Depends on relative order of `/` and `*`.
`'***'` and `'*'`	Depends on relative order of `*` and blank. ■

All relationships not specified are compiler-dependent and are based on the internal code used by the compiler. We described the ASCII code in Section 10.1. It is important that you learn the collating sequence defined for the compiler that you are using. The special functions described next may be of some help.

CHAR and ICHAR

Fortran has a library function, `ICHAR`, which we can use to determine the relative position of a character in the collating sequence. For example, the statement

```
PRINT *, ICHAR(' '), ICHAR('A'), ICHAR('O')
```

prints the relative positions in the collating sequence of the three characters shown (blank, letter `A`, and zero).

The function `CHAR` is the *inverse* of the function `ICHAR`; `CHAR` can be used to determine the character in a specified position of the collating sequence. The statement

```
PRINT *, CHAR(O)
```

will print the first character of the collating sequence (position 0).

The functions `CHAR` and `ICHAR` are described next.

SYNTAX DISPLAY

Function ICHAR

SYNTAX: `ICHAR(`*character*`)`

EXAMPLE: `ICHAR('A')`

INTERPRETATION: The integer function `ICHAR` determines the relative position of *character* in the Fortran collating sequence.

SYNTAX
DISPLAY

Function CHAR

SYNTAX: CHAR(*pos*)

EXAMPLE: CHAR(27)

INTERPRETATION: The character function CHAR determines the character at relative position *pos* in the collating sequence. The value of *pos* must be between 0 and $n - 1$, where n is the number of characters in the collating sequence.

EXAMPLE 10.9

The program in Fig. 10.2 prints the position in the collating sequence of each character in the Fortran character set. The character set is stored in the character variable CHRSET. The PRINT statement prints a character, CHRSET(POS : POS), followed by its position in the collating sequence, ICHAR(CHRSET(POS : POS)). Try this program on your computer. ■

Figure 10.2. *Position of Fortran Characters in the Collating Sequence*

```
      PROGRAM COLLAT
C Prints the relative positions in the collating sequence
C of all characters in the Fortran character set

C Declarations
      INTEGER SETSIZ
      PARAMETER (SETSIZ = 49)
      INTEGER POS
      CHARACTER *(SETSIZ) CHRSET

C FORTRAN character set
      DATA CHRSET
     + /' ABCDEFGHIJKLMNOPQRSTUVWXYZ0123456789+-*/()=$,.'':'/

C Print each character and its relative position
      PRINT *, 'Collating sequence positions for FORTRAN characters'
      PRINT *
      PRINT *, 'Character     Position'
      DO 10 POS = 1, SETSIZ
         PRINT '(5X, A, 11X, I3)',
     +      CHRSET(POS : POS), ICHAR(CHRSET(POS : POS))
  10  CONTINUE

C Exit program
      STOP
      END
```

EXAMPLE 10.10

The program in Fig. 10.3 counts and prints the number of occurrences of each character in an input string (TEXT). The array CHRCNT (subscripts 0 through 255) is used to track the number of occurrences of each character. This array is

Figure 10.3. *Counting Character Occurrences in a String*

```
      PROGRAM OCCURS
C Finds the number of occurrences of each character in text

C Declarations
      INTEGER COLLEN, TXTLEN
      PARAMETER (COLLEN = 255, TXTLEN = 80)
      INTEGER CHRCNT(0 : COLLEN), POS, NEXT
      CHARACTER *(TXTLEN) TEXT
      CHARACTER *1 NEXCHR

C Initialize array of counters and enter data string
      DATA CHRCNT /0, COLLEN * 0/
      PRINT *, 'Enter a string:'
      READ '(A)', TEXT

C Increase count of each character in text
      DO 20 NEXT = 1, TXTLEN
         NEXCHR = TEXT(NEXT : NEXT)
         CHRCNT(ICHAR(NEXCHR)) = CHRCNT(ICHAR(NEXCHR)) + 1
   20 CONTINUE

C Print results
      PRINT *, 'Character        Occurrence'
      DO 30 POS = 0, COLLEN
         IF (CHRCNT(POS) .NE. 0) THEN
            PRINT '(4X, A, 17X, I2)', CHAR(POS), CHRCNT(POS)
         END IF
   30 CONTINUE

C Exit program
      STOP
      END
```

initialized to all zeros. Because `ICHAR(NEXCHR)` is the position of character `NEXCHR` in the collating sequence, the statement

```
CHRCNT(ICHAR(NEXCHR)) = CHRCNT(ICHAR(NEXCHR)) + 1
```

increments the array element corresponding to character `NEXCHR`. The statement

```
PRINT '(4X, A, 17X, I2)', CHAR(POS), CHRCNT(POS)
```

in DO loop 30 prints each character followed by its number of occurrences.

The program shown in Fig. 10.3 works regardless of the collating sequence used on a particular computer. The decision step inside loop 30 ensures that counts are printed only for those characters that actually appear in the text string. A sample run is shown in Fig. 10.4.

Figure 10.4. *Sample Output for Program in Fig. 10.3*

```
Enter a string:
THE QUICK BROWN FOX JUMPED OVER THE LAZY DOG.

Character           Occurrence
                        43
     .                   1
     A                   1
     B                   1
     C                   1
     D                   2
     E                   4
     F                   1
     G                   1
     H                   2
     I                   1
     J                   1
     K                   1
     L                   1
     M                   1
     N                   1
     O                   4
     P                   1
     Q                   1
     R                   2
     T                   2
     U                   2
     V                   1
     W                   1
     X                   1
     Y                   1
     Z                   1
```

10.5 String Length and Search Functions

The Fortran library function LEN determines the length (number of characters) in its character string argument, as described next.

SYNTAX
DISPLAY

String Length Function LEN

SYNTAX: LEN(*string*)

INTERPRETATION: *String* may be any character expression (including character string constants and variables). The value returned is an integer denoting the length of *string*.

NOTES: If *string* is a character string constant, its length is determined by counting the characters inside the enclosing apostrophes [e.g., LEN('ABC') is 3; LEN('A''S') is also 3 (why?)].

If *string* is a character variable (or array element), its length is defined by the variable (or array) declaration statement.

If *string* is a substring of the form $S(exp_1 : exp_2)$, its length is equal to $exp_2 - exp_1 + 1$.

It *string* is a character expression involving the concatenation operator, //, its length is equal to the sum of the individual string lengths of the operands of //.

EXAMPLE 10.11

1. LEN('ABCDE') returns a value of 5.
2. LEN('MY' // 'NAME') returns a value of 6.
3. If WORD is declared as a character variable of length 10, LEN(WORD) always returns a value of 10. Thus the sequence of statements

```
WORD = 'ABCDE'
I = LEN(WORD)
PRINT *, I
```

prints the value 10, the length of the string 'ABCDE   ' that is stored in WORD.

The Function GETLEN

As indicated in the box above, the length of a character variable is independent of the data stored in it. There are times when we would like to know exactly how many characters are stored in a string, excluding any blank padding.

EXAMPLE 10.12

Often we want to disregard any padding characters when determining the length of a string. Standard Fortran does not provide a library function for this purpose, so we must write our own. The user-defined function GETLEN in Fig. 10.5 determines the "actual" length of an input string, excluding any blank padding. It does this by starting with the last character and skipping over blanks until the first nonblank character is reached. If the last character in string S is not a blank, the value of GETLEN(S) is the same as LEN(S). If all

Figure 10.5. *Function GETLEN*

```
      INTEGER FUNCTION GETLEN (STRING)
C Determines length of string excluding any blank padding
C Preconditions : STRING is defined.
C Postconditions: The function result is the actual string length
C                 and includes only the characters preceding the padding.

C Argument Declarations
      CHARACTER *(*) STRING
```

```
C Local Declarations
      CHARACTER *1 BLANK
      PARAMETER (BLANK = ' ')
      INTEGER NEXT

C Start with the last character and find the first nonblank
      DO 10 NEXT = LEN(STRING), 1, -1
          IF (STRING(NEXT : NEXT) .NE. BLANK) THEN
              GETLEN = NEXT
              RETURN
          END IF
   10 CONTINUE

C All characters are blanks
      GETLEN = 0

C Exit function
      RETURN
      END
```

characters are blank, GETLEN returns a value of zero. (The statement

CHARACTER *(*) STRING

in Fig. 10.5 is explained in the next section.)

The GETLEN function is very useful when concatenating strings. If SHORTS is a character variable, there may be a number of extraneous blanks before the letter M in the character string formed by the expression

SHORTS // ' MORE STUFF'

There is only one blank before the letter M in the character string formed by

SHORTS(1 : GETLEN(SHORTS)) // ' MORE STUFF'

Length of Character Arguments

Character arguments in a subprogram call can be character expressions (including character string constants or character variables). Character arguments used in a subprogram call must, of course, correspond to type character dummy arguments.

The type declaration of a character dummy argument specifies its length. The declared length of a character dummy argument may not exceed the length of its associated actual argument. If the length, L, of a dummy argument is less than the actual argument length, then only the leftmost L characters of the actual argument will be associated with the dummy argument.

In most cases, we want the length of a character dummy argument to be the same as its corresponding actual argument. However, the dummy argument lengths cannot be predetermined because the subprogram arguments (and their lengths) change from one call to the next. Consequently, Fortran allows you to use the symbols (*) to declare the length of a character dummy argument. The statement

```
CHARACTER *(*) STRING
```

in Fig. 10.5 indicates that the dummy argument STRING will assume the length of its corresponding actual argument. The actual argument length may vary from one call to the next and can be determined by the function LEN, as illustrated in the DO loop header in Fig. 10.5.

Searching for a Substring

In this section, we introduce a library function that is helpful in examining and manipulating a string stored in memory. The string search function, INDEX, can be used to search a string (the *subject string*) for a desired substring (the *target string*). For example, if SENTNC is the following subject string

SENTNC

| WHAT NEXT |

we could use this function to determine whether a target string 'AT' is a substring in SENTNC; the INDEX function should tell us that 'AT' appears at position 3 (counting from the left). If we tried to locate a target string 'IT', the INDEX function would return a value of zero since 'IT' is not a substring of SENTNC. The function INDEX is described next.

SYNTAX DISPLAY

String Search Function INDEX

SYNTAX: INDEX(*subject*, *target*)

EXAMPLE: INDEX(SENTNC, '.')

INTERPRETATION: The function INDEX returns an integer value indicating the starting position in the character string *subject* of a substring matching the string *target*.

NOTES: If there is more than one occurrence of *target*, the starting position of the first occurrence is returned.

If *target* does not occur in *subject*, the value 0 is returned.

EXAMPLE 10.13

The program in Fig. 10.6 replaces all occurrences of the string 'AIN''T' in SENTNC with the string 'IS NOT'. The statement

```
 COPY = SENTNC( : POSIT-1) //
+       'IS NOT' // SENTNC(POSIT+LEN('AIN''T') : )
```

Figure 10.6. *Program and Output for Example 10.13*

```
      PROGRAM AINT
C Replaces AIN'T with IS NOT

C Declarations
      CHARACTER *80 SENTNC, COPY
      INTEGER POSIT

C Enter data string
      PRINT *, 'Old sentence:'
      READ '(A)', SENTNC

C Find each occurrence of AIN'T in SENTNC
      POSIT = INDEX(SENTNC, 'AIN''T')
      DO WHILE (POSIT .NE. 0)                    9 IF (...) THEN
        COPY = SENTNC( : POSIT-1) //
    +          'IS NOT' // SENTNC(POSIT+LEN('AIN''T') : )
        SENTNC = COPY
        POSIT = INDEX(SENTNC, 'AIN''T')
      END DO                                     GOTO 9
                                                 END IF
C Print results
      PRINT *, 'New sentence:'
      PRINT *, SENTNC

C Exit program
      STOP
      END


Old sentence:
HE AIN'T MY FRIEND.
New sentence:
HE IS NOT MY FRIEND.
```

replaces the substring ('AIN''T') in positions POSIT through POSIT+4 of SENTNC with the string 'IS NOT'. A more general version of a string replacement program is described later in this chapter. ∎

Self-check

1. Evaluate the following:

    a. INDEX ('HAND ME THE CUP AND SAUCER', 'AND')
    b. INDEX ('HAND ME THE CUP AND SAUCER', 'and')
    c. INDEX ('HAND ME THE CUP AND SAUCER', ' AND')
    d. INDEX ('AND', 'HAND ME THE CUP AND SAUCER')

Programming

1. Rewrite function GETLEN so that it has only one RETURN statement. (*Hint:* Use a WHILE loop.)

10.6   Examples of String Manipulation

In previous sections, we introduced the Fortran string manipulation features and provided several examples of their use. Now we illustrate the application of these features in the solution of three sample problems. The first is a program for generating cryptograms; the second involves a subroutine for processing a DO loop header; and the third is a text editor program.

Case Study: Generating Cryptograms

PROBLEM STATEMENT

A cryptogram is a coded message formed by substituting a code character for each letter of an original message. The substitution is performed uniformly throughout the original message, that is, all A's might be replaced by Z, all B's by Y, and so on. We will assume that all punctuation (including blanks between words) remains unchanged.

ANALYSIS

The program must examine each character in a message, MESSAG, and insert the appropriate substitution for that character in the cryptogram, CRYPTO. This can be done by using the position of the original character in the alphabet string ALFBET as an index to the string of code symbols, CODE. For example, the code symbol for the letter A should always be the first symbol in CODE; the code symbol for the letter B should be the second symbol in CODE, etc.

Data Requirements

Program Parameter

the alphabet string (CHARACTER *26 ALFBET = 'ABC...Z')

Problem Inputs

replacement code (CHARACTER *26 CODE)
original message (CHARACTER *80 MESSAG)

Problem Output

the cryptogram (CHARACTER *80 CRYPTO)

Program Variables

position of original character in string ALFBET, used as an index to CODE
    (INTEGER POSCHR)
loop-control variable, which indicates next character in MESSAG to encode
    (INTEGER NEXT)

The algorithm follows:

Algorithm

1. Enter code string (CODE) and message (MESSAG).
2. Form cryptogram (CRYPTO) by replacing each letter in MESSAG with the corresponding code symbol.
3. Print CRYPTO.

Algorithm Refinements

Step 2 Refinement

2.1 DO for each character in MESSAG
    2.2 Locate position, POSCHR, of next message character in alphabet string, ALFBET.
    2.3 IF POSCHR is not equal to 0 THEN
        2.4 Insert corresponding code symbol into CRYPTO.
    ELSE
        2.5 Insert the next message symbol into CRYPTO.
    END IF
END DO

IMPLEMENTATION

Figure 10.7 shows the program. In the figure, the statement

```
POSCHR = INDEX(ALFBET, MESSAG(NEXT : NEXT))
```

locates the current message symbol in the string ALFBET and the statement

```
CRYPTO(NEXT : NEXT) = CODE(POSCHR : POSCHR)
```

inserts the corresponding code symbol in the cryptogram. The statement

```
CRYPTO(NEXT : NEXT) = MESSAG(NEXT : NEXT)
```

inserts any message symbol that is not a letter directly into the cryptogram.

Figure 10.7. *Cryptogram Generator and Sample Cryptogram*

```
      PROGRAM CRYPTO
C Generates cryptograms

C Declarations
      CHARACTER *26 ALFBET
      PARAMETER (ALFBET = 'ABCDEFGHIJKLMNOPQRSTUVWXYZ')
      INTEGER POSCHR, NEXT
      CHARACTER *26 CODE
      CHARACTER *80 MESSAG, CRYPTO
```

```
C Enter code and message
      PRINT *, 'Enter the code symbol for each letter under that letter'
      PRINT *, ALFBET
      READ '(A)', CODE
      PRINT *
      PRINT *, 'Enter a message and I will display its cryptogram:'
      READ '(A)', MESSAG

C Substitute the code symbol for each letter in the message
      DO 10 NEXT = 1, LEN(MESSAG)
C        Locate the current message character in ALFBET
         POSCHR = INDEX(ALFBET, MESSAG(NEXT : NEXT))
         IF (POSCHR .NE. 0) THEN
C           Insert code for letter in CRYPTO
            CRYPTO(NEXT : NEXT) = CODE(POSCHR : POSCHR)
         ELSE
C           Insert non-letter in CRYPTO
            CRYPTO(NEXT : NEXT) = MESSAG(NEXT : NEXT)
         END IF
   10 CONTINUE

C Print the cryptogram
      PRINT *, CRYPTO

C Exit program
      STOP
      END

Enter the code symbol for each letter under that letter
ABCDEFGHIJKLMNOPQRSTUVWXYZ
ZYXWVUTSRQPONMLKJIHGFEDCBA

Enter a message and I will display its cryptogram:
ENCODE THIS *$?+ MESSAGE!
VMXLWV GSRH *$?+ NVHHZTV!
```

TESTING AND VERIFICATION

In the sample run, the code symbol for each letter is entered directly beneath that letter. The sample run ends with two lines of output: The first contains the message; the second contains its cryptogram. For a simple test, try using each letter as its own code symbol. In that case, both lines should be the same. Remember, the program encodes only uppercase letters. Any lowercase letters and special symbols should not be changed.

The next problem involves scanning a character string and extracting substrings.

Case Study: Scanning a DO Loop Header

PROBLEM STATEMENT

The DO loop header has the syntactic form

$$\text{DO } label\ lcv = initial,\ limit,\ step$$

FORTRAN
in Focus

A Team-Building Language

The scientists and engineers at a governmental research organization located in Bedford, Massachusetts, provide research, development, and management consulting services to the federal government. Personnel at this facility work almost exclusively for the Air Force, performing contract research in the field of electronic systems. Fortran is a commonly used tool in the work that they do with radar systems, computers, and other electronic communications systems.

Although administrative systems (such as payroll) are maintained by a central group, research applications are undertaken by the scientists and engineers involved in a particular project. The programming done in many of these applications requires an understanding of the mathematics behind a phenomenon, such as radar propagation, as well as the programming language.

When an application needs to integrate esoteric system functions, or work with an unusual interface, computer system personnel are available to work with the scientific programmers. Fortran makes it easy to build individuals with complementary skills into an applications team; it is simple enough to use for everyday problem solving, powerful enough to accomplish sophisticated tasks, and familiar to most of the research community.

Leonard Bachelder, a lead scientist at this company who has worked in scientific applications, systems work, and as a troubleshooter in the computer center, described one such application. The goal was to create a system that could analyze a radar site, using data about its geographic location, the height of its antenna, and the power and frequency of its radar, and determine what the radar would and would not be able to see.

For example,

```
DO 35 I = FIRST, LAST, 5
```

A compiler must determine whether a program line has this syntactic form. If it does, the compiler must separate the substrings representing the loop parameters *initial*, *limit*, and *step* from the rest of the string and save these

Geographic data from a number of sources provided digital representations of terrain used by the system to determine what the radar could see. For example, the location, height, and relationship of mountainous terrain to the radar in use would be analyzed to determine which portions of the area would be masked by it. To do this, other parts of the application involved mathematical routines and models—for radar propagation or the probability of radar siting a particular target—that were created by scientists specializing in these problems. The final output was graphical: a polar diagram with the radar site in the center and a plot of what the radar could and could not see.

Fortran was chosen for this application first because it was the primary language available on the VAX computer being used for the job. But there were other advantages, too. Many of the math-

ematical routines were taken from code that had already been written on an IBM system. The ease with which Fortran moves from one machine to another meant that 90% of the several thousand lines of code could be ported to the VAX without being adapted. Another major advantage was the ease with which Fortran accessed system services on the VAX. The geographic data used for the application comes on magnetic tape, and a given site may require data from

several different input tapes. By creating a table in the application to correlate tape reel numbers with the geographic locations they cover, the programmers could write Fortran code to call the VAX system services to mount a particular tape. While this is a VAX system function, or a hardware consideration, the VAX Fortran's ability to access it made a difference.

Despite the complexity and sophistication of the application, its input, and output, the entire application was coded in Fortran. And if Leonard Bachelder had all the languages he knows anything about to choose from to do the application again, he thinks he would probably choose Fortran.

We are sincerely grateful to Leonard Bachelder, Lead Scientist at this corporation in Bedford, Massachusetts, for taking the time to tell us about this terrain-masking application.

substrings in separate character variables for later reference. We will write a program to perform this substring separation.

Our program needs to identify and copy the DO loop parameters—*initial, limit,* and *step*—into the character variables INIT, LIMIT, and STEP, respectively.

The most difficult subtask for our program involves determining the starting and ending positions of the loop parameter strings. This, in turn, requires the identification of the positions in the header string of the equal sign (POSEQL) and the first and second commas (POS1CM and POS2CM) beyond the equal sign. If the second comma (and third parameter) in the header statement is missing, the string '1' is stored in STEP. If either the equal sign or the first comma is missing, an error message is printed and program execution is terminated. For simplicity, we will assume that the DO loop parameters contain no array element or function references.

Data Requirements

Program Parameters

the character '=' (EQUAL = '=')
the character ',' (COMMA = ',')
the character '1' (ONE = '1')

Problem Input

DO loop header (CHARACTER *80 HEADER)

Problem Outputs

initial value loop parameter (CHARACTER *80 INIT)
limit value loop parameter (CHARACTER *80 LIMIT)
step value loop parameter (CHARACTER *80 STEP)

Program Variables

position of '=' in HEADER (INTEGER POSEQL)
position of first ',' in HEADER beyond '=' (INTEGER POS1CM)
position of second ',' in HEADER beyond '=' (INTEGER POS2CM)

The algorithm follows:

Algorithm

1. Read HEADER.
2. Locate '=' and save its position in POSEQL. Print an error message and stop if '=' missing.

3. Locate first comma and save its position in POS1CM. Print error message and stop if ',' missing.
4. Locate second comma and save its position in POS2CM.
5. Save loop-parameter substrings and print results.

Algorithm Refinements

Step 5 Refinement

5.1 INIT is the substring between POSEQL and POS1CM.
5.2 IF the second comma is present THEN
       5.3 LIMIT is the substring between POS1CM and POS2CM and STEP is the substring after POS2CM.
  ELSE
       5.4 LIMIT is the substring after POS1CM and STEP is '1'.
  END IF

IMPLEMENTATION

Figure 10.8 shows the program. The statement

```
POS1CM = INDEX(HEADER(POSEQL+1 : ), COMMA) + POSEQL
```

calls function INDEX to search for the first comma in the substring of HEADER following the equal sign. The position of this comma relative to the start of the string HEADER is obtained by adding POSEQL to the result of the substring search. To locate the second comma, INDEX must search the substring HEADER (POS1CM+1 :).

Figure 10.8. *Program and Sample Output for Scanning a DO Loop Header*

```
      PROGRAM DOLOOP
C Separates and saves substrings of DO loop header

C Declarations
      CHARACTER *1 COMMA, EQUAL, ONE
      PARAMETER (COMMA = ',', EQUAL = '=', ONE = '1')
      CHARACTER *80 HEADER
      CHARACTER *80 INIT, LIMIT, STEP
      INTEGER POSEQL, POS1CM, POS2CM

C Enter data
      PRINT *, 'DO loop header:'
      READ '(A)', HEADER

C Search for equal sign — print error message if equal sign missing
      POSEQL = INDEX(HEADER, EQUAL)
      IF (POSEQL .EQ. 0) THEN
         PRINT *, ' = Sign missing'
         STOP
      END IF
```

```
C Search for first comma following = sign
C Print error message if comma is missing
      POS1CM = INDEX(HEADER(POSEQL+1 : ), COMMA) + POSEQL
      IF (POS1CM .EQ. POSEQL) THEN
         PRINT *, 'Comma is missing'
         STOP
      END IF

C Search for second comma following first comma
      POS2CM = INDEX(HEADER(POS1CM+1 : ), COMMA) + POS1CM

C Save loop parameter substrings
      INIT = HEADER(POSEQL+1 : POS1CM-1)
      IF (POS2CM .NE. POS1CM) THEN
         LIMIT = HEADER(POS1CM+1 : POS2CM-1)
         STEP = HEADER(POS2CM+1 : )
      ELSE
         LIMIT = HEADER(POS1CM+1 : )
         STEP = ONE
      END IF

C Print results
      PRINT *
      PRINT *, 'Initial value expression: ', INIT
      PRINT *, 'Limit value expression: ', LIMIT
      PRINT *, 'Step value expression: ', STEP

C Exit program
      STOP
      END

DO Loop header:
DO 20 INDEX = FIRST, LAST-1, 10
Initial value expression:  FIRST
Limit value expression:  LAST-1
Step value expression:   10
```

Once the positions of the equal sign and the commas have been located (using the INDEX function), the substrings *delimited* by them (including all blanks) must be copied into INIT, LIMIT, and STEP. In each case, the copy can be performed using a simple character assignment statement such as

```
INIT = HEADER(POSEQL+1 : POS1CM-1)
```

which assigns to INIT the substring delimited by the equal sign and the first comma.

Ensure the DO loop program processes loop headers with and without a step parameter. The program should work regardless of whether blanks appear after the separator symbol ",". It also should work properly if the loop parameter expressions reference one-dimensional arrays or functions with a single argument. However, it will not be able to process expressions that reference multidimensional arrays or multiargument expressions.

Case Study: Text Editing Problem

A computerized text editing program is useful in many applications. For example, if you are preparing a laboratory report (or a textbook), it would be convenient to be able to modify sections of the report (improve sentence and paragraph structure, change words, correct spelling mistakes, etc.) at a computer terminal and then have a fresh, clean copy of the text typed at the terminal.

A text editor system is a relatively sophisticated system of subprograms that can be used to instruct the computer to perform virtually any kind of text alteration. At the heart of such a system is a subprogram that replaces one substring in the text with another substring. For example, consider the following sentence prepared by an overzealous member of the Addison-Wesley advertising group.

```
'THE BOOK BY KOFFMAN AND FRIEDMEN IN FRACTURED PROGRAMING IS GRREAT?'
```

To correct this sentence, we would want to specify the following edit operations:

1. Replace 'MEN' with 'MAN'.
2. Replace 'IN ' with 'ON '.
3. Replace 'FRAC' with 'STRUC'.
4. Replace 'AM' with 'AMM'.
5. Replace 'RR' with 'R'.
6. Replace '?' with '!'.

The result is now at least grammatically correct, as follows:

```
'THE BOOK BY KOFFMAN AND FRIEDMAN ON STRUCTURED PROGRAMMING IS GREAT!'
```

We will write the replacement program module as the subroutine REPLAC. The data requirements are shown next.

Data Requirements

Input Arguments

maximum length of TEXT (INTEGER MAXLEN)
character string to be replaced (CHARACTER *(*) OLD)
length of OLD (INTEGER OLDLEN)
character string to be inserted (CHARACTER *(*) NEW)
length of NEW (INTEGER NEWLEN)

Input/Output Arguments

character string being edited (CHARACTER *(*) TEXT)
current length of TEXT excluding blank padding (INTEGER CURLEN)

MAXLEN is a text editor system parameter defined to be equal to the maximum length of the text string. CURLEN would be defined when the string to be edited is first placed in TEXT (probably in the main program) and would be redefined each time a change was made to TEXT.

The first task of REPLAC is to locate in TEXT the first occurrence of the substring to be replaced, OLD (: OLDLEN). This is done using the function INDEX.

The additional data requirements for REPLAC are shown next.

Local Variables

the position of the first character of OLD in TEXT if OLD is found (INTEGER POSOLD)
length of edited text (INTEGER REVLEN)
temporary copy of the edited text (CHARACTER *1000 COPY)

DESIGN

The algorithm follows:

Algorithm

1. Search for OLD in TEXT.
2. If OLD is present, replace it with NEW; if not, print a "string missing" message.

Algorithm Refinements

Step 2 Refinement

2.1. IF OLD is found THEN
         2.2. Replace OLD with NEW.
     ELSE
         2.3. Print OLD "not found".
     END IF

Before we can write REPLAC, we need to refine step 2.2 further. If NEWLEN is larger than OLDLEN, it is possible that the length of the revised version of TEXT, REVLEN, would exceed MAXLEN. In this case, an error message should be printed and the replacement operation ignored; otherwise, a copy of TEXT can be made by concatenating the substring preceding OLD (the head of TEXT), NEW, and the substring following OLD (the tail of TEXT). The refinement of step 2.2 follows.

Step 2.2 Refinement

2.2.1 Set REVLEN to the length of the edited text.
2.2.2 IF REVLEN is greater than MAXLEN THEN
   2.2.3 Print "Revised text too long. Replacement ignored".
   ELSE
   2.2.4 Build COPY from NEW and the head and tail of TEXT. Redefine
      TEXT as COPY and CURLEN as REVLEN.
   END IF

In forming COPY (step 2.2.4), the program must check for two special cases: TEXT starts with OLD or TEXT ends with OLD. In the former case, NEW becomes the head of COPY; in the latter case, NEW becomes the tail. Representing the actual character data in NEW, excluding blank padding, is the substring NEW(: NEWLEN).

IMPLEMENTATION

Figure 10.9 shows subroutine REPLAC. A nested IF statement performs the text replacement. The innermost IF statement tests for the special cases mentioned under Step 2.2 Refinement in the preceding paragraph before building COPY from TEXT and NEW.

Figure 10.9. *Subroutine REPLAC*

```
      SUBROUTINE REPLAC (TEXT, MAXLEN, CURLEN,
     +                   OLD, OLDLEN, NEW, NEWLEN)

C Replaces substring OLD with string NEW in TEXT
C Preconditions : CURLEN is actual length of string TEXT, NEWLEN
C    is actual length of string NEW, and OLDLEN is actual length
C    of string OLD.
C Postconditions: First occurrence of NEW in TEXT
C    is replaced by OLD.

C Input Arguments
C    MAXLEN — maximum length of string TEXT
C    OLD — string to be replaced
C    OLDLEN — length of OLD
C    NEW — replacement string
C    NEWLEN — length of NEW
C Input/Output Arguments
C    TEXT — string being edited
C    CURLEN — current length of TEXT
```

```
C Argument Declarations
      CHARACTER *(*) TEXT, OLD, NEW
      INTEGER MAXLEN, CURLEN, OLDLEN, NEWLEN

C Local Declarations
      INTEGER POSOLD, REVLEN
      CHARACTER *1000 COPY

C See if OLD is in TEXT. If so, replace it. If not, ignore request
      POSOLD = INDEX(TEXT, OLD( : OLDLEN))
      IF (POSOLD .NE. 0) THEN
C         Check revised length before replacement
          REVLEN = CURLEN + NEWLEN - OLDLEN
          IF (REVLEN .GT. MAXLEN) THEN
             PRINT *, ' Revised text too long, replacement ignored'
          ELSE
C            Build COPY by replacing OLD with NEW in TEXT
             IF (POSOLD .EQ. 1) THEN
C               Replace head of TEXT with NEW
                COPY = NEW( : NEWLEN) // TEXT(POSOLD+OLDLEN : )
             ELSE IF (POSOLD + OLDLEN .EQ. CURLEN) THEN
C               Replace tail of TEXT with NEW
                COPY = TEXT( : POSOLD-1) // NEW( : NEWLEN)
             ELSE
C               Replace OLD in middle of TEXT with NEW
                COPY = TEXT( : POSOLD-1) // NEW( : NEWLEN) //
     +                 TEXT(POSOLD+OLDLEN : )
             END IF
             TEXT = COPY
             CURLEN = REVLEN
          END IF
      ELSE
          PRINT * , OLD, ' not found, replacement ignored'
      END IF

C Exit subroutine
      RETURN
      END
```

TESTING AND VERIFICATION

To test subroutine REPLAC, write a driver program that reads the three argument strings (TEXT, NEW, OLD) and their actual lengths. Next, your driver program should call the subroutine and display the value returned in TEXT. Ensure you test the special cases discussed in the algorithm refinements. In any string substitution example, you also should check that the program works for substrings at the beginning or the end of the string. Also, see what happens when the target string is not found in the original string. Finally, test REPLAC using the null string (length is 0) as a replacement string (NEW). In this case, the subroutine should simply delete string OLD from TEXT.

Self-check

1. What is the relevance of the assumption made in the discussion of the DO loop header that array element or function references should not appear in the DO loop control parameters?
2. Consider the subroutine in Fig. 10.9. Why is the character variable COPY needed in this program?

Programming

1. For each of the editing operations listed below, write a call statement to REPLAC.

    a. Replace 'FRAC' with 'STRUC'.
    b. Replace the 'I' in 'IN' with an 'O'.
    c. Insert an extra 'M' into 'PROGRAMING'.
    d. Delete an 'R' from 'GRREAT'.

10.7 Common Programming Errors

Now that we know how to manipulate different types of data, we must be careful not to misuse these data types in expressions. Character strings can be operands of the character operator (concatenation, //) and relational operators (.GT., .LE., etc.). Remember that character variables and character constants can be manipulated only with other character data.

1. Misspelling the name of a character variable (or neglecting to declare it) may result in syntax errors because the compiler cannot recognize the type declaration intended for that variable if the variable name is spelled incorrectly. Consequently, the compiler will follow the implied type convention and assume the variable is type INTEGER or REAL. Because arithmetic variables cannot be operands of character operators, diagnostic messages may be generated.
2. When writing substrings such as PRES(I : J), ensure the constraints

$$1 \le I \le J \le LEN(PRES)$$

are satisfied for all possible values of I and J. This means the starting position, I, for the substring must be greater than or equal to 1 and the ending position, J, must be less than or equal to the length of string PRES. Also, the ending position must follow the starting position or at least be the same as the starting position (the latter constraint prevents the definition of substrings of length 0 or less.) A violation of these constraints may be caused by a loop that does not terminate properly or simply by an incorrect

subscript expression. Or if the value assigned to I (or J) is the result of a call to the string search function INDEX, I (or J) may be set to zero. When in doubt, display any suspect substring expressions.
3. As mentioned earlier, an error in character assignment statements also can occur when the same character position is referenced on both sides of the assignment operator ("=" sign). For example, the statement

```
PRES(1 : 5) = PRES(4 : 8)
```

is illegal because positions 4 and 5 are defined and also referenced in this statement.
4. Remember that function LEN counts all character stored in a character variable, including the blank padding. You will need to write your own function GETLEN (see Fig. 10.5) if you want to exclude the blank padding.

Chapter Review

In this chapter, we described character string manipulation, reviewed earlier work with character strings, and introduced several new functions (LEN, INDEX, CHAR, and ICHAR) and a new operator for concatenation (//). We also discussd how to name and search for substrings. The features introduced in this chapter are summarized in Table 10.2.

Table 10.2. *Fortran Statements for Chapter 10*

STATEMENT	EFFECT
Substring	
NEW (1 : NEWLEN)	Denotes the substring of NEW consisting of the first NEWLEN characters
Concatenation	
NEW // OLD	Concatenates (joins) strings NEW and OLD
Functions with Character Arguments or Values	
LEN(NEW)	Returns the declared length of NEW
CHAR(0)	Returns the character in the first position (position zero) of the collating sequence for your compiler
ICHAR('A')	Returns the position of A in the collating sequence
INDEX(SUBJCT, KEY)	Searches the string SUBJCT for the first occurrence of substring KEY. Returns the position of the first character of KEY in SUBJCT if found; otherwise, returns zero

We also presented many examples of these features for manipulating character strings and applied them to generate cryptograms, to solve a problem that might arise in compiler design (processing a DO loop header), and to design a text editor replacement subroutine.

These kinds of problems are called nonnumerical problems and are among the most challenging in computer science. The techniques presented in this chapter should give you a better idea of how to use the computer to solve this type of problem.

Quick-check Exercises

1. The _____ _____ is used to join two strings. Its position in the precedence table is between the _____ and _____ operators.
2. Explain the difference between the terms "character set" and "collating sequence."
3. For each function below, explain its purpose, the type of its argument(s), and the type of its result.

   LEN, INDEX, ICHAR, CHAR

4. Which of the following expressions may return different results on different computers? Evaluate each expression for your computer.

   a. CHAR(32)
   b. INDEX('ABC', 'A')
   c. '9' .LT. 'A'
   d. ICHAR('C') - ICHAR('A')

   e. ICHAR('A')
   f. INDEX('A', 'ABC')
   g. 'A' .GT. 'Z'
   h. ' ' .LE. 'A'

Answer exercises 5–7 assuming the declarations

   CHARACTER STR1 *3, STR2 *5

5. What is the value of LEN(STR1 // STR2)?
6. Write a statement that changes the middle three characters of STR2 to 'ABC'.
7. If STR1 is 'ABC' and STR2 is 'VABCZ', what are the values of the following expressions?

   a. INDEX(STR2, STR1)
   b. INDEX(STR1, STR2)
   c. INDEX(STR1, 'A')
   d. INDEX(STR2, 'A')
   e. INDEX(STR2(2 :), 'B')
   f. INDEX(STR1 // STR2, 'CVA')

Answers to Quick-check Exercises

1. concatenation operator (//); the relational operators and the arithmetic operators
2. The character set is the set of characters that are recognized by the Fortran compiler; each has a unique character code. The collating sequence specifies the relative ordering of the characters in the character set.

3. LEN returns the length (an integer) of its string argument. INDEX returns the starting position (an integer) of the initial occurrence of its second argument (a string) in its first argument (a string). If its second argument is not found in its first argument, INDEX returns 0. ICHAR returns the character code (an integer) of its string argument. CHAR returns the character (a string) that has the character code specified by its integer argument.

4. If the results are computer dependent, we will assume the ASCII Code.

a. blank in ASCII	b. always 1	c. true in ASCII	d. 2 in ASCII
e. 65 in ASCII	f. always 0	g. always false	h. always true

5. 8

6. STR2(2 : 4) = 'ABC'

7. a. 2   b. 0   c. 1   d. 2   e. 2   f. 3

Review Questions

1. The function NOCCUR begins with the statements

```
INTEGER FUNCTION NOCCUR (SUBJCT, TARGET)
CHARACTER *(*) SUBJCT, TARGET
```

For each of the following references to the function NOCCUR, what are the lengths of the dummy arguments SUBJCT and TARGET? Assume TSTRNG and SSTRNG are character variables of size 10 and 20, respectively.

a. NOCCUR(SSTRNG, TSTRNG)
b. NOCCUR(TSTRNG, 'A')
c. NOCCUR(SSTRNG(4 : 12), 'EE')
d. NOCCUR('IS MISSY HERE', 'IS')
e. NOCCUR(SSTRNG // TSTRNG, TSTRNG // 'NO')

2. Given the declarations

```
CHARACTER *10 FLOWER
CHARACTER *24 DESCRP
DATA FLOWER / 'HEATHER' /
DATA DESCRP / 'HEATHER IS A WILD FLOWER' /
```

show the strings formed by the following expressions:

a. FLOWER // DESCRP(9 : 24)
b. DESCRP(1 : 11) // DESCRP(14 : 17)
c. DESCRP(:), DESCRP(1 :), DESCRP(: 24)
d. DESCRP(14 : 18) // 'AS A ROSE'
e. FLOWER(1 : 1) // FLOWER(4 : 5) // FLOWER(7 : 7)
f. FLOWER(7 : 12)

3. For each of the strings below, determine its length using the functions LEN and GETLEN. FLOWER and DESCRP are declared and initialized as in question 2.

   a. FLOWER
   b. DESCRP
   c. FLOWER(1 : GETLEN(FLOWER))
   d. 'MARIGOLD '
   e. DESCRP(4 : 8) // FLOWER(3 : 3)
   f. 'A' // 'B' // 'C'

4. Suppose ADDRES contains the string

   '164 EILEEN DRIVE, ANYCITY, ANYSTATE 16444'

What value is returned for each of the following references to INDEX?

   a. INDEX(ADDRES, 'ANYS')
   b. INDEX(ADDRES, '164')
   c. INDEX(ADDRES(2 :), '164')
   d. INDEX(ADDRES(1 : 10) // ADDRES(11 : 17), 'END')
   e. INDEX(ADDRES, 'CITIES')
   f. INDEX(ADDRES(INDEX(ADDRES, ',') :), 'A')

5. What will be printed by the following program segment?

```
CHARACTER ZERO
PARAMETER (ZERO = '0')
CHARACTER DIGIT
INTEGER NUMBER
READ '(A)', DIGIT
NUMBER = ICHAR(DIGIT) - ICHAR(ZERO)
PRINT *, NUMBER
```

5

   a. 5 (The Integer)   d. 53 (The ASCII code for '5')
   b. 5 (The Character)   e. syntax Error
   c. 48 (The ASCII code for '0')   f. run-time Error

6. What values will be printed for K and L by the program segment at the right?

	K	L
a.	4	2
b.	4	4
c.	4	6
d.	6	2
e.	6	4
f.	6	6

```
CHARACTER *10 CAR, SUB
INTEGER K, L
DATA CAR / 'AUTOMOBILE' /
SUB = CAR (3 : )
K = INDEX (CAR, 'O')
L = INDEX (SUB, 'O')
PRINT *, K, L
```

7. What does the following function do?

```
INTEGER FUNCTION FUN (STRING)
CHARACTER *(*) STRING
CHARACTER BLANK
PARAMETER (BLANK = ' ')
INTEGER K
K  =  LEN (STRING)
DO WHILE  (K .GT. 0)
   IF  (STRING (K : K) .EQ. BLANK)  THEN
      K  =  K - 1
   ELSE
      K  =  -K
   END IF
END DO
K  =  IABS (K)
RETURN
END
```

a. It finds the location of the first nonblank character in STRING.
b. It finds the location of the last nonblank character in STRING.
c. It counts the nonblank characters in STRING.
d. It finds the location of the first blank in STRING.
e. It finds the location of the last blank in STRING.
f. It counts the blanks in STRING.

Programming Projects

1. Write a program to read in a set of words (given below) represented as character strings of 10 characters or fewer and determine whether each word falls between the words in FIRST and LAST (the words DINGBAT and WOMBAT, respectively). Print the words in FIRST and LAST and print each word read in along with the identifiers 'BETWEEN' or 'NOT BETWEEN', whichever applies. Use the following words as test data:

```
HELP      THE
ME        WOMBATS
STIFLE    BEFORE
THE       IT
DINGBAT   IS
AND       TOO
          LATE
```

2. Write a program to read a character string of length 20 into BUFFER and a character string into ITEM. Then search BUFFER for the string contained in ITEM. Print

```
STRING FOUND
```

if the string in ITEM is a substring of BUFFER. Print

STRING NOT FOUND

if the string in ITEM is not a substring of BUFFER. Test your program on the following strings:

BUFFER: IS A MAN IN THE MOON
ITEM: MAN , NUT , N T , MEN, I

BUFFER: IS DUST ON THE MOON
ITEM: THEM, UST , DUST , IN , ON , O

(*Hint:* Use the function GETLEN (Fig. 10.5) to determine the length of each string.)

3. Write a subroutine that will search a subject string for a specified target substring starting with a designated character position in the subject string (three input arguments). The subroutine should determine whether the substring is present and, if found, the position of its first occurrence.

4. Assume a set of data lines is to be processed. Each line contains a single character string that consists of a sequence of words, each separated by one or more blank spaces. Write a program that will read these lines and count the number of words with one letter, two letters, and so on, up to 10 letters.

5. Write a subroutine that will scan a string TEXT of length N and replace all multiple occurrences of a blank with a single occurrence of a blank. You may assume that TEXT and N are input arguments. You also should have an output argument, COUNT, which will be used to return the number of occurrences of multiple blanks found in each call of the subroutine.

6. Write a subprogram BLNKSP that removes all blanks from a character string and "compacts" all nonblank characters in the string. Assume the last character of the input string is a dollar sign. You should have to scan the input string only once from left to right.

7. Write a program to read in a collection of data lines containing character strings of length less than or equal to 80 characters. For each line read, your program should do the following:

   a. Find and print the actual length of the string, excluding trailing blanks.
   b. Count the number of occurrences of four-letter words in each string.
   c. Replace each four-letter word with a string of four asterisks, ****.
   d. Print the new string.

8. Write a program that will process the employee record strings described in Table 10.3 and perform the following tasks:

   a. For each employee compute the gross pay:

   $$gross\ pay\ =\ hours\ worked\ *\ hourly\ pay\ +$$
   $$overtime\ hours\ worked\ *\ hourly\ pay\ *\ 1.5$$

Table 10.3. *Employee Record for Project 8*

COLUMNS	DATA DESCRIPTION
1–6	Employee number (an integer)
7–19	Employee last name
20–27	Employee first name
28–32	Number of hours worked (to the nearest $\frac{1}{2}$ hour) for this employee
33–37	Hourly pay rate for this employee
38	Contains a C if the employee works in the city office and an S for the suburban office
39	Contains an M if the employee is a union member
40–41	Number of dependents
42–46	Number of overtime hours worked (if any) (also to the nearest $\frac{1}{2}$ hour)

b. For each employee compute the net pay as follows:

net pay = gross pay − deductions

Deductions are computed as follows:

*federal tax = (gross pay − 13 * no. of dependents) * .14*
*FICA = gross pay * .065*

$$city\ tax = \begin{cases} \$0.00 \text{ if employee works in the suburbs} \\ 4\% \text{ of } gross\ pay \text{ if employee works in city} \end{cases}$$

$$union\ dues = \begin{cases} \$0.00 \text{ if employee is not a union member} \\ 6.75\% \text{ of } gross\ pay \text{ otherwise} \end{cases}$$

For each employee, print a line of output containing the following:

1. Employee number
2. First and last name
3. Number of hours worked
4. Hourly pay rate
5. Overtime hours
6. Gross pay
7. Federal tax
8. FICA
9. City wage tax (if any)
10. Union dues (if any)
11. Net pay

Also compute and print the following:

1. Number of employees processed
2. Total gross pay
3. Total federal tax withheld
4. Total hours worked
5. Total overtime hours worked

Use formats and provide appropriate column headings for employee output and labels for totals.

9. Following is the layout of a data string that the registrar uses as input for a program to print the end-of-the-semester final grade report for each student:

Columns	Data Description
1–6	Student number
7–18	Last name
20–26	First name
27	Middle initial
28–29	Academic year—FR, SO, JR, SR
30–32	First course—Department ID (3 letters)
33–35	First course—Number (3 digits)
36	First course—Grade A, B, C, D, or F
37	First course—Number of credits: 0–7
40–42 43–45 46 47	Second course: data as described above
50–52 53–55 56 57	Third course data
60–62 63–65 66 67	Fourth course data
70–72 73–75 76 77	Fifth course data

Write a program to print the following grade report sheet for each student:

```
Line    1                MAD RIVER COLLEGE
Line    2                YELLOW GULCH, OHIO
Line    3
Line    4    GRADE REPORT, SPRING SEMESTER 1991
Line    5
Line    6    (student number)    (year)    (student name)
Line    7    - - - - - - -    - - - -    - - - - - - -
Line    8                    GRADE SUMMARY
Line    9            COURSE
Line   10        DEPT    NMBR        CREDITS        GRADE
Line   11    1. - - -    - - -          -             -
Line   12    2. - - -    - - -          -             -
Line   13    3. - - -    - - -          -             -
Line   14    4. - - -    - - -          -             -
Line   15    5. - - -    - - -          -             -
Line   16
Line   17        SEMESTER GRADE POINT AVERAGE =  - - -
```

Compute the grade-point average as follows:

1. Use 4 points for an A, 3 for a B, 2 for a C, 1 for a D, and 0 for an F.
2. Compute the product of points times credits for each course.
3. Add together the products computed in (2).
4. Add together the total number of course credits.
5. Divide (3) by (4) and print the result rounded off to two decimal places. (*Hint:* Rounding is easy when formats are used for printing.)

Use formats for all input and output. Your program should work for students taking anywhere from one to five courses. You will need to determine the number of courses taken by a student from the input data.

10. A file of address labels consists of records that contain the following three lines:

    Line 1: ⟨Title⟩ ⟨First name⟩ ⟨Middle name⟩ ⟨Last name⟩
    Line 2: ⟨Street address⟩
    Line 3: ⟨City⟩, ⟨State⟩, ⟨ZIPcode⟩

    Rewrite each label to a new file that consists of four lines for each record set out in the following form:

    ZIPcode
    State
    Title
    Last name

11. A number expressed in scientific notation is represented by its mantissa (a fraction) and its exponent. Write a subroutine that reads two character strings representing numbers in scientific notation. Write a subroutine that prints the contents of each record as a real value. Also, write a subroutine that computes the sum, product, difference, and quotient of the two numbers. (*Hint:* The string $-0.1234E20$ represents a number in scientific notation. The fraction -0.1234 is the mantissa and the number 20 is the exponent.)

12. Write a program that generates the Morse code equivalent of a sentence. First, read the Morse code for each letter and punctuation character and save it in an array of strings. Next, read and convert the sentence. Your program should print the Morse code for each word on a separate line. The Morse code is as follows:

    A.-, B-..., C-.-., D-.., E., F..-., G--., H...., I.., J.---, K-.-, L.-.., M--, N-., O---,
    P.--., Q--.-, R.-., S..., T-, U..-, V...-, W.--, X-..-, Y-.--, Z--..

13. Write a set of subroutines to do the following:

    a. delete a substring from a source string
    b. insert a new string in a source string at a specified position
    c. indicate where a specified target string occurs in the source string
    d. replace the first occurrence of a specified substring in a source string with another.

Test these procedures by writing a text editor and performing several editing operations. The editor should be driven by the following menu:
 Enter the first letter of an edit operation described as follows:

D—Delete a substring
E—Enter a source string to be edited
I—Insert a substring
L—Locate a substring
P—Print the source string
R—Replace one substring with another
S—Show the menu
Q—Quit

14. Refer to Programming Project 13 and write a more complete text editor that will edit a page of text. Store each line of the page in a separate element of an array of strings. Maintain a pointer (index) to the line currently being edited. In addition to the edit commands, include commands that move the index to the top of the page, to the bottom of the page, or up or down a specified number of lines. Your program also should be able to delete an entire line, insert a new line preceding the current line, and replace the current line with another. The first two of these new operations will require moving a portion of the array of strings up or down by one element.

15. An amusing program consists of a sentence generator that will read a series of four numbers and print out a sentence. Provide three arrays containing eight words each (maximum of 10 characters to each word) called NOUN, VERB, and ADJECT. Fill each of these arrays with some appropriate words and then read four numbers (each in a range from 1–8). Write out a short sentence in which each number is the appropriate subscript from arrays in the following order:

```
NOUN, VERB, ADJECT, NOUN
```

An example would be to read 4, 5, 2, 6. Doing this will print the strings NOUN(4), VERB(5), ADJECT(2), and NOUN(6). If their contents are

```
NOUN(4) is 'JOHN       '
VERB(5) is 'LIKES      '
ADJECT(2) is 'CRAZY        '
NOUN(6) is 'BREAD      '
```

the sentence

```
JOHN LIKES CRAZY BREAD.
```

would be printed. A trailing blank should not be printed; however, there should be one blank between each word and a period at the end.

16. *Right-left justification of text.* Read in text that has arbitrary spacing between words (always at least one blank) and produce output lines that are X columns wide in

which the first word in a line starts in column 1 and the last word ends in column X. The number of blanks separating any two words on a line should differ by no more than one. Note that this is not a one-line-in, one-line-out process; three input lines could, for instance, yield only one output line. Words must not be broken in the middle.

17. Redo the function plotting program in Programming Project 3, Chapter 9, using a string for LINE instead of an array.

18. Write an arithmetic expression translator that compiles fully-parenthesized arithmetic expressions involving the operators *, /, +, and −. For example, given the input string

```
((A+(B*C))-(D/E))
```

the compiler would print out

```
Z = (B*C)
Y = (A+Z)
X = (D/E)
W = (Y-X)
```

Assume only the letters A through F can be used as variable names. (*Hint:* Find the first right parenthesis. Remove it and the four characters preceding it and replace them with the next unused letter (G–Z) at the end of the alphabet.) Print out the assignment statement used. For example, the following is a summary of the sequence of steps required to process the string above:

Expression Status	*Print*
((A+(B*C))-(D/E))	Z = (B*C)
↑	
((A+Z)-(D/E))	Y = (A+Z)
↑	
(Y-(D/E))	X = (D/E)
↑	
(Y-X)	W = (Y-X)
↑	

19. Write a program system (with appropriate documentation) that reads a Fortran program or subprogram and classifies each statement according to the following statement types:

a. Subroutine or function header
b. Type declaration (INTEGER, REAL, LOGICAL, or CHARACTER)
c. Data initialization statement
d. Comment statement
e. Assignment statement
f. Decision structure header IF (−) THEN
g. Loop structure header (DO loop or WHILE)

   h. Structure terminator (`CONTINUE`, `END IF`, `END WHILE`)
   i. `IF` statement
   j. Transfer statement (`GOTO`, `RETURN`, `STOP`)
   k. `END` statement
   l. Decision structure alternative header (`ELSE`, `ELSE IF` (−) `THEN`)
  m. Input/output statement (`READ` or `PRINT`)
   n. Subroutine call
   o. None of the above (possible error)

Assume each statement fits on a single line. Print each statement and its type in a legible form. (*Hint:* You may find the `BLNKSP` subroutine of Programming Project 6 helpful here.)

CHAPTER 11
Plotting Functions and Computer-aided Design

IN THIS chapter, we illustrate several techniques for plotting functions with one variable and parametric equations. We also show how to represent the graph of a function of two variables as a contour plot. Finally, we briefly overview computer facilities for engineering drawing and design.

11.1   Plotting Functions of One Variable

In this and the next two sections, we discuss several ways in which we can get the computer to plot the graphs of functions. Plotting functions of one variable is the focus of this section. In the equation

$$y = F(x),$$

the function F describes a relationship between y, the *dependent variable*, and x, the *independent variable*.

Mapping a Function onto a Screen

The method we are about to describe is very general and will work for any function that has no singularities in the range of x values that we are plotting. A *singularity* exists at x_0 if $|F(x_0)|$ is too large to be represented in the computer. (*Warning*: This definition of singularity differs from the mathematical definition, which is that a singularity exists at x_0 if $F(x_0)$ is undefined at x_0.)

To plot a function of one variable, we compute $F(x)$ on a sequence of equally spaced x-values. Our goal is to develop a program that will allow the user to specify the first and the last of these x-values:

- XINIT: the initial x value
- XFINL: the final x value

The program then will plot $F(x)$ on the interval [XINIT, XFINL]. The number of points plotted will depend on the characteristics of the output device. We will assume the computer screen has 24 rows and 80 columns. Plotting a function of one variable involves mapping a rectangular region of the x-y plane onto our computer screen. Because the x-y plane is a two-dimensional continuum and our computer screen is a two-dimensional arrangement of discrete cells, a considerable amount of information will be lost. Figure 11.1 depicts the function plotting problem. The region shaded in color in the x-y plane is to be mapped onto the computer screen causing the curve $y = F(x)$ to be represented as a finite sequence of characters.

Figure 11.1. *Mapping a Graph onto a Computer Screen*

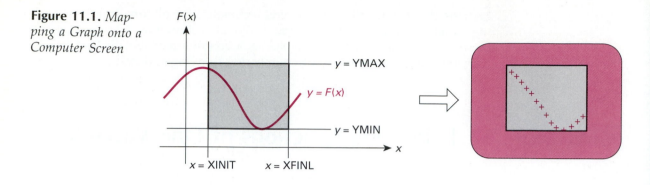

The region of the *x-y* plane that will be mapped onto the computer screen is bounded by four lines as follows:

1. the line x = XINIT on the left
2. the line x = XFINL on the right
3. the line y = YMIN, the minimum computed value for $F(x)$ on the interval [XINIT, XFINL]
4. the line y = YMAX, the maximum computed value for $F(x)$ on the interval [XINIT, XFINL]

The maximum and minimum values of $F(x)$ will be relative to a finite number of tabulation points. We will discuss how these tabulation points are determined later in this section.

Plotting the continuous curve $y = F(x)$ requires imposing a grid structure upon the rectangular region of the *x-y* plane in Fig. 11.1. Suppose we plan to organize our computer screen as shown in Fig. 11.2, so that 20 rows and 70 columns will be devoted to displaying the graph. The rest of the screen will be used to present labeling information. We can use a two-dimensional array, GRAPH, with 20 rows and 70 columns to represent our graph; each element in array GRAPH corresponds to a cell of our grid structure.

Figure 11.2. *Detail of Computer Screen Layout*

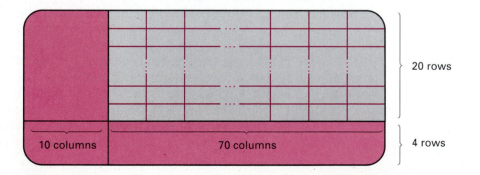

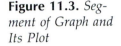

Figure 11.3. *Segment of Graph and Its Plot*

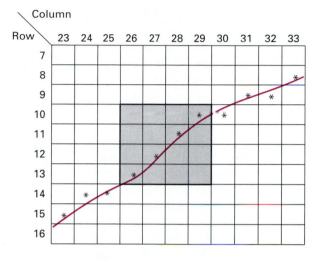

Figure 11.3 shows a portion of the screen in more detail. A 10-cell by 10-cell portion of our screen is superimposed on the corresponding portion of the *x-y* plane. The plotting program requires that the graph of the function, which is a continuous line, be represented by a finite number of characters, one for each column. (We will use the character '*' in plotting the function.) Next we discuss how to determine where to place each asterisk.

Figure 11.4 shows a part of Fig. 11.3, but with additional detail. Our plotting method progresses column by column. In each column, a row is marked with an asterisk. Figure 11.4 shows us at column 27. Columns 1–26 have already been marked. An important observation is that each column corresponds to a particular interval of *x*-values, say [XL, XR]. More significantly for our

Figure 11.4. *Plotting the Point (XM, YV)*

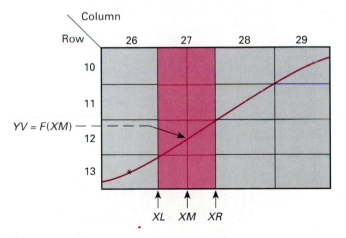

algorithm, these intervals have a midpoint XM. It is at this midpoint, XM, that we will evaluate the function, *F*, yielding a number, YV = *F*(XM). This *y*-value, YV, will then be converted to a row number, and the corresponding cell in array GRAPH will be marked with an asterisk.

The Scaling Problem

The scaling problem is central to plotting functions with a computer. The *scaling problem* is to derive the mathematical relationships between columns and XM values on the one hand and rows and YV values on the other. In terms of Fig. 11.4, the scaling problem is to compute XM, given a particular column number, K, and to compute a row number, R, for a particular function value, YV. (See Section 7.7 for an introduction to scaling.)

Let's first consider how the midpoint, XM, is determined by the column number, K. Figure 11.5 illustrates the decision that XINIT will correspond to the midpoint of the first column and XFINL will correspond to the midpoint of the last column of the graph. (We are giving column numbers relative to the graph and not to the computer screen.) This decision completely determines the relationship between column number, K, and midpoint, XM. There are 69 increments of size XINCR separating XINIT and XFINL. Therefore the increment size is

```
XINCR = (XFINL - XINIT) / 69.0
```

and the midpoint for column K is

```
XM = XINIT + (K - 1) * XINCR
```

This equation is the solution to the scaling problem along the *x*-dimension of the graph. The divisor, 69.0 in this case, will change with the dimensions of the plot, but it will always be one less than the number of columns to be plotted.

Figure 11.5. *Scaling Problem in the x-Dimension*

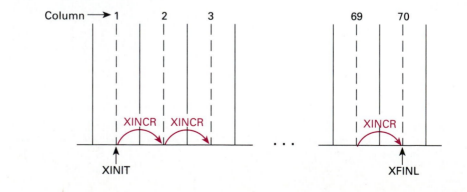

Figure 11.6. *Scaling Problem in the y-Dimension*

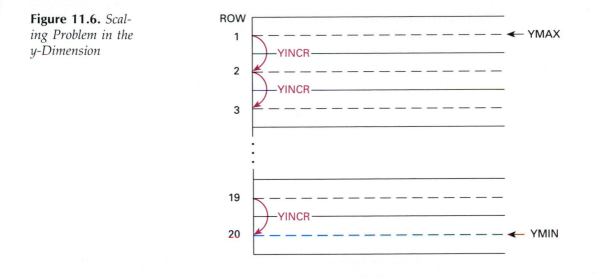

Along the *y*-dimension, we want to be able to compute a row number, R, given the functional value, YV = F(XM). This problem is a little tricky. Figure 11.6 shows a decision to make the midpoint of row 1 correspond to the maximum value for $F(x)$, YMAX, and to make the midpoint of row 20 correspond to the minimum value for $F(x)$, YMIN. This determines that the distance between successive midpoints is

```
YINCR = (YMAX - YMIN) / 19.0
```

The row number, R, for a given *y*-value, YV, depends upon the distance between YV and YMAX measured in terms of *y*-increments, YINCR. This distance, YDIST, is computed as follows:

```
YDIST = (YMAX - YV) / YINCR
```

For example, YDIST is 1.0 means that YV is one *y*-increment away from YMAX, so that YV belongs in row 2. If YDIST is 19.0, then YV is YMIN and belongs in row 20.

Using the Fortran intrinsic function NINT (nearest integer), we can express the relationship between row R and YDIST as

```
R = NINT(YDIST + 1.0)
```

Table 11.1 shows the relationship between YDIST and R imposed by this formula. This table covers all possibilities, since YDIST cannot be less than 0.0 or greater than 19.0.

Table 11.1 *Relationship between YDIST and R*

YDIST	R
YDIST < 0.0	impossible
0.0 ≤ YDIST < 0.5	1
0.5 ≤ YDIST < 1.5	2
1.5 ≤ YDIST < 2.5	3
2.5 ≤ YDIST < 3.5	4
3.5 ≤ YDIST < 4.5	5
. . .	. . .
17.5 ≤ YDIST < 18.5	19
18.5 ≤ YDIST < 19.5	20
YDIST ≥ 19.5	impossible

Having solved the scaling problem, we now can write a program that plots mathematical functions.

A Function Plotting Program

Figure 11.7 is a structure chart of a program system that plots a given function, $F(x)$, on a specified interval [XINIT, XFINL]. The user provides the values for XINIT and XFINL as input. The output consists of a discrete representation of the graph $y = F(x)$.

The main program variables include the two-dimensional array GRAPH. The array GRAPH is declared to be of type CHARACTER *1 and is initialized to all blanks

Figure 11.7. *Structure Chart for Plotting Program*

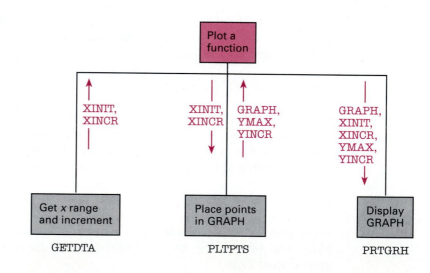

by the statement

```
DATA GRAPH /NCELL * ' '/
```

The subroutine GETDTA reads in the initial and final *x*-values: XINIT and XFINL. In addition, this subroutine computes and returns the value for XINCR, which is needed by two of the other subroutines. Because none of the other subroutines needs its value, XFINL is a local variable.

The subroutine PLTPTS does the actual plotting of the function by marking the appropriate row of each column of the array GRAPH with an asterisk. Doing this forms the heart of the plotting program. The subroutine PLTPTS contains the statement function

```
F(X) = 4.0 * (X - 0.5) ** 2
```

which defines the function we are plotting. To plot a different function, simply replace this one statement with another function statement. However, remember that the subroutine assumes a function that has no singularities on the interval [XINIT, XFINL].

There are two phases in the logic of PLTPTS. First, we must determine the maximum and minimum values for the function $F(x)$ at the 70 evaluation points, XM, given by:

```
XM = XINIT + (K - 1) * XINCR for K = 1, 2, ... , NCOL
```

This involves 70 evaluations of the function $F(x)$. Because we will need these same 70 values during the second phase of our subroutine, we store them in an array YV declared

```
REAL YV(NCOL)
```

Doing this is a matter of saving time by the expenditure of space (or computer storage). Once the maximum and minimum values, YMAX and YMIN, are known, we can compute the increment value, YINCR.

During the second phase of the subroutine PLTPTS, we use the scaling formula derived earlier to convert each of the 70 functional values, YV(K), to a unique row value, R. The cell GRAPH(R,K) is then marked with an asterisk.

The subroutine PRTGRH prints the graph row by row along with appropriate labels. To get the *x*-scale printed at the bottom of the graph, the subroutine uses array XSCALE to store the *x*-values that will be printed.

The complete program system is shown in Fig. 11.8; the output generated by the program is given in Fig. 11.9.

Figure 11.8. *Plotting a Function F(x)*

```
      PROGRAM PLOT1
C Plots the function
C       F(X) = 4.0 * (X - 0.5) ** 2
C on a 20 row by 70 column grid

C Declarations
      INTEGER NROW, NCOL, NCELL
      PARAMETER (NROW = 20, NCOL = 70, NCELL = NCOL * NROW)
      REAL XINIT, XINCR, YMAX, YINCR
      CHARACTER *1 GRAPH(NROW,NCOL)
      DATA GRAPH /NCELL * ' '/

      CALL GETDTA (XINIT, XINCR)
      CALL PLTPTS (GRAPH, XINIT, XINCR, YMAX, YINCR)
      CALL PRTGRH (GRAPH, XINIT, XINCR, YMAX, YINCR)

C Exit program
      STOP
      END


C ────────────────────────────────────────────────────────────

      SUBROUTINE GETDTA (XINIT, XINCR)
C Asks the user for the initial and final X
C values and computes the X increment
C Preconditions : None
C Postconditions: XINIT is provided as data and XINCR is
C     computed so there will be 70 columns between XINIT and XFINL.

C Output Arguments
C   XINIT - The initial X value
C   XINCR - The X increment

C Argument Declarations
      REAL XINIT, XINCR

C Local Declarations
      INTEGER NCOL
      PARAMETER (NCOL = 70)
      REAL XFINL
```

```
C Get initial and final X values from user:
      PRINT *, 'The function is plotted between the values you enter.'
      PRINT *
      PRINT *, 'Enter initial X value:'
      READ *, XINIT
      PRINT *, 'Enter final X value:'
      READ *, XFINL

C Compute X increment and return
      XINCR = (XFINL - XINIT) / REAL(NCOL - 1)
      RETURN
      END


C ─────────────────────────────────────────────────────────

      SUBROUTINE PLTPTS (GRAPH, XINIT, XINCR, YMAX, YINCR)
C Plots the function by marking appropriate
C cells of the array GRAPH with an asterisk
C Preconditions : XINIT and XINCR are defined
C Postconditions: YMAX is largest function value and YINCR is
C     chosen so that the function can be plotted in 20 rows.
C     GRAPH(I, J) is '*' if row I represents the value
C     of the function for the X-value in column J.
C     All other elements of GRAPH contain blanks.

C Input Arguments
C   XINIT, XINCR - The initial X value and X increment
C Output Arguments
C   GRAPH - The grid of points on the X, Y plane
C   YMAX, YINCR - The largest Y value and Y increment
C Argument Declarations
      INTEGER NROW, NCOL
      PARAMETER (NROW = 20, NCOL = 70)
      CHARACTER *1 GRAPH(NROW,NCOL)
      REAL XINIT, XINCR, YMAX, YINCR

C Local Declarations
      REAL YV(NCOL), YDIST, YMIN, XM
      INTEGER R, K

C Function definition:
      F(X) = 4.0 * (X - 0.5) ** 2
```

```
C PHASE ONE: Determine maximum and minimum
C           functional values
      YMAX = -10000.0
      YMIN =  10000.0
      DO 10 K = 1, NCOL
          XM = XINIT + (K - 1) * XINCR
          YV(K) = F(XM)
          IF (YV(K) .GT. YMAX) YMAX = YV(K)
          IF (YV(K) .LT. YMIN) YMIN = YV(K)
   10 CONTINUE

C Compute Y increment
      YINCR = (YMAX - YMIN) / REAL (NROW - 1)

C PHASE TWO: Mark graph column by column
C           using computed functional values
      DO 20 K = 1, NCOL
          YDIST = (YMAX - YV(K)) / YINCR
          R = NINT(YDIST + 1.0)
          GRAPH(R,K) = '*'
   20 CONTINUE

C Exit subroutine
      RETURN
      END


C _____


      SUBROUTINE PRTGRH (GRAPH, XINIT, XINCR, YMAX, YINCR)
C Prints out the graph row by row
C Preconditions : Array GRAPH is defined, as well as
C     XINIT, XINCR, YMAX, YINCR
C Postconditions: GRAPH is displayed along with a
C     horizontal and vertical scale

C Input Arguments
C   GRAPH - The grid of points on the X, Y plane
C   XINIT, XINCR - The initial X value and X increment
C   YMAX, YINCR - The largest Y value and Y increment

C Argument Declarations
      INTEGER NROW, NCOL
      PARAMETER (NROW = 20, NCOL = 70)
      CHARACTER *1 GRAPH(NROW,NCOL)
      REAL XINIT, XINCR, YMAX, YINCR
```

```fortran
C Local Declarations
      INTEGER NXVAL
      PARAMETER (NXVAL = NCOL / 10)
      INTEGER R, K, L
      REAL YVAL, XVAL, XSCALE(NXVAL)

C Print out graph row by row with labels to the left
C of the first row and every fifth row
      PRINT *
      PRINT *, '   Y'
C     Print Row 1 (Y = YMAX)
      PRINT 15, YMAX, (GRAPH(1,K), K = 1, NCOL)
   15 FORMAT (1X, F6.1, 3X, 70A1)
C     Print the rest of the rows
      DO 10 R = 2, NROW
         IF (MOD(R, 5) .EQ. 0) THEN
            YVAL = YMAX - (R - 1) * YINCR
            PRINT 15, YVAL, (GRAPH(R,K), K = 1, NCOL)
         ELSE
            PRINT 25, (GRAPH(R,K), K = 1, NCOL)
   25       FORMAT (10X, 70A1)
         END IF
   10    CONTINUE

C Compute the X scale values (XSCALE)
      K = 10
      KO 20 L = 1, NXVAL
C        XVAL is X value for column K
         XVAL = XINIT + (K - 1) * XINCR
         XSCALE(L)  = XVAL
         K = K + 10
   20    CONTINUE

C Print the X scale at the bottom of the graph
      PRINT 35, '|----------|', ('----------|', L = 1, NXVAL - 1)
   35 FORMAT (10X, 8A)
      PRINT 45, XINIT, (XSCALE(L), L = 1,  NXVAL)
   45 FORMAT (1X, 8(4X, F6.1))
      PRINT 55, 'X -->'
   55 FORMAT (40X, A)

C Exit subroutine
      RETURN
      END
```

Figure 11.9. *Sample Function Plot*

```
The function is plotted between the values you enter.

Enter initial X value:
−10.0
Enter final X value:
10.0

   Y
 441.0   *
          *
           *
            *
 348.2       *
              *
               *
                **
                 *
 232.1            *
                   *
                    **
                   **
                     *
 116.1                **
                       **
                        ***
                        ***
                          ****
   0.0                     ************
         | ——— | ——— | ——— | ——— | ——— | ——— | ——— |
       −10.0   −7.4   −4.5   −1.6   1.3    4.2    7.1   10.0
                              X —>
```

11.2 Plotting Parametric Equations

Parametric equations express the values of a collection of variables as functions of a common parameter. For example, we might express the values of x and y in terms of some parameter t, as follows:

$$x = F(t) \quad \text{and} \quad y = G(t)$$

The parameter t is often viewed as a time parameter. The equations then express the evolution of x- and y-values in terms of time.

Parametric equations for two variables, such as the pair of equations given immediately above, determine a curve in the x-y plane, assuming the functions F and G are continuous. Parametric equations for three variables would determine a curve in three-dimensional space.

The techniques developed in Section 11.1 can be modified easily to plot parametric equations. A two-dimensional array, GRAPH, should be used to store the points to be plotted. You must determine the following:

- The range of values for t [TINIT, TFINL]
- The time interval, TINCR, between points

The algorithm for the subroutine that marks cells in GRAPH follows:

Algorithm for Marking Cells in GRAPH

1. DO for t starting at TINIT and increasing by TINCR
   2. Compute $x(t)$.
   3. Compute $y(t)$.
   4. Find the row number, R, corresponding to $x(t)$.
   5. Find the column number, K, corresponding to $y(t)$.
   6. Place an asterisk in GRAPH(R,K).
   END DO

Steps 4 and 5 correspond to the scaling problem discussed in Section 11.1 and should be solved in the same way. If the range of x- and y-values are known beforehand, then it is an easy matter to compute XINCR and YINCR and use these values in steps 4 and 5 (i.e., compute XDIST, YDIST, and then R and K). Otherwise, it will be necessary to first tabulate and store all values of $x(t)$ and $y(t)$ to find [XMIN, XMAX] and [YMIN, YMAX]. This should be done in a separate step before attempting to mark the cells in GRAPH.

11.3 Plotting Functions of Two Variables

As we continue our discussion of plotting functions using Fortran, we might consider plotting the graph of a function of two variables

$$z = F(x,y).$$

As in Section 11.1, the scaling problem is a central concern. You will be happy to learn that the scaling problem for functions of two variables is essentially solved in the same manner as for functions of one variable.

Many techniques exist to plot the graph of a function of two variables, but most are beyond the scope of this text. (They involve issues of perspective and other sophisticated topics in computer graphics.) However, we will discuss two simple techniques here: displaying the graph plane by plane and using contour plots.

Figure 11.10.
Graph of a Function of One Variable

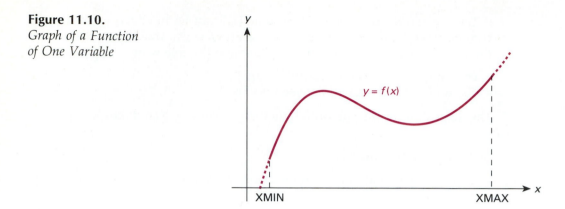

The Information Loss Problem

Graphing a function of two variables presents us with new problems insofar as information loss is concerned. We mentioned in Section 11.1 that when we map a function of one variable onto the computer screen, there is a loss of information because the computer representation is discrete, whereas the actual graph is a continuum. The same sort of consideration holds when we graph a function of two variables.

The graph of a function of one variable defines a curve in two-dimensional space (see Fig. 11.10); the graph of a function of two variables defines a surface in three-dimensional space (see Fig. 11.11). Because our computer screens and printouts are two-dimensional and the graph is three-dimensional, we have a serious problem regarding information loss. How can we map the three-dimensional graph onto the computer screen and yet retain enough information to make our computer representation useful?

Figure 11.11.
Graph of a Function of Two Variables

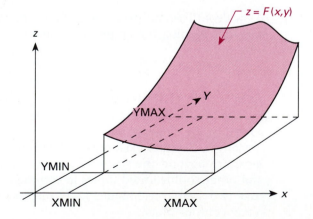

Plotting the Function Plane by Plane

One way to plot the graph of a function of two variables is to project the graph plane by plane onto the computer screen. To do this, a sequence of N y-values $(y_1, y_2, \ldots, y_N)$ is chosen. Each y-value determines a plane, $y = y_j$. Each of these y-values, when substituted into our original function of two variables, $F(x,y)$, will yield a function of one variable $f_j(x)$, as follows:

$$f_j(x) = F_j(x,y)$$

The graph of $z = f_j(x)$ is the intersection of the plane $y = y_j$ with the graph of the original function, $F(x,y)$. Each of these N functions, $f_j(x)$, $j = 1, 2, \ldots, N$, can be plotted using the technique described in Section 11.1. Figure 11.12 suggests what the output of such a program might look like. We can reconstruct the general contours of the original function, $z = F(x,y)$, in our mind's eye by examining these projections.

Contour Plots

Contour plots can be used to represent the graph of a function

$$z = F(x,y)$$

as a whole, not plane by plane. The idea of a contour plot is straightforward. If you have ever worked with a geographical map where heights above and below sea level are color coded, then you already have some familiarity with the basic concept. In a computer-generated contour plot for a function of two variables, the distance of the surface of the graph from the x-y plane is encoded using characters. All points on the surface of the graph within the same range of distances from the x-y plane are assigned the same character.

Figure 11.12. *Representing a Function Graph as a Set of Planes*

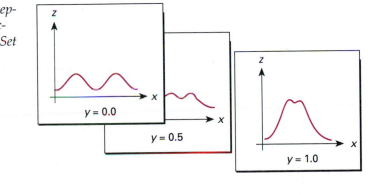
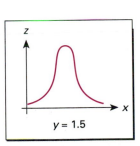

Figure 11.13. *A Contour Plot and Its Key*

```
                 KEY                              plot
    z value         symbol        -----------------------------
                                  -----------------------------
   z ≥ 0.5            +           ----------    ----------
   -0.5 ≤ z < 0.5   blank         -------          --------
   z < -0.5           -           -----        +        -----
                                  ---        +++          ---
                                  -         +++++           -
                                  -        +++++++          -
                                  ---       +++++          ---
                                  -----      +++         ----
                                  -------     +        ------
                                  ---------        --------
                                  -----------   ---------
                                  -----------------------------
```

Figure 11.13 shows a small contour plot where the symbols $+$, $-$, and blank are used to code the value of z. The key to the contour plot is shown on the left. A grid structure consisting of 14 rows and 20 columns has been imposed on a portion of the x-y plane.

The function being plotted is evaluated at each of $14 \times 20 = 280$ grid points, and a symbol is chosen to represent the computed value. The plot in Fig. 11.13 shows a diamond-shaped hill (values of $z \geq 0.5$) rising above a valley (values of $z < -0.5$).

In general, a contour plot such as that shown in Fig. 11.13 is generated by imposing a grid structure on a region of the x-y plane and evaluating the function at a point within each cell of the grid. This region is delimited by the lines $x = $ XMIN, $x = $ XMAX, $y = $ YMIN, and $y = $ YMAX. This region is mapped onto our computer screen as shown in Fig. 11.14, where we have decided to devote 20 rows and 60 columns to the plot, thus allowing a key to be printed on the left side of the screen.

Each of the $20 \times 60 = 1200$ cells on the screen corresponds to a definite region of the x-y plane. That region is a two-dimensional continuum of points.

Figure 11.14. *Mapping a Function of Two Variables onto a Screen*

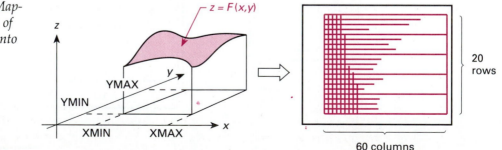

Figure 11.15. *Evaluation of F(x,y) at the Grid Points and Contour Plot for F(x,y)*

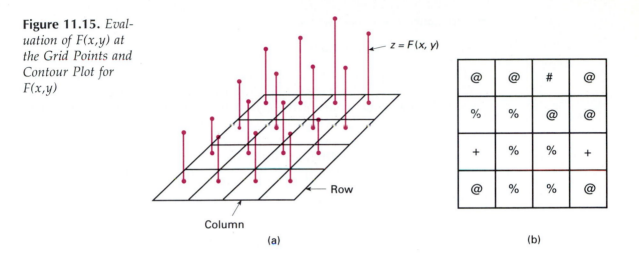

(a)   (b)

The constraints of our computer hardware dictate that the function be represented by only one character at each of these 1200 cells. This discrete sampling of the function is responsible for some of the information loss that occurs in contour plotting. The rest of the information loss is because a continuum of possible functional values is reduced to one of a small collection of characters. The number of characters in the contour plot key is typically in the range of five to ten. If we incorporate too many characters in our key, hoping to counteract the information loss, the result is a plot that is visually confusing. Figure 11.15(a) shows a small section of the x-y plane. The grid is shown as well as the grid points at which the function will be evaluated. Functional values at these grid points are shown as blue lines that are perpendicular to the plane. Figure 11.15(b) shows the corresponding portion of our contour plot.

The Scaling Problem in the x- and y-Dimensions

Contour plotting involves three scaling problems, one in each of the three dimensions: x, y, and z. The scaling in the x-dimension is solved once the decision is made that the midpoint of the first column of our plot will correspond to XMIN and the midpoint of the last column of our plot will correspond to XMAX. If there are NCOL columns (NCOL is 60 in Fig. 11.14), then the midpoints of successive columns are separated by the distance

```
XINCR = (XMAX − XMIN) / (NCOL − 1)
```

Similarly, the scaling problem in the y-dimension is solved once we decide to make the midpoint of the first row correspond to YMAX and the midpoint of the last row correspond to YMIN. Then the midpoints of successive rows will be a distance YINCR apart where

YINCR = (YMAX − YMIN) / (NROW − 1)

and NROW is the number of rows in our contour plot (NROW is 20 in Fig. 11.14).

Our computational strategy is to compute $z = F(x,y)$ at the center point of each cell. The center point of the cell at the top left corner of our plot is (XMIN,YMAX). The nested DO loop below causes x and y to take on the appropriate values so that all grid points are "visited." The grid points will be visited row by row. Note that as we progress from row to row, y decreases because the top of the contour plot corresponds to the maximum y-value.

```
C Compute Z value for each point to be plotted
      Y = YMAX
      DO 10 R = 1, NROW
         X = XMIN
         DO 20 K = 1, NCOL
            Z = F(X,Y)                    (X,Y) is a grid point
            . . . Do what needs to be
                  done with Z . . .
C            Get next X value
            X = X + XINCR
   20    CONTINUE
C        Get next Y value
         Y = Y − YINCR
   10 CONTINUE
```

The Scaling Problem in the z-Dimension

Let us now consider the scaling problem in the z-dimension; that is, we need to associate with every functional value, $z = F(x,y)$, an appropriate symbol based on the key of the contour map. One of two conditions could exist at the outset, as follows:

1. The key is known when we write the program.
2. The key must be computed by the program itself.

We discuss the first of these conditions in detail and the second briefly at the end of this section.

In some cases, the key can be determined by mathematical analysis and so is known before we write the program. For example, in a contour plot of the function

$$z = \sin(a * x) + \cos(b * y)$$

it's a simple matter of analysis to see that z must always lie within the range −2 to 2, since we are adding two sinusoidal functions (sin and cos) with

Table 11.2. *Sample Key for a Contour Plot*

Z-VALUE	SYMBOL
$z \geq 1.5$	#
$1.0 \leq z < 1.5$	@
$0.5 \leq z < 1.0$	%
$0.0 \leq z < 0.5$		
$z < 0.0$	.

amplitude 1. The scaling problem in the z-dimension for this function would require creating a table of correspondences between z-values and characters. (See Table 11.2.) The symbols were chosen so that larger z-values are represented by darker symbols. Furthermore, because we want to highlight the details for positive z-values, we have decided to treat all negative values the same.

It is a simple matter to save this table in a Fortran program and use it to convert a given z-value to a plot symbol. This process is illustrated in the next problem, which deals with writing a computer program that generates a contour plot. We will apply the theory that has been developed so far.

Case Study: Contour Plot for a Hemispherical Surface

PROBLEM STATEMENT

We want to write a program that generates a contour plot of a function whose graph is a hemispherical surface.

ANALYSIS

The function that yields the hemispherical surface is

```
F(X,Y) = SQRT(1.0 - AMIN1(X ** 2 + Y ** 2, 1.0))
```

where AMIN1 is a Fortran library function that returns the minimum of the values in its argument list. Using the key in Table 11.3, we will plot this function for all x-values between -1.0 and 1.0 and all y-values between -1.0 and 1.0. Consequently, the values of $z = F(x,y)$ must lie between 0.0 and 1.0.

The boundary values for z and the plot symbols will be saved in arrays ZBOUND and SYMBOL, respectively. The values for XMIN, XMAX, YMIN, and YMAX are program parameters. We will draw the plot one row at a time, starting with the line $y = $ YMAX. The symbols to be printed in the current row will be stored in the character string RGRAPH (type CHARACTER *NCOL).

Table 11.3. *Key for Hemispherical Contour Plot*

z-VALUE	SYMBOL
$z \geq 0.8$	#
$0.6 \leq z < 0.8$	@
$0.4 \leq z < 0.6$	%
$0.2 \leq z < 0.4$	+
$z < 0.2$	.

Data Requirements

Program Parameters

the minimum x-value (XMIN = −1.0)
the maximum x-value (XMAX = 1.0)
the minimum y-value (YMIN = −1.0)
the maximum y-value (YMAX = 1.0)
the number of symbols in the key (KEYSIZ = 5)
the number of rows in the contour plot (NROW = 20)
the number of columns in the contour plot (NCOL = 60)

Problem Output

each row of the contour plot (CHARACTER *(NCOL) RGRAPH)

Additional Program Variables

the row being plotted (INTEGER R)
the x-value for row R (REAL X)
the increment on the x-axis (REAL XINCR)
the column being defined (INTEGER K)
the y-value for column K (REAL Y)
the increment on the y-axis (REAL YINCR)
the boundary values for the plot key (REAL ZBOUND(KEYSIZ))
the plot symbols (CHARACTER *1 SYMBOL(KEYSIZ))

DESIGN

The algorithm follows:

Algorithm

1. Compute XINCR and YINCR.
2. Define and display each row of the contour plot, starting with the row for which Y is YMAX.

Algorithm Refinements

We discussed the general approach to step 2 earlier. For a given Y value (a row of the plot), we must determine the appropriate plot symbol for each X value along that row. To do this, we first must compute the value of F(X,Y) for each X and then convert this value to the corresponding plot symbol (a character). We will store the plot symbols as individual characters in the string variable RGRAPH.

Step 2 Refinement

2.1 Initialize Y to YMAX.
2.2 DO for each row of the plot
    2.3 Set X to XMIN.
    2.4 DO for each column, K, of the plot
        2.5 Compute Z = F(X,Y).
        2.6 Convert Z to a plot symbol.
        2.7 Store the plot symbol as the Kth character in string RGRAPH
        2.8 Increment X by XINCR.
    END DO
    2.9 Display the string RGRAPH.
    2.10 Decrement Y by YINCR.
END DO

IMPLEMENTATION

Figure 11.16 shows the contour plot program. DO loop 20 corresponds to step 2.4 in the algorithm above. After the value of Z is computed, the IF statement compares Z to the boundary values saved in array ZBOUND to determine the

Figure 11.16. *Generating a Contour Plot for a Hemisphere*

```
      PROGRAM CONTOR
C Generates a contour plot of a hemispherical surface

C Declarations
      INTEGER NCOL, NROW, KEYSIZ
      PARAMETER (NCOL = 60, NROW = 20, KEYSIZ = 5)
      REAL XMIN, XMAX, YMIN, YMAX
      PARAMETER (XMIN = -1.0, XMAX = 1.0)
      PARAMETER (YMIN = -1.0, YMAX = 1.0)

      CHARACTER *(NCOL) RGRAPH
      REAL Z, XINCR, YINCR, ZBOUND(KEYSIZ)
      INTEGER R, K
      CHARACTER *1 SYMBOL(KEYSIZ)
      REAL F, X, Y
```

```
              DATA ZBOUND /0.80, 0.60, 0.40, 0.20, 0.20/
              DATA SYMBOL /'#', '@', '%', '+', '.'/

C Function definition
              F(X,Y) = SQRT(1.0 - AMIN1(X ** 2 + Y ** 2, 1.0))

C Compute X and Y increments
              XINCR = (XMAX - XMIN) / REAL (NCOL - 1)
              YINCR = (YMAX - YMIN) / REAL (NROW - 1)

C Generate contour plot row by row
              Y = YMAX
              DO 10 R = 1, NROW
                 X = XMIN
                 DO 20 K = 1, NCOL
C                   Compute Z value at point (X,Y)
                    Z = F(X,Y)
C                   Place appropriate symbol in RGRAPH
                    IF (Z .GE. ZBOUND(1)) THEN
                       RGRAPH(K:K) = SYMBOL(1)
                    ELSE IF (Z .GE. ZBOUND(2)) THEN
                       RGRAPH(K:K) = SYMBOL(2)
                    ELSE IF (Z .GE. ZBOUND(3)) THEN
                       RGRAPH(K:K) = SYMBOL(3)
                    ELSE IF (Z .GE. ZBOUND(4)) THEN
                       RGRAPH(K:K) = SYMBOL(4)
                    ELSE IF (Z .LT. ZBOUND(5)) THEN
                       RGRAPH(K:K) = SYMBOL(5)
                    END IF

C                   Get next X value
                    X = X + XINCR
   20            CONTINUE
                 PRINT 15, RGRAPH
   15            FORMAT (20X, A60)

C                Get next Y value
                 Y = Y - YINCR
   10         CONTINUE

C Exit program
              STOP
              END
```

corresponding plot symbol. The statement

`RGRAPH(K:K) = SYMBOL(1)`

executes when Z exceeds the largest boundary value. This statement sets the Kth character in string RGRAPH to the symbol that represents the largest Z values.

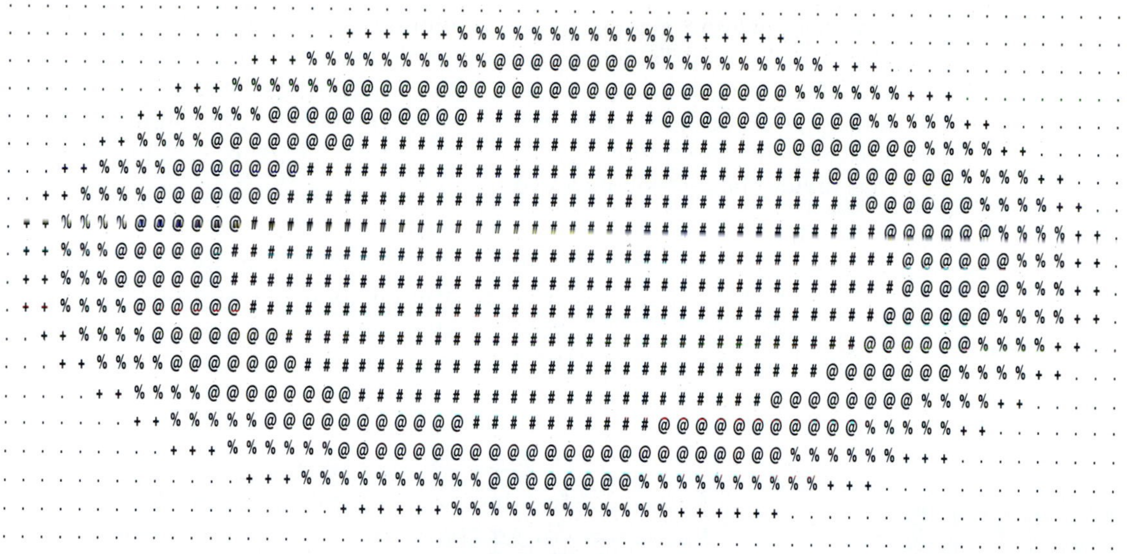

Figure 11.17. *Sample Contour Plot*

This use of substring notation to define a single character in a string was covered in Section 10.2.

TESTING AND IMPLEMENTATION

Figure 11.17 shows a sample contour plot generated for the test function F(X,Y) described earlier. To draw another contour plot, insert a different single-statement function definition for F(X,Y). Ensure you also modify the DATA statement for ZBOUND if the range of function values changes. Alternatively, you could create a separate subroutine to initialize the array ZBOUND, as discussed next.

Computing the Key at Execution Time

Suppose we have decided on a given collection of characters to use in our contour plot, but we don't know the range of z-values that will correspond to a given character (see Table 11.4). The program can determine the desired

Table 11.4. *Key for Unknown Range of z-Values*

Z-RANGE	SYMBOL
$z \geq A$	#
$B \leq z < A$	@
$C \leq z < B$	%
$D \leq z < C$	+
$z < D$	.

z-values once the maximum and minimum z-values (ZMAX and ZMIN, respectively) are known. To determine these two values, the program must compute $z = F(x, y)$ at each grid point; doing this requires nested DO loops that take us row by row through the two-dimensional pattern of grid points. Once ZMAX and ZMIN have been found, we can assign z-values (A, B, C, D) for Table 11.4 that divide the z-range into five regions.

EXERCISE FOR SECTION 11.3

Programming

1. Write a subroutine that defines the values stored in the array ZBOUND for a function $F(x, y)$. (*Hint:* The input arguments to the subroutine should be XMIN, XINCR, YMAX, YINCR, NUMCOL, NUMROW, and KEYSIZ; the output should be the array ZBOUND. Find ZMIN, ZMAX, and then ZINCR.)

FORTRAN *in Focus*

Environmental Simulations Using Fortran
METCALF & EDDY

Metcalf & Eddy, Inc., a subsidiary of Air and Water Technologies, is a worldwide environmental engineering consulting firm. Metcalf & Eddy's clients include government bodies and industrial firms, and jobs range in size from huge multimillion-dollar waste water treatment plant designs to environmental assessments and water supply work for small municipalities.

Employees in the Environmental Quality Division at Metcalf & Eddy's Wakefield, Massachusetts, office depend on Fortran on a regular basis to perform simulations of complex technical situations that allow them to perform analyses and make appropriate recommendations to clients. This division is composed of approximately 30 engineers and scientists of whom only a few do actual Fortran programming. Many

more use models written in Fortran to complete tasks such as simulating ground water flows to evaluate and remediate contamination, determining flood zones, or siting waste water outfalls. Fortran is also used by the Hazardous Waste division of Metcalf & Eddy for similar purposes.

Currently, the Environmental Quality Division is using programs written in Fortran to simulate the water budget of an artificial wetland to be constructed to replace wetlands that will be filled during proposed highway construction. A site for a new wetland was located, and Metcalf & Eddy was called upon to determine whether this site was suitable for a wetland, that is, whether there would be enough ground water discharge to the wetland to keep it saturated.

11.4 Introduction to Computer-aided Design

In addition to using the computer to plot functions, engineers also frequently use the computer as a design tool. Computer graphics systems are widely available to help engineers make engineering drawings whose specifications are saved on disk. Later, the engineer can modify the existing drawing or reuse parts of it in new drawings.

Early graphics systems provided a library of subroutines that the designer could call to draw standard objects such as circles, rectangles, and even poly-

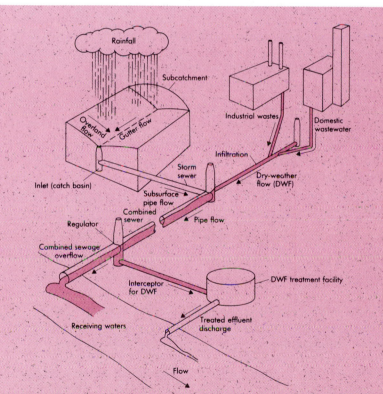

URBAN DRAINAGE SYSTEM. PHILIP BEDIENT/WAYNE HUBER, *HYDROLOGY AND FLOODPLAIN ANALYSIS* © 1992 BY ADDISON-WESLEY PUBLISHING COMPANY, INC. REPRINTED WITH PERMISSION OF THE PUBLISHER. DATA FROM METCALF AND EDDY, INC., UNIVERSITY OF FLORIDA, AND WATER RESOURCES ENGINEERS, INC., 1971, *STORM WATER MANAGEMENT MODEL, VOLUME I: FINAL REPORT,* EPA REPORT 11024DOCO7/71 (NTIS PB-203289), ENVIRONMENTAL PROTECTION AGENCY, WASHINGTON, D.C., JULY.

Using a ground water model called MODFLOW, engineers were able to make these determinations. This model is available through the US Geological Survey (USGS) and is written in Fortran. Information such as soil conditions, depth to bedrock, and recharge rate from precipitation and streams is input into the model, which then calculates ground water elevation and flow using a finite difference method. This model enabled engineers to determine how much they needed to lower the surface of the proposed wetland in order to maintain an adequate ground water supply that would keep the soil saturated.

MODFLOW is a versatile program used by Metcalf & Eddy engineers to model a variety of situations. It is

(continued)

gons. The designer could specify the size and position of each individual object in an engineering drawing. The drawings were printed on line printers with graphics capability or drawn on special output devices called *plotters*.

Today, interactive menu-driven systems are available on personal computers and graphics workstations. The designer uses a mouse to position the cursor at the point where each new object or line is to be drawn and then selects the desired object or line shape from a menu of available objects.

The engineer also can create three-dimensional drawings using a computer-aided design (CAD) system. To create a three-dimensional object, the engineer rotates a two-dimensional object around a specified axis. Once an object has been designed, a CAD system can compute and display certain of its properties such as area, volume, and cross-sections.

When displaying a three-dimensional object, the engineer not only can rotate the object in space and request different views of it, but also select different colors to distinguish among parts of the drawing. For example, in a heating/air-conditioning diagram, components of the heating system could be drawn in one color, components of the cooling system in another color, and components used in both systems in still another color.

CAD systems are widely used in the following engineering fields:

- Aerospace (designing aircraft and space vehicles)
- Automotive (designing automobile bodies, engines, and other components)
- Architecture (creating building designs and room layouts)
- Electronics (drawing circuit-board layouts, integrated circuit fabrications, and wiring diagrams)

commonly used to predict ground water flow in the vicinity of contaminated soils in order to either prevent the spread of hazardous materials or to aid in the remediation of contaminated soil and ground water. This modeling is typically used to aid in the development of remediation strategies by simulating the behavior of ground water in hypothetical situations such as the installation of recovery wells or slurry walls that might be used in a recovery or containment system. Without these Fortran models, such systems could be designed only through intuition and experience.

MODPLOT, another program written in Fortran, was developed by Metcalf & Eddy engineers to display the output from MODFLOW, converting long columns of raw numbers into contour plots that are readily and intuitively comprehensible. Both of these programs are run on IBM compatible personal computers and are maintained by modelers who make necessary alterations to the programs to meet the needs of individual projects.

Dan Wang, an engineer with the Environmental Quality Division, frequently performs simulations using Fortran programs such as MODFLOW, and has written programs to aid in modeling with MODFLOW. As he sees

CAD systems also can be integrated with computer-aided manufacturing (CAD/CAM). In CAD/CAM, the specifications and dimensions created in the design phase are used as inputs in the manufacturing phase to control production tools, thereby automating the manufacturing process.

Computer-aided engineering (CAE) is another extension of CAD. A CAE system can complete an entire design by extrapolating from a few key sections provided by the engineer. It also can decompose an object into its component elements and perform mathematical computations to determine properties, such as stress and temperature, of individual elements.

11.5 Common Programming Errors

Because we did not introduce any new Fortran statements in this chapter, there are no new pitfalls to warn you about. However, this chapter does make extensive use of arrays and subprograms, so you should review the errors common with their use. To avoid argument list errors, continue to be careful about argument list length and the order of arguments. Also, check subscript boundary values in loops that process arrays to ensure each array subscript remains in range for all values of the loop parameters. Finally, ensure you continue to declare the data types of all variables and user-defined functions so errors are not introduced because of implicit (default) types.

it, Fortran is the most common language used for models since it is understood by most engineers and because many current, widely used models are written in Fortran. In this way, the widespread use of Fortran perpetuates itself. It is important to write such models in a language that engineers will understand, and because previous models have been written in Fortran, it is the language these engineers will know. Fortran can do virtually anything a modeler may need and it is simple to use and understand.

As a college student, Wang did not study Fortran, but wishes he had. Once hired as an engineer, he found it necessary to learn Fortran in order to assist in updating the ground water models he uses, and he admits that getting started would have been easier if he had studied the language in college. His advice to students learning Fortran is, "Concentrate on learning how to program rather than on one language . . . developing good programming skills is the most important thing."

Sincere thanks to Dan Wang, Engineer at Metcalf & Eddy's Wakefield, Massachusetts, office for taking the time to explain how Fortran is being used to address many of today's environmental issues.

Chapter Review

In this chapter, we discussed using a computer for plotting functions and described several kinds of function plots, including graphs of parametric equations and contour plots. We also introduced the topic of computer-aided design.

Quick-check Exercises

1. What is a singularity?
2. In a plot of $y = F(x)$, _____ is the dependent variable and _____ is the independent variable.
3. What are parametric equations?
4. How many dimensions can be plotted in a contour plot?
5. Differentiate between CAD, CAD/CAM, and CAE.
6. Name two techniques for plotting a three-dimensional curve.

Answers to Quick-check Exercises

1. A singularity is a point on a curve whose value is too large to be plotted.
2. y, x
3. equations that express the values of a collection of variables as functions of a common parameter
4. three dimensions
5. CAD is used for drawing or drafting. In CAD/CAM, the computer also controls the manufacturing process. In CAE, the computer analyzes properties of a drawing and assists in the engineering process.
6. contour plots and plotting the function plane by plane

Review Questions

1. Explain the scaling problem.
2. What is the scaling problem in a three-dimensional plot?
3. How can you use two-dimensional plots to represent a three-dimensional surface?
4. List three applications of computer-aided design in engineering.
5. Which one of the following is true about the parametric equations $x = F(t)$ and $y = G(t)$?

   a. t is an independent variable   c. x is an independent variable
   b. t is a dependent variable   d. y is an independent variable

6. In the program (see Fig. 11.8) used to plot a function of one variable ($y = F(x)$), the values of y are stored in an array. How many elements are in that array?

   a. One element for each row of the plot (20)
   b. One element for each column of the plot (70)
   c. One element for each row and each column of the plot (20 + 70 = 90)

    d. One element for each grid point of the plot $(20 * 70 = 1400)$
    e. One element for each grid point of the display $(24 * 80 = 1920)$

7. In the program used to plot a function of one variable ($y = F(x)$), the plot is stored in a two-dimensional character array. Which of the following statements could be used to declare that array?

    a. `CHARACTER *(NROW) GRAPH (NCOL)`
    b. `CHARACTER *(NCOL) GRAPH (NROW)`
    c. `CHARACTER *1      GRAPH (NROW, NCOL)`
    d. `CHARACTER *1      GRAPH (NCELL)`
    e. `CHARACTER *1      GRAPH (24, 80)`

8. Which of the following is described by the set of three parametric equations $\{x = F(t), y = G(t), z = H(t)\}$?

    a. A curve in the x-y plane
    b. A region in the x-y plane
    c. A curve in the x-y-z plane
    d. A surface in the x-y-z plane
    e. A volume in the x-y-z plane

Programming Projects

1. Plot each of the following functions over a suitable interval:

    a. $x^4 - 6x^3 - 5x^2 - 70x + 9$
    b. $3 \cos(x) - x$
    c. $\sqrt{|\sin(x)| + |\cos(x)|}$
    d. $e^{-(x^2/2)}$

2. Write a program that will plot two functions on an interval [`XINIT,XFINL`], say

```
Y = F(X)
Y = G(X)
```

Use different symbols for the plot of F and G. Wherever the two functions intersect, use yet a third plotting symbol. Use your program to estimate the two points of intersection for

```
F(X) = SQRT(4.0 - X ** 2)
G(X) = 1.0 + X ** 2
```

3. Modify the program you wrote for Programming Project 2 so that the area between the two functions being plotted will appear shaded (i.e., filled with the symbol/; see Fig. 11.18). Test your program on the functions given in Programming Project 2 and any other functions you might want to try.

Figure 11.18. *Area between Functions*

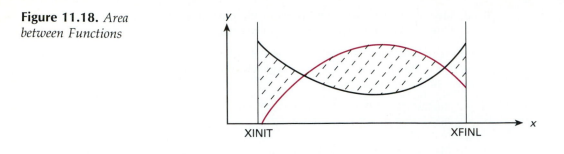

4. Write a parametric equation plotting program and plot the following parametric equations. Each curve must be considered separately. Choose an appropriate x-y scale and time increment in each case.

a. $x = t^2$, $y = t^3$ $-1 \le t \le 2$
b. $x = e^{-t}$, $y = e^t$ $0 \le t \le \ln 3$
c. $x = e^t$, $y = e^{3t}$ $0 \le t \le \ln 2$
d. $x = 3 + 2 \sin(t)$ $\left.\begin{array}{c} \\ \\ \end{array}\right\} -\pi/2 \le t \le \dfrac{\pi}{2}$
   $y = 4 \sin(t)$
e. $x = \cos(t)$ $\left.\begin{array}{c} \\ \\ \end{array}\right\} \ 0 \le t \le 2\pi$
   $y = \sin^2(t)$

5. Write a program to plot the trajectory of a golf ball for various initial velocities, V, and angles of elevation, θ. The user will be asked to enter the values for V (in ft/sec), THETA (in radians), and the distance, H, from the tee (at the origin) to the hole. The equations describing the ball's trajectory are

$$X = (V \cos \theta)t$$
$$Y = -\tfrac{1}{2}gt^2 + (V \sin \theta)t$$

where g is the gravitational acceleration of 32 ft/sec².

In your plot, show the location of the tee and the hole and the trajectory of the ball from the tee to where it first makes landfall (or, water fall, as the case may be). (See Fig. 11.19.)

Figure 11.19. *Golf ball trajectory*

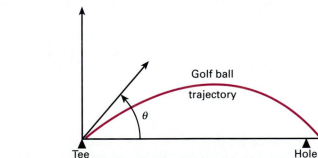

Figure 11.20.

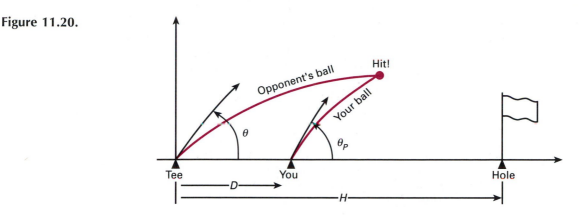

6. You are hidden from view of the golfer in Programming Project 5 at some point on the line between the tee and the hole. The distance between you and the golfer is D. You plan to deflect the golfer's ball by a shot of your own. You will hit your ball with an initial velocity, V_P, at an angle of elevation, θ_P.

Write a program that will accept your opponent's initial velocity, V, and angle of elevation, THETA. Also give the program the values of H (distance from tee to hole) and D (distance between you and your opponent). Once these values have been entered, the program should execute a loop in which it will accept a sequence of VP and THETAP values. For each VP and THETAP value, it should plot your ball's trajectory along with your opponent's. If both balls end up in the same cell of the array GRAPH at the same time, then both trajectories should terminate at that point and that will be considered a hit. (See Fig. 11.20.)

Keep on entering VP and THETAP values until you hit your opponent's ball or get tired.

7. The problem of graphing equations given in polar coordinates duplicates several features of our program to plot parametric equations. An equation in polar coordinates has the form

$$R = F(\theta)$$

where R is interpreted as the distance of a point from the origin and θ (THETA) is the angle (see Fig. 11.21).

Figure 11.21. *Point on a Plane*

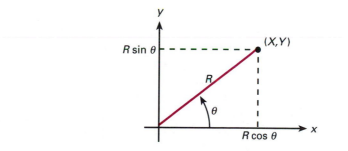

To plot equations given in polar coordinates, we let THETA take on a sequence of values, usually from 0 through $2 * \pi$. A small enough THETA increment must be chosen to obtain sufficient detail. For each THETA, we computed R = F(THETA), then transform the (R, THETA) pair to rectangular coordinates using the equations

```
X = R * COS(THETA)
Y = R * SIN(THETA)
```

These equations can be derived from a consideration of Fig. 11.21. Once we have the (X, Y) pair for the current values of R and THETA, we can mark the appropriate row and column of the array GRAPH.

Implement this technique to plot the following equations given in polar coordinates:

a. $R = \sin(\theta)$
b. $R = \cos(3 * \theta)$
c. $R = \sin(7 * \theta)$
d. $R = 3 - 3 * \sin(\theta)$
e. $R = \tan(\theta)$

8. Apply our contour-plotting technique to each of the following functions in an appropriate region near the origin. In some cases, the function $z = f(x,y)$ is not defined for certain (x,y) (parts a and b). In these cases, have your program print out a blank wherever the function is undefined.

a. $z = 9 - x^2 - y^2$
b. $z = 4 + x^2 - y^2$
c. $z = x^2 + y^2$
d. $z = \sin(x/2) \sin(y/2)$
e. $z = e^{-x} \sin(y)$

9. Write a program that generates a contour plot of the interference pattern produced by two sinusoidal wave generators operating in phase. The amplitude, z, of the disturbance at each point, (x,y), will depend on the distance between (x,y) and the individual generators (or sources). The formula for z in terms of these distances, R1

Figure 11.22. *Location of Generators*

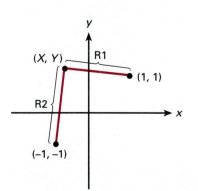

and R2, is

```
Z = COS(R1) + COS(R2)
```

where R1 denotes the distance between the first generator and (x, y) and R2 denotes the distance between the second generator and (x, y).

If the generators are at the points $(1, 1)$ and $(-1, -1)$ (as shown in Fig. 11.22), then R1 and R2 are given by the formulas

```
R1 = SQRT((X - 1.0) ** 2 + (Y - 1.0) ** 2)
R2 = SQRT((X + 1.0) ** 2 + (Y + 1.0) ** 2).
```

Generate the contour plot for z delimited by the lines $x = 10$, $x = -10$, $y = 10$, and $y = -10$.

CHAPTER 12
Introduction to Numerical Methods

IN THIS chapter, we introduce numerical methods and discuss several computational techniques widely used in solving problems in engineering, economics, statistics, business, natural science, and social science. These techniques include finding roots of equations, performing matrix arithmetic, solving simultaneous equations, fitting a line to a data set, and performing numerical integration. We also discuss Fortran features that are important in numerical computation, such as double precision and complex numbers.

The sections in this chapter are fairly independent and may be studied in any order. Because of space limitations, we generally present only one of the several methods for performing a particular numerical operation. A list of references is provided for those wishing to delve deeper into the topic of numerical methods. We've also included an extensive set of programming projects, many of which present alternative methods.

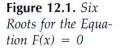

12.1 Finding Roots of Equations

A useful mathematical idea is to compute the roots of an equation

$$F(x) = 0.$$

The roots of the above equation are the values for x that make this equation true. If we graph the function $F(x)$, as shown in Fig. 12.1, the roots of the equation are those points where the x-axis and the graph of the function intersect. The roots of the equation $F(x) = 0$ are also called the *zeros of the function $F(x)$*.

In this section, we discuss two numerical methods for finding approximate real roots of an equation. When a numerical method is successful in finding

Figure 12.1. *Six Roots for the Equation $F(x) = 0$*

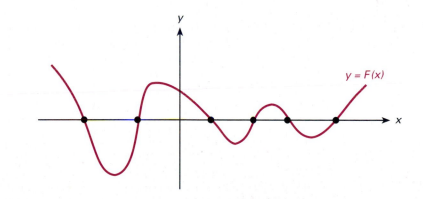

a root, it is said to have *converged* to the root. When a numerical method fails, it is said to have *diverged*. Different root-finding methods have different properties in terms of convergence and divergence. Among the methods we discuss, the bisection method converges relatively slowly (in general) as compared to Newton's method. The speed with which a method converges becomes an important issue when the function, $F(x)$, whose roots we are computing, requires costly computations. This is because finding roots of equations involves repeated evaluations of the function.

Despite its slow convergence properties, the bisection method will be discussed in detail because it does not require calculus, whereas Newton's method does. Newton's method is discussed at the end of this section, and its implementation is presented as an exercise for those students who have studied calculus.

Convergence Criteria

In general, root-finding methods generate a sequence of approximations to a root:

$$x_1, x_2, x_3, \ldots, x_j, \ldots$$

One problem we face when root finding is deciding when to terminate this generation process; that is, when is a given x_j value "good enough" to be accepted as our answer? We can use the following three criteria for judging whether a given x_j is good enough.

Criteria for Convergence to the Root

1. $|F(x_j)| <$ EPSLON
2. $|x_j - \text{RT}| <$ EPSLON
3. $|x_j - x_{j-1}| <$ EPSLON

(*Note:* RT denotes the true root, EPSLON is some predetermined small number, x_j is the latest approximation, and x_{j-1} is the approximation before that.)

Criterion 1 states that x_j is considered a good enough approximation to the root if the value of $|F(x_j)|$ is very small. Criterion 2 states that x_j is considered a good enough approximation to the root if it is very close to the true root. Finally, criterion 3 states that x_j is considered a good enough approximation to the root if it is very close to the previous approximation, x_{j-1}. In other words, we do not expect to gain required accuracy by generating additional approximations. Because the satisfaction of one of these criteria causes the root-finding method to terminate, or converge, these are called *convergence criteria*.

One might wonder how criterion 2 can be applied in practice unless RT is already known. Actually, we do not need to know RT to claim that x_j is within

Figure 12.2. *Showing Nonequivalence of Convergence Criteria 1 and 2*

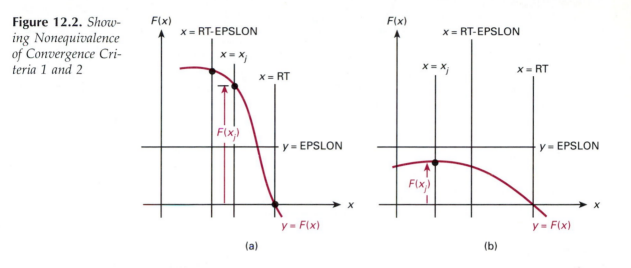

(a)   (b)

EPSLON of RT, as we demonstrate in the next section when we discuss the bisection method. It is sufficient to know that x_j and RT have been isolated to the same sufficiently small interval.

The convergence criteria are not equivalent. For example, Fig. 12.2(a) shows a situation in which x_j is within a distance EPSLON of RT, but $|F(x_j)|$ is greater than EPSLON, and Fig. 12.2(b) shows a situation in which $|F(x_j)| <$ EPSLON but the distance of x_j from RT is greater than EPSLON.

The Bisection Method

The *bisection method* applies the second convergence criterion. We repeatedly generate approximate roots, x_j, until we have an approximation that is certain to be within a distance of EPSLON from the true root, RT. This can be done if we can isolate the true root and the approximate root within the same interval whose length is less than EPSLON. This is exactly what the bisection method does.

When using the bisection method, we first tabulate function values to identify intervals on which changes of sign occur. If a change of sign occurs on an interval, that interval must contain an odd number of roots. Figure 12.3 shows two such intervals. We keep on tabulating the function until we are certain we have isolated each root to a unique interval.

Let's assume that [XL,XR] is an interval on which a change of sign does occur and in which there is exactly one root. Furthermore, assume the function $F(x)$ is continuous on this interval. If we bisect this interval by computing its midpoint, XM, using the formula

$$XM = (XL + XR) / 2.0$$

there are three possible outcomes: The root is in the left-half interval, [XL,XM];

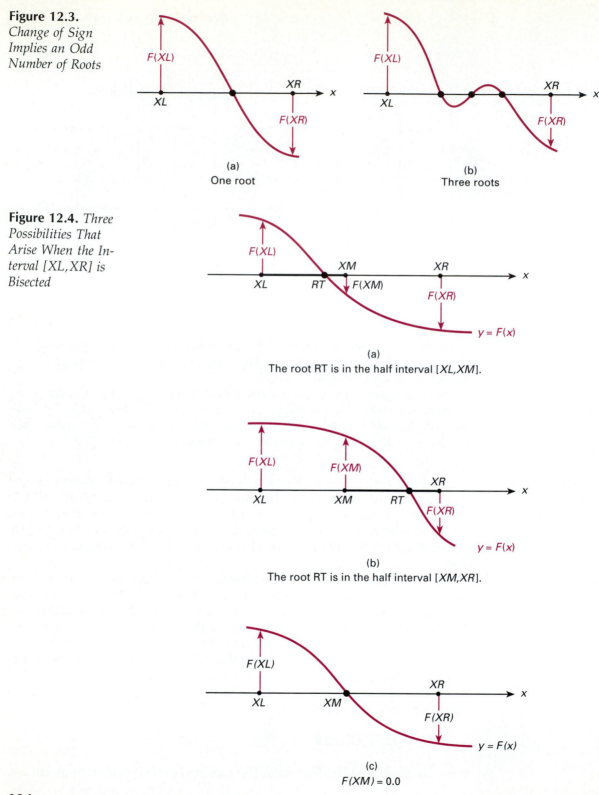

Figure 12.3.
Change of Sign Implies an Odd Number of Roots

(a)
One root

(b)
Three roots

Figure 12.4. *Three Possibilities That Arise When the Interval [XL,XR] is Bisected*

(a)
The root RT is in the half interval [XL,XM].

(b)
The root RT is in the half interval [XM,XR].

(c)
F(XM) = 0.0

the root is in the right-half interval, [XM,XR]; or F(XM) is zero. Figure 12.4 shows these three possibilities graphically.

If F(XM) is zero, there is no claim that XM is an exact root. In this case, we accept XM as an approximate root on the basis of convergence criterion 1 and the process terminates.

If the root is in one of the half intervals and the length of that interval is less than EPSLON, then the midpoint of that half interval must be within EPSLON of the true root. Thus the midpoint of that half interval satisfies convergence criterion 2 and we are done. Otherwise, we make the half interval containing the root the new interval, and we continue by bisecting it. It should be obvious that under the assumptions we have given, if F(XM) never hits zero, then eventually the interval size will become less than EPSLON and the method will converge.

A Bisection Program

The Fortran program in Fig. 12.5 looks for an approximate root for the equation $F(x) = 0$ on the interval [XL,XR] using the bisection method. The endpoints, XL and XR, and the tolerance, EPSLON, are inputs from the user. The main program gets these three inputs, calls subroutine BISECT to perform the bisection procedure, and prints out the final results.

Computing the product F(XL) * F(XR) is the easiest way to detect a change of sign in the interval [XL,XR]. This product is negative when a change of sign occurs.

Figure 12.5. *Finding a Root Using the Bisection Method*

```
      PROGRAM ROOTS
C Finds a root of the equation
C             F(X) = 0
C on a specified interval [XL,XR] using the
C bisection method. The error tolerance is EPSLON.

C Declarations
      EXTERNAL F
      REAL XL, XR, EPSLON, ROOT
      LOGICAL ERR

C Get endpoints and error tolerance from user
      PRINT *, 'Enter left endpoint:'
      READ *, XL
      PRINT *, 'Enter right endpoint:'
      READ *, XR
      PRINT *, 'Enter tolerance:'
      READ *, EPSLON
      PRINT *

      CALL BISECT (XL, XR, EPSLON, F, ERR, ROOT)
```

```
C Report out results
      IF (ERR) THEN
C         No root found
          PRINT *, 'No root in this interval'
      ELSE
C         Root found
          PRINT *, 'Root found in this interval: ', ROOT
          PRINT *, 'Functional value at root:     ', F(ROOT)
      END IF

C Exit program
      STOP
      END


C ——————————————————————————————————————————————————————

      REAL FUNCTION F(X)
C This is the function for which a root is being sought

C Argument Declarations
      REAL X

      F = 5 * X ** 3 — 2 * X ** 2 + 3

      RETURN
      END


C ——————————————————————————————————————————————————————

      SUBROUTINE BISECT (XL, XR, EPSLON, F, ERROR, ROOT)
C Implements the bisection method for finding a root of function F
C Preconditions : XL, XR, and EPSLON are defined; F is a
C     user-defined function.
C Postconditions: If a root is found, it is stored in ROOT and
C     ERROR is .FALSE.; otherwise, ERROR is .TRUE..

C Input Arguments
C   [XL,XR] — The interval being examined
C   EPSLON — The error tolerance
C Output Arguments
C   ERROR — Flag indicating whether or not there is an error
C   ROOT — The root being sought
C Functional Argument
C   F — The function

C Argument Declarations
      REAL XL, XR, EPSLON, F, ROOT
      LOGICAL ERROR

C Local Declarations
      REAL XM, FM, FL, FR
      LOGICAL NTZERO
```

```
C Compute functional values at initial endpoints
      FL = F(XL)
      FR = F(XR)

C Look for root if change of sign occurs on interval.
C Otherwise, no root can be found.
      IF (FL * FR .GT. 0.0) THEN
          ERROR = .TRUE.
      ELSE
C         Go for a root!
C         Compute initial midpoint
          XM = (XL + XR) / 2.0
          NTZERO = .TRUE.

C         Keep on searching so long as interval
C         size is too large and we didn't hit a 0
          DO WHILE (ABS(XR - XL) .GT. EPSLON
     +              .AND. NTZERO)
              FM = F(XM)
              IF (FM .EQ. 0.0) THEN
C                 Zero hit
                  NTZERO = .FALSE.
              ELSE IF (FL * FM .LT. 0.0) THEN
C                 Zero in [XL,XM]
                  XR = XM
              ELSE
C                 Zero in [XM,XR]
                  XL = XM
                  FL = FM
              END IF

C             Print out new interval if there is one
              IF (NTZERO) PRINT *, 'New interval is ', XL, XR
C             New midpoint
              XM = (XL + XR) / 2.0
          END DO

C         Define result
C         Last value of XM is ROOT
          ROOT = XM
          ERROR = .FALSE.
      END IF

C Exit subroutine
      RETURN
      END
```

(annotation boxes)
```
9 IF (...) THEN
```
```
GOTO 9
END IF
```

A sample run of the program is shown in Fig. 12.6. Note that the intermediate values XL and XR are printed by BISECT, showing the convergence to the final answer.

Figure 12.6. *Sample Run of Bisection Method*

```
Enter left endpoint:
-1.0
Enter right endpoint:
1.0
Enter tolerance:
0.001

New interval is  -1.000000      0.0000000E+00
New interval is  -1.000000     -0.5000000
New interval is -0.7500000     -0.5000000
New interval is -0.7500000     -0.6250000
New interval is -0.7500000     -0.6875000
New interval is -0.7500000     -0.7187500
New interval is -0.7343750     -0.7187500
New interval is -0.7343750     -0.7265625
New interval is -0.7304688     -0.7265625
New interval is -0.7304688     -0.7285156
New interval is -0.7294922     -0.7285156
Root found in this interval: -0.7290039
Functional value at root:    -2.6941299E-05
```

Functions as Arguments

Note that the subroutine BISECT contains the function F as a dummy argument. This is the first time we have seen a function used as an argument.

When a function is used as a dummy argument to a subroutine, you must remember to declare that function to be of the correct type within the subroutine. When a program unit passes a function (or subroutine) as an actual argument, that program unit must declare that function (or subroutine) as EXTERNAL. For example, the main program of our root-finding program contains the statement

EXTERNAL F

This allows the compiler to recognize F as a function and not as a variable or named constant. An important rule to remember, however, is that you cannot make a statement function EXTERNAL. Only functions and subroutines, which are independent program units, can be made EXTERNAL.

One final note about the program: The argument ERROR of the subroutine BISECT is used to tell the main program whether a root was found. If ERROR is returned with the value .TRUE., then no root was found. This will happen if the user specifies an interval [XL, XR] on which no change of sign occurs. If the specified interval contains more than one root, only one of them will be found.

Program Style: *Use of Function Arguments*

The use of F as an argument for the subroutine BISECT is not necessary for program correctness. We could have written BISECT without this argument by including a statement function defining F within the subroutine. However, using F as an argument is preferred because it makes subroutine BISECT a more complete, self-contained entity. BISECT will find the root for any function passed as an argument without requiring the programmer to revise BISECT for each new function. Using function F as a dummy argument also makes the intent of the subroutine clearer. Conceptually, the function is more like an argument for the subroutine than an intrinsic part of the subroutine itself.

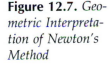

Newton's Method[M]   Newton's method for finding the roots of an equation starts with a guess, x_0, and then generates successive approximate roots $x_1, x_2, \ldots, x_j, x_{j+1}, \ldots$ using the iterative (or open) formula

$$x_{j+1} = x_j - \frac{f(x_j)}{f'(x_j)}$$

where $f'(x_j)$ is the derivative of f evaluated at $x = x_j$. This open formula specifies an iteration by which new approximations are generated from previous ones. In particular, x_{j+1} is to be computed in terms of x_j, $f(x_j)$, and $f'(x_j)$. Figure 12.7 shows the geometric interpretation of Newton's method.

This method uses convergence criterion 3. We will consider x_{j+1} the approximate root when two successive approximations are sufficiently close, that is, when

$$|x_{j+1} - x_j| < \text{EPSLON}.$$

There are famous pathological cases where Newton's method cycles indefinitely. For example, this occurs in trying to find the root of

$$F(x) = x^3 - x$$

Figure 12.7. *Geometric Interpretation of Newton's Method*

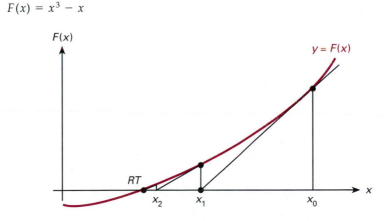

M Sections of this chapter marked with the superscript symbol[M] require calculus.

with an initial guess of $x = 1$ or $x = -1$. In general, Newton's method is more reliable and faster than the bisection method.

EXERCISE FOR SECTION 12.1

Programming

1. Write a subroutine NEWTON to replace subroutine BISECT in Fig. 12.5. (*Hint: Use an external function* DF, *which is the derivative of* $F(x)$, *as an argument.*)

12.2 Vectors and Matrixes

One- and two-dimensional arrays were introduced in Chapter 7. In many technical applications in science, engineering, economics, and business, arrays are used to represent mathematical objects called vectors and matrixes. In this section, we discuss how vectors and matrixes are represented in Fortran and how to write Fortran subroutines that perform basic operations on these objects.

Representing Vectors

A *vector* is a mathematical object consisting of a sequence of numbers (the components of the vector). A vector is said to be of dimension N if it consists of N components. We will use the notation $X(K)$ to denote the Kth component of the vector X. Unfortunately, the use of the word "dimension" in Fortran is not consistent with the standard mathematical usage. The Fortran array x in Fig. 12.8(a) is one-dimensional (in Fortran terms), whereas the vector it represents, shown in Fig. 12.8(b), is three-dimensional (in mathematical terms). An N-dimensional vector is represented in Fortran as a one-dimensional array plus an INTEGER variable that stores the value of N.

The Scalar Product

Two vectors with the same number of components can be multiplied together to form the scalar (dot or inner) product. This is done by computing the sum of the product of corresponding components. Hence, if $X = \langle 1,2,4 \rangle$ and $W =$

Figure 12.8. *Fortran Representation of a Vector*

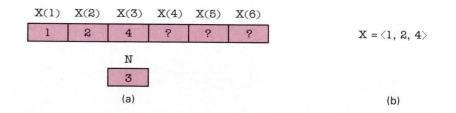

X(1) X(2) X(3) X(4) X(5) X(6)

| 1 | 2 | 4 | ? | ? | ? |

N

| 3 |

(a)

$X = \langle 1, 2, 4 \rangle$

(b)

$\langle 2,3,1 \rangle$, their scalar product is

$$X \cdot W = \langle 1,2,4 \rangle \cdot \langle 2,3,1 \rangle = 1 * 2 + 2 * 3 + 4 * 1 = 12.$$

In general, if $X = \langle x_1, x_2, \ldots, x_N \rangle$ and $W = \langle w_1, w_2, \ldots, w_N \rangle$ are two vectors of dimension N, their scalar product is

$$\sum_{i=1}^{N} x_i * w_i,$$

where x_i and w_i denote the ith components of the vectors X and W, respectively.

Coding the computation of the scalar product of two N-dimensional vectors X and W is straightforward. A DO loop is required to traverse the vectors component by component. A variable SPROD is required to accumulate the sum. The Fortran code for doing this is shown next.

```
    SPROD = 0.0
    DO 10 K = 1, N
        SPROD = SPROD + X(K) * W(K)
10 CONTINUE
```

Many of the subroutines we develop in the rest of this chapter require implementation of some sum, as was required in computing the scalar product. Translating from summation notation to Fortran is a fairly mechanical process. Figure 12.9 shows in some detail the correspondence between the mathematical expression of the scalar product and its implementation in Fortran.

Representing Matrixes

A *matrix* is a mathematical object that consists of a rectangular arrangement of numbers called the *elements* of the matrix. An M-by-N matrix consists of M rows and N columns. Each row is an N-dimensional vector and each column is an M-dimensional vector. The element in the Ith row and Jth column is

Figure 12.9. *Summation Notation and DO Loop Parameters*

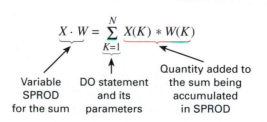

Figure 12.10.
Four-by-three Matrix and Its Implementation as a Two-dimensional Array

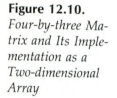

$$A = \begin{bmatrix} 1 & 1 & 1 \\ 2 & 3 & 1 \\ 1 & -1 & -1 \\ 0 & 1 & 2 \end{bmatrix}$$

M $\boxed{4}$

N $\boxed{3}$

	A					
	1	2	3	4	5	6
1	1	1	1	?	?	?
2	2	3	1	?	?	?
3	1	-1	-1	?	?	?
4	0	1	2	?	?	?
5	?	?	?	?	?	?
6	?	?	?	?	?	?

(a)   (b)

denoted by $A(I,J)$. Thus an M-by-N matrix can be implemented in Fortran as a two-dimensional array with M rows and N columns.

Figure 12.10 shows a four-by-three matrix (a) and its implementation as a two-dimensional array (b). Note the necessity of the variables M and N, which specify the number of rows and the number of columns, respectively, in the matrix. The declared dimension of the array must be large enough to accommodate the largest matrix that we expect to use in our application. Thus the array A of Fig.12.10(b) has six rows and six columns, but only four rows and three columns are being used in representing the four-by-three matrix, A.

Multiplying a Matrix by a Vector

If A is an M-by-N matrix and X is an N-dimensional vector, then we can form the product of A and X, denoted by $A * X$, yielding an M-dimensional vector, Y. A matrix with M rows and N columns can be multiplied on the right only by a vector of dimension N. If A is an M-by-N matrix and W is an M-dimensional vector, then we can form the product of W and A, denoted by $W * A$, yielding an N-dimensional vector, Z. A matrix with M rows and N columns can be multipled on the left only by a vector of dimension M. Figure 12.11 shows the multiplication of a four-by-three matrix, A, both on the right (a) and on the left (b). We will restrict our detailed discussion to Fig. 12.11(a).

How were the components of the result vector in Fig. 12.11(a) computed? The answer is that the Ith component of Y, $Y(I)$, is the scalar product of the

Figure 12.11 *Multiplying a Matrix by a Vector*

$$\begin{array}{cccc} A & * \ X & = & Y \\ \begin{bmatrix} 1 & 1 & 1 \\ 2 & 3 & 1 \\ 1 & -1 & -1 \\ 0 & 1 & 2 \end{bmatrix} * \begin{bmatrix} 1 \\ 2 \\ 2 \end{bmatrix} & = & \begin{bmatrix} 5 \\ 10 \\ -3 \\ 6 \end{bmatrix} \end{array}$$

(a) Multiplication on the right

$$\begin{array}{ccccc} W & * & A & = & Z \\ \begin{bmatrix} 2 & 0 & 1 & -1 \end{bmatrix} * \begin{bmatrix} 1 & 1 & 1 \\ 2 & 3 & 1 \\ 1 & -1 & -1 \\ 0 & 1 & 2 \end{bmatrix} & = & \begin{bmatrix} 3 & 0 & -1 \end{bmatrix} \end{array}$$

(b) Multiplication on the left

*I*th row of the matrix *A* and the vector *X*. For example, *Y*(2) is the scalar product of the second row of *A* (considered as a vector) and the vector *X*. These vectors are in color in Fig. 12.11(a). The relevant computation is

$$Y(2) = \langle 2, 3, 1 \rangle \cdot \langle 1, 2, 2 \rangle = 2 * 1 + 3 * 2 + 1 * 2 = 10.$$

The mathematical formula for computing *Y*(*I*) in the general case of the multiplication of an *M*-by-*N* matrix *A* and an *N*-dimensional vector *X* is

$$Y(I) = \sum_{K=1}^{N} A(I,K) * X(K).$$

Note that *A*(*I*,*K*) denotes the *K*th component of the *I*th row of *A* and that *X*(*K*) denotes the *K*th component of the vector *X*. Translating mathematical summation notation into Fortran, we get the following code for computing *Y*(*I*).

```
     Y(I) = 0.0
     DO 20 K = 1, N
         Y(I) = Y(I) + A(I,K) * X(K)
20 CONTINUE
```

Once we have a description of how to compute a typical element of a vector, it is a simple matter to code the computation of the entire vector. All we need to do is embed the computation of the typical element, *Y*(*I*), in a DO loop where *I* is the loop index. The Fortran subroutine MVPROD in Fig. 12.12 uses this idea to compute the product of an *M*-by-*N* matrix *A* and an *N*-dimensional vector *X*. The result is an *M*-dimensional vector, *Y*.

Figure 12.12. *Subroutine MVPROD*

```
      SUBROUTINE MVPROD (M, N, A, X, Y)
C Computes the product of matrix A (M × N) and the
C N-dimensional vector X. The result is stored in vector Y.
C Preconditions : Array A and vector X are defined.
C Postconditions: The first M elements of array Y are defined.
C     Y(I) = A(I,1) * X(1) + A(I,2) * X(2) + . . . + A(I,N) * X(N).

C Input Arguments
C    M - row dimension for matrix A and dimension for vector Y
C    N - column dimension for matrix A and dimension for vector X
C    A - M by N maxtrix
C    X - N-dimensional vector
C Output Argument
C    Y - M-dimensional product vector
```

```
C Argument Declarations
      INTEGER M, N
      REAL A(M,N), X(N), Y(M)

C Local Declarations
      INTEGER I, K

C Compute each component, Y(I), in turn
      DO 10 I = 1, M
         Y(I) = 0.0
         DO 20 K = 1, N
            Y(I) = Y(I) + A(I,K) * X(K)
   20    CONTINUE
   10 CONTINUE

C Exit subroutine
      RETURN
      END
```

Matrix Multiplication

Multiplying a matrix by a vector is just a special case of multiplying a matrix by a matrix, since an N-dimensional vector can be viewed as either a matrix with N rows and 1 column or a matrix with 1 row and N columns. Next, we develop a Fortran subroutine that will multiply any two matrixes, so long as they can be multiplied.

Two matrixes A and B can be multiplied together, yielding a new matrix, $C = A * B$, if the number of columns in A is equal to the number of rows in B. In this case, the matrixes A and B are said to be "conformable" for multiplication. If A is an M-by-N matrix and if B is N by P, then the product matrix C will be M by P. This is consistent with our earlier discussion of multiplying a matrix (M by N) by a vector (N by 1). The result was a new vector (M by 1).

In analyzing the computation of the product of two matrixes, we first consider the computation of a typical element. For example, a typical element in the product matrix C is the element in the Ith row and Jth column. This element is denoted by $C(I,J)$. Once we know how to compute $C(I,J)$, it is a trivial matter to compute the rest of the matrix C. All we have to do is embed the computation of $C(I,J)$ in an appropriate looping mechanism, which allows I and J to take on all relevant values, as shown next.

```
   DO 10 I = 1, M
      DO 20 J = 1, P
         *** Compute C(I,J) ***
20    CONTINUE
10 CONTINUE
```

Figure 12.13. *Multiplying Matrix A by Matrix B*

$$
\begin{array}{ccccccc}
A & * & B & = & C
\end{array}
$$

$$
\begin{bmatrix}
1 & 1 & 1 \\
2 & 3 & 1 \\
1 & -1 & -1
\end{bmatrix}
*
\begin{bmatrix}
2 & 0 & 1 \\
1 & -1 & 0 \\
3 & 1 & -1
\end{bmatrix}
=
\begin{bmatrix}
6 & 0 & 0 \\
10 & -2 & 1 \\
-2 & 0 & 2
\end{bmatrix}
$$

Now we describe the computation of that typical element, $C(I,J)$, of the product matrix, $C = A * B$. The element $C(I,J)$ is just the scalar product of the Ith row of A and the Jth column of B. Figure 12.13 shows the computation of C when the square matrixes A and B are multiplied together. (A matrix is square if it has the same number of rows and columns.) For example, when we compute $C(2,3)$, the second row of A (considered as a vector) is multiplied by the third column of B (considered as a vector). The elements involved are in color in Fig. 12.13.

The mathematical formula for this computation in the general case where A has N columns and B has N rows is

$$
C(I,J) = \sum_{K=1}^{N} A(I,K) * B(K,J).
$$

Note that we are pairing the Kth component of the Ith row of A and the Kth component of the Jth column of B in forming this sum. Routinely translating the above sum into Fortran, we get the following code.

```
C(I,J) = 0.0
DO 30 K = 1, N
    C(I,J) = C(I,J) + A(I,K) * B(K,J)
30 CONTINUE
```

Embedding the above computation into the appropriate nested DO loop structure yields the computation of the entire product matrix. This is done in the subroutine MATMUL of Fig. 12.14, a general subroutine for multiplying any two conformable REAL matrixes.

Figure 12.14. *Subroutine MATMUL*

```
        SUBROUTINE MATMUL (M, N, P, A, B, C)
C Multiplies matrixes A and B yielding the product matrix C
C Preconditions : Array A (M × N) and array B (N × P) are defined.
C Postconditions: Array C (M × P) is defined
C     C(I,J) = A(I,1) * B(1,J) + A(I,2) * B(2,J) + . . . +
C     A(I,N) * B(N,J)
```

```
C Input Arguments
C   M, N, P — dimensions for the matrixes A, B, and C
C   A — M by N matrix
C   B — N by P matrix
C Output Argument
C   C — M by P product matrix

C Argument Declarations
        INTEGER M, N, P
        REAL A(M,N), B(N,P), C(M,P)

C Local Declarations
        INTEGER I, J, K
        REAL CIJ

C Compute each C(I,J) in turn
        DO 10 I = 1, M
          DO 20 J = 1, P
            CIJ = 0.0
            DO 30 K = 1, N
              CIJ = CIJ + A(I,K) * B(K,J)
30          CONTINUE
            C(I,J) = CIJ
20        CONTINUE
10      CONTINUE

C Exit subroutine
        RETURN
        END
```

12.3 Solving Systems of Linear Equations

In the previous section, we saw that if we multiplied a matrix

$$A = \begin{bmatrix} 1 & 1 & 1 \\ 2 & 3 & 1 \\ 1 & -1 & -1 \end{bmatrix}$$

by a vector

$$X = \begin{bmatrix} 1 \\ 2 \\ 1 \end{bmatrix}$$

on the right, then the result is a vector

$$Y = \begin{bmatrix} 4 \\ 9 \\ -2 \end{bmatrix}$$

Now, let's consider another sort of problem. Suppose we know the matrix A and the vector Y, but we don't know the vector X. That is, we want to know which vector, X, when multiplied on the left by the matrix A, will result in the vector Y. The problem is to find the three unknowns, $X(1)$, $X(2)$, and $X(3)$, in the equation

$$\begin{array}{ccccc} A & * & X & = & Y \\ \begin{bmatrix} 1 & 1 & 1 \\ 2 & 3 & 1 \\ 1 & -1 & -1 \end{bmatrix} & * & \begin{bmatrix} X(1) \\ X(2) \\ X(3) \end{bmatrix} & = & \begin{bmatrix} 4 \\ 9 \\ -2 \end{bmatrix} \end{array}$$

To find the values of $X(1)$, $X(2)$, and $X(3)$, we must solve a system of three linear equations in three unknowns. We illustrate this by showing how each component of the vector Y is computed in terms of the matrix A and the vector of unknowns X. For example, $Y(1)$ is the scalar product of the first row of the matrix A and the vector X:

$$Y(1) = A(1,1) * X(1) + A(1,2) * X(2) + A(1,3) * X(3) = 4$$

Replacing the matrix elements $A(I,J)$ with their numerical values, we get the entire system of three linear equations in three unknowns, $X(1)$ $X(2)$, $X(3)$:

$$\begin{array}{r} X(1) + X(2) + X(3) = 4 \\ 2 * X(1) + 3 * X(2) + X(3) = 9 \\ X(1) - X(2) - X(3) = -2 \end{array}$$

In the next section, we use Gaussian elimination to solve these equations.

Gaussian Elimination

In Gaussian elimination, we attempt to reduce the original system of N linear equations to triangular form (also called upper triangular form). In *triangular form*, the coefficients below the diagonal in the matrix of coefficients are all 0 and the diagonal elements are all 1. Figure 12.15 shows the original system of equations in triangular form. Observe that the coefficients above the diagonal (in color) and the components of the constant vector Y no longer have their original values.

Figure 12.15. *Original System of Equations in Triangular Form*

$$\begin{bmatrix} 1 & 1 & 1 \\ 0 & 1 & -1 \\ 0 & 0 & 1 \end{bmatrix} * \begin{bmatrix} X(1) \\ X(2) \\ X(3) \end{bmatrix} = \begin{bmatrix} 4 \\ 1 \\ 1 \end{bmatrix}$$

The three equations that correspond to Fig. 12.15 are shown next.

$$\begin{aligned} X(1) + X(2) + X(3) &= 4 \\ X(2) - X(3) &= 1 \\ X(3) &= 1 \end{aligned}$$

This system can easily be solved for $X(1)$, $X(2)$, and $X(3)$ by solving the last equation for $X(3)$ (i.e., $X(3)$ is 1); substituting this value into the next to last equation and solving for $X(2)$ (i.e., $X(2)$ is 2); and substituting these values into the first equation and solving for $X(1)$ (i.e., $X(1)$ is 1). This process is called *back substitution*. The algorithm for Gaussian elimination follows:

Algorithm for Gaussian Elimination

1. Transform the original system into triangular form.
2. Solve for the $X(i)$ by back substitution.

The Augmented Matrix

Before we can proceed further, we must decide upon appropriate data structures for representing a system of N linear equations in N unknowns. The preferred method of representation for such systems is the augmented matrix. An *augmented matrix* is a single matrix containing the coefficients and constants for each equation, as described next.

Figure 12.16 shows the form of an augmented matrix for a system of N linear equations in N unknowns. The augmented matrix will be represented by a two-dimensional array, AUG. Note that the augmented matrix has N rows and $N + 1$ columns. The last column of the augmented matrix (shown in color) contains the constant vector, Y (e.g., AUG(1,4) is Y(1)). The matrix of coefficients, A, is stored in the rest of the columns of the augmented matrix (e.g., AUG(1,1) is A(1,1)). Note that the vector of unknowns is nowhere to be seen. When a system of linear equations is represented as an augmented matrix, the unknowns are implicit. This particular representation allows for the most concise coding of both triangularization and back substitution.

Figure 12.16. *Original Augmented Matrix AUG*

$$\begin{bmatrix} A(1,1) & A(1,2) & A(1,3) & Y(1) \\ A(2,1) & A(2,2) & A(2,3) & Y(2) \\ A(3,1) & A(3,2) & A(3,3) & Y(3) \end{bmatrix}$$

(a) General form

$$\begin{bmatrix} 1 & 1 & 1 & 4 \\ 2 & 3 & 1 & 9 \\ 1 & -1 & -1 & -2 \end{bmatrix}$$

(b) Our example

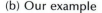

Figure 12.17.
Triangularized
Augmented Matrix

$$\begin{bmatrix} 1 & a'_{12} & a'_{13} & y'_1 \\ 0 & 1 & a'_{23} & y'_2 \\ 0 & 0 & 1 & y'_3 \end{bmatrix} \qquad \begin{bmatrix} 1 & 1 & 1 & 4 \\ 0 & 1 & -1 & 1 \\ 0 & 0 & 1 & 1 \end{bmatrix}$$

(a) General form   (b) Our example

Our first goal is to triangularize the augmented matrix, that is, reduce it to a form in which AUG(1,1), AUG(2,2), and AUG(3,3) are 1 and AUG(2,1), AUG(3,1), and AUG(3,2) are zero, as shown in Fig. 12.17. All other values (shown in color in Fig. 12.17a) are written as symbols such as a'_{ij} and y'_i. The primes are used to emphasize that these values are not the same as those in the original system of equations.

Triangularizing the Augmented Matrix

Let's now turn our attention to the triangularization process, which transforms the original system of equations into a new system in upper triangular form. The rules of linear algebra guarantee that this new system will have the same solution as the original system if we confine ourselves to the following operations upon the augmented matrix, AUG:

- Multiply any row of AUG by a nonzero number.
- Add to any row of AUG a multiple of any other row.
- Swap any two rows.

If the system has a unique solution, we can get the system into triangular form by using just these three operations. If not, our algorithm will determine that there is no unique solution.

We triangularize the augmented matrix by systematically moving down the diagonal, starting at AUG(1,1). When we are working with a particular diagonal element, we call that element the *pivot*. When AUG(L,L) is the pivot, we have two goals:

1. Normalize the pivot row, so that the pivot will take the desired value, 1.
2. Set all coefficients in the column below the pivot to zero, that is, give the elements AUG(L+1,L), AUG(L+2,L), ..., AUG(N,L) the value 0.

The first goal is achieved by multiplying the pivot row (e.g., row L) by an appropriate constant (i.e., 1/AUG(L,L)), which is an application of operation 1. The second goal is achieved by applying operation 2—add to any row of AUG a multiple of any other row—to the rows beneath the pivot row.

Experts recommend that to minimize computational round-off errors during the triangularization process, you should always place the largest possible coefficient (in absolute value) in the pivoting position. That is, when working with the Lth pivot, you should examine all the coefficients in the column beneath the pivot to find the coefficient that has the largest absolute value.

The pivot row and the row containing that largest coefficient should be swapped. This in no way changes the solution of the system of equations because swapping rows is one of the three permissible operations (operation 3—swap any two rows). The process of switching the current row with the one containing the maximum pivot is called *pivoting*.

What if we encounter a maximum pivot whose value is zero? This can happen only when all values beneath the pivot are also zero. If a nonzero value cannot be found in the column beneath the pivot, the given system of equations does not have a unique solution.

The three operations are summarized in the algorithm that follows. The local variable SOLVBL indicates whether the system of equations has a solution.

Local Variables

the current row (INTEGER L)
a flag indicating whether the system has a solution (LOGICAL SOLVBL)

Algorithm for GAUSS

1. Initially assume the system has a solution, SOLVBL = .TRUE.
2. Start with the first row, L = 1.
3. DO WHILE (SOLVBL .AND. (L .LT. N))
     4. Pivot using the maximum pivot strategy.
     5. IF (SOLVBL) THEN
          6. Normalize the pivot row.
          7. Eliminate the coefficients beneath the pivot.
        END IF
     8. Advance to the next row, L = L + 1.
   END DO
9. IF (SOLVBL) THEN
     10. Normalize row N.
   END IF

Subroutine GAUSS is shown in Fig. 12.18. The code for steps 6, 7, and 10 is inserted directly in GAUSS. The loop that performs step 6 simply multiplies each coefficient in row L by 1/AUG(L,L) (stored in RCIPRL). The multiplication starts at column L+1, because the elements in columns 1, 2,..., L−1 should all be zero. In step 10, only the elements in columns N and N+1 need to be changed.

In step 7, each row J beneath the pivot (J = L+1, L+2, ..., N) is modified so that the element in AUG(J,L) becomes zero. This is done by multiplying the pivot row (row L) by −AUG(J,L) (saved in XMULT) and then adding the pivot row to row J. The addition starts at column L+1 of row J because the elements in columns 1, 2, ..., L should all be zero.

Figure 12.18. *Subroutine GAUSS*

```
      SUBROUTINE GAUSS (AUG, N, SOLVBL)
C Triangularizes the augmented matrix AUG
C Preconditions : N is defined and AUG is an N × (N+1) augmented matrix.
C Postconditions: If SOLVBL is .TRUE., AUG is in triangular form;
C    otherwise, SOLVBL is .FALSE..

C Input Argument
C    N — The number of equations
C Input/Output Argument
C    AUG — The system of equations as an augmented matrix
C Output Argument
C    SOLVBL — Flag indicating whether system has a solution (nonsingular)

C Argument Declarations
      INTEGER N
      REAL AUG(N,*)
      LOGICAL SOLVBL

C Local Declarations
      INTEGER J, K, L
      REAL RCIPRL, XMULT

C System is assumed nonsingular; move down the diagonal
      SOLVBL = .TRUE.
      L = 1
      DO WHILE (SOLVBL .AND. (L .LT. N))                9 IF (...) THEN
C        Pivot
         CALL PIVOT (AUG, N, L, SOLVBL)
         IF (SOLVBL) THEN
C           Normalize pivot row
            RCIPRL = 1.0 / AUG(L,L)
            AUG(L,L) = 1.0
            DO 10 K = L+1, N+1
               AUG(L,K) = AUG(L,K) * RCIPRL
 10         CONTINUE

C           Eliminate coefficients beneath pivot
            DO 20 J = L+1, N
               XMULT = −AUG(J,L)
               AUG(J,L) = 0.0
               DO 30 K = L+1, N+1
                  AUG(J,K) = AUG(J,K) + XMULT * AUG(L,K)
 30            CONTINUE
 20         CONTINUE
         END IF
C        Next pivot
         L = L + 1
      END DO                                           GOTO 9
                                                       END IF
```

```
         IF (SOLVBL) THEN
C           Normalize N-th row
            RCIPRL = 1.0 / AUG(N,N)
            AUG(N,N) = 1.0
            AUG(N,N+1) = AUG(N,N+1) * RCIPRL
         END IF

C Exit subroutine
         RETURN
         END
```

Step 4 of GAUSS (the pivot step) is performed by subroutine PIVOT. The data requirements and algorithm for PIVOT follow. The subroutine is shown in Fig. 12.19.

Input Arguments

the number of rows in the augmented matrix (INTEGER N)
the row being normalized (INTEGER L)

Input/Output Arguments

the augmented matrix (REAL AUG)
a flag indicating whether a nonzero pivot was found (LOGICAL FOUND)

Local Variables

the largest absolute value in column L (REAL XMAX)
the row containing the maximum value (INTEGER MAXROW)

Algorithm for PIVOT

1. Starting at row L, find the row, MAXROW, whose element in column L has the largest absolute value.
2. IF the largest absolute value is zero THEN
       3. Set FOUND to .FALSE..
   ELSE IF MAXROW is not row L THEN
       4. Swap rows L and MAXROW.
   END IF

Back Substitution

We now can derive the Fortran code for back substitution in terms of the augmented matrix, AUG. We also will need an array X to represent the vector of unknowns and an INTEGER variable N to store the number of unknowns (three).

Figure 12.19. *Subroutine PIVOT*

```
        SUBROUTINE PIVOT (AUG, N, L, FOUND)
C Performs pivoting with respect to the Lth row and the Lth column
C Preconditions : AUG is an augmented matrix with N rows and
C   1 <= L <= N.
C Postconditions: If AUG(L,L) > 0, AUG(L,L) > AUG(I,L) for L < I <= N
C   and FOUND is .TRUE.; otherwise, FOUND is .FALSE..

C Input Arguments
C   N - The number of equations
C   L - The pivot row and column
C Input/Output Arguments
C   AUG - The augmented matrix
C   FOUND - Set to .FALSE. if search for non-zero pivot fails

C Argument Declarations
        INTEGER N, L
        REAL AUG(N,*)
        LOGICAL FOUND

C Local Declarations
        REAL XMAX, XTEMP
        INTEGER J, K, MAXROW

C Find maximum pivot
        XMAX = ABS(AUG(L,L))
        MAXROW = L
        DO 10 J = L+1, N
            IF (ABS(AUG(J,L)) .GT. XMAX) THEN
                XMAX = ABS(AUG(J,L))
                MAXROW = J
            END IF
   10   CONTINUE

C Swap rows if non-zero pivot was found
        IF (XMAX .EQ. 0.0) THEN
            FOUND = .FALSE.
        ELSE IF (MAXROW .NE. L) THEN
C           Swap rows
            DO 20 K = L, N+1
                XTEMP = AUG(L,K)
                AUG(L,K) = AUG(MAXROW,K)
                AUG(MAXROW,K) = XTEMP
   20       CONTINUE
        END IF

C Exit subroutine
        RETURN
        END
```

The triangularized augmented matrix for our example system (see Fig. 12.17b) is rewritten below on the left with the corresponding storage locations in array AUG shown on the right (e.g., the contents of AUG(1,4) is 4).

$$
\begin{bmatrix}
1 & 1 & 1 & 4 \\
0 & 1 & -1 & 1 \\
0 & 0 & 1 & 1
\end{bmatrix}
\begin{bmatrix}
\text{AUG(1,1)} & \text{AUG(1,2)} & \text{AUG(1,3)} & \text{AUG(1,4)} \\
\text{AUG(2,1)} & \text{AUG(2,2)} & \text{AUG(2,3)} & \text{AUG(2,4)} \\
\text{AUG(3,1)} & \text{AUG(3,2)} & \text{AUG(3,3)} & \text{AUG(3,4)}
\end{bmatrix}
$$

The part of the matrix that is used in back substitution is shown in color.

FORTRAN in Focus

Aerospace Simulations

MCDONNELL DOUGLAS
SPACE SYSTEMS COMPANY

McDonnell Douglas is one of the largest military, commercial, and aerospace companies in the world. Its customers include the United States Department of Defense (the U.S. Air Force, U.S. Army, and U.S. Navy) and NASA. Engineers and scientists at McDonnell Douglas Space Systems Company are involved with many research and development projects. Just a few examples of the many military and aerospace applications being worked on are the design of the Space Station Freedom, the development of the Single Stage Rocket Technology (SSRT) vehicle, and the development of Delta launch vehicles.

Fortran is used heavily throughout the company to support these advanced research programs. An example of a Fortran program used at McDonnell Douglas is the computer code Optimal Trajectories by Implicit Simulation (OTIS), which is funded by the U.S. Air Force and developed by Boeing Aerospace Company and McDonnell Douglas Corporation. This state-of-the-art code is used to analyze system performance and determine system requirements for new advanced military and aerospace vehicles such as space, re-entry, and launch vehicles.

OTIS has been used, for example, to determine the minimum weight for a launch vehicle that delivers a fixed payload to a 100-mile circular orbit. First, vehicle constraints, such as heating limits, loads, and dynamic pressure were determined. Next, the vehicle's propulsion and aerodynamic characteristics were modeled as a function of altitude, Mach number, and angle of attack. An atmosphere subroutine was selected to model the instantaneous atmospheric pressure, density, and speed of sound. The minimum weight of the launch vehicle

Applying the principle of back substitution to the diagram immediately above, we can observe from the last row that

```
X(3) = AUG(3,4) = 1
```

Next, we see from the second row that

```
X(2) = AUG(2,4) - (AUG(2,3) * X(3))  = 1 - (-1 * 1) = 2
```

necessary to deliver the fixed payload to circular orbit was then determined by optimizing the angle of attack. The application was run on a VAX System.

One advantage of Fortran is that many specialty subroutines are available and supported in various Fortran libraries. For example, integrating a set of differential equations is as easy as calling the necessary subroutines from the library. It is not necessary to write an integrator. To solve most problems, it is a matter of coding up and linking to a library. These libraries were created by specialists and are widely available for use. The same is true for OTIS, which used atmospheric, optimizer, and differential equation integrator subroutines.

Principal Engineer/Scientist Rocky Nelson is heavily involved in the use of OTIS, and believes that a key aspect of the language is that it is platform (computer) inde-

pendent. Because Fortran is a common standard between mainframes, it can be converted to different systems easily. Using Fortran when working with many other people is helpful because it is so flexible and everyone has access to it. Nelson finds especially that in his work, the code must be modular and capable of growth. He has also found that if something is done that proves to be useful, somewhere along the line it will require modification. Fortran is the natural language of choice because of its capability of modification, its modular

code, and its portability.

Nelson has been using Fortran for over 30 years and has seen it become more structured and stylish since the 1960s and 1970s when language constructs such as IF, THEN, ELSE weren't available and GO TO's had to be used instead. He believes that the current widespread governmental support for programs in Fortran will continue because it has come to be used so extensively. His advice to students learning Fortran is, "It's not hard to learn, and once you learn it, the next computer language will be easier to learn. . . . Engineers and Fortran are a good match!"

Many thanks to Rocky Nelson, Principal Engineer/Scientist at McDonnell Douglas Space Systems Center, located in Huntington Beach, California, for sharing some of the many ways in which Fortran is being used in aerospace technology.

Finally, we see from the first row that

```
X(1) = AUG(1,4) - (AUG(1,2) * X(2) + AUG(1,3) * X(3))
     = 4 - (1 * 2 + 1 * 1) = 4 - (3) = 1
```

These observations lead to the following algorithm for back substitution:

Algorithm for Back Substitution Using the Augmented Matrix

1. Set X(N) to AUG(N,N+1).
2. For each L = N–1, N–2, ... , 2, 1 in turn compute

$$X(L) = AUG(L, N+1) - \sum_{J=L+1}^{N} AUG(L,J) * X(J)$$

This algorithm is implemented as subroutine BACK shown in Fig. 12.20.

Figure 12.20. *Subroutine BACK*

```
      SUBROUTINE BACK (AUG, N, X)
C Performs back substitution
C Preconditions : AUG is a triangularized augmented matrix.
C Postconditions: Array X contains the solution for the linear system.

C Input Arguments
C   AUG - The triangularized augmented matrix (N by N+1)
C   N - The number of equations
C Output Argument
C   X - The solution vector (X(1) through X(N))

C Argument Declarations
      INTEGER N
      REAL AUG(N,*), X(N)

C Local Declarations
      REAL SUM
      INTEGER L, J

C FIND X(N), X(N-1), and so on
      X(N) = AUG(N,N+1)
      DO 10 L = N-1, 1, -1
         SUM = 0.0
         DO 20 J = L+1, N
            SUM = SUM + AUG(L,J) * X(J)
 20      CONTINUE
         X(L) = AUG(L,N+1) - SUM
 10   CONTINUE

C Exit subroutine
      RETURN
      END
```

The final step in implementing the Gaussian elimination algorithm would be to write a main program. The algorithm for the main program follows:

Algorithm for Main Program

1. Store data in the augmented matrix, AUG.
2. Call subroutine GAUSS to triangularize matrix AUG.
3. IF a solution exists (SOLVBL is .TRUE.) THEN
    4. Call subroutine BACK to find the solution.
    5. Print out the solution.
   ELSE
    6. Print a message indicating there is no solution.
   END IF

Implementing the Main Program

Figure 12.21 shows the main program. The DATA statement initializes AUG to the matrix shown earlier; the sample run displays the solution vector X.

Figure 12.21. *Main Program for Gaussian Elimination*

```
      PROGRAM LINSYS
C Solves a system of linear equations

C Declarations
      INTEGER N
      PARAMETER (N = 3, M = N + 1)
      REAL AUG(N, M), X(N)
      LOGICAL SOLVBL

C Store data in AUG

C         (1  1  1  4)
C   AUG = (2  3  1  9)
C         (1 -1 -1 -2)

      DATA AUG /1.0,2.0,1.0,  1.0,3.0,-1.0,
     +          1.0,1.0,-1.0,  4.0,9.0,-2.0/

C Call subroutine GAUSS to triangularize matrix AUG
      CALL GAUSS (AUG, N, SOLVBL)

C Call BACK and display solution if one exists
      IF (SOLVBL) THEN
         CALL BACK (AUG, N, X)
         PRINT *, 'The values of X are:'
         PRINT '(1X, 3F10.2)', X
      ELSE
         PRINT *, 'NO SOLUTION EXISTS'
      END IF
```

```
C Exit program
      STOP
      END
```

```
The values of X are:
    1.00      2.00      1.00
```

Ill-conditioned Systems

Unfortunately, not every system of N equations in N unknowns has a unique solution. The system may have no solution, in which case it is said to be *singular*, or it may have an infinite number of solutions, in which case it is said to be *degenerate*. The triangularization process will fail if the given system does not have a unique solution. A more serious danger is that our system of equations may be ill-conditioned. In the two-dimensional case (N is 2), this occurs when the two lines whose intersection we are trying to find are nearly parallel.

Another problem that arises in practice is that computational round-off errors can be significant when N is large. The larger N is, the more multiplying gets done in triangularizing the matrix. In large systems, these accumulating round-off errors may make the results obtained from Gaussian elimination useless. In these situations, iterative methods are recommended.

12.4 Linear Regression and Correlation[M]

In this section, we discuss how two important ideas from statistics—linear regression and correlation—are translated into Fortran code. Our discussion will be rather sketchy in that we do not have the space to develop the full rationale behind some of the formulae or to elaborate upon certain issues. We refer the interested reader to the references at the end of the chapter.

The Concept of Regression

Regression is normally used for prediction. Suppose X and Y are two measurable quantities (or *observables*). For example, X might be the annual rainfall and Y might be annual tree ring growth, or X might be a professor's intelligence quotient and Y might be his or her salary. *Regression* means to determine a relationship

$$Y = F(X)$$

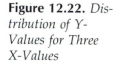

Figure 12.22. *Distribution of Y-Values for Three X-Values*

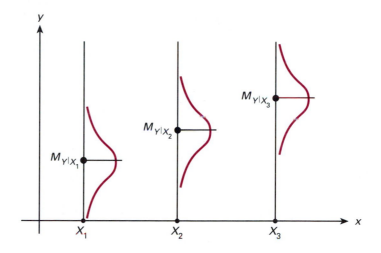

on the basis of a finite sample of X and Y scores. This relationship is then used to predict Y-values for given X-values.

Regression may be linear or nonlinear, depending on whether the relationship, $F(X)$, is linear. We confine our discussion to linear regression, where the relationship $F(X)$ is linear. The linear relationship is then called the *best fit line* through the sample data. This line is of the form

$$Y = A + B * X.$$

To determine the best fit line through sample data, we must make assumptions about X and Y. Different assumptions will yield different solutions for the coefficients A and B. In this case, we assume that Y and not X is the random variable, which means we can measure X exactly and the Y-values for a given X are assumed to be normally distributed about some mean.

Figure 12.22 shows three X-values and the distributions of Y-values for the populations they determine. The mean of the Y-values for a given X-value is denoted by $M_{Y|X}$. We denote the standard deviation of the Y-values for a given X by $S_{Y|X}$.

Figure 12.23 shows the distribution of Y-values for the population associated with a given X-value. The *mean*, $M_{Y|X}$, is a measure of central tendency for the Y-values for this population, and the *standard deviation*, $S_{Y|X}$, is a measure of the dispersion (or spread) of the Y-values for this population. For example, Fig. 12.23 might represent the distribution of intelligence quotients for professors with a given income. The shaded region indicates all professors whose intelligence quotient is within one standard deviation of the mean for this population.

Figure 12.23 *Distribution of Y-Values for a Given X with Mean $M_{Y|X}$ and Standard Deviation $S_{Y|X}$*

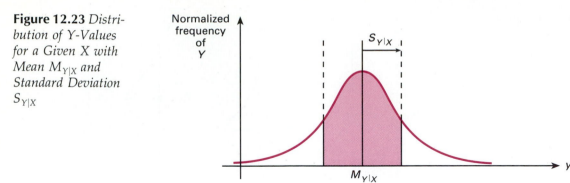

In linear regression, we assume that the means, $M_{Y|X}$, lie on some line

$$M_{Y|X} = \alpha + \beta * X.$$

However, we cannot determine this line exactly because we have only a finite amount of data relating to just some of the X-values. On the basis of this finite sample, we must compute an estimate for the above linear relationship. That estimate is called the best fit line through the sample data. Its equation is

$$Y = A + B * X.$$

As you can see, A is a statistical estimate for α, and B is a statistical estimate for β. Depending upon the statistical properties of our finite sample, the estimates A and B will be more or less reliable. (We won't discuss further this issue as to how confident we can be in the predictions we make with the computed coefficients A and B. However, there are formulae for determining this.)

Figure 12.24 shows a scatter plot for some sample data. A *scatter plot* represents each observed pair of X-Y-values in a sample as a point on a coordinate grid. Superimposed over the scatter plot are lines representing the actual linear relationship

$$M_{Y|X} = \alpha + \beta * X$$

and the best fit line

$$Y = A + B * X$$

based on the data available (11 data points). As shown in Fig. 12.24, the best fit line (in color) is a statistical estimate for the relationship based on a finite sample of data.

Figure 12.24. *Scatter Plot Showing Best Fit and Actual Lines*

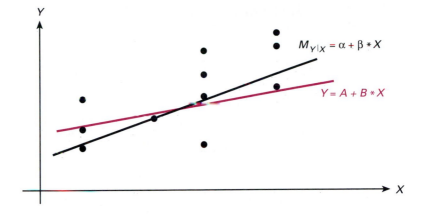

Computing the Linear Regression Coefficients, *A* and *B*

The values *A* and *B* are called *linear regression coefficients*. Next, we discuss how these coefficients are computed on the basis of a finite sample.

Suppose we have a collection of *N* data points. Let's denote the *i*th data point by the pair (X_i, Y_i). That is, Y_i was observed in conjunction with X_i. The best fit line is defined as the unique line that minimizes the sum of the squares of the distances d_i, which are shown in Fig. 12.25. Each d_i is the distance, measured in parallel to the Y-axis, between the point (X_i, Y_i) and the best fit line. Thus

$$d_i = Y_i - (B * X_i + A).$$

It's one of the marvels of calculus that we can discuss the distance d_i to the best fit line when it is the best fit line that we are trying to determine. The

Figure 12.25. *Best Fit Line Minimizes the Sum of the Squares of the Distances d_i*

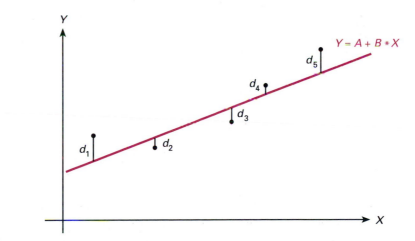

sum that we are trying to minimize,

$$\sum_{i=1}^{N} d_i^2 = \sum_{i=1}^{N} (Y_i - (B * X_i + A))^2 = F(A,B),$$

is a function of the linear regression coefficients. We call this function $F(A,B)$. By computing the partial derivatives of $F(A,B)$ with respect to A and B and setting these partial derivatives to 0, we get two linear equations in two unknowns A and B, as follows:

$$\frac{\partial F(A,B)}{\partial A} = 0$$

$$\frac{\partial F(A,B)}{\partial B} = 0$$

When we solve the resulting system of equations, we get

$$B = \frac{\sum_{i=1}^{N} (X_i - \overline{X})(Y_i - \overline{Y})}{\sum_{i=1}^{N} (X_i - \overline{X})^2}$$

$$A = \overline{Y} - B * \overline{X},$$

where $\overline{X}$ and $\overline{Y}$ denote the means of the observed X- and Y-values, respectively. That is,

$$\overline{X} = \frac{\sum_{i=1}^{N} X_i}{N}$$

$$\overline{Y} = \frac{\sum_{i=1}^{N} Y_i}{N}.$$

The Fortran subroutine in Fig. 12.26 returns the linear regression coefficients A and B for a given collection of data points, (X_i, Y_i). XBAR and YBAR denote the means $\overline{X}$ and $\overline{Y}$, respectively. SUMXY is

$$\sum_{i=1}^{N} (X_i - \overline{X})(Y_i - \overline{Y})$$

Figure 12.26. *Computing the Linear Regression Coefficients A and B*

```
        SUBROUTINE LINREG (X, Y, N, XBAR, YBAR, A, B)
C Computes the linear regression coefficients, A and B
C for the N data points (X(I),Y(I)), given XBAR and YBAR.

C Input Arguments
C   X, Y - array of data points
C   N - number of points
C   XBAR, YBAR - the X and Y mean values
C Output Arguments
C   A, B - the linear regression coefficients

C Argument Declarations
        REAL X(*), Y(*), XBAR, YBAR, A, B
        INTEGER N

C Find A and B
C Local Declarations
        REAL SUMXY, SUMXDS, XDIFF
        INTEGER I

        SUMXY = 0.0
        SUMXDS = 0.0
        DO 10 I = 1, N
            XDIFF = X(I) - XBAR
            SUMXY = SUMXY + XDIFF * (Y(I) - YBAR)
            SUMXDS = SUMXDS + XDIFF ** 2
10   CONTINUE
        B = SUMXY / SUMXDS
        A = YBAR - B * XBAR

C Exit subroutine
        RETURN
        END
```

and SUMXDS is

$$\sum_{i=1}^{N} (X_i - \overline{X})^2$$

XDIFF is introduced so that we don't have to compute (X(I) - XBAR) twice for every execution of DO loop 10.

Correlation

Correlation differs from regression in that it measures the strength of a relationship rather than the actual parameters of that relationship. In computing the correlation between X and Y, we assume that both variables are random. In other words, we do not assume that the X- or Y-values can be determined exactly.

Correlation is said to be high if there is a strong linear relationship between X- and Y-values; otherwise, correlation is said to be low. Figure 12.27 shows four scatter plots along with a qualitative assessment of the correlation between X and Y. Note that in Fig. 12.27(d), although there is obviously a quadratic relationship between X- and Y-values, the correlation is low because correlation is a measure of the strength of linear relationships.

Next, we give a formula for a statistic, r, that is a measure of correlation. This statistic is called the *correlation coefficient*.

We will present this statistic in terms of another statistic called *z-scores*. Z-scores are measured for the X- and Y-values independently. Again, we assume a sample of N data points, (X_i, Y_i). The z-score for a given X_i is its distance from the sample mean, $\overline{X}$, measured in terms of the standard deviation, S_X:

$$Z_{X_i} = \frac{X_i - \overline{X}}{S_X}$$

Figure 12.27.
Scatter Plots with Correlations

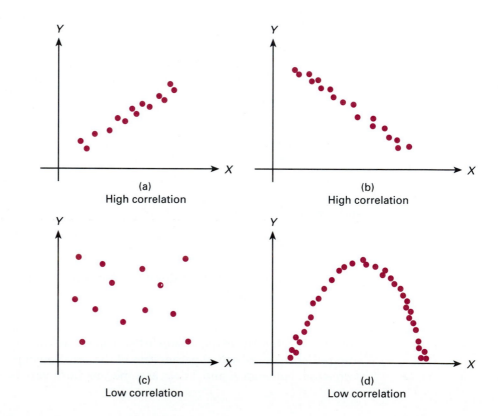

(a)
High correlation

(b)
High correlation

(c)
Low correlation

(d)
Low correlation

An unbiased estimate of the standard deviation for our sample is

$$S_X = \sqrt{\frac{\sum_{i=1}^{N} (X_i - \overline{X})^2}{N - 1}}$$

The z-score for a given Y_i value is

$$Z_{Y_i} = \frac{Y_i - \overline{Y}}{S_Y}$$

where $\overline{Y}$ is the mean and S_Y is the standard deviation for the observed Y-values.

The correlation coefficient, r, is computed in terms of the z-scores as follows:

$$r = \sum_{i=1}^{N} \frac{(Z_{X_i} * Z_{Y_i})}{N - 1}$$

The values for r range between -1 and 1. If $|r| = 1$, then the given data points all lie on a line. If $r = 0$, then the X- and Y-values are said to be uncorrelated. (Again, this means there is absolutely no linear relationship observed between X- and Y-values.)

A Fortran function that computes the correlation coefficient, r, is given in Fig. 12.28. The arguments provided to the function are REAL arrays X and Y, which store the data points, and the INTEGER variable N, which denotes the number of data points in the sample. The variables XBAR and YBAR represent the means, and the variables SX and SY represent the standard deviations. ZXI denotes the z-score for X_i, and ZYI denotes the z-score for Y_i. PS is used to accumulate the sum of the products of ZXI and ZYI.

Figure 12.28. *Function for Computing the Correlation Coefficient*

```
      REAL FUNCTION R (X, Y, N, XBAR, YBAR, SX, SY)
C Computes the correlation coefficient, R, using Z-scores
C for the N data points (X(I),Y(I))
C Preconditions : First N elements of arrays X and Y are defined.
C    XBAR, YBAR are the average values in X, Y. SX, SY are
C    the standard deviations.
C Postconditions: Returns the correlation coefficient.

C Input Arguments
C    X, Y - array of data points
C    N - number of data points
C    XBAR, YBAR - the X and Y mean values
C    SX, SY - the X and Y standard deviations
```

```
C Argument Declarations
      REAL X(*), Y(*), XBAR, YBAR, SX, SY
      INTEGER N

C Local Declarations
      REAL PS, ZXI, ZYI
      INTEGER I

C Find z-scores for each point and sum of their product
      PS = 0.0
      DO 10 I = 1, N
         ZXI = (X(I) - XBAR) / SX
         ZYI = (Y(I) - YBAR) / SY
         PS = PS + ZXI * ZYI
  10  CONTINUE

C Define result and exit function
      R = PS / (N - 1)
      RETURN
      END
```

12.5 Numerical Integration[M]

The definite integral $\int_a^b f(z)\,dz$ denotes the area in the Euclidean plane bounded by the z-axis, the line $z = a$, the line $z = b$, and the curve $y = f(z)$. This area is shown in Fig. 12.29 for two different functions. Note that if the curve $y = f(z)$ dips below the z-axis, the part of the curve below the z-axis makes a negative contribution to the integral.

There are two general classes of solutions to the problem of evaluating definite integrals by computer. Both classes involve evaluating the function

Figure 12.29. *Geometric Meaning of the Definite Integral*

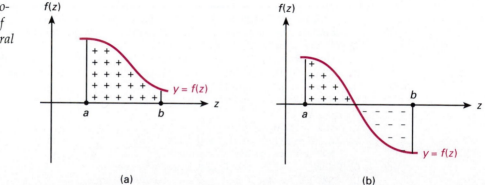

(a)   (b)

Figure 12.30. *Dividing the Interval of Integration into Subintervals*

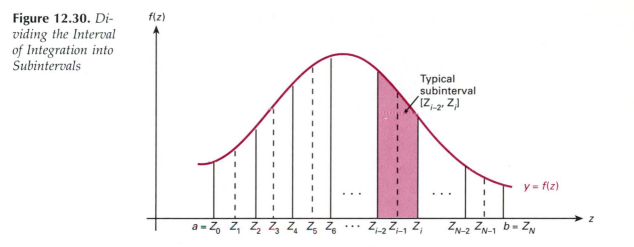

$f(z)$, which we are integrating at a collection of sample points. The *quadrature methods* determine the sampling points by analysis of the function. Simpson's rule and members of its class choose the sampling points independently of the function being integrated. In practice, Simpson's rule is an effective and efficient method for doing numerical integration despite its simplicity.

Derivation of Simpson's Rule

Simpson's rule is derived from the following considerations. Suppose we want to integrate $f(z)$ over the interval $[a,b]$, as shown in Fig. 12.30. Clearly, if we divide the interval $[a,b]$ into an even number, N, of intervals, as shown in Fig. 12.30, then

$$\int_a^b f(z)\,dz = \sum_{\substack{i=2 \\ \text{Step 2}}}^{N} \int_{z_{i-2}}^{z_i} f(z)\,dz. \tag{1}$$

Our notation

$$\sum_{\substack{i=2 \\ \text{Step 2}}}^{N}$$

means that i takes on the values 2, 4, 6, ... , $N-2$, N. (Don't forget that N is assumed to be even.)

Equation (1) says that the original integral equals the sum of the $N/2$ integrals

$$\int_{z_{i-2}}^{z_i} f(z)\,dz.$$

These $N/2$ integrals are computed over the subintervals $[z_{i-2}, z_i]$. Note that z_{i-1} is the midpoint of the subinterval $[z_{i-2}, z_i]$. Furthermore, the subscript $i-1$ of a midpoint is always odd. The subscripts $i-2$ and i at the endpoints are always even.

A typical subinterval $[z_{i-2}, z_i]$ and the integral we are computing on that subinterval are shown in Fig. 12.31. The three points

$$\text{point } 1 = (z_{i-2}, f(z_{i-2}))$$
$$\text{point } 2 = (z_{i-1}, f(z_{i-1}))$$
$$\text{point } 3 = (z_i, f(z_i))$$

determine a unique quadratic polynomial. That is, there is a unique polynomial

$$P_i(z) = r * z^2 + s * z + t$$

that passes through the three given points. This polynomial is called an *interpolating* polynomial. In Fig. 12.31, the polynomial $P_i(z)$ is drawn as a black curve.

The fact that the polynomial $P_i(z)$ passes through three known points gives us enough information to solve for the coefficients r, s, and t. We know that $P_i(z) = f(z)$ when z is z_{i-2}, z_{i-1}, or z_i. This yields three equations in the three unknowns, r, s, and t. This system can be solved for r, s, and t (solution not shown).

Simpson's rule approximates

$$\int_{z_{i-2}}^{z_i} f(z)\, dz$$

Figure 12.31. *Interpolating Polynomial* $P_i(z)$

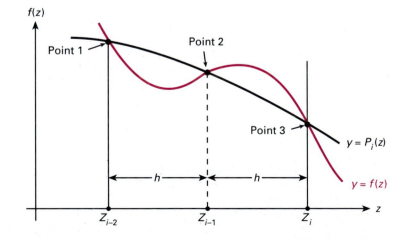

as

$$\int_{z_{i-2}}^{z_i} P_i(z)\,dz.$$

When we substitute the coefficients r, s, and t in $P_i(z)$ and integrate, we get

$$\int_{z_{i-2}}^{z_i} P_i(z)\,dz = \frac{h}{3}(f(z_{i-2}) + 4 \times f(z_{i-1}) + f(z_i))$$

where $h = (b - a)/N$ is the size of one of the N-intervals. This equation approximates the integral of the original function, $f(z)$, over the interval $[z_{i-2}, z_i]$ in terms of the values of $f(z)$ at the endpoints and the midpoint of the interval.

Substituting this equation into Eq. (1), we get Simpson's rule:

$$\int_a^b f(z)\,dz = \sum_{\substack{i=2 \\ \text{Step 2}}}^{N} \int_{z_{i-2}}^{z_i} f(z)\,dz$$

$$\approx \sum_{\substack{i=2 \\ \text{Step 2}}}^{N} \int_{z_{i-2}}^{z_i} P_i(z)\,dz$$

$$= \frac{h}{3} \sum_{\substack{i=2 \\ \text{Step 2}}}^{N} (f(z_{i-2}) + 4 \times f(z_{i-1}) + f(z_i))$$

Recalling that $z_0 = a$ and $z_N = b$, we can rewrite the approximate integral as

$$\int_a^b f(z)\,dz \approx \frac{h}{3}(f(a) + 4 \times f(z_1) + f(z_2) + f(z_2) + 4 \times f(z_3) + f(z_4) + f(z_4)$$

$$+ 4 \times f(z_5) + \cdots + f(z_{N-2}) + 4 \times f(z_{N-1}) + f(b))$$

$$= \frac{h}{3}(f(a) + f(b) + 4 \times \sum_{\substack{i=2 \\ \text{Step 2}}}^{N} f(z_{i-1}) + 2 \times \sum_{\substack{i=2 \\ \text{Step 2}}}^{N-2} f(z_i))$$

Fortran Implementation of Simpson's Rule

Next, we implement in Fortran Simpson's rule as expressed immediately above. We accumulate the sum

$$\sum_{\substack{i=2 \\ \text{Step 2}}}^{N} f(z_{i-1})$$

in the variable SUMODD and the sum

$$\sum_{\substack{i=2 \\ \text{Step 2}}}^{N-2} f(z_i)$$

in the variable SUMEVE. The approximate integral is then

$$(f(a) + f(b) + 4 * \text{SUMODD} + 2 * \text{SUMEVE}) * (h/3.0).$$

In an actual subroutine, f would be replaced by a function call or a statement function that evaluates the desired functional value. Very often, a statement function is adequate for accomplishing this.

Function SIMPSN in Fig. 12.32 computes an approximate value for

$$\int_a^b f(z)\, dz$$

using Simpson's rule for a given value of a, b, and N. For computational purposes, we rewrite the expressions for SUMODD and SUMEVE given above as follows:

$$\text{SUMODD} = \sum_{\substack{i=2 \\ \text{Step 2}}}^{N} f(z_{i-1}) = f(a + h) + f(a + 3 * h) + \cdots + f(a + (N - 1) * h)$$

$$\text{SUMEVE} = \sum_{\substack{i=2 \\ \text{Step 2}}}^{N-2} f(z_i) = f(a + 2 * h) + f(a + 4 * h) + \cdots + f(a + (N - 2) * h)$$

A variable z will denote the value of the current sample point. Each new value of z is determined by adding $2 * h$ to the previous value of z. Because $2 * h$ will be used over and over, we store it in a variable, DELTAZ.

Function SIMPSN in Fig. 12.32 computes the integral of the *standardized normal distribution function* (commonly known as the bell curve)

$$f(z) = \frac{e^{-(z^2/2)}}{\sqrt{2\pi}},$$

which is useful in statistics (see the discussion on correlation in Section 12.4). The Fortran expression

```
SIMPSN(0.0, 2.0, 2)
```

computes the value of this integral for $z = 0.0$ to $z = 2.0$, assuming the interval is divided into two subintervals. The actual value of this integral is 0.4772; the

Figure 12.32. *Computing a Definite Integral Using Simpson's Rule*

```
       REAL FUNCTION SIMPSN (A, B, N)
C Computes the area under the standard normal curve
C between A and B using Simpson's rule with N intervals
C Preconditions : A < B and N is defined.
C Postconditions: Returns the area under F(X) from X = A to X = B.

C Input Arguments
C   A, B — the end points of the integration region [A,B]
C   N — the number of intervals

C Argument Declarations
       REAL A, B
       INTEGER N

C Local Declarations
       REAL PI
       PARAMETER (PI = 3.14159)
       REAL H, DELTAZ, SUMODD, SUMEVE, Z
       INTEGER I

C Statement Function
       F(X) = EXP(-(X ** 2 / 2.0)) / SQRT(2.0 * PI)         .

C Compute required increments
       H = (B — A) / N
       DELTAZ = 2.0 * H

C Compute SUMODD
       SUMODD = 0.0
       Z = A + H
       DO 10 I = 2, N, 2
          SUMODD = SUMODD + F(Z)
          Z = Z + DELTAZ
   10  CONTINUE

C Compute SUMEVE
       SUMEVE = 0.0
       Z = A + DELTAZ
       DO 20 I = 2, N-2, 2
          SUMEVE = SUMEVE + F(Z)
          Z = Z + DELTAZ
   20  CONTINUE

C Compute integral and return
       SIMPSN = (F(A) + F(B) + 4.0 * SUMODD + 2.0 * SUMEVE) * (H / 3.0)
       RETURN
       END
```

function result is 0.4736. When N is increased to 4, the function result is 0.4772. The dependence of the function result on N is discussed in the next subsection. To evaluate the definite integral of another function, it's only necessary to change the statement function definition in function SIMPSN.

Applying Simpson's Rule for a Sequence of N Values

As N increases, the approximate integral becomes closer to the actual integral. However, when using function SIMPSN, there is a point of diminishing return because of computational round-off errors. If you try to compute the integral for a sequence of increasing N-values, say $N = 2, 4, 8, 16, 32, \ldots$, that point of diminishing returns will become readily apparent. Before that point, successive approximations agree to more and more decimal places; beyond that point, the agreement becomes less and less.

In practice, we apply Simpson's rule for a sequence of N-values to identify the point of diminishing return. Usually the sequence of N-values is such that N doubles for each iteration of Simpson's rule. A general rule of thumb is that if the integral we get when $N = 2 * k$ and the integral we get when $N = k$ agree to D decimal places, then the integral we got for $N = 2 * k$ is correct to $D + 1$ decimal places. There is a point, as mentioned above, where the agreement between successive approximations becomes worse. If the number of correct digits we obtain in this manner is not adequate, then we suggest using double precision arithmetic. (See Section 12.7.)

EXERCISE FOR SECTION 12.5

Programming
1. Write a program that calls function SIMPSN in Fig. 12.32 for A = 0.0 and values of B starting at 0.5 and increasing to 5.0 in steps of 0.5. Compute each integral for values of N equal to 2, 4, 8, and 16. Print each result.

12.6 Using Numerical Methods Libraries

So far, we have introduced a number of subroutines for performing highly specialized numerical operations. Some subroutines came with a warning that they will not work in all cases, but there are other techniques that may work. We also saw that it would be fairly time consuming for an engineer or scientist to implement his or her own library of subroutines. For all these reasons, several libraries of numerical subroutines have been developed for use by engineers, scientists, and others who frequently perform numerical operations on data.

One of the most widely used collections of subroutines is the International Mathematics and Statistics Library (IMSL). The IMSL is a collection of thousands of subprograms available on most mainframes and minicomputers and even on some microcomputers.

The IMSL comprises three separate but coordinated libraries of subroutines:

MATH/LIBRARY—subroutines for general applied mathematics
STAT/LIBRARY—subroutines for statistics
SFUN/LIBRARY—subroutines for special functions

Before using one of these libraries, you first must consult the manual for that library. The manual provides documentation for each subroutine along with instructions for using that subroutine and an example of its use. You will need to write a Fortran program that stores the data to be processed and correctly calls the subroutine you select. After the subroutine executes, your program should display the output arguments returned by the subroutine.

EXAMPLE 12.1

LSARG is an IMSL MATH/LIBRARY subroutine that solves a system of linear algebraic equations. Figure 12.33 shows part of the documentation for this subroutine. DLSARG is the double precision version of this subroutine. (Double precision is discussed in the next section.)

The line

```
USAGE: CALL LSARG (N, A, LDA, B, IPATH, X)
```

in Fig. 12.33 shows the order of the arguments in a call to subroutine LSARG. The argument descriptions follow this line.

Figure 12.33. *Partial Documentation for LSARG*

LSARG/DLSARG (Single/Double precision)

PURPOSE: Solve a real general system of linear equations with iterative refinement.

USAGE: CALL LSARG (N, A, LDA, B, IPATH, X)

ARGUMENTS:

N	Number of equations (input)
A	N-by-N matrix containing the coefficients of the linear system (input)
LDA	Leading dimension of A exactly as specified in the dimension statement of the calling program (input)
B	Vector of length N containing the right-hand side of the linear system (input)
IPATH	Path indicator (input) IPATH = 1 means the system $A * X = B$ is solved. IPATH = 2 means the system $trans(A) * X = B$ is solved, where $trans(A)$ is the transpose of A.
X	Vector of length N containing the solution to the linear system (output)

Figure 12.34 is a main program that uses function LSARG to solve the equation

$$A * X = B.$$

The PARAMETER statement,

PARAMETER (N = 3, LDA = 3, IPATH = 1)

defines the subroutine input arguments that are not arrays; the DATA statements define the input argument arrays. The PRINT statements at the end display the output argument, vector X. ■

Figure 12.34. *Using Subroutine LSARG*

```
      PROGRAM USELSA
C Shows how to use subroutine LSARG

C Declarations
      INTEGER N, LDA, IPATH
      PARAMETER (N = 3, LDA = 3, IPATH = 1)
      REAL A(LDA,LDA), B(N), X(N)

C Set values for A and B

C          ( 33.0  16.0  72.0)          ( 129.0)
C      A = (-24.0 -10.0 -57.0)      B = ( -96.0)
C          ( 18.0 -11.0   7.0)          (   8.5)

      DATA A /33.0,-24.0,18.0, 16.0,-10.0,-11.0, 72.0,-57.0,7.0/
      DATA B /129.0, -96.0, 8.5/

C Call the subroutine to solve for X
      CALL LSARG (N, A, LDA, B, IPATH, X)

C Display results
      PRINT *, 'The values of X are:'
      PRINT '(1X, 3F10.2)', X

C Exit program
      STOP
      END


The values of X are:
      1.00      1.50      1.00
```

12.7 Double-Precision and Complex Numbers

In this section, we introduce two new data types: DOUBLE PRECISION and COMPLEX. The DOUBLE PRECISION type enables us to carry more significant digits in computations and thus to improve the accuracy of numerical algorithms.

Complex numbers are numbers of the form

$$x + i * y,$$

where x and y are real numbers and i is the imaginary number $\sqrt{-1}$. Complex numbers have many important applications in science and engineering.

Double Precision   The programs presented in this chapter use type REAL (single precision) numbers to represent numeric quantities. A typical computer might provide seven-digit precision with the REAL data type. However, as we often pointed out in previous sections, not all of these digits will be reliable due to round-off and truncation errors. Typically, only four or five of the seven digits will be accurate. The exact number of reliable digits varies from application to application.

The "double" in double precision refers to the amount of computer storage allocated to the representation of a double-precision number as compared to a single-precision number. A double-precision number, such as DX in Fig. 12.35, occupies two words of computer memory, compared to the one word allocated for the single-precision (REAL) variable X. All of this extra storage is devoted to extending the precision (mantissa) of the number. None of the extra bits are incorporated into the exponent. Therefore, double-precision arithmetic increases only the accuracy, not the range, of computed results.

To use the DOUBLE PRECISION data type, the programmer must know the following:

- How to declare double-precision variables and arrays
- How to form double-precision constants
- How to express operations in double-precision arithmetic
- How double-precision quantities are read and written
- How double-precision functions are used and/or defined

Figure 12.35. *Storage for REAL and DOUBLE PRECISION Numbers*

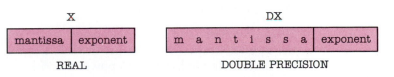

Double-precision variables and arrays are declared in the same way as are variables of other Fortran types.

EXAMPLE 12.2   The statement

```
DOUBLE PRECISION DX, DARR(10)
```

declares a double-precision variable, DX, and a double-precision array, DARR, with 10 elements.

Double-precision two-dimensional arrays may also be declared. There is no automatic implicit typing of double-precision variables.   ■

Double-precision constants are distinguished from single-precision (REAL) constants by the use of the special symbol D in lieu of the symbol E that is used in single-precision constants. The symbol D is used in Fortran scientific notation to denote a double-precision constant.

EXAMPLE 12.3   Assuming our computer allows seven-digit precision for REAL numbers, the following constants would be recognized as being DOUBLE PRECISION constants:

```
1.23456789D3
12.3456789D-5
8.219807654489D2
2.3D-12
0.1D0
```

The constant 2.3D-12 denotes the double-precision representation of the number 2.3×10^{-12}. The constant 0.1D0 denotes the double-precision representation of the number 0.1. It is important to realize that the Fortran constant 0.1 is not the same as the Fortran constant 0.1D0. The former is a single-precision number; the latter is a double-precision number. Furthermore, they are not the same number because the binary representation of 1/10 is not exact. This alerts us to a fundamental problem that arises in the use of double-precision arithmetic: Double-precision arithmetic used incorrectly is no better than single-precision arithmetic.   ■

Double-precision Arithmetic

Single-precision and double-precision arithmetic do not differ in terms of the operations that may be performed. Double-precision numbers may be multiplied, divided, raised to powers, and so forth.

EXAMPLE 12.4   Assuming DX and DY are DOUBLE PRECISION variables, the assignment statement

```
DX = 2.0D0 * DY
```

will store twice the value of DY in DX.   ■

Although mixed-mode arithmetic involving type INTEGER, REAL, and DOUBLE PRECISION numbers is allowed, difficulties arise if an arithmetic expression mixes single-precision and double-precision quantities. In all mixed-mode expressions (except where a double-precision number is being raised to an integer power), the non-double-precision quantities are converted to double precision before the expression is evaluated. However, most compilers will do this conversion in a "stupid" way; that is, they simply pad the mantissa of the single-precision number with trailing zeros.

EXAMPLE 12.5   Assuming DX and DY are double-precision variables, the assignment statements

```
DX = 0.1 * DY
DX = 0.1D0 * DY
```

are not equivalent. The first assignment statement contains a mixed-mode (single- and double-precision) expression on the right side of the assignment operator. As a result, the computation in the first assignment statement is no better than a single-precision computation. (A chain is no stronger than its weakest link!) The second assignment statement is bona fide double-precision arithmetic. The constant 0.1D0 denotes the double-precision representation for the number 0.1.   ■

EXAMPLE 12.6   The condition

```
(0.1 .EQ. 0.1D0)
```

compares the single-precision representation of 0.1 to its double-precision representation. Because of the way the single-precision number is converted to double precision before the comparison, the condition value is false, not true as we might expect.   ■

It is permissible to assign a double-precision value to a type REAL variable. Most compilers simply truncate the extra digits in the mantissa of the double-precision value.

Input and Output of Double-precision Numbers

Double-precision values present no special problems in terms of input. A data value that uses the symbol D will be recognized as a double-precision number. Double-precision values should be read into double-precision variables; otherwise, a loss of precision will occur. In list-directed output, a double-precision number is printed to the precision that the computer allows.

The F and D format codes can be used for formatted input and output of double-precision quantities. The F*w.d* format specification has the same significance whether it is used with single-precision or double-precision quantities. The D*w.d* format specification behaves just like the E*w.d* specification, except that the exponential symbol E is replaced by D.

Using Functions with Double-precision Numbers

Many of the operations performed by the Fortran library functions can be applied to double-precision numbers. For example, the functions DABS and IDINT, which require double-precision arguments, correspond to the functions ABS and INT, which require type REAL arguments. The table of functions in Appendix A includes functions that require double-precision arguments or return double-precision results. Library functions that return double-precision results always begin with the letter D.

Also listed in Appendix A is the function DPROD, which accepts two real arguments and computes their double-precision product. DBLE is the type conversion function that converts from any numerical type (INTEGER, REAL, COMPLEX) to double precision.

The programmer may define double-precision functions not provided by the Fortran library of functions. For example, the function header

```
DOUBLE PRECISION FUNCTION DF (DX, DY)
```

describes a function called DF that returns a double-precision result. DF should be declared as type DOUBLE PRECISION in any program unit that calls it. The function result should be returned to a double-precision variable. If the dummy arguments DX and DY are double precision, they must be declared as type DOUBLE PRECISION within the function definition.

Complex Numbers

The next data type we discuss is type COMPLEX. Complex numbers, of great interest to scientists and engineers, are represented in Fortran, using the data type COMPLEX.

EXAMPLE 12.7

The complex number

$$3.2 - i * 7.8$$

has a *real part* of 3.2 and an *imaginary part* of -7.8. It is written as the COMPLEX constant

$$(3.2, -7.8)$$

in Fortran.   ▪

In general, the form of a COMPLEX constant in Fortran is two real or integer constants enclosed in parentheses and separated by a comma. Double-precision values are not allowed. Hence, (3.2, 0.23D0) is not a legal COMPLEX constant, since the imaginary part is double precision.

COMPLEX variables and arrays are declared just like other variables and arrays.

EXAMPLE 12.8   The declaration

```
COMPLEX SEQ(10), Z
```

instructs the compiler to allocate storage for an array (SEQ) with 10 elements and for a complex variable (Z). Each array element provides storage for two values representing the real and imaginary parts of a complex number. The real and imaginary parts of a complex number are single precision.   ▪

Complex Arithmetic

The rules governing COMPLEX arithmetic in Fortran are consistent with the rules of complex arithmetic, as decribed in Table 12.1. An integer or real operand used with a complex operand will be automatically converted to a complex number with an imaginary part of zero before the operation is performed.

The assignment of a COMPLEX value to a complex variable is allowed, as in

```
Z = (Z1 + Z2) / Z3
```

where Z, Z1, Z2, and Z3 are type COMPLEX. Mixed-mode assignments also are allowed, and the following rules apply. When a COMPLEX number is stored in an INTEGER or REAL variable, it loses its imaginary part. When an INTEGER or REAL

Table 12.1. *Rules of Complex Arithmetic*

OPERATION	RESULT
(a,b) + (c,d)	$(a + c, b + d)$
(a,b) − (c,d)	$(a - c, b - d)$
(a,b) * (c,d)	$(a * c - b * d, a * d + b * c)$
(a,b) / (c,d)	$\left(\dfrac{a * c + b * d}{c^2 + d^2}, \dfrac{b * c - a * d}{c^2 + d^2}\right)$

number is stored in a COMPLEX variable, the imaginary part of the COMPLEX number will be 0.0 and the real part of the COMPLEX number will be the number being assigned (converted to REAL, if necessary).

Using Functions with Complex Numbers

Many of the operations performed by Fortran library functions also can be applied to COMPLEX numbers (see Appendix A). Library functions that return COMPLEX results begin with the letter C. Certain library functions are indispensible when we are working with COMPLEX arithmetic.

Other than .EQ. and .NE., the relational operators cannot be applied to COMPLEX quantities. If Z is COMPLEX, then the following is not a valid LOGICAL expression:

```
(Z .LE. (2.3, 1.0))
```

We must compare the real and imaginary parts separately, as in

```
(REAL(Z) .LE. 2.3 .AND. AIMAG(Z) .LE. 1.0)
```

where the REAL and AIMAG functions extract the real and imaginary parts, respectively, of a COMPLEX value.

Another useful built-in function is CMPLX, which constructs a complex number from two REAL numbers. The first argument of CMPLX becomes the real part of the result; the second argument becomes the imaginary part of the result.

EXAMPLE 12.9

Assuming A and B are type REAL, the statement

```
Z = CMPLX(A, B)
```

stores the complex number $A + i * B$ in the COMPLEX variable Z. The type conversion function CMPLX is necessary, since expressions such as (A, B) are not allowed in Fortran. ◼

The complex conjugate of a complex number

$$z = x + i * y$$

is defined to be the complex number

$$\bar{z} = x - i * y$$

The complex conjugate is important because many applications require computing the absolute value of a complex number, which is defined to be

$$z * \bar{z}$$

Note that $z * \bar{z}$ for $z = x + i * y$ is $x^2 + y^2$, which is a real number. The built-in function CONJG(Z) returns the complex conjugate of the COMPLEX number Z. The built-in function CABS(Z) returns the absolute value of a complex number Z.

COMPLEX function subprograms and statement functions don't differ from other types of functions we have discussed. For example, the type COMPLEX function F would begin with the header

```
COMPLEX FUNCTION F (Z)
```

If Z is a COMPLEX argument, it must be declared as such within the function. Also, it is important to declare F and the variable receiving the function result as type COMPLEX in all program units using F; otherwise, the imaginary part of the result may be lost because F would be type REAL by default in those program units.

Input and Output of Complex Numbers

In list-directed input, a complex data value is written as a complex constant (e.g., (2.31, 0.45E1)) where the parentheses and comma are required. When a COMPLEX value is displayed using list-directed output, the parentheses and the comma appear, as in

```
(0.2310000000E 01, 0.450000000E 00)
```

Because no special format code is provided for the type COMPLEX, the F and E format codes are used to enter and display complex numbers. For each complex number to be read, two real number format codes must be provided and two real numbers must be read from the input file. When a complex number is written using the F or E code, it is displayed as two real numbers. The comma and parentheses that denote a COMPLEX constant should not appear in the input file and will not appear in the output file when formatted output is used.

12.8 Common Programming Errors

The most common errors in programs that perform the numerical techniques discussed in this chapter result from loss of accuracy in mathematical computations. A small round-off error is often magnified when computations are repeated, as is required by many of these algorithms. This loss of accuracy can cause programs to execute forever instead of converging to a result. If the programs do terminate, the results may be so inaccurate as to be useless.

1. Because these programs rely heavily on subroutines and functions, be very careful when writing argument lists. Ensure each argument list has the correct number of arguments and that the arguments are not misspelled or placed incorrectly.
2. We recommend that you use double-precision numbers to gain increased accuracy of representation, thereby reducing the effect of computational error. Ensure you don't combine type REAL or type INTEGER operands with double-precision operands as this will negate the positive effect that otherwise would be realized.

Chapter Review

In this chapter, we discussed several different numerical techniques, including manipulating vectors and matrixes, finding roots (bisection and Newton's methods), solving simultaneous equations (Gaussian elimination), determining linear regression and correlation, and performing numerical integration (Simpson's rule). We also introduced two new data types, DOUBLE PRECISION and COMPLEX.

We have just scratched the surface in our discussion of numerical methods. Dozens of good textbooks have been written on the subject, some of which are listed below.

References on Numerical Methods

1. Carnahan, B., et al. *Applied Numerical Methods.* New York: John Wiley and Sons, Inc., 1964.
2. Conte, S. D., and C. de Boor. *Elementary Numerical Analysis,* 2nd ed. New York: McGraw-Hill, 1972.
3. McCracken, D., and W. S. Dorn. *Numerical Methods and FORTRAN Programming.* New York: John Wiley and Sons, Inc., 1964.
4. Dyck, V. A., et al. *Introduction to Computing: Structured Problem Solving Using WATFIV-S.* Reston, VA: Reston Publishing, 1979.
5. Lentner, Marvin. *Introduction to Applied Statistics.* Boston: Prindle, Weber and Schmidt, Inc., 1975.
6. User's Manual. *STAT/LIBRARY™ FORTRAN SUBROUTINES for Statistical Analysis, Version 1.0.* Houston: IMSL, Inc., April 1987.

Quick-check Exercises

1. Name two methods for finding roots of a function.
2. List the three criteria for converging to a root.
3. What condition must hold in order to multiply matrix A by matrix B?
4. Write the complex number $3 - i \times 5$ as a complex constant in Fortran.

5. Can you represent larger numbers in Fortran using double-precision variables?
6. Can you represent smaller (in absolute value) numbers in Fortran using double-precision variables?
7. Can you declare arrays of double-precision numbers?
8. What is a complex conjugate?
9. What property must a coefficient matrix have in order to be in triangular form?

Answers to Quick-check Exercises

1. Newton's method and the bisection method
2. Assuming EPSLON is a very small value, RT is the actual root, x_j is the current guess for a root, and x_{j-1} was the last guess:

$$\text{ABS}(\text{RT} - x_j) < \text{EPSLON}$$
$$\text{ABS}(F(x_j)) < \text{EPSLON}$$
$$\text{ABS}(x_j - x_{j-1}) < \text{EPSLON}$$

3. The two matrixes must be conformable (i.e., matrix A must have the same number of columns as matrix B has rows).
4. (3.0, -5.0)
5. No, the exponent size is the same as for single precision.
6. Yes, there are more bits in the mantissa, so smaller decimal fractions can be represented more accurately.
7. yes
8. the complex number with the same real part as the original but whose imaginary part is the negative of the original number
9. Only 1's must be along the major diagonal and only 0's below the diagonal.

Review Questions

1. Write the augmented matrix corresponding to the following system of equations:

$$2x_1 + 2x_2 - 4x_3 = 0$$
$$x_1 - 4x_2 + x_3 = 4$$
$$-x_1 + 3x_2 - 2x_3 = -5$$

2. Normalize column 1 of the augmented matrix for question 1.
3. What three operations can be performed on a system of linear equations?
4. How do you tell when you reach a point of diminishing returns in using Simpson's rule to compute an integral?
5. How do double-precision numbers affect the range and accuracy of values that can be represented in computer memory?
6. Explain why you have to be careful when comparing two double-precision numbers and when comparing two complex numbers.

7. Which one of the following is not a criterion for judging if x is a root of the equation $F(x) = 0$?

   a. The value of the function at x is very small.
   b. The value of x is very near to an actual root of the equation.
   c. The value of x is very near to the previous value of x.
   d. The value of the function at x is very near to the value of the function at the previous value of x.

8. Which one of the following conditions will cause the failure of the bisection method for finding a root of a function of one variable? Here LOWER and UPPER represent the endpoints of the interval of interest.

   a. F(LOWER) > 0 and F(UPPER) < 0
   b. F(LOWER) < 0 and F(UPPER) > 0
   c. F(LOWER) $*$ F(UPPER) > 0
   d. F(LOWER) $+$ F(UPPER) > 0
   e. LOWER $>$ UPPER

9. In solving a system of linear equations using Gaussian elimination, determine which one of the following operations may not be applied to the augmented matrix.

   a. Add any row to any other row.
   b. Multiply all the diagonal elements by a nonzero number.
   c. Multiply any row by a nonzero number.
   d. Swap any two rows with each other.

10. In the equation for the linear regression best fit line ($Y = A + B * X$), what are the terms A and B called?

    a. Linear regression coefficients
    b. Central tendency
    c. Observables
    d. Standard deviation
    e. Sum of squares

11. If the random variables X and Y lie along a line, what will be the value of their correlation coefficient, r?

    a. $r = -1$
    b. $r = 0$
    c. $1/r = 0$
    d. $r = 1$
    e. $|r| = 1$

12. Which one of the following is not a valid Fortran constant?

    a. 'text'
    b. (1, 1.0)
    c. 12.34D–1
    d. 5678

e. .TRUE.
f. 9.9
g. 8.76E-2

Programming Projects

1. The polynomial

$$4x^3 - 12.3x^2 - x + 16.2$$

has two zeros between 1 and 2. Use the bisection program to find them. You might want to tabulate the function values first to isolate the zeros in two intervals. Use a tolerance of 0.0005.

2. The polynomial

$$8x^3 + 2x^2 - 5x + 1$$

has three real zeros.

a. First, plot the function to determine appropriate intervals for the root-finding program.
b. Use the bisection program to find the three zeros to within a tolerance of 0.0005.

3. Repeat project 2 for the following functions:

a. $f(x) = x^4 + 3x^3 - 3x^2 - 6x + 1$
b. $f(x) = x^4 - 26x^3 + 131x^2 - 226x + 120$

4. If $x^n = c$, then $x^n - c = 0$ and the nth root of c is a zero of the second equation. Use this idea in conjunction with the bisection routine to compute

a. $\sqrt{2}$
b. $\sqrt[3]{7}$

to six decimal places.

5. In the Regula–Falsi method, the root is isolated to an interval $[XL, XR]$ just as in the bisection method. However, instead of breaking the interval into two subintervals at the midpoint, XM, of the interval, where

$$XM = \frac{XR - XL}{2}$$

we break the interval into two subintervals at the point XG defined by the formula

$$XG = XL - F(XL) * \frac{XR - XL}{F(XR) - F(XL)}$$

Figure 12.36.

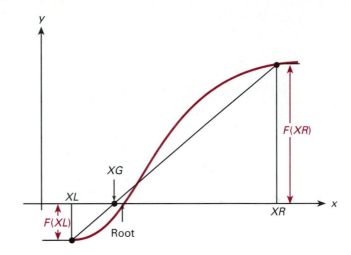

We then isolate the root to the subinterval (either $[XL, XG]$ or $[XG, XR]$) that has the change of signs. Figure 12.36 shows the intuition behind the Regula–Falsi method.

Write a program that will find roots of equations using Regula–Falsi.

6. Write a program that will read in any two rectangular matrixes and multiply them if they are conformable. The program should print out either the product matrix or a message to the effect that the given matrixes are not conformable.

7. Write a program that will input a *square matrix A* (same number of rows and columns) and a nonnegative integer P and compute $A ** P$, the matrix A raised to the power P.
   $A ** P$ is defined as follows:

   $A ** 0 =$ the identity matrix, I
   $A ** P = A * (A ** (P - 1)), P \geq 1$

   (*Note:* The identity matrix I is defined as follows:

   $I(R, R) = 1$ for all R
   $I(R, K) = 0$ for all $R \neq K$

8. Use Gaussian elimination to solve each of the following systems of equations:

   a. $x + 2y + z = 4$
   $\quad 2x + \ y - z = -1$
   $\ -x + \ y + z = 2$

b. $x - y + 2z = 3$
$2x + 3y - 6z = 1$
$4x + y - 2z = 7$

c. $3x - z = 7$
$2x + y = 6$
$3y - z = 7$

9. The inverse of a square matrix A is defined to be the matrix AINV that satisfies

$$A * \text{AINV} = I \text{ (the identity matrix—see project 7).}$$

If AINV exists, then A is said to be invertible. (If A is invertible, then so is AINV and A is the inverse of AINV.) The inverse of a matrix A can be computed using Gaussian elimination. If A is not invertible, this technique will tell us that also.

Let's describe how to set up the data to find the inverse of a matrix A. We do this first with an example. Suppose we want to find the inverse of the following matrix:

$$A = \begin{bmatrix} 1 & 2 & 1 \\ 2 & 1 & -1 \\ -1 & 1 & 1 \end{bmatrix}$$

The problem solution is derived by setting up a work matrix, W, that has the original matrix, A, as its first three columns and the identity matrix as its last three columns:

$$W = \left[\begin{array}{ccc|ccc} 1 & 2 & 1 & 1 & 0 & 0 \\ 2 & 1 & -1 & 0 & 1 & 0 \\ -1 & 1 & 1 & 0 & 0 & 1 \end{array} \right]$$

We now apply Gaussian elimination to the three leftmost columns. However, we modify Gaussian elimination as presented in the text so that the three leftmost columns become the identity matrix. In other words, it is not sufficient to get the three leftmost columns in triangular form. This requires only a slight modification of the subroutine GAUSS. When we eliminate coefficients in the pivot column, we do so both above and beneath the pivot.

The key to this method is that as we apply Gaussian elimination to the left half of W, we apply all row operations throughout the matrix W. When the left side of W is diagonalized, the right side will contain the inverse of A. If Gaussian elimination fails because no nonzero pivot is found for a certain pivot element, then the original matrix A must be noninvertible.

Write a program that will input a square matrix and compute its inverse by this modification of Gaussian elimination.

10. Find the best fit line and the correlation coefficient for the following data set:

Hours of TV Watched per Day, X	Student's Grade Point Average, Y
0.2	3.98
0.8	3.85
1.0	4.00
1.3	3.75
3.0	2.05
4.0	1.56
4.2	1.55
5.0	1.00
6.1	0.98
9.5	0.05

11. Compute the following definite integrals using Simpson's rule.

a. $\int_1^2 \sqrt{2 - (\sin x)^2}\, dx$

b. $\int_1^2 x \cos \frac{x}{2}\, dx$

c. $\int_1^2 (x^3 - 2x^2 + x + 5)\, dx$

d. $\int_{-3}^1 (1 + x^6)\, dx$

12. The transcendental equation

$$x^2(1 - \cos x \cosh x) - \delta \sin x \sinh x = 0$$

is associated with the flexural vibrations of a missile subjected to thrust T. The thrust is directly related to the parameter δ, and the positive roots of the equation determine the configuration and natural frequencies of oscillation of a missile in flight. This information is pertinent to the design of guidance and control systems for such missiles.

Write a Fortran program that uses bisection to determine the first few positive roots for the vibration equation. Although $x = 0$ is an obvious solution, do not begin with 0 and instead start with $x = 0.001$. Perform a stepwise search in increments of 0.5 until a sign change is found or until x exceeds 10. If a sign change is encountered, begin bisection and obtain a root with relative error of less than 0.1%. Then begin your search from that point using the same procedure. Your output must include an echo check of your input data and the relevant roots, clearly labelled.

Run your program for the following values of δ:

$$\delta = .1, \qquad \delta = 2.0, \qquad \text{and} \qquad \delta = .4.$$

13. The electric circuit in Fig. 12.37 shows a nonlinear passive component ρ, the current through which is given by $I = kV^{3/2}$, where k is a constant, V is the potential difference between A and B, R is a linear resistor, and E is a constant voltage source.

Figure 12.37.

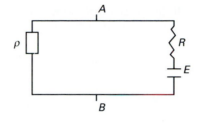

Using the basic relationship for the potential drop, $V = E - IR$, we therefore have

$$V = E - RkV^{3/2}.$$

Write a computer program that will input values for E, R, and k and solve for V using Newton–Raphson. Continue iterations until either the relative error is less than EPS or a maximum of ITMAX iterations have been done. Use an initial guess of E to start the iterations.

Run your program for the following data: EPS $= 0.001$, ITMAX $= 25$, and

E(volts)	R(ohms)	k(amp/volt$^{3/2}$)
100	5000	1.0E-5
10	500	1.0E-3
25.5	300	1.0E-4

 14. An important characteristic of photographic film is the amount of light transmitted through the film after exposure and development. As a function of exposure at a particular point on the film, the proportion of light transmitted ($T(E)$) may be determined by an examination of the H/D curve for the film, given in various film data sheets. A typical plot of T versus E is shown in Fig. 12.38.

Figure 12.38.

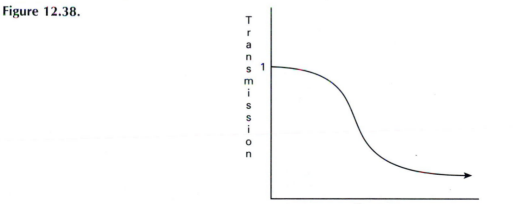

If the exposure is a function of the position on the film ($E(x)$), then the total light transmitted through a film of length L after development is given by

$$H = \int_0^L T(E(x))\,dx.$$

Suppose $E(x) = A/(x^2 + 0.12)$ and write a program to determine H for several values of the parameter A.

Your main program should read and print the tabulated exposure and transmission values (E & T) for a particular film. It also will need a critical exposure value (ECRIT) beyond which transmission is essentially zero. Read and echo check the starting and ending values for position (XBEG and XEND) and the number of points to be used in the integration (N), as well as values for parameter A. The program should then calculate the X vector, an evenly spaced set of N-values with X(1) = XBEG and X(N) = XEND. To calculate the corresponding Y-values, if $(A/(X(I)^2 + 0.12)) >$ ECRIT, then Y(I) = 0. If not, use a subprogram to calculate Y(I) = $T(A/(X(I)^2 + 0.12))$ by linear interpolation using closest points on the E–T table. Finally, use a function subprogram SIMP(N, X, Y, ISIG) to compute the desired integral by Simpson's rule.

SIMP should begin by checking that N is odd. If N is not odd, the error signal ISIG should be set to 1 and an appropriate message printed out in the main program. If N is odd, set ISIG to 0 and proceed with the integration. Run your program on the following data.

Tri-X Film (ECRIT = .095)

Exposure	Transmission
.000	1.000
.005	1.000
.010	1.000
.015	0.986
.020	0.944
.025	0.875
.030	0.778
.035	0.653
.040	0.500
.045	0.347
.050	0.222
.055	0.125
.060	0.0561
.065	0.0142
.070	0.00538
.075	0.00427
.080	0.00292
.090	0.00234
.095	0.00113

XBEG = 0.0; XEND = 1.0

Compute the total transmitted for $A = 0.005, 0.01, 0.1, 0.15$, and $N = 3, 7, 10, 25$ (i.e., for *each* A, you will compute four approximations with corresponding N's).

15. The representation of a periodic signal in terms of its Fourier series is an important tool in electrical engineering. If $f(t)$ is a sufficiently well-behaved periodic function of period P, then its Fourier series representation is given by

$$\frac{a_0}{2} + \sum_{n=1}^{\infty} a_n \cos \frac{2\pi nt}{P} + b_n \sin \frac{2\pi nt}{P},$$

where

$$a_0 = \frac{2}{P} \int_P f(t)\, dt, \qquad a_n = \frac{2}{P} \int_P f(t) \cos \frac{2\pi nt}{P}\, dt,$$

$$b_n = \frac{2}{P} \int_P f(t) \sin \frac{2\pi nt}{P}\, dt.$$

In each case, the integrals are taken over one complete period. With some functions $f(t)$, evaluating these coefficients by analytical methods could be very tedious; in these cases, numerical integration techniques are preferred. Unfortunately, as n increases, the results are often unsatisfactory if the integration technique is taken over the full period P directly. It is better to break up the integral at some *irrational* point Q and apply numerical integration to the resulting subintervals.

Your problem should investigate this for the periodic function $f(t) = 2t + 1$, $0 \leq t < P$, where P will be input to the program. Use function subprograms to define f and the integrands for the coefficients. Have your program calculate the coefficients using a function subprogram for Simpson's rule: SIMP(F, XL, XU, IER), where XL and XU are the lower and upper limits of integration, F is the function subprogram defining the integrand (note that the actual functions will have to be declared EXTERNAL), and IER is an output flag indicating a lack of convergence. Begin with three evenly spaced points and successively double the number of subintervals until approximations differ by less than .0001 or a maximum of seven doublings have been done. If the maximum is reached, do not attempt calculations for larger values of n. Otherwise, try to evaluate the first 20 coefficients (and a_0 of course) in this manner. Do this calculation using Simpson's rule over the interval $[0, P]$; then do it for $[0, P/\sqrt{2}]$ and $[P/\sqrt{2}, P]$, adding the results. Compare the results from these two approaches with the following analytically determined coefficients for this function:

$$a_0 = 2(P + 1), \qquad a_n = 0, \qquad \text{and} \qquad b_n = \frac{-2P}{\pi n}.$$

Your output should be a table as follows:

Exact			Whole Simpson			Broken Simpson		
a_0	a_n	b_n	a_0	a_n	b_n	a_0	a_n	b_n

Run your program for $P = 1$ and $P = 10$.

16. Force transducers are often made by attaching electric resistance strain gages to a section of pipe to make what is called a load cell. A strain indicator is used to measure the change in strain of the gages as loads are applied to the load cell. The device can be calibrated by applying known loads and recording the strain indicator readings. Because loads are kept within the elastic range of the material, there should be a linear relationship between load and strain. Thus we assume that $s = a \cdot l + b$, where s = strain, l = load, and a and b are determined from the calibration data by the "least squares" equations

$$a = \frac{m \sum ls - \sum l \sum s}{m \sum l^2 - (\sum l)^2}$$

$$b = \frac{\sum s \sum l^2 - \sum l \sum ls}{m \sum l^2 - (\sum l)^2},$$

where m = the number of data points and the summations are taken over all of the calibration data. Once a and b are found, the linear equation can be used to find the strains for other imposed loads.

Write a Fortran program that will read a table of calibration data, determine the equation of the least squares line that fits the data, and use that equation to print a table of loads and indicator readings. Input data will include the calibration data, a starting load, load increment, and final load for the table to be generated. Write a subroutine LSQL(M, L, S, A, B) to determine the coefficients A and B from the M calibration values stored in the one-dimensional arrays L and S, as described above. Write a function subprogram STRAIN(LOAD, A, B) to evaluate the strain for LOAD from the linear model using coefficients A and B. Echo check the input data, call LSQL, and print the least squares coefficients. To keep the printed table compact, print it with six columns and the number of rows as determined from input. Assume the number of rows will be such that the entire table will fit on one page. Do *not* store the table to be printed in memory. The generated table should have the following format:

$$\text{Number of rows: } \left(\frac{\text{final load} - \text{starting load}}{\text{increment}} + 1 \right) \Big/ 3$$

Load	Indicator Readings	Load	Indicator Readings	Load	Indicator Readings
1100	XXXX	4100	XXXX	7100	XXXX
1200	XXXX	4200	XXXX	7200	XXXX
⋮	⋮	⋮	⋮	⋮	⋮
3900	XXXX	6900	XXXX	9900	XXXX
4000	XXXX	7000	XXXX	10000	XXXX

Starting load 1100 lb, final load 10,000 lb, load increment 100 lb.

Calibration data:

Load (in. lb.)	Indicator Readings
0	2200
1000	2300
2000	2388
3000	2483
4000	2568
5000	2654
6000	2745
7000	2834
8000	2923

 17. Consider the simple plane framework shown in Fig. 12.39.

We assume the framework is *pin-jointed*, which means the members are connected to the wall and also connected at A, loosely, by pins. This means that if the five members were not connected to the wall, they could rotate quite freely around the point A. With this kind of joint, there is no tendency to bend the members and the only forces present are tensile or compressive forces in the members. Assume also that the weights of the members are negligible and the lengths of the members are such that if the external forces F_1 and F_2 are zero, there are no stresses in the members.

We want to determine the movement of point A when forces are applied to the framework. Let

d_1 = distance moved horizontally
d_2 = distance moved vertically
e_i = extension of ith member, $i = 1, \ldots, 5$
T_i = tension on ith members, $i = 1, \ldots, 5$

Figure 12.39.

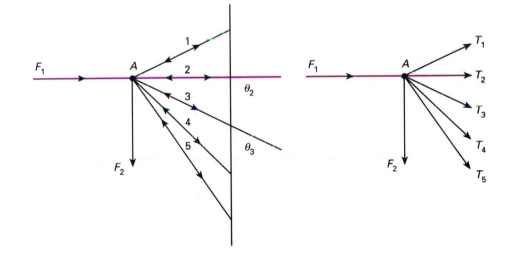

For the 5-pin framework illustrated, we therefore have 12 unknowns, which are related by assuming equilibrium at point A:

$$-T_1 \cos \theta_1 - T_2 \cos \theta_2 - \cdots - T_5 \cos \theta_5 = F_1$$

$$T_1 \sin \theta_1 + T_2 \sin \theta_2 + \cdots + T_5 \sin \theta_5 = F_2$$

$$e_i = -d_1 \cos \theta_i + d_2 \sin \theta_i, \ i = 1, \ \ldots \ , 5;$$

and by Hooke's law for each member:

$$e_i = k_i T_i, \ i = 1, \ \ldots \ , 5,$$

where $k_i = l_i/A_i E$ with l_i = length of pin i, A_i = area of pin i, and E = modulus of elasticity (k_i is called the flexibility of the member). The angles θ_i are the angles made with the horizontal and are negative for members 3, 4, and 5 in the diagram. Assume the changes in θ_i produced by the application of forces are negligible.

Write a Fortran program to determine the distances, extensions, and tensions for such a pin-jointed framework that contains N pins. The program should do this by using Gaussian elimination to solve the above $2N + 2$ system. The input to your program should be the number of pins, the forces F_1 and F_2, and, for each pin, the length, area, and angle. Your program should echo check the input and construct the coefficient and right-hand-side matrixes for the system, then output these matrixes, and use a general Gaussian elimination subroutine to solve for the unknowns, which of course must then be output.

Run your program for the following data: F_1 = 500 N, F_2 = 500 N. (Assume $E = 20.4 \cdot 10^{10}$ N/m^2.)

Pin	θ_i(degrees)	l_i(m)	A_i(m^2)
1	45°	10.2	.785
2	30°	7.3	.785
3	−15°	8.4	.785
4	−30°	9.6	.785
5	−60°	14.8	.785

APPENDIX A
Fortran Library Functions

The table that follows provides the generic and specific names for the Fortran library functions. You can use the generic name for a particular function (e.g., ABS) with arguments of any numeric type; the type of the result is determined by the type of the arguments. If you use the specific name (e.g., IABS), then the type of the function result and the required argument type are specified in the table below (e.g., INTEGER for IABS).

FUNCTION DESCRIPTION	GENERIC NAME	SPECIFIC NAME	NUMBER OF ARGUMENTS	TYPE OF ARGUMENTS	TYPE OF FUNCTION
Conversion of numeric to integer	INT	—	1	Integer	Integer
		INT		Real	Integer
		IFIX		Real	Integer
		IDINT		Double	Integer
		—		Complex	Integer
Conversion of numeric to real	REAL	REAL	1	Integer	Real
		FLOAT		Integer	Real
		—		Real	Real
		SNGL		Double	Real
		—		Complex	Real
Conversion of numeric to double precision	DBLE	—	1	Integer	Double
		—		Real	Double
		—		Double	Double
		—		Complex	Double
Conversion of numeric to complex	CMPLX	—	1 or 2	Integer	Complex
		—		Real	Complex
		—		Double	Complex
		—		Complex	Complex
Conversion of character to integer	—	ICHAR	1	Character	Integer
Conversion of integer to character	—	CHAR	1	Integer	Character

FUNCTION DESCRIPTION	GENERIC NAME	SPECIFIC NAME	NUMBER OF ARGUMENTS	TYPE OF ARGUMENTS	TYPE OF FUNCTION
Truncation	AINT	AINT	1	Real	Real
		DINT		Double	Double
Rounding to nearest integer	ANINT	ANINT	1	Real	Real
		DNINT	1	Double	Double
Rounding to nearest integer	NINT	NINT	1	Real	Integer
		IDNINT	1	Double	Integer
Absolute value	ABS	IABS	1	Integer	Integer
		ABS		Real	Real
		DABS		Double	Double
		CABS		Complex	Real
Remaindering	MOD	MOD	2	Integer	Integer
		AMOD		Real	Real
		DMOD		Double	Double
Transfer of sign	SIGN	ISIGN	2	Integer	Integer
		SIGN		Real	Real
		DSIGN		Double	Double
Positive difference	DIM	IDIM	2	Integer	Integer
		DIM		Real	Real
		DDIM		Double	Double
Double precision product	—	DPROD	2	Real	Double
Maximum value	MAX	MAXO	≥2	Integer	Integer
		AMAX1		Real	Real
		DMAX1		Double	Double
	—	AMAXO		Integer	Real
	—	MAX1		Real	Integer
Minimum value	MIN	MINO	≥2	Integer	Integer
		AMIN1		Real	Real
		DMIN1		Double	Double
	—	AMINO		Integer	Real
	—	MIN1		Real	Integer
Length of character item	—	LEN	1	Character	Integer
Index of a substring	—	INDEX	2	Character	Integer
Imaginary part of a complex value	—	AIMAG	1	Complex	Real
Conjugate of a complex value	—	CONJG	1	Complex	Complex
Square root	SQRT	SQRT	1	Real	Real
		DSQRT		Double	Double
		CSQRT		Complex	Complex
Exponential	EXP	EXP	1	Real	Real
		DEXP		Double	Double
		CEXP		Complex	Complex

FUNCTION DESCRIPTION	GENERIC NAME	SPECIFIC NAME	NUMBER OF ARGUMENTS	TYPE OF ARGUMENTS	TYPE OF FUNCTION
Natural logarithm	LOG	ALOG	1	Real	Real
		DLOG		Double	Double
		CLOG		Complex	Complex
Common logarithm	LOG10	ALOG10	1	Real	Real
		DLOG10		Double	Double
Sine	SIN	SIN	1	Real	Real
		DSIN		Double	Double
		CSIN		Complex	Complex
Cosine	COS	COS	1	Real	Real
		DCOS		Double	Double
		CCOS		Complex	Complex
Tangent	TAN	TAN	1	Real	Real
		DTAN		Double	Double
Arcsine	ASIN	ASIN	1	Real	Real
		DASIN		Double	Double
Arccosine	ACOS	ACOS	1	Real	Real
		DACOS		Double	Double
Arctangent	ATAN	ATAN	1	Real	Real
		DATAN		Double	Double
	ATAN2	ATAN2	2	Real	Real
		DATAN2		Double	Double
Hyperbolic sine	SINH	SINH	1	Real	Real
		DSINH		Double	Double
Hyperbolic cosine	COSH	COSH	1	Real	Real
		DCOSH		Double	Double
Hyperbolic tangent	TANH	TANH	1	Real	Real
		DTANH		Double	Double
Lexically greater than or equal to	—	LGE	2	Character	Logical
Lexically greater than	—	LGT	2	Character	Logical
Lexically less than or equal to	—	LLE	2	Character	Logical
Lexically less than	—	LLT	2	Character	Logical

APPENDIX B
Character Sets

The first chart shows the decimal code values in ASCII (American Standard Code for Information Interchange). Codes 0 through 31 and 126 and 127 represent nonprintable control characters. The code for a blank or space is 32. The next chart shows just the printable characters in EBCDIC (Extended Binary Coded Decimal Interchange Code). The code for a blank or space is 64 in EBCDIC.

ASCII Decimal Equivalence Chart

NUMBER	CHAR	NUMBER	CHAR	NUMBER	CHAR	NUMBER	CHAR
0	NUL	24	CAN	48	0	72	H
1	SOH	25	EM	49	1	73	I
2	STX	26	SUB	50	2	74	J
3	ETX	27	ESC	51	3	75	K
4	EOT	28	FS	52	4	76	L
5	ENQ	29	GS	53	5	77	M
6	ACK	30	RS	54	6	78	N
7	BEL	31	US	55	7	79	O
8	BS	32	□	56	8	80	P
9	HT	33	!	57	9	81	Q
10	LF	34	"	58	:	82	R
11	VT	35	#	59	;	83	S
12	FF	36	$	60	<	84	T
13	CR	37	%	61	=	85	U
14	SO	38	&	62	>	86	V
15	SI	39	'	63	?	87	W
16	DLE	40	(	64	@	88	X
17	DC1	41	)	65	A	89	Y
18	DC2	42	*	66	B	90	Z
19	DC3	43	+	67	C	91	[
20	DC4	44	,	68	D	92	\
21	NAK	45	−	69	E	93	]
22	SYN	46	.	70	F	94	^
23	ETB	47	/	71	G	95	_

ASCII Decimal Equivalence Chart (continued)

NUMBER	CHAR	NUMBER	CHAR	NUMBER	CHAR	NUMBER	CHAR
96	'	104	h	112	p	120	x
97	a	105	i	113	q	121	y
98	b	106	j	114	r	122	z
99	c	107	k	115	s	123	{
100	d	108	l	116	t	124	|
101	e	109	m	117	u	125	}
102	f	110	n	118	v	126	~
103	g	111	o	119	w	127	DEL

EBCDIC Code

LEFT DIGIT(S) \ RIGHT DIGIT	0	1	2	3	4	5	6	7	8	9
6					□					
7					¢	.	<	(	+	|
8	&									
9	!	$	*	)	;	¬				
10							ˆ	,	%	—
11	>	?								
12			:	#	@	'	=	"		a
13	b	c	d	e	f	g	h	i		
14						j	k	l	m	n
15	o	p	q	r						
16			s	t	u	v	w	x	y	z
17								\	{	}
18	[	]								
19				A	B	C	D	E	F	G
20	H	I								J
21	K	L	M	N	O	P	Q	R		
22							S	T	U	V
23	W	X	Y	Z						
24	0	1	2	3	4	5	6	7	8	9

Codes 00–63 and 250–255 are nonprintable control characters.

APPENDIX C

Introduction to MS-DOS, Microsoft Fortran, and Lahey Personal Fortran

The Microsoft Fortran and Lahey Personal Fortran compilers are designed to be used on an IBM PC computer or a compatible computer. To use either compiler, you must be familiar with the MS-DOS operating system (*MicroSoft Disk Operating System*). You must also be able to use an editor to create and modify source files and data files.

Introduction to MS-DOS

When you turn on, or *boot up*, a computer, the operating system is loaded into memory and begins execution. If your computer has a hard disk, the operating system will be on disk drive C (the hard disk) and will issue the prompt

```
C>
```

to inform you that it is ready. Most likely, you will be using a hard disk, and both the operating system and the Fortran compiler will be on disk drive C.

A principal function of an operating system is the maintenance of data files (including Fortran source files) on a floppy disk or a hard disk. In a class situation, you will probably be using a floppy disk for storage of your own Fortran source files and data files. If you are using a new floppy disk for file storage, you must *format* the disk before saving any files on it. If your new floppy disk is in disk drive B, the command

```
C>FORMAT B:
```

instructs MS-DOS to format the disk on drive B.

When you format a disk, you erase any data and files that may already be stored on it. So don't format a disk unless you are sure that it does not contain any important data. Do *not* attempt to format the hard disk, because that will erase your operating system and the Fortran compiler. If you are unsure whether the floppy disk you are

Table C.1. *MS-DOS Commands*

COMMAND	EFFECT
`CD C:\F77EXAMP`	Makes subdirectory `F77EXAMP` on drive C the active directory
`DIR`	Displays the file names in the currently active disk directory
`DIR D.`	Displays the file names in the active directory for disk drive B
`FORMAT B:`	Formats the disk on drive B so it can be used for file storage; erases any existing files on the disk
`ERASE A:EXAMP1.EXE`	Deletes file `EXAMP1.EXE` from disk A
`COPY A:EXAMP1.FOR A:ME.FOR`	Makes a new copy of file `EXAMP1.FOR` on drive A with the file name `ME.FOR`
`RENAME A:ME.FOR PAY.FOR`	Changes the name of file `ME.FOR` on drive A to `PAY.FOR`

using contains any important files, use the command

`C>DIR B:`

to display the directory for drive B. This directory shows the files currently on the floppy disk in drive B.

There are other MS-DOS commands for manipulating files. For example, you can delete a file that is no longer needed (using the `ERASE` command), duplicate a file (using the `COPY` command), list the contents of the file on the screen or the printer (using the `TYPE` command), change a file's name (using the `RENAME` command), or change the active disk directory. Table C.1 summarizes these commands.

Using Microsoft Fortran

The line below should be used to compile source file `EXAMP1.FOR`, which is saved on drive C.

`C>FL EXAMP1.FOR`

The Microsoft Fortran compiler displays the lines

```
Microsoft (R) FORTRAN Optimizing Compiler Version 4.10
Copyright (c) Microsoft Corp 1987, 1988. All rights reserved.
```

`EXAMP1.FOR`

If there are any syntax errors, error messages appear next, along with the number of the source file line containing the error. You should correct the errors and attempt to compile the source file again.

If there are no syntax errors, the system attempts to link the object file (`EXAMP1.OBJ`) created by the compilation step with any necessary library modules. The messages below then appear.

```
Microsoft (R) Segmented-Executable Linker   Version 5.01.20
Copyright (c) Microsoft Corp 1984-1988. All rights reserved.

Object Modules [.OBJ]: EXAMP1.OBJ
Run File [EXAMP1.EXE]: EXAMP1.EXE
List File [NUL.MAP]:NUL
Libraries[.LIB]:
Definitions File [NUL.DEF]: ;
```

If any errors are detected during linking, such as unresolved external references, these error messages appear next. You should go back to the source file, correct the lines in error, and recompile. If there are no errors, you can load and run the *executable file*, EXAMP1.EXE, as often as you wish using the command

C>EXAMP1

Creating a Listing File

If your program contains several syntax errors, it will be difficult to locate and correct the errors using the information displayed during compilation. You will probably want to obtain a listing file to help you debug the program. A listing file shows your source file with each line numbered and with error messages inserted following the line in error. The listing file must be obtained during the compilation step. To get a listing file, use the command below to compile your source file:

C>FL /Fs EXAMP1.FOR

Make sure the second letter F is in uppercase and the letter s is in lowercase.

The compiler then creates a listing file named EXAMP1.LST. You can examine this file and determine the cause of your errors. Make sure that you correct the source file, EXAMP1.FOR, and not the listing file. When you are ready to compile again, you should erase the listing file before compilation.

After running several Fortran programs, your disk may become filled. If you are not likely to rerun a program again, you can delete its object file (.OBJ) and its run file (.EXE) from your disk. However, it is a good idea to retain the source file for future reference.

Sending Output to the Printer

In Microsoft Fortran, you can easily send program output to the printer. In order to do this, you must insert the statement

OPEN (UNIT = 6, FILE = 'LPT1')

after the program declarations. To send a line of program output to the printer, use 6 as the unit number (the first symbol after the left parenthesis) in a WRITE statement:

WRITE (6, *) 'Hello ', USER

This statement prints the contents of variable USER after the string 'Hello'. The symbol * preceding the right parenthesis specifies list-directed output.

To send a line of output to the screen, list * as the unit number in a WRITE statement or use the PRINT statement. The next two statements display a string and the contents of USER on the screen.

```
WRITE (*, *) 'Hello ', USER
PRINT *, 'Hello again ', USER
```

The first symbol * in the WRITE statement denotes the standard system output device (the screen). The symbol * in the PRINT statement and the second symbol * in the WRITE statement specify list-directed output.

Lahey Personal Fortran

The Lahey Personal Fortran compiler is a popular compiler for the IBM personal computer and compatibles. It contains its own editor program called the Blackbeard editor. Programmers have the option of compiling and running programs from within or outside the editor. We cannot provide the details of using the Blackbeard editor here, but we will discuss how to compile your programs both ways.

To compile an existing Fortran program from DOS, enter the command below

```
C>LP77 filename.FOR
```

after the DOS prompt, where *filename* is the name of the source program file. If the program compiles successfully, enter the command

```
C>LINK filename.OBJ
```

to create an executable file. Next, enter the command

```
C>filename
```

to run the executable file.

To enter the Blackbeard editor, type the command

```
C>LB
```

at the DOS prompt. You will receive the prompt

```
Filename:
```

at the bottom of your screen. If you are creating a new program, type in a name for the new source file with the extension .FOR. You will then get an empty screen, and you can begin to type in each line of the program. Use the Tab key to advance to column 7 before typing in each Fortran statement.

If you are trying to retrieve an existing program, either type in the source file name after the prompt above or press Enter. If you press Enter, you will see a list of files in the current directory and you can select your file from this list by moving the highlight bar over it and pressing Enter. In either case, the existing source file will appear on a new screen.

Once you have retrieved an existing file or typed in a new one, you can compile your program by pressing Ctrl-O C [press and hold the Control key (labeled Ctrl), press O, and then press C]. Your screen will be split into two windows: an edit window and a review window. If your program compiles successfully, the line

```
Compiling line 1:   program filename
```

appears in the review window and you can link your program. If your program does not compile successfully, an error message will appear in the review window and the cursor will be moved to the edit window. You can then edit the program and attempt to recompile by pressing Ctrl-O C again.

To link your program, press Ctrl-O L. After the link step, press Ctrl-Z to exit the editor. To run your program, use the command below

C>*filename*

after the DOS prompt.

APPENDIX D
Implementing the WHILE Loop in Standard Fortran

The WHILE loop is not supported in standard Fortran 77. However, it is relatively easy to implement this loop using control statements from standard Fortran. In the WHILE loop below, the loop repetition condition causes the loop body to be repeated while BALANC is still positive.

```
DO WHILE (BALANC .GT. 0.0)
   PRINT *, 'Enter a deposit (positive) or check (negative):'
   READ *, X
   BALANC = BALANC + X
END DO
```

We can use a labeled IF statement with a GOTO statement (see Section 6.3) at the end to implement the WHILE loop in standard Fortran. The IF condition should be identical to the WHILE condition:

```
9 IF (BALANC .GT. 0.0) THEN
     PRINT *, 'Enter a deposit (positive) or check (negative):'
     READ *, X
     BALANC = BALANC + X
   GOTO 9
   END IF
```

The true task executes if the initial value of BALANC is positive; otherwise, the true task is skipped (analogous to an immediate loop exit). The true task updates BALANC, after which the GOTO statement transfers control back to the statement with label 9 (the IF statement header). The IF condition is retested, and the true task is repeated while BALANC is still positive.

Answers to Self-Check Exercises

Chapter 1

Section 1.2

1. -27.2 in cell 0, 75.62 in cell 999. Cell 998 contains the letter 'X', cell 2 contains 0.005.
2. Main memory stores information, including data and program instructions. The CPU performs all arithmetic and logical operations.

   Secondary and main memory are used for storage of data and programs. However, secondary memory (a disk) can store more information and can store it permanently. Information must be transferred into main memory before it can be processed. The disk drive controls the disk; it stores information on the disk and retrieves information from the disk. The keyboard and mouse are input devices; the monitor and printer are output devices.

Section 1.3

1. $X = A + B + C$ means "add the values of A, B, and C together and save the result in X." $X = Y / Z$ means "divide the value of Y by Z and save the result in X." $D = C - B + A$ means "subtract the value of B from C, then add the value of A, and save the result in D." $X = X + 1$ means "add 1 to X and save the result back in X."
2. Pascal was designed for teaching programming.
   COBOL was designed for business applications.
   Fortran was designed for translating scientific formulas.
3. High-level language has instructions such as $X = X + Y$.
   Machine language has instructions that are binary numbers.

Section 1.4

1. A compiler attempts to translate a source file into machine language. If there are syntax errors, the compiler generates error messages. If there are no errors, it creates an object file.

   Syntax errors occur when statements do not follow exactly the syntax rules of the language. They are found in the source file.
2. A file that contains a program is called a source file. The object file, which is the program translated into machine language, is created by the compiler. The load file is created by the linker, which links the new object file with other object files. The source file is created by a programmer. The compiler creates an object file. The

linker creates a load file. The load file is processed by the loader. The linker links the new object file with other object files. The loader places the load file into memory.

Chapter 2

Section 2.1
1. Requirements Specification (Problem Statement), Analysis, Design, Implementation, Testing and Verification
2. algorithm in Design; data requirements in Analysis

Section 2.2
1. Data Requirements

> *Problem Input*
>
> the weight in pounds (REAL POUND)
>
> *Problem Output*
>
> the weight in kilograms (REAL KILOGM)
>
> *Relevant Formulas*
>
> 1 pound = 0.45 kilogram

Algorithm

1. Read the weight in pounds.
2. Convert the weight from pounds to kilograms.
3. Display the weight in kilograms.

> *Step 2 Refinement*
>
> 2.1 Multiply the weight in pounds by 0.45.

2. Data Requirements

three numbers (REAL NUM1, NUM2, NUM3)

> *Problem Outputs*
>
> the sum of the three numbers (REAL SUM)
> the average of the three numbers (REAL AVERAG)

Algorithm

1. Read in the three numbers.
2. Find the sum of the three numbers.
3. Find the average of the three numbers.
4. Print the values of the sum and the average.

> *Step 2 Refinement*
>
> 2.1 Add NUM1, NUM2, and NUM3 and store result in SUM

Step 3 Refinement

3.1 Divide SUM by 3.0 and store result in AVERAG

3. Data Requirements

Problem Inputs

list price of the item (REAL LIST)
percentage of discount (REAL DISPCT)

Problem Outputs

reduced price (REAL PRICE)

Additional Program Variables

the amount of the discount (REAL DISCNT)

Relevant Formulas

discount = list price × discount percentage
reduced price = list price − discount

Algorithm

1. Read in the list price and percentage of discount.
2. Find the reduced price.
3. Print the reduced price.

Step 2 Refinement

2.1 Compute the amount of the discount.
2.2 Compute the reduced price.

Section 2.3
1. Fortran keywords : END, READ, PROGRAM, STOP
   Valid identifiers: END, READ, BILL, RATE, START, BEGIN, STOP, XYZ123
2. Valid Fortran statements : c, e, f, h, j, k
3. The corrected program is listed below:

```
PROGRAM MIXUP
REAL X, Y, Z
Y = 15.0
Z = -Y + 3.5
X = Y + Z
PRINT *, X, Y, Z
STOP
END
```

The first statement identifies MIXUP as the name of the program and the second statement declares the three variables used in the program: X, Y, and Z. The next statement assigns the value of 15.0 to Y. The fourth statement adds the negative value of Y to 3.5, which means that it subtracts -15.0 from 3.5 and assigns the result, -11.5, to Z. The next statement adds the values of Y and Z (15 and -11.5) and assigns the result, 3.5, to X. The sixth statement prints out the values of the three variables, and the next statement stops the program. The last statement instructs the compiler to stop the translation of the source file. The numbers 3.5, 15.0, and -11.5 are printed.

4. Enter two integers:
   5 7
   M = 10
   N = 21

5. My name is:
   Doe, Jane

   I live in Ann Arbor, MI
   and my zip code is 48109

Section 2.4

1. To make the program easier to understand by describing the purpose of the program and each program step

2. 12345678. . . (column numbers)

```
      PROGRAM SPACES
      REAL X, Y
*  Assign values to X and Y
   10 X = 10
   15 Y = 15
C Display X and Y
      PRINT X, Y
      STOP
      END
```

Section 2.5

1. Integer   :   15
   Real   :   15.5E–2, 10E10, 3.45E–5
   Character :   '*', '3.45E–5', '*+'''"'
   Invalid   :   "X"

   The string consisting of the four characters *, +, ', and " would be stored in NAME.

2. 15.5E–2 : 0.155
   10E10   : 100000000000.0
   3.45E–5 : 0.0000345

3. a.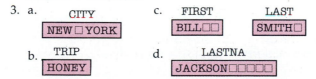

e.
TEAM   TEAM

ORIOLES□□   RED□STOCK

Section 2.6

1.

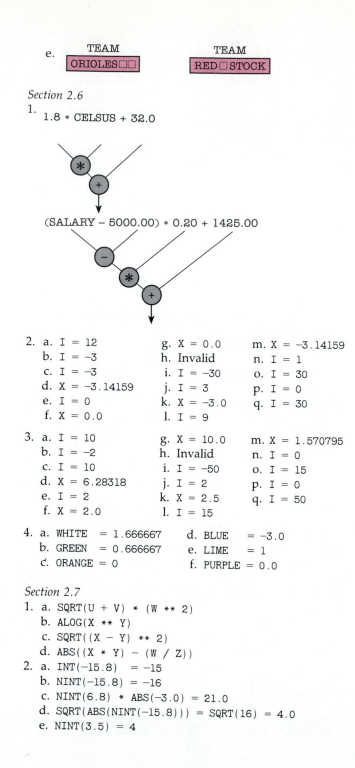

```
1.8 * CELSUS + 32.0
```

```
(SALARY - 5000.00) * 0.20 + 1425.00
```

2. a. I = 12   g. X = 0.0   m. X = -3.14159
   b. I = -3   h. Invalid   n. I = 1
   c. I = -3   i. I = -30   o. I = 30
   d. X = -3.14159 j. I = 3   p. I = 0
   e. I = 0   k. X = -3.0   q. I = 30
   f. X = 0.0   l. I = 9

3. a. I = 10   g. X = 10.0   m. X = 1.570795
   b. I = -2   h. Invalid   n. I = 0
   c. I = 10   i. I = -50   o. I = 15
   d. X = 6.28318 j. I = 2   p. I = 0
   e. I = 2   k. X = 2.5   q. I = 50
   f. X = 2.0   l. I = 15

4. a. WHITE = 1.666667   d. BLUE   = -3.0
   b. GREEN = 0.666667   e. LIME   = 1
   c. ORANGE = 0   f. PURPLE = 0.0

Section 2.7

1. a. SQRT(U + V) * (W ** 2)
   b. ALOG(X ** Y)
   c. SQRT((X - Y) ** 2)
   d. ABS((X * Y) - (W / Z))
2. a. INT(-15.8) = -15
   b. NINT(-15.8) = -16
   c. NINT(6.8) * ABS(-3.0) = 21.0
   d. SQRT(ABS(NINT(-15.8))) = SQRT(16) = 4.0
   e. NINT(3.5) = 4

    f. `REAL(7 / 2) = 3.0`

    g. `REAL(7) / REAL(2) = 3.5`

Chapter 3

Section 3.2

1. `X .NE. Y is .TRUE.`

   `X .LT. X is .FALSE.`

   `X .GE. (Y − X) is .TRUE.`

   `X .EQ. (Y + X − Y) is .TRUE.`

2. a. `.TRUE.`

   b. `.TRUE.`

   c. `.FALSE.`

   d. `.TRUE.`

3.

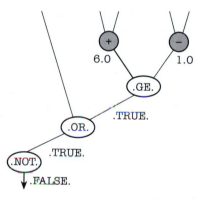

       `.FALSE.`   `4.0 2.0`   `3.0 2.0`

 `.NOT. (FLAG .OR. ((Y + Z) .GE. (X − Z)))`

Section 3.3

1. a. `.TRUE.`

   b. `.FALSE.`

   c. `.TRUE.`

   d. `.FALSE.`

   e. `.FALSE.`

   f. `.TRUE.`

   g. `.FALSE.`

   h. `.TRUE.`

   i. `.TRUE.`

   j. `.FALSE.`

Section 3.4

1. a. Never

   b. O.K.

2. a. If NUM1 < 0, then PRODUC gets the product of NUM1, NUM2, and NUM3 and PRODUC is

displayed; otherwise, NUM1, NUM2, and NUM3 are added and the sum is assigned to SUM and displayed.

b. If X > Y, then the values of X and Y are swapped; otherwise, X gets the value of Y and Y is assigned the new value of X (i.e., Y does not change).

Section 3.5

1. a. X = 12.5 when Y = 15.0
      X = 15.0 when Y = 10.0
   b. X = 30.0 when Y = 15.0
      X = 50.0 when Y = 10.0

Section 3.6

1. Case 2:

Program statement	NUM1	NUM2	NUM3	MINNUM	*Effect*
	?	?	?	?	
PRINT *, 'Enter three...'					Prints a prompt
READ *, NUM1, NUM2, NUM3	10	12	5		Reads the data
IF (NUM1 .LT. NUM2) THEN					Is 10 < 12?
					Value is true
MINNUM = NUM1				10	10 is smallest so far
IF (NUM3 .LT. MINNUM)...					Is 5 < 10?
					Value is true
MINNUM = NUM3				5	5 is smallest
PRINT *, MINNUM...					Prints 5 is the smallest number

Case 3:

Program statement	NUM1	NUM2	NUM3	MINNUM	*Effect*
	?	?	?	?	
PRINT *, 'Enter three...'					Prints a prompt
READ *, NUM1, NUM2, NUM3	5	12	10		Reads the data
IF (NUM1 .LT. NUM2) THEN					Is 5 < 12?
					Value is true
MINNUM = NUM1				5	5 is smallest so far
IF (NUM3 .LT. MINNUM)...					Is 10 < 5?
					Value is false
PRINT *, MINNUM...					Prints 5 is the smallest number

Case 4:

Program statement	NUM1	NUM2	NUM3	MINNUM	Effect
	?	?	?	?	
PRINT *, 'Enter three...'					Prints a prompt
READ *, NUM1, NUM2, NUM3	10	5	12		Reads the data
IF (NUM1 .LT. NUM2) THEN					Is 10 < 5?
					Value is false
MINNUM = NUM2				5	5 is smallest so far
IF (NUM3 .LT. MINNUM)...					Is 12 < 5?
					Value is false
PRINT *, MINNUM...					Prints 5 is the smallest number

When all three numbers are the same:

Program statement	NUM1	NUM2	NUM3	MINNUM	Effect
	?	?	?	?	
PRINT *, 'Enter three...'					Prints a prompt
READ *, NUM1, NUM2, NUM3	5	5	5		Reads the data
IF (NUM1 .LT. NUM2) THEN					Is 5 < 5?
					Value is false
MINNUM = NUM2				5	5 is smallest so far
IF (NUM3 .LT. MINNUM)...					Is 5 < 5?
					Value is false
PRINT *, MINNUM...					Prints 5 is the smallest number

2. Case 1:

Program statement	HOURS	RATE	GROSS	TXTAMT	NET	OVHOUR	Effect
	?	?	?	?	?	?	
PRINT *,'Enter hours...'							Prints a prompt.
READ *, HOURS	30.0						Reads data.
PRINT *,'Enter hourly...'							Prints a prompt.
READ *, RATE		5.00					Reads data.
IF (HOURS .LT. MAXREG)...							Is 30.0 < 40.0? Value is true.
GROSS = HOURS * RATE			150.0				Computes GROSS.
IF (GROSS .LT. TXBRAK)...							Is 150.0 < 100.0? Value is false.
TAXAMT = TAXRAT * GROSS				15.0			Computes TAXAMT.
NET = GROSS − TAXAMT					135.0		Computes NET pay.

Program statement	HOURS	RATE	GROSS	TXTAMT	NET	OVHOUR	Effect
PRINT *,'Gross pay...'							Prints 150.0 as gross pay.
PRINT *,'TAX amount...'							Prints 15.0 as the tax amount.
PRINT *,'NET pay...'							Prints 135.0 as net pay.

Case 2:

Program statement	HOURS	RATE	GROSS	TAXAMT	NET	OVHOUR	Effect
	?	?	?	?	?	?	
PRINT *,'Enter hours...'							Prints a prompt.
READ *, HOURS	20.0						Reads data.
PRINT *,'Enter hourl...'							Prints a prompt.
READ *, RATE		3.00					Reads data.
IF (HOURS .LT. MAXREG)...							Is 20.0 < 40.0? Value is true.
GROSS = HOURS * RATE			60.0				Computes GROSS.
IF (GROSS .LT. TXBRAK)...							Is 60.0 < 100.0? Value is true.
TAXAMT = 0.0				0.0			TAXAMT is 0.0.
NET = GROSS − TAXAMT					60.0		Computes NET.
PRINT *,'Gross pay...'							Prints 60.0 as gross pay.
PRINT *,'TAX amount...'							Prints 0.0 as tax.
PRINT *,'NET pay...'							Prints 60.0 as net pay.

Section 3.8

1. In the inner IF structure, the test for GPA less than 1.0 is made only if the GPA is not less than 2.0. Therefore, the test can never be true, and the case of GPA less than 1.0 (print "Flunked out") will never be handled.

2. The value of DISC is 0.0, so the following output is displayed:

```
There is only one real root
The root is −2.0
```

3. X = 45.0 when Y = 15.0
   X = 50.0 when Y = 10.0
   X = −20.0 when Y = −10.0

Chapter 4

Section 4.1

1. a. I = 1, 2, 3, ... , N–1, N
   b. I = 1, 2, 3, 4, 5, 6, 7, 8, 9, 10
   c. Invalid because of missing label
   d. Invalid because of missing label
   e. I10 = 1, 2, 3, 4, 5, 6, 7, 8, 9, 10
   f. I = 5
   g. Invalid because of missing limit parameter
   h. I = 1, 2, 3, 4, ... 17, 18, 19, 20
   i. Invalid because of missing limit parameter
   j. Invalid because of missing limit parameter

2.

Program statement	COUNT	N	Effect
	?	?	
N = 5	?	5	Assigns 5 to N
DO COUNT = 1, N	1		Initialize COUNT to 1
PRINT *,'*****'			Prints a row of 5 stars
Increment and test COUNT	2		2 ≤ 5 is true
PRINT *,'*****'			Prints a row of 5 stars
Increment and test COUNT	3		3 ≤ 5 is true
PRINT *,'*****'			Prints a row of 5 stars
Increment and test COUNT	4		4 ≤ 5 is true
PRINT *,'*****'			Prints a row of 5 stars
Increment and test COUNT	5		5 ≤ 5 is true
PRINT *,'*****'			Prints a row of 5 stars
Increment and test COUNT	6		Exits loop

3.

Program statement	PROD	I	Effect
	?	?	
PROD = 1	1	?	Initialize PROD to 1
DO 20 I = 1, 5		1	Initialize I to 1
PROD = PROD * I	1		Multiplies PROD by 1
PRINT *, I, PROD			Prints values of I and PROD
Increment and test I		2	2 <= 5 is true
PROD = PROD * I	2		Multiplies PROD by 2
PRINT *, I, PROD			Prints values of I and PROD
Increment and test I		3	3 <= 5 is true
PROD = PROD * I	6		Multiplies PROD by 3
PRINT *, I, PROD			Prints values of I and PROD
Increment and test I		4	4 <= 5 is true
PROD = PROD * I	24		Multiplies PROD by 4

```
    PRINT *, I, PROD                          Prints values of I
                                              and PROD
Increment and test I              5           5 <= 5 is true
    PROD = PROD * I          120              Multiplies PROD by 5
    PRINT *, I, PROD                          Prints values of I
                                              and PROD
Increment and test I              6           Exits loop
```

Section 4.2

1. a. zero times; Nothing would be printed.
   b. nine times; –20, –15, –10, –5, 0, 5, 10, 15, 20
   c. one time; –20
   d. zero times; Nothing would be printed.

2. a. three times; 2, 4, 6
   b. three times; 5, 3, 1
   c. seven times; –3, –2, –1, 0, 1, 2, 3

3. a. The loop would not be executed.
      0 would be printed as a value of K.
   b. L becomes 1, 2, 3;
      2 would be printed as a value of K during the loop.

Section 4.3

1.

Program statement	N	SUM	I	NEXT	*Effect*
	?	?	?	?	
READ *, N	5				Reads in number of data items
SUM = 0		0			Initialize SUM to 0
DO 30 I = 1, N			1		Initialize I to 1
READ *, NEXT				3	Reads data item
IF (NEXT .GE. 0) THEN					Is 3 ≥ 0?
					Value is true
SUM = SUM + NEXT		3			Increments SUM by 3
Increment and test I			2		2 ≤ 5 is true
READ *, NEXT				–5	Reads data item
IF (NEXT .GE. 0) THEN					Is –5 ≥ 0?
					Value is false
SUM = SUM + NEXT		8			Increments SUM by 5
Increment and test I			3		3 ≤ 5 is true
READ *, NEXT				7	Reads data item
IF (NEXT .GE. 0) THEN					Is 7 ≥ 0?
					Value is true
SUM = SUM + NEXT		15			Increments SUM by 7
Increment and test I			4		4 ≤ 5 is true

```
      READ *, NEXT                           0       Reads data item
      IF (NEXT .GE. 0) THEN                          Is 0 ≥ 0?
                                                       Value is true
          SUM = SUM + NEXT          15             Increments SUM by 0
      Increment and test I               5         5 ≤ 5 is true
      READ *, NEXT                          -9       Reads data item
      IF (NEXT .GE. 0) THEN                          Is -9 ≥ 0?
                                                       Value is false
          SUM = SUM + NEXT          24             Increment SUM by 9
      Increment and test I               6         Exits loop
      PRINT *, SUM                                   Prints the SUM, 24
```

Section 4.6

1. All powers of 2 from 2 through 1024 inclusive would be printed.
2. Displays 95, 90, 85, . . . , 5, 0, -5, . . . , -100, -105

```
      DO 10 VAL = 95, -105, -5
          PRINT *, VAL
   10 CONTINUE
```

3.
```
   SUM = 0
   COUNT = 0
   READ *, SCORE
   DO WHILE (SCORE .GT. SENVAL)
       SUM = SUM + SCORE
       COUNT = COUNT + 1
       READ *, SCORE
   END DO
```

4. 295 would be the value of SUM; 4 would be the value of COUNT; AVERGE = REAL(SUM) / REAL(COUNT)

5. a. 5, 4, 3, 2, 1 ; I is 0 after the loop exit
   b. 5, 3, 1   ; I is -1 after the loop exit
   c. 5, 4, 3, 2, 1 ; I is 0 after the loop exit
   d. Infinite loop—executes "forever"
   e. 5, 2, 1   ; I is 0 after the loop exit

Section 4.7

1. a. 1   1

      2   1
      2   2

      3   1
      3   2
      3   3
      .   .   .

      5   5

b. 1   5
   1   4
   1   3
   1   2
   1   1

   2   5
   2   4
   2   3
   2   2

   .   .   .

   4   5
   4   4

   5   5
c. I = 1
        2
        1
   I = 2
        4
        3
        2
   I = 3
        6
        5
        4
        3
   I = 4
        8
        7
        6
        5
        4
   I = 5
       10
        9
        8
        7
        6
        5

Section 4.8
1. Change .GT. in WHILE condition to .GE..

Chapter 5

Section 5.1
1. a. Valid
   b. 4I is invalid; change to I4.
   c. F16.35X is invalid; change to F16.3, 5X.
   d. 2A and F3.3 are invalid; change to A2 and F6.3.
2. a. 1234   555.4567
   b. 1234   555.4567
   c. K = 1234
   d. ALPHA =   555.46
   e. K = 1234   ALPHA =   555.457

Section 5.3
1.

	NAME	X	N
a.	Silly Me	345.67	23
b.	lly Me34	2.3	?
c.	lly Me	34.5	67
d.	lly Me34	5.6	7
e.	lly Me34	5.67	23

2. 30 FORMAT (F7.1 / I5, 2X, A / F6.1, I3)
3. 16312DAWN–321   49
   1 2 3 4 5 6 7 8 9 10111213141516171819

Section 5.4
1. FIRST IS 20

   SECOND IS   0.1222501E+05

Section 5.5
1. a. Reads from unit 15, using the FORMAT statement with label 15, values for the variables X and Y.
   b. Reads from unit 15, using default formatting, values for the variables X and Y.
   c. Reads from the default input device, using the FORMAT statement with label 15, values for the variables X and Y.
   d. Reads from unit 15, using default formatting, values for the variables X and Y. If the end-of-file record is read, a transfer to label 15 occurs.
   e. Invalid; label of FORMAT statement and label of end-of-file control transfer are the same.
   f. Invalid; wrong unit number is used for WRITE.
   g. Writes the values of the variables X and Y to the default output device, using FORMAT statement 15.
   h. Invalid; control list END should not be included in WRITE statement.
   i. Writes the values of the variables X and Y to unit 16, using FORMAT statement 20.
   j. Invalid; wrong unit number is used for READ.
   k. Disconnects the file associated with unit 16.

l. Invalid; wrong unit number.

m. Appends an end-of-file record to the file associated with unit 16.

Section 5.6

1. Both point MIDDLE and point BEFORE are reset to the old point AFTER. Only the first and the last input data items will be displayed on the screen.

Chapter 6

Section 6.1

1.

Statement	X	PLACES	POWER	TEMPX	Effect
	3.14159	2	?	?	
IF (PLACES .GE. 0)					True
POWER = 10.0 ** PLACES			100.0		
TEMPX = X * POWER				314.159	
ROUND = NINT(TEMPX) /POWER					Assigns 314/100.0 to ROUND

2.

Statement	N	I	PRODUC	Effect
	5	?	?	
PRODUC = 1			1	Assigns 1 to PRODUC
DO 10 I = N, 2, -1		5		5 ≥ 2 is True
PRODUC = PRODUC * I			5	
Decrement and test I		4		4 ≥ 2 is True
PRODUC = PRODUC * I			20	
Decrement and test I		3		3 ≥ 2 is True
PRODUC = PRODUC * I			60	
Decrement and test I		2		2 ≥ 2 is True
PRODUC = PRODUC * I			120	
Decrement and test I		1		Exit ioop
FACTRL = PRODUC				Assigns 120 to FACTRL

Section 6.2

1. a. A and B are not declared in main program (implicit REAL). X is declared as REAL (not INTEGER) in main program.
   b. MASSAG is a function, not a variable, so it cannot be an argument.
   f. Needs a third argument.
   h. Third argument is not type INTEGER.

Section 6.3

1. Enter the initial guess for a root:
   0.0
   The approximate root is 0.93750000000E+00
   The function value is 0.39062500000E-02
   4 guesses were made.

Section 6.4

1. Returns and displays the cube of its argument.
2. X = 2 and Y = 0.16589 are returned through the subroutine call; INTEGER data type for X and REAL data type for Y are required. Type mismatch between corresponding arguments.

Section 6.5

1. The three numbers would be stored in ascending order (smallest value first) in A, B, C.
2.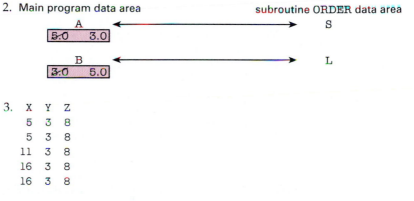

3.
X	Y	Z
5	3	8
5	3	8
11	3	8
16	3	8
16	3	8

Chapter 7

Section 7.1

1. X3 is a simple variable; X(3) is an element of array X.
2. Eleven memory cells that can each store one character.

Section 7.2

1. No

2. *Statement*   *Effect*

```
I = 3                           Assigns 3 to I
X(I) = X(I) + 10.0              Assigns 16.0 (value of X(3) + 10.0) to X(3)
X(I - 1) = X(2 * I - 1)         Assigns 2.5 (value of X(5)) to X(2)
X(I + 1) = X(2 * I) ...         Assigns 26.0 (value of X(6) + X(7)) to X(4);
```

the final contents of array:

X(1)	X(2)	X(3)	X(4)	X(5)	X(6)	X(7)	X(8)
16.0	2.5	16.0	26.0	2.5	12.0	14.0	−54.5

Section 7.3

1. a. Saves I square in the Ith element of array X and displays the values of I and X(I).
   b. Initializes X(I) to zero and stores the value I in X(I).
   c. Shifts array elements 4, 5, 6, and 7 down by one position (i.e., X(4) moves down to X(5), and so on).
   d. Shifts array elements 1, 2, and 3 up by one position (i.e., X(4) moves up to X(3), and so on).
   e. Adds two array elements that are up one and two position(s) and assigns that result to X(I);
      The eighth Fibonacci number is 21.

Section 7.4

1. a. 100; More than one value may appear on a line.
   b. 25; One value per line.
   c. 25; More than one value may appear on a line.
   d. 100; More than one value may appear on a line.
2. a. 100; As many values as will fit appear on each line.
   b. 25; One value per line.
   c. 25; As many values as will fit appear on each line.
   d. 100; As many values as will fit appear on each line.

Section 7.5

1. a. Displays array X, two elements per line, and then displays array Y in the same way.
   b. Prints one element of array X and the corresponding element of array Y on each line.
2. a. This is a String.
   b. This is a String.
   c. T
      h
      i
      s

```
i

s


a


S

t

r

1

n

g

.
```

d. T h i s   i s   a   S t r i n g .
e. Ti saSrn.

Section 7.6
1. It is better to pass the entire array of data rather than individual elements if several elements of the array are being manipulated by a subroutine.
2. a. Invalid: A and B are not declared as arrays in the main program.
   b. Invalid: C(6) is only a single element of the array, not an array.
   c. Valid: stores the sum of arrays C and D in E.
   d. Valid but leads to an error: There is no seventh array element.
   e. Valid: adds only the first five array elements.
   f. Invalid: 6 is not an array, and E is not an integer value.
   g. Valid: stores the sum of arrays D and C in E.
   h. Valid: doubles each element of array C.
   i. Invalid: C(1) is not an integer value.
   j. Valid but could lead to an error if C(1) is greater than 6.
   k. Valid: adds all elements of arrays C and D if C(1) is greater than 6; otherwise, adds only INT(ABS(C(1))) elements.

Section 7.7
1. a. Initializes array X to all zeros.
   b. Initializes array X to all zeros and array Y to all ones.
   c. Initializes array X to all zeros and array Y to all ones.
   d. Initializes the first five elements of arrays X and Y to all zeros and the remaining elements of arrays X and Y to all ones.

Chapter 8

Section 8.1
1. 25 elements in the array MATRIX; 300 elements in the array TABLE.
2. Initializes the first two rows of array MATRIX to all zeros and the last three rows to all ones.
3. a. Prints the entire array MATRIX in column-major order
   b. Prints the entire array MATRIX in column-major order
   c. Prints the entire array MATRIX in row-major order; PRINT statement (c) displays

the array MATRIX one row per output line; PRINT statements (a) and (b) provide the same output.

Section 8.2

1. after the return from subroutine CLEAN:

   1231
   2222
   2334
   5429

   then after the return from subroutine REDUCE:

   0000
   0000
   0101
   1104

Section 8.3

1. The value 1 is returned.

Section 8.4

1. To modify the BUBBLE subroutine to sort an array in descending order, change the IF condition from

   ```
   IF (LIST(FIRST) .GT. LIST(FIRST + 1)) THEN
   ```

   to

   ```
   IF (LIST(FIRST) .LT. LIST(FIRST + 1)) THEN
   ```

Section 8.5

1.

(1)	(2)	(3)	(4)	(5)
B	D	C	D	D

Section 8.7

1. 1.0, 2.0, 4.0
2. The original array NEXT is defined as 1, 3, 5, 7, 9; however, the calls to EXCH switch elements 1 and 4 and elements 2 and 3. The final array printed is 7, 5, 3, 1, 9. The two variables I are unconnected. Subroutine DEFINE has array NEXT as an argument so the subroutine cannot reference COMMON block WHAT.

Chapter 9

Section 9.1

1. 'NEW' is used when a new file is being created, 'OLD' is used when a previously created file is being read, and 'SCRATCH' is used when we do not wish to retain a file that is being created; 'SCRATCH'

2. A formatted file is processed using list-directed or formatted input/output and an unformatted file is not; formatted file; unformatted file; formatted file.
3. a. ACCESS : optional specifier in OPEN statement
 b. FMT : optional specifier in READ statement
 c. UNIT : required specifier in OPEN statement and
      optional specifier in READ statement
 d. FILE : optional specifier in OPEN statement
 e. STATUS : optional specifier in OPEN statement
 f. END . optional specifier in READ statement
 g. REC : required specifier in READ statement for direct access files
 h. RECL : required specifier in OPEN statement for direct access files

Section 9.2
1. They both must be in sequence by key; 1, 2, 3, 4, 5, 7, 12, 14, 15, 16
2. Both records will be copied to file NEWMST.
3. There would be no run-time error. N would be set to zero by subroutine INPOIN. Because N was zero, there would be no computations performed by subroutines COMLEN and COMPCT. Subroutine WRIOUT would display the table heading only.

Section 9.3
1. Use a DO loop whose loop-control variable is used to select the file record being read. For example, if I is the loop-control variable, use the specifier REC = I in the READ statement.

Chapter 10

Section 10.1
1. The ASCII representation would consist of the binary numbers equivalent to the decimal numbers 49, 50, and 51. Each binary number would be written using 8 bits (binary digits).

Section 10.2
1. 042
 , JOHN QUINCY
 ADAMS,
 ADAMS, JOHN QUINCY

Section 10.3
1. JOHN ADAMS
 ADAMS J.Q.
2. a. 'ARE STRUCTURED PROGRAMS' is assigned to QUOTE.
 b. 'RAMS ARE STRUCTURED PROG' is assigned to QUOTE2.
 c. The string in (b) is assigned to QUOTE.
 d. 'HIPS' is assigned to HIPPO.
 e. 'LARGE' is assigned to BIGGER.
 f. The blank string is assigned to BIGGER.
 g. The string 'ST' is inserted in positions 6 and 7 of BIGGER.

Section 10.5
1. a. 2
   b. 0
   c. 16
   d. 0

Section 10.6
1. It is possible for a function reference to have commas in the argument list. Some array references may have commas as well.
2. It would be illegal to assign TEXT a new value by rearranging the substrings of the current TEXT.

Answers to Review Questions

Chapter 1

1. Types of information stored in a computer are character data, real numbers, integer numbers, and program instructions.
2. Functions of the CPU are performing arithmetic operations, logical operations, and the control of all actions performed by the computer.
3. *Input devices:* keyboard and mouse;
   Output devices: monitor and printer;
   Secondary storage: floppy disk and hard disk.
4. False. A computer cannot think.
5. Two categories of programming languages are machine language and high-level language.
6. High-level languages are easier to use, are portable, and resemble English.
7. System software performs tasks required for the operation of the computer system. Application software is written to perform a particular task for the person who is using the computer.
8. Compilation, linking, and loading are needed to transform a Fortran program to a machine language program stored in memory and ready for execution.
9. *Main memory:* stores information, including data and program instructions.
   Secondary memory: provides additional data-storage capability on most computer systems.
   Central processor: manipulates the information in main memory and controls the computer.
10. Secondary memory provides permanent storage for program and data files and is less expensive than main memory. Main memory is limited in size and is volatile.

Chapter 2

1. No, the compiler doesn't translate comments.
2. * or C in column 1
3. A structured program is easier to read, understand, and maintain than an unstructured program.
4. INCOME, CONST, C3PO, R2DTWO
5. A memory cell is allocated to hold a real number identified by the name CELL1.
6. The result of C / (2 * R ** 2) cannot be assigned to PI because PI is defined in the PARAMETER statement as the constant 3.14159.

```
7. CHARACTER * 5 NAME
   PRINT *, 'Enter 5 letters of a name enclosed in apostrophes'
   READ *, NAME
   PRINT *, 'Hello', NAME
   STOP
   END
```
8. `PRINT *, 'The average size of a family is ', FAMSIZ`
9. `INTEGER, REAL, CHARACTER`
10. Operations with integers are faster and always precise, and less storage space is needed to store integers.
11. `10.5`

12.

	Type	Value
X * Y	REAL	14.0
A * B	INTEGER	14
B / Y	REAL	3.5
B / A	INTEGER	3
X / Y	REAL	3.5
MOD(A, B)	INTEGER	2
MOD(X, Y)	invalid arguments	

13. `MOD(11, 2) = 1`   `ABS(-37.5 + 20) = 17.5`
    `INT(-3.5) = -3`   `SQRT(12.0 + 13.0) = 5.0`
    `MAX0(-27, 50, 4) = 50`   `INT(-25.7) = -25`
    `MIN0(-27, 50, 4) = -27` `NINT(-18.7) = -19`
14. `NUM1 = REAL(NINT(NUM1 * 100.0)) / 100.0`
15. *Cancellation error:* When adding a very small number to a very large number, the effect of the small number may be lost. *Arithmetic underflow:* When a number is too small to be represented, it may be stored as zero. *Arithmetic overflow:* A number becomes too large to be represented.
16. b

Chapter 3

1. First, break the problem into a list of subproblems. Then describe the steps needed to solve each subproblem. Refine all the steps, providing greater detail, until the description can be translated directly into a program.
2. `LOGICAL`
3. The six relational operators described are `.LE.` (less than or equal to), `.LT.` (less than), `.GE.` (greater than or equal to), `.GT.` (greater than), `.EQ.` (equal to), and `.NE.` (not equal to).
4. The programmer should hand trace the algorithm.
5.
```
IF (HOURS .GT. 40.0) THEN
    GROSS = (40.0 * RATE) + ((HOURS - 40.0) * 1.5 * RATE)
ELSE
    GROSS = RATE * HOURS
END IF
```

```
6. IF (GENDER .EQ. 'FEMALE') THEN
      IF (AGE .GE. 18) THEN
         STATUS = 'ADULT'
      ELSE
         STATUS = 'CHILD'
      END IF
   ELSE
      IF (AGE .GE. 21) THEN
         STATUS = 'ADULT'
      ELSE
         STATUS = 'CHILD'
      END IF
   END IF
```

7.

Program statement	TEMP	Effect
	?	
PRINT *,'Enter a...'	?	Prints a prompt.
READ *, TEMP	27.34	Reads the data.
IF (TEMP .GT. 32.0) THEN		Is 27.34 > 32.0 ?
		Value is false.
PRINT *,'Ice forming'		Print message 'Ice forming'.

```
8. IF (GRADE .LE. 5) THEN
      PRINT *, 'ELEMENTARY SCHOOL'
   ELSE IF (GRADE .LE. 8) THEN
      PRINT *, 'MIDDLE SCHOOL'
   ELSE IF (GRADE .LE. 12) THEN
      PRINT *, 'HIGH SCHOOL'
   ELSE IF (GRADE .GT. 12) THEN
      PRINT *, 'COLLEGE'
   END IF
```

9. a   10. c   11. b

Chapter 4

1. The IF structure will execute only once, but the WHILE loop body can execute a number of times.

2. For X = 8.0:

IF Structure	WHILE Loop
6.000000	6.000000
	4.000000
	2.000000
	0.000000

For X = 7.0:

5.000000	5.000000
	3.000000
	1.000000
	−1.000000

For X = 0.0, X = −7.0, and X = −8.0, nothing will be printed.

3. a. IF structure
    b. DO loop
    c. IF structure
    d. WHILE loop
    e. DO loop
    f. IF structure
    g. WHILE loop

4. a. ```
    IF (AGE .GE. MINAGE) THEN
        PRINT *, 'Voting age'
    ELSE
        PRINT *, 'Under voting age.'
    END IF
    ```
    b. ```
          DO 10 EMPLOY = 1, 5
                .  .  .
       10 CONTINUE
    ```
    c. ```
    IF (GROSS .LT. RATE1) THEN
          . . .
    ELSE IF (GROSS .LT. RATE2) THEN
          . . .
    ELSE IF (GROSS .LT. RATE3) THEN
          . . .
    ELSE IF (GROSS .LT. RATE4) THEN
          . . .
    ELSE
          . . .
    END IF
    ```
    d. ```
    READ *, ITEM
    DO WHILE (ITEM .NE. FINAL)
        IF (ITEM .EQ. 0.0) THEN
            NUMZER = NUMZER + 1
        END IF
        READ *, ITEM
    END DO
    ```
    e. ```
          DO 10 I = 1, 99, 2
              PRODCT = PRODCT * I
       10 CONTINUE
    ```
    f. ```
    IF (SCORE .LT. 60) THEN
        GRADE = 'F'
    ELSE IF (SCORE .LT. 70) THEN
        GRADE = 'D'
    ELSE IF (SCORE .LT. 80) THEN
        GRADE = 'C'
    ELSE IF (SCORE .LT. 90) THEN
        GRADE = 'B'
    ELSE
        GRADE = 'A'
    END IF
    ```

g. DO WHILE (VALUE .GE. 0.5)
```
   VALUE = VALUE / 2.0
   PRINT *, VALUE
END DO
```

5. A DO loop is for counting; the loop-control variable progresses from one value to another, changing by a certain increment. A WHILE loop is more general; it can be used for counting or for other purpose. It is used when the number of loop repetitions required cannot be determined before executing the program and reading the data.

6. A sentinel value is a value that, when read as input, indicates the end of the data.

7. The READ statements should appear before the WHILE loop and inside the WHILE loop, generally just before END DO.

8.
```
SUM = 0.0
PRINT *,'Enter pay'
READ *, PAY
DO WHILE (PAY .NE. -1.0)
   SUM = SUM + PAY
   PRINT *,'Enter pay'
   READ *, PAY
END DO
```

9. For the first data line, SLOPE is 0.5; for the second data line, SLOPE is 3.0.

10. GOOD, GOOD, POOR, FAIR, POOR

11. The segment will print GOOD "forever."

12. c

13. a

Chapter 5

1.
```
    PRINT 10, 'NAME', 'HOURS', 'RATE', 'PAY'
 10 FORMAT (1X, A4, 11X, A5, 5X, A6, 5X, A8)

    PRINT 20, NAME, HOURS, RATE, PAY
 20 FORMAT (1X, A10, 5X, F5.1, 5X, F6.2, 5X, F8.2)
```

2.
```
    READ 19, NAME, WKSAL, AGE, AUTHOR, NCHILD
 19 FORMAT (A14, F5.2, I2, A8, I1)
```

3. The following lines are printed at the top of a new page:

```
 BOB SOLOMON IS 84 YEARS OLD
HE EARNS 147.63 DOLLARS PER WEEK
HIS FAVORITE AUTHOR IS ARTHUR AND HE HAS 8 CHILDREN
```

4. a. Unit number is not specified.
   b. The Z format descriptor is illegal.
   c. There is no label for the FORMAT statement.

5.
```
    OPEN (UNIT = 1, FILE = 'INPUT', STATUS = 'OLD')
    OPEN (UNIT = 2, FILE = 'OUTPUT', STATUS = 'NEW')
```

```
        PRINT (2, *) 'List of names'
        DO WHILE (.TRUE.)
           READ (1, 5, END = 99) NAME
   5       FORMAT (A)
           PRINT (2, 5) NAME
        END DO

   99 CONTINUE
        PRINT *, 'File Read and Write completed'

        END FILE (UNIT = 2)
        CLOSE (UNIT = 1)
        CLOSE (UNIT = 2)

        STOP
        END
```

6. a.   Spring 17   87.65
   b.   Spring 17   87.65
   c. The following line is printed at the top of a new page:
        Spring 17   87.65
   d. The following line is printed at the top of a new page:
        Spring17   87.65

7. a. 23.45
   b. 2345.6
   c. 23456.
   d. 2.34

8.

	X	I	TEXT
a.	2.345	67	ABCD
b.	12.	3	CDEFGH
c.	12.345	78	ABCDEF
d.	12.345	67	8

9. a

Chapter 6

```
1. INTEGER FUNCTION TOPENY (DOLLAR, CENTS)
   INTEGER DOLLAR, CENTS
   TOPENY = 100 * DOLLAR + CENTS
   RETURN
   END

2. SUBROUTINE OUTGRD (SCORE)
   INTEGER SCORE
   IF (SCORE .GE. 90) THEN
      PRINT *, 'A'
```

```
    ELSE IF (SCORE .GE. 80) THEN
        PRINT *, 'B'
    ELSE IF (SCORE .GE. 70) THEN
        PRINT *, 'C'
    ELSE IF (SCORE .GE. 60) THEN
        PRINT *, 'D'
    ELSE
        PRINT *, 'F'
    END IF
    RETURN
    END
```

3.
```
    CHARACTER *1 OUTGRD (SCORE)
    INTEGER SCORE
    IF (SCORE .GE. 90) THEN
        OUTGRD = 'A'
    ...
    ELSE
        OUTGRD = 'F'
    END IF
    RETURN
    END
```

4. When a subprogram call occurs, all of the subprogram's local variables and parameters are allocated new memory cells (initially undefined). Each dummy argument is associated with the memory cell(s) previously allocated to its corresponding actual argument.

5. A stub is a "dummy subprogram" substituted for an unwritten subprogram that allows the programmer to test the main program and the other completed subprograms.

6. A driver program is used to enter data and to call and test a single subprogram.

7. A structure chart shows the control hierarchy for program units (the main program and the subprograms) and also shows data flow between program units.

8. The structure chart

9. Even though the total number of program lines may increase, each program unit has a small number of lines, which are highly interrelated. Consequently, the program units are short, self-contained, and easier to test, debug, and reuse in new programs. Argument list errors become less likely as you gain more experience in using arguments.

10. 8 will be printed.

11. 4, 9, and 2 will be printed.

Chapter 7

1. The DO loop references array element X(9), which does not exist. The error will be detected during program execution.

2. `REAL SALES(0 : 6)`

3. A real number is assigned to a CHARACTER array element—a syntax error.
4. The statement is syntactically correct; however, an execution error occurs if the integer read into COUNTS(1) is outside the range 1 to 5.
5. Two common ways of selecting an array element are as follows: using a DO loop-control variable as the array subscript so that the array elements are accessed in sequence; reading in the array subscript so that the elements are accessed in random order.
6. Assume MINSUB, MAXSUB, and I are type INTEGER variables.

```
    MINSUB = 1
    MAXSUB = 1
    DO 10 I = 2, 20
        IF (X(I) .LT. X(MINSUB)) MINSUB = I
        IF (X(I) .GT. X(MAXSUB)) MAXSUB = I
 10 CONTINUE
    PRINT *, 'The smallest value has subscript ', MINSUB
    PRINT *, 'The largest value has subscript ', MAXSUB
```

7.
```
       REAL X(100), Y(100)
       INTEGER I, N
       READ *, N
 C Fill array X first and then reverse X in Y
       READ *, (X(I), I = 1, N)
       DO 10 I = 1, N
           Y(I) = X(N - I + 1)
    10 CONTINUE
```

8. d
9. b
10. c
11. a

Chapter 8

1. CHARACTER *20 TITLE(52, 10)
   The array element TITLE(3, 1) will contain the title of the number 1 song for week 3.
2. The array HOURS may be initialized as shown below:

```
REAL HOURS(5, 52, 7)
INTEGER SIZE
PARAMETER (SIZE = 5 * 52 * 7)
INTEGER EMPNO, WEEKNO, DAYNO
DATA HOURS /SIZE * 0.0/
```

or you can replace the DATA statement by the nested loops

```
        DO 10 EMPNO = 1, 5
           DO 20 WEEKNO = 1, 52
              DO 30 DAYNO = 1, 7
                 HOURS(EMPNO, WEEKNO, DAYNO) = 0.0
30            CONTINUE
20         CONTINUE
10 CONTINUE
```

3. The nested loops below display five sums; each value displayed is the summation of three array elements (a row).

```
        DO 10 ROW =  1, 5
           ROWSUM = 0.0
           DO 20 COL = 1, 3
              ROWSUM = ROWSUM + TABLE(ROW, COL)
20         CONTINUE
           PRINT *, ROWSUM
10 CONTINUE
```

4. The nested loops below display three sums; each value displayed is the summation of five array elements (a column).

```
        DO 10 COL =  1, 3
           COLSUM = 0.0
           DO 20 ROW = 1, 5
              COLSUM = COLSUM + TABLE(ROW, COL)
20         CONTINUE
           PRINT *, COLSUM
10 CONTINUE
```

5. 20 30 25 80 40 60   Initial array
   20 25 30 40 60 80   Array after first pass
   20 25 30 40 60 80   Array after second and last pass

6.   LIST(1) = LIST(6)
```
        DO 10 I = 5, 1, -1
           LIST(I + 1) = LIST(I)
10 CONTINUE
```

7. Named common blocks can be used to separate different collections of COMMON data. Data that may be referenced by all or most of the subprograms in a program system are usually placed in blank COMMON rather than named COMMON.

8. a. CALL PSUM (A, MAXSIZ, 1, MAXSIZ, VALID, SUM)
   b. CALL PSUM (A, MAXSIZ, FIRST, LAST, VALID, SUM)
   c. CALL PSUM (A, MAXSIZ, FIRST + 4, LAST, VALID, SUM)
   d. CALL PSUM (A, MAXSIZ, 2, 7, VALID, SUM)
   e. CALL PSUM (A, MAXSIZ, FIRST, LAST * 2, VALID, SUM)

9.   VALID   SUM
   a. .TRUE.   36.2
   b. .TRUE.   12.3
   c. .FALSE.   0.0
   d. .TRUE.   13.4
   e. .FALSE.   0.0

10. COMMON /EMPBLK/ NUMDEP(50), SALARY(100), N, FOUND, X, Y
    INTEGER NUMDEP, N, COUNT
    REAL SALARY, X, Y

11.

```
        SUBROUTINE PSUM(LIST, SIZE, I, J, LEGAL, SUM)
C Computes the sum of elements I through J of LIST
C Preconditions  : I, J, SIZE and array LIST are defined.
C Postconditions : If I <= J <= SIZE, LEGAL is .TRUE.
C     and SUM = LIST(I) +...+ LIST(J); otherwise,
C     LEGAL IS .FALSE.
C Argument Definitions
C   Input Arguments
C     LIST - Array of items to be summed
C     SIZE - Size of the  array
C     I - Index of first array element included in SUM
C     J - Index of last array element included in SUM
C   Output Arguments
C     LEGAL - Indicates whether a illegal index is
C              specified
C     SUM - Sum of the selected array elements
C Argument Declarations
        INTEGER SIZE, I, J
        REAL LIST(SIZE), SUM
        LOGICAL LEGAL

C Local Variables
        INTEGER LCV

C Initialize SUM to zero
        SUM = 0.0

C Determine whether array indices are legal
        LEGAL = (I .LE. J .AND. J .LE. SIZE)
C Computes the sum
        IF (LEGAL) THEN
           DO 10 LCV = I, J
              SUM = SUM + LIST(LCV)
  10       CONTINUE
        END IF
        RETURN
        END
```

Chapter 9

1. a. Unit number is not specified.
   b. The Z format descriptor is invalid.
   c. There is no label on the FORMAT statement.

2.
```
IF (N .GT. 0 .AND. N .LE. MAXNUM) THEN
    READ (UNIT = 2, REC = N) INREC
ELSE
    PRINT *, N, ' IS OUT OF RANGE'
END IF
```

3.
```
    CHARACTER *100 STRING
    DO 10 RECNUM = 10, 50, 10
        READ (UNIT = 3, FMT = 25, REC = RECNUM) STRING
25      FORMAT (A100)
        WRITE (UNIT = 2, FMT = 25) STRING
10  CONTINUE
```

4.
```
    DO 10 RECNUM = 1, 100
        READ (UNIT = 3, FMT = 25, REC = RECNUM) NAME,
    +        ADDRESS, CITY, STATE, ZIP
        ZIP = ZIP * 100
        WRITE (UNIT = 3, FMT = 25, REC = RECNUM) NAME,
    +        ADDRESS, CITY, STATE, ZIP
25      FORMAT (3A30, A2, I8)
10  CONTINUE
```

5. a. REC : READ and WRITE statements
   b. FMT : READ and WRITE statements
   c. UNIT: OPEN, CLOSE, END FILE, READ and WRITE statements
   d. STATUS: OPEN statement
   e. END : READ statement
6. c
7. a
8. d
9. c

Chapter 10

1.

	Length of SUBJCT	Length of TARGET
a.	20	10
b.	10	1
c.	9	2
d.	13	2
e.	30	12

2. a. 'HEATHER   IS A WILD FLOWER'
   b. 'HEATHER IS WILD'
   c. The same string is formed in all three cases,
      'HEATHER IS A WILD FLOWER'
   d. 'WILD AS A ROSE'
   e. 'HTHR'
   f. This substring name is illegal because it attempts to reference character positions
      that are outside the string FLOWER (i.e., character positions 11 and 12).

3.

	Using LEN	Using GETLEN
a.	10	7
b.	24	24
c.	7	7
d.	10	8
e.	5	5
f.	3	3

4. a. 34
   b. 1
   c. 26
   d. 9
   e. 0
   f. 3

5. a
6. a
7. b

Chapter 11

1. The scaling problem consists of mapping the range of X and Y values into the screen width and height, respectively.
2. In a three-dimensional plot, the scaling problem consists of selecting different symbols to represent the range of values for Z.
3. You can use two-dimensional plots to represent a three-dimensional surface by plotting slices in two dimensions. Each slice should be plotted for a fixed value of the third variable. The values of the third variable should run from the minimum to the maximum in fixed increments.
4. Three applications of computer-aided design in engineering are: designing automobile bodies, drawing a wiring diagram for a building, integrated-circuit fabrication.
5. a
6. b
7. c
8. c

Chapter 12

1. $\begin{vmatrix} 2 & 2 & -4 & 0 \\ 1 & -4 & 1 & 4 \\ -1 & 3 & -2 & -5 \end{vmatrix}$

2. $\begin{vmatrix} 1 & 1 & -2 & 0 \\ 0 & -6 & 5 & 4 \\ 0 & 5 & -6 & -5 \end{vmatrix}$

3. Multiplication of a row by a constant, adding or subtracting one row from another, swapping any two rows.

4. If your computer can compute numerical results accurate to d significant digits, you have reached a point of diminishing returns if there is no change in the first d digits when the number of intervals is doubled.

5. Double precision improves the accuracy of numerical computations by increasing the number of significant digits in a result, but it does not affect the range of numbers that may be represented.

6. There is a possibility for error when the double precision representation of a number is compared to its floating point (type REAL) representation. When comparing complex numbers, be sure to compare the real and imaginary parts of the numbers separately.

7. d

8. c

9. b

10. a

11. e

12. b

Index

STATEMENT	EXAMPLE OF USE
Dummy arguments	`INTEGER NUMSTU, SCORE(*)`
	`INTEGER MAXSTU`
	`PARAMETER (MAXSTU = 120)`
COMMON statement	`COMMON STUDNT`
	`CHARACTER * 20 STUDNT(MAXSTU)`
Local variable	`CHARACTER * 20 NAME`
	`C Read each student name from file and score from user`
Assignment	`NUMSTU = 0`
WHILE statement	`DO WHILE (NUMSTU .LT. MAXSTU)`
File READ	`READ (UNIT = 1, FMT = 5, END = 99) NAME`
FORMAT statement	`5    FORMAT (A)`
Format-free PRINT	`PRINT *, 'Enter score for ', NAME`
Increment variable	`NUMSTU = NUMSTU + 1`
Format-free READ	`READ *, SCORE(NUMSTU)`
Array assignment	`STUDNT(NUMSTU) = NAME`
End of WHILE loop	`END DO`
	`C End of file reached`
CONTINUE	`99 CONTINUE`
RETURN	`RETURN`
END subroutine	`END`
	`C———————————————————————————————————————————————`
Subroutine head	`SUBROUTINE DOGRAD(SCORE, NUMSTU, PASSED)`
	`C Assigns a grade, GRADE(I), to student I and resets`
	`C PASSED(I) to .FALSE. if student I has failed.`
Dummy arguments	`INTEGER NUMSTU, SCORE(*)`
	`LOGICAL PASSED(*)`
	`INTEGER MAXSTU`
	`PARAMETER (MAXSTU = 120)`
COMMON statement	`COMMON STUDNT`
	`CHARACTER * 20 STUDNT (MAXSTU)`
Named COMMON	`COMMON /GRD/ GRADE`
	`CHARACTER * 1 GRADE(MAXSTU)`
Local variable	`INTEGER I`
Function declaration	`LOGICAL FAILED`
	`C Assign grades and print results`